A general history and collection of voyages and travels, arranged in systematic order : forming a complete history of the origin and progress of navigation, discovery, and commerce, by sea and land, from the earliest ages to the... Volume 12 of 18

Robert Kerr

\

GENERAL

HISTORY AND COLLECTION

OF

VOYAGES AND TRAVELS,

ARRANGED IN SYSTEMATIC ORDER :

FORMING A COMPLETE HISTORY OF THE ORIGIN AND PROGRESS
OF NAVIGATION, DISCOVERY, AND COMMERCE,
BY SEA AND LAND,
FROM THE EARLIEST AGES TO THE PRESENT TIME.

BY

ROBERT KERR, F. R. S. & F. A. S. EDIN

ILLUSTRATED BY MAPS AND CHARTS.

VOL. XII.

EDINBURGH :

Printed by James Ballantyne and Company,

FOR WILLIAM BLACKWOOD, SOUTH BRIDGE-STREET,
AND JOHN BALLANTYNE AND CO. HIGH-STREET, EDINBURGH
J. MURRAY, ALBEMARLE-STREET, R. BALDWIN, AND GALE,
CURTIS, AND FENNER, PATERNOSTER-ROW, LONDON
AND J. CUMMING, DUBLIN

1814.

CONTENTS

OF

VOL. XII.

———

PART III.

General Voyages and Travels of Discovery, &c.

Page.

BOOK I. An Account of the Voyages undertaken by order of his Majesty, George III., for making Discoveries in the Southern Hemisphere; and successively performed by Commodore Byron, Captains Wallis and Carteret, and Lieutenant Cook, ... 3

General Introduction, ... *ib.*

CHAP. I. An Account of Commodore Byron's Voyage, in 1764, 5, and 6, in his Majesty's ship the Dolphin, 9

SECT. I. The Passage from the Downs to Rio de Janeiro, ... *ib.*

II. Passage from Rio de Janeiro to Port Desire; with some Description of that Place, . 13

III. Course from Port Desire, in search of Pepy's Island, and afterwards to the Coast of Patagonia, with a Description of the Inhabitants, ... 25

IV. Passage up the Streight of Magellan, to Port Famine; with some Account of that Harbour, and the adjacent Coast, . . 33

V. The Course back from Port Famine to Falkland's Islands, with some Account of the Country, ... 40

VI. The Passage through the Strait of Magellan as far as Cape Monday, with a Description of several Bays and Harbours, formed by the Coast on each Side, . . 52

VII. The Passage from Cape Monday, in the Strait of Magellan, into the South Seas; with some general Remarks on the Navigation of that Strait, ... 67

                                                        Page.

SECT. VIII. The Run from the Western Entrance of the
            Strait of Magellan to the Islands of Dis-
            appointment,   .   .   .   75
       IX. The Discovery of King George's Islands,
            with a Description of them, and an Ac-
            count of several Incidents that happened
            there, ...   83
        X. The Run from King George's Islands to the
            Islands of Saypan, Tinian, and Aguigan;
            with an Account of several Islands that
            were discovered in that Track,   .   .   91
       XI. The Arrival of the Dolphin and Tamar at
            Tinian, a Description of the present
            Condition of that Island, and an Ac-
            count of the Transactions there,   .   97
      XII. The Run from Tinian to Pulo Timoan,
            with some Account of that Island, its
            Inhabitants and Productions, and thence
            to Batavia, ...   107
     XIII. Transactions at Batavia, and Departure
            from that Place,   -   -   -   113
      XIV. The Passage from Batavia to the Cape of
            Good Hope, and from thence to Eng-
            land,   -   .   -   -   -   116
CHAP. II. An Account of Captain Wallis's Voyage in 1766,
            7, and 8, in his Majesty's ship the Dolphin, 120
SECT. I. The Passage to the Coast of Patagonia, with
            some Account of the Natives,   .   ib.
       II. The Passage through the Strait of Ma-
            gellan, with some further Account of
            the Patagonians, and a Description of
            the Coast on each Side, and its Inha-
            bitants,   -   -   -   -   -   132
      III. A particular Account of the Places in which
            we anchored during our Passage through
            the Strait, and of the Shoals and Rocks
            that lie near them,   .   .   .   157
       IV. The Passage from the Strait of Magellan,
            to King George the Third's Island, call-
            ed Otaheite, in the South Sea, with an
            Account of the Discovery of several
            other Islands, and a Description of their
            Inhabitants, ...   161
        V. An Account of the Discovery of King
            George the Third's Island, or Otaheite,
            and of several Incidents which happen-
            ed both on board the Ship and on Shore, 175

Page.

SECT. VI. The Sick sent on Shore, and a regular Trade established with the Natives; some Account of their Character and Manners, of their Visits on board the Ship, and a Variety of Incidents that happened during this Intercourse, ... 190

VII. An Account of an Expedition to discover the Inland Part of the Country, and our other Transactions, till we quitted the Island to continue our Voyage, . . 204

VIII. A more particular Account of the Inhabitants of Otaheite, and of their domestic Life, Manners, and Arts, . 210

IX. Passage from Otaheite to Tinian, with some Account of several other Islands that were discovered in the South Seas, 218

X. Some Account of the present State of the Island of Tinian, and our Employment there; with what happened in the Run from thence to Batavia, . . 221

XI. Transactions at Batavia, and an Account of the Passage from thence to the Cape of Good Hope, ... 230

XII. An Account of our Transactions at the Cape of Good Hope, and of the Return of the Dolphin to England, . 234

A Table of the Latitudes and Longitudes West of London, with the Variation of the Needle at several Ports, and Situations at Sea, from Observations made on board his Majesty's Ship the Dolphin; also her Nautical Reckoning during the Voyage, . . 239

CHAP. III. An Account of Captain Carteret's Voyage, in 1766, 7, 8, and 9, in his Majesty's Sloop the Swallow, ... 243

SECT. I. The Run from Plymouth to Madeira, and from thence through the Strait of Magellan, ... ib.

II. The passage from Cape Pillar, at the Western entrance of the Strait of Magellan, to Masafuero; with some Account of that Island, ... 252

III. The Passage from Masafuero to Queen Charlotte's Islands; several Mistakes corrected concerning Davis's Land, and an Account of some small Islands, supposed to be the same that were seen by Quiros, 267

c

                                                    Page.
Sect. IV. An Account of the Discovery of Queen
            Charlotte's Islands, with a Description
            of them and their Inhabitants, and of
            what happened at Egmont Island,   .   275
        V. Departure from Egmont Island, and Passage
            to Nova Britannia; with a Description of
            several other Islands, and their Inhabit-
            ants, ...   287
       VI. Discovery of a Strait dividing the Land
            called Nova Britannia into two Islands,
            with a Description of several small Is-
            lands that lie in the Passage, and the
            Land on each side, with the Inhabitants, 296
      VII. The Passage from Saint George's Channel
            to the Island of Mindanao, with an Ac-
            count of many Islands that were seen,
            and Incidents that happened by the Way, 301
     VIII. Some Account of the Coast of Mindanao,
            and the Islands near it, in which several
            Mistakes of Dampier are corrected,   .   308
       IX. The Passage from Mindanao to the Island
            of Celebes, with a particular Account of
            the Strait of Macassar, in which many
            Errors are corrected,   .   .   .   316
        X. Transactions off Macassar, and the Pas-
            sage thence to Bonthain,   .   .   322
       XI. Transactions at Bonthain, while the vessel
            was waiting for a Wind to carry her to
            Batavia, with some Account of the Place,
            the Town of Macassar and the adja-
            cent Country, ...   328
      XII. Passage from Bonthain Bay, in the Island
            of Celebes, to Batavia.   Transactions
            there, and the Voyage round the Cape
            of Good Hope to England,   .   .   336
A Table of the Variation of the Compass as observed
            on board of the Swallow,   .   .   .   352
CHAP. IV. An Account of Lieutenant Cook's Voyage, in
            1768, 1769, and 1770, in his Majesty's Bark
            the Endeavour, ...   359
    Sect. I. The Passage from Plymouth to Madeira,
            with some Account of that Island,   ib.
        II. The Passage from Madeira to Rio de Ja-
            neiro, with some Account of the Coun-
            try, and the Incidents that happened
            there, ...   368

Page.

Sect. III. The Passage from Rio de Janeiro to the Entrance of the Strait of Le Maire, with a Description of some of the Inhabitants of Terra del Fuego, . . 392

IV. An Account of what happened in ascending a Mountain to search for Plants, 398

V. The Passage through the Strait of Le Maire, and a further Description of the Inhabitants of Terra del Fuego, and its Productions, ... 404

VI. A general Description of the south-east Part of Terra del Fuego, and the Strait of Le Maire; with some Remarks on Lord Anson's Account of them, and Directions for the Passage Westward, round this Part of America, into the South Seas, ... 410

VII. The Sequel of the Passage from Cape Horn to the newly discovered Islands in the South Seas, with a Description of their Figure and Appearance, some Account of the Inhabitants, and several Incidents that happened during the Course, and at the Ship's Arrival among them, ... 416

VIII. The Arrival of the Endeavour at Otaheite, called by Captain Wallis, King George the III.'s Island. Rules established for Traffic with the Natives, and an Account of several Incidents which happened in a Visit to Tootahah and Toubourai Tamaide, two Chiefs, 429

IX. A Place fixed upon for an Observatory and Fort: an Excursion into the Woods, and its Consequences. The Fort erected; a Visit from several Chiefs on Board and at the Fort, with some Account of the Music of the Natives, and the Manner in which they dispose of their Dead, ... 431

X. An Excursion to the Eastward, an Account of several Incidents that happened both on Board and on Shore, and of the first Interview with Oberea, the Person, who, when the Dolphin was here, was supposed to be Queen of the Island, with a Description of the Fort, 4..

Page.

SECT. XI. The Observatory set up; the Quadrant
stolen, and Consequences of the Theft:
A Visit to Tootahah: Description of a
Wrestling match: European Seeds sown:
Names given to our People by the Indians, 448

XII. Some Ladies visit the Fort with very uncommon Ceremonies: The Indians attend Divine Service, and in the Evening exhibit a most extraordinary Spectacle: Toubourai Tamaide falls into
Temptation, ... 458

XIII. Another Visit to Tootahah, with various
Adventures: Extraordinary Amusement
of the Indians, with Remarks upon it:
Preparations to observe the Transit of
Venus, and what happened in the mean
Time at the Fort, . . . 464

XIV. The Ceremonies of an Indian Funeral particularly described: General Observations on the Subject: A Character
found among the Indians to which the
Ancients paid great Veneration: A
Robbery at the Fort, and its Consequences; with a Specimen of Indian
Cookery, and various Incidents, 472

XV. An Account of the Circumnavigation of
the Island, and various Incidents that
happened during the Expedition; with
a Description of a Burying-place and
Place of Worship, called a Morai, 482

XVI. An Expedition of Mr Banks to trace the
River: Marks of subterraneous Fire:
Preparations for leaving the Island:
An Account of Tupia, . . 195

A

GENERAL HISTORY

AND

COLLECTION

OF

VOYAGES AND TRAVELS.

———————→

PART III.

A

GENERAL HISTORY

AND

COLLECTION

OF

VOYAGES AND TRAVELS.

PART III. BOOK I.

CHAPTER I.

AN ACCOUNT OF THE VOYAGES UNDERTAKEN BY THE ORDER OF HIS MAJESTY GEORGE III. FOR MAKING DISCOVERIES IN THE SOUTHERN HEMISPHERE; AND SUCCESSIVELY PERFORMED BY COMMODORE BYRON, CAPTAIN WALLIS, CAPTAIN CARTERET, AND CAPTAIN COOK, IN THE DOLPHIN, THE SWALLOW, AND THE ENDEAVOUR: DRAWN UP FROM THE JOURNALS WHICH WERE KEPT BY THE SEVERAL COMMANDERS, AND FROM THE PAPERS OF SIR JOSEPH BANKS, BART. BY JOHN HAWKESWORTH, LL. D. [TAKEN FROM THE THIRD EDITION, LONDON 1785, VARIOUSLY MODIFIED TO ANSWER THE PURPOSES OF THIS COLLECTION, AS ELSEWHERE EXPLAINED.]

GENERAL INTRODUCTION.

HIS majesty, soon after his accession to the crown, formed a design of sending out vessels for making discoveries of countries hitherto unknown; and, in the year 1764, the kingdom being then in a state of profound peace, he

proceeded

proceeded to put it into execution.' The Dolphin and the
Tamar were dispatched under the command of Commodore
Byron.

The Dolphin was a man-of-war of the sixth rate, mounting twenty-four guns; her complement was 150 men, with
three lieutenants, and thirty-seven petty officers.

The Tamar was a sloop, mounting sixteen guns; her complement was ninety men, with three lieutenants, and two-
and-twenty petty officers, and the command of her was given to Captain Mouat.

Commodore Byron returned in the month of May in the
year 1766, and in the month of August following the Dolphin was again sent out, under the command of Captain
Wallis, with the Swallow, commanded by Captain Carteret.
The equipment of the Dolphin was the same as before. The
Swallow was a sloop mounting fourteen guns; her complement was ninety men, with one lieutenant and twenty-two
petty officers.

These vessels proceeded together till they came within
sight of the South Sea, at the western entrance of the Strait
of Magellan, and from thence returned by different routes to
England.

In the latter part of the year 1767, it was resolved by the
Royal Society, that it would be proper to send persons into
some part of the South Sea to observe a transit of the planet Venus over the sun's disc, which, according to astronomical calculation, would happen in the year 1769; and that
the islands called Marquesas de Mendoza, or those of Rot-
terdam or Amsterdam,[2] were the properest places then
known for making such observation.

In consequence of these resolutions, it was recommended
to his majesty, in a memorial from the Society, dated February, 1768, that he would be pleased to order such an observation to be made; upon which his majesty signified to
the lords commissioners of the Admiralty his pleasure that
a ship should be provided to carry such observers as the society should think fit to the South Seas; and, in the beginning

' In the reign of George II. two voyages of discovery were performed,
viz. by Captain Middleton in 1741, and Captains Smith and Moore in 1746.
They were in search of a north-west passage through Hudson's Bay. Of
these notice will be taken elsewhere.—E.

[2] So called by Tasman, but by the natives Anamooka and Tongataboo;
they belong to that large cluster which Cook named the Friendly Isles.—
E.

ning of April following, the society received a letter from the secretary of the Admiralty, informing them that a bark of three hundred and seventy tons had been taken up for that purpose. This vessel was called the Endeavour, and the command of her given to Lieutenant James Cook,[3] a gentleman of undoubted abilities in astronomy and navigation, who was soon after, by the Royal Society, appointed, with Mr Charles Green, a gentleman who had long been assistant to Dr Bradley at the Royal Observatory at Greenwich, to observe the transit.[4]

While this vessel was getting ready for her expedition, Captain Wallis returned; and it having been recommended to him by Lord Morton, when he went out, to fix on a proper place for this astronomical observation, he, by letter, dated

[3] The gentleman first proposed for this command was Mr Alexander Dalrymple, a member of the Royal Society, and author or publisher of several works in geography. He was anxious for the undertaking, but apprehending that difficulties might arise during the voyage from the circumstance of the crew not being subjected to ordinary naval discipline under him, he made it a condition that he should hold a brevet commission as captain. Sir Edward Hawke, at that time at the head of the Admiralty, did not give his consent to this demand, saying, that his conscience would not permit him to entrust any of his majesty's ships to a person not educated as a seaman; and declaring, in consequence, that he would rather have his right hand cut off than sign any commission to that effect. This brave and spirited man, it is probable, feared the degradation of his profession by such a measure; but, besides this, he knew that in a similar case, where a commission was given to Dr Halley, very serious evils had been occasioned by the sailors refusing to acknowledge the authority thus communicated. Mr Dalrymple remaining equally tenacious of his own opinion, it became necessary either to abandon the undertaking, or to procure another person to command it. Mr Stephens, Secretary to the Admiralty, made mention of our great navigator, as well known to him, and very fit for the office, having been regularly bred in the navy, in which he was that time a master, and having, as marine surveyor of Newfoundland and Labradore, and on several occasions, exhibited very singular marks of good understanding and abilities. Sir Hugh Palliser, applied to by the Board for his opinion on the matter, most warmly, from his own knowledge, espoused Mr Stephens's recommendation of Cook, who was accordingly appointed to the command, and promoted to the rank of lieutenant in the navy, by a commission bearing date 25th of May, 1768. Mr D⸺r⸺le, it may be remarked, took his disappointment very badly. He p⸺⸺ed a petulant letter to Dr Hawkesworth, complaining, among other things, of the ill treatment he had received. Dr H. replied in the second edition of this work, but the controversy betwixt these two gentlemen is unworthy of the reader's patience.—E.

[4] Joseph Banks, Esq. afterwards Sir Joseph Banks, Bart. and Dr Solander, accompanied Cook in this voyage.—E

dated on board the Dolphin the 18th of May, 1768, the day before he landed at Hastings, mentioned Port Royal harbour, in an island which he had discovered, then called George's island, and since Otaheite: the Royal Society, therefore, by letter, dated the beginning of June, in answer to an application from the admiralty to be informed whither they would have their observers sent, made choice of that place.

The Endeavour had been built for the coal trade, and a vessel of that construction was preferred for many reasons, particularly because she was what the sailors called a good sea-boat, was more roomy, would take and lie on the ground better, and might be navigated by fewer men than other vessels of the same burden.

Her complement of officers and men was Lieutenant Cook the commander, with two lieutenants under him, a master and boatswain, with each two mates, a surgeon and carpenter, with each one mate, a gunner, a cook, a clerk and steward, two quarter-masters, an armourer, a sail-maker, three midshipmen, forty-one able seamen, twelve marines, and nine servants, in all eighty-four persons, besides the commander: she was victualled for eighteen months, and took on board ten carriage and twelve swivel guns, with good store of ammunition and other necessaries. The Endeavour also, after the astronomical observation should be made, was ordered to prosecute the design of making discoveries in the South Seas. What was effected by these vessels in their several voyages, will appear in the course of this work, of which it is now necessary to give some account.

It is drawn up from the journals that were kept by the commanders of the several ships, which were put into my hands by the lords commissioners of the admiralty for that purpose: and, with respect to the voyage of the Endeavour, from other papers equally authentic; an assistance which I have acknowledged in an introduction to the account of her voyage.

When I first undertook the work, it was debated, whether it should be written in the first or third person; it was readily acknowledged on all hands, that a narrative in the first person would, by bringing the adventurer and the reader nearer together, without the intervention of a stranger, more strongly excite an interest, and consequently afford more entertainment;

entertainment; but it was objected, that if it was written in
the name of the several commanders, I could exhibit only
a naked narrative, without any opinion or sentiment of my
own, however fair the occasion, and without noting the si-
militude or dissimilitude between the opinions, customs, or
manners of the people now first discovered, and those of nations that have been long known, or remarking on any
other incident or particular that might occur.   In answer to
this objection, however, it was said, that as the manuscript
would be submitted to the gentlemen in whose names it
would be written, supposing the narrative to be in the first
person, and nothing published without their approbation,
it would signify little who conceived the sentiments that
should be expressed, and therefore I might still be at liberty to express my own.   In this opinion all parties acquiesced, and it was determined that the narrative should
be written in the first person, and that I might, notwithstanding, intersperse such sentiments and observations as
my subject should suggest : they are not indeed numerous,
and when they occur, are always cursory and short ; for nothing would have been more absurd than to interrupt an interesting narrative, or new descriptions, by hypothesis and
dissertation.[5] They will, however, be found most frequent

---

[5] It is highly questionable if this substitution of writer for adventurer
have the efficiency ascribed to it, when the reader knows before hand, and
cannot but remember, that it is artificial, and avowedly intended for effect.
This is so obvious, that one cannot help wondering how the parties concerned in the publication of these Voyages should have acquiesced in the
mode of their appearance. The only way of accounting for it, perhaps, is
this ; it was imagined that no one but an author by profession was compe-
tent to fulfil the expectations that had been formed in the public mind.
The opinion generally entertained that Mr Robins was the author of the
Account of Anson's Voyage, might have contributed to this very groundless notion ; and the parties might have hoped, that a person of Dr Hawkesworth's reputation in the literary world, would not fail to fabricate a work
that should at least rival that excellent production. It would be unfair
not to apprise the reader, that this hope was not altogether realised. Public opinion has unquestionably ranked it as inferior, but has not however
been niggard in its praise. The work is read, and always will be read, with
high interest. This, perhaps, is capable of augmentation ; and the Editor
much deceives himself if he has not accomplished this effect by his labours,
as well in pruning off the redundant moralizings and cumbrous ratiocina-
tions of Dr Hawkesworth, as in contributing new but relevant matter to
the mass of amusing and instructive information which that gentleman has
recorded. He confesses that he has far less delicacy in doing either of
these offices in the present case, than he would chuse to avow, had the account emanated purely and directly from the pens of those who performed

in the account of the voyage of the Endeavour; and the principal reason is, that although it stands last in the series, great part of it was printed before the others were written, so that several remarks, which would naturally have been suggested by the incidents and descriptions that would have occurred in the preceding voyages, were anticipated by similar incidents and descriptions which occurred in this.

Some particulars that are related in one voyage will perhaps appear to be repeated in another, as they would necessarily have been if the several commanders had written the account of their voyages themselves; for a digest could not have been made of the whole, without invading the right of each navigator to appropriate the relation of what he had seen : these repetitions, however, taken together, will be found to fill but a few pages of the book.[6]

That no doubt might remain of the fidelity with which I have related the events recorded in my materials, the manuscript account of each voyage was read to the respective commanders at the Admiralty, by the appointment of Lord Sandwich, who was himself present during much the greatest part of the time. The account of the voyage of the Endeavour was also read to Mr Banks and Dr Solander, in whose hands, as well as in those of Captain Cook, the manuscript was left for a considerable time after the reading. Commodore Byron also, Captain Wallis, and Captain Carteret, had the manuscripts of their respective voyages to peruse, after they had been read at the Admiralty in their presence, and such emendations as they suggested were made. In order thus to authenticate the voyage of Captain Cook, the account of it was first written, because it was expected when his journal was put into my hand, that he would have sailed on his second voyage in less than five months.

[Some

---

the voyages; nor can he help feeling a regret, that such persons as Byron and Cook, both of whom have given most satisfactory proofs of their possessing every literary requisite, were not permitted to edify the public as they thought good, without the officious instrumentality of an editor. These men needed no such interference, though their modesty and good sense availed them, undoubtedly, in profiting by the merely verbal corrections of friendship; and their own productions have the charm of simplicity and genuineness of narrative, which, it is certain, the ability acquired by mere drudgery in composition is by no means adequate to produce.—E.

6 These repetitions have been studiously avoided in this work, wherever omission could be practised, or reference to different parts of the collection seemed unembarrassing.—E.

[Some paragraphs, containing reasons or apologies for certain minute specifications of courses, bearings, &c. &c. are here omitted, as unnecessary where the things themselves, to which objections were anticipated, are not given. Some cuts also alluded to are of course unsuitable to this work, and the references to them are in consequence left out. Dr Hawkesworth occupies the remainder of this introduction in discussing two subjects, about which it is thought unadvisable to take up the reader's attention at present—the controversy respecting the existence of giants in Patagonia, asserted by Byron, Wallis, and Carteret; and the justifiableness of attempting discoveries, where, in prosecution of them, the lives of human beings in a savage state are of necessity sacrificed.]

AN ACCOUNT OF A VOYAGE ROUND THE WORLD, IN THE YEARS 1764, 1765, AND 1766, BY THE HONOURABLE COMMODORE BYRON, IN HIS MAJESTY'S SHIP THE DOLPHIN.

SECTION I.

The Passage from the Downs to Rio de Janeiro.

[The longitude in this voyage is reckoned from the meridian of London, west to 180 degrees, and east afterwards.]

ON the 21st of June, 1764, I sailed from the Downs, with his majesty's ship the Dolphin, and the Tamar frigate, under my command. In coming down the river, the Dolphin got a-ground; I therefore put into Plymouth, where she was docked, but did not appear to have received any damage.[c] At this place, having changed some of our men, and paid the people two months wages in advance, I hoisted the broad pendant, and sailed again on the 3d of July; on the 4th we were off the Lizard, and made the best of our way with a fine breeze, but had the mortification to find the Tamar a very

---

[1] In a well-drawn-up account of this voyage, published 1767, by an officer of the Dolphin, it is said that " her bottom was sheathed with copper, as were likewise the braces and pintles for the use of the rudder, which was the first experiment of the kind that had ever been made on any vessel " This work will be referred to occasionally, and is certainly deserving of that notice.—E.

very heavy sailer. In the night of Friday the 6th, the officer of the first watch saw either a ship on fire, or an extraordinary phenomenon which greatly resembled it, at some
distance : It continued to blaze for about half an hour, and
then disappeared. In the evening of July the 12th, we saw
the rocks near the island of Madeira, which our people call
the Deserters, from Desertes, a name which has been given
them from their barren and desolate appearance : The next
day we stood in for the road of Funchiale, where, about
three o'clock in the afternoon, we came to an anchor. In
the morning of the 14th, I waited upon the governor, who
received me with great politeness, and saluted me with eleven
guns, which I returned from the ship. The next day, he
returned my visit at the house of the consul, upon which I
saluted him with eleven guns, which he returned from the
fort. I found here his majesty's ship the Crown, and the
Ferret sloop, who also saluted the broad pendant.

Having completed our water, and procured all the refreshment I was able for the companies of both the ships, every
man having twenty pounds weight of onions for his sea-stock,
we weighed anchor on Thursday the 19th, and proceeded
on our voyage. On the 21st, we made the island of Palma,
one of the Canaries, and soon after examining our water,
we found it would be necessary to touch at one of the Cape
de Verd islands for a fresh supply. During the whole of our
course from the Lizard, we observed that no fish followed
the ship, which I judged to be owing to her being sheathed
with copper. By the 26th, our water was become foul, and
stunk intolerably, but we purified it with a machine, which
had been put on board for that purpose : It was a kind of
ventilator, by which air was forced through the water in a
continual stream, as long as it was necessary.

In the morning of the 27th, we made the island of Sal,
one of the Cape de Verds, and seeing several turtle upon
the water, we hoisted out our jolly-boat, and attempted to
strike them, but they all went down before our people could
come within reach of them. On Monday the 30th, we came
to an anchor in Port Praya bay, the principal harbour in
St Jago, the largest of the Cape de Verd Islands. The rainy
season was already set in, which renders this place very unsafe ; a large swell that rolls in from the southward, makes
a frightful surf upon the shore, and there is reason every
hour to expect a tornado, of which, as it is very violent, and

blows

blows directly in, the consequences are likely to be fatal; so that after the 15th of August no ship comes hither till the rainy season is over, which happens in November; for this reason I made all possible haste to fill my water and get away. I procured three bullocks for the people, but they were little better than carrion, and the weather was so hot, that the flesh stunk in a few hours after they were killed.

On Thursday the 2d of August, we got again under sail, with a large cargo of fowls, lean goats, and monkies, which the people contrived to procure for old shirts, jackets, and other articles of the like kind.[2] The intolerable heat, and almost incessant rain, very soon affected our health, and the men began to fall down in fevers, notwithstanding all my attention and diligence to make them shift themselves before they slept, when they were wet.

On Wednesday the 8th, the Tamar fired a gun, upon which we shortened sail till she came up: We found that she had suffered no damage but the carrying away of her top-sail-yard; however, as we were obliged to make an easy sail till she had got up another, and the wind seemed to be coming again to the southward, we lost a good deal of way. We continued, to our great mortification, to observe that no fish would come near enough to our copper bottom for us to strike, though we saw the sea as it were quickened with them at a little distance. Ships in these hot latitudes generally take fish in plenty, but, except sharks, we were not able to catch one.

On the 11th of September, we made the coast of Brazil; and on the 13th, anchored in eighteen fathom, in the great road of Rio de Janeiro. The city, which is large, and makes a handsome appearance, is governed by the viceroy of Brazil, who is perhaps, in fact, as absolute a sovereign as any upon earth. When I visited him, he received me in great form; above sixty officers were drawn up before the palace, as well as a captain's guard, who were men of a good appearance, and extremely well clothed: His excellency, with a number of persons of the first distinction, belonging to the place, met me at the head of the stairs, upon which

---

[2] " Clothes, particularly those that are black, however mean, are here an object of ambition and vanity, rendered less necessary by the warmth of the climate."

which fifteen guns were fired from the nearest port : We then entered the room of state, and, after conversing about a quarter of an hour in French, I took my leave, and was dismissed with the same form that had been used at my reception.   He offered to return my visit at a house which I had hired on shore, but this I declined, and soon after he returned it on board.

The people in my own ship, who had as much fresh meat and greens as they could eat every day, were very healthy, but there being many sick on board the Tamar, I procured a place for them on shore, where they soon recovered.   As the seams of both the ships were very open, some Portuguese caulkers were engaged, who, after having worked some time, rendered them perfectly tight.[3]

While we lay here, Lord Clive, in the Kent Indiaman, came to the port.   This ship had sailed from England a month before us, and had not touched any where, yet she came in a month after us ; so that her passage was just two months longer than ours, notwithstanding the time we lost in waiting for the Tamar, which, though the Dolphin was by no means a good sailer, sailed so much worse, that we seldom spread more than half our canvas.   The Kent had many of her people down in the scurvy.

On Tuesday the 16th of October, we weighed anchor, being impatient to get to sea, for the heat here was intolerable ; but we lay four or five days above the bar, waiting for the land-breeze to carry us out, for there is no getting out with the sea-breeze, and the entrance between the two first forts is so narrow, and so great a sea breaks in upon them, that it was not without much danger and difficulty we got out at last, and if we had followed the advice of the Portuguese pilot, we had certainly lost the ship.[4]   As this
                                      narrative

---

[3] " We had six, who were paid at the rate of six shillings sterling a day ; though it is certain that one of our English caulkers would do as much in one day as they could in three ; but though they are slow and inactive, they perform their work very completely, or else their vessels could not run so many voyages in a shattered condition as they frequently do."

[4] The harbour of Rio de Janeiro is uncommonly good, and spacious enough for a large fleet, but the entrance is very narrow, and requires to be entered with the assistance of a sea-breeze, which fortunately blows daily from before noon till sun-set. According to Captain Krusenstern, the harbour of St Catharines in the island of that name near the Brazil coast, is " infinitely preferable to Rio Janeiro," for ships going round Cape Horn.—See his reasons in the account of his voyage p. 76.—E.

narrative is published for the advantage of future navigators, particularly those of our own nation, it is also necessary I should observe, that the Portuguese here, carrying on a great trade, make it their business to attend every time a boat comes on shore, and practise every artifice in their power to entice away the crew : if other methods do not succeed, they make them drunk, and immediately send them up the country, taking effectual care to prevent their return, till the ship to which they belong has left the place ; by this practice I lost five of my men, and the Tamar nine : Mine I never recovered, but the Tamar had the good fortune to learn where her's were detained, and by sending out a party in the night, surprised them, and brought them back.

Section II.

Passage from Rio de Janeiro to Port Desire; with some Description of that Place.

ON Monday the 22d, being now once more at sea, I called all hands upon deck, and informed them, that I was not, as they imagined, bound immediately to the East Indies, but upon certain discoveries, which it was thought might be of great importance to our country; in consideration of which, the lords commissioners of the Admiralty had been pleased to promise them double pay, and several other advantages, if during the voyage they should behave to my satisfaction. They all expressed the greatest joy imaginable upon the occasion, and assured me, that there was no danger or difficulty that they would not with the utmost cheerfulness undergo in the service of their country, nor any order that I could give them which they would not implicitly and zealously obey.[1]

We continued our course till Monday the 29th, having frequently hard gales with sudden gusts, which obliged us

to

[1] " We had all the reason possible to believe that we were bound to the East Indies, and that we should now steer to the Cape of Good Hope, the scheme being so well concerted by our commodore, as even to deceive Lord Clive, who pressed him with great importunity to allow him to take his passage in the Dolphin, we being in much greater readiness for sea than the Kent; but to this the commodore could not consent; but flattered his lordship with the hopes of his taking him on board on their meeting at the Cape."

to strike our top-gallant-masts, and get up our stumps; but this day it blew a storm, with a terrible sea, and the ship laboured so much, that, to ease her, I ordered the two foremost and two aftermost guns to be thrown overboard. The gale continued with nearly equal violence all the rest of the day, and all night, so that we were obliged to lie-to under a double-reefed main-sail; but in the morning, it being more moderate, and veering from N.W. to S. by W. we made sail again, and stood to the westward. We were now in latitude 35° 50' S. and found the weather as cold as it is at the same season in England, although the month of November here is a spring month, answering to our May, and we were near twenty degrees nearer the Line: To us, who within little more than a week had suffered intolerable heat, this change was most severely felt: And the men who, supposing they were to continue in a hot climate during the whole voyage, had contrived to sell not only all their warm clothes, but their bedding, at the different ports where we had touched, now applied in great distress for slops, and were all furnished for the climate.

On Friday the 2d of November, after administering the proper oaths to the lieutenants of both ships, I delivered them their commissions; for till this time they acted only under verbal orders from me, and expected to receive their commissions in India, whither they imagined we were bound. We now began to see a great number of birds about the ship, many of them very large, of which some were brown and white, and some black: There were among them large flocks of pintadoes, which are somewhat larger than a pigeon, and spotted with black and white. On the 4th, we saw a great quantity of rock weed, and several seals: The prevailing winds were westerly, so that being continually driven to the eastward, we foresaw that it would not be easy to get in with the coast of Patagonia. On the 10th, we observed the water to change colour, but we had no ground with one hundred and forty fathom. The next day we stood in for the land till eight in the evening, when we had ground of red sand with forty-five fathom. We steered S.W. by W. all night, and the next morning had fifty-two fathom with the same ground: Our latitude now being 42° 34' S., longitude 58° 17' W., the variation 11°¼ E.

On Monday the 12th, about four o'clock in the afternoon, as I was walking on the quarter-deck, all the people upon

the

the forecastle called out at once, " Land right a-head ;" it
was then very black almost round the horizon, and we had
had much thunder and lightning; I looked forward under
the fore-sail, and upon the lee-bow, and saw what at first
appeared to be an island, rising in two rude craggy hills,
but upon looking to leeward I saw land joining to it, and
running a long way to the south-east: We were then steering S.W. and I sent officers to the mast-head to look out
upon the weather-beam, and they called out that they saw
land also a great way to the windward. I immediately
brought to, and sounded; we had still fifty-two fathom, but
I thought that we were embayed, and rather wished than
hoped that we should get clear before night. We made
sail and steered E.S.E. the land still having the same appearance, and the hills looking blue, as they generally do
at a little distance in dark rainy weather, and now many of
the people said that they saw the sea break upon the sandy
beaches; but having steered out for about an hour, what
we had taken for land vanished all at once, and to our astonishment appeared to have been a fog-bank. Though I
had been almost continually at sea for seven-and-twenty
years, I had never seen such a deception before; others,
however, have been equally deceived; for the master of a
ship not long since made oath, that he had seen an island
between the west end of Ireland and Newfoundland, and
even distinguished the trees that grew upon it. Yet it is
certain that no such island exists, at least it could never be
found, though several ships were afterwards sent out on
purpose to seek it. And I am sure, that if the weather had
not cleared up soon enough for us to see what we had taken
for land disappear, every man on board would freely have
made oath, that land had been discovered in this situation.

The next day, at four o'clock in the afternoon, the weather being extremely fine, the wind shifted at once to the
S.W. and began to blow fresh, the sky at the same time becoming black to windward: In a few minutes all the people
that were upon the deck were alarmed with a sudden and
unusual noise, like the breaking of the sea upon the shore.
I ordered the top-sails to be handed immediately; but before it could be done, I saw the sea approaching at some
distance, in vast billows covered with foam; I called to the
people to haul up the fore-sail, and let go the main-sheet
instantly;

instantly; for I was persuaded that if we had any sail out when the gust reached us, we should either be overset, or lose all our masts. It reached us, however, before we could raise the main tack, and laid us upon our beam-ends; the main tack was then cut, for it was become impossible to cast it off; and the main sheet struck down the first lieutenant, bruised him dreadfully, and beat out three of his teeth: the main-topsail, which was not quite handed, was split to pieces. If this squall, which came on with less warning and more violence than any I had ever seen, had taken us in the night, I think the ship must have been lost. When it came on we observed several hundred of birds flying before it, which expressed their terror by loud shrieks; it lasted about twenty minutes, and then gradually subsided. The Tamar split her main-sail, but as she was to leeward of us, she had more time to prepare. In a short time it began to blow very hard again, so that we reefed our main-sail, and lay-to all night. As morning approached the gale became more moderate, but we had still a great sea, and the wind shifting to S. by W. we stood to the westward under our courses. Soon after it was light, the sea appeared as red as blood, being covered with a small shell-fish of that colour, somewhat resembling our cray-fish, but less, of which we took up great quantities in baskets.

At half an hour past four in the morning of the 15th of November, we saw land, which had the appearance of an island about eight or nine leagues long, there being no land in sight either to the northward or southward, though by the charts it should be Cape Saint Helena, which projects from the coast to a considerable distance, and forms two bays, one to the north, and the other to the south. As the weather was very fine, I tacked and stood in for it about ten o'clock; but as there were many sunken rocks at about two leagues distance from it, upon which the sea broke very high, and the wind seemed to be gradually dying away, I tacked again and stood off. The land appeared to be barren and rocky, without either tree or bush: When I was nearest to it I sounded, and had forty-five fathom, with black muddy ground. To my great misfortune, my three lieutenants and the master were at this time so ill as to be incapable of duty, though the rest of the ship's company were in good health.

The next day I shaped my course by the chart in the account

count of Lord Anson's voyage, for Cape Blanco. In the evening it blew extremely hard at S.W. by S. so that we brought to for the night under our main-sail In the morning we made sail again, but we had a great sea; and although it was now almost Midsummer in these parts, the weather was, in every respect, much worse than it is in the Bay of Biscay at the depth of winter. About six in the evening, having carried all the sail I could, we made land, bearing about S.S.W. which, as we had a good observation of the sun, we knew to be Cape Blanco; but it now began to blow with more violence than ever, and the storm continued all night, with a sea that was continually breaking over us, so that the ship laboured very much. At four in the morning, we sounded and had forty fathom, with rocky ground; having stood off in the night, we now wore and stood in again, the storm still continuing with hail and snow; and about six o'clock we saw the land again, bearing S.W. by W. The ship was now so light, that in a gale of wind she drove bodily to leeward; so that I was very solicitous to get into Port Desire,² that I might put her hold in order, and take in sufficient ballast, to avoid the danger of being caught upon a lee-shore in her present trim. We steered in for the land with the wind at N.E. and in the evening brought to; but the wind coming to the westward, we were driven off in the night. At seven the next morning, we stood in again, steering S.W. by S. by the compass, and soon perceived the sea to break right a-head of us; we immediately sounded, and shoaled our water from thirteen to seven fathom, soon after deepening it again from seventeen to forty-two; so that we went over the end of a shoal, which a little farther to the northward might have been fatal to us. Cape Blanco at this time bore W.S.W. ½ S. distant four leagues: But we were still at a loss for Port Desire, it being impossible that any description should be more confused than that which Sir John Narborough has given of this harbour. I stood into a bay to the southward of the cape, as he directs, but could find no such place; I therefore stood along the shore to the southward, the wind blowing off the land very hard, and saw several large co-

² So called after the name of his ship, the Desire, by Sir Thomas Candish, or Cavendish, who put in there on the 27th of November, 1586. See vol. x. p. 70.—E.

lumns of smoke rising in many places, but no tree or bush, the country resembling in appearance the barren downs of England. We observed also that the water was frequently very shallow at the distance of seven or eight miles from the shore, for we had many times not more than ten fathom.

We continued to stand along the shore all day as near as possible, and in the evening we saw an island at the distance of about six leagues; in the morning we stood in for it, and found that it corresponded with Narborough's description of Penguin Island. As Port Desire is said to lie about three leagues north-west of this island, I sent the boat to look for it, and when she returned, having found it, I stood in for the land. There were thousands of seals and penguins about the ship, and near Penguin Island several smaller islands, or rather rocks. In the evening we saw a remarkable rock, rising from the water like a steeple, on the south side of the entrance of Port Desire; this rock is an excellent mark to know the harbour, which it would otherwise be difficult to find. At night, there being little wind, we anchored at the distance of four or five miles from the shore; and in the morning, with a breeze from the land, we turned up the harbour's mouth; we found it very narrow, with many rocks and shoals about it, and the most rapid tide I had ever known. I came to an anchor off the harbour in nine fathom, the entrance of the river being open, and bearing W.S.W. Penguin Island S.E. ½ E. distant about three leagues; the Steeple Rock S.W. by. W. the northermost land N.N.W. and two rocks, which are covered at half tide, and lie at the southermost extremity of a reef which runs from the same land, N.E. by N. I mention all these bearings particularly, because I think it may be of importance to future navigators, especially as the descriptions that have been given of this place by the few who have already visited it, are extremely defective. The wind blew very hard the greater part of this day, and there ran an ugly sea where we were stationed, yet I ordered our two boats to sound the harbour, and attended in my own boat myself. We found it very narrow for near two miles, with a tide running at the rate of eight miles an hour; we found also many rocks and shoals, but all the danger shows itself above water. When we came to the shore I landed, and walked a little way into the country, which as far as I could see was all downs, without a single tree or shrub. We saw the

dung

dung of many beasts, and had a glimpse of four, which ran away as soon as we came in sight, so that we could not certainly determine what they were; but we believed them to be guanicoes, many of which we afterwards saw come down to the water-side; they resemble our deer, but are much larger, the height of some being not less than thirteen hands; they are very shy and very swift. After I returned to my boat, I went farther up the harbour, and landed upon an island that was covered with seals, of which we killed above fifty, and among them many that were larger than a bullock, having before half-loaded our boat with different kinds of birds, of which, and seals, there are enough to supply the navy of England. Among the birds one was very remarkable; the head resembled that of an eagle, except that it had a large comb upon it; round the neck there was a white ruff, exactly resembling a lady's tippet; the feathers on the back were as black as jet, and as bright as the finest polish could render that mineral; the legs were remarkably strong and large, the talons were like those of an eagle, except that they were not so sharp, and the wings, when they were extended, measured from point to point no less than twelve feet.

The Tamar worked into the harbour with the tide of flood, but I kept my station with the Dolphin till I should have a leading wind, and the wind shifting to the eastward, I weighed about five o'clock in the afternoon, intending to go up with the evening flood: Before I could get under sail, however, the wind shifted again to N.W. by N. and it being low water, the ship lying but just within the harbour, and there being no tide to assist us, we were obliged to anchor near the south shore. The wind came off the land in very hard flaws, and in a short time our anchor coming home, the ship tailed on shore against a steep gravelly beach. The anchoring ground, indeed, as far as we had yet sounded, was bad, being very hard; so that, in this situation, if the wind blows fresh, there is always the greatest reason to fear that the anchor should come home before the ship can be brought up. While we were on shore, it began to blow very hard, and the tide running like a sluice, it was with the utmost difficulty that we could carry an anchor to heave us off; however, after about four hours hard labour, this was effected, and the ship floated in the stream. As there was only about six or seven feet of the after-part of her that

touched

touched the ground, there was reason to hope that she had suffered no damage ; however, I determined to unhang the rudder, that it might be examined.

During all this night and the next morning the wind blew with great violence, and we had let go our best bower anchor when we were near the shore, in hopes it would have brought us up, and had not yet been able to weigh it. We now rode in a very disagreeable situation with our small bower, and that unfortunately came home again ; we therefore got a hawser out of the Tamar, who lay in the stream, and after weighing the small bower, we got out by her assistance, and then dropped it again, most ardently wishing for fair weather, that we might get the ship properly moored.

The next day we sounded the harbour higher up, and found the ground softer, and the water not so deep ; yet the wind continued to blow so hard that we could not venture to change our station. We had found a small spring of water about half a mile inland, upon the north side of the bay, but it had a brackish taste ; I had also made another excursion of several miles into the country, which I found barren and desolate, in every direction, as far as the eye could reach. We had seen many guanicoes at a distance, but we could not get near enough to have a shot at them ; we tracked beasts of several kinds in the soil, near a pond of salt water, and among them a very large tyger : We found also a nest of ostrich's eggs, which we eat, and thought very good. It is probable that all the animals which had left marks of their feet near the salt pond, drank the water, and indeed we saw no fresh water for them. The spring that we had found, which was not perfectly fresh, was the only one of the kind that we had been able to discover ; and for that we had been obliged to dig, there being no appearance of it except a slight moisture of the ground.

On the 24th, upon slack water, we carried both the ships higher up and moored them : The extreme points of the harbour's mouth at low water bore from E. by S $\frac{1}{4}$ S. to E. ; and the Steeple rock S.E. $\frac{1}{4}$ E. We had here, at low water, but six fathom ; but at spring tides the water rises no less than four fathom and a half, which is seven-and-twenty feet. The tide indeed in this place is such as perhaps it is not in

any

any other ? It happened by some accident that one of our
men fell overboard; the boats were all alongside, and the
man was an exceeding good swimmer, yet before any assistance could be sent after him, the rapidity of the stream
had hurried him almost out of sight; we had however at
last the good fortune to save him. This day I was again
on shore, and walked six or seven miles up the country : I
saw several hares as large as a fawn; I shot one of them
which weighed more than six and twenty pounds, and if I
had had a good greyhound, I dare say the ship's company
might have lived upon hare two days in the week. In the
mean time the people on board were busy in getting up all
the cables upon deck, and clearing the hold, that a proper
quantity of ballast might be taken in, and the guns lowered
into it, except a few which it might be thought necessary
to keep above.

On the 25th, I went a good way up the harbour in the
boat, and having landed on the north side, we soon after
found an old oar of a very singular make, and the barrel of
a musket, with the king's broad arrow upon it. The mus-
ket-barrel had suffered so much from the weather, that it
might be crumbled to dust between the fingers : I imagined
it had been left there by the Wager's people, or perhaps
by Sir John Narborough. Hitherto we had found no kind
of vegetables except a species of wild peas; but though we
had seen no inhabitants, we saw 'places where they had
made their fires, which however did not appear to be recent. While we were on shore we shot some wild ducks
and a hare; the hare ran two miles after he was wounded,
though it appeared when he was taken up that a ball had
passed quite through his body. I went this day many miles
up the country, and had a long chace after one of the guanicoes, which was the largest we had seen : He frequently
stopped to look at us, when he had left us at a good dis-
　　　　　　　　　　　　　　　　　　　　　　　　　　　tance

---

³ " The harbour itself is not much more than half a mile over. On the
south shore is a remarkable rock in the form of a tower, which appears on
entering the harbour's mouth. Abreast of this rock we lay at anchor in
seven or eight fathom water, moored to the east and west, with both bow-
ers, which we found extremely necessary, on account of the strong tide
that regularly ebbs and flows every twelve hours. Indeed the ebb is so rapid, that we found by our log-line it continued to run five or six knots an
hour; and in ten minutes after the ebb is past, the flood returns with equal
velocity; besides, the wind generally blows during the whole night out of
the harbour."

tance behind, and made a noise that resembled the neighing of a horse; but when we came pretty near him he set out again, and at last, my dog being so tired that he could not run him any longer, he got quite away from us, and we saw him no more. We shot a hare however, and a little ugly animal which stunk so intolerably that none of us could go near him. The flesh of the hares here is as white as snow, and nothing can be better tasted. A serjeant of marines, and some others who were on shore at another part of the bay, had better success than fell to our share, for they killed two old guanicoes and a fawn; they were however obliged to leave them where they fell, not being able to bring them down to the water side, near six miles, without farther assistance, though they were but half the weight of those that are mentioned by Sir John Narborough; some however I saw, which could not weigh less than seven or eight and thirty stone, which is about three hundred pounds. When we returned in the evening it blew very hard, and the deck being so full of lumber that we could not hoist the boats in, we moored them astern. About midnight, the storm continuing, our six-oared cutter filled with water and broke adrift; the boat-keeper, by whose neglect this accident happened, being on board her, very narrowly escaped drowning by catching hold of the stern ladder. As it was tide of flood when she went from the ship, we knew that she must drive up the harbour; yet as the loss of her would be an irremediable misfortune, I suffered much anxiety till I could send after her in the morning, and it was then some hours before she was brought back, having driven many miles with the stream. In the mean time, I sent another party to fetch the guanicoes which our people had shot the night before; but they found nothing left except the bones, the tygers having eaten the flesh, and even cracked the bones of the limbs to come at the marrow. Several of our people had been fifteen miles up the country in search of fresh water, but could not find the least rill: We had sunk several wells to a considerable depth where the ground appeared moist, but upon visiting them, I had the mortification to find that, altogether, they would not yield more than thirty gallons in twenty-four hours: This was a discouraging circumstance, especially as our people, among other expedients, had watched the guanicoes, and seen them drink at the salt ponds. I therefore
determined

determined to leave the place as soon as the ship could be got into a little order, and the six-oared cutter repaired, which had been hauled up upon the beach for that purpose.

On the 27th, some of our people, who had been ashore on the north side of the bay to try for more guanicoes, found the skull and bones of a man, which they brought off with them, and one young guanicoe alive, which we all agreed was one of the most beautiful creatures we had ever seen: It soon grew very tame, and would suck our fingers like a calf; but, notwithstanding all our care and contrivances to feed it, it died in a few days. In the afternoon of this day it blew so hard that I was obliged to keep a considerable number of hands continually by the sheet-anchor, as there was too much reason to fear that our cables would part, which however did not happen. In the mean time, some of our people that were on shore with the carpenters, who were repairing the cutter on the south side of the bay, found two more springs of tolerable water about two miles from the beach, in a direct line from the ship's station. To these springs I sent twenty hands early in the morning with some small casks called barecas, and in a few turns they brought on board a tun of water, of which we began to be in great want. In the mean time, I went myself about twelve miles up the river in my boat, and the weather then growing bad, I went on shore: The river, as far as I could see, was very broad; there were in it a number of islands, some of which were very large, and I make no doubt but that it penetrates the country for some hundreds of miles. It was upon one of the islands that I went on shore, and I found there such a number of birds, that when they rose they literally darkened the sky, and we could not walk a step without treading upon their eggs. As they kept hovering over our heads at a little distance, the men knocked down many of them with stones and sticks, and carried off several hundreds of their eggs. After some time I left the island and landed upon the main, where our men dressed and eat their eggs, though there were young birds in most of them. I saw no traces of inhabitants on either side of the river, but great numbers of guanicoes, in herds of sixty or seventy together: They would not however suffer us to approach them, but stood and gazed at us from the hills. In this excursion the surgeon, who was of my party,

shot

shot a tyger cat, a small but very fierce animal ; for, though it was much wounded, it maintained a very sharp contest with my dog for a considerable time before it was killed.[*]

On the 29th, we completed our ballast, which the strength of the tide, and the constant gales of wind, rendered a very difficult and laborious task ; we also got on board another tun of water. On the morning of the 30th, the weather was so bad that we could not send a boat on shore ; but employed all hands on board in setting up the rigging. It grew more moderate however about noon, and I then sent a boat to procure more water. The two men who first came up to the well found there a large tyger lying upon the ground ; having gazed at each other some time, the men, who had no fire-arms, seeing the beast treat them with as much contemptuous neglect as the lion did the knight of La Mancha, began to throw stones at him : Of this insult, however, he did not deign to take the least notice, but continued stretched upon the ground in great tranquillity till the rest of the party came up, and then he very leisurely rose and walked away.

On the first of December, our cutter being thoroughly repaired, we took her on board, but the weather was so bad that we could not get off any water : The next day we struck the tents which had been set up at the watering-place, and got all ready for sea. The two wells from which we got our water bear about S.S.E. of the Steeple rock, from which they are distant about two miles and a half ; but I fixed a mark near them, that they might be still more easily found than by their bearings. During our stay in this harbour, we sounded every part of it with great care, as high as a ship could go, and found that there is no danger but what may be seen at low water ; so that now fresh water is found, though at some distance from the beach, it would be a very convenient place for ships to touch at, if it were not for the rapidity of the tide. The country about the bay
　　　　　　　　　　　　　　　　　　　　　abounds

---

[*] " On the south shore the rocks are not so numerous as on the north side ; and there are more hills and deep vallies ; but they are covered only by high grass and a few small shrubs. Hence this is but a bad place to touch at, by any ship that is under the necessity of wooding and watering. Our commodore, in order to clear the ground of the overgrown grass, which grew in some places in great quantities, and also to improve the soil, which appeared to be of a barren sandy nature, gave orders for the grass to be set on fire in different places, which was no sooner done, than the flames ran so fast, that in less than half an hour they spread several miles round."

abounds with guanicoes, and a great variety of wild fowl, particularly ducks, geese, widgeon, and sea-pies, besides many others for which we have no name. Here is also such plenty of excellent mussels, that a boat may be loaded with them every time it is low water. Wood indeed is scarce; however in some parts of this coast there are bushes, which in a case of necessity might produce a tolerable supply of fuel.

On Wednesday the 5th of December, I unmoored, in order to get out, but the best bower came up foul, and before we could heave short upon the small bower, the tide of ebb made strong; for at this place slack water scarcely continues ten minutes; so that we were obliged to wait till it should be low water. Between five and six in the evening, we weighed, and steered out E.N.E. with a fresh gale at N.N.W.

Section III.

*Course from Port Desire, in search of Pepys' Island, and af-
terwards to the Coast of Patagonia, with a Description of the
Inhabitants.*

As soon as we were out of the bay, we steered for Pepys' Island, which is said to lie in latitude 47° S. Our latitude was now 47° 22′ S. longitude 65° 49′ W.; Port Desire bore S. 66° W. distant twenty-three leagues; and Pepys' Island, according to Halley's chart, E. ¼ N. distant thirty-four leagues. The variation here was 19° E.

We continued our course the next day with a pleasant gale and fine weather, so that we began to think that this part of the world was not wholly without a summer. On the 7th, I found myself much farther to the northward than I expected, and therefore supposed the ship's way had been influenced by a current. I had now made eighty degrees easting, which is the distance from the main at which Pepys' Island is placed in Halley's chart, but unhappily we have no certain account of the place. The only person who pretends to have seen it, is Cowley,[1] the account of whose voyage

---

[1] For an account of his voyage, and of his supposed discovery, see vol. x. page 217. It seems impossible to reconcile the veracity of his narration with the non-existence of the island here spoken of, which is not now al-

age is now before me; and all he says of its situation is, that
it lies in latitude 47° S.; for he says nothing of its longitude: He says, indeed, that it has a fine harbour; but he
adds, that the wind blew so hard he could not get into it,
and that he therefore stood away to the southward. At
this time I also was steering southward; for the weather
being extremely fine, I could see very far to the northward
of the situation in which it is laid down. As I supposed it
must lie to the eastward of us, if indeed it had any existence,
I made the Tamar signal to spread early in the afternoon;
and as the weather continued to be very clear, we could see,
between us, at least twenty leagues. We steered S.E. by
the compass, and at night brought-to, being, by my account, in latitude 47° 18′ S. The next morning it blew very
hard at N.W. by N. and I still thought the island might lie
to the eastward; I therefore intended to stand about thirty
leagues that way, and if I found no island, to return into
the latitude of 47° again. But a hard gale coming on, with
a great sea, I brought-to about six o'clock in the evening
under the main-sail; and at six o'clock the next morning,
the wind being at W.S.W. we made sail again under our
courses to the northward. I now judged myself to be about
sixteen leagues to the eastward of the track I had run before: Port Desire bore S. 80° 53′ W. distant ninety-four
leagues; and in this situation I saw a great quantity of
rock-weed, and many birds. We continued to stand to the
northward the next day under our courses, with a hard gale
from S.W. to N.W. and a great sea. At night, being in
latitude 46° 50′ S. I wore ship, and stood in to the westward again, our ships having spread every day as far as they
could be seen by each other: And on the 11th at noon, being now certain that there could be no such island as is
mentioned by Cowley, and laid down by Halley under the
name of Pepys' Island, I resolved to stand in for the main,
and take in wood and water, of which both ships were in
great want, at the first convenient place I could find, especially as the season was advancing very fast, and we had
no time to lose. From this time we continued to haul in
for the land as the winds would permit, and kept a look-out
                                                        for

lowed to hold a place in our maps. But the reader will be better able to
form a correct opinion on this subject, after he has read the 5th Section,
where the discovery of Cowley is pretty fully discussed.—E.

for the islands of Sebald de Wert,[2] which, by all the charts
we had on board, could not be far from our track : A great
number of birds were every day about the ship, and large
whales were continually swimming by her.   The weather
in general was fine, but very cold, and we all agreed, notwithstanding the hope we had once formed, that the only
difference between the middle of summer here, and the middle of winter in England, lies in the length of the days.   On
Saturday the 15th, being in latitude 50° 33′ S. longitude
66° 59′ W. we were overtaken about six in the evening by
the hardest gale at S.W. that I was ever in, with a sea still
higher than any I had seen in going round Cape Horn with
Lord Anson : I expected every moment that it would fill
us, our ship being much too deep-waisted for such a voyage : It would have been safest to put before it under our
bare poles, but our stock of fresh water was not sufficient,
and I was afraid of being driven so far off the land as not
to be able to recover it before the whole was exhausted ;
we therefore lay-to under a balanced mizen, and shipped
many heavy seas, though we found our skreen bulk-heads
of infinite service.

The storm continued with unabated violence the whole
night, but about eight in the morning began to subside.
At ten, we made sail under our courses, and continued to
steer for the land till Tuesday the 18th, when, at four in the
morning, we saw it from the mast-head.   Our latitude was
now 51° 8′ S. our longitude 71° 4′ W. and Cape Virgin Mary, the north entrance of the Streights of Magellan, bore S.
19° 50′ W. distant nineteen leagues.   As we had little or no
wind, we could not get in with the land this day ; the next
morning, however, it being northerly, I stood in to a deep
bay, at the bottom of which there appeared to be a harbour, but I found it barred, the sea breaking quite from
one side of it to the other ; and at low water I could perceive that it was rocky, and almost all dry : The water was
shoal at a good distance from it, and I was in six fathom
before I stood out again.   In this place there seemed to be
plenty of fish, and we saw many porpoises swimming after
them

[2] These may be considered the same as what are now called Falkland's
Islands, the name said to have been given them by Captain Strong, in 1639;
but they had been frequently seen before that period, as by Sir Richard
Hawkins in 1594, and Davis in 1592. They have various other names, and
are pretty well known.—E.

them, that were as white as snow, with black spots; a very uncommon and beautiful sight. The land here has the same appearance as about Port Desire, all downs, without a single tree.

At break of day, on the 20th, we were off Cape Fairweather, which bore about west at the distance of four leagues, and we had here but thirteen fathom water, so that it appears necessary to give that cape a good birth. From this place I ran close on shore to Cape Virgin Mary, but I found the coast to lie S. S. E. very different from Sir John Narborough's description, and a long spit of sand running to the southward of the cape for above a league: In the evening I worked up close to this spit of sand, having seen many guanicoes feeding in the vallies as we went along, and a great smoke all the afternoon, about four or five leagues up the strait, upon the north shore.[5]   At this place I came to an anchor in fifteen fathom water, but the Tamar was so far to leeward, that she could not fetch the anchoring ground, and therefore kept under way all night.

The next morning, at day-break, I got again under sail, and seeing the same smoke that I had observed the day before, I stood in for it, and anchored about two miles from the shore. This is the place where the crew of the Wager, as they were passing the strait in their boat, after the loss of the vessel, saw a number of horsemen, who waved what appeared to be white handkerchiefs, inviting them to come on shore, which they were very desirous to have done, but it blew so hard that they were obliged to stand out to sea.   Bulkeley, the gunner of the Wager, who has published some account of her voyage, says, that they were in doubt whether these people were Europeans who had been shipwrecked upon the coast, or native inhabitants of the country about the river Gallagoes.   Just as we came to an anchor, I saw with my glass exactly what was seen by the people in the Wager, a number of horsemen riding backward and forward, directly abreast of the ship, and waving somewhat white, as an invitation for us to come on shore.   As I was very desirous to know what these people were, I ordered out my twelve-oared boat, and went towards the beach,
                                                                with

----

[5] " At eight we discovered a good deal of smoke issuing from different quarters, and on our nearer approach, could plainly perceive a number of people on horseback."

with Mr Marshall, my second lieutenant, and a party of men, very well armed; Mr Cumming, my first lieutenant, following in the six-oared cutter.[6] When we came within a little distance of the shore, we saw, as near as I can guess, about five hundred people, some on foot, but the greater part on horseback : They drew up upon a stony spit, which ran a good way into the sea, and upon which it was very bad landing, for the water was shallow, and the stones very large. The people on shore kept waving and hallooing, which, as we understood, were invitations to land ; I could not perceive that they had any weapons among them, however I
made

[6] Now for the goblins, the giants of Patagonia! Some account of the controversy about them is reserved for another place. In the mean time the reader may amuse himself with the following notices in addition to the substance of the text ; they are extracted from the account of this voyage, already referred to in the preceding notes. " On our first approaching the coast, evident signs of fear appeared among those in the boat, on seeing men of such enormous size, while some, perhaps to encourage the rest, observed that these gigantic people were as much surprised at the sight of our muskets, as we were at seeing them, though it is highly probable they did not know their use, and had never heard the report of a gun. But this was sufficient to remind us, that our fire-arms gave us an advantage much superior to that derived from height of stature and personal strength."— " The commodore and chief officers entered upon a short consultation on the propriety of landing. The first officer, fired with the thoughts of making a full discovery in regard to these Indians, who have been so much the subject of conversation among the English, made a motion to approach nearer and jump on shore ; but the commodore objected to it, and would not suffer any man to go before himself."—" Immediately on our landing, they came about us to the number of two hundred or more, looking at us with evident marks of surprise, and smiling, as it should seem, at the great disproportion of our stature."—" They were so delighted with the different trinkets, which they had an opportunity of viewing, as they hung round their necks, and fell down before their bosoms, that the commodore could scarcely restrain them from caressing him, particularly the women, whose large and masculine features corresponded with the enormous size of their bodies. *Their middle stature seemed to be about 8 feet ; their extreme 9 and upwards ;* though he did not measure them by *any standard,* and had *reason* to believe them rather more than less."—" The commodore himself measures full six feet, and though he stood on tip toe, he could but just reach the crown of one of the Indians' heads, who was not, *by far,* the tallest among them."—" They seemed particularly pleased with Lieutenant Cumming, on account of his stature, he being 6 feet 2 inches high, and some of them patted him on the shoulder, but their hands fell with such force, that it affected his whole frame." The two last paragraphs, with more to the same effect, are given in a note, and are said to have been communicated by gentlemen who were present on this occasion. It is right to add that their names are not mentioned. So much at present for these monsters.—E.

made signs that they should retire to a little distance, with which they immediately complied : They continued to shout with great vociferation, and in a short time we landed, though not without great difficulty, most of the boat's crew being up to the middle in water.   I drew up my people upon the beach, with my officers at their head, and gave orders that none of them should move from that station, till I should either call or beckon to them.   I then went forward alone, towards the Indians, but perceiving that they retired as I advanced, I made signs that one of them should come near : As it happened, my signals were understood, and one of them, who afterwards appeared to be a chief, came towards me : He was of a gigantic stature, and seemed to realize the tales of monsters in a human shape : He had the skin of some wild beast thrown over his shoulders, as a Scotch highlander wears his plaid, and was painted so as to make the most hideous appearance I ever beheld : Round one eye was a large circle of white, a circle of black surrounded the other, and the rest of his face was streaked with paint of different colours : I did not measure him, but if I may judge of his height by the proportion of his stature to my own, it could not be much less than seven feet. When this frightful Colossus came up, we muttered somewhat to each other as a salutation, and I then walked with him towards his companions, to whom, as I advanced, I made signs that they should sit down, and they all readily complied : There were among them many women, who seemed to be proportionably large ; and few of the men were less than the chief who had come forward to meet me.   I had heard their voices very loud at a distance, and when I came near, I perceived a good number of very old men, who were chanting some unintelligible words in the most doleful cadence I ever heard, with an air of serious solemnity, which inclined me to think that it was a religious ceremony : They were all painted and clothed nearly in the same manner ; the circles round the two eyes were in no instance of one colour, but they were not universally black and white, some being white and red, and some red and black : Their teeth were as white as ivory, remarkably even and well set ; but except the skins, which they wore with the hair inwards, most of them were naked, a few only having upon their legs a kind of boot, with a short pointed stick fastened to each heel, which served as a spur.   Having looked round upon these

enormous

enormous goblins with no small astonishment, and with some difficulty made those that were still galloping up sit down with the rest, I took out a quantity of yellow and white beads, which I distributed among them, and which they re-ceived with very strong expressions of pleasure : I then took out a whole piece of green silk ribband, and giving the end of it into the hands of one of them, I made the person that sat next take hold of it, and so on as far as it would reach : All this while they sat very quietly, nor did any of those that held the ribband attempt to pull it from the rest, though I perceived that they were still more delighted with it than with the beads. While the ribband was thus extended, I took out a pair of scissars, and cut it between each two of the Indians that held it, so that I left about a yard in the possession of every one, which I afterwards tied about their heads, where they suffered it to remain without so much as touching it while I was with them. Their peaceable and orderly beha-viour on this occasion certainly did them honour, especial-ly as my presents could not extend to the whole company : Neither impatience to share the new finery, nor curiosity to gain a nearer view of me and what I was doing, brought any one of them from the station that I had allotted him.

These people, however, were not wholly strangers to Eu-ropean commodities, for upon a closer attention, I percei-ved among them one woman who had bracelets either of brass, or very pale gold, upon her arms, and some beads of blue glass, strung upon two long queues of hair, which be-ing parted at the top, hung down over each shoulder be-fore her: She was of a most enormous size, and her face was, if possible, more frightfully painted than the rest. I had a great desire to learn where she got her beads and bracelets, and enquired by all the signs I could devise, but found it impossible to make myself understood. One of the men shewed me the bowl of a tobacco-pipe, which was made of a red earth, but I soon found that they had no tobacco among them ; and this person made me understand that he wanted some : Upon this I beckoned to my people, who re-mained upon the beach, drawn up as I had left them, and three or four of them ran forward, imagining that I wanted them. The Indians, who, as I had observed, kept their eyes almost continually upon them, no sooner saw some of them advance, than they all rose up with a great clamour, and were leaving the place, as I supposed to get their arms,

which

which were probably left at a little distance : To prevent
mischief, therefore, and put an end to the alarm, which had
thus accidentally been spread among them, I ran to meet
the people who were, in consequence of my signal, coming
from the beach, and as soon as I was within hearing I hallooed to them, and told them that I would have only one
come up with all the tobacco that he could collect from the
rest.   As soon as the Indians saw this, they recovered from
their surprise, and every one returned to his station, except
a very old man, who came up to me, and sung a long song,
which I much regretted my not being able to understand : Before the song was well finished, Mr Cumming came up with
the tobacco, and I could not but smile at the astonishment
which I saw expressed in his countenance, upon perceiving
himself, though six feet two inches high, become at once a
pigmy among giants ; for these people may indeed more
properly be called giants than tall men : Of the few among
us who are full six feet high, scarcely any are broad and
muscular in proportion to their stature, but look rather like
men of the common bulk, run up accidentally to an unusual
height ; and a man who should measure only six feet two
inches, and equally exceed a stout well-set man of the common stature in breadth and muscle, would strike us rather
as being of a gigantic race, than as an individual accidentally anomalous ; our sensations therefore, upon seeing five
hundred people, the shortest of whom were at least four
inches taller, and bulky in proportion, may be easily imagined.   After I had presented the tobacco, four or five of
the chief men came up to me, and, as I understood by the
signs they made, wanted me to mount one of the horses,
and go with them to their habitations, but as it would upon
every account have been imprudent to comply, I made signs
in return that I must go back to the ship ; at this they expressed great concern, and sat down in their stations again.
During our pantomimical conference, an old man often laid
his head down upon the stones, and shutting his eyes for
about half a minute, afterwards pointed first to his mouth,
and then to the hills, meaning, as I imagined, that if I
would stay with them till the morning they would furnish me
with some provisions, but this offer I was obliged to decline.
When I left them, not one of them offered to follow us, but
as long as I could see them continued to sit quietly in their
places.   I observed that they had with them a great number

ber of dogs, with which I suppose they chase the wild animals which serve them for food. The horses were not large,
nor in good case, yet they appeared to be nimble and well
broken. The bridle was a leathern thong, with a small piece
of wood that served for a bit, and the saddles resembled the
pads that are in use among the country people in England.
The women rode astride, and both men and women without
stirrups; yet they galloped fearlessly over the spit upon which
we landed, the stones of which were large, loose, and slippery.

SECTION IV.

*Passage up the Strait of Magellan to Port Famine; with some
Account of that Harbour, and the adjacent Coast.*

SOON after I returned on board I got under way, and
worked up the strait, which is here about nine leagues
broad, with the flood, not with a view to pass through it,
but in search of some place where I might get a supply of
wood and water, not chusing to trust wholly to the finding
of Falkland's Islands, which I determined afterwards to seek.
About eight in the evening, the tide of ebb beginning to
make, I anchored in five-and-twenty fathoms. Point Possession bore N.N.E. at about three miles distance, and some
remarkable hummocks on the north, which Bulkeley, from
their appearance, has called the Asses Ears, W. ½ N.

At three in the morning of the 22d we weighed with the
wind at E. and steered S.W. by W. about twelve miles.
During this course we went over a bank, of which no notice has hitherto been taken : At one time we had but six
fathoms and a half, but in two or three casts we had thirteen. When our water was shallowest, the Asses Ears bore
N.W. by W. ¼ W. distant three leagues, and the north
point of the first narrow W. by S. distant between five and
six miles. We then steered S.W. by S. near six miles to
the entrance of the first narrow, and afterwards S.S.W. about
six miles, which brought us through : The tide here was so
strong that the passage was very rapid.[1] During this course
we saw a single Indian upon the south shore, who kept wa-

[1] " This narrow is about three miles over, and is the narrowest part of
the straits." Wallis agrees as to the former remark.—E.

ving to us as long as we were in sight; we saw also some guanicoes upon the hills, though Wood, in the account of his voyage, says there were none upon that shore. As soon as we had passed the first narrow we entered a little sea, for we did not come in sight of the entrance of the second narrow till we had run two leagues. The distance from the first to the second narrow is about eight leagues, and the course S.W. by W.² The land is very high on the north side of the second narrow, which continues for about five leagues, and we steered through it S.W. ½ W. with soundings from twenty to five-and-twenty fathoms: We went out of the west end of this narrow about noon, and steered south about three leagues for Elizabeth's island; but the wind then coming right against us, we anchored in seven fathoms. The island bore S.S.E. distant about a mile, and Bartholomew's island bore E.S.E. In the evening, six Indians upon the island came down to the water side, and continued waving and hallooing to us for a long time; but as my people wanted rest, I was unwilling to employ them in hoisting out a boat, and the Indians, seeing their labour fruitless, at length went away. While we were steering from Point Possession to the first narrow, the flood set to the southward, but as soon as we entered the narrow, it set strongly over to the north shore: It flows here at the full and change of the moon about ten o'clock. Between the first and the second narrow the flood sets to the S.W. and the ebb to the N.E.; after the west end of the second narrow is past, the course, with a leading wind, is S. by E. three leagues. Between the islands of Elizabeth and Saint Bartholomew the channel is about half a mile over,³ and the water is deep. We found the flood set very strongly to the southward, with a great rippling, but round the islands the tides set many different ways.

In the morning of the 23d we weighed with the wind at S. by W. and worked between Elizabeth and Bartholomew's island: Before the tide was spent we got over upon the north shore,

---

² " At the entrance, or east end of the second narrow, lies Cape Gregory, which is a white cliff of a moderate height, and a little to the northward of it is a sandy bay, in which you may ride in eight fathoms water, with very good anchorage." " At the west end of the second narrow on the south shore, is a white headland, called Sweepstakes Foreland." See also Wallis.—E.

³ The other work says a mile and a half.—E.

shore, and anchored in ten fathom. Saint George's island
then bore N.E. by N. distant three leagues; a point of land,
which I called *Porpois Point*, N. by W. distant about five
miles, and the southermost land S. by E. distant about two
miles. In the evening we weighed and steered S. by E.
about five miles along the north shore, at about one mile's
distance, with regular soundings, from seven to thirteen fathom, and every where good ground. At ten o'clock at
night we anchored in thirteen fathom; Sandy Point then
bearing S. by E. distant four miles; Porpois Point W.N.W.
three leagues; and Saint George's island N.E. four leagues.
All along this shore the flood sets to the southward; at the
full and change of the moon it flows about eleven o'clock,
and the water rises about fifteen feet.

The next morning I went out in my boat in search of
Fresh Water Bay; I landed with my second lieutenant upon Sandy Point, and having sent the boat along the shore,
we walked abreast of her.[4] Upon the point we found plenty
of wood, and very good water, and for four or five miles the
shore was exceedingly pleasant. Over the point there is a
fine level country, with a soil that, to all appearance, is extremely rich; for the ground was covered with flowers of
various kinds, that perfumed the air with their fragrance;
and among them there were berries, almost innumerable,
where the blossoms had been shed: we observed that the
grass was very good, and that it was intermixed with a great
number of peas in blossom. Among this luxuriance of herbage we saw many hundreds of birds feeding, which, from
their form, and the uncommon beauty of their plumage, we
called painted geese. We walked more than twelve miles,
and found great plenty of fine fresh water, but not the bay
that we sought; for we saw no part of the shore, in all our
walk from Sandy Point, where a boat could land without
the utmost hazard, the water being very shoal, and the sea
breaking very high. We fell in with a great number of the
huts or wigwams of the Indians, which appeared to have
been

---

[4] " We sent the boat to sound between Elizabeth's and St Bartholomew's Islands, and found it a very good channel, with very deep water. On
this occasion we saw a number of Indians, that hallooed to us from Elizabeth's Island. Both the men and the women were of the middle size, well-
made, and with smooth black hair; they appear to be of an olive-coloured
complexion, but rendered more red than they are naturally, by rubbing a
red earth mixed with grease all over their bodies. They are very active and
swift of foot," &c.

been very lately deserted, for in some of them the fires which they had kindled were scarcely extinguished; they were in little recesses of the woods, and always close to fresh water. In many places we found plenty of wild celery, and a variety of plants, which probably would be of great benefit to seamen after a long voyage. In the evening we walked back again, and found the ships at anchor in Sandy Point Bay, at the distance of about half a mile from the shore. The keen air of this place made our people so voraciously hungry that they could have eaten three times their allowance; I was therefore very glad to find some of them employed in hauling the seine, and others on shore with their guns; sixty very large mullets were just taken with the seine as I came up; and the gunners had good sport, for the place abounded with geese, teale, snipes, and other birds, that were excellent food.

On the 25th, Christmas day, we observed by two altitudes, and found the latitude of Sandy Point to be 53° 10' S. At eight in the morning we weighed, and having sailed five leagues from Sandy Point, in the direction of S. by E. ½ E. we anchored again in thirty-two fathom, about a mile from the shore; the south point of the Fresh Water Bay then bearing N.N.W. distant about four miles; and the southermost land S.E. by S. As we sailed along the shore, at about two miles distance, we had no ground with sixty fathom; but at the distance of one mile we had from twenty to thirty-two fathom. At the full and change of the moon, the tide flows off Fresh Water Bay at twelve o'clock; it runs but little, yet flows very much by the shore.

On the 26th, at eight o'clock in the morning, we weighed, with the wind at E.N.E. and steered S.S.E. for Port Famine. At noon, St Anne's Point, which is the northermost point of that port, bore S. by E. ½ E. distant three leagues. Along this shore, at the distance of two or three miles, we had very deep water; but within a mile had ground with twenty-five or thirty fathom. From St Anne's Point a reef of rocks runs out S.E. by E. about two miles; and at the distance of two cables' length from this reef the water will suddenly shoal from sixty-five to thirty-five and twenty fathom. The point itself is very steep, so that there is no sounding till it is approached very near, and great care must be taken in standing into Port Famine, especially if the ship is as far southward as Sedger river, for the water
will

will shoal at once from thirty to twenty, fifteen, and twelve fathom ; and at about two cables' length farther in, at more than a mile from the shore, there is but nine feet water when the tide is out. By hauling close round St Anne's Point, soundings will soon be got ; and as the water shoals very fast, it is not safe to go farther in, when there is no more than seven fathom ; the strait here is not more than four leagues wide.

The next day at noon, having had little wind and calms, we anchored at Port Famine, close to the shore, and found our situation very safe and convenient ; we had shelter from all winds except the S.E. which seldom blows, and if a ship should be driven ashore in the bottom of the bay, she could receive no damage, for it is all fine soft ground. We found drift-wood here sufficient to have furnished a thousand sail, so that we had no need to take the trouble of cutting green. The water of Sedger river is excellent, but the boats cannot get in till about two hours flood, because at low water it is very shallow for about three quarters of a mile. I went up it about four miles in my boat, and the fallen trees then rendered it impossible to go farther : I found it, indeed, not only difficult but dangerous to get up thus far. The stream is very rapid, and many stumps of trees lie hidden under it : One of these made its way through the bottom of my boat, and in an instant she was full of water. We got on shore as well as we could ; and afterwards, with great difficulty, hauled her up upon the side of the river : Here we contrived to stop the hole in her bottom, so as that we made a shift to get her down to the river's mouth, where she was soon properly repaired by the carpenter. On each side of this river there are the finest trees I ever saw, and I make no doubt but that they would supply the British navy with the best masts in the world. Some of them are of a great height, and more than eight feet in diameter, which is proportionably more than eight yards in circumference ; so that four men, joining hand in hand, could not compass them : Among others, we found the pepper tree, or Winter's bark, in great plenty.[5] Among these woods, notwithstanding the
coldness

---

[3] " In this part may be found a considerable quantity of excellent wood, either green or dry, the latter lying along the shore on both sides the straits, which are almost covered with the trees, that, having grown on the banks, have been blown down by the high winds. These trees are some-what like our birch, but are of so considerable a size, that the trunks of

coldness of the climate, there are innumerable parrots, and other birds of the most beautiful plumage. I shot every day geese and ducks enough to serve my own table and several others, and every body on board might have done the same : We had, indeed, great plenty of fresh provisions of all kinds, for we caught as much fish every day as served the companies of both ships. As I was much on shore here, I tracked many wild beasts in the sand, but never saw one ; we also found many huts or wigwams, but never met with an Indian. The country between this port and Cape Forward, which is distant about four leagues, is extremely fine, the soil appears to be very good, and there are no less than three pretty large rivers, besides several brooks.[6]

While we lay here, I went one day to Cape Forward, and when I set out I intended to have gone farther ; but the weather became so bad, with heavy rain, that we were glad to stop there, and make a great fire to dry our clothes, which were wet through. From the place where we stopped, the Indians had been gone so lately, that the wood, which lay half burnt, where they had made their fire, was still warm ; and soon after our fire was kindled, we perceived that another was kindled directly opposite to it, on the Terra del Fuego shore ; probably as a signal, which, if we had been Indians, we should have understood. After we were dried and refreshed at our fire, the rain having abated, I walked cross the Cape, to see how the Streight ran, which I found to be about W.N.W. The hills, as far as I could see, were of an immense height, very craggy, and covered with snow quite from the summit to the base. I made also another excursion along the shore to the northward, and found the country for many miles exceedingly pleasant, the ground being, in many places, covered with flowers, which were not inferior to those that are commonly found in our gardens, either in beauty or fragrance ; and if
it

some of them are two feet (surely an error, yards must be intended) and a half in diameter, and sixty feet in length. Many of these we cut down for our carpenters use, and found that, when properly dried, they were very serviceable, though not fit for masts." The bark named Winter's in the text, is so called after Captain Winter, who discovered it in 1567. It was long held a specific for scurvy, and is now commended in certain cases as an article in diet-drinks. According to the work just now quoted, the sailors often used it in pies instead of spice, and found it palatable.—E.

[6] The other account gives a very spirited description of the scenery of this agreeable spot—but it is too long for insertion here.—E.

it were not for the severity of the cold in winter, this country might, in my opinion, be made, by cultivation, one of
the finest in the world.   I had set up a small tent at the
bottom of this bay, close to a little rivulet, and just at the
skirts of a wood, soon after the ship came to an anchor,
where three men were employed in washing: They slept
on shore ; but soon after sunset were awakened out of their
first sleep by the roaring of some wild beasts, which the
darkness of the night, and the solitariness of their situation
in this pathless desert, rendered horrid beyond imagination :
the tone was hollow and deep, so that the beasts, of whatever kind, were certainly large, and the poor fellows perceived that they drew nearer and nearer, as the sound every
minute became more loud.   From this time sleep was renounced for the night, a large fire was immediately kindled,
and a constant blaze kept up : This prevented the beasts
from invading the tent; but they continued to prowl round
it at a little distance, with incessant howlings, till the day
broke, and then, to the great comfort of the affrighted sailors, they disappeared.

At this place, not far from where the ship lay, there is a
hill that has been cleared of wood, and we supposed this
to be the spot where the Spaniards formerly had a settlement.[7]   One of the men, as he was passing over this hill,
perceived that, in a particular part, the ground returned the
sound of his foot, as if it was hollow : He therefore repass-
ed it several times, and finding the effect still the same, he
conceived a strong notion that something was buried there ;
when he came on board, he related what he had remarked
to me, and I went myself to the spot, with a small party,
furnished with spades and pickaxes, and saw the spot opened to a considerable depth, but we found nothing, nor did
there appear to be any hollow or vault as was expected.
As we were returning through the woods, we found two
very large skulls, which, by the teeth, appeared to have belonged to some beasts of prey, but of what kind we could
not guess.

Having continued here till Friday the 4th of January,
and completed the wood and water of both ships, for which
purpose I had entered the streight, I determined to steer back
again in search of Falkland's Islands.

SECTION

---

[7] See some account of this settlement in the Voyage of Captain Wallis,
Section III.

SECTION V.

The Course back from Port Famine to Falkland's Islands, with some Account of the Country.

WE weighed anchor at four o'clock in the morning, and worked to windward out of the harbour: The wind continued contrary at N.N.E. till about one o'clock the next day, when it shifted to W.S.W. and blew a fresh gale. We steered N.W. by N. four leagues, and then three leagues north, between Elizabeth and Bartholomew Islands: We then steered from the islands N. by E. three leagues, to the second narrow; and steered through N.E.¼E. continuing the same course from the second narrow to the first, which was a run of eight leagues. As the wind still continued to blow fresh, we steered through the first narrow against the flood, in the direction of N.N.E.; but about ten o'clock at night, the wind dying away, the flood set us back again into the entrance of the first narrow, where we were obliged to anchor, in forty fathom, within two cables' length of the shore. The tide flows here, at the full and change of the moon, about two o'clock, and runs full six knots an hour.

At one o'clock the next morning, we weighed, with a light northerly breeze; and about three, we passed the first narrow a second time. Having now seen the ship safe through, and being quite exhausted with fatigue, as I had been upon the deck all the preceding day, and all night, I went into my cabin to get some rest. I lay down, and soon fell asleep; but in less than half an hour, I was awakened by the beating of the ship upon a bank: I instantly started up, and ran upon the deck, where I soon found that we had grounded upon a hard sand. It was happy for us, that at this time it was stark calm; and I immediately ordered out the boats to carry an anchor astern, where the water was deepest: The anchor took the ground, but before we could work the capstern, in order to heave the ship off to it, she went off, by the mere rising of the tide. It happened fortunately to be just low water when she went aground, and there was fifteen feet forward, and six fathom a very little way astern. The master told me, that at the

last

last cast of the lead, before we were aground, he had thirteen fathom; so that the water shoaled at once no less than sixty-three feet.

This bank, which has not been mentioned by any navigator who has passed the streight, is extremely dangerous; especially as it lies directly in the fair way between Cape Virgin Mary and the first narrow, and just in the middle between the south and north shores. It is more than two leagues long, and full as broad; in many places also it is very steep. When we were upon it, Point Possession bore N.E. distant three leagues; and the entrance of the narrow S.W. distant two leagues. I afterwards saw many parts of it dry, and the sea breaking very high over other parts of it, where the water was shallow. A ship that should ground upon this shoal in a gale of wind, would probably be very soon beaten to pieces.

About six o'clock in the morning, we anchored in fifteen fathom, the shoal bearing N.N.W.¼W. at the distance of about half a mile. At noon, we weighed with a light breeze at N.E. and worked with the ebb tide till two; but finding the water shoal, we anchored again in six fathom and a half, at about the distance of half a mile from the south side of the shoal; the Asses' Ears then bearing N.W. by W. distant four leagues, and the south point of the entrance of the first Narrow W.S.W. distant about three leagues. At this time the opening of the narrow was shut in, and upon sending out the boats to sound, they discovered a channel between the shoal and the south shore of the streight. The Tamar in the mean time, as she was endeavouring to come near us, was very near going on shore, having once got into three fathom, but soon after came to an anchor in the channel between the shoal and the north shore.

The next morning, about eight o'clock, we weighed, with little wind at W.S.W. and steered about half a mile S.E. by E. when, having deepened our water to thirteen fathom, we steered between the E. and E.N.E. along the south side of the shoal, at the distance of about seven miles from the south shore, keeping two boats at some distance, one on each bow, to sound. The depth of water was very irregular, varying continually between nine and fifteen fathom; and upon hauling nearer to the shoal, we had very soon no more than seven fathom: The boats went over a bank, up-

on

on which they had six fathom and a half; it being then low water, but within the bank, they had thirteen fathom. At noon, we were to the eastward of the shoal, and as we hauled over to the north shore, we soon deepened our water to twenty fathom. Point Possession at this time bore N.N.W. distant between four and five leagues, the Asses' Ears W.N.W. distant six leagues, and Cape Virgin Mary N.E.½E. distant about seven leagues. From this situation we steered N.E. by E. for the south end of the spit which runs to the southward of the Cape, and had no soundings with five and twenty fathom. At four in the afternoon, Cape Virgin Mary bore N.E. and the south end of the spit N.E. by E. distant three leagues. At eight the next morning, the Cape bore N. by W. distant two leagues. Our latitude was 51° 50', and our soundings were eleven and twelve fathom. We now brought-to for the Tamar, who had come through the north channel, and was some leagues astern of us, and while we were waiting for her coming up, the officer of the watch informed me that the head of the main-mast was sprung: I immediately went up to look at it myself, and found it split almost in a straight line perpendicularly for a considerable length, but I could not discover exactly how far the fissure went, for the cheeks that were upon the mast. We imagined this to have happened in the very hard gale that had overtaken us some time before; but as it was of more importance to contrive how to repair the damage, than discover how it happened, we immediately put on a strong fish, and woolded it so well, that we had reason to hope the mast would be as serviceable as ever. Cape Virgin Mary now bore S. 62° W. distant twenty-one leagues, and our latitude was 51° 50' S. longitude 69° 56' W.; the variation 20° E.

On the 9th, having sailed S. 67° E. our latitude was 52° 8' S. our longitude 68° 31' W. and Cape Virgin Mary bore S. 83° W. distant thirty-three leagues.

On the 10th, there having been little wind for the last twenty-four hours, between the north and east, with thick foggy weather, our course was N. 18° W. for thirty-nine miles. Our latitude was 51° 31' S. longitude 68° 44' W.; variation 20° E. and Cape Virgin Mary bore S. 60° W. distant thirty-three leagues.

On the 11th, we had strong gales at S.W. with a great sea; Our course was N. 87° E. for ninety-nine miles. Our

latitude

latitude was 51° 24' S. longitude 66° 10' W.   Cape Virgin
Mary bore S. 73° 8' W. distant sixty-five leagues, and Cape
Fair-weather W. 2° S. distant seventy leagues; the variation
was now 19° E.   About seven in the evening, I thought I
saw land a-head of us, but the Tamar being some leagues
astern, I wore ship, and made an easy sail off: The next
morning, at break of day, I stood in again, the wind having
shifted in the night to N.W. and about four o'clock I recovered sight of the land a-head, which had the appearance of three islands: I imagined they might be the islands
of Sebald de Wert, but intending to stand between them,
I found that the land which had appeared to be separated,
was joined by some very low ground, which formed a deep
bay.   As soon as I had made this discovery, I tacked and
stood out again, and at the same time saw land a great way
to the southward, which I made no doubt was the same that
is mentioned in the charts by the name of the New Islands.
As I was hauling out of this bay, I saw a long, low shoal of
rocks, stretching out for more than a league to the northward of us, and another of the same kind lying between
that and what we had taken for the northernmost of De
Wert's Islands.   This land, except the low part, which is
not seen till it is approached near, consists of high, craggy,
barren rocks, which in appearance very much resemble
Staten Land.   When I had got so near as to discover the
low land, I was quite embayed, and if it had blown hard at
S.W. so great a sea must have rolled in here as would have
rendered it almost impossible to claw off the shore; all
ships, therefore, that may hereafter navigate these parts,
should avoid falling in with it.   The seals and birds here
are innumerable; we saw also many whales spouting about
us, several of which were of an enormous size.   Our latitude now was 51° 27' S. longitude 63° 54' W.; the variation was 23° 30' E.   In the evening we brought-to, and at
day-break the next morning, stood in for the north part of
the island by the coast of which we had been embayed:
When we had got about four miles to the eastward, it fell
calm, and rained with great violence, during which there
arose such a swell as I never remember to have seen   It
came from the westward, and ran so quick and so high, that
I expected every moment it would break: It set us very
fast towards the shore, which is as dangerous as any in the
world, and I could see the surge breaking at some distance
from

from it, mountains high : Happily for us a fresh gale
sprung up at south-east, with which, to our great joy, we
were able to stand off; and it behoves whoever shall afterwards come this way, to give the north part of this island
a good birth.   After I had got to some distance, the weather being thick, and it raining very hard, I brought-to.
Our latitude was now 51° S. and longitude 63° 22' W.

On Monday the 14th, the weather having cleared up, and
the wind shifted to the S.S.W. we steered along the shore
S.E. by E. four miles, and saw a low flat island full of high
tufts of grass, resembling bushes, bearing south, at the distance of two or three leagues, the northermost land at the
same time bearing west, distant about six leagues: We had
here thirty-eight fathom, with rocky ground. We continued our course along the shore six leagues farther, and then
saw a low rocky island bearing S E. by E. distant about five
miles : Here we brought-to, and having sounded, we had
forty fathom water, with a bottom of white sand. This
island is about three leagues distant from the land we were
coasting, which here forms a very deep bay, and bears E.
by N. of the other i land on which we had seen the long
tufts of grass : We saw the sea break at a good distance from
the shore, and during the night stood off and on. The next
morning at three o'clock we made sail, and stood in for the
land to look for a harbour. At six, the east end of the rocky
island bore W.S.W. distant about three miles, and our
soundings then were sixteen fathom, with rocky ground;
but when we got within the island we had twenty fathom,
with fine white sand.   The coast from this rocky island lies
E. by S. distant about seven or eight leagues, where there
are two low islands, which make the eastermost land in sight.
At eight o'clock we saw an opening, which had the appearance of an harbour, bearing E.S.E. and being between two
and three leagues distant. Upon this discovery we brought
to, and sent a boat from each of the ships to examine the
opening ; but it beginning to blow very hard soon after,
and the weather growing thick, with heavy rain, we were
obliged to stand out to sea with both the ships, and it was
not without great difficulty that we cleared the two rocky
islands which were to the eastward of us. We had now a
great sea, and I began to be under much concern lest we
should be blown off, and our people in the boats left behind :
However, about three in the afternoon, the weather clearing
up.

up, I tacked and stood in again, and presently after had the satisfaction to see one of the boats, though it was a long way to leeward of us. I immediately bore down to her, and found her to be the Tamar's boat, with Mr Hindman, the second lieutenant, on board, who having been on shore in the opening, had ventured off, notwithstanding the great sea and bad weather, to inform me that he had found a fine harbour: We immediately stood in for it, and found it equally beyond his report and our expectations; the entrance is about a mile over, and every part of it is perfectly safe, the depth of water, close to the shore, being from ten to seven fathom. We found this harbour to consist of two little bays on the starboard side, where ships may anchor in great safety, and in each of which there is a fine rivulet of fresh water. Soon after we entered an harbour of much greater extent, which I called Port Egmont, in honour of the earl, who was then first lord of the Admiralty; and I think it is one of the finest harbours in the world. The mouth of it is S.E. distant seven leagues from the low rocky island, which is a good mark to know it by: Within the island, and at the distance of about two miles from the shore, there is between seventeen and eighteen fathom water; and about three leagues to the westward of the harbour, there is a remarkable white sandy beach, off which a ship may anchor till there is an opportunity to run in. In standing in for this sandy beach, the two low rocky islands, which we found it difficult to clear when the weather obliged us to stand off, appear to the eastward, and Port Egmont is about sixteen leagues from the north end of these islands. We moored in ten fathom, with fine holding ground. The northermost point of the western shore was distant two miles and a half, the watering-place on that shore bore W.N.W.¼ W. and was distant half a mile, and the islands on the east side bore E. by S. and were distant four miles. The whole navy of England might ride here in perfect security from all winds. Soon after the ship came to an anchor, the other boat which had remained on shore when Mr Hindman put off, came on board. In the southermost part of the harbour there are several islands, but there is no passage out for a ship; I went, however, through in my boat, about seven leagues distant from where the ship lay, and entered a large sound, which is too much exposed to a westerly wind for ships to lie in it safely; and the master of the Tamar, who had been

round

round in her boat, and entered this sound from without, reported that many shoals lay off it, so that if the harbour was
ever so good, it would not be prudent to attempt getting in.
In every part of Port Egmont there is fresh water in the
greatest plenty, and geese, ducks, snipes, and other birds are
so numerous, that our people grew tired of them : It was a
common thing for a boat to bring off sixty or seventy fine
geese, without expending a single charge of powder and
shot, for the men knocked down as many as they pleased
with stones : Wood, however, is wanting here, except a
little that is found adrift along the shore, which I imagined
came from the Straits of Magellan.   Among other refreshments, which are in the highest degree salutary to those
who have contracted scorbutic disorders, during a long
voyage, here are wild celery, and wood sorrel, in the greatest abundance; nor is there any want of mussels, clams,
cockles, and limpets : The seals and penguins are innumerable, so that it is impossible to walk upon the beach without first driving them away : And the coast abounds with
sea-lions, many of which are of an enormous size.   We
found this animal very formidable ; I was once attacked by
one of them very unexpectedly, and it was with the utmost
difficulty that I could disengage myself from him : At other
times we had many battles with them, and it has sometimes
afforded a dozen of us an hour's work to dispatch one of
them : I had with me a very fine mastiff dog, and a bite of
one of these creatures almost tore him to pieces.   Nor were
these the only dangerous animals that we found here, for
the master having been sent out one day to sound the coast
upon the south shore, reported, at his return, that four creatures of great fierceness, resembling wolves, ran up to their
bellies in the water to attack the people in his boat, and
that as they happened to have no fire-arms with them, they
had immediately put the boat off into deep water.   The
next morning after this happened, I went upon the southern
shore myself, where we found one of the largest sea-lions I
had ever seen : As the boat's crew were now well armed,
they immediately engaged him, and during the contest one
of the other animals was seen running towards us : He was
fired at before he came up, and was presently killed, though
I afterwards wished that we had endeavoured to take him
alive, which, if we had been aware of his attack, I dare say
might easily have been done. When any of these creatures

got

got sight of our people, though at ever so great a distance, they ran directly at them ; and no less than five of them were killed this day. They were always called wolves by the ship's company, but, except in their size, and the shape of the tail, I think they bore a greater resemblance to a fox. They are as big as a middle-sized mastiff, and their fangs are remarkably long and sharp. There are great numbers of them upon this coast, though it is not perhaps easy to guess how they first came hither, for these islands are at least one hundred leagues distant from the main : They burrow in the ground like a fox, and we have frequently seen pieces of seal which they have mangled, and the skins of penguins, lie scattered about the mouth of their holes. To get rid of these creatures, our people set fire to the grass, so that the country was in a blaze as far as the eye could reach, for several days, and we could see them running in great numbers to seek other quarters I dug holes in many places, about two feet deep, to examine the soil, which I found first a black mold, and then a light clay. While we lay here, we set up the armourer's forge on shore, and completed a great deal of iron-work that was much wanted. Our people had every morning an excellent breakfast made of portable soup, and wild celery, thickened with oatmeal : Neither was our attention confined wholly to ourselves, for the surgeon of the Tamar surrounded a piece of ground near the watering-place with a fence of turf, and planted it with many esculent vegetables as a garden, for the benefit of those who might hereafter come to this place.[1] Of this harbour, and all the neighbouring islands, I took possession for his majesty King George the Third of Great Britain, by the name of *Falkland's Islands;* and there is, I think, little reason to doubt that they are the same land to which Cowley gave the name of Pepys's Island.

In the printed account of Cowley's voyage, he says, " we held our course S.W. till we came into the latitude of forty-seven degrees, where we saw land, the same being an island, not before known, lying to the westward of us : It was not inhabited, and I gave it the name of Pepys's Island. We found it a very commodious place for ships to water at, and take

---

[1] " Many of them began to spring up very fast, and we have since heard, that some persons who arrived there after our departure, eat of those roots and sallad."

take in wood, and it has a very good harbour, where a thousand sail of ships may safely ride.   Here is great plenty of fowls, and, we judge, abundance of fish, by reason of the ground's being nothing but rocks and sands."

To this account there is annexed a representation of Pepys's Island, in which names are given to several points and head-lands, and the harbour is called Admiralty Bay; yet it appears that Cowley had only a distant view of it, for he immediately adds, " the wind being so extraordinary high that we could not get into it to water, we stood to the southward, shaping our course S.S.W. till we came into the latitude of 53°;" and though he says that " it was commodious to take in wood," and it is known that there is no wood on Falkland's Islands, Pepys's Island and Falkland's Islands may notwithstanding be the same; for upon Falkland's Islands there are immense quantities of flags with narrow leaves, reeds and rushes which grow in clusters, so as to form bushes about three feet high, and then shoot about six or seven feet higher: These at a distance have greatly the appearance of wood, and were taken for wood by the French, who landed there in the year 1764, as appears by Pernetty's account of their voyage.' It has been suggested that the latitude of Pepys's Island might, in the MS. from which the account of Cowley's voyage was printed, be expressed in figures, which, if ill made, might equally resemble forty-seven, and fifty-one; and therefore as there is no island in these seas in latitude forty-seven, and as Falkland's Islands lie nearly in fifty-one, that fifty-one might reasonably be concluded to be the number for which the figures were intended to stand: Recourse therefore was had

---

[2] Bougainville, who had the command of the expedition here referred to, says, " The same illusion which made Hawkins, Woods Rogers, and others believe that these isles were covered with wood, acted likewise upon my fellow voyagers. We were surprised when we landed, to see that what we took for woods as we sailed along the coast, was nothing but bushes of a tall rush, standing very close together. The bottom of its stalks being dried, got the colour of a dead leaf to the height of about five feet; and from thence springs the tuft of rushes, which crown this stalk; so that at a distance, these stalks together have the appearance of a wood of middling height. These rushes only grow near the sea side, and on little isles; the mountains on the main land are, in some parts, covered all over with heath, which are easily mistaken for bushes."—Forster's Translation, where a pretty interesting account of these islands (called Malouines) is to be found.—E.

had to the British Museum, and a manuscript journal of Cowley's was there found. In this manuscript no mention is made of an island not before known, to which he gave the name of Pepys's Island, but land is mentioned in latitude forty seven degrees forty minutes, expressed in words at length, which exactly answers to the description of what is called Pepys's Island in the printed account, and which here, he says, he supposed to be the islands of Sebald de Weit. This part of the manuscript is in the following words: "January, 1683, This month we were in the latitude of forty-seven degrees and forty minutes, where we espied an island bearing west from us, we having the wind at east north-east, we bore away for it; it being too late for us to go on shore, we lay by all night. The island seemed very pleasant to the eye, with many woods, I may as well say the whole land was woods. There being a rock lying above water to the eastward of it, where an innumerable company of fowls, being of the bigness of a small goose, which fowls would strike at our men as they were aloft: Some of them we killed and eat: They seemed to us very good, only tasted somewhat fishly. I sailed along that island to the southward, and about the south-west side of the island there seemed to me to be a good place for ships to ride; I would have had the boat out to have gone into the harbour, but the wind blew fresh, and they would not agree to go with it. Sailing a little further, keeping the lead, and having six and-twenty and seven-and-twenty fathoms water, until we came to a place where we saw the weeds ride, heaving the lead again, found but seven fathoms water. Fearing danger went about the ship there; were then fearfull to stay by the land any longer, it being all rocky ground, but the harbour seemed to be a good place for shipps to ride there; in the island, seeming likewise to have water enough, there seemed to me to be harbour for five hundred sail of ships. The going in but narrow, and the north side of the entrance shallow water that I could see, but I verily believe that there is water enough for any ship to go in on the south side, for there cannot be so great a lack of water, but must needs scoure a channel away at the ebb deep enough for shipping to go in. I would have had them stood upon a wind all night, but they told me they were not come out to go upon discovery. We saw likewise another island by this that night, which made me think them to be the Sibble D'wards.

" The same night we steered our course againe west south
west, which was but our south west, the compasse having
two and twenty degrees variation eastwardly, keeping that
course till we came in the latitude of three and fifty degrees."

In both the printed and manuscript account, this land is
said to lie in latitude forty-seven, to be situated to the westward of the ship when first discovered, to appear woody, to
have an harbour where a great number of ships might ride
in safety, and to be frequented by innumerable birds.   It
appears also by both accounts, that the weather prevented
his going on shore, and that he steered from it W. S. W.
till he came into latitude fifty-three : There can therefore
be little doubt but that Cowley gave the name of Pepys's
Island after he came home, to what he really supposed to
be the island of Sebald de Wert, for which it is not difficult to assign several reasons ; and though the supposition
of a mistake of the figures does not appear to be well grounded, yet, there being no land in forty-seven, the evidence
that what Cowley saw was Falkland's Islands is very strong.
The description of the country agrees in almost every particular, and even the map is of the same general figure, with
a strait running up the middle.   The chart of Falkland's
that accompanies my narrative, was laid down from the
journals and drawings of Captain Macbride, who was dispatched thither after my return, and circumnavigated the
whole coast : The two principal islands were probably called Falkland's Islands by Strong, about the year 1689, as he
is known to have given the name of Falkland's Sound to
part of the strait which divides them.   The journal of this
navigator is still unprinted in the British Museum.   The
first who saw these islands is supposed to be Captain Da-
vies, the associate of Cavendish, in 1692.   In 1594, Sir Richard Hawkins saw land, supposed to be the same, and in
honour of his mistress, Queen Elizabeth, called them Hawkins's Maiden Land.   Long afterwards, they were seen by
some French ships from Saint Maloes, and Frezier, probably for that reason, called them the Malouins, a name which
has been since adopted by the Spaniards.

Having continued in the harbour which I had called Port
Egmont till Sunday the 27th of January, we sailed again at
eight o'clock in the morning with the wind at S. S. W. ;
but we were scarcely got out of the port before it began to
blow very hard, and the weather became so thick that we
                                                        could

could not see the rocky islands. I now most heartily wished myself again at anchor in the harbour we had quitted;
but in a short time we had the satisfaction to see the weather become clear, though it continued to blow very hard
the whole day. At nine the entrance of Port Egmont harbour bore E. S. E. distant two leagues; the two low islands
to the northward E. by N. distant between three and four
miles; and the rocky island W. ¼ N. distant four leagues.
At ten the two low islands bore S. S. E. distant four or five
miles; and we then steered along the shore east by the
compass, and after having run about five leagues, we saw a
remarkable head-land, with a rock at a little distance from
it, bearing E. S. E. ½ E. distant three leagues. This head-
land I called *Cape Tamar.* Having continued the same
course five leagues farther, we saw a rock about five miles
from the main bearing N. E. at the distance of four or five
leagues: This rock I called the *Edistone,* and then steered
between it and a remarkable head-land which I called *Cape
Dolphin,* in the direction of E. N. E. five leagues farther.
From Cape Tamar to Cape Dolphin, a distance of about
eight leagues, the land forms, what I thought, a deep sound,
and called it *Carlisle Sound,* but what has since appeared to
be the northern entrance of the strait between the two principal islands. In the part that I supposed to be the bottom
of the sound, we saw an opening, which had the appearance of a harbour. From Cape Dolphin we steered along
the shore E. ¼ N. sixteen leagues, to a low flat cape or head-
land, and then brought-to. In this day's run the land, for
the most part, resembled the east side of the coast of Patagonia, not having so much as a single tree, or even a bush,
being all downs, with here and there a few of the high tufts
of grass that we had seen at Port Egmont; and in this account I am sure I am not mistaken, for I frequently sailed
within two miles of the shore; so that if there had been a
shrub as big as a gooseberry bush, I should have seen it.
During the night we had forty fathom water with rocky
ground.

The next morning, at four o'clock, we made sail, the low
flat cape then bearing S. E. by E. distant five leagues: At
half an hour after five it bore S. S. E. distant two leagues
and we then steered from it E. S. E. five leagues, to three
low rocky islands, which lie about two miles from the main.
From these islands we steered S. S. E. four leagues, to two
other

other low islands, which lie at a distance of about one mile from the main. Between these islands the land forms a very deep sound, which I called *Berkeley's Sound.* In the south part of this sound there is an opening, which has the appearance of a harbour; and about three or four miles to the southward of the south point of it, at the distance of about four miles from the main, some rocks appear above the water, upon which the sea breaks very high, there being here a great swell from the southward. When we were abreast of these breakers, we steered S. W. by S. about two leagues, when the southermost land in sight, which I took to be the southermost part of Falkland's Islands, bore W. S. W. distant five leagues. The coast now began to be very dangerous, there being, in all directions, rocks and breakers at a great distance from the shore. The country also inland had a more rude and desolate appearance; the high ground, as far as we could see, being all barren, craggy rocks, very much resembling that part of Terra del Fuego which lies near Cape Horn. As the sea now rose every moment, I was afraid of being caught here upon a lee-shore, in which case there would have been very little chance of my getting off, and therefore I tacked, and stood to the northward; the latitude of the southermost point in sight being about 52° 3¼ S. As we had now run no less than seventy leagues along the coast of this island, it must certainly be of very considerable extent. It has been said by some former navigators to be about two hundred miles in circumference, but I made no doubt of its being nearer seven. Having hauled the wind, I stood to the northward about noon; the entrance of Berkeley's Sound at three o'clock bore S. W. by W. distant about six leagues. At eight in the evening, the wind shifting to the S. W. we stood to the westward.

SECTION VI.

The Passage through the Strait of Magellan as far as Cape Monday, with a Description of several Bays and Harbours, formed by the Coast on each Side.

WE continued to make sail for Port Desire till Wednesday the 6th of February, when about one o'clock in the afternoon we saw land, and stood in for the port. During the

run

run from Falkland's Islands to this place, the number of whales about the ship was so great as to render the navigation dangerous; we were very near striking upon one, and another blew the water in upon the quarter-deck; they were much larger than any we had seen. As we were standing in for Port Desire, we saw the Florida, a store-ship that we expected from England; and at four we came to an anchor off the harbour's mouth.

The next morning, Mr Dean, the master of the storeship, came on board; and finding from his report that his foremast was sprung, and his ship little better than a wreck, I determined to go into the harbour, and try to unload her there, although the narrowness of the place, and the rapidity of the tides, render it a very dangerous situation. We got in in the evening, but it blowing very hard in the night, both the Tamar and the store-ship made signals of distress; I immediately sent my boats to their assistance, who found that, notwithstanding they were moored, they had been driven up the harbour, and were in the greatest danger of being on shore. They were brought back, not without great difficulty, and the very next night they drove again, and were again saved by the same efforts, from the same danger. As I now found that the store-ship was continually driving about the harbour, and every moment in danger of being lost, I gave up, with whatever reluctance, my design of taking the provisions out of her, and sent all our carpenters on board, to fish the mast, and make such other repairs as they could. I also lent her my forge to complete such iron-work as they wanted, and determined, the moment she was in a condition to put to sea, to take her with us into the strait of Magellan, and unload her there. While this was doing, Captain Mouat, who commanded the Tamar, informed me that his rudder was sprung, and that he had reason to fear it would in a short time become wholly unserviceable. Upon this I ordered the carpenter of the Dolphin on board the Tamar, to examine the rudder, and he reported it to be so bad, that in his opinion the vessel could not proceed on her voyage without a new one. A new one, however, it was not in our power to procure at this place, and I therefore desired Captain Mouat to get his forge on shore, and secure his rudder with iron clamps in the best manner he could, hoping that in the strait a

piece

piece of timber might be found which would furnish him with a better.

On Wednesday the 13th, the store-ship being ready for sea, I put on board of her one of my petty officers, who was well acquainted with the strait, and three or four of my seamen to assist in navigating her; I also lent her two of my boats, and took those belonging to her, which were staved, on board to get them repaired, and then I ordered her master to put to sea directly, and make the best of his way to Port Famine; though I did not doubt but that I should come up with her long before she got thither, as I intended to follow her as soon as the Tamar was ready, and Captain Mouat had told me that the rudder having been patched together by the joint labour and skill of the carpenter and smith, he should be in a condition to proceed with me the next morning.

The next morning we accordingly put to sea, and a few hours afterwards being abreast of Penguin island, we saw the store-ship a long way to the eastward.

On Saturday the 16th, about six o'clock in the morning, we saw Cape Fair-weather, bearing W. S. W. at the distance of five or six leagues; and at nine, we saw a strange sail to the N. W. standing after us.

On the 17th, at six in the morning, Cape Virgin Mary bearing south, distant five miles, we hauled in for the strait, and the strange ship still followed us.

On the 18th we passed the first narrow, and as I perceived the strange ship to have shaped the same course that we had, from the time she had first seen us, shortening or making sail as we did, she became the subject of much speculation; and as I was obliged, after I had got through the first narrow, to bring-to for the store-ship, which was a great way astern, I imagined she would speak with us, and therefore I put the ship in the best order I could. As soon as he had passed the narrow, and saw me lying-to, he did the same about four miles to windward of me. In this situation we remained till night came on, and the tide setting us over to the south shore, we came to an anchor; the wind however shifted before morning, and at day-break I saw our satellite at anchor about three leagues to leeward of us. As it was then tide of flood, I thought of working through the second narrow; but seeing the stranger get under way, and

work

work up towards us, I ran directly over into Gregory Bay, and brought the ship to an anchor, with a spring upon our cable : I also got eight of our guns, which were all we could get at, out of the hold, and brought them over on one side. In the mean time, the ship continued to work up towards us, and various were our conjectures about her, for she shewed no colours, neither did we. It happened about this time that the store-ship, as she was endeavouring to come to an anchor near us, ran aground ; upon which the stranger came to an anchor a little way astern, at the same time hoisting French colours, and sending his launch, and another boat, with an anchor to assist her. Still, however, I showed no colours, but sent my own boats, and a boat of the Tamar's, to assist the store-ship, giving orders at the same time to the officers, not to suffer the French boats to come on board her, but to thank them in polite terms for the assistance they intended. These orders were punctually obeyed, and with the assistance of our own boats only, the store-ship was soon after got off : My people reported that the French ship was full of men, and seemed to have a great number of officers on board.

At six o'clock in the evening, I made the signal and weighed; we worked through the second narrow, and at ten o'clock passed the west end of it : at eleven we anchored in seven fathom off Elizabeth's Island, and the French ship at the same time anchored in a bad situation, to the southward of Saint Bartholomew's Island, which convinced me that she was not acquainted with the channel.

At six o'clock the next morning, I weighed and sailed between Elizabeth and Bartholomew Islands, with the wind at N.W. and after steering S.S.W. five or six miles, we crossed a bank, where among the weeds we had seven fathom water. This bank lies W.S.W. five or six miles from the middle of George's Island, and it is said in some former accounts that in many places there is not three fathom water upon it ; the danger here therefore is considerable, and to avoid it, it is necessary to keep near Elizabeth's Island till the western shore is but at a short distance, and then a southern course may be steered with great safety, till the reef, which lies about four miles to the northward of Saint Anne's Point, is in sight. At noon this day, the north point of Fresh Water Bay bore W. by N. and Saint Anne's Point S. by E. ¼ E. The French ship still steered after us, and

we

we imagined that she was either from Falkland's Islands, where the French had then a settlement, to get wood, or upon a survey of the strait. The remaining part of this day, and the next morning, we had variable winds with calms; in the afternoon therefore I hoisted out the boats, and towed round Saint Anne's Point into Port Famine; at six in the evening we anchored, and soon after the French ship passed by us to the southward.

Here we continued till Monday the 25th, when both the Dolphin and Tamar having taken out of the store-ship as much provision as they could stow, I gave the master of her orders to return to England as soon as he could get ready, and with the Tamar sailed from Port Famine, intending to push through the streight before the season should be too far advanced. [1] At noon we were three leagues distant from Saint Anne's Point, which bore N.W. and three or four miles distant from Point Shutup, which bore S.S.W. Point Shutup bears from Saint Anne's Point S. ½ E. by the compass, and they are about four or five leagues asunder. Between these two points there is a flat shoal, which runs from Port Famine before Sedger river, and three or four miles to the southward.

We steered S.S.W. with little wind along the shore, from Point Shutup towards Cape Forward; and about three o'clock in the afternoon we passed by the French ship, which we saw in a little cove, about two leagues to the southward of Point Shutup. She had hauled her stern close into the woods, and we could see large piles of the wood which she had cut down, lying on each side of her; so that I made no doubt of her having been sent out to procure that necessary for their new settlement, though I could not conceive why they should have come so far into the strait for that purpose. After my return to England, I learnt that this vessel was the Eagle, commanded by M. Bougainville, and that her business in the strait was, as I conjectured, to cut wood for the French settlement in the Falkland's Islands. From Cape Shutup to Cape Forward,
the

---

[1] " At taking our leave of the store-ship, our boatswain, and all that were sick on board the Dolphin and Tamar, obtained leave to return in her to England; the commodore in the mean time openly declaring to the men in general, that if any of them were averse to proceeding on the voyage, they had free liberty to return; an offer which only one of our men accepted."

the course by compass is S.W. by S. and the distance is seven leagues. At eight o'clock in the evening, Cape Forward bore N.W. ½ W. and was distant about a mile, and we brought-to for the night. This part of the strait is about eight miles over, and off the cape we had forty fathom within half a cable's length of the shore. About four o'clock in the morning we made sail, and at eight, having had light airs almost quite round the compass, Cape Forward bore N.E. by E. distant about four miles; and Cape Holland W.N.W. ½ W. distant about five leagues. At ten we had fresh gales at W.N.W. and at intervals sudden squalls, so violent as to oblige us to clue all up every time they came on. We kept, however, working to windward, and looking out for an anchoring-place, endeavouring at the same time to reach a bay about two leagues to the westward of Cape Forward. At five o'clock I sent a boat with an officer into this bay to sound, who finding it fit for our purpose, we entered it, and about six o'clock anchored in nine fathom: Cape Forward bore E. ½ S. distant five miles; a small island which lies in the middle of the bay, and is about a mile distant from the shore, W. by S. distant about half a mile; and a rivulet of fresh water N.W. by W. distant three quarters of a mile.

At six o'clock the next morning, we weighed and continued our course through the strait; from Cape Holland to Cape Gallant, which are distant about eight leagues, the coast lies W. ½ S. by the compass: Cape Gallant is very high and steep, and between this and Cape Holland lies a reach about three leagues over, called English Reach About five miles south of Cape Gallant lies a large island, called Charles's Island, which it is necessary to keep to the northward of: We sailed along the north shore of it, at about two miles distance, and sometimes much less. A little to the eastward of Cape Holland is a fair sandy bay, called Wood's Bay, in which there is good anchoring. The mountains on each side the strait are, I think, higher, and of a more desolate appearance, than any other in the world, except perhaps the Cordeliers, both being rude, craggy, and steep, and covered with snow from the top to the bottom.

From Cape Gallant to Passage Point, which are distant about three leagues, the coast lies W. by N. by compass. Passage Point is the east point of Elizabeth's Bay, and is

low

low land, with a rock lying off it.   Between this and Cape
Gallant there are several islands. Some of them are very
small; but the eastermost, which is Charles's Island, that
has been just mentioned, is two leagues long; the next is
called Monmouth's Island, and the westermost Rupert's Island: Rupert's Island lies S. by E. of Point Passage. These
islands make the strait narrow; between Point Passage and
Rupert's Island it is not more than two miles over, and it is
necessary to go to the northward of them all, keeping the
north shore on board : We sailed within two cables' length
of it, and had no ground with forty fathom.   At six in the
evening, the wind shifted to the westward, upon which we
stood in for Elizabeth's Bay, and anchored in ten fathom
with very good ground; the best anchoring, however, is in
thirteen fathom, for there was but three or four fathom about
a cable's length within us.   In this bay there is a good rivulet of fresh water.   We found the flood here set very
strong to the eastward; and according to our calculation,
it flows at the full and change of the moon about twelve
o'clock.   We found the variation two points easterly.

At two o'clock in the afternoon, on Thursday the 28th,
the wind being between the N.W. and W. with fresh gales
and squalls, we made the signal to weigh, and just as we
had got the ship over the anchor, a violent gust brought it
home; the ship immediately drove into shoal water, within two cables' length of the shore, upon which we let go
the small bower in four fathom, and had but three fathom
under our stern : The stream anchor was carried out with
all possible expedition, and by applying a purchase to the
capstern, the ship was drawn towards it; we then heaved
up both the bower anchors, slipt the stream cable, and with
the jib and stay-sails ran out into ten fathom, and anchored with the best bower exactly in the situation from which
we had been driven.

At five o'clock the next morning, the wind being northerly, and the weather moderate, we weighed again, and at seven passed Muscle Bay, which lies on the southern shore,
about a league to the westward of Elizabeth's Bay. At eight
we were abreast of Bachelor's River, which is on the north
shore, about two leagues W. by N. from Elizabeth's Bay.
At nine we passed St Jerom's Sound, the entrance of which
is about a league from Bachelor's River : When St Jerom's
Sound was open, it bore N.W. We then steered W.S.W.

by

by the compass for Cape Quod, which is three leagues distant from the southermost point of the sound.   Between
Elizabeth Bay and Cape Quod is a reach about four miles
over, called Crooked Reach.   At the entrance of Jerom's
Sound, on the north side, we saw three or four fires, and
soon afterwards perceived two or three canoes paddling after us.   At noon Cape Quod bore W S.W. ½ W. distant
four or five miles, and soon after having light airs and
calms, we drove to the eastward with the flood tide; in the
mean time the canoes came up, and after having paddled
about us some time, one of them had the resolution to come
on board.   The canoe was of bark, very ill made, and the
people on board, which were four men, two women, and a
boy, were the poorest wretches I had ever seen.   They were
all naked, except a stinking seal skin that was thrown loosely over their shoulders; they were armed, however, with
bows and arrows, which they readily gave me in return for
a few beads, and other trifles.   The arrows were made of a
reed, and pointed with a green stone; they were about two
feet long, and the bows were three feet; the cord of the
bow was the dried gut of some animal.[2]   In the evening
we anchored abreast of Bachelor's River, in fourteen fathom.   The entrance of the river bore N. by E. distant one
mile, and the northermost point of Saint Jerom's Sound
W.N.W. distant three miles.   About three quarters of a
mile eastward of Bachelor's River, is a shoal, upon which
there is not more than six feet water when the tide is out:
it is distant about half a mile from the shore, and may be
known by the weeds that are upon it.   The tide flows here,
at the full and change of the moon, about one o'clock.
Soon after we were at anchor, several Indians came on
board us, and I made them all presents of beads, ribbands,
                                                        and

[2] " They have also javelins.   These people seem to be very poor and
perfectly harmless, coming forth to their respective callings, as soon as the
morning dawns, and as soon as the sun sets retiring to their different habitations."—" They are very dexterous in striking the fish with their javelins, though they lie some feet under water.   In these instances they
seem to shew the utmost extent of their ingenuity; for we found them
incapable of understanding things the most obvious to their senses.
For instance, on their first coming on board, amongst the trinkets we presented them were some knives and scissars, and in giving them these, we
tried to make them sensible of their use; but after our repeated endeavours, by shewing the manner of using them, they continued as inflexible as
at first, and could not learn to distinguish the blades from the handles."

and other trifles, with which they appeared to be greatly delighted. This visit I returned by going on shore among
them, taking only a few people with me in my jolly boat,
that I might not alarm them by numbers. They received
us with great expressions of kindness, and to make us welcome, they brought us some berries which they had gathered for that purpose, and which, with a few muscles, seem
to be a principal part, if not the whole of their subsistence.

At five o'clock in the morning of the 2d, we weighed and
towed with the tide, but at ten, having no wind, and finding that we drove again to the eastward, we anchored with
the stream anchor in fifteen fathom, upon a bank which
lies about half a mile from the north shore; after veering
about two-thirds of a cable, we had five-and-forty fathom
along-side and still deeper water at a little distance. The
south point of Saint Jerom's Sound bore N.N.E. distant two
miles, and Cape Quod W.S W. distant about eight miles.
From the south point of Saint Jerom's Sound to Cape Quod
is three leagues, in the direction of S.W by W. The tides
in this reach are exceedingly strong, though very irregular;
we found them set to the eastward from nine o'clock in the
morning till five o'clock the next morning, and the other
four hours, from five to nine, they set to the westward.[3] At
twelve o'clock at night, it began to blow very hard at
W N.W. and at two in the morning the ship drove off the
bank: We immediately hove the anchor up, and found
both the flukes broken off; till three o'clock we had no
ground, and then we drove into sixteen fathom, at the entrance of Saint Jerom's Sound; as it still blew a storm, we
immediately let go the best bower, and veered to half a cable. The anchor brought the ship up at so critical a moment, that we had but five fathom, and even that depth was
among breakers. We let go the small bower under foot,
and at five, finding the tide set to the westward, and the weather more moderate, we got up both the anchors, and kept
working to windward. At ten we found the tide setting
again

---

3 " The streights are here four leagues over, and it is difficult to get
any anchorage, on account of the unevenness and irregularity of the bottom, which in several places close to the shore has from twenty to fifty fathoms water, and in other parts no ground is to be found with a line of a
hundred and fifty fathoms."

again strongly to the eastward, and we therefore sent the boat back to seek for an anchoring-place, which she found in a bay on the north shore, about four miles to the eastward of Cape Quod, and a little way within some small islands : We endeavoured to get into this bay, but the tide rushed out of it with such violence, that we found it impossible, and at noon bore away for York Road, at the entrance of Bachelor's River, where we anchored about an hour afterwards.

At six o'clock the next morning, we weighed and worked with the tide, which set the same as the day before, but we could not gain an anchoring-place, so that at noon we bore away for York Road again. I took this opportunity to go up Bachelor's River in my jolly-boat, as high as I could, which was about four miles: In some places I found it very wide and deep, and the water was good, but near the mouth it is so shallow at low water, that even a small boat cannot get into it.

At six o'clock on the 5th we weighed again, and at eight, it being stark calm, we sent the boats a-head to tow; at eleven, however, the tide set so strong from the westward, that we could not gain the bay on the north shore, which the boat had found for us on the 4th, and which was an excellent harbour, fit to receive five or six sail: We were therefore obliged to anchor upon a bank, in forty-five fathom, with the stream anchor, Cape Quod bearing W.S.W. distant five or six miles, the south point of the island that lies to the east of the cape, being just in one with the pitch of it, and a remarkable stone patch on the north shore, bearing N ½ W. distant half a mile. Close to the shore here, the depth of water was seventy-five fathom. As soon as we were at anchor, I sent an officer to the westward to look out for a harbour, but he did not succeed. It was calm the rest of the day, and all night, the tide setting to the eastward from the time we anchored till six o'clock the next morning, when we weighed, and were towed by the boats to the westward. At eight a fresh breeze sprung up at W.S.W. and W. and at noon Cape Quod bore E. by S. at the distance of about five miles. In this situation I sent the boats out again to look for an anchoring-place, and about noon, by their direction, we anchored in a little bay on the south shore, opposite to Cape Quod, in five and twenty fathom,

with

with very good ground.[4]   A small rocky island bore W. by
N. at the distance of about two cables' length, the eastermost point E. ½ S. and Cape Quod N.E. by N. distant about
three miles: In this place we had shell-fish of various kinds
in great plenty.   The Tamar not being able to work up to
us, anchored about two o'clock in the bay on the north
shore, about six miles to the eastward of Cape Quod, which
has been mentioned already. During the night it was stark
calm, but in the morning, having little airs of wind westerly, I weighed about eight o'clock, and worked with the
tide.   At noon Cape Quod bore E. by S. distant between
two and three leagues, and Cape Monday, which is the

westermost

---

[4] " We here saw a great number of islands, and many Indians dispersed in several quarters, amongst whom we found a family which struck our
attention. It was composed of a decrepid old man, his wife, two sons, and
a daughter.   The latter appeared to have tolerable features, and an English face, which they seemed to be desirous of letting us know; they making a long harangue, not a syllable of which we understood, though we
plainly perceived it was in relation to this woman, whose age did not exceed thirty, by their pointing first at her, and then at themselves.   Various were the conjectures we formed in regard to this circumstance, though
we generally agreed, that their signs plainly shewed that they offered her
to us, as being of the same country."   It is scarcely uncharitable to imagine that this young lady's mother had once been unfaithful to her lord
and master, preferring the addresses of some favoured European.   A little
of our northern pride would have concealed this family disgrace.   But in
those distant regions, where such occurrences must have been rare, perhaps vanity would gratify itself by transmuting it into an honour.   After
all, however, it is very difficult to divine who was or could be the " gay de-
ceiver."   A fanciful reader, indeed, who was acquainted with Byron's narrative of the loss of the Wager, might be tempted to conjecture that the
good mother, being on an expedition to the northward of the straits, was
one of the wives whom, as he says, the crew, at that time subject to no
controul, endeavoured to seduce, a conduct which gave the Indians great
offence.   There are undoubtedly some strong marks of identity, betwixt
the Indians described in that narrative and the inhabitants found in the
straits.   They resembled in stature, in complexion, in hair, in dress, viz.
the skin of some unknown beast; they used the same diet, living principally on fish, (muscles are particularly mentioned in both accounts;) they
were both very dexterous in the management of the javelin; and the former, it is clear from Byron's words, came from the south.   Their canoes
also, it may be added, were of very similar materials and structure. Of the
jealousy of these Indians, Byron relates some striking evidences, from what
he himself had the unhappiness to experience.   Who knows what some
waggish spectator of the young lady might surmise about her English features, if he had ever heard of the gallant commodore's adventure in the
wigwam, &c., so feelingly introduced and dilated in his interesting narrative !—E.

westermost land in sight on the south shore, W. by N. distant about ten or eleven leagues. This part of the strait lies W.N.W. ½ W. by the compass, and is about four miles over; so that the craggy mountains which bound it on each side, towering above the clouds, and covered with everlasting snow, give it the most dreary and desolate appearance that can be imagined. The tides here are not very strong; the ebb sets to the westward, but with an irregularity for which it is very difficult to account. About one o'clock, the Tamar anchored in the bay on the south shore, opposite to Cape Quod, which we had just left, and we continued working to windward till seven in the evening, when we anchored in a small bay on the north shore, about five leagues to the westward of Cape Quod, with very good ground. This bay may be known by two large rocks that appear above water, and a low point which makes the east part of the bay. The anchoring-place is between the two rocks, the eastermost bearing N.E. ½ E. distant about two cables' length, and the westermost, which is near the point, W.N.W. ½ W. at about the same distance: There is also a small rock which shows itself among the weeds at low water, and bears E. ½ N. distant about two cables' length. If there are more ships than one, they may anchor farther out in deeper water. During the night it was calm, and the weather became very foggy; but about ten in the morning it cleared up, and I went on shore. I found abundance of shell-fish, but saw no traces of people. In the afternoon, while the people were filling water, I went up a deep lagoon, which lies just round the westermost rock: At the head of it I found a very fine fall of water, and on the east side several little coves, where ships of the greatest draught may lie in perfect security. We saw nothing else worthy of notice, and therefore having filled our boat with very large muscles, we returned.

At seven o'clock the next morning, we weighed and towed out of the bay, and at eight saw the Tamar very far astern, steering after us. At noon we had little wind at E.N.E. but at five o'clock it shifted to W.N.W. and blew fresh. At six we were abreast of Cape Monday, and at six the next morning, Cape Upright bore E. by S. distant three leagues. From Cape Monday to Cape Upright, which are both on the south shore, and distant from each other about five leagues, the course is W. by N. by the compass: The

shore

shore on each side is rocky, with broken ground. At about half an hour after seven, we had a very hard squall, and the weather being then exceedingly thick, we suddenly perceived a reef of rocks close under our lee-bow, upon which the sea broke very high: We had but just time to tack clear of them, and if the ship had missed stays, every soul on board must inevitably have perished. These rocks lie at a great distance from the south shore, and are about three leagues to the north of Cape Upright. At nine the weather cleared a little, and we saw the entrance of Long Reach, upon which we bore away, keeping nearest the south shore, in hopes of finding an anchoring-place. At ten we had strong gales and thick weather, with hard rain, and at noon we were again abreast of Cape Monday, but could find no anchoring-place, which, however, we continued to seek, still steering along the south shore, and were soon after joined by the Tamar, who had been six or seven leagues to the eastward of us all night. At six in the evening we anchored in a deep bay, about three leagues to the eastward of Cape Monday: We let go the anchor in five-and-twenty fathom, near an island in the bottom of the bay; but before we could bring up the ship, we were driven off, and the anchor took the ground in about fifty fathom. The extreme points of the bay bore from N.W. to N. E. by E. and the island W. ½ S. We veered to a whole cable, and the anchor was about a cable's length from the nearest shore. In the night we had fresh gales westerly, with sudden squalls and hard rain; but in the morning the weather became more moderate, though it was still thick, and the rain continued. As a great swell set into this place, and broke very high upon the rocks, near which we lay, I got up the anchor, and warped the ship to a bank where the Tamar was riding: We let go our anchor in fourteen fathom, and moored with the stream anchor to the eastward, in forty-five fathom. In the bottom of this bay there is a bason, at the entrance of which there is but three fathom and a half at low water, but within there is ten fathom, and room enough for six or seven sail to lie where no wind can hurt them.

We continued here till Friday the 15th, and during all that time had one continued storm, with impenetrable fogs, and incessant rain. On the 12th, I sent out the boat, with an officer to look for harbours on the southern shore: The
boat

boat was absent till the 14th, and then returned, with an
account that there were five bays between the ship's station
and Cape Upright, where we might anchor in great safety.
The officer told me, that near Cape Upright he had fallen
in with a few Indians, who had given him a dog, and that
one of the women had offered him a child which was suck-
ing at her breast.   It is scarcely necessary to say that he
refused it, but the offer seems to degrade these poor forlorn
savages more than any thing in their appearance or manner of life : It must be a strange depravity of nature that
leaves them destitute of affection for their offspring, or a
most deplorable situation that impresses necessities upon
them by which it is surmounted.   Some hills, which, when
we first came to this place, had no snow upon them, were
now covered, and the winter of this dreary and inhospitable
region seemed to have set in at once: The poor seamen
not only suffered much by the cold, but had scarcely ever
a dry thread about them : I therefore distributed among
the crews of both the ships, not excepting the officers, two
bales of a thick woollen stuff, called Fearnought, which is
provided by the government, so that every body on board
had now a warm jacket, which at this time was found both
comfortable and salutary.

At eight o'clock in the morning of the 15th, we weighed
and made sail, and at three o'clock in the afternoon, we
were once more abreast of Cape Monday, and at five we
anchored in a bay on the east side of it.   The pitch of the
cape bore N.W. distant half a mile, and the extreme points
of the bay from E. to N. by W.   We lay at about half a
cable's length from the nearest shore, which was a low island between the ship and the cape.

At six o'clock the next morning we weighed, and found
that the palm was gone from the small bower anchor.   The
wind was at W.N.W. with hard rain: At eight o'clock we
found a strong current setting us to the eastward, and at
noon, Cape Monday bore W.N.W. distant two miles.   The
Tamar being to windward of us, fetched into the bay, and
anchored again.   We continued to lose ground upon every
tack, and therefore, at two o'clock, anchored upon the
southern shore in sixteen fathom, about five miles to the
eastward of Cape Monday.   At three, however, I weighed
again, for the boat having sounded round the ship, found
the ground rocky. The wind was N.W. with hard rain, and

we continued working all the rest of the day, and all night, every man on board being upon deck the whole time, and every one wet to the skin; for the rain, or rather sheets of water, that came down, did not cease a moment.

In the morning, we had again the mortification to find that, notwithstanding all our labour, we had lost ground upon every tack, in consequence of the current, which continued to set with great force to the eastward. At eight o'clock we bore away, and at nine anchored in the same bay from which we sailed on the 15th.

The wind continued W. and W.N.W. without any tide to the westward, all the 18th and 19th, and the weather was exceedingly bad, with hard squalls and heavy rain. In the mean time I had sent an officer with a boat to sound a bay on the north shore, but he found no anchorage in it. On the 20th, at six o'clock in the morning, a hard squall coming on, the ship drove, and brought the anchor off the bank into forty fathom, but by heaving up the bower, and carrying out the kedge anchor, we got the ship on the bank again. At eight the day following, though the wind was from W.N.W. to S.W. we weighed, and once more stood out of the bay; the current still set very strongly to the eastward, but at noon we found that we had gained about a mile and a half in a contrary direction. The wind now became variable, from S.W. to N.W. and at five in the afternoon, the ship had gained about four miles to the westward; but not being able to find an anchoring-place, and the wind dying away, we drove again very fast to the eastward with the current. At six, however, we anchored in forty fathom, with very good ground, in a bay about two miles to the westward of that from which we sailed in the morning. A swell rolled in here all night, so that our situation was by no means desirable, and therefore, although the wind was still at W.S.W. we weighed and made sail about eight o'clock the next day: We had likewise incessant rain, so that the people were continually wet, which was a great aggravation of their fatigue; yet they were still cheerful, and, what was yet less to be expected, still healthy. This day, to our great joy, we found the current setting to the westward, and we gained ground very fast. At six in the evening, we anchored in the bay on the east side of Cape Monday, where the Tamar lay in eighteen fathom,

the

the pitch of the cape bearing W. by N. distant half a mile. We found this place very safe, the ground being excellent, and there being room enough for two or three ships of the line to moor.

SECTION VII.

The Passage from Cape Monday, in the Streight of Magellan, into the South Seas; with some general Remarks on the Navigation of that Strait.

AT eight the next morning we weighed, and soon after we made sail opened the South Sea, from which such a swell'rolled in upon us as I have seldom seen. At four o'clock in the afternoon, we anchored in a very good bay, with a deep sound at the bottom of it, by which it may be known, about a league to the eastward of Cape Upright, in fourteen fathom. The extreme point of the bay bore from N.W. to N.E. by E. and Cape Upright 'W.N.W. about a cable's length to the eastward of a low island which makes the bay.

At three o'clock in the morning of the 24th, I sent a boat with an officer from each ship, to look for anchoring-places to the westward; but at four in the afternoon they returned without having been able to get round Cape Upright.

The next morning I sent the boats again to the westward, and about six in the evening they returned, having been about four leagues, and found two anchoring-places, but neither of them were very good. We made sail, however, about eight in the forenoon of the next day, and at three, Cape Upright bore E.S.E. distant about three leagues, a remarkable cape on the north shore at the same time bearing N.E. distant four or five miles. This cape, which is very lofty and steep, lies N.N.W. by compass from Cape Upright, at the distance of about three leagues. The south shore in this place had a very bad appearance, many sunken rocks lying about it to a considerable distance, upon which the sea breaks very high. At four the weather became very thick, and in less than half an hour we saw the south shore at the distance of about a mile, but could get no anchoring-place; we therefore tacked, and stood over

to

to the north shore. At half an hour after six, I made the Tamar signal to come under our stern, and ordered her to keep a-head of us all night, and to show lights, and fire a gun every time she changed her tack. At seven it cleared up for a moment just to show us the north shore, bearing W. by N. We tacked immediately, and at eight the wind shifted from N.N.W. to W.N.W. and blew with great violence. Our situation was now very alarming; the storm increased every minute, the weather was extremely thick, the rain seemed to threaten another deluge, we had a long dark night before us, we were in a narrow channel, and surrounded on every side by rocks and breakers. We attempted to clue up the mizen top-sail, but before this service could be done it was blown all to rags: We then brought-to, with the main and fore-topsail close-reefed, and upon the cap, keeping the ship's head to the south-west; but there being a prodigious sea, it broke over us so often that the whole deck was almost continually under water. At nine, by an accidental breaking of the fog, we saw the high cape on the north shore that has been just mentioned, bearing east, at about a mile distance; but we had entirely lost sight of the Tamar. At half an hour after three in the morning, we suddenly perceived ourselves close to a high land on the south shore, upon which we wore, and brought to the northward. The gale still continued, if possible, with increasing violence, and the rain poured down in torrents, so that we were in a manner immersed in water, and expected every moment to be among the breakers. The long-wished-for day at length broke, but the weather was still so thick that no land was to be seen, though we knew it could not be far distant, till after six, when we saw the south shore at about the distance of two miles; and soon after, to our great satisfaction, we saw the Tamar: At this time Cape Monday bore S. E. distant about four miles, and the violence of the gale not abating, we bore away. About seven, both ships came to an anchor in the bay which lies to the eastward of Cape Monday, notwithstanding the sea that rolled in; for we were glad to get anchorage any where.' We had now been twice within four leagues of

Tuesday's

' " The straits are here four or five leagues over, and the mountains seem to be ten times as high as the mast-head of our ships; but not much covered with snow, or encompassed with trees."

Tuesday's Bay, at the western entrance of the streight, and had been twice driven back ten or twelve leagues by such storms as we had now just experienced. When the season is so far advanced as it was when we attempted the passage of this streight, it is a most difficult and dangerous undertaking, as it blows a hurricane incessantly night and day, and the rain is as violent and constant as the wind, with such fogs as often render it impossible to discover any object at the distance of twice the ship's length. This day our best bower cable being quite rubbed to pieces, we cut it into junk, and bent a new one, which we rounded with old rigging, eight fathom from the anchor.

In the afternoon of the day following, the Tamar parted a new best bower cable, it being cut by the rock, and drove over to the east side of the bay, where she was brought up at a very little distance from some rocks, against which she must otherwise have been dashed to pieces.

At seven o'clock in the morning of the 29th, we weighed, and found our small bower-cable very much rubbed by the foul ground, so that we were obliged to cut no less than six-and-twenty fathom of it off, and bend it again. In about half an hour, the Tamar, being very near the rocks, and not being able to purchase her anchor, made signals of distress. I was therefore obliged to stand into the bay again, and having anchored, I sent hawsers on board the Tamar, and heaved her up while she purchased her anchor, after which we heaved her to windward, and at noon, being got into a proper birth, she anchored again. We continued in our station all night, and the next morning a gale came on at W.N.W. which was still more violent than any that had preceded it; the water was torn up all around us, and carried much higher than the mast heads, a dreadful sea at the same time rolling in; so that, knowing the ground to be foul, we were in constant apprehension of parting our cables, in which case we must have been almost instantly dashed to atoms against the rocks that were just to leeward of us, and upon which the sea broke with inconceivable fury, and a noise not less loud than thunder. We lowered all the main and fore-yards, let go the small bower, veered a cable and a half on the best bower, and having bent the sheet-cable, stood by the anchor all the rest of the day, and till midnight, the sea often breaking half way up our main shrouds. About one in the morning, the weather became

somewhat

somewhat more moderate, but continued to be very dark, rainy, and tempestuous, till midnight, when the wind shifted to the S.W. and soon afterwards it became comparatively calm and clear.

The next morning, which was the first of April, we had a stark calm, with now and then some light airs from the eastward ; but the weather was again thick with hard rain, and we found a current setting strongly to the eastward. At four o'clock we got up the lower yards, unbent the sheet-cable, and weighed the small bower ; at eight we weighed the best bower, and found the cable very much rubbed in several places, which we considered as a great misfortune, it being a fine new cable, which never had been wet before. At eleven, we hove short on the stream-anchor ; but soon after, it being calm, and a thick fog coming on with hard rain, we veered away the stream-cable, and with a warp to the Tamar, heaved the ship upon the bank again, and let go the small bower in two-and-twenty fathom.

At six in the evening, we had strong gales at W.N.W. with violent squalls and much rain, and continued in our station till the morning of the 3d, when I sent the Tamar's boat, with an officer from each ship, to the westward, in search of anchoring-places on the south shore ; and at the same time I sent my own cutter with an officer to seek anchoring-places on the north shore.

The cutter returned the next morning, at six o'clock, having been about five leagues to the westward upon the north shore, and found two anchoring-places. The officer reported, that having been on shore, he had fallen in with some Indians, who had with them a canoe of a construction very different from any that they had seen in the strait before : This vessel consisted of planks sewed together, but all the others were nothing more than the bark of large trees, tied together at the ends, and kept open by short pieces of wood, which were thrust in transversely between the two sides, like the boats which children make of a bean-shell. The people, he said, were the nearest to brutes in their manner and appearance of any he had seen : They were, like some which we had met with before, quite naked, notwithstanding the severity of the weather, except part of a seal-skin which was thrown over their shoulders ; and they eat their food, which was such as no other animal but
a hog

a hog would touch, without any dressing : They had with them a large piece of whale blubber, which stunk intolerably, and one of them tore it to pieces with his teeth, and gave it about to the rest, who devoured it with the voracity of a wild beast.   They did not, however, look upon what they saw in the possession of our people with indifference; for while one of them was asleep, they cut off the hinder part of his jacket with a sharp flint which they use as a knife.

About eight o'clock, we made sail, and found little or no current.   At noon, Cape Upright bore **W.S.W.** distant three leagues; and at six in the evening, we anchored in the bay, on the southern shore, which lies about a league to the eastward of the cape, and had fifteen fathom water.

While we were lying here, and taking in wood and water, seven or eight Indians in a canoe came round the western point of the bay, and having landed opposite to the ship, made a fire.   We invited them to come on board by all the signs we could devise, but without success; I therefore took the jolly-boat, and went on shore to them.   I introduced myself by making them presents of several trifles, with which they seemed to be much gratified, and we became very intimate in a few minutes: After we had spent some time together, I sent away my people, in the boat, for some bread, and remained on shore with them alone. When the boat returned with the bread, I divided it among them, and I remarked with equal pleasure and surprise, that if a bit of the biscuit happened to fall, not one of them offered to touch it till I gave my consent.   In the mean time some of my people were cutting a little grass for two or three sheep which I had still left on board, and at length the Indians perceiving what they were doing, ran immediately, and tearing up all the weeds they could get, carried them to the boat, which in a very short time was filled almost up to her gunwale.   I was much gratified by this token of their good-will, and I could perceive that they were pleased with the pleasure that I expressed upon the occasion: They had indeed taken such a fancy to us, that when I returned on board the boat, they all got into their canoe, and followed me.   When we came near the ship, however, they stopped, and gazed at her as if held in surprise by a mixture of astonishment and terror; but at last,
though

though not without some difficulty, I prevailed upon four
or five of them to venture on board. As soon as they entered the ship I made them several presents, and in a very
little time they appeared to be perfectly at ease. As I was
very desirous to entertain them, one of the midshipmen
played upon the violin, and some of my people danced; at
this they were so much delighted, and so impatient to show
their gratitude, that one of them went over the ship's side
into the canoe, and fetched up a seal-skin bag of red paint,
and immediately smeared the fiddler's face all over with it:
He was very desirous to pay me the same compliment,
which, however, I thought fit to decline; but he made
many very vigorous efforts to get the better of my modesty,
and it was not without some difficulty that I defended myself from receiving the honour he designed me in my own
despight. After having diverted and entertained them several hours, I intimated to them that it would be proper for
them to go on shore; but their attachment was such, that
it was by no means an easy matter to get them out of the
ship. Their canoe was not of bark, but of planks sewed together.

On Sunday the 7th, at six o'clock in the morning, we
weighed, with a moderate breeze at E.N.E. and fine weather. At seven, we were abreast of Cape Upright; and at
noon, it bore E.S.E. distant four leagues: Soon after we
tried the current, and found it set to the eastward at the
rate of a knot and a half an hour. At three it fell calm,
and the current driving us to the eastward very fast, we
dropped an anchor, which before it took the ground was in
one hundred and twenty fathom.

This day, and not before, the Tamar's boat returned from
the westward: She had been within two or three leagues
of Cape Pillar, and had found several very good anchoring-
places on the south shore.

At one o'clock the next morning, having a fresh gale at
west, we weighed, notwithstanding the weather was thick,
and made sail; at eleven it blew very hard, with violent
rain and a great sea, and as we perceived that we rather
lost than gained ground, we stood in for a bay on the south
shore, about four leagues to the westward of Cape Upright,
and anchored in twenty fathom: The ground was not good,
but in other respects this was one of the best harbours that
we had met with in the streight, for it was impossible that any
wind

wind should hurt us. There being less wind in the afternoon, and it inclining a little towards the south, we unmoored at two, and at four, the wind having then come
round to the S.S.E. and being a moderate breeze, we weighed and steered to the westward: We made about two
leagues and a half, but night then coming on, we anchored,
not without great difficulty, in a very good bay on the south
shore in twenty fathom. As very violent gusts came from
the land, we were very near being driven off before we
could let go an anchor, and if we had not at last succeeded
we must have passed a dreadful night in the strait; for it
blew a hurricane from the time we came to an anchor till
the morning, with violent rain, which was sometimes inter-
mingled with snow.

At six o'clock, the wind being still fresh and squally at
S.S.E. we weighed and steered W. by N. along the south
shore. At eleven, we were abreast of Cape Pillar, which
by compass is about fourteen leagues W.$\frac{1}{4}$N. from Cape
Upright. Cape Pillar may be known by a large gap upon
the top, and when it bears W.S.W. an island appears off
it which has an appearance somewhat like a hay-stack, and
about which lie several rocks. The strait to the eastward
of the cape is between seven and eight leagues over; the
land on each side is of a moderate height, but it is lowest
on the north shore, the south shore being much the boldest,
though both are craggy and broken. Westminster Island
is nearer to the north than the south shore; and, by the
compass, lies N.E. from Cape Pillar. The land on the
north shore, near the west end of the strait, makes in many
islands and rocks, upon which the sea breaks in a tremendous manner. The land about Cape Victory is distant from
Cape Pillar about ten or eleven leagues, in the direction of
N. W. by N. From the cape westward, the coast trends
S. S. W. $\frac{1}{2}$ W. to Cape Deseada, a low point, off which lie
innumerable rocks and breakers. About four leagues W.
S. W. from Cape Deseada, lie some dangerous rocks, called by Sir John Narborough the Judges, upon which a mountainous surf always breaks with inconceivable fury. Four
small islands, called the Islands of Direction, are distant
from Cape Pillar about eight leagues, in the direction of
N. W. by W. When we were off this cape it was stark
calm; but I never saw such a swell as rolled in here, nor such
a surge as broke on each shore. I expected every moment
that

that the wind would spring up from its usual quarter, and that the best which could happen to us would be to be driven many leagues up the streight again. Contrary, however, to all expectation, a fine steady gale sprung up at S. E. to which I spread all the sail that it was possible for the ship to bear, and ran off from this frightful and desolate coast at the rate of nine miles an hour; so that by eight o'clock in the evening we had left it twenty leagues behind us. And now, to make the ship as stiff as possible, I knocked down our after bulk-head, and got two of the boats under the half-deck; I also placed my twelve-oared cutter under the boom; so that we had nothing upon the skids but the jolly-boat; and the alteration which this made in the vessel is inconceivable: For the weight of the boats upon the skids made her crank, and in a great sea they were also in danger of being lost.

It is probable, that whoever shall read this account of the difficulties and dangers which attended our passage through the Streight of Magellan, will conclude, that it ought never to be attempted again; but that all ships which shall hereafter sail a western course from Europe into the South Seas ought to go round Cape Horn. I, however, who have been twice round Cape Horn, am of a different opinion. I think that at a proper season of the year, not only a single vessel, but a large squadron might pass the streight in less than three weeks; and I think, to take the proper season, they should be at the eastern entrance some time in the month of December.[2] One great advantage of this passage, is the
facility

[2] Bougainville gives the same advice as to preferring the passage through the streights, from the month of September till the end of March, but at all other periods he recommends to go round Cape Horn. He was 52 days in going the whole length of the streights, reckoning from Cape Virgin Mary to Cape Pillar, a distance of 342 miles, and he says that 36 hours of fair wind were sufficient to carry him from Port Gallant to the Pacific Ocean. Captain Wallis, we shall see, did not realize this opinion, or the hopes formed on it—he was almost four months in getting through the streights, although he attempted the passage at the very time recommended by Byron. On the other hand, Captain Krusenstern doubled the cape in four weeks only, after his leaving St Catharine's Island, which the reader will observe is considerably northward of the river La Plata, " a voyage," says he, " which perhaps was never made in a shorter time." In weathering the cape, he took the advice of Cook, not to approach the land nearer than 30 or 36 miles, by which means he avoided the strong currents which, according to our great navigator's assertion, seem to lose all their force at that distance.—E.

facility with which fish is almost every where to be procured, with wild celery, scurvy-grass, berries, and many other
vegetables in great abundance; for to this I impute the
healthiness of my ship's company, not a single man being
affected with the scurvy in the slightest degree, nor upon
the sick list for any other disorder, notwithstanding the
hardship and labour which they endured in the passage,
which cost us seven weeks and two days, as we entered the
streight on Sunday the 17th of February, and quitted it on
Tuesday the 9th of April. Wood and water are also to be
procured almost at every anchoring-place beyond Fresh-
water Bay. Our sufferings I impute wholly to our passing
the streight just as the sun approached the equinox, when,
in this high latitude, the worst weather was to be expected;
and indeed the weather we had was dreadful beyond all
description.

Section VIII.

The Run from the Western Entrance of the Streight of Magellan to the Islands of Disappointment.

Having cleared the streight, we pursued our course to
the westward, till Friday, April the 26th, when we discovered the island of Massafuero, bearing W. N. W. ¼ W. distant about sixteen leagues; but as to the northward it was
hazy, the island of Don Juan Fernandez was not in sight.
During this run, the variation had gradually decreased from
22° to 9° 36'. E.

We bore away for Masafuero,[3] and at sun-set, being within about seven leagues of it, we brought-to, and afterwards
kept the wind all night. At day-break the next day, we
bore away again for the island, at the same time sending an
officer, with a boat from each ship, to sound the eastern side
of it. About noon, the middle of the island bore W. distant about three miles, and as I saw the boats run along the
shore, without being able to land any where for the surf, I
bore

---

[3] " The commodore thought it more advisable to touch at this island
than at Juan Fernandez; it being rather more secure than the latter, from
any discoveries which the Spaniards might make of our designs; in consequence of which our voyage, and all our farther discoveries, might have
been prevented."

bore down to the north part of the island, off which a reef runs for the distance of about two miles, and lay by for them. This island is very high, and the greater part of it is covered with wood; but towards the north end, where I lay, some spots seemed to have been cleared, upon which great numbers of goats were feeding, and they had a green and pleasant appearance. When the boats returned, the officer informed me that he had found a bank, on the east side of the island nearest to the south point, at a considerable distance from the shore, where we might anchor, and opposite to which there was a fine fall of fresh water; but near the north point, he said, he could find no anchorage. The boats brought off a great quantity of very fine fish, which they had caught with hook and line near the shore; and as soon as we had taken them on board, which was late in the afternoon, we made sail, and worked to windward in the night.

At seven o'clock in the morning, we anchored with the small bower, on the bank which the boats had discovered, in twenty-four fathom, with black sandy ground. The extreme points bore from S. to N. W. and the fall of water bore S. S. W. distant about a mile from the ship's station. This part of the island lies north and south, and is about four miles long: The soundings are very regular, from twenty to fifteen fathom, within two cables' length of the shore. Soon after we were come to an anchor, I sent out the boats to endeavour to get some wood and water, but as I observed the shore to be rocky, and a surf to break with great violence upon it, I ordered all the men to put on cork-jackets, which had been sent with us to be made use of upon such occasions. By the help of these jackets, which not only assisted the men in swimming, but prevented their being bruised against the rocks, we got off a considerable quantity of water and wood, which, without such assistance, we could not have done: There was, however, another species of danger here, against which cork-jackets afforded no defence, for the sea abounded with sharks of an enormous size, which, when they saw a man in the water, would dart into the very surf to seize him: Our people, however, happily escaped them, though they were many times very near: One of them, which was upwards of twenty feet long, came close to one of the boats that was watering, and having seized a large seal, instantly devoured it at one mouthful; and

I my-

I myself saw another of nearly the same size do the same thing under the ship's stern. Our people killed and sent off several of the goats, which we thought as good as the best venison in England; and I observed, that one of them appeared to have been caught and marked, its right ear being slit in a manner that could not have happened by accident.[4] We had also fish in such plenty, that one boat would, with hooks and lines, catch, in a few hours, as much as would serve a large ship's company two days: They were of various sorts, all excellent in their kind, and many of them weighed from twenty to thirty pounds.

This evening, the surf running very high, the gunner and one of the seamen who were on shore with the waterers, were afraid to venture off, and the boat therefore, when she came on board the last time, left them behind her.

The next day we found a more convenient watering-place about a mile and a half to the northward of the ship, and about the middle-way between the north and south points of the island, there being at this place less surf than where the boats first went on shore. The tide here set twelve hours to the northward, and twelve to the southward, which we found very convenient, for as the wind was southerly, with a great swell, the boats could not otherwise have got on board with their water. We got off ten tons of water from the new watering-place this day, and in the afternoon I sent a boat to fetch off the gunner and seaman, who had been left on shore at the old watering-place the night before; but the surf was still so great, that the seaman, who could not swim, was afraid to venture: He was therefore again left behind, and the gunner stayed with him.

As soon as this was reported to me, I sent another boat to inform them, that as, by the appearances of the weather, there was reason to believe it would soon blow hard, I was afraid I might be driven off the bank in the night, the consequence of which would be that they must be left behind upon the island. When the boat came to the surf, the people on board delivered my message, upon which the gunner swam

---

[4] The other account says the same of two of the goats caught here, and conjectures, as no traces of inhabitants were then to be discovered in the island, that " some solitary Selkirk had dwelt there, who, like his namesake at Juan Fernandez, when he caught more than he wanted, marked them and let them go." Captain Carteret gives some particulars respecting this island, to which the reader is referred.—E.

swam through the surf, and got on board her; but the seaman, though he had a cork-jacket on, said he was sure he
should be drowned if he attempted to get off to the boat,
and that, chusing rather to die a natural death, he was determined at all events to remain upon the island : He then
took an affectionate leave of the people, wishing them all
happiness, and the people on board returned his good wishes.
One of the midshipmen, however, just as the boat was about
to return, took the end of a rope in his hand, jumped into
the sea, and swam through the surf to the beach, where
poor John still continued ruminating upon his situation, in
a dejected attitude, and with a most disconsolate length of
countenance.   The midshipman began to expostulate with
him upon the strange resolution he had taken, and in the
mean time having made a running knot in his rope, he dexterously contrived to throw it round his body, calling out
to his companions in the boat, who had hold of the other
end of it, to haul away; they instantly took the hint, and
the poor seceder was very soon dragged through the surf
into the boat : He had, however, swallowed so great a quantity of water that he was to all appearance dead, but, being
held up by the heels, he soon recovered his speech and motion, and was perfectly well the next day.   In the evening
I removed Captain Mouat from the Tamar, and appointed
him captain of the Dolphin under me ; Mr Cumming, my
first lieutenant, I appointed captain of the Tamar, taking
Mr Carteret, her first lieutenant, on board in his room, and
gave Mr Kendal, one of the mates of the Dolphin, a commission as second lieutenant of the Tamar.

On the 30th, at seven o'clock in the morning, we weigh
ed, and steered, to the northward, along the east and north-
east side of the island, but could find no anchoring-place ;
we bore away, therefore, with a fresh gale at S.E. and hazy weather, and at noon, the middle of the island was distant eight leagues, in the direction of S.S.E.   I continued
to steer N. 3° W. the next day, and at noon on the 2d of
May I changed my course, and steered W. intending, if
possible, to make the land, which is called Davis's Land in
the charts, and is laid down in latitude 27° 30′ S. and about
500 leagues west of Copiapo in Chili; but on the 9th, finding little prospect of getting to the westward, in the latitude
which I at first proposed, being then in latitude 26° 46′ S.
longitude 94° 45′ W. and having a great run to make, I determined

termined to steer a north-west course till I got the true trade-wind, and then to stand to the westward till I should fall in with Solomon's Islands, if any such there were, or make some new discovery.

On the 10th we saw several dolphins and bonnettas about the ship, and the next day some straggling birds, which were brown on the back and the upper part of their wings, and white on the rest of the body, with a short beak, and a short pointed tail. The variation was now decreased to 4° 45' E. our latitude was 24° 30' S. our longitude 97° 45' W.

On the 14th we saw several grampuses, and more of the birds which have just been described, so that, imagining we might be near some land, we kept a good look-out, but saw nothing. In latitude 23° 2' S. longitude 101° 28' W. the variation, by azimuth, was 3° 20' E.

On the morning of the 16th we saw two very remarkable birds; they flew very high, were as large as geese, and all over as white as snow, except their legs, which were black: I now began to imagine that I had passed some land, or islands, which lay to the southward of us, for the last night we observed, that, although we had generally a great swell from that quarter, the water became quite smooth for a few hours, after which the swell returned.

On the 22d, being in latitude 20° 52' S. longitude 115° 38' W. with a faint breeze at E.S.E. we had so great a swell from the southward, that we were in perpetual danger of our masts rolling over the ship's side, so that I was obliged to haul more to the northward, as well to ease the ship, as in hopes of getting the true trade-wind, which we had not yet; and now, to my great concern, some of my best men began to complain of the scurvy. This day, for the first time, we caught two bonnettas; we also saw several tropic birds about the ship, and observed that they were larger than any we had seen before; their whole plumage was white, and they had two long feathers in the tail. The variation now had changed its direction, and was 19' W.

On the 26th we saw two large birds about the ship, which were all black, except the neck and the beak, which were white; they had long wings, and long feathers in their tails, yet we observed that they flew heavily, and therefore imagined that they were of a species which did not usually fly far from the shore. I had flattered myself, that, before we had run six degrees to the northward of Masafuero, we

should

should have found a settled trade-wind to the S.E. but the winds still continued to the north, though we had a mountainous swell from the S.W. Our latitude was now 16° 55' S. longitude 127° 55' W. and here the needle, at this time, had no variation.

On the 28th we saw two fine large birds about the ship, one of which was brown and white, and the other black and white; they wanted much to settle upon the yards, but the working of the ship frighted them.

On the 31st the wind shifted from N. by W. to N.W. by W. and the number of birds that were now about the ship was very great; from these circumstances, and our having lost the great south-west swell, I imagined some land to be near, and we looked out for it with great diligence, for our people began now to fall down with the scurvy very fast.

We saw no land, however, till one o'clock in the morning of Friday the 7th of June, when we were in latitude 14° 5' S. longitude 144° 58' W. and observed the variation to be 4° 30' E. After making the land, I hauled upon a wind under an easy sail till the morning, and then a low small island bore from us W.S.W. at the distance of about two leagues. In a very short time we saw another island to windward of us, bearing E.S.E. distant between three and four leagues : This appeared to be much larger than that which we first discovered, and we must have passed very near it in the night.

I stood for the small island, which, as we drew near it, had a most beautiful appearance; it was surrounded by a beach of the finest white sand, and within, it was covered with tall trees, which extended their shade to a great distance, and formed the most delightful groves that can be imagined, without underwood. We judged this island to be about five miles in circumference, and from each end of it we saw a spit running out into the sea, upon which the surge broke with great fury; there was also a great surf all round it. We soon perceived that it was inhabited, for many of the natives appeared upon the beach, with spears in their hands that were at least sixteen feet long. They presently made several large fires, which we supposed to be a signal; for we immediately perceived several fires upon the larger island that was to windward of us, by which we knew that also to be inhabited. I sent the boat with an officer to look for an anchoring-place, who, to our great regret and disappointment,

pointment, returned with an account that he had been all
round the island, and that no bottom could be found within
less than a cable's length of the shore, which was surrounded close to the beach with a steep coral rock.[5] The scurvy
by this time had made dreadful havock among us, many of
my best men being now confined to their hammocks; the
poor wretches who were able to crawl upon the deck, stood
gazing at this little paradise, which Nature had forbidden
them to enter, with sensations which cannot easily be conceived; they saw cocoa-nuts in great abundance, the milk
of which is, perhaps, the most powerful antiscorbutic in the
world: They had reason to suppose that there were limes,
bananas, and other fruits which are generally found between
the tropics; and, to increase their mortification, they saw
the shells of many turtle scattered about the shore. When
I knew the soundings, I could not forbear standing close
round the island with the ship, though I also knew it was
impossible to procure any of the refreshments which it produced. The natives ran along the shore abreast of the ship,
shouting and dancing; they also frequently brandished their
long spears, and then threw themselves backward, and lay
a few minutes motionless, as if they had been dead: This
we understood as a menace that they would kill us, if we
ventured to go on shore. As we were sailing along the coast,
we took notice that in one place the natives had fixed upright in the sand two spears, to the top of which they had
fastened several things that fluttered in the air, and that
some of them were every moment kneeling down before
them, as we supposed invoking the assistance of some invi-
sible being to defend them against us. While I was thus
circumnavigating the island with the ship, I sent the boats
out again to sound, and when they came near the shore, the
Indians set up one of the most hideous yells I had ever

VOL. XII.   F   heard,

---

[5] " Other objections stood also in our way; for the Indians had surrounded the shore with staves and javelins 16 feet long, with a piece of
bone at the end in the form of a harpoon, in their hands, hallooing and
shouting in the most hideous manner, at the same time making signs with
their hands for us to be gone; always taking care, as the boat sailed along
the shore, to move in the same direction and accompany it; and though
the men saw some turtle at a distance, they could get at none, as those
Indians still kept opposite to them."—" They altogether amounted to about
50 in number, including women and children; and to the south-west we
could perceive their huts, under the shade of the most lovely grove we ever
saw."

heard, pointing at the same time to their spears, and poising in their hands large stones which they took up from the beach. Our men on the contrary made all the signs of amity and good-will that they could devise, and at the same time threw them bread and many other things, none of which they vouchsafed so much as to touch, but with great expedition hauled five or six large canoes, which we saw lying upon the beach, up into the wood. When this was done, they waded into the water, and seemed to watch for an opportunity of laying hold of the boat, that they might drag her on shore: The people on board her, apprehending that this was their design, and that if they got them on shore they would certainly put them to death, were very impatient to be before-hand with them, and would fain have fired upon them; but the officer on board, having no permission from me to commit any hostilities, restrained them. I should indeed have thought myself at liberty to have obtained by force the refreshments, for want of which our people were dying, if it had been possible to have come to an anchor, supposing we could not have made these poor savages our friends; but nothing could justify the taking away their lives for a mere imaginary or intentional injury, without procuring the least advantage to ourselves. They were of a deep copper colour, exceedingly stout and well-limbed, and remarkably nimble and active, for I never saw men run so fast in my life. This island lies in latitude 14° 5′ S., longitude 145° 4′ W. from the meridian of London. As the boats reported a second time that there was no anchoring ground about this island, I determined to work up to the other, which was accordingly done all the rest of the day and the following night.

At six o'clock in the morning of the 8th, we brought-to on the west side of it, at the distance of about three quarters of a mile from the shore, but we had no soundings with one hundred and forty fathom of line. We now perceived several other low islands, or rather peninsulas, most of them being joined one to the other by a neck of land, very narrow, and almost level with the surface of the water, which breaks high over it. In approaching these islands the cocoa-nut trees are first discovered, as they are higher than any part of the surface. I sent a boat with an officer from each ship to sound the lee-side of these islands for an anchoring-place; and as soon as they left the ship, I saw the

Indians

Indians run down to the beach in great numbers, armed with long spears and clubs ; they kept abreast of the boats as they went sounding along the shore, and used many threatening gestures to prevent their landing ; I therefore fired a nine-pound shot from the ship over their heads, upon which they ran into the woods with great precipitation.[6] At ten o'clock the boats returned, but could get no soundings close in with the surf, which broke very high upon the shore. The middle of this cluster of islands lies in latitude 14° 10′ S., longitude 144° 52′ W. ; the variation of the compass was here 4° 30′ E.

At half an hour after ten, we bore away and made sail to the westward, finding it impossible to procure at these islands any refreshment for our sick, whose situation was becoming more deplorable every hour, and I therefore called them the *Islands of Disappointment.*

Section IX.

The Discovery of King George's Islands, with a Description of them, and an Account of several Incidents that happened there.

At half an hour after five o'clock in the afternoon of the 9th, we saw land again, bearing W. S. W. at the distance of six or seven leagues ; and at seven we brought-to for the night. In the morning, being within three miles of the shore, we discovered it to be a long low island, with a white beach, of a pleasant appearance, full of cocoa-nut and other trees, and surrounded with a rock of red coral. We stood along

[6] " They were in much greater number than at the other island, and followed us in the same manner, several hundreds of them running along the coast in great disorder."—" They had many canoes, which, on our approaching the shore, they dragged into the woods, and at the same time the women came with great stones in their hands to assist the men in preventing our landing."—" We had now 30 sick on board, to whom the land air, the fruit and vegetables, that appeared so beautiful and attractive, would doubtless have afforded immediate relief." It seems very probable, from the conduct of these islanders, and of the others mentioned in the next section, that some former visitants had used them so ill, as to unite them in determined opposition to the entrance of all strangers. Would it be unfair to imagine, from a circumstance afterwards narrated, that these visitants were Dutch ? All the seafaring nations of Europe, alas ! are too deeply implicated in the animosities and miseries of the South Sea inhabitants.—E.

along the north-east side of it, within half a mile of the
shore; and the savages, as soon as they saw us, made great
fires, as we supposed, to alarm the distant inhabitants of the
island, and ran along the beach, abreast of the ship, in great
numbers, armed in the same manner as the natives of the
Islands of Disappointment. Over the land on this side of
the island we could see a large lake of salt water, or lagoon,
which appeared to be two or three leagues wide, and to
reach within a small distance of the opposite shore. Into
this lagoon we saw a small inlet about a league from the
south-west point, off which we brought-to. At this place
the natives have built a little town, under the shade of a
fine grove of cocoa-nut trees. I immediately sent off the
boats, with an officer in each, to sound; but they could find
no anchorage, the shore being every where as steep as a
wall, except at the very mouth of the inlet, which was scarcely a ship's length wide, and there they had thirteen fathom,
with a bottom of coral rock. We stood close in with the
ships, and saw hundreds of the savages, ranged in very good
order, and standing up to their waists in water; they were
all armed in the same manner as those that we had seen at
the other islands, and one of them carried a piece of mat
fastened to the top of a pole, which we imagined was an ensign. They made a most hideous and incessant noise, and
in a short time many large canoes came down the lake to
join them. Our boats were still out, and the people on
board them made all the signs of friendship that they could
invent, upon which some of the canoes came through the
inlet and drew near them. We now began to hope that a
friendly intercourse might be established; but we soon discovered that the Indians had no other design than to haul
the boats on shore: Many of them leaped off the rocks,
and swam to them; and one of them got into that which
belonged to the Tamar, and in the twinkling of an eye seized a seaman's jacket, and jumping over board with it, never once appeared above water till he was close in shore
among his companions. Another of them got hold of a
midshipman's hat, but not knowing how to take it off, he
pulled it downward instead of lifting it up; so that the owner had time to prevent its being taken away, otherwise it
would probably have disappeared as suddenly as the jacket.
Our men bore all this with much patience, and the Indians
seemed to triumph in their impunity.

About

About noon, finding there was no anchorage here, I bore away and steered along the shore to the westermost point of the island : The boats immediately followed us, and kept sounding close to the beach, but could get no ground.

When we came to the westermost point of this island, we saw another, bearing S. W. by W. about four leagues distant. We were at this time about a league beyond the inlet where we had left the natives, but they were not satisfied with having got rid of us quietly ; for I now perceived two large double canoes sailing after the ship, with about thirty men in each, all armed after the manner of their country. The boats were a good way to leeward of us, and the canoes passing between the ship and the shore, seemed very eagerly to give them chace. Upon this I made the signal for the boats to speak with the canoes, and as soon as they perceived it; they turned, and made towards the Indians, who, seeing this, were seized with a sudden panic, and immediately hauling down their sails, paddled back again at a surprising rate. Our boats however came up with them ; but notwithstanding the dreadful surf that broke upon the shore, the canoes pushed through it, and the Indians immediately hauled them up upon the beach. Our boats followed them, and the Indians, dreading an invasion of their coast, prepared to defend it with clubs and stones, upon which our men fired, and killed two or three of them : One of them received three balls which went quite through his body; yet he afterwards took up a large stone, and died in the action of throwing it against his enemy. This man fell close to our boats, so that the Indians who remained unhurt did not dare to attempt the carrying off his body, which gave us an opportunity to examine it; but they carried off the rest of their dead, and made the best of their way back to their companions at the inlet. Our boats then returned, and brought off the two canoes which they had pursued. One of them was thirty-two feet long, and the other somewhat less, but they were both of a very curious construction, and must have cost those who made them infinite labour. They consisted of planks exceedingly well wrought, and in many places adorned with carving; these planks were sewed together, and over every seam there was a stripe of tortoise-shell, very artificially fastened, to keep out the weather : Their bottoms were as sharp as a wedge, and they were very narrow; and therefore two of them

were

were joined laterally together by a couple of strong spars,
so that there was a space of about six or eight feet between
them : A mast was hoisted in each of them, and the sail
was spread between the masts : The sail, which I preserved,
and which is now in my possession, is made of matting,
and is as neat a piece of work as ever I saw : their paddles
were very curious, and their cordage was as good and as
well laid as any in England, though it appeared to be made
of the outer covering of the cocoa-nut. When these vessels
sail, several men sit upon the spars which hold the canoes
together.

As the surf, which broke very high upon the shore, rendered it impossible to procure refreshments for the sick
in this part of the island, I hauled the wind, and worked
back to the inlet, being determined to try once more what
could be done there.

I recovered that station in the afternoon, and immediately sent the boats to sound the inlet again, but they confirmed the account which had been made before, that it afforded no anchorage for a ship. While the boats were absent,
I observed a great number of the natives upon the point
near the spot where we had left them in the morning, and
they seemed to be very busy in loading a great number of
large canoes which lay close to the beach. As I thought
they might be troublesome, and was unwilling that they
should suffer by another unequal contest with our people, I
fired a shot over their heads, which produced the effect I intended, for they all disappeared in a moment.

Just before the evening closed in, our boats landed, and
got a few cocoa-nuts, which they brought off, and saw none
of the inhabitants. In the night, during which we had
rain and hard squalls, I stood off and on with the ships, and
at seven o'clock in the morning brought-to off the inlet. I
immediately sent the boats on shore in search of refreshments, and made all the men who were not so ill of the
scurvy as to be laid up, go in them ; I also went on shore
myself, and continued there the whole day. We saw many
houses or wigwams of the natives, but they were totally deserted, except by the dogs, who kept an incessant howling
from the time we came on shore till we returned to the ship :
They were low mean hovels, thatched with cocoa-nut branches ; but they were most delightfully situated in a fine grove
of stately trees, many of which were the cocoa-nut, and

many

many such as we were utterly unacquainted with. The cocoa-nut trees seem to furnish them with almost all the necessaries of life ; particularly food, sails, cordage, timber,
and vessels to hold water ; so that probably these people always fix their habitations where the trees abound. We observed the shore to be covered with coral, and the shells of
very large pearl oysters ; so that I make no doubt but that
as profitable a pearl fishery might be established here as any
in the world. We saw but little of the people, except at a
distance ; we could however perceive that the women had
a piece of cloth of some kind, probably fabricated of the
same stuff as their sail, hanging from the waist as low as the
knee ; the men were naked.

Our people, in rummaging some of the huts, found the
carved head of a rudder, which had manifestly belonged to
a Dutch long-boat, and was very old and worm-eaten. They
found also a piece of hammered iron, a piece of brass, and
some small iron tools, which the ancestors of the present inhabitants of this place probably obtained from the Dutch
ship to which the long-boat had belonged, all which I
brought away with me. Whether these people found
means to cut off the ship, or whether she was lost upon the
island, or after she left it, cannot be known ; but there is
reason to believe that she never returned to Europe, because
no account of her voyage, or of any discoveries that she
made, is extant. If the ship sailed from this place in safety, it is not perhaps easy to account for her leaving the rudder of her long-boat behind her : And if she was cut off by
the natives, there must be much more considerable remains
of her in the island, especially of her iron-work, upon which
all Indian nations, who have no metal, set the highest value ; we had no opportunities however to examine this matter farther. The hammered-iron, brass, and iron tools, I
brought away with me ; but we found a tool exactly in the
form of a carpenter's adze, the blade of which was a pearl
oyster-shell ; possibly this might have been made in imitation of an adze which had belonged to the carpenter of the
Dutch ship, for among the tools that I brought away there
was one which seemed to be the remains of such an implement, though it was worn away almost to nothing.

Close to the houses of these people, we saw buildings of
another kind, which appeared to be burying-places, and
from which we judged that they had great veneration for
their

their dead. They were situated under lofty trees, that gave
a thick shade; the sides and tops were of stone; and in
their figure they somewhat resembled the square tombs,
with a flat top, which are always to be found in our country church-yards. Near these buildings we found many
neat boxes full of human bones, and upon the branches of
the trees which shaded them, hung a great number of the
heads and bones of turtle, and a variety of fish, inclosed in
a kind of basket-work of reeds: Some of the fish we took
down, and found that nothing remained but the skin and
the teeth; the bones and entrails seemed to have been extracted, and the muscular flesh dried away.

We sent off several boat-loads of cocoa-nuts, and a great
quantity of scurvy-grass, with which the island is covered;
refreshments which were of infinite service to us, as by this
time I believe there was not a man among us wholly un-
touched by the scurvy.

The fresh water here is very good, but it is scarce; the
wells which supply the natives are so small, that when two
or three cocoa-nut shells have been filled from them, they
are dry for a few minutes; but as they presently fill again,
if a little pains were taken to enlarge them, they would
abundantly supply any ship with water.

We saw no venomous creature here; but the flies were
an intolerable torment, they covered us from head to foot,
and filled not only the boat, but the ships. We saw great
numbers of parrots and paroquets, and several other birds
which were altogether unknown to us; we saw also a beautiful kind of dove, so tame that some of them frequently
came close to us, and even followed us into the Indian huts.

All this day the natives kept themselves closely concealed, and did not even make a smoke upon any part of the
islands as far as we could see; probably fearing that a smoke
might discover the place of their retreat. In the evening,
we all returned on board the ship.

This part of the island lies in latitude 14° 29' S., longitude 148° 50' W. and after I got on board, I hauled a little
way farther from the shore, intending to visit the other island
in the morning, which had been seen to the westward of that
before which the ship lay, and which is distant about sixty-
nine leagues from the Islands of Disappointment, in the direction of W. ¼ S.

The next morning at six o'clock, I made sail for the
island

island which I intended to visit, and when I reached it, I
steered S. W. by W. close along the north-east side of it,
but could get no soundings : This side is about six or seven
leagues long, and the whole makes much the same appearance as the other, having a large salt-water lake in the middle of it.   As soon as the ship came in sight, the natives
ran down to the beach in great numbers : They were armed in the same manner as those that we had seen upon the
other island, and kept abreast of the ship for several leagues.
As the heat of this climate is very great, they seemed to
suffer much by running so far in the sun, for they sometimes
plunged into the sea, and sometimes fell flat upon the sand,
that the surf might break over them, after which they renewed the race with great vigour.   Our boats were at this
time sounding along the shore, as usual, but I had given
strict orders to the officers who commanded them never to
molest the natives, except it should become absolutely necessary for their own defence, but to try all possible means
to obtain their confidence and good will : Our people therefore went as near to the shore as they durst for the surf, and
made signs that they wanted water ; the Indians readily understood them, and directed them to run down farther along
the shore, which they did, till they came abreast of such a
cluster of houses as we had just left upon the other island ;
to this place the Indians still followed them, and were there
joined by many others : The boats immediately hauled close
into the surf, and we brought-to, with the ships, at a little
distance from the shore, upon which a stout old man, with
a long white beard, that gave him a very venerable appearance, came down from the houses to the beach.   He was
attended by a young man, and appeared to have the authority of a chief or king : The rest of the Indians, at a signal which he made, retired to a little distance, and he then
advanced quite to the water's edge ; in one hand he held
the green branch of a tree, and in the other he grasped his
beard, which he pressed to his bosom ; in this attitude he
made a long oration, or rather song, for it had a musical cadence which was by no means disagreeable.   We regretted
infinitely that we could not understand what he said to us,
and not less that he could not understand any thing which
we should say to him ; to shew our good-will, however, we
threw him some trifling presents, while he was yet speaking,
but he would neither touch them himself, nor suffer them to
be

be touched by others till he had done : He then walked into
the water, and threw our people the green branch, after
which he took up the things which had been thrown from
the boats.   Every thing now having a friendly appearance,
our people made signs that they should lay down their
arms, and most of them having complied, one of the midshipmen, encouraged by this testimony of confidence and
friendship, leaped out of the boat with his clothes on, and
swam through the surf to shore.   The Indians immediately
gathered round him, and began to examine his clothes with
great curiosity;   they seemed particularly to admire his
waistcoat, and being willing to gratify his new friends, he
took it off, and presented it to them ;   this courtesy, however, produced a disagreeable effect, for he had no sooner
given away his waistcoat, than one of the Indians very inge-
niously untied his cravat, and the next moment snatched it
from his neck, and ran away with it.   Our adventurer,
therefore, to prevent his being stripped by piece-meal,
made the best of his way back again to the boat: Still,
however, we were upon good terms, and several of the Indians swam off to our people, some of them bringing a cocoa-nut, and others a little fresh water in a cocoa-nut shell.
But the principal object of our boats was to obtain some
pearls ; and the men, to assist them in explaining their
meaning, had taken with them some of the pearl oyster-
shells which they had found in great numbers upon the
coast; but all their endeavours were ineffectual, for they
could not, even with this assistance, at all make themselves
understood.   It is indeed probable that we should have succeeded better, if an intercourse of any kind could have been
established between us, but it was our misfortune that no
anchorage could be found for the ships.   As all Indians are
fond of beads, it can scarcely be supposed that the pearls,
which the oysters at this place contained, were overlooked
by the natives, and it is more than probable that if we could
have continued here a few weeks, we might have obtained
some of great value in exchange for nails, hatchets, and bill-
hooks, upon which the natives, with more reason, set a much
higher value.   We observed, that in the lake, or lagoon,
there were two or three very large vessels, one of which had
two masts, and some cordage aloft to support them.

  To these two islands, I gave the name of *King George's
Islands,* in honour of his majesty. That which we last visited,

ed lies in latitude 14° 41' S., longitude 149° 15' W.; the variation of the compass here was 5° E.

Section X.

The Run from King George's Islands to the Islands of Saypan, Tinian, and Aguigan; with an Account of several Islands that were discovered in that Track.

We pursued our course to the westward the same day, and the next, about three o'clock in the afternoon, we saw land again, bearing S.S.W. distant about six leagues. We immediately stood for it, and found it to be a low and very narrow island, lying east and west: we ran along the south side of it, which had a green and pleasant appearance, but a dreadful surf breaks upon every part of it, with foul ground at some distance, and many rocks and small islands scattered at about three leagues from the shore. We found it about twenty leagues in length, and it appeared to abound with inhabitants, though we could only get a transient glance of them as we passed along. To this place I gave the name of the *Prince of Wales's Island.* It lies in latitude 15° S. and the westermost end of it in longitude 151° 53' W. It is distant from King George's Islands about eight-and-forty leagues, in the direction of S. 80 W. the variation here was 5° 30' E.

From the western extremity of this island, we steered N. 82 W. and at noon on the 16th, were in latitude 14° 28' S. longitude 156° 23' W. the variation being 7° 40' E. The wind was now easterly, and we had again the same mountainous swell from the southward that we had before we made the Islands of Direction, and which, from that time to this day, we had lost: When we lost that swell, and for some days before, we saw vast flocks of birds, which we observed always took their flight to the southward when evening was coming on.[1] These appearances persuaded me

that

---

[1] No doubt to the Navigators' Islands, so called by Bougainville. Captain Wallis touched at one of them, and named them Boscawen's and Keppel's Islands. Peyrouse has given a very curious, but not a pleasing account of their inhabitants. To the south of them again are the Friendly Islands.—E.

that there was land in the same direction, and I am of opinion, that if the winds had not failed me in the higher latitudes, I should have fallen in with it: I would indeed at this time have hauled away to the southward, and attempted the discovery, if our people had been healthy, for having observed that all the islands we had seen were full of inhabitants, I was still more confirmed in my opinion; as I could account for their being peopled only by supposing a chain of islands reaching to a continent; but the sickness of the crews, in both ships, was an insuperable impediment.

The next day we again saw many birds of various sorts about the ship, and therefore supposed that some other island was not far distant, for the swell continuing, I concluded that the land was not of very great extent: I proceeded, however, with caution, for the islands in this part of the ocean render the navigation very dangerous, they being so low, that a ship may be close in with them before they are seen. We saw nothing, however, on the 18th, the 19th, nor the 20th, during which we continued to steer the same course, though the birds still continued about the vessel in great numbers. Our latitude was now 12° 33′ S. longitude 167° 47′ W. The Prince of Wales's Island was distant 313 leagues, and the variation of the needle was 9° 15′ E. The next morning about seven o'clock, we discovered a most dangerous reef of breakers, bearing S.S.W. and not farther distant than a single league. In about half an hour afterwards, land was seen from the mast-head, bearing W.N.W. and distant about eight leagues; it had the appearance of three islands, with rocks and broken ground between them. The south-east side of these islands lies N.E. by N. and S.W. by S. and is about three leagues in length between the extreme points, from both which a reef runs out, upon which the sea breaks to a tremendous height. We sailed round the north end, and upon the north-west and west side, saw innumerable rocks and shoals, which stretched near two leagues into the sea, and were extremely dangerous. The islands themselves had a more fertile and beautiful appearance than any we had seen before, and, like the rest, swarmed with people, whose habitations we saw standing in clusters all along the coast. We saw also a large vessel under sail, at a little distance from the shore; but to our unspeakable regret we were obliged to leave the place without farther examination, for it was surrounded in every direction by rocks and breakers, which rendered the hazard more than equivalent to every advantage we might procure. At this time I took these for part of the islands called Solomon's Islands, and was in hopes that I should fall in with others of them, in some of which we might find an harbour.

The reef of rocks which we first saw as we approached these islands, lies in latitude 10° 15' S. longitude 169° 28' W. and it bears from Prince of Wales's Island N. 76° 48' W. distant 352 leagues. The islands bear from the reef W.N.W. distant nine leagues: I called them the *Islands of Danger*, and steered from them N.W. by W. allowing for the variation.

After having seen the breakers soon after it was light in the morning, I told my officers that I apprehended we should have frequent alarms in the night; at night, therefore, every body was upon the watch, which a very hard squall of wind, with rain, rendered the more necessary. About nine o'clock, having just gone down into my cabin, I heard a great noise above, and when I enquired what was the matter, I was told that the Tamar, who was a-head, had fired a gun, and that our people saw breakers to leeward: I ran instantly upon deck, and soon perceived that what had been taken for breakers was nothing more than the undulating reflection of the moon, which was going down, and shone faintly from behind a cloud in the horizon; we therefore bore away after the Tamar, but did not get sight of her till an hour afterwards.

Nothing worthy of notice happened till Monday the 24th, when, about ten o'clock in the morning, we discovered another island, bearing S.S.W. distant about seven or eight leagues: We steered for it, and found it to be low, but covered with wood, among which were cocoa-nut trees in great abundance. It had a pleasant appearance, and a large lake in the middle, like King George's Island: It is near thirty miles in circumference, a dreadful sea breaks upon almost every part of the coast, and a great deal of foul ground lies about it. We sailed quite round it, and when we were on the lee-side, sent out boats to sound, in hopes of finding anchorage: No soundings, however, were to be got near the shore, but I sent the boats out a second time, with orders

ders to land, if it were possible, and procure some refreshments for the sick: they landed with great difficulty, and
brought off about two hundred cocoa-nuts, which, to persons
in our circumstances, were an inestimable treasure. The
people who were on shore, reported that there were no signs
of its having ever been inhabited, but that they found thousands of sea fowl sitting upon their nests, which were built
in high trees: These birds were so tame that they suffered
themselves to be knocked down without leaving their nests:
The ground was covered with land crabs, but our people
saw no other animal. At first I was inclined to believe that
this island was the same that in the Neptune François is
called Maluita, and laid down about a degree to the eastward of the great island of Saint Elizabeth, which is the
principal of the Solomon's Islands; but being afterwards
convinced to the contrary, I called it the *Duke of York's
Island,* in honour of his late royal highness, and I am of
opinion that we were the first human beings who ever saw
it. There is indeed great reason to believe that there is no
good authority for laying down Solomon's Islands in the
situation that is assigned to them by the French: The only
person who has pretended to have seen them is Quiros, and
I doubt whether he left behind him any account of them
by which they might be found by future navigators.[2]

We continued our course till the 29th, in the track of
these islands, and being then ten degrees to the westward
of their situation in the chart, without having seen any
thing of them, I hauled to the northward, in order to cross
the equinoxial, and afterwards shape my course for the
Ladrone Islands, which, though a long run, I hoped to accomplish before I should be distressed for water, notwithstanding it now began to fall short. Our latitude, this day,
was 8° 13′ S., longitude 176° 20′ E. and the variation was
10° 10′ E.

On Tuesday the 2d of July, we again saw many birds
about the ship, and at four o'clock in the afternoon, discovered

vered

---

[2] The opinion here stated is now pretty generally confided in. Byron
we see sailed over the northern, and Captain Carteret (as we shall find)
the southern limits of these supposed islands, but could not find them.
The name is now given to a cluster of islands lying betwixt the north of
Queen Charlotte's Archipelago, discovered by Carteret, and the south-east
coast of New Britain, &c.—E.

vered an island bearing north, and distant about six leagues:
We stood for it till sun-set, when it was distant about four
leagues, and then kept off and on for the night. In the
morning, we found it a low flat island, of a most delightful
appearance, and full of wood, among which the cocoa-nut
tree was very conspicuous: We saw, however, to our great
regret, much foul ground about it, upon which the sea
broke with a dreadful surf. We steered along the south-
west side of it, which we judged to be about four leagues
in length, and soon perceived not only that it was inhabited, but very populous; for presently after the ship came in
sight, we saw at least a thousand of the natives assembled
upon the beach, and in a very short time more than sixty
canoes, or rather proas, put off from the shore, and made
towards us. We lay by to receive them, and they were
very soon ranged in a circle round us. These vessels were
very neatly made, and so clean that they appeared to be
quite new: None of them had fewer than three persons on
board, nor any of them more than six.³ After these Indians had gazed at us some time, one of them suddenly
jumped out of his proa, swam to the ship, and ran up the
side like a cat: As soon as he had stepped over the gunwale, he sat down upon it, and burst into a violent fit of
laughter, then started up, and ran all over the ship, attempting to steal whatever he could lay his hands upon,
but without success, for, being stark naked, it was impossible to conceal his booty for a moment. Our seamen put
on him a jacket and trowsers, which produced great merriment, for he had all the gestures of a monkey newly
dressed: We also gave him bread, which he eat with a voracious appetite, and after having played a thousand antic
tricks, he leaped overboard, jacket and trowsers and all,
and swam back again to his proa; after this several others
swam to the ship, ran up the side of the gun-room ports,
and having crept in, snatched up whatever lay in their
reach, and immediately leaped again into the sea, and
swam away at a great rate, though some of them, having
both

³ " These have some resemblance to the proas used by the Indians of
the Ladrone Islands, they having what is termed an outrigger, that is, a
frame laid out to the windward, to balance this little vessel, and prevent
its oversetting, which would otherwise infallibly happen, from its small
breadth in proportion to its length."

7

both hands full, held up their arms quite out of the water, to prevent their plunder from being spoiled. These people are tall, well-proportioned, and clean-limbed : Their skin is a bright copper-colour, their features are extremely good, and there is a mixture of intrepidity and cheerfulness in their countenances that is very striking. They have long black hair, which some of them wore tied up behind in a great bunch, others in three knots : Some of them had long beards, some only whiskers, and some nothing more than a small tuft at the point of the chin. They were all of them stark naked, except their ornaments, which consisted of shells, very prettily disposed and strung together, and were worn round their necks, wrists, and waists : All their ears were bored, but they had no ornaments in them when we saw them : Such ornaments as they wear, when they wear any, are probably very heavy, for their ears hang down almost to their shoulders, and some of them were quite split through.[4] One of these men, who appeared to be a person of some consequence, had a string of human teeth about his waist, which was probably a trophy of his military prowess, for he would not part with it in exchange for any thing I could offer him. Some of them were unarmed, but others had one of the most dangerous weapons I had ever seen : It was a kind of spear, very broad at the end, and stuck full of sharks' teeth, which are as sharp as a lancet, at the sides, for about three feet of its length. We shewed them some cocoa-nuts, and made signs that we wanted more; but instead of giving any intimation that they could supply us, they endeavoured to take away those we had.

I sent out the boats to sound soon after we brought-to off the island, and when they came back, they reported that there was ground at the depth of thirty fathom, within two cables' length of the shore; but as the bottom was coral rock, and the soundings much too near the breakers for a ship to lie in safety, I was obliged again to make sail without procuring any refreshments for the sick. This island, to which my officers gave the name of *Byron's Island,* lies
in

[4] " Though we saw upwards of a hundred of them in their proas, there was but one woman among them, and of her they seemed to take great notice; she was distinguished by wearing something about her waist."

in latitude 1° 18′ S., longitude 173° 46′ E., the variation of the compass here was one point E.

In our course from this place, we saw, for several days, abundance of fish, but we could take only sharks, which were become a good dish even at my own table. Many of the people now began to fall down with fluxes, which the surgeon imputed to the excessive heat and almost perpetual rains.

By the 21st, all our cocoa-nuts being expended, our people began to fall down again with the scurvy. The effect of these nuts alone, in checking this disease, is astonishing: Many whose limbs were become as black as ink, who could not move without the assistance of two men, and who, besides total debility, suffered excruciating pain, were in a few days, by eating these nuts, although at sea, so far recovered as to do their duty, and could even go aloft as well as they did before the distemper seized them. For several days about this time, we had only faint breezes, with smooth water, so that we made but little way, and as we were now not far from the Ladrone Islands, where we hoped some refreshments might be procured, we most ardently wished for a fresh gale, especially as the heat was still intolerable, the glass for a long time having never been lower than eighty-one, but often up to eighty-four; and I am of opinion that this is the hottest, the longest, and most dangerous run that ever was made.

On the 18th, we were in latitude 13° 9′ N., longitude 158° 50′ E., and on the 22d, in latitude 14° 25′ N., longitude 153° 11′ E. during which time we had a northerly current. Being now nearly in the latitude of Tinian, I shaped my course for that island.

Section XI.

The Arrival of the Dolphin and Tamar at Tinian, a Description of the present Condition of that Island, and an Account of the Transactions there.

On the 28th, we saw a great number of birds about the ship, which continued till the 30th, when about two o'clock in the afternoon we saw land, bearing W. ½ N. which proved to be the islands Saypan, Tinian, and Aiguigan. At

sun-set, the extremes of them bore from N. W. ⅓ N. westward to S. W.; and the three islands had the appearance
of one. At seven, we hauled the wind, and stood off and
on all night; and at six the next morning, the extremes of
the islands, which still made in one, bore from N. W. by N.
to S. W. by S. distant five leagues. The east side of these
islands lies N. E. by N. and S. W. by S. Saypan is the
northermost; and from the north-east point of that island
to the south-west point of Aiguigan, the distance is about
seventeen leagues. These three islands are between two
and three leagues distant from each other; Saypan is the
largest, and Aguigan, which is high and round, the smallest.
We steered along the east side of them, and at noon hauled
round the south point of Tinian, between that island and
Aiguigan, and anchored at the south-west end of it, in sixteen fathom water, with a bottom of hard sand and coral
rock, opposite to a white sandy bay, about a mile and a
quarter from the shore, and about three quarters of a mile
from a reef of rocks that lies at a good distance from the
shore, in the very spot where Lord Anson lay in the Centurion. The water at this place is so very clear that the bottom is plainly to be seen at the depth of four-and-twenty
fathom, which is no less than one hundred and forty-four
feet.

As soon as the ship was secured, I went on shore, to fix
upon a place where tents might be erected for the sick,
which were now very numerous; not a single man being
wholly free from the scurvy, and many in the last stage of
it. We found several huts which had been left by the
Spaniards and Indians the year before; for this year none
of them had as yet been at the place, nor was it probable
that they should come for some months, the sun being now
almost vertical, and the rainy season set in. After I had
fixed upon a spot for the tents, six or seven of us endeavoured to push through the woods, that we might come at
the beautiful lawns and meadows of which there is so luxuriant a description in the Account of Lord Anson's Voyage,
and if possible kill some cattle. The trees stood so thick,
and the place was so overgrown with underwood, that we
could not see three yards before us, we therefore were obliged to keep continually hallooing to each other, to prevent
our being separately lost in this trackless wilderness. As
the weather was intolerably hot, we had nothing on besides
our

our shoes, except our shirts and trowsers, and these were
in a very short time torn all to rags by the bushes and
brambles; at last, however, with incredible difficulty and
labour, we got through; but, to our great surprise and disappointment, we found the country very different from the
account we had read of it: The lands were entirely overgrown with a stubborn kind of reed or brush, in many
places higher than our heads, and no where lower than our
middles, which continually entangled our legs, and cut us
like whipcord; our stockings perhaps might have suffered
still more, but we wore none. During this march we were
also covered with flies from head to foot, and whenever we
offered to speak we were sure of having a mouthful, many
of which never failed to get down our throats. After we
had walked about three or four miles, we got sight of a bull,
which we killed, and a little before night got back to the
beach, as wet as if we had been dipt in water, and so fatigued that we were scarcely able to stand. We immediately sent out a party to fetch the bull, and found that
during our excursion some tents had been got up, and the
sick brought on shore.

The next day our people were employed in setting up
more tents, getting the water-casks on shore, and clearing
the well at which they were to be filled. This well I imagined to be the same that the Centurion watered at; but
it was the worst that we had met with during the voyage,
for the water was not only brackish, but full of worms.
The road also where the ships lay was a dangerous situation
at this season, for the bottom is hard sand and large coral
rocks, and the anchor having no hold in the sand, the
cable is in perpetual danger of being cut to pieces by the
coral; to prevent which as much as possible, I rounded
the cables, and buoyed them up with empty water-casks.
Another precaution also was taught me by experience, for
at first I moored, but finding the cables much damaged, I
resolved to lie single for the future, that by veering away
or heaving in, as we should have more or less wind, we
might always keep them from being slack, and consequently from rubbing, and this expedient succeeded to my wish.
At the full and change of the moon, a prodigious swell
tumbles in here, so that I never saw ships at anchor roll
so much as ours did while we lay here; and it once drove
in from the westward with such violence, and broke so high

upon

upon the reef, that I was obliged to put to sea for a week ;
for if our cable had parted in the night, and the wind had
been upon the shore, which sometimes happens for two or
three days together, the ship must have inevitably been
lost upon the rocks.

As I was myself very ill with the scurvy, I ordered a tent
to be pitched for me, and took up my residence on shore ;
where we also erected the armourer's forge, and began to
repair the iron-work of both the ships. I soon found that
the island produced limes, sour oranges, cocoa-nuts, bread-
fruit,[1] guavas, and paupas in great abundance ; but we
found no water-melons, scurvy-grass, or sorrel.

Notwithstanding the fatigue and distress that we had endured, and the various climates we had passed through,
neither of the ships had yet lost a single man since their
sailing from England ; but while we lay here two died of
fevers, a disease with which many were seized, though we
all recovered very fast from the scurvy. I am indeed of
opinion that this is one of the most unhealthy spots in the
world, at least during the season in which we were here.
The rains were violent, and almost incessant, and the heat
was so great as to threaten us with suffocation. The thermometer, which was kept on board the ship, generally
stood at eighty-six, which is but nine degrees less than the
heat of the blood at the heart ; and if it had been on shore
it would have risen much higher. I had been upon the
coast of Guinea, in the West Indies, and upon the island
of Saint Thomas, which is under the Line, but I had never
felt any such heat as I felt here. Besides the inconvenience
which we suffered from the weather, we were incessantly
tormented by the flies in the day, and by the musquitos in
the night. The island also swarms with centipedes and
scorpions, and a large black ant, scarcely inferior to either
in the malignity of its bite. Besides these, there were
venomous insects without number, altogether unknown to
us, by which many of us suffered so severely, that we were
afraid to lie down in our beds ; nor were those on board
in a much better situation than those on shore, for great
numbers of these creatures being carried into the ship with
the wood, they took possession of every birth, and left the
poor seamen no place of rest either below or upon the deck.

A-

---

[1] See a particular description of the bread-fruit, in the 8th chapter o
Lieut. Cook's voyage.

As soon as we were settled in our new habitations, I sent out parties to discover the haunts of the cattle, some of which were found, but at a great distance from the tents, and the beasts were so shy that it was very difficult to get a shot at them. Some of the parties which, when their haunts had been discovered, were sent out to kill them, were absent three days and nights before they could succeed; and when a bullock had been dragged seven or eight miles through such woods and lawns as have just been described, to the tents, it was generally full of fly-blows, and stunk so as to be unfit for use: Nor was this the worst, for the fatigue of the men in bringing down the carcase, and the intolerable heat they suffered from the climate and the labour, frequently brought on fevers which laid them up.[2] Poultry however we procured upon easier terms: There was great plenty of birds, and they were easily killed; but the flesh of the best of them was very ill-tasted, and such was the heat of the climate that within an hour after they were killed it was as green as grass, and swarmed with maggots. Our principal resource for fresh meat was the wild hog, with which the island abounds. These creatures are very fierce, and some of them so large that a carcase frequently weighed two hundred pounds. We killed them without much difficulty, but a black belonging to the Tamar contrived a method to snare them, so that we took great numbers of them alive, which was an unspeakable advantage, for it not only ensured our eating the flesh while it was sweet, but enabled us to send a good number of them on board as sea-stores.

In the mean time we were very desirous of procuring some beef in an eatable state, with less risk and labour, and Mr Gore, one of our mates, at last discovered a pleasant spot upon the north-west part of the island, where cattle were in great plenty, and whence they might be brought to the tents by sea. To this place, therefore, I dispatched a party, with a tent for their accommodation, and sent the boats every day to fetch what they should kill; sometimes however there broke such a sea upon the rocks, that it was impossible to approach them, and the Tamar's boat unhappily lost three of her best men by attempting it. We were
now,

[2] " But we had cast anchor on the *wrong side* of the island, and, to our great disappointment, found cattle very scarce, ' &c. &c.

now, upon the whole, pretty well supplied with provisions,; especially as we baked fresh bread every day for the sick and the fatigue of our people being less, there were fewer ill with the fever : But several of them were so much disordered by eating of a very fine-looking fish which we caught here, that their recovery was for a long time doubtful. The author of the Account of Lord Anson's Voyage says, that the people on board the Centurion thought it prudent to abstain from fish, as the few which they caught at their first arrival surfeited those who eat of them. But not attending sufficiently to this caution, and too hastily taking the word *surfeit* in its literal and common acceptation, we imagined that those who tasted the fish when Lord Anson first came hither, were made sick merely by eating too much; whereas, if that had been the case, there would have been no reason for totally abstaining afterwards, but only eating temperately. We however bought our knowledge by experience, which we might have had cheaper; for though all our people who tasted this fish, eat sparingly, they were all soon afterwards dangerously ill.

Besides the fruit that has been mentioned already, this island produces cotton and indigo in abundance, and would certainly be of great value if it were situated in the West Indies. The surgeon of the Tamar enclosed a large spot of ground here, and made a very pretty garden; but we did not stay long enough to derive any advantage from it.[4]

                                                      While

___

[3] The other account indicates a little more gratitude :—" Our people had as much good beef and broth as we could possibly expend; with guavas, oranges, lemons, limes, plenty of excellent cabbages, which grow on the cocoa-trees, and the bread-fruit, for which these islands are justly famous; and not only poultry like those in England, but wild fowl of various sorts."

[4] The descriptions of this island given by the author of Anson's Voyage, and in the other account of this one, so often referred to, are both more favourable than Byron's; a circumstance which may, perhaps, be accounted for on very common principles, without any impeachment of the respective authorities. The former description was purposely omitted in our 10th volume, as it was judged advisable to introduce it in this place, so that the reader might directly compare it with that which is given in the text. Here it follows entire :—

" Its length is about twelve miles, and its breadth about half as much; it extending from the S S.W to N.N.E. The soil is every where dry and healthy, and somewhat sandy, which being less disposed than other soils

While we lay here, I sent the Tamar to examine the island of Saypan, which is much larger than Tinian, rises higher, and, in my opinion, has a much pleasanter appearance.

to a rank and over luxuriant vegetation, occasions the meadows and the bottoms of the woods to be much neater and smoother than is customary in hot climates. The land rises by easy slopes, from the very beach where we watered to the middle of the island; though the general course of its ascent is often interrupted and traversed by gentle descents and vallies; and the inequalities that are formed by the different combinations of these gradual swellings of the ground, are most beautifully diversified with large lawns, which are covered with a very fine trefoil, intermixed with a variety of flowers, and are skirted by woods of tall and well-spread trees, most of them celebrated either for their aspect or their fruit. The turf of the lawns is quite clean and even, and the bottoms of the woods in many places clear of all bushes and underwoods; and the woods themselves usually terminate on the lawns with a regular outline, not broken, nor confused with straggling trees, but appearing as uniform as if laid out by art. Hence arose a great variety of the most elegant and entertaining prospects formed by the mixture of these woods and lawns, and their various intersections with each other, as they spread themselves differently through the vallies, and over the slopes and declivities with which the place abounds. The fortunate animals too, which for the greatest part of the year are the sole lords of this happy soil, partake in some measure of the romantic cast of the island, and are no small addition to its wonderful scenery. For the cattle, of which it is not uncommon to see herds of some thousands feeding together in a large meadow, are certainly the most remarkable in the world, for they are all of them milk-white, except their ears, which are generally black. And though there are no inhabitants here, yet the clamour and frequent parading of domestic poultry, which range the woods in great numbers, perpetually excite the ideas of the neighbourhood of farms and villages, and greatly contribute to the cheerfulness and beauty of the place. The cattle on the island we computed were at least ten thousand; and we had no difficulty in getting near them, as they were not shy of us. Our first method of killing them was shooting them; but at last, when by accidents to be hereafter recited, we were obliged to husband our ammunition, our men ran them down with ease. Their flesh was extremely well tasted, and was believed by us to be much more easily digested, than any we had ever met with. The fowls too were exceeding good, and were likewise run down with little trouble; for they could scarce fly further than an hundred yards at a flight, and even that fatigued them so much, that they could not readily rise again; so that, aided by the openness of the woods, we could at all times furnish ourselves with whatever number we wanted. Besides the cattle and the poultry, we found here abundance of wild hogs: These were most excellent food; but as they were a very fierce animal, we were obliged either to shoot them, or to hunt them with large dogs, which we found upon the place at our landing, and which belonged to the detachment which was then upon the island amassing provisions for the garrison of Guam. As these dogs had been purposely trained to the killing of the wild hogs, they followed us very readily, and hunted for us; but though they were a large bold breed, the hogs

ance.   She anchored to the leeward of it, at the distance of
a mile from the shore, and in about ten fathom water, with
much the same kind of ground as we had in the road of Tinian.

fought with so much fury, that they frequently destroyed them, so that we
by degrees lost the greatest part of them.

  " But this place was not only extremely grateful to us from the plenty
and excellency of its fresh provisions, but was as much perhaps to be admired for its fruits and vegetable productions, which were most fortunately adapted to the cure of the sea scurvy, which had so terribly reduced us.
For in the woods there were inconceivable quantities of cocoa-nuts, with
the cabbages growing on the same tree: There were besides guavoes,
limes, sweet and sour oranges, and a kind of fruit peculiar to these islands,
called by the Indians *Rima*, but by us the *Bread-fruit*, for it was constantly eaten by us during our stay upon the island instead of bread, and so universally preferred to it, that no ship's bread was expended during that
whole interval.   It grew upon a tree which is somewhat lofty, and which,
towards the top, divides into large and spreading branches.   The leaves of
this tree are of a remarkable deep green, are notched about the edges, and
are generally from a foot to eighteen inches in length.   The fruit itself
grows indifferently on all parts of the branches; it is in shape rather elip-
tical than round, is covered with a rough rind, and is usually seven or
eight inches long; each of them grows singly and not in clusters.   This
fruit is fittest to be used when it is full grown, but is still green; in which
state its taste has some distant resemblance to that of an artichoke bottom,
and its texture is not very different, for it is soft and spungy.   As it ripens
it grows softer and of a yellow colour, and then contracts a luscious taste,
and an agreeable smell, not unlike a ripe peach; but then it is esteemed
unwholesome, and is said to produce fluxes.   Besides the fruits already
enumerated, there were many other vegetables extremely conducive to the
cure of the malady we had long laboured under, such as water-melons,
dandelion, creeping purslain, mint, scurvy-grass, and sorrel; all which, together with the fresh meats of the place, we devoured with great eagerness, prompted thereto by the strong inclination which nature never fails
of exciting in scorbutic disorders for these powerful specifics.

  " It will easily be conceived from what hath been already said, that our
cheer upon this island was in some degree luxurious, but I have not yet recited all the varieties of provision which we here indulged in.   Indeed we
thought it prudent totally to abstain from fish, the few we caught at our
first arrival having surfeited those who eat of them; but considering how
much we had been inured to that species of food, we did not regard this
circumstance as a disadvantage, especially as the defect was so amply supplied by the beef, pork, and fowls already mentioned, and by great plenty
of wild fowl; for I must observe, that near the centre of the island there
were two considerable pieces of fresh water, which abounded with duck,
teal, and curlew: Not to mention the whistling plover, which we found
there in prodigious plenty.

  " And now perhaps it may be wondered at, that an island so exquisitely
furnished with the conveniences of life, and so well adapted, not only to the
subsistence, but likewise to the enjoyment of mankind, should be entirely
destitute of inhabitants, especially as it is in the neighbourhood of other
islands,

nian. Her people landed upon a fine sandy beach which is six or seven miles long, and walked up into the woods, where they saw many trees which were fit for top-masts.
They

islands, which in some measure depend upon this for their support. To obviate this difficulty, I must observe, that it is not fifty years since the island was depopulated. The Indians we had in our custody assured us, that formerly the three islands of Tinian, Rota, and Guam, were all full of inhabitants; and that Tinian alone contained thirty thousand souls   But a sickness raging amongst these islands, which destroyed multitudes of the people, the Spaniards, to recruit their numbers at Guam, which were greatly diminished by this mortality, ordered all the inhabitants of Tinian thither; where, languishing for their former habitations, and their customary method of life, the greatest part of them in a few years died of grief. Indeed, independent of that attachment which all mankind have ever shown to the places of their birth and bringing up, it should seem from what has been already said, that there were few countries more worthy to be regretted than this of Tinian.

" These poor Indians might reasonably have expected, at the great distance from Spain, where they were placed, to have escaped the violence and cruelty of that haughty nation, so fatal to a large proportion of the whole human race: But it seems their remote situation could not protect them from sharing in the common destruction of the western world, all the advantage they received from their distance being only to perish an age or two later. It may perhaps be doubted, if the number of the inhabitants of Tinian, who were banished to Guam, and who died there pining for their native home, was so great, as what we have related above; but, not to mention the concurrent assertion of our prisoners, and the commodiousness of the island, and its great fertility, there are still remains to be met with on the place, which evince it to have been once extremely populous. For there are, in all parts of the island, a great number of ruins of a very particular kind, they usually consist of two rows of square pyramidal pillars, each pillar being about six feet from the next, and the distance between the rows being about twelve feet; the pillars themselves are about five feet square at the base, and about thirteen feet high; and on the top of each of them there is a semi-globe, with the flat part upwards; the whole of the pillars and semi-globe is solid, being composed of sand and stone cemented together, and plastered over. If the account our prisoners gave us of these structures was true, the island must indeed have been extremely populous; for they assured us, that they were the foundations of particular buildings set apart for those Indians only who had engaged in some religious vow; and monastic institutions are often to be met with in many Pagan nations. However, if these ruins were originally the bases of the common dwelling-houses of the natives, their numbers must have been considerable; for in many parts of the island they are extremely thick planted, and sufficiently evince the great plenty of former inhabitants. But to return to the present state of the island.

" Having mentioned the conveniences of this place, the excellency and quantity of its fruits and provisions, the neatness of its lawns, the stateliness, freshness, and fragrance of its woods, the happy inequality of its surface, and the variety and elegance of the views it afforded, I must now observe

They saw no fowls, nor any tracks of cattle; but of hogs
and guanicoes there was plenty. They found no fresh water near the beach, but saw a large pond inland, which they
did not examine. They saw large heaps of pearl oyster-
shells thrown up together, and other signs of people having
been there not long before: Possibly the Spaniards may go
thither at some season of the years, and carry on a pearl
fishery. They also saw many of those square pyramidal pillars

serve, that all these advantages were greatly enhanced by the healthiness
of its climate, by the almost constant breezes which prevail there, and by
the frequent showers which fall, and which, though of a very short and
almost momentary duration, are extremely grateful and refreshing, and are
perhaps one cause of the salubrity of the air, and of the extraordinary influence it was observed to have upon us, in increasing and invigorating our
appetites and digestion. This was so remarkable, that those amongst our
officers, who were at all other times spare and temperate eaters, who, besides a slight breakfast, made but one moderate repast a day, were here, in
appearance, transformed into gluttons; for instead of one reasonable flesh
meal, they were now scarcely satisfied with three, and each of them so
prodigious in quantity, as would at another time have produced a fever or
a surfeit: And yet our digestion so well corresponded with the keenness
of our appetites, that we were neither disordered nor even loaded by this
repletion; for after having, according to the custom of the island, made a
large beef breakfast, it was not long before we began to consider the approach of dinner as a very desirable, though somewhat tardy incident.

" And now having been thus large in my encomiums on this island, in
which, however, I conceive I have not done it justice, it is necessary I
should speak of those circumstances in which it is defective, whether in
point of beauty or utility.

" And first, with respect to its water. I must own, that before I had
seen this spot, I did not conceive that the absence of running water, of
which it is entirely destitute, could have been so well replaced by any
other means, as it is in this island; for though there are no streams, yet
the water of the wells and springs, which are to be met with every where
near the surface, is extremely good; and in the midst of the island there
are two or three considerable pieces of excellent water, whose edges are as
neat and even, as if they had been basons purposely made for the decoration of the place. It must, however, be confessed, that with regard to the
beauty of the prospects, the want of rills and streams is a very great defect, not to be compensated either by large pieces of standing water, or by
the neighbourhood of the sea, though that, by reason of the smallness of
the island, generally makes a part of every extensive view.

" As to the residence upon the island, the principal inconvenience attending it is the vast numbers of musquitoes, and various other species of
flies, together with an insect called a tick, which, though principally attached to the cattle, would yet frequently fasten upon our limbs and bodies,
and if not perceived and removed in time, would bury its head under the
skin, and raise a painful inflammation. We found here, too, centipedes
and scorpions, which we supposed were venomous, but none of us ever received any injury from them."

lars which are to be found at Tinian, and which are particularly described in the account of Lord Anson's voyage.

On Monday the 30th of September, having now been here nine weeks, and our sick being pretty well recovered, I ordered the tents to be struck, and with the forge and oven carried back to the ship; I also laid in about two thousand cocoa-nuts, which I had experienced to be so powerful a remedy for the scurvy, and the next day I weighed, hoping, that before we should get the length of the Bashé Island, the N.E. monsoon would be set in. I stood along the shore to take in the beef-hunters; but we had very little wind this day and the next till the evening, when it came to the westward and blew fresh: I then stood to the northward till the morning of the 3d, when we made Anatacan, an island that is remarkably high, and the same that was first fallen in with by Lord Anson.

SECTION XII.

The Run from Tinian to Pulo Timoan, with some Account of that Island, its Inhabitants and Productions, and thence to Batavia.

WE continued our course till Thursday the 10th, when being in latitude 18° 33′ N. longitude 136° 50′ E. we found the ship two-and-twenty miles to the southward of her account, which must have been the effect of a strong current in that direction. The variation here was 5° 10′ E. and for some time we found it regularly decreasing, so that on the 19th, being in latitude 21° 10′ N. longitude 124° 17′ E. the needle pointed due north.

On the 18th, we had found the ship eighteen miles to the northward of her account, and saw several land-birds about the ship, which appeared to be very much tired: We caught one as it was resting upon the booms, and found it very remarkable. It was about as big as a goose, and all over as white as snow, except the legs and beak which were black; the beak was curved, and of so great a length and thickness, that it is not easy to conceive how the muscles of the neck, which was about a foot long, and as small as that of a crane, could support it. We kept it about four months upon biscuit and water, but it then died, apparently for

want

want of nourishment, being almost as light as a bladder. It was very different from every species of the toucan that is represented by Edwards, and I believe has never been described. These birds appeared to have been blown off some island to the northward of us, that is not laid down in the charts.

The needle continued to point due north till the 22d, when, at six o'clock in the morning, Grafton's Island, the northermost of the Bashee Islands, bore south, distant six leagues. As I had designed to touch at these islands, I stood for that in sight; but as the navigation from hence to the strait of Banca is very dangerous, and we had now both a fine morning and a fine gale, I thought it best to proceed on our way, and therefore steered westward again. The principal of these islands are five in number, and by a good observation Grafton's Island lies in latitude 21° 8′ N. longitude 118° 14′ E. The variation of the compass was now 1° 20′ W.

On the 24th, being in latitude 16° 59′ N. longitude 118° 1′ E. we kept a good look-out for the Triangles, which lie without the north end of the Prasil, and form a most dangerous shoal.[1] On the 30th we saw several trees and large bamboos floating about the ship, and upon sounding had three-and-twenty fathom, with dark brown sand, and small pieces of shells. Our latitude was now 7° 17′ N. longitude 104° 21′ E. the variation was 30° W. The next day we found the ship thirteen miles to the northward of her account, which we judged to be the effect of a current; and on the 2d of November, we found her thirty-eight miles to the southward of her account. Our latitude by observation was 3° 54′ N. longitude 103° 20′ E. We had here soundings at forty-two and forty-three fathom, with soft mud.

At seven o'clock the next morning, we saw the island of Timoan, bearing S.W. by W. distant about twelve leagues. As Dampier has mentioned Pulo Timoan as a place where some refreshments are to be procured, I endeavoured to touch there, having lived upon salt provisions, which were now become bad, ever since we were at Tinian; but light airs,

---

[1] The Prasil, or Pracels, is a congeries of rocks and small islands, about sixty miles eastward of the coast of Cochin China, and reckoned very dangerous to navigators, on account of breakers and counter currents.—E.

airs, calms, and a southerly current, prevented our coming to an anchor till late in the evening of the 5th. We had sixteen fathom at about the distance of two miles from the shore, on a bay on the east side of the island.

The next day I landed to see what was to be got, and found the inhabitants, who are Malays, a surly insolent set of people. As soon as they saw us approaching the shore, they came down to the beach in great numbers, having a long knife in one hand, a spear headed with iron in the other, and a cressit or dagger by their side. We went on shore, however, notwithstanding these hostile appearances, and a treaty soon commenced between us; but all we could procure, was about a dozen of fowls, and a goat and kid. We had offered them knives, hatchets, bill-hooks, and other things of the same kind; but these they refused with great contempt, and demanded rupees: As we had no rupees, we were at first much at a loss how to pay for our purchase; but at last we bethought ourselves of some pocket-handkerchiefs, and these they vouchsafed to accept, though they would take only the best.

These people were of a small stature, but extremely well made, and of a dark copper-colour. We saw among them one old man who was dressed somewhat in the manner of the Persians, but all the rest were naked, except a handkerchief, which they wore as a kind of turban upon their heads, and some pieces of cloth which were fastened with a silver plate or clasp round their middles. We saw none of their women, and probably some care was taken to keep them out of our sight. The habitations are very neatly built of slit bamboo, and are raised upon posts about eight feet from the ground. Their boats are also well made, and we saw some of a large size, in which we supposed that they carried on a trade to Malacca.

The island is mountainous and woody, but we found it pleasant when we were ashore; it produces the cabbage and cocoa-nut tree in great plenty, but the natives did not chuse to let us have any of the fruit. We saw also some rice grounds, but what other vegetable productions Nature has favoured them with, we had no opportunity to learn, as we stayed here but two nights and one day. In the bay where the ship rode, there is excellent fishing, though the surf runs very high: We hauled our seine with great success, but could easily perceive that it gave umbrage to the inhabitants,

bitants, who consider all the fish about these islands as their own. There are two fine rivers that run into this bay, and the water is excellent : It was indeed so much better than what we had on board, that I filled as many casks with it as loaded the boat twice. While we lay here, some of the natives brought down an animal which had the body of a hare, and the legs of a deer; one of our officers bought it, and we should have been glad to have kept it alive, but it was impossible for us to procure for it such food as it would eat; it was therefore killed, and we found it very good food. All the while we lay here, we had the most violent thunder, lightning, and rain, that I had ever known; and, finding that nothing more was to be procured, we sailed again on Thursday morning, with a fine breeze off the land. In the afternoon, we tried the current, and found it set S.E. at the rate of a mile an hour. The variation here was 38′ W. We certainly made this passage at an improper season of the year; for after we came into the latitude of Pulo Condore, we had nothing but light airs, calms, and tornadoes, with violent rain, thunder, and lightning.

At seven o'clock in the morning of Sunday the 10th, we saw the east end of the island of Lingen, bearing S.W. by W. distant eleven or twelve leagues. The current set E.S.E. at the rate of a mile an hour. At noon it fell calm, and I anchored with the kedge in twenty fathom. At one o'clock, the weather having cleared up, we saw a small island bearing S.W. ½ S. distant ten or eleven leagues.

At one o'clock the next morning, we weighed and made sail ; and at six the small island bore W.S.W. distant about seven leagues, and some very small islands, which we supposed to be Domines Islands, W. ½ N. distant about seven or eight leagues, a remarkable double peak on the island of Lingen, bearing at same time W. by N. distant about ten or twelve leagues. Our latitude by observation was now 18′ S. The latitude of the east end of Lingen is 10′ S. longitude 105° 15′ E. Pulo Taya bears from it nearly S. by W. and is distant about twelve leagues.

At ten o'clock in the morning of Tuesday the 12th, we saw a small Chinese junk to the north-east; and at seven the next morning a small island, called Pulo Toté, bearing S.E. by E. distant about twelve leagues. A little to the northward of Pulo Taya, is a very small island, called Pulo Toupoa.

The

The next day, at four in the afternoon, there being no wind, we came to an anchor in fourteen fathom with soft ground, Pulo Taya bearing N.W. distant about seven leagues. We tried the current, and found it set E. by S. at the rate of two knots two fathoms an hour. We saw a sloop at anchor about four miles from us, which hoisted Dutch colours. In the night we had violent rain, with hard squalls, during one of which we parted the stream cable, and therefore let go the small bower. At eight in the morning, the wind became moderate and variable, from N.N.W. to W.S.W. We got out our long-boat and weighed the stream anchor, and at nine made sail. We found the current still very strong to the eastward; and at two we anchored again in fourteen fathom, Pulo Taya bearing N.W. ½ N. distant between seven and eight leagues. The vessel which we had seen the day before under Dutch colours, still lying at anchor in the same place, I sent a boat with an officer to speak with her: The officer was received on board with great civility; but was extremely surprised to find that he could not make himself understood, for the people on board were Malays, without a single white man among them: They made tea for our men immediately, and behaved with great cheerfulness and hospitality. The vessel was of a very singular construction; her deck was of slit bamboo, and she was steered, not by a rudder, but by two large pieces of timber, one upon each quarter.

The next morning, at six o'clock, we weighed and made sail; at two Monopin Hill bore S. by E. distant about ten or eleven leagues, and had the appearance of a small island. It bears S. by W. from the Seven Islands, and is distant from them about twelve leagues: Its latitude is 2° S. From the Seven Islands we steered S.W. by S. and had regular soundings from twelve to seven fathom, and soon after saw the coast of Sumatra, bearing from W.S.W. to W. by N. at the distance of about seven leagues. In the evening, we anchored in seven fathom; and the next morning at four we made sail again, and continued our course S. by E. till the peak of Monopin Hill bore east, and Batacarang Point, on the Sumatra shore, S.W. to avoid a shoal, called Frederick Hendrick, which is about midway between the Banca and Sumatra shore: The soundings were thirteen and fourteen fathom. We then steered E.S.E. and kept mid channel to avoid the banks of Palambam river, and that which lies

lies off the westermost point of Banca.   When we were
abreast of Palambam river, we regularly shoaled our water
from fourteen to seven fathom ; and when we had passed
it, we deepened it again to fifteen and sixteen fathom. We
continued to steer E.S.E. between the third and fourth
points of Sumatra, which are about ten leagues distant from
each other : The soundings, nearest to the Sumatra shore,
were all along from eleven to thirteen fathom ; and the high
land of Queda Banca appeared over the third point of Sumatra, bearing E.S.E. From the third point to the Second,
the course is S.E. by S. at the distance of about eleven or
twelve leagues.   The high land of Queda Banca, and the
second point of Sumatra, bear E.N.E. and W.S.W. of each
other. The strait is about five leagues over, and in the mid-
channel there is twenty-four fathom.   At six o'clock in the
evening we anchored in thirteen fathom, Monopin Hill
bearing N. ½ W. and the third point of Sumatra, S.E. by E.
distant between two and three leagues. Many small vessels
were in sight, and most of them hoisted Dutch colours. In
the night we had fresh gales and squalls, with thunder and
lightning, and hard rain; but as our cables were good, we
were in no danger, for in this place the anchor is buried in
a stiff clay.

In the morning the current or tide set to the S.E. at the
rate of three knots; at five we weighed, with a moderate
gale at west and hazy weather, and in the night the tide
shifted, and ran as strongly to the N.W. so that it ebbs and
flows here twelve hours.

On the 19th we spoke with an English snow, belonging
to the East India company, which was bound from Bencoo-
len to Malacca and Bengal.   We had now nothing to eat
but the ship's provisions, which were become very bad, for all
our beef and pork stunk intolerably, and our bread was rotten and full of worms; but as soon as the master of this
snow learnt our situation, he generously sent me a sheep, a
dozen fowls, and a turtle, which I verily believe was half
his stock, besides two gallons of arrack, and would accept
nothing but our thanks in return.   It is with great pleasure
that I pay this tribute to his liberality, and am very sorry
that I cannot recollect his name, or the name of his vessel.
In the afternoon we worked round the first point of Sumatra, and our soundings on the north side, at the distance of
about a mile and a half from the shore, were fourteen fa-
                                                    thom.

thom. At half an hour after three we anchored, and sent a boat to sound for the shoals which lie to the northward of the island called Lasipara, which bore from us S.E. by S. distant about six leagues. Little wind, and a strong tide of flood to the northward, prevented our working between these shoals and the coast of Sumatra till the afternoon of the 20th; the soundings were very regular, being nine or ten fathom as we stood over to the island, and five or six when we stood over to Sumatra. As this strait has been often navigated, and is well known, it is not necessary to insert all the particulars of our passage through it; I shall therefore only say, that at six o'clock in the evening of Tuesday the 27th, we steered between the islands Edam and Horn, and entered the road of Batavia. At eight we anchored without the ships, Onrust bearing W.N.W. distant five or six miles.

SECTION XIII.

Transactions at Batavia, and Departure from that Place.

THE next day, which by our account was the 28th, but by the account of the Dutch at this place, was the 29th, we having lost a day by having steered westward a year, we anchored nearer to the town, and saluted the water-fort with eleven guns, which were returned. We found here above a hundred sail great and small, and among others, a large English ship belonging to Bombay, which saluted us with thirteen guns.

There is always lying here a Dutch commodore belonging to the company, who, among his countrymen, is a person of very great consequence. This gentleman thought fit to send his boat on board of me, with only the cockswain in her, who was a very dirty ragged fellow: As soon as he was brought to me, he asked whence I came, whither I was bound, and many other questions, which I thought equally impertinent, at the same time pulling out a book, and pen and ink, that he might set down the answers; but as I was impatient to save him this trouble, he was desired immediately to walk over the ship's side, and put off his boat, with which he was graciously pleased to comply.

When we came to this place, we had not one man sick

in either of the ships; but as I knew it to be more unhealthy than any other part of the East Indies, as the rainy
season was at hand, and arrack was to be procured in great
plenty, I determined to make my stay here as short as possible. I went on shore to wait upon the Dutch governor,
but was told that he was at his country-house, about four
miles distant from the town. I met however with an officer, called a shebander, who is a kind of master of the ceremonies, and he acquainted me, that if I chose to go to the
governor immediately, rather than wait for his coming to
town, he would attend me; I accepted his offer, and we
set out together in his chariot. The governor received me
with great politeness, and told me, that I might either take
a house in any part of the city that I should like, or be provided with lodgings at the hotel. This hotel is a licensed
lodging-house, the only one in the place, and kept by a
Frenchman, an artful fellow, who is put in by the governor
himself. It has indeed more the appearance of a palace
than a house of entertainment, being the most magnificent
building in Batavia; nor would a small edifice answer the
purpose, for as there is a penalty of five hundred dollars
upon any person in the city who shall suffer a stranger to
sleep a single night at his house, the strangers who make
it their residence are never few: All the houses indeed have
a stately appearance on the outside, and are elegantly fitted
up within, and we were told that the Chinese, of whom there
are great numbers at this place, were the architects. The
city is large, and the streets well laid out, but they have
greatly the appearance of those in the cities of Holland, for
a canal runs through most of them, with a row of trees
planted on each side: This is convenient for the merchants,
who have every thing brought up to their own doors by
water, but it probably contributes to the unhealthiness of
the place; the canal, indeed, as the city is built in a swamp,
might be necessary as a drain, but the trees, though they
have a pleasant appearance, must certainly prevent the
noxious vapours that are perpetually arising, from being
dispersed, by obstructing the circulation of the air.

The number of people here is incredible, and they are of
almost every nation in the world, Dutch, Portuguese, Chinese, Persians, Moors, Malays, Javanese, and many others:
The Chinese, however, have a large town to themselves,
without the walls, and carry on a considerable trade, for
they

they have annually ten or twelve large junks from China; and to these the opulence of the Dutch at Batavia is in a great measure owing. The beef here is bad, and the mutton scarce, but the poultry and fish are excellent and in great plenty. Here are also the greatest variety and abundance of the finest fruit in the world, but the musquitos, centipedes, scorpions, and other noxious vermin, which are innumerable, are extremely troublesome, especially to strangers. The roads, for many miles about the city, are as good as any in England: They are very broad, and by the side of them runs a canal, shaded by tall trees, which is navigable for vessels of a very large size: On the other side of the canal are gardens of a very pleasant appearance, and country-houses of the citizens, where they spend as much of their time as possible, the situation being less unwholesome than the city; and there are so few of them who not keep a carriage, that it is almost a disgrace to be seen on foot.

At this place I continued from the 28th of November to the 10th of December, when, having procured what refreshments I could for my people, and taken on board a sufficient quantity of rice and arrack, to serve for the rest of the voyage, I weighed anchor and made sail. The fort saluted me with eleven guns, and the Dutch commodore with thirteen, which I returned; we were saluted also by the English ship. We worked down to Prince's Island, in the strait of Sunda, and came to an anchor there on the 14th. In this passage, the boats came off to us from the Java shore, and supplied us with turtle in such plenty, that neither of the ship's companies eat any thing else. We lay at Prince's Island till the 19th, and during all that time we subsisted wholly upon the same food, which was procured from the inhabitants at a very reasonable rate. Having now taken on board as much wood and water as we could stow, we weighed, and got without Java Head before night: But by this time a dangerous putrid fever had broken out among us; three of my people had died, and many others now lay in so dangerous a condition that there were little hopes of their recovery: We did not, however, bury one at Batavia, which, notwithstanding our stay was so short, was thought to be a very extraordinary instance of good fortune; and our sick gradually recovered after we had been a week or two at sea.

SECTION

SECTION XIV.

*The Passage from Batavia to the Cape of Good Hope, and
from thence to England.*

WE continued our course, without any event worthy of
notice, (except that one of my best men unhappily fell
overboard and was drowned,) till Monday the 10th of February, when, at six o'clock in the morning, we saw the
coast of Africa, bearing from N.N.W. to N.E. distant
about seven leagues: It made in several high hills, and
white sandy cliffs, and its latitude was 34° 15′ S. longitude
21° 45′ E.; the variation here was 22° W. and our depth
of water fifty-three fathom, with a bottom of coarse brown
sand.

I stood in for the land, and when I was within about two
leagues of it, I saw a great smoke rising from a sandy beach.
I imagined the smoke to be made by the Hottentots; yet
I was astonished at their chusing this part of the coast for
their residence, for it consisted of nothing but sand-banks
as far as we could see, without the least bush or a single
blade of verdure, and so heavy a sea broke upon the coast,
that it was impossible to catch any fish.

On Wednesday the 12th, at three o'clock in the afternoon, we were abreast of Cape Lagullas, from which the
coast lies W.N.W. to the Cape of Good Hope, which is
distant about thirty leagues. The next day we passed between Penguin Island and Green Point, and worked into
Table Bay with our top-sails close reefed, there being a
strong gale, with hard squalls, at S.S.E. At three o'clock
in the afternoon, we anchored, and saluted the fort, which
was returned. The Dutch told me, that none of their ships
could have worked in such a gale of wind, and that we
seemed to come in faster than they were generally able to
do when the wind was fair.

The next morning, I waited upon the governor, who had
sent his coach and six to the water-side for me. He was
an old man, but a favourite with all ranks of people: He
received me with the greatest politeness, and not only offered me the company's house in the garden for my residence while I should continue at the Cape, but his coach
                                                      whenever

whenever I should think fit to use it. As I was one day at
dinner with him, and some other gentlemen, I took occasion
to mention the smoke that I had seen upon one of the sandy
beaches on a desolate part of the coast, and the surprise
with which it had struck me: They then told me that another ship, some time before, had fallen in with that part of
the coast, and had seen large smokes as I had done, although the place was uninhabited, and supposed to be an
island: To account for the smokes, however, they told me
also, that two Dutch East Indiamen had, about two years
before, sailed from Batavia for the Cape, and had never afterwards been heard of; and it was supposed that one or
both of them had been shipwrecked there, and that the
smokes which had been seen, were made by some of the
unfortunate crew: They added, that they had more than
once sent out vessels to look for them, but that there broke
so dreadful a sea upon the coast, they were obliged to return without attempting to go on shore. When I heard
this melancholy account, I could only regret that I had not
known it before, for I would then certainly have made every
effort in my power to have found these unhappy wretches,
and taken them from a place where, in all probability, they
would miserably perish.

The cape is certainly a most excellent place for ships to
touch at; it is a healthy climate, a fine country, and abounds
with refreshments of every kind. The company's garden
is a delightful spot, and at the end of it there is a paddock
belonging to the governor, in which are kept a great number of rare and curious animals, and among others, when
I was there, there were three fine ostriches, and four zebras
of an uncommon size. I gave all the people leave to go
on shore by turns, and they always contrived to get very
drunk with cape wine before they came back. Many ships
came in while we lay here; some were Dutch, some French,
some Danes, but all were outward-bound.

Having continued here three weeks, and during that time
refreshed our men, and completed our water, I took leave
of the good old governor on the 6th of March, and on the
7th, sailed out of the bay, with a fine breeze at S.E.

On Sunday the 16th, at six in the morning, we saw the
island of St Helena, bearing W. by N. at the distance of
about sixteen leagues, and about noon, a large ship, which
shewed French colours. We pursued our course, and a
few

few days afterwards, as we were sailing with a fine gale, and at a great distance from land, the ship suddenly received a rude shock, as if she had struck the ground: This instantly brought all who were below upon the deck in great consternation, and upon looking out we saw the water to a very large extent, tinged with blood; this put an end to our fears, and we concluded that we must have struck either a whale or a grampus, from which the ship was not likely to receive much damage, nor in fact did she receive any. About this time also we had the misfortune to bury our carpenter's mate, a very ingenious and diligent young man, who had never been well after our leaving Batavia.[1]

On the 25th, we crossed the equator, in longitude 17° 10′ W. and the next morning, Captain Cumming came on board, and informed me that the Tamar's three lower rudder-braces on the stern were broken off, which rendered the rudder unserviceable. I immediately sent the carpenter on board, who found the condition of the braces even worse than had been reported, so that the rudder could not possibly be new hung; he therefore went to work upon a machine, like that which had been fixed to the Ipswich, and by which she was steered home: This machine in about five days he completed, and with some little alterations of his own, it was an excellent piece of work. The Tamar steered very well with it, but thinking that it might not be sufficient to secure her in bad weather, or upon a lee-shore, I ordered Captain Cumming to run down to Antigua, that he might there heave the ship down, and get the rudder new hung, with a fresh set of braces which he had with him for that purpose; for the braces with which the ship went out, being of iron, were not expected to last as

long

---

[1] " By the tenderness and care of the Honourable Mr Byron, our excellent commodore, in causing the crews to be served with portable soup, and with the greatest humanity distributing provisions to the sick from his own table, that dreadful disease the sea-scurvy was rendered less inveterate and fatal, and we lost a less number of men, than any other ship in such a voyage: For, to the honour of that humane commander, let it be known to posterity, that under him the Dolphin and Tamar encompassed the earth, and in so long a voyage through various seas and climates, and after sailing several thousand leagues under the torrid zone, lost six men only out of each ship, including those that were drowned: A number so inconsiderable, that it is highly probable more of them would have died had they staid on shore."

long as ours, the lower ones, with the sheathing, being of copper.

Pursuant to these orders, the Tamar parted company with us on the 1st of April, and steered for the Caribbee Islands. When we came into latitude 34° N. longitude 35° W. we had strong gales from W.S.W. to W.N.W. with a great sea, which broke over us continually for six days successively, and run us into latitude 48° N. longitude 14° W. On the 7th of May, at seven o'clock in the morning, we made the islands of Scilly, having been just nine weeks coming from the Cape of Good Hope, and somewhat more than two-and-twenty months upon the voyage; the 9th, the ship came to anchor in the Downs, and on the same day I landed at Deal, and set out for London.

———

[The reader will find a short but interesting memoir of Byron prefixed, for the first time, to the Narrative of the Shipwreck of the Wager, published at Edinburgh by Ballantyne, 1812. All that it is thought necessary to quote from it here is, that in 1769, about three years after his return from this circumnavigation, he was appointed governor of Newfoundland, which office he held till 1775, that then he was promoted to the rank of rear-admiral of the blue, and successively to that of rear-admiral of the white and red; that he was appointed to command the squadron directed to watch and oppose the French fleet under Count d'Estaign, over which, however, owing to circumstances no prudence or bravery could controul, he obtained no decisive advantages; that in 1779, he was promoted to the rank of vice-admiral of the white; and that he died in 1786, at the age of 73, generally respected and beloved for his eminent professional and moral qualities.—E.]

CHAPTER

CHAPTER II.

AN ACCOUNT OF A VOYAGE ROUND THE WORLD, IN THE
YEARS 1766, 1767, AND 1768, BY SAMUEL WALLIS, ESQ.
COMMANDER OF HIS MAJESTY'S SHIP THE DOLPHIN.

SECTION II.

*The Passage to the Coast of Patagonia, with some Account of
the Natives.*

[The longitude in this voyage is reckoned from the meridian of London.]

HAVING received my commission, which was dated
the 19th of June 1766, I went on board the same
day, hoisted the pendant, and began to enter seamen, but,
according to my orders, took no boys either for myself or
any of the officers.

The ship was fitted for the sea with all possible expedition, during which the articles of war and the act of parliament were read to the ship's company: On the 26th of
July we sailed down the river, and on the 16th of August,
at eight o'clock in the morning, anchored in Plymouth
Sound.

On the 19th I received my sailing orders, with directions
to take the Swallow sloop, and the Prince Frederick store-
ship, under my command: And this day I took on board,
among other things, three thousand weight of portable
soup, and a bale of cork jackets. Every part of the ship
was filled with stores and necessaries of various kinds, even
to the steerage and state-room, which were allotted to the
slops and portable soup. The surgeon offered to purchase
an extraordinary quantity of medicines, and medical necessaries, which, as the ship's company might become sickly, he said would in that case be of great service, if room
could

could be found to stow them in; I therefore gave him leave to put them into my cabin, the only place in the ship where they could be received, as they consisted of three large boxes.

On the 22d, at four o'clock in the morning, I weighed and made sail in company with the Swallow and Prince Frederick, and had soon the mortification to find that the Swallow was a very bad sailer.

We proceeded in our voyage, without any remarkable incident, till Sunday the 7th of September, when, about eight o'clock in the morning, we saw the island of Porto Santo, bearing west; and about noon saw the east end of the island of Madeira.

About five o'clock we ran between this end of the island and the Deserters. On the side next the Deserters is a low flat island, and near it a needle rock; the side next to Madeira is full of broken rocks, and for that reason it is not safe to come within less than two miles of it.

At six in the evening we anchored in Madeira road, about two-thirds of a mile from the shore, in twenty-four fathom with a muddy bottom: About eight the Swallow and Prince Frederick also came to an anchor; and I sent an officer on shore to the governor, to let him know that I would salute him, if he would return an equal number of guns, which he promised to do; the next morning, therefore, at six o'clock, I saluted him with thirteen guns, and he returned thirteen as he had promised.

Having taken in a proper quantity of water at this place, with four pipes and ten puncheons of wine, some fresh beef, and a large quantity of onions, we weighed anchor on the 12th, and continued our voyage.

At six o'clock in the morning of Tuesday the 16th, we saw the island of Palma, and found the ship fifteen miles to the southward of her reckoning. As we were sailing along this island, at the rate of no less than eight miles an hour, with the wind at east, it died away at once; so that within less than two minutes the ship had no motion, though we were at least four leagues distant from the shore. Palma lies in lat. 28° 40′ N. long. 17° 48′ W.

On the 20th we tried the current, and found it set S.W. by W. one mile an hour. This day we saw two herons flying to the eastward, and a great number of bonnettos about the ship, of which we caught eight.

In

In the night between the 21st and 22d we lost our companion the Swallow, and about eight in the morning we saw the island of Sal, bearing S. ½ W., at noon it bore S. ¾ W. distant eight leagues; and at noon on the 23d, the nearest land of the island of Bonavista bore from S. to W.S.W. distant seven or eight miles, the east end, at the same time, bearing W. distant two leagues. In this situation we sounded, and had only fifteen fathom, with rocky ground; at the same time we saw a very great rippling, which we supposed to be caused by a reef, stretching off the point about E.S.E. three miles, and the breakers without us, distant also about three miles in the direction of S.E. We steered between the rippling and the breakers, but after hauling the ship off about half a mile, we had no soundings. The Prince Frederick passed very near the breakers, in the S.E., but had no soundings; yet these breakers are supposed to be dangerous. The middle of the isle of Sal is in lat. 16° 55′ N. long. 21° 59′ W.; the middle of Bonavista is in lat. 16° 10′ long. 23° W.

On the next day, at six in the morning, the isle of May bore from W. to S. W. six leagues; and soon after the Swallow again joined company. At half an hour after ten the west end of the isle of May bore north at the distance of five miles, and we found a current here, setting to the southward at the rate of twenty miles in four-and-twenty hours. The latitude of this island is 15° 10′ N. longitude 22° 25′ W.

At noon the south end of the island of St Iago bore S.W. by W. distant four leagues; and the north end N.W. distant five leagues. At half an hour after three we anchored in Port Praya, in that island, in company with the Swallow and Prince Frederick, in eight fathom water, upon sandy ground. We had much rain and lightning in the night, and early in the morning I sent to the commanding officer at the fort, for leave to get off some water, and other refreshments, which he granted.

We soon learnt that this was the sickly season, and that the rains were so great as to render it extremely difficult to get any thing down from the country to the ships: It happened also, unfortunately, that the small-pox, which is extremely fatal here, was at this time epidemic; so that I permitted no man to go ashore who had not had that distemper,

per, and I would not suffer even those that had to go into any house.

We procured, however, a supply of water and some cattle from the shore, and caught abundance of fish with the seine, which was hauled twice every day : We found also in the valley where we got our water, a kind of large purslain, growing wild in amazing quantities : This was a most welcome refreshment both raw as a sallad, and boiled with the broth and pease ; when we left the place we carried away enough of it to serve us a week.

On the 28th, at half an hour after twelve, we weighed and put to sea ; at half an hour after six in the evening the peak of Fuego bore W.N.W. distant twelve leagues, and in the night the burning mountain was very visible.

This day I ordered hooks and lines to be served to all the ship's company, that they might catch fish for themselves ; but at the same time I also ordered that no man should keep his fish more than four-and-twenty hours before it was eaten, for I had observed that stale, and even dried fish, had made the people sickly, and tainted the air in the ship.

On the first of October, in lat. 10° 37′ N. we lost the true trade-wind, and had only light and variable gales ; and this day we found that the ship was set twelve miles to the northward by a current ; on the third we found a current run S. by E. at the rate of six fathom an hour, or about twenty miles and a half a day : On the seventh we found the ship nineteen miles to the southward of her reckoning.

On the 20th, our butter and cheese being all expended, we began to serve the ship's company with oil, and I gave orders that they should also be served with mustard and vinegar once a fortnight during the rest of the voyage.

On the 22d we saw an incredible number of birds, and among the rest a man-of-war bird, which inclined us to think that some land was not more than sixty leagues distant : This day we crossed the equator in longitude 23° 40′ W.

On the 24th, I ordered the ship's company to be served with brandy, and reserved the wine for the sick and convalescent. On the 26th the Prince Frederick made signals of distress, upon which, we bore down to her, and found that she had carried away her fore-top-sail-yard, and to supply this loss, we gave her our sprit-sail top-sail-yard, which we could spare, and she hoisted it immediately.

On

On the 27th she again made signals of distress, upon which I brought-to, and sent the carpenter on board her, who returned with an account that she had sprung a leak under the larboard cheek forward, and that it was impossible to do any thing to it till we had better weather. Upon speaking with Lieutenant Brine, who commanded her, he informed me that the crew were sickly; that the fatigue of working the pumps, and constantly standing by the sails, had worn them down; that their provisions were not good, that they had nothing to drink but water, and that he feared it would be impossible for him to keep company with me except I could spare him some assistance. For the badness of their provision I had no remedy, but I sent on board a carpenter and six seamen to assist in pumping and working the ship.

On the eighth of November, being in latitude 25° 52' S. longitude 39° 38', we sounded with 160 fathom, but had no ground: On the ninth, having seen a great number of birds, called albatrosses, we sounded again with 180 fathom, but had no ground.

On the 11th, having by signal brought the store-ship under our stern, I sent the carpenter, with proper assistants, on board to stop the leak; but they found that very little could be done: We then completed our provisions, and those of the Swallow, from her stores, and put on board her all our staves, iron hoops, and empty oil jars. The next day I sent a carpenter and six seamen to relieve the men that had been sent to assist her on the 27th of October, who, by this time, began to suffer much by their fatigue. Several of her crew having the appearance of the scurvy, I sent the surgeon on board her with some medicines for the sick. This day, having seen some albatrosses, turtles, and weeds, we sounded, but had no ground with 180 fathom.

On the 12th, being now in latitude 30 south, we began to find it very cold; we therefore got up our quarter cloths, and fitted them to their proper places, and the seamen put on their thick jackets. This day we saw a turtle, and several albatrosses, but still had no ground with 180 fathom.

We continued to see weeds and birds on board the ship, but had no ground till the 18th, when we found a soft muddy bottom at the depth of fifty-four fathom. We were now in lat. 35° 40' S. long. 49° 54' W.; and this was the first sounding we had after our coming upon the coast of Brazil.

On the 19th, about eight o'clock in the evening, we saw a meteor of a very extraordinary appearance in the north-east, which, soon after we had observed it, flew off in a horizontal line to the south-west, with amazing rapidity: It was near a minute in its progress, and it left a train of light behind it so strong, that the deck was not less illuminated than at noon-day. This day we saw a great number of seals about the ship, and had soundings at fifty-five fathom, with a muddy bottom. The next day the seals continued, and we had soundings at fifty-three fathom, with a dark-coloured sand; upon which we bent our cables.

On the 21st we had no ground with 150 fathom. Our lat. at noon was 37° 40' S. long 51° 24' W.

On the 22d we had soundings again at seventy fathom, with a dark brown sand, and saw many whales and seals about the ship, with a great number of butterflies, and birds, among which were snipes and plovers. Our lat. at noon was 38° 55' long. 56° 47' W.

Our soundings continued from forty to seventy fathom, till the eighth of December, when, about six o'clock in the morning, we saw land bearing from S. W. to W. by S. and appearing like many small islands. At noon it bore from W. by S. to S. S. W. distant eight leagues; our latitude then being 47° 16' S. long. 64° 58' W. About three o'clock Cape Blanco bore W. N. W. distant six leagues, and a remarkable double saddle W. S. W. distant about three leagues. We had now soundings from twenty to sixteen fathom, sometimes with coarse sand and gravel, sometimes with small black stones and shells. At eight in the evening the Tower rock at Port Desire bore S. W. by W. distant about three leagues; and the extremes of the land from S. by E. to N. W. by N. At nine, Penguin Island bore S. W. by W. ½ W. distant two leagues; and at four o'clock in the morning of the ninth, the land seen from the mast-head bore from S. W. to W. by N.

At noon, Penguin island bore S. by E. distant fifty-seven miles; our latitude being 48° 56' S. longitude 65° 6' W. This day we saw such a quantity of red shrimps about the ship that the sea was coloured with them.

At noon the next day, Wednesday the 10th, the extremes of the land bore from S. W. to N. W. and Wood's Mount,

near

near the entrance of St Julian's, bore S. W. by W. distant three or four leagues. Our latitude was 49° 16′ S. our longitude 66° 48′ W. ; and our soundings were from forty to forty-five fathom, sometimes fine sand, sometimes soft mud.

At noon, on Thursday the 11th, Penguin Island bore N.N.E. distant fifty-eight leagues. Our latitude was 50° 48′ S. our longitude 67° 10′ W.

We continued our course till Saturday the 13th, when our latitude being 50° 34′ S. and our longitude 68° 15′ W. the extremes of the land bore from N. ¼ E. to S. S. W. ½ W. and the ship was about five or six miles distant from the shore. Cape Beachy-head, the northermost cape, was found to lie in latitude 50° 16′ S. and Cape Fairweather, the southermost cape, in latitude 50° 50′ S.

On Sunday the 14th, at four in the morning, Cape Beachy-head bore N. W. ½ N. distant about eight leagues ; and at noon, our latitude being 50° 52′ S. and longitude 68° 10′ W. Penguin island bore N. 35° E. distant 68 leagues. We were six leagues from the shore, and the extremes of the land were from N. W. to W. S. W.

At eight o'clock in the morning of Monday the 15th, being about six miles from the shore, the extremes of the land bore from S. by E. to N. by E. and the entrance of the river St Croix S. W. ½ W. We had twenty fathom quite cross the opening, the distance from point to point being about seven miles, and afterwards keeping at the distance of about four miles from each cape, we had from twenty-two to twenty-four fathom. The land on the north shore is high, and appears in three capes ; that on the south shore is low and flat. At seven in the evening, Cape Fairweather bore S. W. ½ S. distant about four leagues, a low point running out from it S. S. W. ¾ W. We stood off and on all night, and had from thirty to twenty-two fathom water, with a bottom of sand and mud. At seven the next morning, Tuesday the 16th, we shoaled gradually into twelve fathom, with a bottom of fine sand, and soon after into six ; we then hauled off S. E. by S. somewhat more than a mile : then steered east five miles, then E. by N. and deepened into twelve fathom. Cape Fairweather at this time bore W. ½ S. distant four leagues, and the northermost extremity of the land W. N. W. When we first came into shoal water, Cape Fairweather bore W. ½ N. and a low point without it W. S. W. distant about four miles.

At

At noon Cape Fairweather bore W. N. W. ½ W. distant six leagues, and a large hummock S. W. ½ W. distant seven leagues. At this time our lat. was 51° 52' W. long. 68° W.

At one o'clock, being about two leagues distant from the shore, the extremes of three remarkable round hills bore from S. W. by W. to W. S. W. At four, Cape Virgin Mary bore S. E. by S. distant about four leagues. At eight, we were very near the Cape, and upon the point of it saw several men riding, who made signs for us to come on shore. In about half an hour we anchored in a bay, close under the south side of the Cape, in ten fathom water, with a gravelly bottom. The Swallow and store-ship anchored soon after between us and the Cape, which then bore N. by W. ½ W. and a low sandy point like Dungeness S. by W. From the Cape there runs a shoal, to the distance of about half a league, which may be easily known by the weeds that are upon it. We found it high water at half an hour after eleven, and the tide rose twenty feet.

The natives continued abreast of the ship all night, making several great fires, and frequently shouting very loud. As soon as it was light, on Wednesday morning the 17th, we saw great numbers of them in motion, who made signs for us to land. About five o'clock I made the signal for the boats belonging to the Swallow and the Prince Frederick to come on board, and in the meantime hoisted out our own. These boats being all manned and armed, I took a party of marines, and rowed towards the shore, having left orders with the master to bring the ship's broad-side to bear upon the landing place, and to keep the guns loaded with round shot. We reached the beach about six o'clock, and before we went from the boat, I made signs to the natives to retire to some distance : They immediately complied, and I then landed with the Captain of the Swallow, and several of the officers : The marines were drawn up, and the boats were brought to a grappling near the shore. I then made signs to the natives to come near, and directed them to sit down in a semicircle, which they did with great order and cheerfulness. When this was done, I distributed among them several knives, scissars, buttons, beads, combs, and other toys, particularly some ribbands to the women, which they received with a very becoming mixture of pleasure and respect. Having distributed my presents, I endeavoured to make them understand that I had other

things

things which I would part with, but for which I expected
somewhat in return. I shewed them some hatchets and
bill-hooks, and pointed to some guanicoes, which happened to be near, and some ostriches which I saw dead among
them; making signs at the same time I wanted to eat; but
they either could not, or would not understand me: For
though they seemed very desirous of the hatchets and the
bill-hooks, they did not give the least intimation that they
would part with any provisions; no traffic therefore was
carried on between us.

Each of these people, both men and women, had a horse,
with a decent saddle, stirrups, and bridle. The men had
wooden spurs, except one, who had a large pair of such as
are worn in Spain, brass stirrups, and a Spanish scymitar,
without a scabbard; but notwithstanding these distinctions,
he did not appear to have any authority over the rest; the
women had no spurs. The horses appeared to be well-made,
and nimble, and were about fourteen hands high. The people had also many dogs with them, which, as well as the
horses, appeared to be of a Spanish breed.

As I had two measuring rods with me, we went round
and measured those that appeared to be tallest among them.
One of these was six feet six inches high, several more
were six feet five, and six feet six inches; but the stature
of the greater part of them was from five feet ten to six
feet. Their complexion is a dark copper-colour, like that
of the Indians in North America; their hair is straight, and
nearly as harsh as hog's bristles: It is tied back with a cotton string, but neither sex wears any head-dress. They are
well-made, robust, and bony; but their hands and feet are
remarkably small. They are clothed with the skins of the
guanico, sewed together into pieces about six feet long and
five wide: These are wrapped round the body, and fastened with a girdle, with the hairy side inwards; some of them
had also what the Spaniards have called a *puncho*, a square
piece of cloth made of the downy hair of the guanico,
through which a hole being cut for the head, the rest hangs
round them about as low as the knee. The guanico is an
animal that in size, make, and colour, resembles a deer, but
it has a hump on its back, and no horns. These people wear
also a kind of drawers, which they pull up very tight, and
buskins, which reach from the mid-leg to the instep before,
and behind are brought under the heel; the rest of the foot

is

is without any covering. We observed that some of the men had a circle painted round the left eye, and that others were painted on their arms, and on different parts of the face; the eye-lids of all the young women were painted black. They talked much, and some of them called out Ca-pi-ta-ne; but when they were spoken to in Spanish, Portuguese, French, and Dutch, they made no reply. Of their own language we could distinguish only one word, which was *chevow*: We supposed it to be a salutation, as they always pronounced it when they shook hands with us, and when, by signs, they asked us to give them any thing. When they were spoken to in English, they repeated the words after us as plainly as we could do; and they soon got by heart the words, " Englishmen come on shore." Every one had a missile weapon of a singular kind, tucked into the girdle. It consisted of two round stones, covered with leather, each weighing about a pound, which were fastened to the two ends of a string about eight feet long. This is used as a sling, one stone being kept in the hand, and the other whirled round the head till it is supposed to have acquired sufficient force, and then discharged at the object. They are so expert in the management of this double-headed shot, that they will hit a mark, not bigger than a shilling, with both the stones, at the distance of fifteen yards; it is not their custom, however, to strike either the guanico or the ostrich with them in the chase, but they discharge them so that the cord comes against the legs of the ostrich, or two of the legs of the guanico, and is twisted round them by the force of the swing of the balls, so that the animal being unable to run, becomes an easy prey to the hunter.

While we stayed on shore, we saw them eat some of their flesh-meat raw, particularly the paunch of an ostrich, without any other preparation or cleaning than just turning it inside out, and shaking it. We observed among them several beads, such as I gave them, and two pieces of red baize, which we supposed had been left there, or in the neighbouring country, by Commodore Byron.

After I had spent about four hours with these people, I made signs to them that I was going on board, and that I would take some of them with me if they were desirous to go. As soon as I had made myself understood, above an hundred eagerly offered to visit the ship; but I did not chuse to indulge more than eight of the number. They jumped into the boats with the joy and alacrity of children going to a fair, and, having no intention of mischief against us, had not the least suspicion that we intended any mischief against them.   They sung several of their country songs while they were in the boat, and when they came on board did not express either the curiosity or wonder which the multiplicity of objects, to them equally strange and stupendous, that at once presented themselves, might be supposed to excite.   I took them down into the cabin, where they looked about them with an unaccountable indifference, till one of them happened to cast his eyes upon a looking-glass: This, however, excited no more astonishment than the prodigies which offer themselves to our imagination in a dream, when we converse with the dead, fly in the air, and walk upon the sea, without reflecting that the laws of nature are violated ; but it afforded them infinite diversion : They advanced, retreated, and played a thousand tricks before it, laughing violently, and talking with great emphasis to each other.   I gave them some beef, pork, biscuit, and other articles of the ship's provisions: They eat indiscriminately whatever was offered to them, but they would drink nothing but water.   From the cabin I carried them all over the ship, but they looked at nothing with much attention, except the animals which we had on board as live stock: They examined the hogs and sheep with some curiosity, and were exceedingly delighted with the Guinea hens and turkies; they did not seem to desire any thing that they saw except our apparel, and only one of them, an old man, asked for that: We gratified him with a pair of shoes and buckles, and to each of the others I gave a canvass bag, in which I put some needles ready threaded, a few slips of cloth, a knife, a pair of scissars, some twine, a few beads, a comb, and a looking-glass, with some new sixpences and half-pence, through which a hole had been drilled, that was fitted with a ribband to hang round the neck.   We offered them some leaves of tobacco, rolled up into what are called segars, and they smoked a little, but did not seem fond of it.   I showed them the great guns, but they did not appear to have any notion of their use.   After I had carried them through the ship, I ordered the marines to be drawn up, and go through part of their exercise.   When the first volley was fired, they were struck with astonishment and terror; the old man, in particular, threw himself down upon

the

the deck, pointed to the muskets, and then striking his breast with his hand, lay some time motionless, with his eyes shut: By this we supposed he intended to shew us that he was not unacquainted with fire-arms, and their fatal effect. The rest, seeing our people merry, and finding themselves unhurt, soon resumed their cheerfulness and good humour, and heard the second and third volley fired without much emotion; but the old man continued prostrate upon the deck some time, and never recovered his spirits till the firing was over. About noon, the tide being out, I acquainted them by signs that the ship was proceeding farther, and that they must go on shore: This I soon perceived they were very unwilling to do; all, however, except the old man and one more, were got into the boat without much difficulty; but these stopped at the gang-way, where the old man turned about, and went aft to the companion ladder, where he stood some time without speaking a word; he then uttered what we supposed to be a prayer; for he many times lifted up his hands and his eyes to the heavens, and spoke in a manner and tone very different from what we had observed in their conversation: His orison seemed to be rather sung than said, so that we found it impossible to distinguish one word from another. When I again intimated that it was proper for him to go into the boat, he pointed to the sun, and then moving his hand round to the west, he paused, looked in my face, laughed, and pointed to the shore: By this it was easy to understand that he wished to stay on board till sun-set, and I took no little pains to convince him that we could not stay so long upon that part of the coast, before he could be prevailed upon to go into the boat; at length, however, he went over the ship's side with his companion, and when the boat put off they all began to sing, and continued their merriment till they got on shore. When they landed, great numbers of those on shore pressed eagerly to get into the boat; but the officer on board, having positive orders to bring none of them off, prevented them, though not without great difficulty, and apparently to their extreme mortification and disappointment.

When the boat returned on board, I sent her off again with the master, to sound the shoal that runs off from the point: He found it about three miles broad from north to south, and that to avoid it, it was necessary to keep four miles off the cape, in twelve or thirteen fathom water.

SECTION

Section II.

*The Passage through the Streight of Magellan, with some fur-
ther Account of the Patagonians, and a Description of the
Coast on each side, and its Inhabitants.*

About one o'clock, on Wednesday the 17th of December, I made the signal and weighed, ordering the Swallow
to go a-head, and the store-ship to bring up the rear. The
wind was right against us, and blew fresh, so that we were
obliged to turn into the Streight of Magellan with the
flood-tide, between Cape Virgin Mary and the Sandy Point
that resembles Dungeness. When we got a-breast of this
Point, we stood close into the shore, where we saw two
guanicoes, and many of the natives on horseback, who
seemed to be in pursuit of them : When the horsemen came
near, they ran up the country at a great rate, and were
pursued by the hunters, with their slings in their hands
ready for the cast; but neither of them was taken while
they were within the reach of our sight.

When we got about two leagues to the west of Dungeness, and were standing off shore, we fell in with a shoal
upon which we had but seven fathom water at half flood :
This obliged us to make short tacks, and keep continually
heaving the lead. At half an hour after eight in the evening, we anchored about three miles from the shore, in 20
fathom, with a muddy bottom : Cape Virgin Mary then
bearing N. E. by E. ½ E. ; Point Possession W. ½ S. at the
distance of about five leagues.

About half an hour after we had cast anchor, the natives
made several large fires a-breast of the ship, and at break
of day we saw about four hundred of them encamped in
a fine green valley, between two hills, with their horses
feeding beside them. About six o'clock in the morning,
the tide being done, we got again under sail : Its course
here is from east to west; it rises and falls thirty feet, and
its strength is equal to about three knots an hour. About
noon there being little wind, and the ebb running with
great force, the Swallow, which was a-head, made the signal
and came to an anchor; upon which I did the same, and
so did the store-ship that was a-stern.

As

As we saw great numbers of the natives on horseback a-breast of the ship, and as Captain Carteret informed me that this was the place where Commodore Byron had the conference with the tall men, I sent the lieutenants of the Swallow and the store-ship to the shore, but with orders not to land, as the ships were at too great a distance to protect them. When these gentlemen returned, they told me, that the boat having lain upon her oars very near the beach, the natives came down in great numbers, whom they knew to be the same persons they had seen the day before, with many others, particularly women and children; that when they perceived our people had no design to land, they seemed to be greatly disappointed, and those who had been on board the ship waded off to the boat, making signs for it to advance, and pronouncing the words they had been taught, " Englishmen come on shore," very loud, many times; that when they found they could not get the people to land, they would fain have got into the boat, and that it was with great difficulty they were prevented. That they presented them with some bread, tobacco, and a few toys, pointing at the same time to some guanicoes and ostriches, and making signs that they wanted them as provisions, but that they could not make themselves understood; that finding they could obtain no refreshment, they rowed along the shore in search of fresh water, but that, seeing no appearance of a rivulet, they returned on board.

At six o'clock the next morning, we weighed, the Swallow being still a-head, and at noon we anchored in Possession Bay, having twelve fathom, with a clean sandy bottom. Point Possession at this time bore east, distant three leagues; the Asses Ears west, and the entrance of the Narrows S. W. ½ W.: The bottom of the bay, which was the nearest land to the ship, was distant about three miles. We saw a great number of Indians upon the Point, and at night, large fires on the Terra del Fuego shore.

From this time, to the 22d, we had strong gales and heavy seas, so that we got on but slowly; and we now anchored in 18 fathom, with a muddy bottom. The Asses Ears bore N. W. by W. ½ W. Point Possession N. E. by E. and the point of the Narrows, on the south side, S. S. W. distant between three and four leagues. In this situation, our longitude, by observation, was 70° 20′ W. latitude 52° 30′ S. The tide here sets S. E. by S. and N. E. by N. at

the

the rate of about three knots an hour; the water rises four-and-twenty feet, and at this time it was high water at four in the morning.

In the morning of the 23d, we made sail, turning to windward, but the tide was so strong, that the Swallow was set one way, the Dolphin another, and the store-ship a third: There was a fresh breeze, but not one of the vessels would answer her helm We had various soundings, and saw the rippling in the middle ground: In these circumstances, sometimes backing, sometimes filling, we entered the first Narrows. About six o'clock in the evening, the tide being done, we anchored on the south shore, in forty fathom with a sandy bottom; the Swallow anchored on the north shore, and the store-ship not a cable's length from a sand-bank, about two miles to the eastward. The streight here is only three miles wide, and at midnight, the tide being slack, we weighed and towed the ship through. A breeze sprung up soon afterwards, which continued till seven in the morning, and then died away. We steered from the first Narrows to the second S. W. and had nineteen fathom, with a muddy bottom. At eight we anchored two leagues from the shore, in 24 fathom, Cape Gregory bearing W. ½ N. and Sweepstakes Foreland S. W. ½ W. The tide here ran seven knots an hour, and such *bores* sometimes came down, with immense quantities of weeds, that we expected every moment to be adrift.

The next day, being Christmas day, we sailed through the second Narrows. In turning through this part of the Streight we had twelve fathom within half a mile of the shore on each side, and in the middle seventeen fathom, twenty-two fathom, and no ground. At five o'clock in the evening, the ship suddenly shoaled from seventeen fathom to five, St Bartholomew's island then bearing S. ½ W. distant between three and four miles, and Elizabeth's Island S. S. W. ½ W. distant five or six miles. About half an hour after eight o'clock, the weather being rainy and tempestuous, we anchored under Elizabeth's island in twenty-four fathom, with hard gravelly ground. Upon this island we found great quantities of celery, which, by the direction of the surgeon, was given to the people, with boiled wheat and portable soup, for breakfast every morning. Some of the officers who went a-shore with their guns, saw two small dogs, and several places where fires had been recently made,
with

with many fresh shells of mussels and limpets lying about them : They saw also several wigwams or huts, consisting of young trees, which, being sharpened at one end, and thrust into the ground in a circular form, the other ends were brought to meet, and fastened together at the top; but they saw none of the natives.

From this place we saw many high mountains, bearing from S. to W. S. W.; several parts of the summits were covered with snow, though it was the midst of summer in this part of the world : They were clothed with wood about three parts of their height, and above with herbage, except where the snow was not yet melted. This was the first place where we had seen wood in all South America.

At two o'clock in the morning of the 26th, we weighed, and, having a fair wind, were a-breast of the north end of Elizabeth's Island at three : At half an hour after five, being about mid-way between Elizabeth's Island and St George's Island, we suddenly shoaled our water from seventeen fathom to six : We struck the ground once, but the next cast had no bottom with twenty fathom. When we were upon this shoal, Cape Porpoise bore W. S. W. ½ W. the south end of Elizabeth's island W. N. W. ½ W. distant three leagues, the south end of Saint George's Island N.E. distant four leagues. The store-ship, which was about half a league to the southward of us, had once no more than four fathom, and for a considerable time not seven; the Swallow, which was three or four miles to the southward, had deep water, for she kept near to St George's Island. In my opinion it is safest to run down from the north end of Elizabeth's Island, about two or three miles from the shore, and so on all the way to Port Famine. At noon a low point bore E. ½ N.; Fresh-water Bay S.W. ½ W. At this time we were about three miles distant from the north shore, and had no ground with eighty fathom. Our longitude, by observation, which was made over the shoal, was 71° 20' W. our latitude 53° 12' S.

About four o'clock we anchored in Port Famine Bay, in thirteen fathom, and there being little wind, sent all the boats, and towed in the Swallow and Prince Frederick.

The next morning, the weather being squally, we warped the ship farther into the harbour, and moored her with a cable each way in nine fathom. I then sent a party of men to pitch two large tents in the bottom of the bay, for the sick, the wooders, and the sail-makers, who were soon after

sent

sent on shore, with the surgeon, the gunner, and some midshipmen. Cape St Anne now bore N.E. by E. distant three quarters of a mile, and Sedger river S. ½ W.

On the 28th we unbent all the sails, and sent them on shore to be repaired, erected tents upon the banks of Sedger river, and sent all the empty casks on shore, with the coopers to trim them, and a mate and ten men to wash and fill them. We also hauled the seine, and caught fish in great plenty: Some of them resembled a mullet, but the flesh was very soft; and among them were a few smelts, some of which were twenty inches long, and weighed four-and-twenty ounces.

During our whole stay in this place we caught fish enough to furnish one meal a-day both for the sick and the well: We found also great plenty of celery and pea-tops, which were boiled with the pease and portable soup. Besides these, we gathered great quantities of fruit that resembled the cranberry, and the leaves of a shrub somewhat like our thorn, which were remarkably sour. When we arrived, all our people began to look pale and meagre; many had the scurvy to a great degree, and upon others there were manifest signs of its approach; yet in a fortnight there was not a scorbutic person in either of the ships. Their recovery was effected by their being on shore, eating plenty of vegetables, being obliged to wash their apparel, and keep their persons clean by daily bathing in the sea.

The next day we set up the forge on shore; and from this time, the armourers, carpenters, and the rest of the people, were employed in refitting the ship, and making her ready for the sea.

In the mean time a considerable quantity of wood was cut, and put on board the store-ship, to be sent to Falkland's Island; and as I well knew there was no wood growing there, I caused some thousands of young trees to be carefully taken up with their roots, and a proper quantity of earth; and, packing them in the best manner I could, I put them also on board the store-ship, with orders to deliver them to the commanding officer at Port Egmont, and to sail for that place with the first fair wind, putting on board two of my seamen, who, being in an ill state of health when they first came on board, were now altogether unfit to proceed in the voyage.

On Wednesday the 14th of January we got all our peo-

ple

ple and tents on board; having taken in seventy-five tons of water from the shore, and twelve months provisions of all kinds, at whole allowance for ourselves, and ten months for the Swallow, from on board the store-ship, I sent the master in the cutter, which was victualled for a week, to look out for anchoring-places on the north shore of the streight.

After several attempts to sail, the weather obliged us to continue in our old station till Saturday the 17th, when the Prince Frederick victualler sailed for Falkland's Island, and the master returned from his expedition. The master reported that he had found four places in which there was good anchorage, between the place were we lay and Cape Froward: That he had been on shore at several places, where he had found plenty of wood and water close to the beach, with abundance of cranberries and wild celery. He reported also, that he had seen a great number of currant bushes full of fruit, though none of it was ripe, and a great variety of beautiful shrubs in full blossom, bearing flowers of different colours, particularly red, purple, yellow, and white, besides great plenty of the Winter's bark, a grateful spice which is well known to the botanists of Europe. He shot several wild ducks, geese, gulls, a hawk, and two or three of the birds which the sailors call a race-horse.

At five o'clock in the morning of Sunday the 18th we made sail, and at noon, being about two miles from the shore, Cape Froward bore N. by E. a bluff point N.N.W. and Cape Holland W. ½ S. Our latitude at this place, by observation, was 54° 3' S. and we found the streight to be about six miles wide. Soon after I sent a boat into Snug Bay, to lie at the anchoring-place, but the wind coming from the land, I stood off again all night; and at a mile from the shore we had no ground with 140 fathom.

In the morning of Monday the 19th, the Swallow having made the signal for anchoring under Cape Holland, we ran in, and anchored in ten fathom, with a clear sandy bottom. Upon sending the boats out to sound, we discovered that we were very near a reef of rocks; we therefore tripped the anchor, and dropped farther out, where we had twelve fathom, and were about half a mile from the shore, just opposite to a large stream of water, which falls with great rapidity from the mountains, for the land here is of a stupendous height. Cape Holland bore W.S.W. ½ W. distant two miles, and Cape Froward E. Our latitude, by observation, was 53° 58' S.

The

The next morning we got off some water, and great plenty of wild celery, but could get no fish except a few mussels. I sent off the boats to sound, and found that there was good anchorage at about half a mile from the shore, quite from the cape to four miles below it; and close by the cape a good harbour, where a ship might refresh with more safety than at Port Famine, and avail herself of a large river of fresh water, with plenty of wood, celery, and berries; though the place affords no fish except mussels.

Having completed our wood and water, we sailed from this place on the 22d, about three o'clock in the afternoon. At nine in the evening, the ship being about two miles distant from the shore, Cape Gallant bore W.¼N. distant two leagues, Cape Holland E. by N. distant six leagues; Cape Gallant and Cape Holland being nearly in one: A white patch in Monmouth's Island bore S.S.W.¼W. Rupert's Island W.S.W. At this place the strait is not more than five miles over; and we found a tide which produced a very unusual effect, for it became impossible to keep the ship's head upon any point.

At six the next morning, the Swallow made the signal for having found anchorage; and at eight we anchored in a bay under Cape Gallant, in ten fathom, with a muddy bottom. The east point of Cape Gallant bore S.W. by ¼ W. the extreme point of the easternmost land E. by S. a point making the mouth of a river N. by W. and the white patch on Charles' Island S.W. The boats being sent out to sound, found good anchorage every-where, except within two cables' length S.W. of the ship, where it was coral, and deepened to sixteen fathom. In the afternoon I sent out the master to examine the bay and a large lagoon; and he reported that the lagoon was the most commodious harbour we had yet seen in the strait, having five fathom at the entrance, and from four to five in the middle; that it was capable of receiving a great number of vessels, had three large fresh-water rivers, and plenty of wood and celery. We had here the misfortune to have a seine spoiled, by being entangled with the wood that lies sunk at the mouth of these rivers; but though we caught but little fish, we had an incredible number of wild ducks, which we found a very good succedaneum.

The mountains are here very lofty, and the master of the Swallow climbed one of the highest, hoping that from the summit

summit he should obtain a sight of the South Sea ; but he found his view intercepted by mountains still higher on the southern shore : Before he descended, however, he erected a pyramid, within which he deposited a bottle containing a shilling, and a paper on which was written the ship's name, and the date of the year ; a memorial which possibly may remain there as long as the world endures.

In the morning of the 24th we took two boats and examined Cordes bay, which we found very much inferior to that in which the ship lay ; it had indeed a larger lagoon, but the entrance of it was very narrow, and barred by a shoal, on which there was not sufficient depth of water for a ship of burden to float : The entrance of the bay also was rocky, and within it the ground was foul.

In this place we saw an animal that resembled an ass, but it had a cloven hoof, as we discovered afterwards by tracking it, and was as swift as a deer. This was the first animal we had seen in the streight, except at the entrance, where we found the guanicoes that we would fain have trafficked for with the Indians. We shot at this creature, but we could not hit it ; probably it is altogether unknown to the naturalists of Europe.

The country about this place has the most dreary and forlorn appearance that can be imagined ; the mountains on each side the streight are of an immense height : About one-fourth of the ascent is covered with trees of a considerable size ; in the space from thence to the middle of the mountain there is nothing but withered shrubs ; above these are patches of snow, and fragments of broken rock ; and the summit is altogether rude and naked, towering above the clouds in vast crags that are piled upon each other, and look like the ruins of nature devoted to everlasting sterility and desolation.

We went over in two boats to the Royal Islands, and sounded, but found no bottom : A very rapid tide set through wherever there was an opening ; and they cannot be approached by shipping without the most imminent danger. Whoever navigates this part of the streight, should keep the north shore close on board all the way, and not venture more than a mile from it till the Royal Islands are passed. The current sets easterly through the whole tour-and-twenty hours, and the indraught should by all means be avoided. The latitude of Cape Gallant road is 53° 50′ S.

We

We continued in this station, taking in wood and water, and gathering mussels and herbs, till the morning of the 27th, when a boat that had been sent to try the current, returned with an account that it set nearly at the rate of two miles an hour, but that, the wind being northerly, we might probably get round to Elizabeth Bay or York Road before night; we therefore weighed with all expedition. At noon on the 28th, the west point of Cape Gallant bore W.N.W. distant half a mile, and the white patch on Charles' Island S E. by S. We had fresh gales and heavy flaws off the land; and at two o'clock the west point of Cape Gallant bore E. distant three leagues, and York Point W.N.W. distant five leagues. At five, we opened York Road, the point bearing N.W. at the distance of half a mile: At this time the ship was taken a-back, and a strong current with a heavy squall drove us so far to leeward, that it was with great difficulty we got into Elizabeth Bay, and anchored in twelve fathom near a river. The Swallow being at anchor off the point of the bay, and very near the rocks, I sent all the boats with anchors and hausers to her assistance, and at last she was happily warped to windward into good anchorage. York Point now bore W. by N. a shoal with weeds upon it W.N.W. at the distance of a cable's length. Point Passage S.E.¼E. distant half a mile, a rock near Rupert's Isle S.¼E. and a rivulet on the bay N.E. by E. distant about three cables' length. Soon after sun-set we saw a great smoke on the southern shore, and another on Prince Rupert's Island.

Early in the morning I sent the boats on shore for water, and soon after our people landed, three canoes put off from the south shore, and landed sixteen of the natives on the east point of the bay. When they came within about a hundred yards of our people they stopt, called out, and made signs of friendship: Our people did the same, shewing them some beads and other toys. At this they seemed pleased, and began to shout; our people imitated the noise they made, and shouted in return: The Indians then advanced, still shouting and laughing very loud. When the parties met they shook hands, and our men presented the Indians with several of the toys which they had shewn them at a distance. They were covered with seal-skins, which stunk abominably, and some of them were eating the rotten flesh and blubber raw, with a keen appetite and great seem-

I   ing

ing satisfaction. Their complexion was the same as that
of the people we had seen before, but they were low of stature, the tallest of them not being more than five foot six:
They appeared to be perishing with cold, and immediately
kindled several fires. How they subsist in winter, it is not
perhaps easy to guess, for the weather was at this time so
severe, that we had frequent falls of snow. They were
armed with bows, arrows, and javelins; the arrows and javelins were pointed with flint, which was wrought into the
shape of a serpent's tongue; and they discharged both with
great force and dexterity, scarce ever failing to hit a mark
at a considerable distance. To kindle a fire they strike a
pebble against a piece of mundic, holding under it, to catch
the sparks, some moss or down, mixed with a whitish earth,
which takes fire like tinder: They then take some dry grass,
of which there is every-where plenty, and, putting the lighted moss into it, wave it to and fro, and in about a minute
it blazes.

When the boat returned she brought three of them on
board the ship, but they seemed to regard nothing with
any degree of curiosity, except our clothes and a looking-
glass; the looking-glass afforded them as much diversion
as it had done the Patagonians, and it seemed to surprise
them more: When they first peeped into it they started
back, first looking at us, and then at each other; they then
took another peep, as it were by stealth, starting back as
before, and then eagerly looking behind it: When by degrees they became familiar with it, they smiled, and seeing
the image smile in return, they were exceedingly delighted,
and burst into fits of the most violent laughter. They left
this however, and every thing else, with perfect indifference, the little they possessed being to all appearance equal
to their desires. They eat whatever was given them, but
would drink nothing but water.

When they left the ship I went on shore with them, and
by this time several of their wives and children were come
to the watering-place. I distributed some trinkets among
them, with which they seemed pleased for a moment, and
they gave us some of their arms in return; they gave us
also several pieces of mundic, such as is found in the tin
mines of Cornwall: They made us understand that they
found it in the mountains, where there are probably mines
of tin, and perhaps of more valuable metal. When they

left us and embarked in their canoes, they hoisted a seal-skin for a sail, and steered for the southern shore, where we saw many of their hovels; and we remarked that not one of them looked behind, either at us or at the ship, so little impression had the wonders they had seen made upon their minds, and so much did they appear to be absorbed in the present, without any habitual exercise of their power to reflect upon the past.

In this station we continued till Tuesday the 3d of February. At about half an hour past twelve we weighed, and in a sudden squall were taken a-back, so as that both ships were in the most imminent danger of being driven ashore on a reef of rocks; the wind however suddenly shifted, and we happily got off without damage. At five o'clock in the afternoon, the tide being done, and the wind coming about to the west, we bore away for York Road, and at length anchored in it: The Swallow at the same time being very near Island Bay, under Cape Quod, endeavoured to get in there, but was by the tide obliged to return to York Road. In this situation Cape Quod bore W.½S. distant 19 miles, York Point E.S.E. distant one mile, Bachelor's River N.N.W. three quarters of a mile, the entrance of Jerom's Sound N.W. by W. and a small island on the south shore W. by S. We found the tide here very rapid and uncertain; in the stream it generally set to the eastward, but it sometimes, though rarely, set westward six hours together. This evening we saw five Indian canoes come out of Bachelor's River, and go up Jerom's Sound.

In the morning, the boats which I had sent out to sound both the shores of the streight and all parts of the bay, returned with an account that there was good anchorage within Jerom's Sound, and all the way thither from the ship's station at the distance of about half a mile from the shore; also between Elizabeth and York Point, near York Point, at the distance of a cable and a half's length from the weeds, in sixteen fathom, with a muddy bottom. There were also several places under the islands on the south shore where a ship might anchor; but the force and uncertainty of the tides, and the heavy gusts of wind that came off the high lands, by which these situations were surrounded, rendered them unsafe. Soon after the boats returned, I put fresh hands into them, and went myself up Bachelor's River: We found a bar at the entrance, which at certain times

times of the tide must be dangerous. We hauled the seine, and should have caught plenty of fish if it had not been for the weeds and stumps of trees at the bottom of the river. We then went ashore, where we saw many wigwams of the natives, and several of their dogs, who, as soon as we came in sight, ran away. We also saw some ostriches, but they were beyond the reach of our pieces: We gathered mussels, limpets, sea-eggs, celery, and nettles, in great abundance. About three miles up this river, on the west side, between Mount Misery and another mountain of a stupendous height, there is a cataract which has a very striking appearance: It is precipitated from an elevation of above four hundred yards; half the way it rolls over a very steep declivity, and the other half is a perpendicular fall. The sound of this cataract is not less awful than the sight.

In this place contrary winds detained us till 10 o'clock in the morning of Saturday the 14th, when we weighed, and in half an hour the current set the ship towards Bachelor's River: We then put her in stays, and while she was coming about, which she was long in doing, we drove over a shoal where we had little more than sixteen feet water with rocky ground; so that our danger was very great, for the ship drew sixteen feet nine inches aft, and fifteen feet one inch forward: As soon as the ship gathered way, we happily deepened into three fathom; within two cables' length we had five, and in a very short time we got into deep water. We continued plying to windward till four o'clock in the afternoon, and then finding that we had lost ground, we returned to our station, and again anchored in York Road.

Here we remained till five o'clock in the morning of the 17th, when we weighed, and towed out of the road. At nine, though we had a fine breeze at west, the ship was carried with great violence by a current towards the south shore: The boats were all towing a-head, and the sails asleep, yet we drove so close to the rock, that the oars of the boats were entangled in the weeds. In this manner we were hurried along near three quarters of an hour, expecting every moment to be dashed to pieces against the cliff, from which we were seldom farther than a ship's length, and very often not half so much. We sounded on both sides, and found that next the shore we had from fourteen to twenty fathom, and on the other side of the

ship

ship no bottom : As all our efforts were ineffectual, we resigned ourselves to our fate, and waited the event in a state
of suspense very little different from despair. At length,
however, we opened Saint David's Sound, and a current
that rushed out of it set us into the mid-channel. During
all this time the Swallow was on the north shore, and consequently could know nothing of our danger till it was
past. We now sent the boats out to look for an anchoring-place; and at noon Cape Quod bore N.N.E. and Saint
David's head S.E.

About one o'clock the boats returned, having found an
anchoring-place in a small bay, to which we gave the name
of Butler's Bay, it having been discovered by Mr Butler,
one of the mates. It lies to the west of Rider's Bay on the
south shore of the streight, which is here about two miles
wide. We ran in with the tide which set fast to the westward, and anchored in sixteen fathom water. The extremes of the bay from W. by N. to N.½W. are about a
quarter of a mile asunder; a small rivulet, at the distance
of somewhat less than two cables' length, bore S.¼W. and
Cape Quod N. at the distance of four miles. At this time
the Swallow was at anchor in Island Bay on the north
shore, at about six miles distance.

I now sent all the boats out to sound round the ship and
in the neighbouring bays; and they returned with an account that they could find no place fit to receive the ship,
neither could any such place be found between Cape Quod
and Cape Notch.

In this place we remained till Friday the 20th, when
about noon the clouds gathered very thick to the westward,
and before one it blew a storm, with such rain and hail as
we had scarcely ever seen. We immediately struck the
yards and top-masts, and having run out two hausers to a
rock, we hove the ship up to it : We then let go the small
bower, and veered away, and brought both cables a-head;
at the same time we carried out two more hausers, and
made them fast to two other rocks, making use of every expedient in our power to keep the ship steady. The gale
continued to increase till six o'clock in the evening, and
to our great astonishment the sea broke quite over the fore-
castle in upon the quarter-deck, which, considering the
narrowness of the streight, and the smallness of the bay in
which we were stationed, might well have been thought
impossible.

impossible. Our danger here was very great, for if the cables had parted, as we could not run out with a sail, and as we had not room to bring the ship up with any other anchor, we must have been dashed to pieces in a few minutes, and in such a situation it is highly probable that every soul would immediately have perished, however, by eight o'clock the gale was become somewhat more moderate, and, gradually decreasing during the night, we had tolerable weather the next morning. Upon heaving the anchor, we had the satisfaction to find that our cable was sound, though our hawsers were much rubbed by the rocks, notwithstanding they were parcelled with old hammacoes, and other things The first thing I did after performing the necessary operations about the ship, was to send a boat to the Swallow to enquire how she had fared during the gale: The boat returned with an account that she had felt but little of the gale, but that she had been very near being lost, in pushing through the islands two days before, by the rapidity of the tide: That notwithstanding an alteration which had been made in her rudder, she steered and worked so ill, that every time they got under way they were apprehensive that she could never safely be brought to an anchor again; I was therefore requested, in the name of the captain, to consider that she could be of very little service to the expedition, and to direct what I thought would be best for the service. I answered, that as the Lords of the Admiralty had appointed her to accompany the Dolphin, she must continue to do it as long as it was possible; that as her condition rendered her a bad sailer, I would wait her time, and attend her motions; and that if any disaster should happen to either of us, the other should be ready to afford such assistance as might be in her power.

We continued here eight days, during which time we completed our wood and water, dried our sails, and sent great part of the ship's company on shore, to wash their clothes and stretch their legs, which was the more necessary, as the cold, snowy, and tempestuous weather had confined them too much below. We caught mussels and limpets, and gathered celery and nettles in great abundance. The mussels were the largest we had ever seen, many of them being from five to six inches long: We caught also great plenty of fine, firm, red fish, not unlike a gurnet, most of

which

which were from four to five pounds weight. At the same
time we made it part of the employment of every day to
try the current, which we found constantly setting to the
eastward.

The master having been sent out to look for anchoring-
places, returned with an account that he could find no shelter, except near the shore, where it should not be sought
but in cases of the most pressing necessity. He landed
upon a large island on the north side of Snow Sound, and
being almost perished with cold, the first thing he did was
to make a large fire, with some small trees which he found
upon the spot. He then climbed one of the rocky mountains, with Mr Pickersgill, a midshipman, and one of the
seamen, to take a view of the streight, and the dismal regions that surround it. He found the entrance of the sound
to be full as broad as several parts of the streight, and to
grow but very little narrower, for several miles inland on
the Terra del Fuego side. The country on the south of it
was still more dreary and horrid than any he had yet seen :
It consisted of craggy mountains, much higher than the
clouds, that were altogether naked from the base to the
summit, there not being a single shrub, nor even a blade of
grass to be seen upon them ; nor were the vallies between
them less desolate, being entirely covered with deep beds
of snow, except here and there where it had been washed
away, or converted into ice, by the torrents which were
precipitated from the fissures and crags of the mountain
above, where the snow had been dissolved ; and even these
vallies, in the patches that were free from snow, were as
destitute of verdure as the rocks between which they lay.

On Sunday the first of March, at half an hour after four
o'clock in the morning, we saw the Swallow under sail, on
the north shore of Cape Quod. At seven we weighed, and
stood out of Butler's Bay, but it falling calm soon afterwards, the boats were obliged to take the vessel in tow,
having with much difficulty kept clear of the rocks : The
passage being very narrow, we sent the boats, about noon,
to seek for anchorage on the north shore. At this time,
Cape Notch bore W. by N. ½ N. distant between three
and four leagues, and Cape Quod E. ½ N. distant three
leagues.

About three o'clock in the afternoon, there being little
wind, we anchored, with the Swallow, under the north
shore,

shore, in a small bay, where there is a high, steep, rocky mountain, the top of which resembles the head of a lion, for which reason we called the bay Lion's Cove. We had here forty fathom, with deep water close to the shore, and at half a cable's length without the ship, no ground. We sent the boats to the westward in search of anchoring-places, and at midnight they returned with an account that there was an indifferent bay at the distance of about four miles, and that Goodluck Bay was three leagues to the westward.

At half an hour after twelve the next day, the wind be-ing northerly, we made sail from Lion's Cove, and at five anchored in Goodluck Bay, at the distance of about half-a-cable's length from the rocks, in twenty-eight fathom wa-ter. A rocky island at the west extremity of the bay bore N.W. by W distant about a cable's length and a half, and a low point, which makes the eastern extremity of the bay, bore E.S.E. distant about a mile. Between this point and the ship, there were many shoals, and in the bottom of the bay two rocks, the largest of which bore N.E. by N. the smallest N. by E. From these rocks, shoals run out to the S.E. which may be known by the weeds that are upon them; the ship was within a cable's length of them: When she swung with her stern in shore, we had sixteen fathom, with coral rock; when she swung off, we had fifty fathom, with sandy ground. Cape Notch bore from us W. by S. $\frac{1}{2}$ W. distant about one league; and in the intermediate space there was a large lagoon which we could not sound, the wind blowing too hard all the while we lay here. After we had moored the ship, we sent two boats to assist the Swallow, and one to look out for anchorage beyond Cape Notch. The boats that were sent to assist the Swallow, towed her into a small bay, where, as the wind was souther-ly, and blew fresh, she was in great danger, for the cove was not only small, but full of rocks, and open to the south-easterly winds.

All the day following, and all the night, we had hard gales, with a great sea, and much hail and rain. The next morning, we had gusts so violent, that it was impossible to stand the deck; they brought whole sheets of water all the way from Cape Notch, which was a league distant, quite over the deck. They did not last more than a minute, but were so frequent, that the cables were kept on a constant

strain,

strain, and there was the greatest reason to fear that they would give way. It was a general opinion that the Swallow could not possibly ride it out, and some of the men were so strongly prepossessed with the notion of her being lost, that they fancied they saw some of her people coming over the rocks towards our ship. The weather continued so bad, till Saturday the 7th, that we could send no boat to enquire after her; but the gale being then more moderate, a boat was dispatched about four o'clock in the morning, which, about the same hour in the afternoon, returned with an account that the ship was safe, but that the fatigue of the people had been incredible, the whole crew having been upon the deck near three days and three nights. At midnight the gusts returned, though not with equal violence, with hail, sleet, and snow. The weather being now extremely cold, and the people never dry, I got up, the next morning, eleven bales of thick woollen stuff, called fearnought, which is provided by the government, and set all the tailors to work to make them into jackets, of which every man in the ship had one.

I ordered these jackets to be made very large, allowing, one with another, two yards and thirty-four inches of the cloth to each jacket. I sent also seven bales of the same cloth to the Swallow, which made every man on board a jacket of the same kind; and I cut up three bales of finer cloth, and made jackets for the officers of both ships, which I had the pleasure to find were very acceptable.

In this situation we were obliged to continue a week, during which time, I put both my own ship, and the Swallow, upon two-thirds allowance, except brandy; but continued the breakfast as long as greens and water were plenty.

On Sunday the 15th, about noon, we saw the Swallow under sail, and it being calm, we sent our launch to assist her. In the evening the launch returned, having towed her into a very good harbour on the south shore, opposite to where we lay. The account that we received of this harbour, determined us to get into it as soon as possible; the next morning therefore, at eight o'clock, we sailed from Goodluck Bay, and thought ourselves happy to get safe out of it. When we got a-breast of the harbour where the Swallow lay, we fired several guns, as signals for her boats to assist us in getting in; and in a short time the master

came

came on board us, and piloted us to a very commodious station, where we anchored in twenty-eight fathom, with a muddy bottom. This harbour, which is sheltered from all winds, and excellent in every respect, we called *Swallow Harbour*. There are two channels into it, which are both narrow, but not dangerous, as the rocks are easily discovered by the weeds that grow upon them.

At nine o'clock the next morning, the wind coming easterly, we weighed, and sailed from Swallow Harbour. At noon we took the Swallow in tow, but at five, there being little wind, we cast off the tow. At eight in the evening, the boats which had been sent out to look for anchorage, returned with an account that they could find none: At nine we had fresh gales, and at midnight Cape Upright bore S.S.W. ¼ W.

At seven the next morning, we took the Swallow again in tow, but were again obliged to cast her off and tack, as the weather became very thick, with a great swell, and we saw land close under our lee. As no place for anchorage could be found, Captain Carteret advised me to bear away for Upright Bay, to which I consented; and as he was acquainted with the place, he went a-head: The boats were ordered to go between him and the shore, and we followed. At eleven o'clock, there being little wind, we opened a large lagoon, and a current setting strongly into it, the Swallow was driven among the breakers close upon the lee-shore: To aggravate the misfortune, the weather was very hazy, there was no anchorage, and the surf ran very high. In this dreadful situation she made signals of distress, and we immediately sent our launch, and other boats, to her assistance: The boats took her in tow, but their utmost efforts to save her would have been ineffectual, if a breeze had not suddenly came down from a mountain and wafted her off.

As a great swell came on about noon, we hauled over to the north shore. We soon found ourselves surrounded with islands, but the fog was so thick, that we knew not where we were, nor which way to steer. Among these islands the boats were sent to cast the lead, but no anchorage was to be found; we then conjectured that we were in the Bay of Islands, and that we had no chance to escape shipwreck, but by hauling directly out: This, however, was no easy task, for I was obliged to tack almost continually,

tinually, to weather some island or rock. At four o'clock in the afternoon, it happily cleared up for a minute, just to shew us Cape Upright, for which we directly steered, and at half an hour after five anchored, with the Swallow, in the bay. When we dropped the anchor, we were in twenty-four fathom, and after we had veered away a whole cable, in forty-six, with a muddy bottom. In this situation, a high bluff on the north shore bore N.W ½ N. distant five leagues, and a small island within us S. by E. ½ E. Soon after we had anchored, the Swallow drove to leeward, notwithstanding she had two anchors a-head, but was at last brought up, in seventy fathom, about a cable's length a-stern of us. At four o'clock in the morning I sent the boats, with a considerable number of men, and some hawsers and anchors, on board her, to weigh her anchors, and warp her up to windward. When her best-bower anchor was weighed, it was found entangled with the small one; I therefore found it necessary to send the stream-cable on board, and the ship was hung up by it. To clear her anchors, and warp her into a proper birth, cost us the whole day, and was not at last effected without the utmost difficulty and labour.

On the 18th we had fresh breezes, and sent the boats to sound cross the streight. Within half-a-mile of the ship, they had forty, forty-five, fifty, seventy, one hundred fathom, and then had no ground, till within a cable's length of the lee-shore, where they had ninety fathom. We now moored the ship in seventy-eight fathom, with the stream-anchor.

The next morning, while our people were employed in getting wood and water, and gathering celery and mussels, two canoes, full of Indians, came alongside of the ship. They had much the same appearance as the poor wretches whom we had seen before in Elizabeth's Bay. They had on board some seal's flesh, blubber, and penguins, all which they eat raw. Some of our people, who were fishing with a hook and line, gave one of them a fish, somewhat bigger than a herring, alive, just as it came out of the water. The Indian took it hastily, as a dog would take a bone, and instantly killed it, by giving it a bite near the gills: He then proceeded to eat it, beginning with the head, and going on to the tail, without rejecting either the bones, fins, scales, or entrails. They eat every thing that was given them, indifferently,

differently, whether salt or fresh, dressed or raw, but would drink nothing but water. They shivered with cold, yet had nothing to cover them but a seal-skin, thrown loosely over their shoulders, which did not reach to their middle; and we observed, that when they were rowing, they threw even this by, and sat stark naked. They had with them some javelins, rudely pointed with bone, with which they used to strike seals, fish, and penguins, and we observed that one of them had a piece of iron, about the size of a common chissel, which was fastened to a piece of wood, and seemed to be intended rather for a tool than a weapon. They had all sore eyes, which we imputed to their sitting over the smoke of their fires, and they smelt more offensively than a fox, which perhaps was in part owing to their diet, and in part to their nastiness. Their canoes were about fifteen feet long, three broad, and nearly three deep: They were made of the bark of trees, sewn together, either with the sinews of some beast, or thongs cut out of a hide. Some kind of rush was laid into the seams, and the outside was smeared with a resin or gum, which prevented the water from soaking into the bark. Fifteen slender branches, bent into an arch, were sewed transversely to the bottom and sides, and some straight pieces were placed across the top, from gunwale to gunwale, and securely lashed at each end: Upon the whole, however, it was poorly made, nor had these people any thing among them in which there was the least appearance of ingenuity. I gave them a hatchet or two, with some beads, and a few other toys, with which they went away to the southward, and we saw no more of them.

While we lay here, we sent out the boats, as usual, in search of anchoring-places, and having been ten leagues to the westward, they found but two : One was to the westward of Cape Upright, in the Bay of Islands, but was very difficult to enter and get out of; the other was called Dolphin Bay, at ten leagues distance, which was a good harbour, with even ground in all parts. They saw several small coves, which were all dangerous, as in them it would be necessary to let go the anchor within half-a-cable's length of the lee-shore, and steady the ship with hawsers fastened to the rocks. The people belonging to one of the boats spent a night upon an island, upon which, while they were there, six canoes landed about thirty Indians. The Indians ran immediately

to the boat, and were carrying away every thing they found
in her: Our people discovered what they were doing just
time enough to prevent them. As soon as they found themselves opposed they went to their canoes, and armed themselves with long poles, and javelins pointed with the bones
of fish. They did not begin an attack, but stood in a threatening manner: Our people, who were two-and-twenty in
number, acted only on the defensive, and by parting with a
few trifles to them, they became friends, and behaved peaceably the rest of the time they staid.

For many days we had hail, lightning, rain, and hard
gales, with a heavy sea, so that we thought it impossible for
the ship to hold, though she had two anchors a-head, and
two cables an-end. The men, however, were sent frequently
on shore for exercise, which contributed greatly to their
health, and procured an almost constant supply of mussels
and greens. Among other damages that we had sustained,
our fire-place was broken to pieces; we therefore found it necessary to set up the forge, and employ the armourers to
make a new back, we also made lime of burnt shells, and
once more put it into a useful condition

On Monday the 30th we had the first interval of moderate weather, and we improved it in drying the sails, which,
though much mildewed, we had not before been able to
loose, for fear of setting the ship adrift: We also aired the
spare sails, which we found much injured by the rats, and
employed the sail-makers to mend them. Captain Carteret having represented that his fire-place, as well as ours,
had been broken to pieces, our armourers made him also a
new back, and set it up with lime that we made upon the
spot, in the same manner as had been done on board our
own ship   This day we saw several canoes, full of Indians,
put to shore on the east side of the bay, and the next morning several of them came on board, and proved to be the
same that our people, who were out in the boat, had met
with on shore.   They behaved very peaceably, and we dismissed them with a few toys, as usual.

The day following, several other Indians came off to the
ship, and brought with them some of the birds called Race-
Horses.   Our people purchased the birds for a few trifles,
and I made them a present of several hatchets and knives.

On Thursday, the 2d of April, the master of the Swallow,
who had been sent out to seek for anchoring-places, returned,

ed, and reported that he had found three on the north shore, which were very good; one about four miles to the eastward of Cape Providence, another under the east-side of Cape Tamar, and the third about four miles to the eastward of it; but he said that he found no place to anchor under Cape Providence, the ground being rocky.

This day two canoes came on board, with four men and three young children in each. The men were somewhat more decently dressed than those that we had seen before, but the children were stark naked. They were somewhat fairer than the men, who seemed to pay a very tender attention to them, especially in lifting them in and out of the canoes. To these young visitors I gave necklaces and bracelets, with which they seemed mightily pleased. It happened that while some of these people were on board, and the rest waiting in their canoes by the ship's side, the boat was sent on shore for wood and water. The Indians who were in the canoes, kept their eyes fixed upon the boat while she was manning, and the moment she put off from the ship, they called out with great vociferation to those that were on board, who seemed to be much alarmed, and hastily handing down the children, leaped into their canoes, without uttering a word. None of us could guess at the cause of this sudden emotion, but we saw the men in the canoes pull after the boat with all their might, hallooing and shouting with great appearance of perturbation and distress. The boat out-rowed them, and when she came near the shore, the people on board discovered some women gathering mussels among the rocks. This at once explained the mystery; the poor Indians were afraid that the strangers, either by force or favour, should violate the prerogative of a husband, of which they seemed to be more jealous than the natives of some other countries, who in their appearance are less savage and sordid. Our people, to make them easy, immediately lay upon their oars, and suffered the canoes to pass them. The Indians, however, still continued to call out to their women, till they took the alarm and ran out of sight, and as soon as they got to land, drew their canoes upon the beach, and followed them with the utmost expedition.

We continued daily to gather mussels till the 5th, when several of the people being seized with fluxes, the surgeon desired that no more mussels might be brought into the ship.

The

The weather being still tempestuous and unsettled, we remained at anchor till ten o'clock in the morning of Friday, the 10th, and then, in company with the Swallow, we made sail.   At noon, Cape Providence bore N.N.W. distant four or five miles; at four in the afternoon Cape Tamar bore N.W. by W ⅓ W distant three leagues, Cape Upright E.S E. ½ S., distant three leagues, and Cape Pillar W. distant ten leagues. We steered about W. ½ N. all night, and at six o'clock in the morning, had run eight and thirty miles by the log. At this time Cape Pillar bore S.W. distant half a mile, and the Swallow was about three miles a-stern of us. At this time there being but little wind, we were obliged to make all the sail we could, to get without the streight's mouth. At eleven o'clock I would have shortened sail for the Swallow, but it was not in my power, for as a current set us strongly down upon the Isles of Direction, and the wind came to the west, it became absolutely necessary for me to carry sail, that I might clear them. Soon after we lost sight of the Swallow, and never saw her afterwards.[1] At first I was inclined to have gone back into the streight; but a fog coming on, and the sea rising very fast, we were all of opinion that it was indispensably necessary to get an offing as soon as possible; for except we pressed the ship with sail, before the sea rose too high, it would be impracticable either to weather Terra del Fuego on one tack, or Cape Victory on the other.   At noon, the Islands of Direction bore N. 21' W. distant three leagues, Saint Paul's cupola and Cape Victory in one, N. distant seven leagues, and Cape Pillar E. distant six leagues.

Our latitude, by observation, was 52° 38', and we computed our longitude to be 76° W.

Thus we quitted a dreary and inhospitable region, where we were in almost perpetual danger of shipwreck for near four months, having entered the streight on the 17th of December 1766, and quitted it on the 11th of April 1767: a region where, in the midst of summer, the weather was cold, gloomy, and tempestuous, where the prospects had more the appearance of a chaos than of nature, and where, for the most part, the vallies were without herbage, and the hills without wood.

SECTION

---

[1] How very vexatious this was to the Swallow's crew, the reader has to learn from the account of Carteret's voyage.—E.

SECTION III.

A particular Account of the Places in which we anchored du-
ring our Passage through the Streight, and of the Shoals and
Rocks that lie near them.

HAVING cleared the streight, we steered a western course.
But before I continue the narrative of our voyage, I shall
give a more particular account of the several places where
we anchored, plans of which are deposited in the Admiralty-
office for the use of future navigators, with the shoals and
rocks that lie near them, the latitude, longitude, tides, and
variation of the compass.

I. CAPE VIRGIN MARY. The bay under this cape is a
good harbour, when the wind is westerly. There is a shoal
lying off the cape, but that may easily be known by the
rock-weed that grows upon it: The cape is a steep white
cliff, not unlike the South Foreland. Its latitude, by observation, is 52° 24′ S. and its longitude, by account, 68° 22′
W. The variation of the needle, by the medium of five
azimuths and one amplitude, was 24° 30′ E. In this place
we saw no appearance either of wood or water. We anchored in ten fathom, with coarse sandy ground, about a
mile from the shore, Cape Virgin Mary bearing N. by W.
½ W. distant about two miles, and Dungeness Point S.S.W.
distant four miles. We anchored here on the 17th of December, and sailed the next day. There is good landing,
on a fine sandy beach, all along the shore.

II. POSSESSION BAY. In sailing into this bay, it is necessary to give the point a good birth, because there is a
reef that runs right off it about a short mile. The soundings are very irregular all over the bay, but the ground is
every where a fine soft mud and clay, so that the cables can
come to no damage. The point lies in latitude 52° 23′ S.
longitude, by account, 68° 57′ W.: The variation is two
points easterly. In the bay the tide rises and falls between
four and five fathom, and runs at the rate of about a mile
an hour; in the mid-channel without the bay, it runs nearly three miles an hour. In this place we saw no appearance either of wood or water. The landing appeared to be
good,

good, but we did not go on shore. We anchored here on the 19th of December, and sailed again on the 22d.

III. Port Famine. At this place, the Spaniards, in the year 1581, built a town, which they called Phillippeville, and left in it a colony, consisting of 400 persons. When our celebrated navigator, Cavendish, arrived here in 1587, he found one of these unhappy wretches, the only one that remained, upon the beach : They had all perished for want of subsistence, except twenty-four; twenty-three of these set out for the river Plata, and were never afterwards heard of. This man, whose name was Hernando, was brought to England by Cavendish, who called the place where he had taken him up, Port Famine. It is a very fine bay, in which there is room and conveniency for many ships to moor in great safety. We moored in nine fathom, having brought Cape St Anne N.E. by E. and Sedger River S. ½ W. which perhaps is the best situation, though the whole bay is good ground. In this place there is very good wooding and watering; we caught many fine small fish with a hook and line off the ship's side, and hauled the seine with great success, in a fine sandy bay, a little to the southward of Sedger River : We also shot a great number of birds, of various kinds, particularly geese, ducks, teal, snipes, plover, and race-horses, and we found wild celery in great plenty. The latitude of this place is 53° 42′ S., longitude, by observation, 71° 28′ W.: The variation is two points easterly. We anchored here the 27th of December 1766, and sailed again the 18th of January 1767.

IV. Cape Holland Bay. There is no danger in sailing into this bay, and there is good anchoring ground in every part of it. We lay at about three cables' length from the shore, in ten fathom, the ground coarse sand and shells, Cape Holland bearing W.S.W. ¼ W. distant three miles, Cape Froward a little to the N. of the E. Right a-breast of the ship there was a very fine rivulet, and close under Cape Holland a large river, navigable for boats many miles : The shore also affords fire-wood in great plenty. We found abundance of wild celery and cranberries, mussels and limpets, but caught very little fish, either with hook and line, or the seine. We killed some geese, ducks, teal, and race-horses, but they were not plenty. This bay lies in latitude 53° 57′ S., longitude, by account, 72° 34′ W.; the variation

is

is two points easterly. The water rose about eight feet; we found, however, no regular tide, but for the most part a strong current setting to the eastward. We anchored here on the 19th of January, and sailed again on the 23d.

V. CAPE GALLANT BAY. In this bay, which may be entered with great safety, there is a fine large lagoon, where a fleet of ships may moor in perfect security. There is a depth of four fathom in every part of it, with a soft muddy ground. In the bay, the best anchoring is on the east side, where there is from six to ten fathom. Here is good watering from two rivers, and plenty of wood. The lagoon abounded with wild fowl, and we found wild celery, mussels, and limpets in plenty. We did not haul the seine, having torn one to pieces, and the other being unpacked; but if we had, there is reason to believe that we should have been well supplied with fish. The landing is good. The latitude of the bay and lagoon is 53° 50′ S., longitude, by account, 73° 9′ W.; the variation is two points easterly. I observed the water to rise and fall about nine feet, but the tide was very irregular. We anchored here the 23d of January, and sailed again the 28th.

VI. ELIZABETH's BAY. At the entrance of this bay there are two small reefs, which appear above water. The most dangerous lies off the east point of the bay; but this may easily be avoided, by keeping at the distance of about two cables' length from the point. There is good landing all round the bay, but it is much exposed to the westerly winds. The best place for anchoring is Passage Point, at half a mile distance, bearing S.E. and the river bearing N. E. by E. distant three cables' length; in this situation, a bank or shoal, which may be known by the weeds, bears W. N.W. distant a cable's length: The ground is coarse sand, with shells. Sufficient wood is to be procured here for the use of ships, and there is good watering at a small river. We found a little celery and a few cranberries, but neither fish nor fowl. The latitude of this place is 53° 43′ S. the longitude, by account, 73° 24′ W.; the variation is two points easterly. We anchored here the 29th of January, and sailed the 4th of February.

VII. YORK ROAD. The only danger of sailing into the bay, that is formed by two points in this road, arises from a reef that runs off to about a cable's length from the western point, which, once known, may be easily avoided. To anchor choi in this bay, it is safest to bring York Point E.S.E. Bachelor's River N. by W. ¼ W. the west point of the bay or reef N.W. ¼ W. and St Jerom's Sound W.N.W. at the distance of half a mile from the shore. There is good watering about a mile up Bachelor's River, and good wooding all round the bay, where the landing also is, in all parts, very good. We found plenty of celery, cranberries, mussels, and limpets, many wild fowl, and some fish, but not enough to supply the ship's company with a fresh meal. The latitude here is 53° 39′ S., longitude, by account, 73° 52′ W.; the variation two points easterly. The water rises and falls about eight feet, but the tide is irregular. The master, who crossed the streight many times to examine the bays, frequently found the current setting in three different directions. We anchored here on the 4th of February, and sailed again the 11th.

VIII. Butler's Bay. This is a small bay, entirely surrounded by rocks, so that no ship should anchor here if she can possibly avoid it. We found, however, sufficient wood and water to keep up our stock, mussels and limpets in plenty, some good rock fish, and a few wild fowl, but celery and cranberries were very scarce. This bay lies in latitude 53° 37′ S., longitude, by account, 74° 9′ W.; the variation is two points easterly. The water rises and falls here about four feet, but the current always sets to the eastward. We anchored here the 18th of February, and sailed the 1st of March.

IX. Lion Cove. This is a small bay, and surrounded by rocks. The water is deep, but the ground is good. It is not a bad place for one ship, nor a good one for two. Here is good watering up a small creek, but no wood. There is good landing at the watering-place, but no where else. We found no refreshment but a few mussels, limpets, and rock-fish, with a little celery. The latitude is 53° 26′ S., longitude, by account, 74° 25′ W.; the variation was two points easterly. The water, as far as we could judge by the appearance of the rocks, rises and falls about five feet, and the current sets at the rate of about two knots an hour. We anchored here on the 2d of March, and sailed the next day.

X. Good-luck Bay. This is a small bay, and, like several others in this streight, entirely surrounded by rocks. The ground is very coarse, and the cable of our best-bower anchor was so much rubbed, that we were obliged to condemn

demn it, and bend a new one. At this place there is a little
wood, and plenty of good water, but the rocks render it very
difficult of access. No man that sees this part of the coast,
can expect to find any kind of refreshment upon it; and indeed we caught nothing except a few rock-fish, with hook
and line. There may be circumstances in which it may be
good luck to get into this bay, but we thought it very good
luck to get out of it. It lies in latitude 53° 23' S., longitude,
by account, 74° 33' W.; the variation is two points easterly. The water rises and falls between three and four feet,
though, whenever we had an opportunity of trying the current, we found it run easterly. We anchored here the 3d of
March, and sailed the 15th.

XI. SWALLOW HARBOUR. This harbour, when once entered, is very safe, being sheltered from all winds, but the
entrance is narrow and rocky; the rocks, however, may be
easily avoided by keeping a good look-out, as there are large
bunches of rock-weed upon them all. We found here a sufficient supply of wood and water, the wood however was
very small. As the water is constantly smooth here, the
landing is every where good; but we found no supply of
provisions, except a few mussels and rock-fish. The mountains round it have the most horrid appearance, and seem to
be altogether deserted by every thing that has life. The
latitude is 53° 29' S., the longitude, by account, 74° 35' W;
the variation is two points easterly, and the tide rises and
falls between four and five feet. We anchored here the
15th of March, and left the place the next day.

XII. UPRIGHT BAY. This bay may be safely entered,
as there is no obstruction but what is above water. The wood
here is very small, but we found sufficient to keep up our
stock. The water is excellent, and in great plenty. As to
provisions, we got only a few wild fowl, rock-fishes, and mussels. The landing is bad. The latitude of this place is 53°
8' S., longitude 75° 35' W.; the variation two points easterly. The water rises and falls about five feet, but the tide
or current is very irregular. We anchored here on the 18th
of March, and sailed again on the 10th of April.

There are three very good bays a little beyond Cape Shutup, which we called *River Bay, Lodging Bay,* and *Wallis's
Bay.* Wallis's Bay is the best.

About half way between Elizabeth's Bay and York Road,
lies Mussel Bay, where there is very good anchorage with

a west-a westerly wind. There is also a bay, with good anchorage, opposite to York Road, and another to the eastward of Cape Cross-tide, but this will hold only a single ship. Between Cape Cross and Saint David's Head, lies Saint David's Sound, on the south side of which we found a bank of coarse sand and shells, with a depth of water from nineteen to thirty fathom, where a ship might anchor in case of necessity; and the master of the Swallow found a very good small bay a little to the eastward of Saint David's Head. A little to the eastward of Cape Quod, lies Island Bay, where the Swallow lay some time, but it is by no means an eligible situation. The ground of Chance Bay is very rocky and uneven, and for that reason should be avoided.

As all the violent gales by which we suffered in this navigation, blew from the westward, it is proper to stand about a hundred leagues or more to the westward, after sailing out of the streight, that the ship may not be endangered on a lee-shore, which at present is wholly unknown.

The following table shews the courses and distances, from point to point, in the streight of Magellan, by compass.[1]

[1] Bougainville, in the account of his voyage, has given a tolerably minute chart of the streight of Magellan, but the names do not correspond with those used here, or by the English navigators in general. Perhaps the fullest and most accurate chart of this very intricate and unsafe passage ever published, is to be found in the American Atlas of Jefferys, London, 1775. It is enlarged from one published at Madrid in 1769, improved from the surveys and observations of Byron, Wallis, and Carteret, and compared with those of Bougainville. Like all the works of Jefferys, the Arrowsmith of his day, it exhibits most commendable diligence and attention to every source of information. After all, however, it seems unlikely that this streight will ever become well known to Europeans, the inducement to navigate it being indeed very inconsiderable at any time, and the dangers it presents always highly formidable.—E.

Courses and Distances from Point to Point, in the Streight of Magellan by Compass.

Cape Virgin Mary lies in latitude 52° 24′ S., and longitude 68° 22′ W.

From	Courses.	Miles.	Latitude.	Long.
Cape Virgin Mary to Dungeness Point	S. by W. -	5	52° 28′	68° 28′
Dungeness Point to Point Possession	W. ¾ S. -	18	52 23	68 57
Point Possession to the S. side of the 1st Narrows - - -	S.W. ¼ S. -	27	52 35	69 38
The N. to the S. end of the Narrows	S.S.W. - -	9	—	—
The S. end of the Narrows to Cape Gregory - - -	W.S.W. ¼ W.	25	52 39	70 31
Cape Gregory to Sweepstakes Foreland	S. 30° W. -	12⅓	—	—
Cape Gregory to Dolphin's Foreland	S.W. ½ W. -	14	52 43	70 53
Dolphin's Foreland to the N. end of Elizabeth's Island - - -	S. ½ W. -	14⅔	52 56	71 6
The N. end of Elizabeth's Island to St Bartholomew's Island - -	E.N.E. - -	1½	52 56	71 4
The N. end of Elizabeth's Island to St George's Island - -	S.E. - - -	8	—	—
The N. end of Elizabeth's Island to Porpus Point - - -	S. by W. -	12	53 6	71 17
Porpus Point to Fresh-water Bay -	S. ½ E. - -	22⅔	—	—
Fresh-water Bay to Cape St Ann, or Port Famine - - -	S.S.E. ¼ E. -	13⅔	53 42	71 28
Cape St Ann to the entry of a great sound on the south shore -	N.E.	—	—	—
Cape St Ann to Cape Shut-up -	S. by E. -	12	53 54	71 32
Cape Shut-up to Dolphin's Island	S.S.W. - -	7	53 59	71 41
Dolphin's Island to Cape Froward, the southermost in all America -	S. 47 W. -	11	54 3	71 59
Cape Froward to Snug Bay Point -	W. ½ N. -	8	—	—
Snug Bay Point to Cape Holland -	W. by S. -	13⅔	53 57	72 34
Cape Holland to Cape Gallant -	W. ¼ S. - -	21½	53 50	73 9
Cape Gallant to Elizabeth's Bay -	W.N.W. ½ W.	11⅔	53 43	73 24
Elizabeth's Bay to York Point -	W.N.W. ½ W.	6⅓	53 39	73 32
York Road to Cape Cross-tide -	W. ¼ S. -	10	—	—
York Road to Cape Quod -	W. ½ S. - -	21	53 33	74 6
Cape Quod to St David's Head -	S.E. - - -	4⅓	—	—
Cape Quod to Butler's Bay -	S. ¼ W. -	4	53 37	74 9
Cape Quod to Chance Bay -	S.S.W. - -	5	—	—
Cape Quod to Great Mussel Bay -	S W. ½ S. -	6	—	—
Cape Quod to Snow Sound -	W.S.W. ½ W.	10	—	—
Cape Quod to Lion's Cove -	W.N.W. ¾ W	12	53 26	74 25
Lion's Cove to Good-Luck Bay -	W.N.W. ¾ W.	6	53 23	74 33
Cape Quod to Cape Notch -	W.N.W. ¾ W.	21	53 22	74 36
Cape Notch to Swallow Harbour -	S.S.E. - -	7	53 29	74 36
Cape Notch to Piss-pot Bay -	W. ¼ S. -	23	—	—
Cape Notch to Cape Monday -	W. - - -	23	53 12	75 20

From	Courses.	Miles.	Latitude.	Long.
Cape Monday to Cape Upright -	W. by N. - -	13	53° 6'	75° 38'
Cape Monday to a great Sound on the N. shore - - - - -	N. - - - -	7		
Cape Upright to Cape Providence -	N. by W. ½ W.	9	52 57	75 37
Cape Upright to Cape Tamar -	N.W. by W. ½ W.	18		
Cape Upright to Cape Pillar -	W. ½ N. -	50	52 43	76 52
Cape Pillar to Westminster Island	N. E. ½ N. -	15		
Cape Pillar to Cape Victory -	N.W. ½ N. - -	28		
Cape Pillar to the Islands of Direction	W.N.W. - -	23	52 27	77 19

SECTION IV.

The Passage from the Streight of Magellan to King George the Third's Island, called Otaheite, in the South Sea, with an Account of the Discovery of several other Islands, and a Description of their Inhabitants.

As we continued our course to the westward, after having cleared the streight, we saw a great number of gannets, sheerwaters, pintado birds, and many others, about the ship, and had for the most part strong gales, hazy weather, and heavy seas, so that we were frequently brought under our courses, and there was not a dry place in the ship for some weeks together.

At eight in the morning of the 22d, we had an observation, by which we found our longitude to be 95° 46' W. and at noon our latitude was 42° 24' S. and the variation, by azimuth, 11° 6' E.

By the 24th, the men began to fall down very fast in colds and fevers, in consequence of the upper works being open, and their clothes and beds continually wet.

On the 26th, at four in the afternoon, the variation, by azimuth, was 10° 20' E. and at six in the morning of the next day, it was 9° 8' E. Our latitude, on the 27th at noon, was 36° 54' S. our longitude, by account, 100° W. This day, the weather being moderate and fair, we dried all the people's clothes, and got the sick upon deck, to whom we gave salop, and wheat boiled with portable soup, every morning for breakfast, and all the ship's company had as much vinegar and mustard as they could use; portable soup was also constantly boiled in their pease and oatmeal.

The hard gales, with frequent and violent squalls, and a heavy sea, soon returned, and continued with very little intermission.

termission. The ship pitched so much, that we were afraid she would carry away her masts, and the men were again wet in their beds.

On the 30th, the variation, by azimuth, was 8° 30′ E. our latitude was 32° 50; longitude, by account, 100 W. I began now to keep the ship to the northward, as we had no chance of getting westing in this latitude; and the surgeon was of opinion, that in a little time the sick would so much increase, that we should want hands to work the ship, if we could not get into better weather.

On the third of May, about four in the afternoon, we had an observation of the sun and moon, by which we found our longitude to be 96° 26′ W. the variation by the azimuth was 5° 44′ E. at six in the evening, and at six the next morning, it was 5° 58′ E. Our latitude, this day at noon, was 28° 20′ S. At four in the afternoon, we had several observations for the longitude, and found it to be 96° 21′ W.; at seven in the evening, the variation was 6° 40′ E. by the azimuth, and the next morning at ten it was, by amplitude, 5° 48′ E.; at three in the afternoon, the variation, by amplitude, was 7° 40′ E. This day we saw a tropic bird.

At six o'clock in the morning of Friday the eighth of May, the variation of the needle, by amplitude, was 7° 11′ E. In the afternoon we saw several sheer-waters and sea-swallows. At eight in the morning of the 9th, the variation, by azimuth, was 6° 34′ E. and in the morning of the 11th, by azimuth and amplitude, it was 4° 40′ E. Our latitude was 27° 20′ S. longitude, by account, 106° W. This day and the next we saw several sea-swallows, sheer-waters, and porpoises, about the ship.

On the 14th of May, the variation, by four azimuths, was 2° E. About four o'clock in the afternoon, we saw a large flock of brown birds, flying to the eastward, and something which had the appearance of high land, in the same quarter. We bore away for it till sun-set, and it still having the same appearance, we continued our course; but at two in the morning, having run eighteen leagues without making it, we hauled the wind, and at day-light nothing was to be seen. We had now the satisfaction to find our ailing people mend apace. Our latitude was 24° 50′ S. our longitude, by account, 106° W. During all this time, we were looking out for the Swallow.[1]

At

[1] This is very liable to be controverted. Captain W. well knew the bad

At four in the afternoon of the 16th, the variation, by azimuth and amplitude, was 6° E. and at six the next morning, by four azimuths, it was 3° 20′.

The carpenters were now employed in caulking the upper works of the ship, and repairing and painting the boats, and on the 18th I gave a sheep among the people that were sick and recovering.

On Wednesday the 20th, we found our longitude, by observation, to be 106° 47′ W. and our latitude 20° 52′ S. The next day we saw several flying fish, which were the first we had seen in these seas.

On the 22d, our longitude, by observation, was 111° W. and our latitude 20° 18′ S. and this day we saw some bonettoes, dolphins, and tropic birds.

The people, who had been recovering from colds and fevers, now began to fall down in the scurvy, upon which, at the surgeon's representation, wine was served to them; wort was also made for them of malt, and each man had half a pint of pickled cabbage every day. The variation from 4 to 5 E.

On the 26th we saw two grampuses; on the 28th we saw another, and the next day several birds, among which was one about the size of a swallow, which some of us thought was a land bird.

Our men now began to look very pale and sickly, and to fall down very fast in the scurvy, notwithstanding all our care and attention to prevent it. They had vinegar and mustard without limitation, wine instead of spirits, sweet wort and salop. Portable soup was still constantly boiled in their peas and oatmeal; their birth and clothes were kept perfectly clean; the hammocks were constantly brought upon the deck at eight o'clock in the morning, and carried down at four in the afternoon. Some of the beds and hammocks were washed every day; the water was rendered wholesome

condition and insufficiency of that vessel, and had, in consequence, promised to *wait* on her. But did he so, after he cleared the streights? Did he even appoint a rendezvous or place of meeting with her, after getting into the South Sea?—a thing so common for vessels sailing in concert. He has assigned his reasons for not doing the former, in Section II. Of his neglect of the latter, no satisfactory account perhaps can be given. The reader will have some cause of wonder and displeasure at more persons than one, when he peruses what Captain Carteret has to say as to the propriety of sending out the Swallow on this voyage. One can scarcely help inferring from his words, that he had been intended as a mere forlorn hope, in navigating the difficult and dangerous passage betwixt the two oceans.—E.

wholesome by ventilation, and every part between decks frequently washed with vinegar.

On Sunday the 31st of May, our longitude, by observation, was 127° 45′ W. our latitude 29° 38′ S. and the variation, by azimuth and amplitude, 5° 9′ E.

The next day, at three in the afternoon, our longitude, by observation, was 129° 15′ W. and our latitude 19° 34′ S. We had squally weather, with much lightning and rain, and saw several man-of-war birds.

On the 3d we saw several gannets, which, with the uncertainty of the weather, inclined us to hope that land was not very far distant. The next day a turtle swam close by the ship; on the 5th we saw many birds, which confirmed our hope that some place of refreshment was near, and at eleven o'clock in the forenoon of the 6th, Jonathan Puller, a seaman, called out from the mast-head, " Land in the W.N.W." At noon it was seen plainly from the deck, and found to be a low island, at about five or six leagues distance. The joy which every one on board felt at this discovery, can be conceived by those only who have experienced the danger, sickness, and fatigue of such a voyage as we had performed.

When we were within about five miles of this island, we saw another, bearing N.W. by W. About three o'clock in the afternoon, being very near the island that was first discovered, we brought-to, and I sent Mr Furneaux, my second lieutenant, my first lieutenant being very ill, with the boats manned and armed, to the shore. As he approached it, we saw two canoes put off, and paddle away with great expedition towards the island that lay to leeward. At seven in the evening the boats returned, and brought with them several cocoa-nuts, and a considerable quantity of scurvy-grass; they brought also some fish-hooks, that were made of oyster-shells, and some of the shells of which they were made. They reported that they had seen none of the inhabitants, but had visited three huts, or rather sheds, consisting only of a roof, neatly thatched with cocoa-nut and palm-leaves, supported upon posts, and open all round. They saw also several canoes building, but found no fresh water, nor any fruit but cocoa-nuts. They sounded, but found no anchorage, and it was with great difficulty they got on shore, as the surf ran very high. Having received this account, I stood off and

on

on all night, and, early the next morning, I sent the boats
out again to sound, with orders, if possible, to find a place
where the ship might come to an anchor; but at eleven
o'clock they returned, with no better success than before.
The people told me that the whole island was surrounded
by a reef, and that although on the weather side of the
island there was an opening through it, into a large bason,
that extended to the middle of the island, yet they found
it so full of breakers, that they could not venture in; neither indeed had they been able to land on any part of the
island, the surf running still higher than it had done the
day before.   As it would therefore answer no purpose to
continue here, I hoisted the boats in, and stood away for.
the other island, which bore S. 22° E. distant about four
leagues   The island which I now quitted, having been
discovered on Whitsun-eve, I called it *Whitsun Island.* It
is about four miles long, and three wide. Its latitude is
19° 26′ S., and its longitude, by observation, 157° 56′ W.

When we came under the lee of the other island, I sent
Lieutenant Furneaux, with the boats manned and armed,
to the shore, where I saw about fifty of the natives armed
with long pikes, and several of them running about with
fire-brands in their hands. I ordered Mr Furneaux to go
to that part of the beach where we saw the people, and
endeavour to traffic with them for fruit and water, or whatever else might be useful; at the same time being particularly careful to give them no offence. I ordered him also
to employ the boats in sounding for anchorage. About
seven o'clock he returned, and told me that he could find
no ground with the line, till he came within half-a-cable's
length of the shore, and that there it consisted of sharp
rocks, and lay very deep.

As the boat approached the shore, the Indians thronged
down towards the beach, and put themselves upon their
guard with their long pikes, as-if to dispute landing. Our
men then lay upon their oars, and made signs of friendship,
shewing at the same time several strings of beads, ribbands,
knives, and other trinkets. The Indians still made signs to
our people that they should depart, but at the same time
eyed the trinkets with a kind of wishful curiosity. Soon
after, some of them advanced a few steps into the sea, and
our people making signs that they wanted cocoa-nuts and
water, some of them brought down a small quantity of
                                                        both

both, and ventured to hand them into the boat: the water was in cocoa-nut shells, and the fruit was stripped of its outward covering, which is probably used for various purposes. For this supply they were paid with the trinkets that had been shewed them, and some nails, upon which they seemed to set a much greater value. During this traffic, one of the Indians found means to steal a silk handkerchief, in which some of our small merchandise was wrapped up, and carried it clear off, with its contents, so dexterously, that nobody observed him. Our people made signs that a handkerchief had been stolen, but they either could not or would not understand them. The boat continued about the beach, sounding for anchorage, till it was dark; and having many times endeavoured to persuade the natives to bring down some scurvy-grass, without success, she returned on board.

I stood off and on with the ship all night, and as soon as the day broke, I sent the boats again, with orders to make a landing, but without giving any offence to the natives, that could possibly be avoided. When our boats came near the shore, the officer was greatly surprised to see seven large canoes, with two stout masts in each, lying just in the surf, with all the inhabitants upon the beach, ready to embark. They made signs to our people to go higher up; they readily complied, and as soon as they went ashore, all the Indians embarked, and sailed away to the westward, being joined by two other canoes at the west end of the island. About noon, the boats returned, laden with cocoa-nuts, palm-nuts, and scurvy-grass. Mr Furneaux, who commanded the expedition, told me that the Indians had left nothing behind them but four or five canoes. He found a well of very good water, and described the island as being sandy and level, full of trees, but without underwood, and abounding with scurvy-grass. The canoes, which steered about W.S.W. as long as they could be seen from the mast-head, appeared to be about thirty feet long, four feet broad, and three and an half deep. Two of these being brought along-side of each other, were fastened together, at the distance of about three feet asunder, by cross beams, passing from the larboard gunwale of one, to the starboard gunwale of the other, in the middle and near to each end.

The inhabitants of this island were of a middle stature, and dark complexion, with long black hair, which hung

loose

loose over their shoulders. The men were well made, and the women handsome. Their clothing was a kind of coarse cloth or matting, which was fastened about their middle, and seemed capable of being brought up round their shoulders.

In the afternoon, I sent Lieutenant Furneaux with the boats again on shore. He had with him a mate and twenty men, who were to make a rolling-way for getting the casks down to the beach from the well. I gave orders that he should take possession of the island, in the name of King George the Third, and give it the name of *Queen Charlotte's Island*, in honour of her majesty. The boats returned freighted with cocoa-nuts and scurvy-grass,-and the officer told me that he had found two more wells of good water, not far from the beach. I was at this time very ill, yet I went ashore with the surgeon, and several of the people, who were enfeebled by the scurvy, to take a walk. I found the wells so convenient, that I left the mate and twenty men on shore to fill the water, and ordered a week's provisions to be sent them from the ship, they being already furnished with arms and ammunition. In the evening I returned on board, with the surgeon and the sick, leaving only the waterers on shore. As we had not been able to find any anchorage, I stood off and on all night.

In the morning, I sent all the empty water casks on shore: the surgeon and the sick were also sent for the benefit of another airing, but I gave them strict orders that they should keep near the water-side, and in the shade; that they should not pull down or injure any of the houses, nor, for the sake of the fruit, destroy the cocoa-trees, which I appointed proper persons to climb. At noon, the rolling-way being made, the cutter returned laden with water, but it was with great difficulty got off the beach, as it is all rock, and the surf that breaks upon it is often very great. At four, I received another boat-load of water, and a fresh supply of cocoa-nuts, palm-nuts, and scurvy-grass; the surgeon also returned with the sick men, who received much benefit from their walk. The next morning, as soon as it was light, I dispatched orders to the mate, to send all the water that was filled on board, and to be ready to come off with his people when the boats should return again, bringing with them as many cocoa-nuts, and as much scurvy-grass, as they could procure. About eight o'clock, all the

the boats and people came on board, with the water and refreshments, but the cutter, in coming off, shipped a sea, which almost filled her with water : The barge was happily near enough to assist her, by taking great part of her crew on board, while the rest freed her, without any other damage than the loss of the cocoa-nuts and greens that were on board. At noon, I hoisted the boats in, and there being a great sea, with a dreadful surf rolling in upon the shore, and no anchorage, I thought it prudent to leave this place, with such refreshments as we had got. The people who had resided on shore, saw no appearance of metal of any kind, but several tools, which were made of shells and stones, sharpened and fitted into handles, like adzes, chissels, and awls. They saw several canoes building, which were formed of planks, sewed together, and fastened to several small timbers, that passed transversely along the bottom and up the sides. They saw several repositories of the dead, in which the body was left to putrefy under a canopy, and not put into the ground.

When we sailed, we left a union jack flying upon the island, with the ship's name, the time of our being here, and an account of our taking possession of this place, and Whitsun Island, in the name of his Britannic Majesty, cut on a piece of wood, and in the bark of several trees. We also left some hatchets, nails, glass bottles, beads, shillings, sixpences, and halfpence, as presents to the natives, and an atonement for the disturbance we had given them. Queen Charlotte's Island is about six miles long, and one mile wide, lies in latitude 19° 18' S., longitude, by observation, 138° 4' W. ; and we found the variation here to be 4° 46' E.

We made sail with a fine breeze, and, about one o'clock, saw an island W. by S., Queen Charlotte's Island at this time bearing E. by N. distant fifteen miles. At half an hour after three, we were within about three quarters of a mile of the east end of the island, and ran close along the shore, but had no soundings. The east and west ends are joined to each other by a reef of rocks, over which the sea breaks into a lagoon, in the middle of the island, which, therefore, had the appearance of two islands, and seemed to be about six miles long, and four broad. The whole of it is low land, full of trees, but we saw not a single cocoa-nut, nor any huts : We found, however, at the westermost

most end, all the canoes and people who had fled, at our approach, from Queen Charlotte's Island, and some more. We counted eight double canoes, and about fourscore people, women, and children. The canoes were drawn up on the beach, the women and children were placed near them, and the men advanced with their pikes and firebrands, making a great noise, and dancing in a strange manner. We observed that this island was sandy, and that under the trees there was no verdure. As the shore was every where rocky, as there was no anchorage, and as we had no prospect of obtaining any refreshment here, I set sail at six o'clock in the evening, from this island, to which I gave the name of *Egmont Island*, in honour of the Earl of Egmont, who was then first Lord of the Admiralty. It lies in latitude 19° 20′ S., longitude, by observation, 138° 30′ W.

At one o'clock, on the 11th, we saw an island in the W. S.W. and stood for it. At four in the afternoon, we were within a quarter of a mile of the shore, and ran along it, sounding continually, but could get no ground. It is surrounded on every side by rocks, on which the sea breaks very high. It is full of trees, but not one cocoa-nut, and has much the same appearance with Egmont Island, but is much narrower. Among the rocks, at the west end, we saw about sixteen of the natives, but no canoes: They carried long pikes or poles in their hands, and seemed to be, in every respect, the same kind of people that we had seen before. As nothing was to be had here, and it blew very hard, I made sail till eight in the evening, and then brought to. To this island, which is about six miles long, and from one mile to one quarter of a mile broad, I gave the name of *Gloucester Island*, in honour of his royal highness the Duke. It lies in latitude 19° 11′ S., and longitude, by observation, 140° 4′ W.

At five o'clock in the morning, we made sail, and soon after saw another island. At ten o'clock, the weather being tempestuous, with much rain, we saw a long reef, with breakers on each side of the island, and therefore brought the ship to, with her head off the shore. To this island, which lies in latitude 19° 18′ S., longitude, by observation, 140° 36′ W., I gave the name of *Cumberland Island*, in honour of his royal highness the Duke. It lies low, and is about the same size as Queen Charlotte's Island. We found the variation of the needle here to be 7° 10′ E. As

I had

I had no hope of finding any refreshment here, I stood on to the westward.

At day-break, on Saturday the 13th, we saw another small low island, in the N.N.W. right to windward. It had the appearance of small flat keys. This place I called *Prince William Henry's Island,* in honour of his majesty's third son. It lies in latitude 19° S., longitude, by observation, 141° 6' W. I made no stay here, hoping that to the westward I should find higher land, where the ship might come to an anchor, and such refreshments as we wanted be procured.

Soon after day-light, on the 17th, we saw land bearing W. by N. and making in a small round hummock. At noon, when it bore N. 64° W. distant about five leagues, its appearance greatly resembled the Mewstone in Plymouth Sound, but it seemed to be much larger. We found the ship this day twenty miles to the northward of her reckoning, which I imputed to a great S.W. swell.

At five in the evening, this island bore N.W. distant about eight miles. I then hauled the wind, and stood on and off all night. At ten, we saw a light upon the shore, which, though the island was small, proved that it was inhabited, and gave us hopes that we should find anchorage near it. We observed with great pleasure, that the land was very high, and covered with cocoa-trees; a sure sign that there was water.

The next morning, I sent Lieutenant Furneaux to the shore, with the boats manned and armed, and all kinds of trinkets, to establish a traffic with the natives, for such refreshment as the place would afford. I gave him orders also to find, if possible, an anchoring-place for the ship. While we were getting out the boats, several canoes put off from the island, but as soon as the people on board saw them make towards the shore, they put back. At noon, the boats returned, and brought with them a pig and a cock, with a few plantains and cocoa-nuts. Mr Furneaux reported, that he had seen at least an hundred of the inhabitants, and believed there were many more upon the island; but that, having been all round it, he could find no anchorage, nor scarcely a landing-place for the boat. When he reached the shore, he came to a grappling, and threw a warp to the Indians upon the beach, who caught it and held it fast. He then began to converse with them

by

by signs, and observed that they had no weapon among
them, but that some of them had white sticks, which seemed to be ensigns of authority, as the people who bore them
kept the rest of the natives back. In return for the pig
and the cock, he gave them some beads, a looking-glass,
a few combs, with several other trinkets, and a hatchet.
The women, who had been kept at a distance, as soon as
they saw the trinkets, ran down in a crowd to the beach,
with great eagerness, but were soon driven away by the
men, at which they expressed much disappointment and
vexation. While this traffic was carrying on, a man came
secretly round a rock, and diving down, took up the boat's
grappling, and at the same time the people on shore who
held the warp, made an effort to draw her into the surf.
As soon as this was perceived by the people on board, they
fired a musket over the man's head who had taken up the
grappling, upon which he instantly let it go, with marks
of great terror and astonishment; the people on shore also
let go the rope. The boats, after this, lay some time upon
their oars, but the officer, finding that he could get nothing
more, returned on board. Mr Furneaux told me, that
both the men and women were clothed, and he brought a
piece of their cloth away with him. The inhabitants appeared to him to be more numerous than the island could
support, and for this reason, especially as he saw some
large double canoes upon the beach, he imagined there
were islands of larger extent, not far distant, where refreshments in greater plenty might be procured, and hoped that
they might be less difficult of access. As I thought this a
reasonable conjecture, I hoisted in the boats, and determined to run farther to the westward. To this place, which
is nearly circular, and about two miles over, I gave the
name of *Osnaburgh Island*, in honour of Prince Frederick,
who is bishop of that see. It lies in latitude 17° 51′ S.,
and longitude 147° 30′ W.; the variation here was 7° 10′
E.[2]

SECTION

[2] The islands spoken of in this section, with several more, constitute
a pretty considerable cluster, to which Bougainville gave the name of
Dangerous Archipelago; and by this name they are usually designated in
modern maps.—E.

SECTION V.

An Account of the Discovery of King George the Third's Is-
land, or Otaheite, and of several Incidents which happened
both on board the Ship, and on Shore.

AT two o'clock, the same day, we bore away, and in
about half an hour, discovered very high land in the W.
S.W.   At seven in the evening, Osnaburgh Island bore E.
N.E. and the new discovered land, from W.N.W. to W.
by S.   As the weather was thick and squally, we brought
to for the night, or at least till the fog should break away.
At two in the morning, it being very clear, we made sail
again; at day-break we saw the land, at about five leagues
distance, and steered directly for it; but at eight o'clock,
when we were close under it, the fog obliged us again to
lie to, and when it cleared away, we were much surprised
to find ourselves surrounded by some hundreds of canoes.
They were of different sizes, and had on board different
numbers, from one to ten, so that in all of them together,
there could not be less than eight hundred people. When
they came within pistol-shot of the ship, they lay by, gazing at us with great astonishment, and by turns conferring
with each other.   In the mean time we shewed them trinkets of various kinds, and invited them on board. Soon after, they drew together, and held a kind of council, to determine what should be done : Then they all paddled round
the ship, making signs of friendship, and one of them
holding up a branch of the plantain-tree, made a speech
that lasted near a quarter of an hour, and then threw it into the sea. Soon after, as we continued to make signs of
invitation, a fine, stout, lively young man ventured on
board : He came up by the mizen chains, and jumped
out of the shrouds upon the top of the awning. We made
signs to him to come down upon the quarter-deck, and
handed up some trinkets to him : He looked pleased, but
would accept of nothing till some of the Indians came
along-side, and after much talk, threw a few branches of
plantain-tree on board the ship; he then accepted our presents, and several others very soon came on board, at different

ferent parts of the ship, not knowing the proper entrance. As one of these Indians was standing near the gang-way, on the larboard side of the quarter-deck, one of our goats butted him upon the haunches: Being surprised at the blow, he turned hastily about, and saw the goat raised upon his hind-legs, ready to repeat the blow. The appearance of this animal, so different from any he had ever seen, struck him with such terror, that he instantly leaped over-board; and all the rest, upon seeing what had happened, followed his example with the utmost precipitation: They recovered, however, in a short time, from their fright, and returned on board. After having a little reconciled them to our goats and sheep, I shewed them our hogs and poultry, and they immediately made signs that they had such animals as these. I then distributed trinkets and nails among them, and made signs that they should go on shore and bring us some of their hogs, fowls, and fruit, but they did not seem to understand my meaning: They were, in the mean time, watching an opportunity to steal some of the things that happened to lie in their way, but we generally detected them in the attempt. At last, however, one of the midshipmen happened to come where they were standing, with a new laced hat upon his head, and began to talk to one of them by signs: While he was thus engaged, another of them came behind him, and suddenly snatching off the hat, leaped over the taffarel into the sea, and swam away with it.

As we had no anchorage here, we stood along the shore, sending the boats at the same time to sound at a less distance. As none of these canoes had sails, they could not keep up with us, and therefore soon paddled back towards the shore. The country has the most delightful and romantic appearance that can be imagined: Towards the sea it is level, and is covered with fruit trees of various kinds, particularly the cocoa-nut. Among these are the houses of the inhabitants, consisting only of a roof, and at a distance having greatly the appearance of a long barn. The country within, at about the distance of three miles, rises into lofty hills, that are crowned with wood, and terminate in peaks, from which large rivers are precipitated into the sea. We saw no shoals, but found the island skirted by a reef of rocks, through which there are several openings into deep water. About three o'clock in the afternoon, we
brought-to

brought-to a-breast of a large bay, where there was an appearance of anchorage. The boats were immediately sent to sound it, and while they were thus employed, I observed a great number of canoes gather round them. I suspected that the Indians had a design to attack them; and as I was very desirous to prevent mischief, I made the signal for the boats to come on board, and at the same time, to intimidate the Indians, I fired a nine-pounder over their heads. As soon as the cutter began to stand towards the ship, the Indians in their canoes, though they had been startled by the thunder of our nine-pounder, endeavoured to cut her off. The boat, however, sailing faster than the canoes could paddle, soon got clear of those that were about her; but some others, that were full of men, way-laid her in her course, and threw several stones into her, which wounded some of the people. Upon this, the officer on board fired a musket, loaded with buck-shot, at the man who threw the first stone, and wounded him in the shoulder. The rest of the people in the canoe, as soon as they perceived their companion wounded, leapt into the sea, and the other canoes paddled away in great terror and confusion. As soon as the boats reached the ship, they were hoisted on board, and just as she was about to stand on, we observed a large canoe, under sail, making after us. As I thought she might have some chief on board, or might have been dispatched to bring me a message from some chief, I determined to wait for her. She sailed very fast, and was soon alongside of the ship, but we did not observe, among those on board, any one that seemed to have an authority over the rest. One of them, however, stood up, and having made a speech, which continued about five minutes, threw on board a branch of the plantain-tree. We understood this to be a token of peace, and we returned it, by handing over one of the branches of plantain that had been left on board by our first visitors: With this and some toys, that were afterwards presented to him, he appeared to be much gratified, and after a short time, went away.

The officers who had been sent out with the boats, informed me that they had sounded close to the reef, and found as great a depth of water as at the other islands: However, as I was now on the weather-side of the island, I had reason to expect anchorage in running to leeward. I therefore took this course, but finding breakers that ran off to a great distance from the south end of the island, I hauled the wind, and continued turning to windward all night, in order to run down on the east side of the island.

At five o'clock in the morning, we made sail, the land bearing N.W. by W. distant ten leagues; and there seemed to be land five leagues beyond it, to the N.E.; a remarkable peak, like a sugar loaf, bore N.N.E. when we were about two leagues from the shore, which afforded a most delightful prospect, and was full of houses and inhabitants. We saw several large canoes near the shore, under sail, but they did not steer towards the ship. At noon, we were within two or three miles of the island, and it then bore from S.$\frac{1}{4}$W. to N.W. by N. We continued our course along the shore, sometimes at the distance of half a mile, and sometimes at the distance of four or five miles, but hitherto had got no soundings. At six o'clock in the evening, we were a-breast of a fine river, and the coast having a better appearance here than in any other part that we had seen, I determined to stand off and on all night, and try for anchorage in the morning. As soon as it was dark, we saw a great number of lights all along the shore. At daybreak, we sent out the boats to sound, and soon after, they made the signal for twenty fathom. This produced an universal joy, which it is not easy to describe, and we immediately ran in, and came to an anchor in seventeen fathom, with a clear sandy bottom. We lay about a mile distant from the shore, opposite to a fine run of water; the extremes of the land bearing from E.S.E. to N.W. by W. As soon as we had secured the ship, I sent the boats to sound along the coast, and look at the place where we saw the water. At this time, a considerable number of canoes came off to the ship, and brought with them hogs, fowls, and fruit in great plenty, which we purchased for trinkets and nails. But when the boats made towards the shore, the canoes, most of which were double, and very large, sailed after them. At first they kept at a distance, but as the boats approached the shore, they grew bolder, and at last three of the largest ran at the cutter, staved in her quarter, and carried away her out-rigger, the Indians preparing at the same time to board her, with their clubs and paddles in their hands. Our people being thus pressed, were obliged to fire, by which one of the assailants was killed, and another much wounded. Upon receiving the

shot,

shot, they both fell overboard, and all the people who were
in the same canoe instantly leaped into the sea after them :
The other two canoes dropped a-stern, and our boats went
on without any farther interruption. As soon as the Indians, who were in the water, saw that the boats stood on
without attempting to do them any further hurt, they recovered their canoe, and hauled in their wounded companions. They set them both upon their feet to see if they
could stand, and finding they could not, they tried whether they could sit upright : One of them could, and him
they supported in that posture, but perceiving that the
other was quite dead, they laid the body along at the bottom of the canoe. After this some of the canoes went
ashore, and others returned again to the ship to traffic,
which is a proof that our conduct had convinced them that
while they behaved peaceably they had nothing to fear,
and that they were conscious they had brought the mischief, which had just happened, upon themselves.

The boats continued sounding till noon, when they returned with an account that the ground was very clear; that
it was at the depth of five fathom, within a quarter of a
mile of the shore; but that there was a very great surf
where we had seen the water. The officers told me, that
the inhabitants swarmed upon the beach, and that many of
them swam off to the boat with fruit, and bamboos filled
with water. They said that they were very importunate
with them to come on shore, particularly the women, who
came down to the beach, and stripping themselves naked,
endeavoured to allure them by many wanton gestures, the
meaning of which could not possibly be mistaken. At this
time, however, our people resisted the temptation.

In the afternoon, I sent the boats again to the shore, with
some barecas, or small casks, which are filled at the head,
and have a handle by which they are carried, to endeavour to procure some water, of which we began to be in
great want. In the mean time many of the canoes continued about the ship, but the Indians had been guilty of
so many thefts, that I would not suffer any more of them
to come on board.

At five in the evening, the boats returned with only two
barecas of water, which the natives had filled for them;
and as a compensation for their trouble, they thought fit
to detain all the rest. Our people, who did not leave their

boat, tried every expedient they could think of to induce the Indians to return their water-vessels, but without success; and the Indians, in their turn, were very pressing for our people to come on shore, which they thought it prudent to decline. There were many thousands of the inhabitants of both sexes, and a great number of children on the beach, when our boats came away.

The next morning, I sent the boats on shore again for water, with nails, hatchets, and such other things as I thought most likely to gain the friendship of the inhabitants. In the mean time, a great number of canoes came off to the ship, with bread-fruit, plantains, a fruit resembling an apple, only better, fowls, and hogs, which we purchased with beads, nails, knives, and other articles of the like kind, so that we procured pork enough to serve the ship's company two days, at a pound a man.

When the boats returned, they brought us only a few calibashes of water, for the number of people on the beach was so great, that they would not venture to land, though the young women repeated the allurements which they had practised the day before, with still more wanton, and, if possible, less equivocal gestures. Fruit and provisions of various kinds were brought down and ranged upon the beach, of which our people were also invited to partake, as an additional inducement for them to leave the boat. They continued, however, inexorable, and shewing the Indians the barecas on board, made signs that they should bring down those which had been detained the day before: To this the Indians were inexorable in their turn, and our people therefore weighed their grapplings, and sounded all round the place, to see whether the ship could come in near enough to cover the waterers, in which case they might venture on shore, in defiance of the whole island. When they put off, the women pelted them with apples and bananas, shouting, and shewing every mark of derision and contempt that they could devise. They reported, that the ship might ride in four fathom water, with sandy ground, at two cables' length from the shore, and in five fathom water at three cables' length. The wind here blew right along the shore, raising a great surf on the side of the vessel, and on the beach.

At day-break, the next morning, we weighed, with a design to anchor off the watering-place. As we were standing
ing

ing off, to get farther to windward, we discovered a bay
about six or eight miles to leeward, over the land, from the
mast-head, and immediately bore away for it, sending the
boats a-head to sound.   At nine o'clock, the boats making
the signal for twelve fathom, we hauled round a reef, and
stood in, with a design to come to an anchor ; but when
we came near the boats, one of which was on each bow,
the ship struck.   Her head continued immoveable, but her
stern was free ; and, upon casting the lead, we found the
depth of water, upon the reef or shoal, to be from seventeen fathom to two and a half: We clewed all up as fast as
possible, and cleared the ship of what lumber there happened to be upon the deck, at the same time getting out
the long-boat, with the stream and kedge anchors, the
stream-cable and hauser, in order to carry them without the
reef, that when they had taken ground, the ship might be
drawn off towards them, by applying a great force to the
capstern, but unhappily without the reef we had no bottom.   Our condition was now very alarming, the ship continued beating against the rock with great force, and we
were surrounded by many hundred canoes, full of men ;
they did not, however, attempt to come on board us, but
seemed to wait in expectation of our shipwreck.   In the
anxiety and terror of such a situation we continued near
an hour, without being able to do any thing for our deliverance, except staving some water-casks in the fore-hold,
when a breeze happily springing up from the shore, the
ship's head swung off.   We immediately pressed her with
all the sail we could make ; upon which she began to
move, and was very soon once more in deep water.

We now stood off, and the boats being sent to leeward,
found that the reef ran down to the westward about a mile
and a half, and that beyond it there was a very good harbour.   The master, after having placed a boat at the end
of the reef, and furnished the long-boat with anchor and
hausers, and a guard to defend her from an attack of the
Indians, came on board, and piloted the ship round the reef
into the harbour, where, about twelve o'clock, she came to
an anchor in seventeen fathom water, with a fine bottom
of black sand.

The place where the ship struck appeared, upon farther
examination, to be a reef of sharp coral rock, with very
unequal soundings, from six fathom to two ; and it happened

pened unfortunately to lie between the two boats that were placed as a direction to the ship, the weathermost boat having twelve fathom, and the leewardmost nine. The wind freshened almost as soon as we got off, and though it soon became calm again, the surf ran so high, and broke with such violence upon the rock, that if the ship had continued fast half an hour longer, she must inevitably have been beaten to pieces. Upon examining her bottom, we could not discover that she had received any damage, except that a small piece was beaten off the bottom of her rudder. She did not appear to admit any water, but the trussel-trees, at the head of all the masts, were broken short, which we supposed to have happened while she was beating against the rock. Our boats lost their grapplings upon the reef, but as we had reason to hope that the ship was sound, they gave us very little concern. As soon as the ship was se-cured, I sent the master, with all the boats manned and armed, to sound the upper part of the bay, that if he found good anchorage we might warp the ship up within the reef, and anchor her in safety. The weather was now very plea-sant, a great number of canoes were upon the reef, and the shore was crowded with people.

About four in the afternoon the master returned, and re-ported, that there was every-where good anchorage; I therefore determined to warp the ship up the bay early in the morning, and in the mean time, I put the people at four watches, one watch to be always under arms; loaded and primed all the guns, fixed musquetoons in all the boats, and ordered all the people who were not upon the watch, to repair to the quarters assigned them, at a moment's warning, there being a great number of canoes, some of them very large, and full of men, hovering upon the shore, and many smaller venturing to the ship, with hogs, fowls, and fruit, which we purchased of them, much to the satis-faction of both parties; and at sun-set, all the canoes rowed in to the shore.

At six o'clock the next morning, we began to warp the ship up the harbour, and soon after, a great number of canoes came under her stern. As I perceived that they had hogs, fowls, and fruit on board, I ordered the gunner, and two midshipmen, to purchase them for knives, nails, beads, and other trinkets, at the same time prohibiting the trade to all other persons on board. By eight o'clock, the number

number of canoes was greatly increased, and those that
came last up were double, of a very large size, with twelve
or fifteen stout men in each. I observed, with some con
cern, that they appeared to be furnished rather for war
than trade, having very little on board except round pebble
stones; I therefore sent for Mr Furneaux, my first lieutenant being still very ill, and ordered him to keep the
fourth watch constantly at their arms, while the rest of the
people were warping the ship. In the mean time more
canoes were continually coming off from the shore, which
were freighted very differently from the rest, for they had
on board a number of women, who were placed in a row,
and who, when they came near the ship, made all the wanton gestures that can be conceived. While these ladies
were practising their allurements, the large canoes, which
were freighted with stones, drew together very close round
the ship, some of the men on board singing in a hoarse
voice, some blowing conchs, and some playing on a flute.
After some time, a man who sat upon a canopy that was
fixed on one of the large double canoes, made signs that
he wished to come up to the ship's side; I immediately intimated my consent, and when he came alongside, he gave
one of the men a bunch of red and yellow feathers, making
signs that he should carry it to me. I received it with expressions of amity, and immediately got some trinkets to
present him in return, but to my great surprise he had put
off to a little distance from the ship, and upon his throwing up the branch of a cocoa-nut tree, there was an universal shout from all the canoes, which at once moved towards
the ship, and a shower of stones was poured into her on
every side. As an attack was now begun, in which our
arms only could render us superior to the multitude that
assailed us, especially as great part of the ship's company
was in a sick and feeble condition, I ordered the guard to
fire; two of the quarter-deck guns, which I had loaded with
small shot, were also fired nearly at the same time, and the
Indians appeared to be thrown into some confusion: In a
few minutes, however, they renewed the attack, and all our
people that were able to come upon deck, having by this
time got to their quarters, I ordered them to fire the great
guns, and to play some of them constantly at a place on
shore, where a great number of canoes were still taking in
men, and pushing off towards the ship with the utmost expedition

pedition. When the great guns began to fire, there were not less than three hundred canoes about the ship, having on board at least two thousand men; many thousands were also upon the shore, and more canoes coming from every quarter: The firing, however, soon drove away the canoes that were about the ship, and put a stop to the coming off of others. As soon as I saw some of them retreating, and the rest quiet, I ordered the firing to cease, hoping that they were sufficiently convinced of our superiority, not to renew the contest. In this, however, I was unhappily mistaken: A great number of the canoes that had been dispersed, soon drew together again, and lay some time on their paddles, looking at the ship from the distance of about a quarter of a mile, and then suddenly hoisting white streamers, pulled towards the ship's stern, and began again to throw stones, with great force and dexterity, by the help of slings, from a considerable distance: Each of these stones weighed about two pounds, and many of them wounded the people on board, who would have suffered much more, if an awning had not been spread over the whole deck to keep out the sun, and the hammocks placed in the nettings. At the same time several canoes, well manned, were making towards the ship's bow, having probably taken notice that no shot had been fired from this part: I therefore ordered some guns forward, to be well pointed and fired at these canoes; at the same time running out two guns abaft, and pointing them well at the canoes that were making the attack. Among the canoes that were coming toward the bow, there was one which appeared to have some chief on board, as it was by signals made from her that the others had been called together: It happened that a shot, fired from the guns forward, hit this canoe so full as to cut it asunder. As soon as this was observed by the rest, they dispersed with such haste that in half an hour there was not a single canoe to be seen; the people also who had crowded the shore, immediately fled over the hills with the utmost precipitation.

Having now no reason to fear any further interruption, we warped the ship up the harbour, and by noon, we were not more than half a mile from the upper part of the bay, within less than two cables' length of a fine river, and about two and a half of the reef. We had here nine fathom water, and close to the shore there were five. We moored
the

the ship, and carried out the stream-anchor, with the two
shroud-hawsers, for a spring, to keep the ship's broadside
abreast of the river; we also got up and mounted the eight
guns which had been put into the hold. As soon as this
was done, the boats were employed in sounding all around
the bay, and in examining the shore where any of the inhabitants appeared, in order to discover, whether it was
probable that they would give us any further disturbance.
All the afternoon, and part of the next morning, was spent
in this service; and about noon, the master returned, with
a tolerable survey of the place, and reported, that there
were no canoes in sight; that there was good landing on
every part of the beach; that there was nothing in the bay
from which danger could be apprehended, except the reef,
and some rocks at the upper end, which appeared above
water; and that the river, though it emptied itself on the
other side of the point, was fresh water.

Soon after the master had brought me this account, I
sent Mr Furneaux again, with all the boats manned and
armed, the marines being also put on board, with orders to
land opposite to our station, and secure himself, under cover of the boats and the ship, in the clearest ground he
could find. About two o'clock the boats landed without
any opposition, and Mr Furneaux stuck up a staff, upon
which he hoisted a pendant, turned a turf, and took possession of the island in his majesty's name, in honour of
whom he called it *King George the Third's Island:*[1] He
then went to the river, and tasted the water, which he
found excellent, and, mixing some of it with rum, every
man drank his majesty's health. While he was at the river, which was about twelve yards wide, and fordable, he
saw two old men on the opposite side of it, who perceiving
that they were discovered, put themselves in a supplicatory
posture, and seemed to be in great terror and confusion.
Mr Furneaux made signs that they should come over the
river, and one of them complied. When he landed, he
came forward, creeping upon his hands and knees, but Mr
Furneaux raised him up, and, while he stood trembling,
shewed

---

[1] This island is much better known by the name given it by its inhabitants—Otaheite. The reader need scarcely to be informed that a description of it, and an account of many interesting particulars respecting it,
must occupy no small place in the pages devoted to the history of Cook's
Voyages.—E.

shewed him some of the stones that were thrown at the ship, and endeavoured to make him apprehend that if the natives attempted no mischief against us, we should do no harm to them. He ordered two of the water-casks to be filled, to shew the Indian that we wanted water, and produced some hatchets, and other things, to intimate that he wished to trade for provisions. The old man, during this pantomimical conversation, in some degree recovered his spirits; and Mr Furneaux, to confirm his professions of friendship, gave him a hatchet, some nails, beads, and other trifles; after which he re-embarked on board the boats, and left the pendant flying. As soon as the boats were put off, the old man went up to the pendant, and danced round it a considerable time : He then retired, but soon after returned with some green boughs, which he threw down, and retired a second time : It was not long, however, before he appeared again, with about a dozen of the inhabitants, and putting themselves in a supplicating posture, they all approached the pendant in a slow pace, but the wind happening to move it, when they were got close to it, they suddenly retreated with the greatest precipitation. After standing some time at a distance, and gazing at it, they went away, but in a short time came back, with two large hogs alive, which they laid down at the foot of the staff, and at length, taking courage, they began to dance. When they had performed this ceremony, they brought the hogs down to the water-side, launched a canoe, and put them on board. The old man, who had a large white beard, then embarked with them alone, and brought them to the ship : When he came alongside, he made a set speech, and afterwards handed in several green plantain-leaves, one by one, uttering a sentence, in a solemn slow tone, with each of them as he delivered it; after this he sent on board the two hogs, and then, turning round, pointed to the land. I ordered some presents to be given him, but he would accept of nothing; and soon after put off his canoe, and went on shore.

At night, soon after it was dark, we heard the noise of many drums, with conchs, and other wind-instruments, and saw a multitude of lights all along the coast. At six in the morning, seeing none of the natives on shore, and observing that the pendant was taken away, which probably they had learnt to despise, as the frogs in the fable did King Log,

Log, I ordered the lieutenant to take a guard on shore, and, if all was well, to send off, that we might begin watering: In a short time, I had the satisfaction to find that he had sent off for water-casks, and by eight o'clock, we had four tons of water on board. While our people were employed in filling the casks, several of the natives appeared on the opposite side of the river, with the old man whom the officer had seen the day before; and soon after he came over, and brought with him a little fruit, and a few fowls, which were also sent off to the ship. At this time, having been very ill for near a fortnight, I was so weak that I could scarcely crawl about; however, I employed my glasses to see what was doing on shore. At near half an hour after eight o'clock, I perceived a multitude of the natives coming over a hill at about the distance of a mile, and at the same time a great number of canoes making round the western point, and keeping close along the shore. I then looked at the watering-place, and saw at the back of it, where it was clear, a very numerous party of the natives creeping along behind the bushes; I saw also many thousands in the woods, pushing along towards the watering-place, and canoes coming very fast round the other point of the bay to the eastward. Being alarmed at these appearances, I dispatched a boat, to acquaint the officer on shore with what I had seen, and order him immediately to come on board with his men, and leave the casks behind him: He had, however, discovered his danger, and embarked before the boat reached him. Having perceived the Indians that were creeping towards him under shelter of the wood, he immediately dispatched the old man to them, making signs that they should keep at a distance, and that he wanted nothing but water. As soon as they perceived that they were discovered, they began to shout, and advanced with greater speed. The officer immediately repaired to the boats with his people, and the Indians, in the mean time, having crossed the river, took possession of the water-casks, with great appearance of exultation and joy. The canoes now pulled along the shore, towards the place, with the utmost expedition, all the people on land keeping pace with them, except a multitude of women and children, who seated themselves upon a hill which overlooked the bay and the beach. The canoes from each point of the bay, as they drew nearer to that part of it where the ship

was

was at anchor, put on shore, and took in more men, who had great bags in their hands, which afterwards appeared to be filled with stones. All the canoes that had come round the points, and many others that had put off from the shore within the bay, now made towards the ship, so that I had no doubt but that they intended to try their fortune in a second attack. As to shorten the contest would certainly lessen the mischief, I determined to make this action decisive, and put an end to hostilities at once; I therefore ordered the people, who were at all their quarters, to fire first upon the canoes, which were drawn together in groups: this was immediately done so effectually, that those which were to the westward made towards the shore as fast as possible, and those to the eastward, getting round the reef, were soon beyond the reach of our guns. I then directed the fire into the wood in different parts, which soon drove the Indians out of it, who ran up the hill where the women and children had seated themselves to see the battle. Upon this hill there were now several thousands who thought themselves in perfect security; but to convince them of the contrary, and hoping that when they saw the shot fall much farther than they could think possible, they would suppose it could reach them at any distance, I ordered some of the guns to be let down as low as they would admit, and fired four shot towards them. Two of the balls fell close by a tree where a great number of these people were sitting, and struck them with such terror and consternation, that in less than two minutes not one of them was to be seen. Having thus cleared the coast, I manned and armed the boats, and putting a strong guard on board, I sent all the carpenters with their axes, and ordered them to destroy every canoe that had been run ashore. Before noon, this service was effectually performed, and more than fifty canoes, many of which were sixty feet long, and three broad, and lashed together, were cut to pieces. Nothing was found in them but stones and slings, except a little fruit, and a few fowls and hogs, which were on board two or three canoes of a much smaller size.

At two o'clock in the afternoon, about ten of the natives came out of the wood with green boughs in their hands, which they stuck up near the water side, and retired. After a short time, they appeared again, and brought with them several hogs, with their legs tied, which they placed near

the

the green boughs, and retired a second time. After this
they brought down several more hogs, and some dogs, with
their fore-legs tied over their heads, and going again into
the woods, brought back several bundles of the cloth which
they use for apparel, and which has some resemblance to
Indian paper. These they placed upon the beach, and called to us on board to fetch them away. As we were at the
distance of about three cables' length, we could not then
perfectly discover of what this peace-offering consisted; we
guessed at the hogs and the cloth, but seeing the dogs,
with their fore-legs appearing over the hinder part of the
neck, rise up several times, and run a little way in an erect
posture, we took them for some strange unknown animal,
and were very impatient to have a nearer view of them.
The boat was therefore sent on shore with all expedition,
and our wonder was soon at an end. Our people found nine
good hogs, besides the dogs and the cloth: the hogs were
brought off, but the dogs were turned loose, and with the
cloth left behind. In return for the hogs, our people left
upon the shore some hatchets, nails, and other things, making signs to some of the Indians who were in sight, to take
them away with their cloth. Soon after the boat had come
on board, the Indians brought down two more hogs, and
called to us to fetch them; the boat therefore returned,
and fetched off the two hogs, but still left the cloth, though
the Indians made signs that we should take it. Our people
reported, that they had not touched any of the things
which they had left upon the beach for them, and somebody
suggesting that they would not take our offering because we
had not accepted their cloth, I gave orders that it should
be fetched away. The event proved that the conjecture was
true, for the moment the boat had taken the cloth on
board, the Indians came down, and, with every possible demonstration of joy, carried away all I had sent them into
the wood. Our boats then went to the watering-place, and
filled and brought off all the casks, to the amount of about
six tons. We found that they had suffered no injury while
they had been in the possession of the Indians, but some
leathern buckets and funnels, which had been taken away
with the casks, were not returned.

The next morning I sent the boats on shore, with a guard,
to fill some more casks with water, and soon after the people were on shore, the same old man who had come over
the

the river to them the first day, came again to the farther side of it, where he made a long speech, and then crossed the water. When he came up to the waterers, the officer shewed him the stones that were piled up like cannon balls upon the shore, and had been brought thither since our first landing, and some of the bags that had been taken out of the canoes, which I had ordered to be destroyed, filled with stones, and endeavoured to make him understand that the Indians had been the aggressors, and that the mischief we had done them was in our own defence. The old man seemed to apprehend his meaning, but not to admit it: he immediately made a speech to the people, pointing to the stones, slings, and bags, with great emotion, and sometimes his looks, gestures, and voice were so furious as to be frightful. His passions, however, subsided by degrees, and the officer, who, to his great regret, could not understand one word of all that he had said, endeavoured to convince him, by all the signs he could devise, that we wished to live in friendship with them, and were disposed to shew them every mark of kindness in our power. He then shook hands with him, and embraced him, giving him at the same time several such trinkets as he thought would be most acceptable. He contrived also to make the old man understand that we wished to traffic for provisions, that the Indians should not come down in great numbers, and that they should keep on one side of the river and we on the other. After this the old man went away with great appearance of satisfaction, and before noon a trade was established, which furnished us with hogs, fowls, and fruit in great abundance, so that all the ship's company, whether sick or well, had as much as they could use.

SECTION VI.

The Sick sent on Shore, and a regular Trade established with the Natives; some Account of their Character and Manners, of their Visits on board the Ship, and a Variety of Incidents that happened during this Intercourse.

MATTERS being thus happily settled, I sent the surgeon, with the second lieutenant, to examine the country, and fix upon some place where the sick might take up their residence

dence on shore. When they returned, they said, that with
respect to health and convenience, all the places they had
seen upon the island seemed to be equally proper; but that
with respect to safety, they could recommend none but the
watering-place, as they would be there under the protection
of the ship and the guard, and would easily be prevented
from straggling into the country, and brought off to their
meals. To the watering-place therefore I sent them, with
those that were employed in filling the casks, and appointed the gunner to command the party that was to be their
guard. A tent was erected for them as a shelter both from
the sun and the rain, and the surgeon was sent to superintend their conduct, and give his advice if it should be
wanted. It happened that walking out with his gun, after
he had seen the sick properly disposed of in the tent, a wild
duck flew over his head, which he shot, and it fell dead
among some of the natives who were on the other side of
the river. This threw them into a panic, and they all ran
away; when they got to some distance they stopped, and
he made signs to them to bring the duck over: This one of
them at last ventured to do, and, pale and trembling, laid it
down at his feet. Several other ducks happening at the instant to fly over the spot where they were standing, he fired
again, and fortunately brought down three more. This incident gave the natives such a dread of a gun, that if a
musket was pointed at a thousand of them, they would all
run away like a flock of sheep; and probably the ease with
which they were afterwards kept at a distance, and their orderly behaviour in their traffic, was in a great measure owing to their having upon this occasion seen the instrument,
of which before they had only felt the effects.

As I foresaw that a private traffic would probably com-
mence between such of our people as were on shore, and
the natives, and that if it was left to their own caprice, perpetual quarrels and mischief would ensue, I ordered that all
matters of traffic should be transacted by the gunner on behalf of both parties, and I directed him to see that no injury was done to the natives, either by violence or fraud,
and by all possible means to attach the old man to his interest. This service he performed with great diligence and
fidelity, nor did he neglect to complain of those who trans-
gressed my orders, which was of infinite advantage to all
parties; for as I punished the first offenders with a neces-

sary

sary severity, many irregularities, that would otherwise have
produced the most disagreeable consequences, were prevented: we were also indebted for many advantages to the
old man, whose caution kept our people perpetually upon
their guard, and soon brought back those who straggled
from the party. The natives would indeed sometimes pil-
fer, but by the terror of a gun, without using it, he always
found means to make them bring back what was stolen. A
fellow had one day the dexterity and address to cross the river unperceived, and steal a hatchet; the gunner, as soon
as he missed it, made the old man understand what had
happened, and got his party ready, as if he would have
gone into the woods after the thief: the old man, however,
made signs that he would save him the trouble, and, immediately setting off, returned in a very short time with the
hatchet. The gunner then insisted that the offender should
be delivered up, and with this also the old man, though not
without great reluctance, complied. When the fellow was
brought down, the gunner knew him to be an old offender,
and therefore sent him prisoner on board. I had no intention to punish him otherwise, than by the fear of punishment, and therefore, after great entreaty and intercession, I
gave him his liberty, and sent him on shore. When the natives saw him return in safety, it is hard to say whether
their astonishment or joy was greatest; they received him
with universal acclamations; and immediately carried him
off into the woods: the next day, however, he returned,
and as a propitiation to the gunner, he brought him a considerable quantity of bread-fruit, and a large hog, ready
roasted.

At this time, the people on board were employed in caulking and painting the weather-work, over-hauling the rigging, stowing the hold, and doing other necessary business;
but my disorder, which was a bilious cholic, increased so
much, that this day I was obliged to take to my bed; my
first lieutenant also still continued very ill, and the purser
was incapable of his duty. The whole command devolved
upon Mr Furneaux, the second lieutenant, to whom I gave
general directions, and recommended a particular attention
to the people on shore. I also ordered that fruit and fresh
provisions should be served to the ship's company as long
as they could be procured, and that the boats should never
be

be absent from the ship after sunset. These directions were fulfilled with such prudence and punctuality, that during all my sickness I was not troubled with any business, nor had the mortification to hear a single complaint or appeal. The men were constantly served with fresh pork, fowls, and fruit, in such plenty, that when I left my bed, after having been confined to it near a fortnight, my ship's company looked so fresh and healthy, that I could scarcely believe them to be the same people.

Sunday the 28th was marked by no incident; but on Monday the 29th, one of the gunner's party found a piece of saltpetre near as big as an egg. As this was an object of equal curiosity and importance, diligent enquiry was immediately made from whence it came. The surgeon asked every one of the people on shore, separately, whether he had brought it from the ship; every one on board also was asked whether he had carried it on shore, but all declared that they had never had such a thing in their possession. Application was then made to the natives, but the meaning of both parties was so imperfectly conveyed by signs, that nothing could be learnt of them about it : during our whole stay here, however, we saw no more than this one piece.

While the gunner was trafficking for provisions on shore, we sometimes hauled the seine, but we caught no fish; we also frequently trawled, but with no better success : the disappointment, however, was not felt, for the produce of the island enabled our people to " fare sumptuously every day."

All matters continued in the same situation till the 2d of July, when, our old man being absent, the supply of fresh provisions and fruit fell short; we had, however, enough to serve most of the messes, reserving plenty for the sick and convalescent.

On the 3d, we heeled the ship, and looked at her bottom, which we found as clean as when she came out of dock, and, to our great satisfaction, as sound. During all this time, none of the natives came near our boats, or the ship, in their canoes. This day, about noon, we caught a very large shark, and when the boats went to fetch the people on board to dinner, we sent it on shore. When the boats were putting off again, the gunner seeing some of the natives on the other side of the river, beckoned them to come

come over; they immediately complied, and he gave them the shark, which they soon cut to pieces, and carried away with great appearance of satisfaction.

' On Sunday the 5th, the old man returned to the market-tent, and made the gunner understand that he had been up the country, to prevail upon the people to bring down their hogs, poultry, and fruit, of which the parts near the watering-place were now nearly exhausted. The good effects of his expedition soon appeared, for several Indians, whom our people had never seen before, came in with some hogs that were larger than any that had been yet brought to market. In the mean time, the old man ventured off in his canoe to the ship, and brought with him, as a present to me, a hog ready roasted. I was much pleased with his attention and liberality, and gave him, in return for his hog, an iron pot, a looking-glass, a drinking-glass, and several other things, which no man in the island was in possession of but himself.

While our people were on shore, several young women were permitted to cross the river, who, though they were not averse to the granting of personal favours, knew the value of them too well not to stipulate for a consideration: The price, indeed, was not great, yet it was such as our men were not always able to pay, and under this temptation they stole nails and other iron from the ship. The nails that we brought for traffic were not always in their reach, and therefore they drew several out of different parts of the vessel, particularly those that fastened the cleats to the ship's side. This was productive of a double mischief; damage to the ship, and a considerable rise at market. When the gunner offered, as usual, small nails for hogs of a middling size, the natives refused to take them, and produced large spikes, intimating that they expected such nails as these. A most diligent enquiry was set on foot to discover the offenders, but all to no purpose; and though a large reward was offered to procure intelligence, none was obtained. I was mortified at the disappointment, but I was still more mortified at a fraud which I found some of our people had practised upon the natives. When no nails were to be procured, they had stolen lead, and cut it up in the shape of nails. Many of the natives who had been paid with this base money, brought their leaden nails, with great simplicity, to the gunner, and requested him to give them iron in

their

their stead. With this request, however reasonable, he would not comply; because, by rendering lead current, it would have encouraged the stealing it, and the market would have been as effectually spoiled by those who could not procure nails, as by those who could; it was therefore necessary, upon every account, to render this leaden currency of no value, though for our honour I should have been glad to have called it in.

On Tuesday the 7th, I sent one of the mates, with thirty men, to a village at a little distance from the market, hoping that refreshments might there be bought at the original price; but here they were obliged to give still more than at the water-side. In the mean time, being this day able to get up for the first time, and the weather being fine, I went into a boat, and rowed about four miles down the coast. I found the country populous, and pleasant in the highest degree, and saw many canoes on the shore; but not one came off to us, nor did the people seem to take the least notice of us as we passed along. About noon I returned to the ship.

The commerce which our men had found means to establish with the women of the island, rendered them much less obedient to the orders that had been given for the regulation of their conduct on shore, than they were at first. I found it necessary therefore to read the articles of war, and I punished James Proctor, the corporal of marines, who had not only quitted his station, and insulted the officer, but struck the master at arms such a blow as brought him to the ground.

The next day, I sent a party up the country to cut wood, and they met with some of the natives, who treated them with great kindness and hospitality. Several of these friendly Indians came on board in our boat, and seemed, both by their dress and behaviour, to be of a superior rank. To these people I paid a particular attention, and to discover what present would most gratify them, I laid down before them a Johannes, a guinea, a crown piece, a Spanish dollar, a few shillings, some new halfpence, and two large nails, making signs that they should take what they liked best. The nails were first seized, with great eagerness, and then a few of the halfpence, but the silver and gold lay neglected. Having presented them, therefore, with some nails and halfpence, I sent them on shore superlatively happy.

From

From this time our market was very ill supplied, the Indians refusing to sell provisions at the usual price, and making signs for large nails. It was now thought necessary to look more diligently about the ship, to discover what nails had been drawn; and it was soon found that all the belaying cleats had been ripped off, and that there was scarcely one of the hammock nails left. All hands were now ordered up, and I practised every artifice I could think of to discover the thieves, but without success. I then told them, that till the thieves were discovered, not a single man should go on shore: This however produced no effect, except that Proctor the corporal behaved in a mutinous manner, for which he was instantly punished.

On Saturday the 11th, in the afternoon, the gunner came on board with a tall woman, who seemed to be about five-and-forty years of age, of a pleasing countenance and majestic deportment. He told me that she was but just come into that part of the country, and that seeing great respect paid her by the rest of the natives, he had made her some presents; in return for which she had invited him to her house, which was about two miles up the valley, and gave him some large hogs; after which she returned with him to the watering-place, and expressed a desire to go on board the ship, in which he had thought it proper, on all accounts, that she should be gratified. She seemed to be under no restraint, either from diffidence or fear, when she first came into the ship; and she behaved, all the while she was on board, with an easy freedom, that always distinguishes conscious superiority and habitual command. I gave her a large blue mantle, that reached from her shoulders to her feet, which I threw over her, and tied on with ribbands; I gave her also a looking-glass, beads of several sorts, and many other things, which she accepted with a very good grace, and much pleasure. She took notice that I had been ill, and pointed to the shore. I understood that she meant I should go thither to perfect my recovery, and I made signs that I would go thither the next morning. When she intimated an inclination to return, I ordered the gunner to go with her, who, having set her on shore, attended her to her habitation, which he described as being very large and well built. He said, that in this house she had many guards and domestics, and that she had another at a little distance, which was enclosed in lattice-work.

The

The next morning I went on shore for the first time; and my princess, or rather queen, for such by her authority she appeared to be, soon after came to me, followed by many of her attendants. As she perceived that my disorder had left me very weak, she ordered her people to take me in their arms, and carry me not only over the river, but all the way to her house; and observing that some of the people who were with me, particularly the first lieutenant and purser, had also been sick, she caused them also to be carried in the same manner, and a guard, which I had ordered out upon the occasion, followed. In our way, a vast multitude crowded about us, but upon her waving her hand, without speaking a word, they withdrew, and left us a free passage. When we approached near her house, a great number of both sexes came out to meet her: These she presented to me, after having intimated by signs that they were her relations, and taking hold of my hand, she made them kiss it. We then entered the house, which covered a piece of ground 327 feet long, and forty-two feet broad. It consisted of a roof, thatched with palm leaves, and raised upon thirty-nine pillars on each side, and fourteen in the middle. The ridge of the thatch, on the inside, was thirty feet high, and the sides of the house, to the edge of the roof, were twelve feet high; all below the roof being open. As soon as we entered the house, she made us sit down, and then calling four young girls, she assisted them to take off my shoes, draw down my stockings, and pull off my coat, and then directed them to smooth down the skin, and gently chafe it with their hands: The same operation was also performed upon the first lieutenant and purser, but upon none of those who appeared to be in health. While this was doing, our surgeon, who had walked till he was very warm, took off his wig to cool and refresh himself: A sudden exclamation of one of the Indians who saw it, drew the attention of the rest, and in a moment every eye was fixed upon the prodigy, and every operation was suspended: the whole assembly stood some time motionless, in silent astonishment, which could not have been more strongly expressed if they had discovered that our friend's limbs had been screwed on to the trunk; in a short time, however, the young women who were chafing us, resumed their employment, and having continued it for about half an hour, they dressed us again, but in this they were, as may easily be imagined, very awkward; I found great bene-

ß

fit, however, from the chafing, and so did the lieutenant and purser. After a little time, our generous benefactress ordered some bales of Indian cloth to be brought out, with which she clothed me, and all that were with me, according to the fashion of the country. At first I declined the acceptance of this favour, but being unwilling not to seem pleased with what was intended to please me, I acquiesced. When we went away, she ordered a very large sow, big with young, to be taken down to the boat, and accompanied us thither herself. She had given directions to her people to carry me, as they had done when I came, but as I chose rather to walk, she took me by the arm, and whenever we came to a plash of water or dirt, she lifted me over with as little trouble as it would have cost me to have lifted over a child if I had been well.

The next morning I sent her by the gunner, six hatchets, six bill-hooks, and several other things; and when he returned, he told me, that he found her giving an entertainment to a great number of people, which, he supposed, could not be less than a thousand. The messes were all brought to her by the servants that prepared them, the meat being put into the shells of cocoa-nuts, and the shells into wooden trays, somewhat like those used by our butchers, and she distributed them with her own hands to the guests, who were seated in rows round the great house. When this was done, she sat down herself, upon a place somewhat elevated above the rest, and two women, placing themselves one on each side of her, fed her, she opening her mouth as they brought their hands up with the food. When she saw the gunner, she ordered a mess for him; he could not certainly tell what it was, but he believed it to be fowl picked small, with apples cut among it, and seasoned with salt water; it was, however, very well tasted. She accepted the things that I sent her, and seemed to be much pleased with them. After this correspondence was established with the queen, provisions of every kind became much more plenty at market; but though fowls and hogs were every day brought in, we were still obliged to pay more for them than at the first, the market having been spoiled by the nails which our men had stolen and given to the women; I therefore gave orders that every man should be searched before he went on shore, and that no woman should be suffered to cross the river.

On

On the 14th, the gunner being on shore to trade, perceived an old woman on the other side of the river, weeping
bitterly: When she saw that she had drawn his attention
upon her, she sent a young man, who stood by her, over the
river to him, with a branch of the plantain tree in his hand.
When he came up, he made a long speech, and then laid
down his bough at the gunner's feet: After this he went
back and brought over the old woman, another man at the
same time bringing over two large fat hogs. The woman
looked round upon our people with great attention, fixing
her eyes sometimes upon one, and sometimes upon another,
and at last burst into tears. The young man who brought
her over the river, perceiving the gunner's concern and astonishment, made another speech, longer than the first:
Still, however, the woman's distress was a mystery; but at
length she made him understand that her husband, and
three of her sons, had been killed in the attack of the ship.
During this explanation, she was so affected, that at last
she sunk down unable to speak, and the two young men
who endeavoured to support her, appeared to be nearly in
the same condition: They were probably two more of her
sons, or some very near relations. The gunner did all in his
power to sooth and comfort her, and when she had in some
measure recovered her recollection, she ordered the two
hogs to be delivered to him, and gave him her hand in token of friendship, but would accept nothing in return,
though he offered her ten times as much as would have purchased the hogs at market.

The next morning, I sent the second lieutenant, with all
the boats, and sixty men, to the westward, to look at the
country, and try what was to be got. About noon he returned, having marched along the shore near six miles.
He found the country very pleasant and populous, and
abounding as well with hogs and fowls, as fruit, and other
vegetables of various kinds. The inhabitants offered him
no molestation, but did not seem willing to part with any
of the provisions which our people were most desirous to
purchase: They gave them, however, a few cocoa-nuts and
plantains, and at length sold them nine hogs and a few
fowls. The lieutenant was of opinion, that they might be
brought to trade freely by degrees, but the distance from
the ship was so great, that too many men would be necessary for a guard. He saw a great number of very large canoes

noes upon the beach, and some that were building. He observed that all their tools were made of stone, shells, and bone, and very justly inferred, that they had no metal of any kind. He found no quadrupeds among them, besides hogs and dogs, nor any earthen vessel, so that all their food is either baked or roasted. Having no vessel in which water could be subjected to the action of fire, they had no more idea that it could be made hot, than that it could be made solid. As the queen was one morning at breakfast with us on board the ship, one of her attendants, a man of some note, and one of those that we thought were priests, saw the surgeon fill the tea-pot by turning the cock of an urn that stood upon the table: Having remarked this with great curiosity and attention, he presently turned the cock, and received the water upon his hand: As soon as he felt himself scalded, he roared out, and began to dance about the cabin with the most extravagant and ridiculous expressions of pain and astonishment: The other Indians not being able to conceive what was the matter with him, stood staring at him in amaze, and not without some mixture of terror. The surgeon, however, who had innocently been the cause of the mischief, applied a remedy, though it was some time before the poor fellow was easy.

On Thursday the 16th, Mr Furneaux, my second lieutenant, was taken very ill, which distressed me greatly, as the first lieutenant was not yet recovered, and I was still in a very weak state myself: I was this day also obliged once more to punish Proctor, the corporal of marines, for mutinous behaviour. The queen had now been absent several days, but the natives made us understand, by signs, that the next day she would be with us again.

Accordingly the next morning she came down to the beach, and soon after a great number of people, whom we had never seen before, brought to market provisions of every kind; and the gunner sent off fourteen hogs, and fruit in great plenty.

In the afternoon of the next day, the queen came on board, with a present of two large hogs, for she never condescended to barter, and in the evening she returned on shore. I sent a present with her, by the master, and as soon as they landed, she took him by the hand, and having made a long speech to the people that flocked round them, she

led

led him to her house, where she clothed him, as she had before done me, according to the fashion of the country.

The next morning he sent off a greater quantity of stock than we had ever procured in one day before; it consisted of forty-eight hogs and pigs, four dozen of fowls, with bread-fruit, bananas, apples, and cocoa-nuts, almost without number.

On the 20th, we continued to trade with good success, but in the afternoon it was discovered that Francis Pinckney, one of the seamen, had drawn the cleats to which the main sheet was belayed, and, after stealing the spikes, thrown them overboard. Having secured the offender, I called all the people together upon the deck, and after taking some pains to explain his crime, with all its aggravations, I ordered that he should be whipt with nettles, while he ran the gauntlet thrice round the deck: My rhetoric, however, had very little effect, for most of the crew being equally criminal with himself, he was handled so tenderly, that others were rather encouraged to repeat the offence by the hope of impunity, than deterred by the fear of punishment. To preserve the ship, therefore, from being pulled to pieces, and the price of refreshments from being raised so high as soon to exhaust our articles of trade, I ordered that no man except the wooders and waterers, with their guard, should be permitted to go on shore.

On the 21st, the queen came again on board, and brought several large hogs as a present, for which, as usual, she would accept of no return. When she was about to leave the ship, she expressed a desire that I should go on shore with her, to which I consented, taking several of the officers with me. When we arrived at her house, she made us all sit down, and taking off my hat, she tied to it a bunch or tuft of feathers of various colours, such as I had seen no person on shore wear but herself, which produced by no means a disagreeable effect. She also tied round my hat, and the hats of those who were with me, wreaths of braided or plaited hair, and gave us to understand that both the hair and workmanship were her own: She also presented us with some matts, that were very curiously wrought. In the evening she accompanied us back to the beach, and when we were getting into the boat, she put on board a fine large sow, big with young, and a great quantity of fruit. As we

were

were parting, I made signs that I should quit the island in seven days: She immediately comprehended my meaning, and made signs that I should stay twenty days; that I should go two days journey into the country, stay there a few days, bring down plenty of hogs and poultry, and after that leave the island. I again made signs that I must go in seven days; upon which she burst into tears, and it was not without great difficulty that she was pacified.

The next morning, the gunner sent off no less than twenty hogs, with great plenty of fruit. Our decks were now quite full of hogs and poultry, of which we killed only the small ones, and kept the other for sea-stores; we found, however, to our great mortification, that neither the fowls nor the hogs could, without great difficulty, be brought to eat any thing but fruit, which made it necessary to kill them faster than we should otherwise have done; two, however, a boar and a sow, were brought alive to England, of which I made a present to Mr Stephens, secretary to the Admiralty, the sow afterwards died in pigging, but the boar was alive at the date of this publication.

On the 23d, we had very heavy rain, with a storm of wind that blew down several trees on shore, though very little of it was felt where the ship lay.

The next day, I sent the old man, who had been of great service to the gunner at the market-tent, another iron pot, some hatchets and bills, and a piece of cloth. I also sent the queen two turkies, two geese, three Guinea hens, a cat big with kitten, some china, looking-glasses, glass-bottles, shirts, needles, thread, cloth, ribbands, pease, some small white kidney beans, called callivances, and about sixteen different sorts of garden seeds, and a shovel, besides a considerable quantity of cutlery wares, consisting of knives, scissars, bill-hooks, and other things. We had already planted several sorts of the garden seeds, and some pease in several places, and had the pleasure to see them come up in a very flourish-ing state; yet there were no remains of them when Captain Cook left the island. I sent her also two iron pots, and a few spoons. In return for these things, the gunner brought off eighteen hogs, and some fruit.

In the morning of the 25th, I ordered Mr Gore, one of the mates, with all the marines, forty seamen, and four mid-shipmen, to go up the valley by the river as high as they could, and examine the soil and produce of the country,

noting,

noting the trees and plants which they should find, and
when they saw any stream from the mountains, to trace it
to its source, and observe whether it was tinctured with any
mineral or ore   I cautioned them also to keep continually
upon their guard against the natives, and directed them to
make a fire, as a signal, if they should be attacked.   At
the same time I took a guard on shore, and erected a tent
on a point of land, to observe an eclipse of the sun, which,
the morning being very clear, was done with great accuracy.

	Hours.	Min.	Sec.
The immersion began, by true time, at -	6	51	50
The emersion, by true time, was at - - -	8	1	0
The duration of the eclipse was - - - -	1	9	10

The latitude of the point, on which the observation was
made, was 17° 30′ S., the sun's declination was 19° 40′ N.,
and the variation of the needle 5° 36′ E.

After the observation was taken, I went to the queen's
house, and shewed her the telescope, which was a reflector.
After she had admired its structure, I endeavoured to make
her comprehend its use, and fixing it so as to command
several distant objects, with which she was well acquainted,
but which could not be distinguished with the naked eye, I
made her look through it.   As soon as she saw them, she
started back with astonishment, and, directing her eye as the
glass was pointed, stood some time motionless and silent;
she then looked through the glass again, and again sought
in vain, with the naked eye, for the objects which it discovered.   As they by turns vanished and re-appeared, her
countenance and gestures expressed a mixture of wonder and
delight which no language can describe.   When the glass
was removed, I invited her, and several of the chiefs that
were with her, to go with me on board the ship, in which I
had a view to the security of the party that I had sent out;
for I thought that while the queen and the principal people were known to be in my power, nothing would be attempted against any person belonging to the ship on shore.'
When we got on board, I ordered a good dinner for their
entertainment, but the queen would neither eat nor drink;
the people that were with her eat very heartily of whatever
was set before them, but would drink only plain water.

In the evening our people returned from their excursion,
and came down to the beach, upon which I put the queen
and

and her attendants into the boats, and sent them on shore. As she was going over the ship's side, she asked, by signs, whether I still persisted in my resolution of leaving the island at the time I had fixed ; and when I made her understand that it was impossible I should stay longer, she expressed her regret by a flood of tears, which for a while took away her speech. As soon as her passion subsided, she told me that she would come on board again the next day ; and thus we parted.

Section VII.

An Account of an Expedition to discover the Inland Part of the Country, and our other Transactions, till we quitted the Island to continue our Voyage.

After the mate came on board, he gave me a written account of his expedition, to the following effect :

" At four o'clock in the morning of Saturday the 25th of June, I landed, with four midshipmen, a serjeant and twelve marines, and twenty-four seamen, all armed, besides four, who carried hatchets and other articles of traffic, and four who were loaded with ammunition and provisions, the rest being left with the boat : Every man had his day's allowance of brandy, and the hatchet-men two small kegs, to give out when I should think proper.

" As soon as I got on shore, I called upon our old man, and took him with us : We then followed the course of the river in two parties, one marching on each side. For the first two miles it flowed through a valley of considerable width, in which were many habitations, with gardens walled in, and abundance of hogs, poultry, and fruit ; the soil here seemed to be a rich fat earth, and was of a blackish colour. After this the valley became very narrow, and the ground rising abruptly on one side of the river, we were all obliged to march on the other. Where the stream was precipitated from the hills, channels had been cut to lead the water into gardens and plantations of fruit-trees : In these gardens we found an herb which had never been brought down to the water-side, and which we perceived the inhabitants eat raw. I tasted it, and found it pleasant, its flavour somewhat resembling that of the West Indian spin-
nage,

nage, called *Calleloor,* though its leaf was very different.
The ground was fenced off so as to make a very pretty appearance; the bread-fruit and apple-trees were planted in
rows on the declivity of the hills, and the cocoa-nut and
plantain, which require more moisture, on the level ground:
Under the trees, both on the sides and at the foot of the
hills, there was very good grass, but no underwood. As we
advanced, the windings of the stream became innumerable,
the hills on each side swelled into mountains, and vast crags
every where projected over our heads. Travelling now became difficult, and when we had proceeded about four miles,
the road for the last mile having been very bad, we sat down
to rest ourselves, and take the refreshment of our breakfast;
we ranged ourselves upon the ground under a large apple
tree, in a very pleasant spot; but just as we were about to
begin our repast, we were suddenly alarmed by a confused
sound of many voices, and a great shouting, and presently
afterwards saw a multitude of men, women, and children,
upon the hill above us; our old man seeing us rise hastily,
and look to our arms, beckoned to us to sit still, and immediately went up to the people that had surprised us. As
soon as he joined them they were silent, and soon after disappeared; in a short time, however, they returned, and
brought with them a large hog ready roasted, with plenty
of bread-fruit, yams, and other refreshments, which they
gave to the old man, who distributed them among our people. In return for this treat, I gave them some nails, buttons, and other things, with which they were greatly delighted. After this we proceeded up the valley as far as we could,
searching all the runs of water, and all the places where water had run, for appearances of metal or ore, but could find
none, except what I have brought back with me. I shewed all the people that we met with, the piece of saltpetre
which had been picked up in the island, and which I had
taken with me for that purpose, but none of them took any
notice of it, nor could I learn from them any thing about
it. The old man began now to be weary, and there being
a mountain before us, he made signs that he would go home:
Before he left us, however, he made the people who had so
liberally supplied us with provisions, take the baggage, with
the fruit that had not been eaten, and some cocoa-nut shells
full of fresh water, and made signs that they should follow
us up the side of the mountain. As soon as he was gone,
they

they gathered green branches from the neighbouring trees, and with many ceremonies, of which we did not know the meaning, laid them down before us : After this they took some small berries with which they painted themselves red, and the bark of a tree that contained a yellow juice, with which they stained their garments in different parts. We began to climb the mountain while our old man was still in sight, and he, perceiving that we made our way with difficulty through the weeds and brush-wood, which grew very thick, turned back, and said something to the natives in a firm loud tone; upon which twenty or thirty of the men went before us, and cleared us a very good path ; they also refreshed us with water and fruit as we went along, and assisted us to climb the most difficult places, which we should otherwise have found altogether impracticable. We began to ascend this hill at the distance of about six miles from the place where we landed, and I reckoned the top of it to be near a mile above the river that runs through the valley below. When we arrived at the summit, we again sat down to rest and refresh ourselves. While we were climbing we flattered ourselves that from the top we should command the whole island, but we now saw mountains before us so much higher than our situation, that with respect to them we appeared to be in a valley ; towards the ship indeed the view was enchanting : The sides of the hills were beautifully clothed with wood, villages were every where interspersed, and the vallies between them afforded a still richer prospect ; the houses stood thicker, and the verdure was more luxuriant. We saw very few habitations above us, but discovered smoke in many places ascending from between the highest hills that were in sight, and therefore I conjectured that the most elevated parts of the country are by no means without inhabitants. As we ascended the mountain, we saw many springs gush from fissures on the side of it, and when we had reached the summit, we found many houses that we did not discover as we passed them. No part of these mountains is naked ; the summits of the highest that we could see were crowned with wood, but of what kind I know not: Those that were of the same height with that which we had climbed, were woody on the sides, but on the summit were rocky and covered with fern. Upon the flats that appeared below these, there grew a sedgy kind of grass and weeds: In general the soil here, as well as in the valley, seemed to

be

be rich. We saw several bushes of sugar-cane, which was very large and very good, growing wild, without the least culture. I likewise found ginger and turmerick, and have brought samples of both, but could not procure seeds of any tree, most of them being in blossom. After traversing the top of this mountain to a good distance, I found a tree exactly like a fern, except that it was 14 or 15 feet high. This tree I cut down, and found the inside of it also like a fern: I would have brought a piece of it with me, but found it too cumbersome, and I knew not what difficulties we might meet with before we got back to the ship, which we judged to be now at a great distance. After having recruited our strength by refreshment and rest, we began to descend the mountain, being still attended by the people to whose care we had been recommended by our old man. We kept our general direction towards the ship, but sometimes deviated a little to the right and left in the plains and vallies, when we saw any houses that were pleasantly situated, the inhabitants being every where ready to accommodate us with whatever they had. We saw no beasts except a few hogs, nor any birds, except parrots, parroquets, and green doves; by the river, however, there was plenty of ducks, and every place that was planted and cultivated, appeared to flourish with great luxuriance, though in the midst of what had the appearance of barren ground. I planted the stones of peaches, cherries, and plumbs, with a great variety of garden seeds, where I thought it was most probable they would thrive, and limes, lemons, and oranges, in situations which resembled those in which they are found in the West Indies. In the afternoon, we arrived at a very pleasant spot, within about three miles of the ship, where we procured two hogs and some fowls, which the natives dressed for us very well, and with great expedition. Here we continued till the cool of the evening, and then made the best of our way for the ship, having liberally rewarded our guides, and the people who had provided us so good a dinner. Our men behaved through the whole day with the greatest decency and order, and we parted with our Indian friends in perfect good humour with each other."

About 10 o'clock the next morning, the queen came on board according to her promise, with a present of hogs and fowls, but went on shore again soon afterwards. This day, the gunner sent off near thirty hogs, with great plenty of fowls and fruit. We completed our wood and water, and got all ready for sea. More inhabitants came down to the beach, from the inland country, than we had seen before, and many of them appeared, by the respect that was paid them, to be of a superior rank. About three o'clock in the afternoon, the queen came again down to the beach, very well dressed, and followed by a great number of people. Having crossed the river with her attendants and our old man, she came once more on board the ship. She brought with her some very fine fruit, and renewed her solicitation, that I would stay ten days longer, with great earnestness, intimating that she would go into the country and bring me plenty of hogs, fowls, and fruit. I endeavoured to express a proper sense of her kindness and bounty, but assured her that I should certainly sail the next morning. This, as usual, threw her into tears, and after she recovered, she enquired by signs when I should return: I endeavoured to express fifty days, and she made signs for thirty: But the sign for fifty being constantly repeated, she seemed satisfied. She stayed on board till night, and it was then with the greatest difficulty that she could be prevailed upon to go on shore. When she was told that the boat was ready, she threw herself down upon the arm-chest, and wept a long time with an excess of passion that could not be pacified; at last, however, though with great reluctance, she went into the boat, and was followed by her attendants and the old man. The old man had often intimated that his son, a lad about fourteen years of age, should go with us, and the boy seemed to be willing: He had, however, now disappeared for two days; I enquired after him when I first missed him, and the old man gave me to understand that he was gone into the country to see his friends, and would return time enough to go with us; but I have reason to think that, when the time drew near, the father's courage failed, and that to keep his child he secreted him till the ship was gone, for we never saw him afterwards.

At break of day, on Monday the 27th, we unmoored, and at the same time I sent the barge and cutter to fill the few water-casks that were now empty. When they came near the shore, they saw, to their great surprise, the whole beach covered with inhabitants, and having some doubt whether it would be prudent to venture themselves among such a multitude, they were about to pull back again for the ship.

As

As soon as this was perceived from the shore, the queen
came forward, and beckoned them; at the same time
guessing the reason of what had happened, she made the
natives retire to the other side of the river; the boats then
proceeded to the shore, and filled the casks; in the mean
time she put some hogs and fruit on board, and when they
were putting off would fain have returned with them to the
ship. The officer, however, who had received orders to
bring off none of the natives, would not permit her; upon
which she presently launched a double canoe, and was rowed off by her own people. Her canoe was immediately followed by fifteen or sixteen more, and all of them came up
to the ship. The queen came on board, but not being able
to speak, she sat down and gave vent to her passion by weeping. After she had been on board about an hour, a breeze
springing up, we weighed anchor and made sail. Finding
it now necessary to return into her canoe, she embraced us
all in the most affectionate manner, and with many tears;
all her attendants also expressed great sorrow at our departure. Soon after it fell calm, and I sent the boats a-head to
tow, upon which all the canoes returned to the ship, and
that which had the queen on board came up to the gun-
room port, where her people made it fast. In a few minutes
she came into the bow of her canoe, where she sat weeping
with inconsolable sorrow. I gave her many things which I
thought would be of great use to her, and some for ornament; she silently accepted of all, but took little notice of
any thing. About 10 o'clock we were got without the reef,
and a fresh breeze springing up, our Indian friends, and
particularly the queen, once more bade us farewell, with such
tenderness of affection and grief, as filled both my heart
and my eyes.[1]

At noon, the harbour from which we sailed bore S. E. ¼ E.
distant about twelve miles. It lies in latitude 17° 30′ S,
longitude 150° W., and I gave it the name of Port Royal
Harbour.

SECTION

---

[1] Of this queen, as Captain W. calls her, the reader will see more particulars in the account of Cook's visit to this island. Her name was Obe-
rēa. She was wife to Oammo, who governed the greater part of Otaheite
in behalf of his son, according to the custom of the place; but at the time
of Wallis's arrival, she cohabited with Toopāea, a native of Ulietēa, and remarkable among these islanders for his wisdom and information.—E.

Section VIII.

A more particular Account of the Inhabitants of Otaheite, and of their domestic Life, Manners, and Arts.

HAVING lain off this island from the 24th of June to the 27th of July, I shall now give the best account of its inhabitants, with their manners and arts, that I can; but having been in a very bad state of health the whole time, and for great part of it confined to my bed, it will of necessity be much less accurate and particular than I might otherwise have made it.

The inhabitants of this island are a stout, well-made, active, and comely people. The stature of the men, in general, is from five feet seven to five feet ten inches, though a few individuals are taller, and a few shorter; that of the women from five feet to five feet six. The complexion of the men is tawney, but those that go upon the water are much redder than those who live on shore. Their hair in general is black, but in some it is brown, in some red, and in others flaxen, which is remarkable, because the hair of all other natives of Asia, Africa, and America, is black, without a single exception. It is generally tied up, either in one bunch, in the middle of the head, or in two, one on each side, but some wear it loose, and it then curls very strongly: In the children of both sexes it is generally flaxen. They have no combs, yet their hair is very neatly dressed, and those who had combs from us, made good use of them. It is a universal custom to anoint the head with cocoa-nut oil, in which a root has been scraped that smells something like roses. The women are all handsome, and some of them extremely beautiful. Chastity does not seem to be considered as a virtue among them, for they not only readily and openly trafficked with our people for personal favours, but were brought down by their fathers and brothers for that purpose: They were, however, conscious of the value of beauty, and the size of the nail that was demanded for the enjoyment of the lady, was always in proportion to her charms. The men who came down to the side of the river, at the same time that they presented the girl, shewed a

stick

stick of the size of the nail that was to be her price, and if
our people agreed, she was sent over to them, for the men
were not permitted to cross the river.   This commerce was
carried on a considerable time before the officers discovered it, for while some straggled a little way to receive the
lady, the others kept a look-out.   When I was acquainted
with it, I no longer wondered that the ship was in danger
of being pulled to pieces for the·nails and iron that held
her together, which I had before puzzled myself to account
for in vain, the whole ship's company having daily as much
fresh provision and fruit as they could eat.   Both men and
women are not only decently but gracefully clothed, in a
kind of white cloth, that is made of the bark of a shrub,
and very much resembles coarse China paper.   Their dress
consists of two pieces of this cloth : One of them, a hole ha
ving been made in the middle to put the head through
hangs down from the shoulders to the mid leg before and
behind ; another piece, which is between four and five yards
long, and about one yard broad, they wrap round the body
in a very easy manner.   This cloth is not woven, but is
made, like paper, of the macerated fibres of an inner bark
spread out and beaten together.   Their ornaments are feathers, flowers, pieces of shells, and pearls : The pearls are
worn chiefly by the women, from whom I purchased about
two dozen of a small size : They were of a good colour, but
were all spoiled by boring.   Mr Furneaux saw several in his
excursion to the west, but he could purchase none with any
thing he had to offer.   I observed, that it was here a universal custom both for men and women to have the hinder
part of their thighs and loins marked very thick with black
lines in various forms.   These marks were made by striking
the teeth of an instrument, somewhat like a comb, just
through the skin, and rubbing into the punctures a kind of
paste made of soot and oil, which leaves an indelible stain.
The boys and girls under twelve years of age are not marked : But we observed a few of the men whose legs were
marked in chequers by the same method, and they appeared to be persons of superior rank and authority. One of the
principal attendants upon the queen appeared much more
disposed to imitate our manners than the rest ; and our people, with whom he soon became a favourite, distinguished
him by the name of Jonathan.   This man, Mr Furneaux
clothed completely in an English dress, and it sat very easy

upon him. Our officers were always carried on shore, it being shoal water where we landed, and Jonathan, assuming
new state with his new finery, made some of his people carry him on shore in the same manner He very soon attempted to use a knife and fork at his meals, but at first, when
he had stuck a morsel upon his fork, and tried to feed himself with that instrument, he could not guide it, but by the
mere force of habit his hand came to his mouth, and the
victuals at the end of the fork went away to his ear.

Their food consists of pork, poultry, dog's flesh, and fish,
bread-fruit, bananas, plantains, yams, apples, and a sour
fruit, which, though not pleasant by itself, gives an agreeable relish to roasted bread-fruit, with which it is frequently beaten up. They have abundance of rats, but, as far as
I could discover, these make no part of their food. The
river affords them good mullet, but they are neither large
nor in plenty. They find conchs, mussels, and other shell-
fish on the reef, which they gather at low-water, and eat
raw with bread-fruit before they come on shore. They have
also very fine cray-fish, and they catch with lines, and hooks
of mother-of-pearl, at a little distance from the shore, par-
rot-fish, groopers, and many other sorts, of which they are
so fond that we could seldom prevail upon them to sell us
a few at any price. They have also nets of an enormous
size, with very small meshes, and with these they catch
abundance of small fish about the size of sardines; but
while they were using both nets and lines with great success,
we could not catch a single fish with either. We procured
some of their hooks and lines, but for want of their art we
were still disappointed.

The manner in which they dress their food is this: They
kindle a fire by rubbing the end of one piece of dry wood
upon the side of another, in the same manner as our carpenters whet a chissel; then they dig a pit about half a
foot deep, and two or three yards in circumference: They
pave the bottom with large pebble stones, which they lay
down very smooth and even, and then kindle a fire in it
with dry wood, leaves, and the husks of the cocoa-nut.
When the stones are sufficiently heated, they take out the
embers, and rake up the ashes on every side; then they cover the stones with a layer of green cocoa-nut tree leaves,
and wrap up the animal that is to be dressed in the leaves
of the plantain; if it is a small hog they wrap it up whole;

if

if a large one they split it. When it is placed in the pit,
they cover it with the hot embers, and lay upon them
bread-fruit and yams, which are also wrapped up in the
leaves of the plantain . Over these they spread the remainder of the embers, mixing among them some of the hot
stones, with more cocoa-nut tree leaves upon them, and
then close all up with earth, so that the heat is kept in.
After a time proportioned to the size of what is dressing,
the oven is opened, and the meat taken out, which is tender, full of gravy, and, in my opinion, better in every respect than when it is dressed any other way. Excepting the
fruit, they have no sauce but salt water, nor any knives but
shells, with which they carve very dexterously, always cutting from them.   It is impossible to describe the astonishment they expressed when they saw the gunner, who, while
he kept the market, used to dine on shore, dress his pork
and poultry by boiling them in a pot. Having, as I have before observed, no vessel that would bear the fire, they had
no idea of hot water or its effects : But from the time that
the old man was in possession of an iron pot, he and his
friends eat boiled meat every day. The iron pots which I
afterwards gave to the queen and several of the chiefs, were
also in constant use, and brought as many people together,
as a monster or a puppet-show in a country fair. They appeared to have no liquor for drinking but water, and to be
happily ignorant of the art of fermenting the juice of any
vegetable, so as to give it an intoxicating quality . They
have, as has been already observed, the sugar-cane, but they
seemed to make no other use of it than to chew, which
they do not do habitually, but only break a piece off when
they happen to pass by a place where it is growing.
   Of their domestic life and amusements, we had not sufficient opportunity to obtain much knowledge; but they appear sometimes to have wars with each other, not only
from their weapons, but the scars with which many of them
were marked, and some of which appeared to be the remains of very considerable wounds, made with stones, bludgeons, or some other obtuse weapon: By these scars also
they appear to be no inconsiderable proficients in surgery
of which indeed we happened to have more direct evidence
One of our seamen, when he was on shore, run a large
splinter into his foot, and the surgeon being on board, one
of his comrades endeavoured to take it out with a penknife

but after putting the poor fellow to a good deal of pain, was obliged to give it over. Our good old Indian, who happened to be present, then called over one of his countrymen that was standing on the opposite side of the river, who, having looked at the seaman's foot, went immediately down to the beach, and, taking up a shell, broke it to a point with his teeth; with this instrument, in little more than a minute, he laid open the place, and extracted the splinter; in the mean time the old man, who, as soon as he had called the other over, went a little way into the wood, returned with some gum, which he applied to the wound upon a piece of the cloth that was wrapped round him, and in two days time it was perfectly healed. We afterwards learned that this gum was produced by the apple tree, and our surgeon procured some of it, and used it as a vulnerary balsam with great success.

The habitations of these happy people I have described already; and besides these, we saw several sheds inclosed within a wall, on the outside of which there were several uncouth figures of men, women, hogs, and dogs, carved on posts, that were driven into the ground. Several of the natives were from time to time seen to enter these places, with a slow pace and dejected countenance, from which we conjectured that they were repositories of the dead. The area within the walls of these places was generally well paved with large round stones, but it appeared not to be much trodden, for the grass every where grew up between them. I endeavoured with particular attention to discover whether they had a religious worship among them, but never could find the least traces of any.

The boats or canoes of these people are of three different sorts. Some are made out of a single tree, and carry from two to six men: These are used chiefly for fishing, and we constantly saw many of them busy upon the reef: Some were constructed of planks, very dexterously sewed together: These were of different sizes, and would carry from ten to forty men. Two of them were generally lashed together, and two masts set up between them; if they were single, they had an out-rigger on one side, and only one mast in the middle. With these vessels they sail far beyond the sight of land, probably to other islands, and bring home plantains, bananas, and yams, which seem also to be more plenty upon other parts of this island, than that off which
the

the ship lay. A third sort seem to be intended principally for pleasure and show: They are very large, but have no sail, and in shape resemble the gondolas of Venice: The middle is covered with a large awning, and some of the people sit upon it, some under it None of these vessels came near the ship, except on the first and second day after our arrival; but we saw, three or four times a week, a procession of eight or ten of them passing at a distance, with streamers flying, and a great number of small canoes attending them, while many hundreds of people ran a-breast of them along the shore. They generally rowed to the outward point of a reef which lay about four miles to the westward of us, where they stayed about an hour, and then returned. These processions, however, are never made but in fine weather, and all the people on board are dressed; though in the other canoes they have only a piece of cloth wrapped round their middle. Those who rowed and steered were dressed in white; those who sat upon the awning and under it in white and red, and two men who were mounted on the prow of each vessel were dressed in red only. We sometimes went out to observe them in our boats, and though we were never nearer than a mile, we saw them with our glasses as distinctly as if we had been upon the spot.

The plank of which these vessels are constructed, is made by splitting a tree, with the grain, into as many thin pieces as they can. They first fell the tree with a kind of hatchet, or adze, made of a tough greenish kind of stone, very dexterously fitted into a handle; it is then cut into such lengths as are required for the plank, one end of which is heated till it begins to crack, and then with wedges of hard wood they split it down: Some of these planks are two feet broad, and from fifteen to twenty feet long. The sides are smoothed with adzes of the same materials and construction, but of a smaller size. Six or eight men are sometimes at work upon the same plank together, and, as their tools presently lose their edge, every man has by him a cocoa-nut shell filled with water, and a flat stone, with which he sharpens his adze almost every minute. These planks are generally brought to the thickness of about an inch, and are afterwards fitted to the boat with the same exactness that would be expected from an expert joiner. To fasten these planks together, holes are bored with a piece of bone that is fixed into a stick for that purpose, a use to which our nails were

afterwards

afterwards applied with great advantage, and through these holes a kind of plaited cordage is passed, so as to hold the planks strongly together : The seams are caulked with dried rushes, and the whole outside of the vessed is paid with a gummy juice, which some of their trees produce in great plenty, and which is a very good succedaneum for pitch.

The wood which they use for their large canoes, is that of the apple-tree, which grows very tall and straight. Several of them that were measured, were near eight feet in the girth, and from twenty to forty to the branches, with very little diminution in the size. Our carpenter said, that in other respects it was not a good wood for the purpose, being very light. The small canoes are nothing more than the hollow trunk of the bread-fruit tree, which is still more light and spongy. The trunk of the bread-fruit tree is six feet in girth, and about twenty feet to the branches.

Their principal weapons are stones, thrown either with the hand or sling, and bludgeons ; for though they have bows and arrows, the arrows are only fit to knock down a bird, none of them being pointed, but headed only with a round-stone.

I did not see one turtle all the while I lay off this island ; but, upon shewing some small ones which I brought from Queen Charlotte's Island, to the inhabitants, they made signs that they had them of a much larger size. I very much regretted my having lost our he-goat, which died soon after we left St Iago, and that neither of our she-goats, of which we had two, were with kid. If the he-goat had lived, I would have put them all on shore at this place, and I would have left a she-goat here if either of them had been with kid ; and I doubt not, but that in a few years they would have stocked the island.

The climate here appears to be very good, and the island to be one of the most healthy as well as delightful spots in the world. We saw no appearance of disease among the inhabitants. The hills are covered with wood, and the vallies with herbage ; and the air in general is so pure, that, notwithstanding the heat, our flesh meat kept very well two days, and our fish one. We met with no frog, toad, scorpion, centipied, or serpent of any kind : And the only troublesome insects that we saw were ants, of which there were but few.

The south-east part of the island seems to be better cultivated

tivated and inhabited than where we lay, for we saw every day boats come round from thence laden with plantains and other fruit, and we always found greater plenty, and a lower price, soon after their arrival, than before.

The tide rises and falls very little, and, being governed by the winds, is very uncertain; though they generally blow from the E. to the S. E., and for the most part a pleasant breeze.

The benefit that we received while we lay off this island, with respect to the health of the ship's company, was beyond our most sanguine expectations, for we had not now an invalid on board, except the two lieutenants and myself, and we were recovering, though still in a very feeble condition.

It is certain that none of our people contracted the venereal disease here, and therefore, as they had free commerce with great numbers of the women, there is the greatest probability that it was not then known in the country. It was, however, found here by Captain Cook, in the Endeavour, and as no European vessel is known to have visited this island before Captain Cook's arrival, but the Dolphin, and the Boudeuse and Etoil, commanded by M. Bougainville, the reproach of having contaminated, with that dreadful pest, a race of happy people, to whom its miseries had till then been unknown, must be due either to him or to me, to England or to France; and I think myself happy to be able to exculpate myself and my country beyond the possibility of doubt.

It is well known that the surgeon on board his majesty's ships keeps a list of the persons who are sick on board, specifying their diseases, and the times when they came under his care, and when they were discharged. It happened that I was once at the pay-table on board a ship, when several sailors objected to the payment of the surgeon, alleging, that although he had discharged them from the list, and reported them to be cured, yet their cure was incomplete. From this time, it has been my constant practice when the surgeon reported a man to be cured, who had been upon the sick-list, to call the man before me, and ask him whether the report was true: If he alleged that any symptoms of his complaint remained, I continued him upon the list; if not, I required him, as a confirmation of the surgeon's report, to sign the book, which was always done

done in my presence. A copy of the sick-list on board the
Dolphin, during this voyage, signed by every man in my
presence, when he was discharged well, in confirmation of
the surgeon's report, written in my own hand, and confirmed by my affidavit, I have deposited in the Admiralty ; by
which it appears, that the last man on board the ship, in
her voyage outward, who was upon the sick-list for the
venereal disease, except one who was sent to England in
the store-ship, was discharged cured, and signed the book
on the 27th of December, 1766, near six months before our
arrival at Otaheite, which was on the 19th of June, 1767 ;
and that the first man who was upon the list for that disease, in our return home, was entered on the 26th of February, 1768, six months after we left the island, which was
on the 26th of July, 1767, so that the ship's company was
entirely free fourteen months within one day, the very middle of which time we spent at Otaheite ; and the man who
was first entered as a venereal patient, on our return home,
was known to have contracted the disease at the Cape of
Good Hope, where we then lay.

SECTION IX.

*Passage from Otaheite to Tinian, with some Account of several
other Islands that were discovered in the South Seas.*

HAVING made sail from King George the Third's Island,
we proceeded along the shore of the Duke of York's Island,
at the distance of about two miles. There appeared to be
good bays in every part of it, and in the middle a fine harbour ; but I did not think it worth while to go on shore.
The middle and west end is very mountainous, the east
end is lower, and the coast, just within the beach, is covered with cocoa-nut, bread-fruit, apple, and plantain trees.

At day-light, the next morning, we saw land, for which
we made sail, and ran along the lee-side of it. On the weather-side there were very great breakers, and the lee-side
was rocky, but in many places there appeared to be good
anchorage. We saw but few inhabitants, and they appeared to live in a manner very different from those of
King George's Island, their habitations being only small
huts. We saw many cocoa-nut and other trees upon the
shore ;

shore ; but all of them had their heads blown away, probably in a hurricane. This island is about six miles long,
and has a mountain of considerable height in the middle,
which seems to be fertile   It lies in latitude 17° 28' S.,
and longitude, by our last observation, 151° 4' W. and I
called it *Sir Charles Saunders's Island.*

On the 29th, the variation of the compass, by azimuth,
was 7° 52' E.; and early the next morning, at day-break,
we saw land bearing from N. by E. to N.W. We stood
for it, but could find no anchorage, the whole island being
surrounded by breakers. We saw smoke in two places,
but no inhabitants. A few cocoa-nut trees were growing
on the lee-part of it, and I called it *Lord Howe's Island.* It
is about ten miles long, and four broad, and lies in latitude
16° 46' S., longitude, by observation, 154° 13' W.

In the afternoon, we saw land bearing W. by N. and
stood for it. At five o'clock, we saw breakers running a
great way out to the southward, and soon after, low land
to the S.W. and breakers all about it in every direction.

We turned to windward all night, and as soon as it was
light, crowded sail to get round these shoals. At nine we
got round them, and named them *Scilly Islands.* They
are a group of islands or shoals extremely dangerous ; for
in the night, however clear the weather, and by day, if it is
hazy, a ship may run upon them without seeing land. They
lie in latitude 16° 28' S. longitude 155° 30' W.

We continued to steer our course westward, till day-
break on the 13th of August, when we saw land bearing
W. by S. and hauled towards it. At eleven o'clock in the
forenoon, we saw more land in the W.S.W. At noon, the
first land that we saw, which proved to be an island, bore
W. $\frac{1}{4}$ S. distant about five leagues, and had the appearance
of a sugar-loaf; the middle of the other land, which was
also an island, and appeared in a peak, bore W.S.W. distant
six leagues. To the first, which is nearly circular, and
three miles over, I gave the name of *Boscawen's Island ;*
and the other, which is three miles and a half long, and
two broad, I called *Keppel's Isle.* Port Royal at this time
bore E. 4° 10' S. distant 478 leagues.

At two o'clock, being about two miles distant from Boscawen's Island, we saw several of the inhabitants ; but
Keppel's Isle being to windward, and appearing more likely
to afford us anchorage, we hauled up for it. At six, it was

not

not more than a mile and a half distant, and, with our glasses, we saw many of the inhabitants upon the beach; but there being breakers at a considerable distance from the shore, we stood off and on all night.

At four o'clock the next morning, we sent off the boats to sound, and visit the island; and as soon as it was light, we ran down and lay over-against the middle of it. At noon, the boats returned, and reported that they had run within a cable's length of the island, but could find no ground: That seeing a reef of rocks lie off it, they had hauled round it, and got into a large deep bay which was full of rocks. That they then sounded without the bay, and found anchorage from fourteen to twenty fathom, with a bottom of sand and coral: That afterwards they went again into the bay, and found a rivulet of good water, but the shore being rocky, went in search of a better landing-place, which they found about half a mile farther, and went ashore. They reported also, that from the water to this landing-place, a good rolling-way might be made for supplying the ship, but that a strong guard would be necessary, to prevent molestation from the inhabitants. They saw no hogs, but brought off two fowls and some cocoa-nuts, plantains, and bananas. While the boats were on shore, two canoes came up to them with six men: They seemed to be peaceably inclined, and were much the same kind of people as the inhabitants of King George's Island, but they were clothed in a kind of matting, and the first joint of their little fingers had been taken off; at the same time about fifty more came down from the country, to within about an hundred yards of them, but would advance no farther. When our people had made what observations they could, they put off, and three of the natives from the canoes came into one of the boats, but when she got about half a mile from the shore, they all suddenly jumped overboard, and swam back again.

Having received this account, I considered that the watering here would be tedious, and attended with great fatigue: That it was now the depth of winter in the southern hemisphere, that the ship was leaky, that the rudder shook the stern very much, and that what other damage she might have received in her bottom could not be known. That for these reasons, she was very unfit for the bad weather which she would certainly meet with either in going round

Cape

Cape Horn, or through the streight of Magellan: That if she should get safely through the streight, or round the cape, it would be absolutely necessary for her to refresh in some port, but in that case no port would be in her reach; I therefore determined to make the best of my way to Tinian, Batavia, and so to Europe by the Cape of Good Hope. By this route, as far as we could judge, we should sooner be at home; and if the ship should prove not to be in a condition to make the whole voyage, we should still save our lives, as from this place to Batavia we should probably have a calm sea, and be not far from a port.

In consequence of this resolution, at noon I bore away, and passed Boscawen's Island without visiting it. It is a high round island, abounding in wood, and full of people; but Keppel's Isle is by far the largest and the best of the two.

Boscawen's Island lies in latitude 15° 50′ S. longitude 175° W. and Keppel's Isle in latitude 15° 55′ S. longitude 175° 3′ W.

We continued a W.N.W. course till ten o'clock in the morning of Sunday the 16th, when we saw land bearing N. by E. and hauled up for it. At noon, we were within three leagues of it: The land within shore appeared to be high, but at the water-side it was low, and had a pleasant appearance; the whole seemed to be surrounded by reefs, that ran two or three miles into the sea. As we sailed along the shore, which was covered with cocoa-nut trees, we saw a few huts, and smoke in several parts up the country. Soon after we hauled without a reef of rocks, to get round the lee-side of the island, and at the same time sent out the boats to sound, and examine the coast.

The boats rowed close along the shore, and found it rocky, with trees growing close down to the water-side. These trees were of different sorts, many of them very large, but had no fruit: On the lee-side, however, there were a few cocoa-nuts, but not a single habitation was to be seen. They discovered several small rills of water, which, by clearing, might have been made to run in a larger stream. Soon after they had got close to the shore, several canoes came up to them, each having six or eight men on board. They appeared to be a robust, active people, and were quite naked, except a kind of mat that was wrapped round their middle. They were armed with large

maces

maces or clubs, such as Hercules is represented with, two of
which they sold to the master for a nail or two, and some
trinkets.   As our people had seen no animal, either bird or
beast, except sea-fowl, they were very desirous to learn of
the natives whether they had either, but could not make
themselves understood.   It appears, that during this conference, a design was formed to seize our cutter, for one of
the Indians suddenly laid hold of her painter, and hauled
her upon the rocks.   Our people endeavoured, in vain, to
make them desist, till they fired a musket cross the nose
of the man that was most active in the mischief.   No hurt
was done; but the fire and report so affrighted them, that
they made off with great precipitation.   Both our boats
then put off, but the water had fallen so suddenly that they
found it very difficult to get back to the ship; for when
they came into deep water they found the points of rocks
standing up, and the whole reef, except in one part, was
now dry, and a great sea broke over it.   The Indians probably perceived their distress, for they turned back, and
followed them in their canoes all along the reef till they
got to the breach, and then seeing them clear, and making
way fast towards the ship, they returned.

About six in the evening, it being then dark, the boats
returned, and the master told me, that all within the reef
was rocky, but that in two or three places, at about two
cables' length without it, there was anchorage in eighteen,
fourteen, and twelve fathom, upon sand and coral.   The
breach in the reef he found to be about sixty fathom broad,
and here, if pressed by necessity, he said a ship might anchor or moor in eight fathom; but that it would not be
safe to moor with a greater length than half a cable.

When I had hoisted the boats in, I ran down four miles
to leeward, where we lay till the morning; and then, finding that the current had set us out of sight of the island, I
made sail.   The officers did me the honour to call this
island after my name.   *Wallis's Island* lies in latitude 13°
18' S. longitude 177° W.

As the latitudes and longitudes of all these islands are
accurately laid down, and plans of them delivered in to the
Admiralty, it will be easy for any ship, that shall hereafter
navigate these seas, to find any of them, either to refresh
or to make farther discoveries of their produce.

I thought it very remarkable, that although we found no
kind

kind of metal in any of these islands, yet the inhabitants of all of them, the moment they got a piece of iron in their possession, began to sharpen it, but made no such attempt on brass or copper.

We continued to steer N. westerly, and many birds were from time to time seen about the ship, till the 28th, when her longitude being, by observation, 187° 24' W. we crossed the Line into north latitude. Among the birds that came about the ship, one which we caught exactly resembled a dove in size, shape, and colour. It had red legs, and was web-footed. We also saw several plantain leaves and cocoa-nuts pass by the ship.

On Saturday the 29th, about two o'clock in the afternoon, being in latitude 2° 50' N. longitude 188° W. we crossed a great rippling, which stretched from the N. E. to the S. W. as far as the eye could reach from the mast-head. We sounded, but had no bottom with a line of two hundred fathoms.

On Thursday the 3d of September, at five o'clock in the morning, we saw land bearing E. N. E. distant about five miles: In about half an hour we saw more land in the N. W. and at six, saw in the N. E. an Indian proa, such as is described in the account of Lord Anson's voyage. Perceiving that she stood towards us, we hoisted Spanish colours; but when she came within about two miles of us, she tacked, and stood from us to the N.N.W. and in a short time was out of sight.

At eight o'clock, the islands which I judged to be two of the Piscadores, bore from S. W. by W. to W. and to windward, from N. by E. to N. E. and had the appearance of small flat keys. They were distant about three leagues; but many others, much farther off, were in sight. The latitude of one of those islands is 11° N. longitude 192° 30' W., and the other 11° 20' N., longitude 192° 58' W.

On the 7th, we saw a curlieu and a pewit, and on the 9th we caught a land-bird, very much resembling a starling.

On the 17th, we saw two gannets, and judged the island of Tinian to bear west, at about one and-thirty leagues distance; our latitude being 15° N., and our longitude 212° 30' W. At six o'clock the next morning, we saw the island of Saypan, bearing W. by N. distant about ten leagues. In the afternoon, we saw Tinian, and made sail for the road; where, at nine o'clock in the morning, of Saturday the 19th,

we

we came to an anchor in two-and-twenty fathom, sandy ground, at about a mile distant from the shore, and half a mile from the reef.

SECTION X.

Some Account of the present State of the Island of Tinian, and our Employment there; with what happened in the Run from thence to Batavia.

As soon as the ship was secured, I sent the boats on shore to erect tents, and bring off some refreshments ; and about noon they returned, with some cocoa-nuts, limes, and oranges.

In the evening, the tents being erected, I sent the surgeon and all the invalids on shore, with two months provisions, of every kind, for forty men, the smith's forge, and a chest of carpenter's tools. I then landed myself, with the first lieutenant, both of us being in a very sickly condition, taking with us also a mate, and twelve men, to go up the country and hunt for cattle.

When we first came to an anchor, the north part of the bay bore N. 39° W. Cocoa point N. 7° W. the landing-place N. E. by N. and the south end of the island S. 28° E. ; but next morning, the master having sounded all the bay, and being of opinion that there was a better situation to the southward, we warped the ship a little way up, and moored with a cable each way.

At six in the evening, the hunters brought in a fine young bull, of near four hundred weight: Part of it we kept on shore, and sent the rest on board with bread-fruit, limes, and oranges.

Early the next morning, the carpenters were set at work to caulk the ship all over, and put every thing in repair as far as possible. All the sails were also got on shore, and the sail-makers employed to mend them : The armourers at the same time were busy in repairing the iron-work, and making new chains for the rudder. The number of the people now on shore, sick and well, was fifty-three.

In this place we got beef, pork, poultry, papaw apples, bread-fruit, limes, oranges, and every refreshment that is mentioned in the account of Lord Anson's voyage. The

sick

sick began to recover from the day they first went on shore: The air, however, was so different here from what we found it in King George's Island, that flesh meat, which there kept sweet two days, could here be scarcely kept sweet one. There had been many cocoa-nut trees near the landing-place, but they had been all wastefully cut down for the fruit, and none being grown up in their stead, we were forced to go three miles into the country before a single nut could be procured. The hunters also suffered incredible fatigue, for they were frequently obliged to go ten or twelve miles through one continued thicket, and the cattle were so wild that it was very difficult to come near them, so that I was obliged to relieve one party by another; and it being reported that cattle were more plenty at the north end of the island, but that the hunters being quite exhausted with fatigue when they got thither, were not able to kill them, much less to bring them down, I sent Mr Gore, with fourteen men, to establish themselves in that part of the island, and ordered that a boat should go every morning, at day-break, to bring in what they should kill. In the mean time the ship was laid by the stern to get at some of the copper sheathing which had been much torn; and in repairing the copper, the carpenter discovered and stopped a large leak under the lining of the knee of the head, by which we had reason to hope most of the water that the vessel had lately admitted in bad weather, came in. During our stay here, I ordered all the people on shore by turns, and by the 15th of October, all the sick being recovered, our wood and water completed, and the ship made fit for the sea, we got every thing off the shore, and embarked all our men from the watering-place, each having, at least, five hundred limes, and there being several tubs full on the quarter-deck, for every one to squeeze into his water as he should think fit.

At break of day, on Friday the 16th, we weighed, and sailed out of the bay, sending the boats at the same time to the north end of the island, to bring off Mr Gore and his hunters. At noon, we received them and their tents on board, with a fine large bull, which they had just killed.

While we lay at anchor in this place, we had many observations for the latitude and longitude, from which we drew up the following table:

Latitude

Latitude of the ship, as she lay at anchor   14° 55′ N. long. 214° 15′ W.
Latitude of the watering-place   -   -   14   59 N.
Longitude of the body of Tinian   -   -   2 4   W.
Longitude of the Tinian Road   -   -   214   8 W.
Medium of Longitude, observed at Tinian 214   7

We continued a westerly course, inclining somewhat to the north, till the 21st, when Tinian bearing S. 71° 40′ E. distant 277 leagues, we saw many birds; and the next day, saw three, resembling gannets, of the same kind that we had seen when we were within about thirty leagues of Tinian.

On the 23d, we had much thunder, lightning, and rain, with strong gales, and a great sea. The ship laboured very much, and the rudder being loose again, shook the stern as much as ever. The next day, we saw several small land birds, and the gales continuing, we split the gib and main-top-mast-stay-sail; the wind increased all the remainder of the day, and all night, and on Sunday it blew a storm. The fore-sail and mizen-sail were torn to pieces, and lost; and having bent others, we wore and stood under a reefed fore-sail, and balanced mizen. We had the mortification to find the ship admit more water than usual. We got the top-gallant masts down upon the deck, and took the gib-boom in; soon after which a sea struck the ship upon the bow, and washed away the round houses, with all the rails of the head, and every thing that was upon the fore-castle: We were, however, obliged to carry as much sail as the ship would bear, being, by Lord Anson's account, very near the Bashee Islands, and, by Mr Byron's, not more than thirty leagues, with a lee-shore.

The next morning, we saw several ducks and shags, some small land birds, and a great number of horse-flies about the ship; but had no ground with 160 fathom. The incessant and heavy rain had kept every man on board constantly wet to the skin for more than two days and two nights; the weather was still very dark, and the sea was continually breaking over the ship.

On the 27th, the darkness, rain, and tempest continuing, a mountainous sea that broke over us, staved all the half-ports to pieces on the starboard side, broke all the iron stanchions on the gunwale, washed the boat off the skids, and carried many things overboard. We had, however, this day, a gleam of sunshine, sufficient to determine our latitude, which we found to be 20° 50′ N., and the ship appeared to be fifty minutes north of her reckoning.

The

The weather now became more moderate. At noon, on the 28th, we altered our course, steering S. by W.; and at half an hour after one, we saw the Bashee Islands bearing from S. by E. to S.S.E. distant about six leagues. These islands are all high, but the northermost is higher than the rest. By an observation made this day, we found Grafton Island to lie in the longitude of 239° W. and in latitude of 21° 4′ N. At midnight, the weather being very dark, with sudden gusts of wind, we missed Edmund Morgan, a marine tailor, whom we supposed to have fallen overboard, having reason to fear that he had drunk more than his allowance.

From this time, to the 3d of November, we found the ship every day from ten to fifteen miles north of her reckoning. The day before we had seen several gannets; but upon sounding many times during the day and the next night, we had no ground with 160 fathom. This morning, at seven o'clock, we saw a ledge of breakers bearing S.W. at the distance of about three miles: We hauled off from them, and at eleven saw more breakers bearing S.W. by S. distant about five miles. At noon, we hauled off the east end of them, from which we were not distant more than a quarter of a mile.

The first shoal lies in latitude 11° 8′ N.; longitude, from Bashee Islands, 8° W.

The second shoal lies in latitude 10° 46′ N.; longitude of the N.E. end, from Bashee Islands, 8° 15′ W.

We saw much foul ground to the S. and S.S.E. but had no bottom with 150 fathom. Before one, however, we saw shoal water on the larboard bow, and standing from it, passed another ledge at two. At three, we saw a low sandy point, which I called *Sandy Isle*, bearing N. ¼ E. distant about two miles. At five, we saw a small island, which I called *Small Key*, bearing N. by E. distant about five miles; and soon after, another larger, which I called *Long Island*, beyond it. At six in the evening, the largest island being distant between two and three leagues, we brought-to, and stood off and on from mid-night till break of day, continually sounding, but having no ground.

At seven in the morning, of Wednesday the 4th, we saw another island, which I called *New Island*, bearing S.E. by E., and a large reef of rocks, bearing S. ½ W. distant six miles. At ten, we saw breakers from W.S.W. to W. by N.

At noon, the north end of the great reef bore S.E. by E. distant two leagues, and another reef bore W.N.W. at about the same distance.

The latitudes and longitudes of these islands and shoals, appear by the following table:

		Lat. N.	Long. W.
Sandy Isle	-	10° 40'	247° 12'
Small Key	- -	10 37	247 16
Long Island	- -	10 20	247 24
New Island	- -	10 10	247 40
First Shoal	- -	10 14	247 36
Second Shoal	-	10 4	247 45
Third Shoal	- -	10 5	247 50

Soon after, we saw another reef in latitude 10° 15', longitude 248°.

The next day we found the ship, which had for some time been to the northward of her reckoning, eight miles to the southward.

We continued our course, often sounding, but finding no bottom. On the 7th, we passed through several ripplings of a current, and saw great quantities of drift-wood, cocoa-nut leaves, things like cones of firs, and weed, which swam in a stream N.E. and S.W. We had now soundings at sixty-five fathom, with brown sand, small shells, and stones; and at noon, found the ship again to the northward of her reckoning ten miles, and had decreased our soundings to twenty-eight fathom, with the same ground. Our latitude was 8° 36' N.; longitude 253° W. At two o'clock, we saw the island of Condore, from the mast-head, bearing W. ½ N. At four, we had ground with twenty fathom; the island bearing from W. to N.W. by W. distant about thirteen leagues, and having the appearance of high hummocks. The latitude of this island is 8° 40' N.; longitude, by our reckoning, 254° 15'.

We now altered our course; and the next morning, I took from the petty officers and seamen, all the log and journal books relative to the voyage.

On the 10th, being in latitude 5° 20' N., longitude 255° W. we found a current setting four fathom an hour S. by W.; and during our course to the islands Timoun, Aros, and Pesang, which we saw about six in the afternoon of the 13th, we were every day from ten to twenty miles southward of our reckoning.

On

On the 16th, at ten in the morning, we crossed the Line again into south latitude, in longitude 255°; and soon after we saw two islands, one bearing S. by E. distant five leagues, and the other S. by W. distant seven leagues.

The next morning, the weather became very dark and tempestuous, with heavy rain; we therefore clewed all up, and lay by till we could see about us. The two islands proved to be Pulo Toté, and Pulo Weste; and having made sail till one o'clock, we saw the Seven Islands. We continued our course till two the next morning, the weather being very dark, with heavy squalls of wind, and much lightning and rain. While one of these blasts was blowing with all its violence, and the darkness was so thick that we could not see from one part of the ship to the other, we suddenly discovered, by a flash of lightning, a large vessel close aboard of us. The steersman instantly put the helm a-lee, and the ship answering her rudder, we just cleared each other. This was the first ship we had seen since we parted with the Swallow; and it blew so hard, that not being able to understand any thing that was said, we could not learn to what nation she belonged.

At six, the weather having cleared up, we saw a sail at anchor in the E.S.E.; and at noon, we saw land in the W.N.W. which proved to be Pulo Taya, Pulo Toté bearing S. 35° E. Pulo Weste S. 13° E. At six in the evening, we anchored in fifteen fathom, with sandy ground; and observed a current running E.N.E. at the rate of five fathom an hour.

At six in the morning, we weighed and made sail, and soon after saw two vessels a-head; but at six in the evening, finding that we lost much ground, we came again to an anchor in fifteen fathom, with a fine sandy bottom.

At six o'clock the next morning, the current being slack, we hove short on the small bower, which soon after parted at a third from the clench. We immediately took in the cable, and perceived that, although we had sounded with great care before we anchored, and found the bottom clear, it had been cut through by the rocks. After some time, the current becoming strong, a fresh gale springing up, and the ship being a great way to the leeward, I made sail, in hopes to get up and recover the anchor; but I found at last that it was impossible, without anchoring again; and being afraid of the consequences of doing that in foul ground, I determined

mined to stand on, especially as the weather was become squally.

We were, however, able to make very little way till the next day, when, about three in the afternoon, we saw Monopin Hill bearing S. ⅞ E and advancing very little, saw the coast of Sumatra at half an hour after six the next morning. We continued to suffer great delay by currents and calms, but on Monday the 30th of November, we anchored in Batavia Road.

SECTION XI.

Transactions at Batavia, and an Account of the Passage from thence to the Cape of Good Hope.

WE found here fourteen sail of Dutch East-India ships, a great number of small vessels, and his majesty's ship the Falmouth, lying upon the mud in a rotten condition.

I sent an officer on shore, to acquaint the governor of our arrival, to obtain his permission to purchase refreshments, and to tell him that I would salute him, if he would engage to return an equal number of guns. The governor readily agreed; and at sun-rise, on Tuesday the 1st of December, I saluted him with thirteen guns, which he returned with fourteen from the fort. Soon after, the purser sent off some fresh beef, and plenty of vegetables, which I ordered to be served immediately; at the same time I called the ship's company together, and told them that I would not suffer any liquor to come on board, and would severely punish those who should attempt to bring any: And I took some pains to reconcile them to this regulation, by assuring them that in this country, intemperance would inevitably destroy them. As a further preservative, I suffered not a man to go on shore, except those who were upon duty; and took care that none even of these straggled into the town.

On the 2d, I sent the boatswain and the carpenter, with the carpenter of the Falmouth, to look at such of her stores as had been landed at Onrust, with orders, that if any were fit for our use they should be bought. At their return, they informed me that all the stores they had seen were rotten, and unfit for use, except one pair of tacks, which they brought with them: The masts, yards, and cables were all

dropping

dropping to pieces, and even the iron work was so rusty that it was worth nothing. They also went on board the Falmouth to examine her hulk, and found her in so shattered a condition, that in their opinion she could not be kept together during the next monsoon. Many of her ports were washed into one, the stern-post was quite decayed, and there was no place in her where a man could be sheltered from the weather. The few people who belonged to her were in as bad a state as their vessel, being quite broken and worn down, and expecting to be drowned as soon as the monsoon should set in.

Among other necessaries, we were in want of an anchor, having lost two, and of three-inch rope for rounding the cables; but the officers whom I had sent to procure these articles, reported, that the price which had been demanded for them was so exorbitant, that they had not agreed to give it. On Saturday the 5th, therefore, I went on shore myself, for the first time, and visited the different storehouses and arsenals, but found it impossible to make a better bargain than my officers. I suspected that the dealers took advantage of our apparent necessity, and supposing that we could not sail without what we had offered to purchase, determined to extort from us more than four times its value. I was, however, resolved to make any shift rather than submit to what I thought a shameful imposition, and therefore told them that I should certainly sail on the next Tuesday; that if they would agree to my terms in the mean time, I would take the things I had treated for; if not, that I would sail without them.

Soon after I returned on board, I received a petition from the warrant-officers of the Falmouth, representing, that there was nothing for them to look after: That the gunner had been long dead, and his stores spoiled, particularly the powder, which, by order of the Dutch, had been thrown into the sea: That the boatswain, by vexation and distress, had lost his senses, and was then a deplorable object in a Dutch hospital: That all his stores had been long spoiled and rotten, the roof of the storehouse having fallen in during a wet monsoon, and left them exposed many months, all endeavours to procure another place to put them in being ineffectual: That the carpenter was in a dying condition, and the cook a wounded cripple. For these reasons they requested that I would take them home, or at least dismiss them from their charge.

charge. It was with the greatest regret and compassion that I told these unhappy people it was not in my power to relieve them, and that as they had received charge of stores, they must wait orders from home. They replied, that they had never received a single order from England since they had been left here, and earnestly entreated that I would make their distress known, that it might be relieved. They had, they said, ten years pay due, in the expectation of which they were grown old, and which now they would be content to forfeit, and go home sweepers, rather than continue to suffer the miseries of their present situation, which were indeed very great. They were not suffered to spend a single night on shore, whatever was their condition, and when they were sick, no one visited them on board; they were, besides, robbed by the Malays, and in perpetual dread of being destroyed by them, as they had a short time before burnt the Siam prize. I assured them that I would do my utmost to procure them relief, and they left me with tears in their eyes.

As I heard nothing more of the anchor and rope for which I had been in treaty, I made all ready for sea. The ship's company had continued healthy and sober, and been served with fresh beef every day, from the time of our first coming to an anchor in the Road; we had also some beef, and a live ox, to carry out with us. We had now only one man upon the sick list, except a seaman, who had been afflicted with rheumatic pains ever since our leaving the Streight of Magellan: And at six o'clock in the morning, of Tuesday the 8th of December, after a stay of just one week, we set sail.

On the 11th, at noon, we were off a small island called the Cap, between the coasts of Sumatra and Java, and several of our people fell down with colds and fluxes. The next day, a Dutch boat came on board, and sold us some turtle, which was served to the ship's company. At night, being at the distance of about two miles from the Java shore, we saw an incredible number of lights upon the beach, which we supposed were intended to draw the fish near it, as we had seen the same appearance at other places.

On Monday the 14th, we anchored off Prince's Island, and began to take in wood and water. The next morning, the natives came in with turtle, poultry, and hog-deer, which we bought at a reasonable price. We continued here, fitting

ting the ship for the sea, till the 19th, during which time many of the people began to complain of intermitting disorders, something like an ague. At six o'clock the next morning, having completed our wood, and taken on board seventy-six tons of water, we made sail.

While we lay here, one of the seamen fell from the mainyard into the barge, which lay along-side the ship. His body was dreadfully bruised, and many of his bones were broken: It happened also, that in his fall he struck two other men, one of whom was so much hurt that he continued speechless till the 24th, and then died, though the other had only one of his toes broken. We had now no less than sixteen upon the sick list, and by the 1st of January, the number was increased to forty; we had buried three, among whom was the quarter-master, George Lewis, who was a diligent, sober man, and the more useful, as he spoke both the Spanish and Portuguese languages. The diseases by which we suffered, were fluxes, and fevers of the putrid kind, which are always contagious, and, for that reason alone, would be more fatal on board a ship than any other. The surgeon's mate was very soon laid up, and those who were appointed to attend the sick, were always taken ill in a day or two after they had been upon that service. To remedy this evil, as much as it was in my power, I made a very large birth for the sick, by removing a great number of people from below to the half deck, which I hung with painted canvas, keeping it constantly clean, and directing it to be washed with vinegar, and fumigated once or twice a day. Our water was well tasted, and was kept constantly ventilated; a large piece of iron, also, used for the melting of tar, and called a loggerhead, was heated red-hot, and quenched in it before it was given out to be drank. The sick had also wine instead of grog, and salep or sago every morning for breakfast: Two days in a week they had mutton broth, and had a fowl or two given them on the intermediate days; they had, besides, plenty of rice and sugar, and frequently malt meshed; so that perhaps people in a sickly ship had never so many refreshments before: The surgeon also was indefatigable; yet, with all these advantages, the sickness on board gained ground. In the mean time, to aggravate our misfortune, the ship made more than three feet water in a watch; and all her upper works were very open and loose.

By

By the 10th of January, the sickness began, in some degree, to abate, but more than half the company were so feeble, that they could scarcely crawl about.   On this day, being in latitude 22° 41' S., longitude, by account, 300° 47' W. we saw many tropic birds about the ship.

On the 17th, being in latitude 27° 32' S., longitude 310° 36' W., we saw several albatrosses, and caught some bonettas.   The ship was this day ten miles to the southward of her account.

On the 24th, in latitude 33° 40' S., longitude, by account, 328° 17' W., we met with a violent gale, which split the main-top-sail and the main-top-mast-stay-sail all to pieces. The sea broke over the ship in a dreadful manner, the starboard rudder chain was broken, and many of the booms were washed overboard.   During the storm we saw several birds and butterflies; and our first attention, after it was subsided, was to dry the bedding of the sick : At the same time, every one on board who could handle a needle was employed in repairing the sails, which were now in a shattered condition.

On the 26th and 27th, being in latitude 34° 16', and becalmed, we had several observations, by which we determined the longitude of the ship to be 323 30'; and it appeared that we were several degrees to the eastward of our reckoning.

At six in the evening, of the 30th of January, we saw land, and on the 4th of February, we anchored in Table Bay, at the Cape of Good Hope.

Our run from Prince's Island to the Cape was, by our reckoning, 89 degrees longitude, which makes the longitude of the Cape 345° W.; but the longitude of the Cape being, by observation, 342° 4', it appeared that the ship was three degrees to the eastward of her reckoning.

Section XII.

*An Account of our Transactions at the Cape of Good Hope,
and of the Return of the Dolphin to England.*

As soon as the ship was at anchor, I sent an officer on shore, with the usual compliments to the governor, who received him with great civility, telling him that we were welcome

come to all the refreshments and assistance that the Cape afforded, and that he would return our salute with the same number of guns.

We found riding here a Dutch commodore, with sixteen sail of Dutch East Indiamen, a French East India ship, and the Admiral Watson, Captain Griffin, an East India packet-boat, for Bengal. We saluted the governor with thirteen guns, and he returned the same number; the Admiral Watson saluted us with eleven guns, and we returned nine; the French ship afterwards saluted us with nine guns, and we returned seven.

Having got off some mutton for the ship's company, with plenty of greens, I sent the surgeon on shore to hire quarters for the sick, but he could procure none for less than two shillings a day, and a stipulation to pay more, if any of them should take the small-pox, which was then in almost every house, in proportion to the malignity of the disease. The first expence being great, and it appearing, upon enquiry, that many of our people had never had the small-pox, so that the increase was likely to be considerable, besides the danger, I requested the governor's permission to erect a tent upon a spacious plain, at about two miles distance from the town, called Green Point, and to send my people on shore thither during the day, under the care of an officer, to prevent their straggling. This permission the governor immediately granted, and gave orders that they should suffer no molestation.

In this place, therefore, I ordered tents to be erected, and the surgeon and his mate, with proper officers, to attend; at the same time strictly charging that no man should be suffered to go into the town, and that no liquor should be brought to the tents. All the sick, except two, left the ship early in the morning, with their provisions and firing; and for those that were reduced to great weakness, I ordered the surgeon to procure such extraordinary provisions as he should think proper, particularly milk, though it was sold at an excessive price. About six in the evening they returned on board, and seemed to be greatly refreshed. At the same time, being extremely ill myself, I was obliged to be put on shore, and carried about eight miles up the country, where I continued all the time the ship lay here; and when she was ready to sail, returned on board without having received the least benefit.

No

No time, however, was lost in refitting the vessel: The sails were all unbent, the yards and top-masts struck, the forge was set up, the carpenters were employed in caulking, the sail-makers in mending the sails, the cooper in repairing the casks, the people in overhauling the rigging, and the boats in filling water.

By the 10th of February, the heavy work being nearly dispatched, twenty of the men who had had the small-pox, were permitted to go ashore at the town, and others, who were still liable to the distemper, were landed at some distance, with orders to go into the country, and return in the evening, which they punctually obeyed: This liberty, therefore, was continued to them all the while the vessel lay at this port, which produced so good an effect, that the ship's company, except the sick, who recovered very fast, had a more healthy and vigorous appearance than when they left England. We purchased here the necessaries that we endeavoured to procure at Batavia, at a reasonable price, besides canvass and other stores; we also procured fresh water by distillation, principally to shew the captains of the Indiamen, and their officers, that, upon an emergency, wholesome water might be procured at sea. At five o'clock in the morning, we put fifty-six gallons of salt water into the still, at seven it began to run, and in about five hours and a quarter afforded us two-and-forty gallons of fresh water, at an expence of nine pounds of wood, and sixty-nine pounds of coals. Thirteen gallons and two quarts remained in the still, and that which came off had no ill taste, nor, as we had often experienced, any hurtful quality. I thought the shewing this experiment of the more consequence, as the being able to allow plenty of water not only for drink, but for boiling any kind of provision, and even for making tea and coffee, especially during long voyages, and in hot climates, conduces greatly to health, and is the means of saving many lives. I never once put my people to an allowance of water during this whole voyage, always using the still when we were reduced to five-and-forty tons, and preserving the rain water with the utmost diligence. I did not, however, allow water to be fetched away at pleasure, but the officer of the watch had orders to give such as brought provisions of any kind, water sufficient to dress it, and a proper quantity also to such as brought tea and coffee.

On the 25th, the wood and water being nearly completed,

ted, and the ship almost ready for sea, I ordered every body to go on board, and the sick tents to be brought off; the people being so well recovered, that in the whole ship's company there were but three men unable to do duty, and happily, since our leaving Batavia, we had lost but three. The next day, and the day following, the carpenters finished caulking all the out-works, the fore-castle, and the main-deck; we got all our bread on board from the shore, with a considerable quantity of straw, and thirty-four sheep for sea-stores. In the mean time I came on board, and having unmoored, lay waiting for a wind till the evening of Thursday the 3d of March, when a breeze springing up, we got under sail. While we were on shore at Green Point, we had an opportunity of making many celestial observations, by which we determined Table Bay to lie in latitude 34° 2' S., longitude, from Greenwich, 18° 8' E. The variation of the needle, at this place, was 19° 30' W.

On the 7th, being in latitude 29° 33' S., longitude, by account, 347° 38', the ship was eight miles to the northward of her dead reckoning.

On the 13th, having sailed westward 360 degrees from the meridian of London, we had lost a day; I therefore called the latter part of this day Monday, March 14th.

At six o'clock in the evening, of Wednesday the 16th, we saw the island of St Helena, at the distance of about fourteen leagues; and at one the next morning, brought-to. At break of day, we made sail for the island, and at nine, anchored in the bay. The fort saluted us with thirteen guns, and we returned the same number. We found riding here the Northumberland Indiaman, Captain Milford, who saluted us with eleven guns, and we returned nine. We got out all the boats as soon as possible, and sent the empty casks to be filled with water; at the same time several of the people were employed to gather purslain, which grows here in great plenty. About two o'clock, I went on shore myself, and was saluted by the fort with thirteen guns, which I returned. The governor and the principal gentlemen of the island did me the honour to meet me at the water-side, and having conducted me to the fort, told me, that it was expected I should make it my home during my stay.

By noon the next day, our water was completed, and the ship was made ready for sea; soon after, she was unmoored, to take advantage of the first breeze, and at five in the afternoon,

ternoon, I returned on board.   Upon my leaving the shore,
I was saluted with thirteen guns, and soon after, upon getting under way, I was saluted with thirteen more, both which
I returned; the Northumberland Indiaman then saluted me
with thirteen guns, so did the Osterley, which arrived here
the evening before I made sail, and I returned the compliment with the same number.

On the 21st, in the evening, we saw several men of war
birds; and at midnight, heard many birds about the ship.
At five o'clock in the morning of the 23d, we saw the Island
of Ascension; and at eight, discovered a ship to the eastward, who brought-to, and hoisted a jack at her main-top-
mast-head, upon which we shewed our colours, and she then
stood in for the land again.   We ran down close along the
north-east side of the island, and looked into the bay, but
seeing no ship there, and it blowing a stiff gale, I made the
best of my way.

On Monday the 28th, we crossed the equator, and got
again into north latitude.

On Wednesday, the 13th of April, we passed a great
quantity of gulph weed; and on the 17th, we passed a great
deal more.   On the 19th, we saw two flocks of birds, and
observing the water to be discoloured, we thought the
ground might be reached, but, upon sounding, could find
no bottom.

At five o'clock in the morning of Sunday the 24th, we
saw the peak of the island of Pico bearing N. N. E. at the
distance of about eighteen leagues.   We found, by observation, that Fyal lies in latitude 38° 20′ N., longitude 28°
30′ W. from London.

No incident worth recording happened till about noon
on the 11th of May, when, being in latitude 48° 44′ N.,
longitude 7° 16′ W. we saw a ship in chace of a sloop, at
which she fired several guns.   We bore away, and at three,
fired a gun at the chace, and brought her to; the ship to
windward, being near the chace, immediately sent a boat
on board her, and soon after, Captain Hammond, of his
majesty's sloop the Savage, came on board of me, and told
me, that the vessel he had chaced, when he first saw her,
was in company with an Irish wherry, and that as soon as
they discovered him to be a man of war, they took different
ways; the wherry hauled the wind, and the other vessel
bore

bore away. That he at first hauled the wind, and stood after the wherry, but finding that he gained no ground, he bore away after the other vessel, which probably would also have escaped, if I had not stopped her, for that he gained very little ground in the chace. She appeared to be laden with tea, brandy, and other goods, from Roscoe in France; and though she was steering a south-west course, pretended to be bound to Bergen in Norway. She belonged to Liverpool, was called the Jenny, and commanded by one Robert Christian. Her brandy and tea were in small kegs and bags; and all appearances being strongly against her, I detained her, in order to be sent to England.

At half an hour after five, on the 13th, we saw the islands of Scilly; on the 19th, I landed at Hastings in Sussex; and at four the next morning, the ship anchored safely in the Downs, it being just 637 days since her weighing anchor in Plymouth Sound. To this narrative, I have only to add, that the object of the voyage being discovery, it was my constant practice, during the whole time of my navigating those parts of the sea which are not perfectly known, to lie-to every night, and make sail only in the day, that nothing might escape me.

A Table of the Latitudes and the Longitudes West of London, with the Variation of the Needle, at several Ports, and Situations at Sea, from Observations made on board his Majesty's Ship the Dolphin; and her Nautical Reckoning during the Voyage which she made round the World in the Years 1766, 1767, 1768, under the Command of Captain Samuel Wallis.

NAMES OF PLACES.	Time when.	Latitude in	Longitude supposed.	Long. observed by Dr Maskeline's Method.	Variation.
	1766.				
Lizard - -	Aug. 22.	50° 0′ N	5° 14′ W	————	21° 0′ W
Funchall R. Madeira	Sept. 8.	32 35 N.	18 0 W	16° 40′ W	14 10 W.
Port Praja St Jaga	Sept. 24.	14 53 N	23 50 W.	————	8 20 W.
Port Desire -	Dec. 8.	47 56 S.	67 20 W	66 24 W.	23 15 E.
Cape Virgin Mary	Dec. 17.	52 24 S.	70 4 W	69 6 W.	23 0 E.

A Table of the Latitudes and Longitudes &c. continued.

Names of Places.	Time when.	Latitude in.	Longitude supposed.	Long. observed by Dr Maskeline's Method.	Variation.
	1766.				
Point Possession	Dec. 23.	52 30 S.	70 11 W	69 50 W	22 40 E.
Point Porpass -	Dec 26	53 8 S	71 0 W	71 30 W	22 50 E.
Port Famine -	Dec. 27	53 43 S	71 0 W.	71 32 W	22 30 E.
	1767.				
Cape Froward -	Jan. 19.	54 5 S.	————	————	22 40 E.
Cape Holland -	Jan. 20	53 58 S.	————	————	22 40 E.
Cape Gallant -	Jan. 23.	53 50 S.	————	————	22 40 E.
York Road -	Feb. 4.	53 40 S.	————	————	22 30 E.
Cape Quod -	Feb. 17.	53 33 S.	————	————	32 35 E.
Cape Notch -	Mar. 4.	53 22 S.	————	————	23 0 E.
Cape Upright -	Mar. 18	53 5 S	————	————	22 40 E.
Cape Pillar -	April 11	52 46 S.	76 0 W	————	23 0 E
At Sea - -	April 21	42 30 S.	96 30 W.	95 46 W	12 0 E.
At Sea - -	May 4.	28 12 S	99 0 W	96 30 W.	6 0 E.
At Sea - -	May 20.	21 0 S	110 0 W.	106 47 W.	5 0 E.
At Sea - -	May 23.	20 20 S	116 54 W.	112 64 W.	5 0 E.
At Sea - -	June 1.	20 38 S.	132 0 W.	127 45 W.	5 9 E.
At Sea - -	June 3.	19 30 S	132 30 W.	129 50 W	5 40 E.
Whitsunday Island	June 7.	19 26 S.	141 0 W.	137 56 W	6 0 E.
Q Charlotte's Isl.	June 8.	19 18 S.	141 4 W.	138 4 W	5 20 E.
Egmont Island -	June 11	19 30 S.	141 27 W	138 30 W	6 0 E.
D. of Glouces. Isl.	June 12.	19 11 S.	143 8 W	140 6 W	7 10 E.
D. of Cumberl. Isl.	June 13.	19 18 S	143 44 W.	140 34 W	7 0 E.
Pr. Wm. Henry's Isl	June 13.	19 0 S.	144 4 W.	141 6 W.	7 0 E
Osnaburgh Island	June 17.	17 51 S.	150 27 W.	147 30 W	6 0 E.
K. Geo. ⟩ S. E end	June 19.	17 48 S.	151 30 W.	149 15 W	6 0 E.
III.'s Isl. ⟨ N. W. end	July 4.	17 30 S.	152 0 W.	150 0 W	5 30 E.
D. of York's Island	July 27.	17 28 S.	152 12 W	150 16 W	6 0 E
Sir C. Saunders's Isl	July 28.	17 28 S.	153 2 W	151 4 W	6 30 E.
Lord Howe's Island	July 30	16 46 S.	156 38 W	154 13 W	7 40 E
Scilly Island	July 31.	16 28 S.	157 22 W.	155 30 W	8 0 E.
Boscawen's Island	Aug. 13	15 50 S	177 20 W.	175 10 W.	9 0 E
Aug Keppel's Island	Aug. 13.	15 53 S.	177 23 W.	175 13 W	10 0 E.
Wallis's Island	Aug. 17.	13 18 S.	180 0 W.	177 0 W.	10 0 E
Piscadores ⟩ S. end	Sept. 3.	11 0 N	195 0 W	192 30 W	10 0 E.
Islands ⟨ N. end		11 20 N	195 25 W	193 0 W	10 0 E.
Timan - -	Sept. 30.	14 58 N	215 40 W.	214 10 W	6 20 E.
At Sea - -	Oct. 17.	16 10 N	218 0 W	216 25 W	5 15 E.
Grafton's Island	Oct. 29.	21 4 N	241 0 W	239 0 W	1 3 W.
Pulo Aroe -	Nov. 15	2 28 N	258 0 W	255 0 W	1 0 W.
Lucipará -	Nov. 26	4 10 S		254 46 W	None.
Batavia -	Dec. 1.	6 8 S		254 30 W	1 25 W.
Prince's Island	Dec. 16	6 41 S	256 0 W	256 30 W	1 0 W

A Table of the Latitudes and Longitudes, &c. concluded.

NAMES OF PLACES.	Time when.	Latitude in	Longitude supposed	Long ob served by Dr Maskeline s Method	Variation.
	1768.				
At Sea - -	Jan. 26.	34 24 S.	328 0 W	328 30 W	24 0 W
At Sea - -	Jan. 27.	34 14 S	324 0 W.	323 13 W.	24 0 W
Cape of Good Hope	Feb. 11.	34 0 S.	345 0 W	342 0 W	19 30 W
At Sea - -	Mar. 15.	16 44 S.	3 0 W.	2 0 W	13 0 W
At Sea - -	Mar. 15	16 36 S.	2 0 W.	2 5 W	12 50 W.
St Helena -	Mar. 19	15 57 S.	5 49 W	5 40 W	12 47 W.
Ascension -	Mar. 23.	7 28 S.	14 18 W	14 4 W.	9 53 W
At Sea - -	Mar. 24	7 58 S	14 °0 W	14 38 W.	10 0 W
At Sea - -	April 8	15 4 N	30 0 W	34 30 W	4 48 W.
At Sea - -	April 11.	21 28 N	36 0 W	36 37 W	4 30 W
At Sea - -	April 21	33 55 N	32 0 W	33 0 W	11 34 W
At Sea - -	April 23.	36 15 N.	30 0 W	29 31 W	11 30 W
At Sea - -	May 10.	49 43 N	6 0 W	7 52 W	22 30 W.
At Sea - -	May 11	48 48 N	7 30 W	8 19 W	
St Agnus's Light-h.	May 13.	49 58 N	7 14 W	7 8 W.	20 0 W

CHAPTER III.

AN ACCOUNT OF A VOYAGE ROUND THE WORLD, IN THE YEARS 1766, 1767, 1768, AND 1769, BY PHILIP CARTERET, ESQ. COMMANDER OF HIS MAJESTY'S SLOOP THE SWALLOW.

SECTION I.

The Run from Plymouth to Madeira, and from thence through the Streight of Magellan.

[The longitude of this voyage is reckoned from London westward to 180, and eastward afterwards]

SOON after I returned from a voyage round the world with the Honourable Commodore Byron, I was appointed to the command of his majesty's sloop the Swallow, by a commission bearing date the first of July, 1766; the Swallow then lay at Chatham, and I was ordered to fit her out with all possible expedition. She was an old ship, having been in the service thirty years, and was, in my opinion, by no means fit for a long voyage, having only a slight thin sheathing upon her bottom, which was not even filled with nails to supply the want of a covering that would more effectually keep out the worm. I had been given to understand that I was to go out with the Dolphin; but the disparity of the two ships, and the difference in their equipment, made me think that they could not be intended for the same duty; the Dolphin, which was sheathed with copper, being supplied with every thing that was requisite for a long and dangerous navigation; and the Swallow having only a scanty supply of common necessaries. However, I ventured to apply for a forge, some iron, a small skiff, and several other things which I knew by experience would be of the utmost importance, if it was intended that I should make another voyage round the world; but I was told that the vessel and her equipment were very fit for the service she was to perform, and none of the requisites for which I applied were allowed me. I was therefore confirmed in my opinion, that, if the Dolphin was to go round the world, it could never be intended that I should go farther than Falkland's islands, where the Jason, a fine frigate, which was, like the Dolphin, sheathed with copper, and amply equipped, would supply my place. I was, however, deficient in junk, an article which is essentially necessary in every voyage, and for this I applied when I got to Plymouth, but I was told that a quantity sufficient for both the ships had been put on board the Dolphin.

On Friday the 22d of August, 1766, the ship's company having the evening before received two months pay, I weighed, and made sail from Plymouth Sound in company with the Dolphin, under the command of Captain Wallis, and the Prince Frederick store-ship, commanded by Lieutenant James Brine. We proceeded together without any remarkable incident till the 7th of September, when we came to an anchor in Madeira road.

While I lay at this place, not being yet acquainted with my destination, I represented my want of junk, and the reply that had been made to my application for a supply by the commissioner at Plymouth, in a letter to Captain Wallis, who sent me five hundred weight. This quantity however was so inadequate to my wants, that I was soon afterwards reduced to the disagreeable necessity of cutting off some of my cables to save my rigging.

On the 9th, very early in the morning, the lieutenant acquainted me that, in the night, nine of my best men had secretly set off from the ship to swim on shore, having stripped themselves naked and left all their clothes behind them, taking only their money, which they had secured in a handkerchief that was tied round their waist; that they proceeded together till they came very near the surf, which breaks high upon the shore, and that one of them, being then terrified at the sound, had swum back again to the ship, and been taken on board, but that the rest had ventured through. As the loss of these men would have been very severely felt, I immediately sat down to write a letter to the consul, entreating his assistance to recover them; but, before I had finished it, he sent me word, that all of them having, to the great astonishment of the natives, been found naked on the beach, they had been taken into custody, and would be delivered

livered up to my order. The boat was dispatched immediately, and as soon as I heard they were on board, I went
upon the deck. I was greatly pleased to see a contrition in
their countenances, which at once secretly determined me
not to inflict the punishment by which they seemed most
heartily willing to expiate their fault; but I asked them what
could have induced them to quit the ship, and desert the
service of their country, at the risk of being devoured by
sharks, or dashed to pieces by the surf against the shore.
They answered, that though they had indeed, at such risks,
ventured to swim on shore, they never had any intention of
deserting the ship, which they were determined to stand by
as long as she could swim; but that being well assured they
were going a long voyage, and none being able to tell who
might live, or who might die, they thought it hard not to
have an opportunity of spending their own money, and therefore determined, as they said, once more to get a skinful of
liquor, and then swim back to the ship, which they hoped
to have done before they were missed. As I had resolved
to remit their punishment, I did not too severely scrutinize
their apology, which the rest of the ship's company, who
stood round them, seemed very much to approve; but, observing that with a skinful of liquor they would have been
in a very unfit condition to swim through the surf to the
ship, I told them that, hoping they would for the future expose their lives only upon more important occasions, and
that their conduct would thenceforward give me no cause
of complaint, I would for this time be satisfied with the
shame and regret which I perceived they suffered from a
sense of their misbehaviour: I then admonished them to
put on their clothes, and lie down, as I was confident they
wanted rest; and added, that as I might possibly during the
course of the voyage have occasion for good swimmers, I
was very glad that I knew to whom I might apply. Having
thus dismissed these honest fellows from their fears, I was
infinitely gratified by the murmur of satisfaction which instantly ran through the ship's company; and was afterwards
amply rewarded for my lenity, there being no service during
all the toils and dangers of the voyage which they did not
perform with a zeal and alacrity that were much to their
honour and my advantage, as an example to the rest.

We sailed again on the 12th, and I was then first acquainted with the particulars of our voyage by Captain
Wallis,

Wallis, who gave me a copy of his instructions, and appointed Port Famine, in the Streight of Magellan, to be the place of rendezvous, if we should happen to be separated.

I was now convinced that I had been sent upon a service to which my vessel and her equipment were by no means equal, but I determined at all events to perform it in the best manner I was able.

We proceeded on our voyage without any remarkable event till we anchored off Cape Virgin Mary, where we saw the Patagonians, of which I have given some account in a letter to Dr Matty, which was published in the sixtieth volume of the Transactions of the Royal Society, and which it is not necessary here to repeat, as it is in general the same as those which have been given by Commodore Byron and Captain Wallis.

When we entered the Streight, I was ordered to keep ahead of the Dolphin and the store-ship, to pilot them through the shoals; but my ship worked so ill, that we could but very seldom make her tack without the help of a boat to tow her round: However, with much labour, and at no inconsiderable risk, we anchored in Port Famine, on Friday the 26th of December. At this place we unhung our rudder, and added a piece of wood to it, in hopes that by making it broader, we should obtain some advantage in working the ship; in which, however, we were altogether disappointed.

After many difficulties and dangers, we got into Island Bay on the 17th of February; and before we made sail again, I represented the condition of my ship by letter to Captain Wallis, and requested him to consider what was best for his majesty's service, whether she should be dismissed, or continue the voyage. Captain Wallis replied, that as the lords of the Admiralty had ordered the Swallow on this service, with the nature of which I was well acquainted, he did not think himself at liberty to alter her destination.[1]

We

---

[1] This seems quite irrational. Would Captain W. have thought himself bound " to his destination," in circumstances, which, to the judgment of his own mind, and in the unanimous opinion of his officers, rendered success beyond the accomplishment of human agents? Surely not—Then why judge by any other rule than that of practicability, when another person, one under his command, was concerned? Some discretionary power is obviously implied in every system of orders intended for rational and ac-

We continued therefore for some time to navigate the Streight together, and as I had passed it before, I was ordered to keep a-head and lead the way, with liberty to anchor and weigh when I thought proper; but, perceiving that the bad sailing of the Swallow would so much retard the Dolphin as probably to make her lose the season for getting into high southern latitudes, and defeat the intention of the voyage, I proposed to Captain Wallis that he should lay the Swallow up in some cove or bay, and that I should attend and assist him with her boats till the Streight should be passed, which would probably be in much less time than if he continued to be retarded by my ship; and I urged, as an additional advantage, that he might complete, not only his stock of provisions and stores, but his company, out of her, and then send her back to England, with such of his crew as sickness had rendered unfit for the voyage: Proposing also, that in my way home I would examine the eastern coast of Patagonia, or attempt such other discoveries as he should think proper. If this was not approved, and my knowledge of the South Seas was thought necessary to the success of the voyage, I offered to go with him on board the Dolphin, and give up the Swallow to be commanded by his first lieutenant, whose duty I would perform during the rest of the voyage, or to make the voyage myself with only the Dolphin, if he would take the Swallow back to Europe; but Captain Wallis was still of opinion, that the voyage should be prosecuted by the two ships jointly, pursuant to the orders that had been given.

The

countable beings. The use made of it is one of the data, on which the determination of the degrees of merit or demerit as to conduct, must be founded. On no other principle than one involving some liberty, nay some duty of judging, can the intelligence of mankind be availing in the execution of projects. Divine authority alone, unequivocally made known, can dispense with acquiescence to the demands of reason, or render inefficient the most glaringly insuperable difficulties. How even the *Lords* of the Admiralty, or their delegate, Capt. W. should assume such dispensing prerogatives, it is impossible to comprehend. They relied, it is probable, on the honour, as it is called, of their subject. This alters the case entirely no doubt. A mighty convenient thing this *honour* in all well-established monarchies! One cannot help desiring, nevertheless, that *men of honour* should have the management of it. Were they men of *humane feeling* too, it would be so much the better. Is it possible to predicate these things of the persons who gave poor Carteret his orders? Is it possible to believe he was expected to circumnavigate the world in the Swallow? An opinion has already been hazarded on this nice point.—E.

The Swallow was now become so foul, that with all the sail she could set, she could not make so much way as the Dolphin, with only her top-sails and a reef in them: We continued in company, however, till Friday the 10th of April, when the western entrance of the Streight was open, and the Great South Sea in sight. Hitherto I had, pursuant to my directions, kept a-head, but now the Dolphin being nearly a-breast of us, set her foresail, which soon carried her a-head of us; and before nine o'clock in the evening, as she shewed no lights, we lost sight of her. We had a fine eastern breeze, of which we made the best use we could during the night, carrying all our small sails even to the top-gallant studding sails, notwithstanding the danger to which it exposed us; but at day-break the next morning, we could but just see the Dolphin's top-sails above the horizon: we could perceive, however, that she had studding-sails set, and at nine o'clock we had entirely lost sight of her; we judged that she was then clear of the Streight's mouth, but we, who were still under the land, had but light and variable airs. From this time, I gave up all hope of seeing the Dolphin again till we should arrive in England, no plan of operation having been settled, nor any place of rendezvous appointed, as had been done from England to the Streight. I thought myself the more unfortunate in this separation, as no part of the woollen cloth, linen, beads, scissars, knives, and other cutlery-ware, and toys, which were intended for the use of both ships, and were so necessary to obtain refreshments from Indians, had, during the nine months we had sailed together, been put on board the Swallow, and as we were not provided either with a forge or iron, which many circumstances might render absolutely necessary to the preservation of the ship: I had the satisfaction, however, to see no marks of despondency among my people, whom I encouraged, by telling them, that although the Dolphin was the best ship, I did not doubt but that I should find more than equivalent advantages in their courage, ability, and good conduct.

At noon, this day, we were abreast of Cape Pillar, when, a gale springing up at S.W., we were obliged to take down our small sails, reef our top-sails, and haul close to the wind: Soon after it freshened to the W.S.W. blowing right in from the sea, and after making two boards, we had the mortification to find that we could not weather the land on either
tack.

tack. It was now almost dark, the gale increased, driving
before it a hollow swell, and a fog came on, with violent
rain; we therefore got close under the south shore, and sent
our boat a-head to find out Tuesday's Bay, which is said by
Sir John Narborough to lie about four leagues within the
Streight, or to find out any other place in which we might
come to an anchor. At five o'clock, we could not see the
land, notwithstanding its extreme height, though we were
within less than half a mile of it, and at six, the thickness
of the weather having rendered the night so dark that we
could not see half the ship's length, I brought-to for the
boat, and was indeed, with good reason, under great concern for her safety: We hoisted lights, and every now and
then made a false fire, but still doubting whether they could
be seen through the fog and rain, I fired a gun every half
hour, and at last had the satisfaction to take her on board,
though she had made no discovery, either of Tuesday's Bay,
or any other anchoring-place. We made sail the rest of
the night, endeavouring to keep near the south shore, and
our ground to the westward as much as possible; and as
soon as it was light the next morning, I sent the master
again, out in the cutter, in search of an anchorage on the
south shore. I waited in a state of the most painful suspense for her return, till five o'clock in the afternoon, fearing that we should be obliged to keep out in this dangerous
pass another night, but I then saw her sounding a bay, and
immediately stood in after her: In a short time the master
came on board, and to our unspeakable comfort, reported
that we might here come safely to an anchor; this, with the
help of our boat, was effected about six o'clock, and I went
down into my cabin to take some rest: I had, however,
scarcely lain down, before I was alarmed with a universal
shout and tumult among the people, all that were below
running hastily upon the deck, and joining the clamour of
those above: I instantly started up, imagining that a gust
had forced the ship from her anchor, and that she was driving out of the bay, but when I came upon the deck, I
heard the people cry out, The Dolphin! the Dolphin! in a
transport of surprise and joy which appeared to be little
short of distraction: A few minutes, however, convinced us,
that what had been taken for a sail was nothing more than
the water which had been forced up, and whirled about in
the air, by one of the violent gusts that were continually
coming

coming off the high land, and which, through the haze, had a most deceitful appearance. The people were for a few minutes somewhat dejected by their disappointment, but before I went down, I had the pleasure to see their usual fortitude and cheerfulness return.

The little bay where we were now at anchor, lies about three leagues E. by S. from Cape Pillar: It is the first place which has any appearance of a bay within that Cape, and bears S. by E., about four leagues from the island which Sir John Narborough called Westminster Hall, from its resemblance to that building in a distant view. The western point of this bay makes a very remarkable appearance, being a perpendicular plane like the wall of a house. There are three islands about two cables' length within its entrance, and within those islands a very good harbour, with anchorage in between twenty-five and thirty fathom, with a bottom of soft mud. We anchored without the islands, the passage on each side of them being not more than one-fourth of a cable's length wide. Our little bay is about two cables' length broad, the points bearing east and west of each other: In the inner part there is from sixteen to eighteen fathom, but where we lay it is deeper; we had one anchor in seventeen fathom, and the other in forty-five, with great over-falls between them, and rocks in several places. Here we rode out a very hard gale, and the ground being extremely uneven, we expected our cables to be cut in two every minute, yet when we weighed, to our great surprise, they did not appear to have been rubbed in any part, though we found it very difficult to heave them clear of the rocks. The land round this bay and harbour is all high, and as the current sets continually into it, I doubt not but it has another communication with the sea to the south of Cape Deseada. The master said he went up it four miles in a boat, and could not then be above four miles from the Western Ocean, yet he still saw a wide entrance to the S.W. The landing is every where good, there is plenty of wood and water, and mussels and wild geese in abundance.

From the north shore of the western end of the Streight of Magellan, which lies in about latitude 52° ½ S. to latitude 48°, the land which is the western coast of Patagonia runs nearly north and south, and consists wholly of broken islands, among which are those that Sharp has laid by the name of the Duke of York's Islands; he has indeed placed them at a

considerable

considerable distance from the coast, but if there had been many islands in that situation, it is impossible but that the Dolphin, the Tamar, or the Swallow, must have seen them, as we ran near their supposed meridian, and so did the Dolphin and the Tamar the last voyage. Till we came into this latitude, we had tolerable weather, and little or no current in any direction, but when we came to the northward of 48°, we found a current setting strongly to the north, so that probably we then opened the great bay, which is said to be ninety leagues deep. We found here a vast swell from the N.W. and the winds generally blew from the same quarter; yet we were set every day twelve or fifteen miles to the northward of our account.

On Wednesday the 15th, at about four o'clock in the morning, after surmounting many dangers and difficulties, we once more got abreast of Cape Pillar, with a light breeze at S.E. and a great swell. Between five and six o'clock, just as we opened Cape Deseada, the wind suddenly shifted to S. and S. by W. and blew so hard that it was with great difficulty we could carry the reefed top-sails: The sudden changing of the wind, and its excessive violence, produced a sea so dreadfully hollow, that great quantities of water were thrown in upon our deck, so that we were in the utmost danger of foundering; yet we did not dare to shorten sail, it being necessary to carry all we could spread, in order to weather the rocky islands, which Sir John Narborough has called the Islands of Direction, for we could not now run back again into the Streight, without falling down among the broken land, and incurring the dangers of the northern shore, which was to leeward; towards this broken land, however, and lee-shore, the ship settled very fast, notwithstanding our utmost efforts: In this pressing emergency we were obliged to stave all the water-casks upon the deck, and between decks, to clear the vessel, and to make her carry better sail, and at length, happily escaped the danger which threatened us. After we got clear of those islands, and drew off from the Streight's mouth and the land, we found the sea run more regularly from the S.W. and the wind soon after coming from S.S.W. to S.S.E. we had by noon got a pretty good offing, about nine leagues from Cape Victory, which is on the north shore. Thus we cleared the western entrance of the Streight, which, in my opinion, is too dangerous for navigation; a deliverance which happened

ed in the very crisis of our fate, for almost immediately afterwards, the wind came again to the S.W., and if it had
continued in that quarter, our destruction would have been
inevitable.

SECTION II.

*The Passage from Cape Pillar, at the Western Entrance of
the Streight of Magellan, to Masafuero; with some Account
of that Island.*

I TOOK my departure from Cape Pillar, which I make to
lie in the latitude of 52° 45′ S., and in the longitude 75°
10′ W. of the meridian of London, and as soon as I got
clear of the streight, steered to the northward along the
coast of Chili. Upon examining what quantity of fresh
water we had now on board, I found that it amounted only
to between four and five and twenty tons, which I thought
not sufficient for so long a voyage as was probably before
us; I therefore hauled to the northward, intending to make
the island of Juan Fernandes, or Masafuero, that we might
increase our stock before we sailed to the westward.

In the middle of the night of the 16th, we had the wind
first to the S.S.E. and then to the S.E. with which we kept
away N.W. and N.N.W. in high spirits, hoping that in a
short time we should be in a more temperate climate: We
had the misfortune, however, very soon to find ourselves
disappointed, for on the 18th, the wind came to the
N.N.W. and blew directly from the point upon which we
were steering. We had now got about a hundred leagues
from the streight's mouth; our latitude was 48° 39′ S., and
we were, by account, 4° 33′ W. of Cape Pillar; but from
this time, till the 8th of May, the wind continued unfavourable, and blew a continued storm, with sudden gusts
still more violent, and much rain and hail, or rather fragments of half-melted ice: At intervals also we had thunder and lightning, more dreadful than all the past, and a
sea which frequently laid the whole vessel under water.

From the time of our clearing the streight, and during
our passage along this coast, we saw a great number of
sea-birds, particularly albatrosses, gannets, sheerwaters, and
a thick lumpish bird, about as big as a large pigeon, which
the

the sailors call a Cape-of-Good-Hope hen : They are of a dark-brown or blackish colour, and are therefore some-times called the black gull : We saw also a great many pintado birds, of nearly the same size, which are prettily spotted with black and white, and constantly on the wing, though they frequently appear as if they were walking up-on the water, like the peterels, to which sailors have given the name of Mother Carey's chickens ; and we saw also many of these.

In the evening of Monday the 27th, which was very dark, as we were standing to the westward under our courses, and a close-reefed top-sail, the wind, in a hard squall, suddenly shifted, and took the vessel right a-head ; the violent jerk with which the sails were instantly thrown a-back, was very near carrying the masts away by the board, and oversetting the ship ; the sails being at this time extremely wet, and the gale in the highest degree violent, they clung so fast to the masts and rigging, that it was scarcely possible to get them either up or down ; yet by the dexterous activity of our people, we got the main-sail up, clewed up the main top-sail, and got the ship's head round without receiving much damage. The vio-lence of the wind continued several hours, but before morn-ing it veered again to the N.W. and continued in that quarter till the afternoon of the 29th, when it died away, and we had a dead calm for six hours. During this time we had a high sea, which ran in great confusion from all quarters, and broke against the ship in a strange manner, making her roll with so violent and sudden a motion, that I expected every moment to lose our masts. The wind afterwards sprung up at W.S.W. which was fair, and we carried all the sail we could set to make the most of it. It blew very hard in this direction, with heavy rain for a few hours, but by noon on the 30th, it returned to its usual quarter the N.W., and was so violent as to bring us again under our courses, there being at the same time a prodi-gious swell, which frequently broke over us. At five o'clock the next morning, as we were lying-to under the reefed main-sail and balanced mizen, a vast sea broke over the quarter where the ship's oars were lashed, and carried away six of them, with the weather-cloth ; it also broke the mi-zen-gaff close where the sail was reefed, and the iron-strap of one of the main dead eyes, laying the whole vessel for

some

some time under water: We were however fortunate enough to haul up the main-sail without splitting, though it blew a hurricane, and a deluge of rain, or rather of half-melted ice, at the same time poured down upon us. The wind soon after shifted again from N.W. to S.W. and for about an hour blew, if possible, stronger than ever. This wind made the ship come up with her head right against the vast sea which the north-west wind had raised, and at every pitch which she made against it, the end of the bowsprit was under water, and the surge broke over the forecastle as far aft as the main-mast, in the same manner as it would have broke over a rock, so that there was the greatest reason to apprehend she would founder. With all her defects she was indeed a good sea-boat, and if she had not, it would have been impossible for her to have outlived this storm, in which, as well as on several other occasions, we experienced the benefit of the bulk-heads which we had fixed on the fore-part of the half-deck, and to the after-part of the fore-castle.

Notwithstanding this wind was fair, we durst not venture to put the ship before it, for if in wearing, any of these enormous seas had broken on her side, it would inevitably have carried away all before it. After some time, however, it became more moderate, and we then got up our yards and made sail, steering N. by W.; and now the men having been up all night, and being wet to the skin, I ordered every one of them a dram.

By the next morning, the 2d of May, the wind came again to the N.W. and N.N.W. but by this time we had got down the broken mizen-gaff, repaired it as well as we could, got it up again in its place, and bent the sail to it; but we now most sensibly felt the want of a forge and iron.

On the 3d, at day-break, we found the rudder-chain broken, and upon this occasion we again most feelingly regretted the want of a forge; we made, however, the best shift we could, and the next day, the weather being more moderate, though the wind was still contrary, we repaired our rigging, and the carpenters fixed a new dead eye where the old one had been broken; the sail-maker also was busy in mending the sails that had been split.

On the 5th, we were again brought under our courses by a hurricane from the N. by W. and N.N.W. and the ship was tossed about with such violence that we had no com-

mand

mand of her.   During this storm, two of our chain-plates
were broken, and we continued toiling in a confused hollow sea till midnight, when a light gale sprung up at N.W.
which soon blew very hard ; but at two in the morning, we
were again taken right a-head by a sudden and violent
squall at west, which at once threw all our sails aback, and
before we could get the ship round, was very near carrying
all by the board.   With this gale we stood north, and in the
forenoon the carpenters fixed new chain-plates to the main
shrouds, and one to the fore shrouds, in the place of those
which had been broken in the squall during the night.   This
was another occasion on which it was impossible not to regret the want of a forge and iron.

The gale continued in this direction till eight in the
morning of the 7th, when it returned to the N.W. with unsettled weather.   On the 8th, it came to south, and this was
a fine day, the first we had seen after our leaving the
Streight of Magellan.   Our latitude at noon was 36° 39′S.
and we were about five degrees to the westward of Cape
Pillar.   The next day we made the island of Masafuero,
and on the 10th, the island of Juan Fernandes : In the afternoon we got close to the eastermost part of it, and soon
after hauled round the north end, and opened Cumberland
Bay.   As I did not know that the Spaniards had fortified
this island, I was greatly surprised to see a considerable
number of men about the beach, with a house and four
pieces of cannon near the water-side, and a fort about three
hundred yards farther from the sea, just upon the rising of
the hill, with Spanish colours flying on the top of it.   This
fort, which is faced with stone, has eighteen or twenty em-
brasures, and within it a long house, which I supposed to
be barracks for the garrison : Five-and-twenty or thirty
houses of different kinds are scattered round it, and we saw
much cattle feeding on the brow of the hills, which seemed to be cultivated, as many spots were divided by enclosures from each other ; we saw also two large boats lying on
the beach.   The gusts of wind which came right out of
this bay, prevented my going so near as I intended, for
they were so violent as to oblige us many times to let fly
our top-sail sheets, though the sails were close reefed ; and
I think it is impossible to work a ship into this bay when
the wind blows hard from the southward. As we stood cross
the bay to the westward, one of the boats put off from the
shore

shore, and rowed towards us; but perceiving that the gusts or flaws made us lie at a considerable distance from the land, she went in again. We then opened West Bay, on the east part of which, close to the sea side, is a small house, which I took for a guard-house, and two pieces of cannon mounted upon their carriages, without any works about them.— We now wore, and stood again for Cumberland Bay, but as soon as we opened it, the boat again put off, and made towards us: As the hard gusts would not permit us to come any nearer to the land than before, we stood along it to the eastward, the boat still making after us till she was very far out of the bay: At length it grew dark, and we lost sight of her, upon which we made all the sail we could to the eastward.

During all this time I hoisted no colours, having none but English on board, which at this time I did not think it proper to shew.

As I was disappointed of wood and water at this place, and of the refreshments, of which, after the dangers and fatigue of our voyage through the Streight, and our passage from it, we stood in the most pressing need, I made all the sail I could for the island of Masafuero. On the 12th of May we arrived off the south eastermost part of it, but it blowing hard, with a great sea, we did not dare to come near it on this side, and therefore went round to the west side, where, in the evening, we cast anchor upon an excellent bank, fit to receive a fleet of ships, which, in the summer, might ride here with great advantage. I sent out both the boats to endeavour to get some water, but they found it impossible to land, for the beach is rocky, and the surf at this time was so great, that the swimmers could not get through the breakers: This was the more mortifying, as we saw a fine run of fresh water from the ship, with plenty of trees fit for fire-wood, and a great number of goats upon the hills.

The next morning, as soon as it was light, I sent the boats out again, to examine any place where they could get on shore. They returned with a few casks of water, which they had filled at a small rill, and reported, that the wind being at S.E. blew so strong on the east side of the island, and raised so great a sea, that they could not come near the shore.

We continued here till the 15th, at day-break, and then, the

the weather becoming more moderate, we weighed, and in the evening, just at sun-set, we anchored on the east side of the island, in the same place where Commodore Byron had anchored about two years before. We lost no time, but immediately got off fifteen casks of water, and sent a number of men on shore with others, that were empty, to be filled against the next morning, and a strong party to cut wood : But it happened that about two o'clock in the morning a hard gale of wind came on from the N.W. with violent gusts from the shore, which drove us off the bank, though we had two anchors a-head, which were in the utmost danger of being lost; we got them up, however, with great difficulty, and immediately set the sails, and worked under the lee of the island, keeping as near the shore as we could; the weather soon afterwards became more moderate, so that we could carry double-reefed sails; we had also very smooth water, yet we could not make the ship tack, and were forced to wear her every time we wanted to go about.

At day-break, though we were at a good distance from the shore, I sent the cutter to get off a load of water, before the surf should be so great upon the beach as to prevent her landing. About ten o'clock, the wind came to the N.N.E. which enabled us to get within a little distance of the watering-place, and we might have recovered our anchoring ground upon the bank from which we had been driven, but the weather had so bad an appearance, and the gale freshened so fast, that we did not think it prudent to venture: We brought-to, however, as near the shore as possible, for the advantage of smooth water to unload the cutter, which soon after came alongside with twelve casks of water. As soon as we had taken these on board, I sent the cutter again for another freight, and as we were at a very little distance from land, I ventured to send our long-boat, a clumsy, heavy, four-oared vessel, with provisions for the people on shore, and orders to bring back a load of water, if she could get it : As soon as these boats were dispatched, we made a tack off to keep our ground. At noon it blew hard, with heavy rain and thick weather; and at one, as we were standing in again, we saw the boats running along the shore, for the lee-part of the island, this side being open to the wind; we therefore followed them, and brought-to as near the shore as possible, to favour their coming on board:

board: They presently made towards us, and we hoisted them in, but the sea was now risen so high, that in doing it they received considerable damage, and we soon learnt that they found the surf so great as not to be able even to land their empty water-casks. We continued to lie-to, under a balanced mizen, off the lee-part of the island all the afternoon, and although all hands had been constantly employed ever since the ship had been driven off her anchoring-ground, the carpenters worked all night in repairing the boats.

At four o'clock in the morning, the island bore west of us, being four leagues distant, and right to windward: We had now a fine gale and smooth water, and about ten o'clock we fetched very near to the south part of it, and with the help of the boat made the ship tack. As it was not probable that with such a vessel we could regain the anchoring-ground, I took advantage of our being so near the shore, though at a good distance from the watering-place, to send the cutter for another load. In the mean time I stood on and off with the ship, and about four o'clock in the afternoon the cutter brought her freight of water on board. I enquired of the lieutenant after the people on shore, and he told me, that the violent rain which had fallen in the night, had suddenly brought down such torrents of water through the hollow or gulley where they had taken up their station, that they were in the utmost danger of being swept away before it, and though with great difficulty they saved themselves, several of the casks were entirely lost. It was now too late for the boat to make another turn to the place where we had hitherto got our water; but Mr Erasmus Gower, the lieutenant, whose diligence and ability in all our dangers and distress I cannot sufficiently commend, having, as he returned with the cutter, observed that many runs of water had been made by the night's rain, on that part of the island which was nearest to us, and knowing how impatient I was of delay, offered to go thither with the boat, and fill as many casks as she could bring back. I gladly accepted this offer; Mr Gower went away in the boat, and in the mean time I made a tack off with the ship; but before they had been gone an hour, the weather began to grow gloomy, and the wind to freshen, a heavy black cloud at the same time settled over the island so as to hide the tops of the hills,

hills, and soon after it began to thunder and lighten at a dreadful rate: As these appearances were very threatening, I stood in again towards the island in hopes of meeting with the boat, but though we ran in as close as we dared, we saw nothing of her. In the mean time night came on, which the thickness of the weather rendered extremely dark, the gale increased, and it began to rain with great violence: In this situation I lay to under a balanced mizen, firing guns, and burning false fires, as a guide to the boat; and not being able to account for her delay, I suffered the most distressful anxiety, and had indeed but too much reason to fear that she was lost. About seven o'clock, however, to my unspeakable satisfaction, she came safe alongside, and as I had long seen a storm gathering, which I expected every moment to burst upon us, we got her in with all possible expedition. It was indeed happy for us all that no time was lost; for before she could be got into her place the squall came on, which in a moment laid the ship down in a surprising manner, and broke the mizen gaff just where the sail was reefed; so that if another minute had passed before the boat had been got in, we must inevitably have lost her, and every soul on board would have perished. This wind and weather continued till midnight, when it became somewhat more moderate, so that we were able to set our courses and top-sails. In the mean time I had enquired of Mr Gower how it came to be so long before he returned to the ship, and he told me, that after he had got to the place where he intended to fill the casks, three of the boat's crew had swam ashore with them for that purpose; but that within a few minutes the surf had risen so high, and broke with such fury on the shore, that it was impossible for them to get back to the boat; that being unwilling to leave them behind, especially as they were stark naked, he had waited in hopes that an opportunity might be found for their coming on board; but that, being intimidated by the appearance of the weather, and the uncommon darkness of the night, he had at last, with whatever reluctance, been obliged to come on board without them. The situation of these poor fellows now furnished another subject of solicitude and anxiety; they were naked, upon a desolate island, at a great distance from the watering-place where their shipmates had a tent, without food and without shelter, in a night of violent and incessant rain, with such thunder and lightning as in Europe is altogether unknown. In the evening of the 19th, however, I had the satisfaction to receive them on board, and to hear an account of their adventures from their own lips. As long as it was light, they flattered themselves, like their friends in the boat, that they should find an opportunity to return on board her; but afterwards, when the darkness of the night was broken only by the flashes of lightning, and the tempest became every moment more violent, they knew that to reach the boat was impossible, if it still remained in its station; and that most probably the people on board had provided for their own safety, by returning on board the ship: To reach the tent of their shipmates, during the darkness and tempest, was equally beyond their power, and they were reduced to the necessity of passing such a night, in such a place, without the least defence against either the rain or the cold, which now began to be severely felt. Necessity is said to be ingenious; and they contrived to procure a temporary succedaneum both for apparel and a shed, by lying one upon another, each man alternately placing himself between the other two; in this situation it may easily be believed that they longed most ardently for the dawn, and as soon as it appeared they set out for the tent: They were obliged, however, to make their way along the seashore, for the inland country was impassable; nor was this the worst, for they were frequently stopped by high steep bluff points, which they were obliged to swim round at a considerable distance; for if they had not taken a compass, they would' have been dashed to pieces against the rocks by the surf, and as it was, they were every moment in danger of being devoured by a shark. About ten o'clock in the morning, however, they reached the tents, almost perished with hunger and cold, and were received with equal surprise and, joy by their shipmates, who immediately shared with them such provisions and clothes as they had. When they came on board, I gave orders that they should have such refreshments as were proper, and remain in their hammocks the whole night. The next day they were as hearty as if nothing had happened, nor did they suffer any farther inconvenience from the accident. These were three of the honest fellows who had swam naked from the ship at the island of Madeira to get a skinful of liquor. I now return to my narrative in the order of time.

On

On the 18th, the weather was moderate, and in the evening we were within half a mile of the anchoring-ground, from which we had been driven; but the wind suddenly failing, and a current making against us, we could not reach it: We took advantage, however, of being so near the waterers' tent to send a boat on shore to enquire after the three men whose adventure has been just related, and soon after she brought them on board. The carpenters were all this time employed in making a new mizen-gaff, out of a gibboom, and in the mean while we were obliged to make shift with the old one, keeping the sail balanced. It continued a stark calm all the night, so that in the morning we found the current and the swell had driven us no less than nine miles from the land: The weather, however, being good, I sent the cutter for a load of water, which she brought on board about one o'clock. Soon after a breeze sprung up at N.N.W. and as we now approached the land very fast, I sent the boat on shore again for water; it happened, however, that before we could reach our anchoring-ground, it again fell calm, and we were again kept off by the current: The boat in the meantime, as she rowed along the shore, caught as much fish with hook and line as served all the ship's company, which was some alleviation of our disappointment. At eight o'clock in the evening, it began again to blow hard with sudden squalls, so that we passed another toilsome and dangerous night. In the morning, having a stiff gale at N.W. we made towards our anchoring-ground with all the sail we could spread, and happily regained it about four o'clock in the afternoon, when we anchored, at two cables' length from the beach, in eighteen fathom, with a bottom of fine sand, and moored with a small anchor in shore. By the time the ship was properly secured, it was too late to proceed with our watering; the long-boat however was sent along the shore to fish, and though before seven o'clock it blew so hard that she was obliged to return, she brought fish enough on board to serve all the people. In the night we had foul weather, with hard squalls and much rain; and in the morning, the wind blowing with great violence along the shore, we frequently drove, though we had not less than two hundred fathom of cable out; for the bank is a loose fine sand that easily gives way. We rode out the storm, however, without damage, but the rain was so violent, and the sea ran so high, that nothing could

be

be done with the boats, which was the more mortifying, as it was for the sake of completing our watering that we had endured almost incessant labour for five days and nights to regain the situation in which we now lay.　About eight in the evening, the wind became more moderate, and though it was then too late to fetch off any water, we got out one of the boats, and sent three men on shore, right abreast of the ship, to kill seals, and make oil of their fat, for burning in lamps and other uses on board the ship.

The wind blew very hard the next morning, as it had done all night, but being at W.N W. which was off the land, we sent the boats away soon after it was light, and about ten, they returned with each of them a load of water, and a great number of pintado birds : These birds they got from the people on shore, who told them, that when a gale of wind happened in the night they flew faster into their fire than they could well take them out, so that during the gale of the last night, they got no less than seven hundred of them.　The boats were employed in getting water on board all this day, although the surf was so great that several of the casks were staved and lost : They were sent out again a little before it was light the next day, and by seven o'clock a few casks only were wanting to complete our stock.　The threatening appearances of the weather made me now very impatient to get the people on board, with the casks that were still at the watering-place ; as soon, therefore, as the boats were cleared of their loading, I dispatched them again, with orders to bring off all the hands, with the tent, and every thing else that was on shore, with all possible expedition.　From this time the wind increased very fast, and by eleven o'clock it blew so hard, with violent gusts from the land, that the ship began to drive off the bank : We heaved the small anchor up, and got it in out of the way of the other ; the gale still increased, but as it was right off the land, I was in no pain about the ship, which continued to drive, still dragging the anchor through the sand, with two hundred fathom of cable out ; being very solicitous to give the boats time to bring all on board before we were quit of the bank, I would not weigh. At two o'clock, however, the anchor was quite off the ground, and the ship was in deep water ; we were now therefore obliged to bring the cable to the capstern, and with great difficulty we got the anchor up. The gusts off the land were so violent, that,

not

not daring to show any canvas, we lay-to under our bare poles, and the water was frequently torn up, and whirled round in the air much higher than our mast heads. As the ship now drove from the island at a great rate, and night was coming on, I began to be in great pain for the boats, in which, besides my lieutenant, there were eight-and-twenty of my best men; but just in the dusk of the evening, I perceived one of them scudding before the seas, and making towards the ship: This proved to be the long-boat, which, in spite of all the efforts of those on board, had been forced from her grappling, and driven off the land. We took the best opportunity that offered to get her on board, but notwithstanding all our care, she received considerable damage as we were hoisting her in. She had on board ten of my people, who informed me, that when they were first driven from the shore, they had some fire-wood on board, but that they were obliged to throw that, and every thing else, into the sea, to lighten the boat. As we had yet seen nothing of the cutter, and had reason to fear that she also, with the tents, and the other eighteen people, besides the lieutenant, had been driven off the island, I gave her up for lost; knowing that if the night, which was now at hand, should overtake her in such a storm, she must inevitably perish. It was however possible that the people might be ashore, and therefore that, if the boat should be lost, they might still be preserved; for this reason I determined to regain the land as soon as possible. At midnight the weather became more moderate, so that we could carry our courses and topsails, and at four o'clock in the morning we crowded all the sail we could make. At ten o'clock, we were very near the shore; to our great concern, we saw nothing of the cutter, yet we continued to stand on till about noon, when we happily discovered her at a grappling, close under the land: We immediately ran to our glasses, by the help of which we saw the people getting into her, and about three o'clock, to our mutual and inexpressible joy, she came safe on board with all her people: They were however so exhausted with fatigue, that they could scarcely get up the ship's side. The lieutenant told me, that the night before he had attempted to come off, but that as soon as he had left the shore, a sudden squall so nearly filled the boat with water, that she was very near going to the bottom; but that all hands bailing with the utmost diligence and activity, they happily cleared

her:

her: That he then made for the land again, which, with the utmost difficulty, he regained, and having left a sufficient number on board the boat, to watch her, and keep her free from water, he with the rest of the people went on shore. That having passed the night in a state of inexpressible anxiety and distress, they looked out for the ship with the first dawn of the morning, and seeing nothing of her, concluded that she had perished in the storm, which they had never seen exceeded. They did not, however, sit down torpid in despair, but began immediately to clear the ground near the beach of brushes and weeds, and cut down several trees of which they made rollers to assist them in hauling up the boat, in order to secure her; intending, as they had no hope of the ship's return, to wait till the summer season, and then attempt to make the island of Juan Fernandes. They had now better hopes, and all sense of the dangers that were before us was for a while obliterated by the joy of our escape from those that were past.

From the 16th, when we were first driven from our anchoring-ground, to this time, we suffered an uninterrupted series of danger, fatigue, and misfortunes. The ship worked and sailed very ill, the weather was dark and tempestuous, with thunder, lightning, and rain, and the boats, which I was obliged to keep always employed, even when we were under sail, to procure us water, were in continual danger of being lost, as well by the hard gales which constantly blew, as by the sudden gusts which frequently rushed upon us with a violence that is scarcely to be conceived. This distress was the more severe as it was unexpected, for I had experienced very different weather in these parts about two years before with Commodore Byron. It has generally been thought, that upon this coast the winds are constantly from the S. to the S.W., though Frezier mentions his having had strong gales and high seas from the N.N.W. and N.W. quarter, which was unhappily my case.

Having once more got my people and boats safe on board, I made sail from this turbulent climate, and thought myself fortunate not to have left any thing behind me except the wood, which our people had cut for firing.

The island of Masafuero lies in latitude 33° 45′ S., longitude 80° 46′ W. of London. Its situation is west of Juan Fernandes, both being nearly in the same latitude, and by the globe, it is distant about thirty-one leagues. It is very high

high and mountainous, and at a distance appears like one hill or rock: It is of a triangular form, and about seven or eight leagues in circumference. The south part, which we saw when we first made the island, at a distance of three-and-twenty leagues, is much the highest: On the north end there are several spots of clear ground, which perhaps might admit of cultivation.

The author of the account of Lord Anson's voyage mentions only one part of this island as affording anchorage, which is on the north side, and in deep water, but we saw no part where there was not anchorage: On the west side in particular, there is anchorage at about a mile from the shore in twenty fathom, and at about two miles and a half in forty and forty-five fathom, with a fine black sand at the bottom. This author also says, that " there is a reef of rocks running off the eastern point of the island about two miles in length, which may be seen by the sea's breaking over them ;" but in this he is mistaken, there is no reef of rocks, or shoal running off the eastern point, but there is a reef of rocks and sand running off the western side, near the south end of it. He is also mistaken as to the distance of this island from Juan Fernandes, and its direction, for he says the distance is twenty-two leagues, and the direction W. by S., but we found the distance nearly one-third more, and the direction is due west, for, as I have before observed, the latitude of both islands is nearly the same. The goats that he mentions we found upon it in the same abundance, and equally easy to be caught.

On the south-west point of the island there is a remark-able rock with a hole in it, which is a good mark to come to an anchor on the western side, where there is the best bank of any about the place. About a mile and a half to the northward of this hole, there is a low point of land, and from this point runs the reef that has been just mentioned, in the direction of W. by S. to the distance of about three quarters of a mile, where the sea continually breaks upon it. To anchor, run in till the hole in the rock is shut in, about a cable's length upon this low point of land, then bearing S. by E.½E. and anchor in twenty and twenty-two fathom, fine black sand and shells: There is anchorage also at several places on the other sides of the island, particular-ly off the north point, in fourteen and fifteen fathom, with fine sand.

There

There is plenty of wood and water all round the island, but they are not to be procured without much difficulty. A great quantity of stones, and large fragments of the rock, have fallen from the high land all round the island, and upon these there breaks such a surf that a boat cannot safely come within a cable's length of the shore; there is therefore no landing here but by swimming from the boat, and then mooring her without the rocks, nor is there any method of getting off the wood and water but by hauling them to the boat with ropes: There are, however, many places where it would be very easy to make a commodious landing by building a wharf, which it would be worth while even for a single ship to do if she was to continue any time at the island.

This part of Masafuero is a very good place for refreshment, especially in the summer season: The goats have been mentioned already, and there is all round the island such plenty of fish, that a boat may, with three hooks and lines, catch as much as will serve an hundred people: Among others we caught excellent coal-fish, cavallies, cod, hallibut, and cray-fish. We took a king-fisher that weighed eighty-seven pounds, and was five feet and a half long, and the sharks were so ravenous, that when we were sounding one of them swallowed the lead, by which we hauled him above water, but as he then disgorged it, we lost him. The seals were so numerous, that I verily think if many thousands of them were killed in a night, they would not be missed in the morning: We were obliged to kill great numbers of them, as, when we walked the shore, they were continually running against us, making at the same time a most horrible noise. These animals yield excellent train oil, and their hearts and plucks are very good eating, being in taste something like those of a hog, and their skins are covered with the finest fur I ever saw of the kind. There are many birds here, and among others some very large hawks. Of the pintado birds, our people, as I have before observed, caught no less than seven hundred in one night. We had not much opportunity to examine the place for vegetable productions, but we saw several leaves of the mountain cabbage, which is a proof that the tree grows here.

SECTION

SECTION III.

The Passage from Masafuero to Queen Charlotte's Islands; several Mistakes corrected concerning Davis's Land, and an Account of some small Islands, supposed to be the same that were seen by Quiros.

WHEN we took our departure from Masafuero, we had a great sea from the N. W. with a swell of long billows from the southward, and the wind, which was from the S. W. to the W. N. W., obliged me to stand to the northward, in hope of getting the south-east trade-wind, for the ship was so dull a sailer, that there was no making her go without a strong wind in her favour. Having thus run farther to the northward than at first I intended, and finding myself not far from the parallel of latitude which has been assigned to two islands called Saint Ambrose, and Saint Felix or Saint Paul, I thought I should perform an acceptable service by examining if they were fit for shipping to refresh at, especially as the Spaniards having fortified Juan Fernandes, they might be found convenient for Great Britain, if she should hereafter be engaged in a Spanish war. These islands are laid down in Green's charts, which were published in the year 1753, from latitude 26° 20′ to 27° S., and from 1°¼ to 2°½ W. of Masafuero; I therefore hauled up with a design to keep in that latitude, but soon afterwards, consulting Robertson's Elements of Navigation, I found the island of Saint Ambrose there laid down in latitude 25° 30′ S., and 82° 20′ longitude west of London, and supposing that islands of so small an extent might be laid down with more exactness in this work than in the chart, I bore away more northward for that latitude; the event, however, proved that I should not have trusted him so far: I missed the islands, and as I saw great numbers of birds and fish, which are certain indications of land not far off, there is the greatest reason to conclude that I went to the northward of them. I am sorry to say that upon a farther examination of Robertson's tables of latitudes and longitudes, I found them erroneous in many particulars: This censure, however, if I had not thought it necessary to prevent future mischief, should have been suppressed.

Upon

Upon examining the account that is given by Wafer,
who was surgeon on board Captain Davis's ship, I think it
is probable that these two islands are the land that Davis
fell in with in his way to the southward from the Gallapago
islands, and that the land laid down in all the sea charts under the name of Davis's Land, has no existence, notwithstanding what is said in the account of Roggewein's voyage,
which was made in 1722, of land that they called Eastern
Island, which some have imagined to be a confirmation of
Davis's discovery, and the same land to which his name has
been given.

It is manifest from Wafer's narrative, that little credit is
due to the account kept on board Davis's ship, except with
respect to the latitude, for he acknowledges that they had
like to have perished by their making an allowance for the
variation of the needle westward, instead of eastward : He
tells us also that they steered S. by E. ¼ E. from the Gallapagos, till they made land in latitude 27° 20′ S., but it is
evident that such a course would carry them not to the
westward but to the eastward of the Gallapagos, and set
them at about the distance of two hundred leagues from
Capiapo, and not five hundred leagues, as he has alleged ;
for the variation here is not more than half a point to the
eastward now, and it must have been still less then, it having been increasing to the eastward on all this coast. The
course that Davis steered therefore, if the distance between
the islands of St Ambrose and St Felix, and the Gallapagos, as laid down in all our sea charts, is right, must have
brought him within sight of St Ambrose and St Felix,
when he had run the distance he mentions. The truth is,
that if there had been any such place as Davis's Land in
the situation which has been allotted to it in our sea charts,
I must have sailed over it, or at least have seen it, as will
appear in the course of this narrative.

I kept between the latitude 25° 50′ and 25° 30′, in search
of the islands I intended to examine, till I got five degrees
to the westward of our departure, and then seeing no land,
and the birds having left us, I hauled more to the southward, and got into latitude 27° 20′ S. where I continued till
we got between seventeen and eighteen degrees to the
westward of our departure. In this parallel we had light
airs and foul winds, with a strong northerly current, which
made me conjecture that we were near this Davis's Land,

for

for which we looked out with great diligence, but a fair wind springing up again, we steered west by south, which gradually brought us into the latitude of 28° ¼ S., so that it is evident I must have sailed over this land, or at least have seen it if there had been any such place. I afterwards kept in the latitude of 28° for forty degrees to the westward of my departure, or, according to my account, 121 degrees west of London, this being the highest south latitude the winds and weather would permit me to keep, so that I must have gone to the southward of the situation assigned to the supposed continent called Davis's Land in all our charts.[1]

We continued our search till Wednesday the 17th of June, when, in latitude 28° S., longitude 112° W., we saw many sea-birds, which flew in flocks, and some rock-weed, which made me conjecture that we were approaching, or had passed by, some land. At this time the wind blew hard from the northward, which made a great sea, but we had notwithstanding long rolling billows from the southward, so that whatever land was in that quarter, could be only small rocky islands; and I am inclined to believe that if there was land at all it was to the northward, possibly it might be Roggewein's eastern island, which he has placed in latitude 27° S., and which some geographers have supposed to be about seven hundred leagues distant from the continent of South America, if indeed any credit is to be given to his account.

It was now the depth of winter in these parts, and we had hard gales and high seas that frequently brought us under our courses and low sails: The winds were also variable, and though we were near the tropic, the weather was dark, hazy, and cold, with frequent thunder and lightning, sleet and rain. The sun was above the horizon about ten hours in the four-and-twenty, but we frequently passed many days together without seeing him; and the weather was so thick, that when he was below the horizon the darkness was dreadful: The gloominess of the weather was indeed not only a disagreeable, but a most dangerous circumstance, as we were often long without being able to make

an

---

[1] This was really the case, as will be seen in the account of one of Cook's Voyages. For there seems reason to believe, that the island called Easter Island, and sometimes Teapy, is the land which Captain Davis saw in 1686, and Roggewein visited in 1722. See what is said on this subject in vol. xi, p. 90, of this collection.—E.

an observation, and were, notwithstanding, obliged to carry all the sail we could spread, day and night, our ship being so bad a sailer, and our voyage so long, to prevent our perishing by hunger, which, with all its concomitant horrors, would otherwise be inevitable.

We continued our course westward till the evening of Thursday the 2d of July, when we discovered land to the northward of us. Upon approaching it the next day, it appeared like a great rock rising out of the sea: It was not more than five miles in circumference, and seemed to be uninhabited; it was, however, covered with trees, and we saw a small stream of fresh water running down one side of it. I would have landed upon it, but the surf, which at this season broke upon it with great violence, rendered it impossible. I got soundings on the west side of it at somewhat less than a mile from the shore, in twenty-five fathom, with a bottom of coral and sand; and it is probable that in fine summer weather landing here may not only be practicable but easy. We saw a great number of sea-birds hovering about it, at somewhat less than a mile from the shore, and the sea here seemed to have fish. It lies in latitude 25° 2′ S., longitude 133° 21′ W., and about a thousand leagues to the westward of the continent of America. It is so high that we saw it at the distance of more than fifteen leagues, and it having been discovered by a young gentleman, son to Major Pitcairn of the marines, who was unfortunately lost in the Aurora, we called it PITCAIRN'S ISLAND.

While we were in the neighbourhood of this island, the weather was extremely tempestuous, with long rolling billows from the southward, larger and higher than any I had seen before. The winds were variable, but blew chiefly from the S.S.W.W. and W.N.W. We had very seldom a gale to the eastward, so that we were prevented from keeping in a high south latitude, and were continually driving to the northward.

On the 4th, we found that the ship made a good deal of water, for having been so long labouring in high and turbulent seas, she was become very crazy; our sails also being much worn, were continually splitting, so that it was become necessary to keep the sail-maker constantly at work. The people had hitherto enjoyed good health, but they now began to be affected with the scurvy. While we

were

were in the Strait of Magellan, I caused a little awning to be made, which I covered with a clean painted canvas, that had been allowed me for a floor-cloth to my cabin, and with this we caught so much rain water, with but little trouble or attendance, that the people were never put to a short allowance of this important article : The awning also afforded shelter from the inclemency of the weather, and to these precautions I imputed our having escaped the scurvy so long, though perhaps it was in some measure owing to the mixture of spirit of vitriol with the water that was thus preserved, our surgeon putting a small quantity into every cask when it was filled up.

On Saturday the 11th, we discovered a small, low, flat island, which appeared to be almost level with the water's edge, and was covered with green trees: As it was to the south, and directly to windward of us, we could not fetch it. It lies in latitude 22° S., and longitude 141° 34' W.; and we called it the BISHOP OF OSNABURGH'S ISLAND, in honour of his majesty's second son.[2]

On the 12th, we fell in with two more small islands, which were covered with green trees, but appeared to be uninhabited. We were close in with the southermost, which proved to be a slip of land in the form of a half-moon, low, flat, and sandy: From the south end of it a reef runs out to the distance of about half a mile, on which the sea breaks with great fury. We found no anchorage, but the boat landed. It had a pleasant appearance, but afforded neither vegetables nor water; there were however many birds upon it, so tame that they suffered themselves to be taken by hand. The other island very much resembles this, and is distant from it about five or six leagues: They lie W.N.W. and E.S.E of each other. One of them is in latitude 20° 38' S., longitude 146° W.; the other 20° 34' S., longitude 146' 15' W., and we called them the DUKE OF GLOUCESTER'S ISLANDS; the variation here is five degrees east. These islands are probably the land seen by Quiros, as the situation is nearly the same; but if not, the land he saw could not be more considerable: Whatever it was, he went to the southward of it, and the long billows we had here, convinced us that there was no land near us in that direction.

[2] There is another island of this name, among those that were discovered by Captain Wallis.

direction. The wind here being to the eastward, I hauled to the southward again, and the next day, Monday the 13th, in the evening, as we were steering W. S. W. we observed that we lost the long southerly billows, and that we got them again at seven o'clock the next day. When we lost them we were in latitude 21° 7′ S., longitude 147° 4′ W.; and when we got them again we were in latitude 21° 43 S., longitude 149° 48′ W; so that I imagine there was some land to the southward, not far distant. [3]

From this time to the 16th, the winds were variable from N. E. round by the N. the N. W. and S. W. and blew very hard, with violent gusts, one of which was very near being fatal to us, with thick weather and hard rain. We were then in latitude 22° S., and 70° 30′ W. of our departure, where we found the variation 6° 30′ E. and the tempestuous gales were succeeded by a dead calm. After some time, however, the wind sprung up again at west, and at length settled in the W. S. W. which soon drove us again to the northward, so that on the 20th we were in latitude 19° S., longitude 75° 30′ W. of our departure : The variation was here 6° E.

On the 22d, we were got into latitude 18° S., longitude 161° W., which was about one thousand eight hundred leagues to the westward of the continent of America, and in all this track we had no indication of a continent. The men now began to be very sickly, the scurvy having made great progress among them, and as I found that all my endeavours to keep in a high southern latitude at this time were ineffectual, and that the badness of the weather, the variableness of the winds, and above all, the defects of the ship, rendered our progress slow, I thought it absolutely necessary to fix upon that course which was most likely to preserve the vessel and the crew; instead therefore of attempting to return back by the south-east, in which, considering our condition, and the advanced season of the year, it was scarcely possible that we should succeed, I bore away to the northward, that I might get into the trade-wind, keeping still in such a track, as if the charts were to be trusted, was most likely to bring me to some island, where the refreshments of which we stood so much in need might
be

[3] The Islands called Oheteroa, Toobouai, Vabouai, Vavitoo, lie a little to the south of this part of Carteret's track.—E.

be procured intending then, if the ship could be put in a proper condition, to have pursued the voyage to the southward, when the fit season should return, to have attempted farther discoveries in this track ; and, if I should discover a continent, and procure a sufficient supply of provisions there, to keep along the coast to the southward till the sun had crossed the equinoctial, and then, getting into a high southern latitude, either have gone west about to the Cape of Good Hope, or returned to the eastward, and having touched at Falkland's Islands, if necessary, made the best of my way from thence back to Europe.

When I got into latitude 16° S. and not before, I found the true trade-wind ; and as we proceeded to the northwest, and the northward, we found the variation increase very fast ; for when we had advanced to latitude 18° 15' S. and were in longitude 80°¼ W. of our departure, it was 7° 30' E. We had bad weather, with hard gales, and a great sea from the eastward till the 25th, when, being in latitude 12° 15' S., we saw many birds flying in flocks, and supposed ourselves to be near some land, particularly several islands that are laid down in the charts, and one which was seen by Commodore Byron in 1765, and called the Island of Danger ; none of these islands, however, could we see. At this time it blew so hard, that, although we went before the wind, we were obliged to reef our top-sails, and the weather was still very thick and rainy. The next morning, being in latitude 10° S., longitude 167° W., we kept nearly in the same parallel, in hopes to have fallen in with some of the islands called Solomon's Islands, this being the latitude in which the southermost of them is laid down. We had here the trade-wind strong, with violent squalls and much rain, and continuing our course till Monday the 3d of August, we were then in latitude 10° 18' S. longitude, by account, 177° ¼ E. ; our distance west from the continent of America about twenty-one hundred leagues, and we were five degrees to the westward of the situation of those islands in the charts. It was not our good fortune, however, to fall in with any land ; probably we might pass near some, which the thick weather prevented our seeing ; for in this run great numbers of sea birds were often about the ship : However, as Commodore Byron in his last voyage sailed over the northern limits of that part of the ocean in which the Islands of Solomon are said to lie, and as I sailed

ed over the southern limits without seeing them, there is great reason to conclude, that, if there are any such islands, their situation in all our charts is erroneously laid down.[4]

From the latitude 14° S., longitude 168° 46' W., we had a strong gale from the S.E. which made a great sea after us, and from that time I did not observe the long billows from the southward till we got into latitude 10° 18' S., longitude 177° 30' E., and then it returned from the S.W. and S.S.W. and we found a current setting to the southward, although a current in the contrary direction had attended us almost all the way from the Streight of Magellan; I conjectured therefore that here the passage opened between New Zealand and New Holland. The variation here was 11° 14' E. On the 5th, being in latitude 10° ½ S., longitude 175° 44' E., the variation was 11° 15' E.; and on the 8th, in latitude 11° S., longitude 171° 14' E. it was 11° ½ E.

About this time we found our stock of log-lines nearly expended, though we had already converted all our fishing lines to the same use. I was some time in great perplexity how to supply this defect, but, upon a very diligent enquiry, found that we had, by chance, a few fathom of thick untarred rope. This, which in our situation was an inestimable treasure, I ordered to be untwisted; but as the yarns were found to be too thick for our purpose, it became necessary to pick them into oakham; and when this was done, the most difficult part of the work remained; for this oakham could not be spun into yarn, till, by combing, it was brought into hemp, its original state. This was not seamen's work, and if it had, we should have been at a loss how to perform it for want of combs; one difficulty therefore arose upon another, and it was necessary to make combs, before we could try our skill in making hemp. Upon this trying occasion we were again sensible of the danger to which we were exposed by the want of a forge: Necessity, however, the fruitful mother of invention, suggested an expedient. The armourer was set to work to file nails down to a smooth point, with which we produced a tolerable succedaneum for a comb; and one of the quarter-masters was found sufficient-

ly

---

[4] See what is said on this subject in the account of Byron's voyage. It will be resumed when we come to speak of some of Cook's discoveries.—E.

ly skilled in the use of this instrument to render the oakham so smooth and even, that we contrived to spin it into yarn, as fine as our coarse implements would admit; and thus we made tolerable log-lines, although we found it much more difficult than to make cordage of our old cables, after they had been converted into junk, which was an expedient that we had been obliged to practise long before. We had also long before used all our sewing sail-twine, and if, knowing that the quantity with which I had been supplied was altogether inadequate to the wants of such a voyage, I had not taken the whole quantity that had been put on board to repair the seine into my own custody, this deficiency might have been fatal to us all.

SECTION IV.

An Account of the Discovery of Queen Charlotte's Islands, with a Description of them and their Inhabitants, and of what happened at Egmont Island.

THE scurvy still continued to make great progress among us, and those hands that were not rendered useless by disease, were worn down by excessive labour; our vessel, which at best was a dull sailer, had been long in so bad a condition that she would not work; and on the 10th, to render our condition still more distressful and alarming, she sprung a leak in the bows, which being under water, it was impossible to get at while we were at sea. Such was our situation, when, on the 12th, at break of day, we discovered land: The sudden transport of hope and joy which this inspired, can perhaps be equalled only by that which a criminal feels who hears the cry of a reprieve at the place of execution. The land proved to be a cluster of islands, of which I counted seven, and believe there were many more. We kept on for two of them, which were right a-head when land was first discovered, and seemed to lie close together; in the evening we anchored on the north-east side of one of them, which was the largest and the highest of the two, in about thirty fathom, with a good bottom, and at the distance of about three cables' length from the shore. We soon after saw two of the natives, who were black, with woolly heads, and stark naked; I immediately sent the master out with the boat to fix upon a watering-place, and speak to them, but they disappeared before she could reach the shore. The boat soon after returned with an account that there was a fine run of fresh water a-breast of the ship and close to the beach, but that the whole country in that part being an almost impenetrable forest quite to the water's edge, the watering would be very difficult, and even danger-ous, if the natives should come down to prevent it: That there were no esculent vegetables, for the refreshment of the sick, nor any habitations as far as the country had been examined, which was wild, forlorn, and mountainous.

Having considered this account, and finding that a swell, which came round the eastern part of the bay, would ren-der watering troublesome and inconvenient, exclusive of the danger that might be apprehended from the natives, if they should attack us from ambushes in the wood, I deter-mined to try whether a better situation could not be found.

The next morning, therefore, as soon as it was light, I dispatched the master, with fifteen men in the cutter, well armed and provided, to examine the coast to the westward, our present situation being on the lee of the island, for a place where we might more conveniently be supplied with wood and water, and at the same time procure some refresh-ments for the sick, and lay the ship by the stern to examine and stop the leak. I gave him some beads, ribbons, and other trifles, which by chance I happened to have on board, to conciliate the good-will of the natives, if he should hap-pen to meet with any of them; but at the same time enjoin-ed him to run no risk, and gave him particular orders im-mediately to return to the ship, if any number of canoes should approach him which might bring on hostilities; and if he should meet the Indians in small parties, either at sea or upon shore, to treat them with all possible kindness, so as to establish a friendly intercourse with them; charging him on no account to leave the boat himself, nor to suffer more than two men to go on shore at a time, while the rest stood ready for their defence; recommending to him, in the strongest terms, an application to his duty, without regard-ing any other object, as the finding a proper place for the ship was of the utmost importance to us all; and conjuring him to return as soon as this service should be performed, with all possible speed.

Soon after I had dispatched the cutter on this expedition,

I sent

I sent the long-boat with ten men on board well armed to the shore, who before eight o'clock brought off a tun of water. About nine, I sent her off again, but soon after seeing some of the natives advancing along the shore towards the place where the men landed, I made the signal for them to return, not knowing to what number they would be exposed, and having no boat to send off with assistance if they should be attacked.

Our men had not long returned on board, when we saw three of the natives sit down under the trees a-breast of the ship. As they continued there gazing at us till the afternoon, as soon as the cutter came in sight, not caring that both the boats should be absent at the same time, I sent my lieutenant in the long-boat, with a few beads, ribbons, and trinkets, to endeavour to establish some kind of intercourse with them, and by their means, with the rest of the inhabitants; these men, however, before the boat could reach the shore, quitted their station, and proceeded along the beach. As the trees would soon prevent their being seen by our people, who were making towards the land, we kept our eyes fixed upon them from the ship, and very soon perceived that they were met by three others. After some conversation, the first three went on, and those who met them proceeded towards the boat with a hasty pace. Upon this, I made the signal to the lieutenant to be upon his guard, and as soon as he saw the Indians, observing that there were no more than three, he backed the boat into the shore, and making signs of friendship, held up to them the beads and ribbons which I had given him as presents, our people at the same time carefully concealing their arms. The Indians, however, taking no notice of the beads and ribbons, resolutely advanced within bow-shot, and then suddenly discharged their arrows, which happily went over the boat without doing any mischief; they did not prepare for a second discharge, but instantly ran away into the woods, and our people discharged some musquets after them, but none of them were wounded by the shot. Soon after this happened, the cutter came under the ship's side, and the first person that I particularly noticed was the master, with three arrows sticking in his body. No other evidence was necessary to convict him of having acted contrary to my orders, which appeared indeed more fully from his own account of the matter, which it is reasonable to suppose was as favourable

able to himself as he could make it. He said, that having seen some Indian houses with only five or six of the inhabitants, at a place about fourteen or fifteen miles to the westward of the ship's station, where he had sounded some bays, he came to a grappling, and veered the boat to the beach, where he landed with four men, armed with musquets and pistols; that the Indians at first were afraid of him, and retired, but that soon after they came down to him, and he gave them some beads and other trifles, with which they seemed to be much pleased: That he then made signs to them for some cocoa-nuts, which they brought him, and with great appearance of friendship and hospitality, gave him a broiled fish and some boiled yams: That he then proceeded with his party to the houses, which, he said, were not more than fifteen or twenty yards from the water-side, and soon after saw a great number of canoes coming round the western point of the bay, and many Indians among the trees: That being alarmed at these appearances, he hastily left the house where they had been received, and with the men, made the best of his way towards the boat; but that, before he could get on board, the Indians attacked as well those that were with him as those that were in the boat, both from the canoes and the shore. Their number, he said, was between three and four hundred: Their weapons were bows and arrows, the bows were six feet five inches long, and the arrows four feet four, which they discharged in platoons, as regularly as the best disciplined troops in Europe: That it being necessary to defend himself and his people when they were thus attacked, they fired among the Indians to favour their getting into their boat, and did great execution, killing many and wounding more: That they were not however discouraged, but continued to press forward, still discharging their arrows by platoons in almost one continued flight: That the grappling being foul, occasioned a delay in hauling off the boat, during which time he, and half of the boat's crew, were desperately wounded: That at last they cut the rope, and ran off under their foresail, still keeping up their fire with blunderbusses, each loaded with eight or ten pistol balls, which the Indians returned with their arrows, those on shore wading after them breast-high into the sea: When they had got clear of these, the canoes pursued them with great fortitude and vigour, till one of them was

sunk,

sunk, and the numbers on board the rest greatly reduced by the fire, and then they returned to the shore.

Such was the story of the master, who, with three of my best seamen, died some time afterwards of the wounds they had received; but culpable as he appears to have been by his own account, he appears to have been still more so by the testimony of those who survived him. They said, that the Indians behaved with the greatest confidence and friendship till he gave them just cause of offence, by ordering the people that were with him, who had been regaled in one of their houses, to cut down a cocoa-nut tree, and insisting upon the execution of his order, notwithstanding the displeasure which the Indians strongly expressed upon the occasion: As soon as the tree fell, all of them except one, who seemed to be a person of authority, went away; and in a short time a great number of them were observed to draw together into a body among the trees, by a midshipman who was one of the party that were on shore, and who immediately acquainted the master with what he had seen, and told him, that from the behaviour of the people he imagined an attack was intended: That the master made light of the intelligence, and instead of repairing immediately to the boat, as he was urged to do, fired one of his pistols at a mark: That the Indian who had till that time continued with them left them abruptly, and joined the body in the wood: That the master, even after this, by an infatuation that is altogether unaccountable, continued to trifle away his time on shore, and did not attempt to recover the boat till the attack was begun.

As the expedition to find a better place for the ship had issued thus unhappily, I determined to try what could be done where we lay; the next day, therefore, the ship was brought down by the stern, as far as we could effect it, and the carpenter, the only one of the crew who was in tolerable health, caulked the bows, as far down as he could come at the bottom; and though he did not quite stop the leak, he very much reduced it. In the afternoon a fresh gale set right into the bay, which made the ship ride with her stern very near the shore, and we observed a great number of the natives sculking among the trees upon the beach, who probably expected that the wind would have forced the ship on shore.

The next morning, the weather being fine, we veered the
ship

ship close in shore, with a spring upon our cable, so that we brought our broadside to bear upon the watering-place, for the protection of the boats that were to be employed there. As there was reason to suppose that the natives whom we had seen among the trees the night before, were not now far distant, I fired a couple of shot into the wood, before I sent the waterers ashore; I also sent the lieutenant in the cutter, well manned and armed, with the boat that carried them, and ordered him and his people to keep on board, and lie close to the beach, to cover the watering-boat while she was loading, and to keep discharging muskets into the wood on each side of the party that were filling the water. These orders were well executed, the beach was steep, so that the boats could lie close to the people that were at work, and the lieutenant from the cutter fired three or four vollies of small arms into the woods before any of the men went on shore, and none of the natives appearing, the waterers landed and went to work. But notwithstanding all these precautions, before they had been on shore a quarter of an hour, a flight of arrows was discharged among them, one of which dangerously wounded a man that was filling water in the breast, and another stuck into a bareca on which Mr Pitcairn was sitting. The people on board the cutter immediately fired several vollies of small arms into that part of the wood from which the arrows came, and I recalled the boats that I might more effectually drive the Indians from their ambuscades with grape-shot from the ship's guns. When the boats and people were on board, we began to fire, and soon after saw about two hundred men rush out of the woods, and run along the beach with the utmost precipitation. We judged the coast to be now effectually cleared, but in a little time we perceived that a great number had got together on the westermost point of the bay, where they probably thought themselves beyond our reach: To convince them therefore of the contrary, I ordered a gun to be fired at them with round shot; the ball just grazing the water rose again, and fell in the middle of them, upon which they dispersed with great hurry and confusion, and we saw no more of them. After this we watered without any farther molestation, but all the while our boats were on shore, we had the precaution to keep firing the ship's guns into the wood on both sides of them, and the cutter, which lay close to the beach, as she did before,

kept

kept up a constant fire of small arms in platoons, at the same time. As we saw none of the natives during all this firing, we should have thought that none of them had ventured back into the wood, if our people had not reported that they heard groans from several parts of it, like those of dying men.

Hitherto, though I had been long ill of an inflammatory and bilious disorder, I had been able to keep the deck; but this evening the symptoms became so much more threatening that I could keep up no longer, and I was for some time afterwards confined to my bed. The master was dying of the wounds he received in his quarrel with the Indians, the lieutenant also was very ill, the gunner and thirty of my men incapable of duty, among whom were seven of the most vigorous and healthy, that had been wounded with the master, and three of them mortally, and there was no hope of obtaining such refreshments as we most needed in this place. These were discouraging circumstances, and not only put an end to my hopes of prosecuting the voyage farther to southward, but greatly dispirited the people; except myself, the master, and the lieutenant, there was nobody on board capable of navigating the ship home; the master was known to be a dying man, and the recovery of myself and the lieutenant was very doubtful. I would however have made a further effort to obtain refreshments here, if I had been furnished with any toys, iron tools, or cutlery-ware, which might have enabled me to recover the goodwill of the natives, and establish a traffic with them for such necessaries as they could have furnished us with; but I had no such articles, and but very few others fit for an Indian trade; and not being in a condition to risk the loss of any more of the few men who were capable of doing duty, I weighed anchor at day-break on Monday the 17th, and stood along the shore for that part of the island to which I had sent the cutter. To the island I had given the name of *Egmont Island*, in honour of the Earl: It certainly is the same to which the Spaniards have given the name of Santa Cruz, as appears by the accounts which their writers have given of it, and I called the place in which we had lain, *Swallow Bay*. From the easternmost point of this bay, which I called *Swallow Point*, to the north-east point of the island, which I called *Cape Byron*, is about seven miles east, and from the westernmost point of the bay, which I called *Han-*

way's

way's Point, to Cape Byron, is about ten or eleven miles.
Between Swallow Point and Hanway's Point, in the bottom
of the bay, there is a third point, which does not run out so
far, and a little to the westward of this point is the best anchoring-place, but it is necessary to give it birth, as the
ground near it is shoaly. When we were at anchor in this
bay, Swallow Point bore E. by N. and Hanway's Point
W.N.W. From this Point there runs a reef, on which the
sea breaks very high: The outer part of this reef bore N.W.
by W. and an island which has the appearance of a volcano,
was just over the breakers. Soon after we had passed Hanway's Point, we saw a small village, which stands upon the
beach, and is surrounded by cocoa-nut trees. It is situated in a bay between Hanway's Point and another, to which
I gave the name of *Howe's Point.* The distance from Hanway's Point to Howe's Point is between four and five miles.
Close to the shore there is about thirty fathom of water;
but in crossing the bay, at the distance of about two miles,
we had no bottom. Having passed Howe's Point, we opened another bay or harbour, which had the appearance of a
deep lagoon, and which we called *Carlisle Harbour.* Over-
against the entrance of Carlisle Harbour, and north of the
coast, we found a small island, which we called *Portland's
Island.* On the west side of this island there is a reef of
rocks that runs to the main; the passage into the harbour,
therefore, is on the east side of it, and runs in and out E.
N.E. and W.S.W. it is about two cables' length wide, and
has about eight fathom water. I believe the harbour within it to be good; but a ship would be obliged to warp both
in and out, and would after all be in danger of an attack
by the natives, who are bold even to temerity, and have a
perseverance which is not common among undisciplined
savages. When the ship was a mile from the shore, we had
no ground with fifty fathom. About four or five miles west
from Portland's Island, is a fine, small, round harbour, just
big enough to receive three ships, which we called *Byron's
Harbour.* When we were abreast of the entrance of it, it
bore from us S. by E. ½ E. and the Volcano Island bore
N.W. ¼ W. Our boat entered it, and found two runs of
water, one fresh and the other salt; by the run of salt water we judged that it had a communication with Carlisle
Harbour. When we had proceeded about three leagues
from the harbour, we opened the bay where the cutter had
been

been attacked by the Indians, to which, for that reason, we gave the name of *Bloody Bay*. In this bay is a small rivulet of fresh water, and here we saw many houses regularly built: Close to the water-side stood one much longer than any of the rest, which seemed to be a kind of common-hall, or council-house, and was neatly built and thatched. This was the building in which our people had been received who were on shore here with the master; and they told me that both the sides and floor were lined with a kind of fine matting, and a great number of arrows, made up into bundles, were hung up in it ready for use. They told me also, that at this place there were many gardens, or plantations, which are enclosed by a fence of stone, and planted with cocoa-nut trees, bananas, plantains, yams, and other vegetables. The cocoa-nut trees we saw from the ship in great numbers, among the houses of the village. About three miles to the westward of this town we saw another of considerable extent; in the front of which, next to the water-side, there was a breast-work of stone, about four feet six inches high, not in a straight line, but in angles, like a fortification; and there is great reason to suppose, from the weapons of these people, and their military courage, which must in great measure be the effect of habit, that they have frequent wars among themselves. As we proceeded westward from this place, we found, at the distance of two or three miles, a small bight, forming a kind of bay, in which a river empties itself. Upon taking a view of this river from the mast-head, it appeared to run very far into the country, and at the entrance, at least, to be navigable for small vessels. This river we called *Granville's River,* and to the westward of it is a point, to which we gave the name of *Ferrer's Point.* From this point the land forms a large bay, and near it is a town of great extent, which seemed to swarm like a bee-hive: An incredible multitude came out of it as the ship passed by, holding something in their hands which looked like a wisp of green grass, with which they seemed to stroke each other, at the same time dancing, or running in a ring. About seven miles to the westward of Point Ferrers, is another that was called *Carteret Point,* from which a reef of rocks, that appears above water, runs out to the distance of about a cable's length. Upon this point we saw a large canoe, with an awning or shade built over it; and a little to the westward, another

another large town, fronted, and probably surrounded, with a breastwork of stone, like the last.   Here also the people thronged to the beach as the ship was passing, and performed the same kind of circular dance. After a little time they launched several canoes, and made towards us ; upon which we lay-to, that they might have time to come up, and we conceived great hopes that we should prevail upon them to come on board ; but when they came near enough to have a more distinct view of us, they lay upon their paddles and gazed at us, but seemed to have no design of advancing farther ; and therefore we made sail and left them behind us.   About half a mile from **Carteret Point,** we had sixty fathom, with a bottom of sand and coral. From this point the land trends away W.S.W. and S.W. forming a deep lagoon, at the mouth of which lies an island, that with the main forms two entrances into it. The island we called *Trevanion's Island.*   This entrance is about two miles wide, and the lagoon, if there is anchorage in it, is certainly a fine harbour for shipping.   After crossing the first entrance, and coming off the north-west part of Trevanion's Island, which we called *Cape Trevanion,* we saw a great rippling, and therefore sent the boat off to sound. We had, however, no bottom with fifty fathom ; the rippling being caused only by the meeting of the tides.   Having hauled round this cape, we found the land trend to the southward ; and we continued to stand along the shore till we opened the western passage into the lagoon between Trevanion's Island and the main.   In this place, both the main and the island appeared to be one continued town, and the inhabitants were innumerable.   We sent a boat to examine this entrance or passage, and found the bottom to be coral and rock, with very irregular soundings over it. As soon as the natives saw the boat leave the ship, they sent off several armed canoes to attack her. The first that came within bow-shot discharged her arrows at the people on board, who, being ready, fired a volley, by which one of the Indians was killed, and another wounded ; at the same time we fired a great gun from the ship, loaded with grape-shot, among them ; upon which they all pulled back to the shore with great precipitation, except the canoe which began the attack ; and that being secured by the boat's crew, with the wounded man in her, was brought to the ship.   I immediately ordered the Indian to be taken on board, and
the

the surgeon to examine his wounds. It appeared that one shot had gone through his head, and that his arm was broken by another: The surgeon was of opinion that the wound in his head was mortal; I therefore ordered him to be put again into his canoe, and, notwithstanding his condition, he paddled away towards the shore. He was a young man, with a woolly head, like that of the negroes, and a small beard, but he was well-featured, and not so black as the natives of Guinea. He was of the common stature, and, like all the rest of the people whom we had seen upon this island, quite naked. His canoe was very small, and of rude workmanship, being nothing more than part of the trunk of a tree made hollow; it had, however, an outrigger, but none of them had sails.

We found this place to be the western extremity of the island on the north side, and that it lay in exactly the same latitude as the eastern extremity on the same side. The distance between them is about fifty miles due east and west, and a strong current sets westward along the shore.

I was still confined to my bed, and it was with infinite regret that I gave up the hopes of obtaining refreshments at this place, especially as our people told me they saw hogs and poultry in great plenty as we sailed along the shore, with cocoa-nut trees, plantains, bananas, and a variety of other vegetable productions, which would soon have restored to us the health and vigour we had lost, by the fatigue and hardships of a long voyage; but no friendly intercourse with the natives could now be expected, and I was not in a situation to obtain what I wanted by force. I was myself dangerously ill, great part of my crew, as I have already observed, was disabled, and the rest dispirited by disappointment and vexation, and if the men had been all in health and spirits, I had not officers to lead them on or direct them in any enterprise, nor even to superintend the duties that were to be performed on board the ship. These disadvantages, which prevented my obtaining refreshments at this island, prevented me also from examining the rest that were near it. Our little strength was every minute becoming less; I was not in a condition to pursue the voyage to the southward, and was in danger of losing the monsoon, so that no time was now to be lost; I therefore gave orders to steer northward, hoping to refresh at the country which Dampier has called *Nova Britannia.* I shall, however,
ever,

ever, give the best account I can of the appearance and situation of the islands that I left behind me.

I gave the general name of *Queen Charlotte's Islands* to
the whole cluster, as well to those I did not see distinctly,
as to those that I did; and I gave several of them particular names as I approached them.

To the southermost of the two, which when we first discovered land were right a-head, I gave the name of *Lord
Howe's Island*, and the other was Egmont Island, of which
some account has already been given. The latitude of Lord
Howe's Island is 11° 10′ S. longitude 164° 43′ E. The latitude of Cape Byron, the north-east point of Egmont Island,
is 10° 40′ S. longitude 164° 49′ E. The east sides of these
two islands, which lie exactly in a line with each other,
about N. by W. and S. by E. including the passage between
them, extend about eleven leagues, and the passage is
about four miles broad; both of them appear to be fertile,
and have a pleasant appearance, being covered with tall
trees, of a beautiful verdure. Lord Howe's Island, though
more flat and even than the other, is notwithstanding high
land. About thirteen leagues W.N.W. ¾ N. by compass,
from Cape Byron, there is an island of a stupendous height,
and a conical figure. The top of it is shaped like a funnel, from which we saw smoke issue, though no flame; it
is, however, certainly a volcano, and therefore I called it
Volcano Island. To a long flat island that, when Howe's
and Egmont's islands were right a-head, bore N.W. I gave
the name of *Keppel's Island.* It lies in latitude 10° 15′ S.
longitude, by account, 165° 4′ E. The largest of two others
to the S.E. I called *Lord Edgcumb's Island.* The small
one I called *Ourry's Island.* Edgcumb's Island has a fine
pleasant appearance, and lies in latitude 11° 10′ S. longitude 165° 14′ E. The latitude of Ourry's Island is 11° 10′
S. longitude 165° 19′ E. The other islands, of which there
were several, I did not particularly name.

The inhabitants of Egmont island, whose persons have
been described already, are extremely nimble, vigorous,
and active, and seem to be almost as well qualified to live
in the water as upon the land, for they were in and out of
their canoes almost every minute. The canoes that came
out against us from the west end of the island, were all like
that which our people brought on board, and might probably, upon occasion, carry about a dozen men, though
three or four manage them with amazing dexterity: We
saw,

saw, however, others of a large size upon the beach, with awnings or shades over them.

We got two of their bows, and a bundle of their arrows, from the canoe that was taken with the wounded man; and with these weapons they do execution at an incredible distance. One of them went through the boat's washboard, and dangerously wounded a midshipman in the thigh. Their arrows were pointed with flint, and we saw among them no appearance of any metal. The country in general is woody and mountainous, with many vallies intermixed; several small rivers flow from the interior part of the country into the sea, and there are many harbours upon the coast. The variation here was about 11° 15′ E.

SECTION V.

Departure from Egmont Island, and Passage to Nova Britannia; with a Description of several other Islands, and their Inhabitants.

WE made sail from this island in the evening of Tuesday the 18th of August, with a fresh trade-wind from the eastward, and a few squalls at times. At first we only hauled up W.N.W. for I was not without hope of falling in with some other islands, where we might be more fortunate than we had been at those we left, before we got the length of Nova Britannia.

On the 20th, we discovered a small, flat, low island, and got up with it in the evening. It lies in latitude 7° 56′ S. longitude 158° 56′ E. and I gave it the name of *Gower's Island.* To our great mortification we found no anchorage here, and could procure only a few cocoa-nuts from the inhabitants, (who were much the same kind of people that we had seen at Isle Egmont,) in exchange for nails, and such trifles as we had; they promised, by signs, to bring us more the next day, and we kept off and on all night. The night was extremely dark; and the next morning at day-break, we found that a current had set us considerably to the southward of the island, and brought us within sight of two more. They were situated nearly east and west of each other, and were distant about two miles. That to the eastward is much the smallest, and this we called *Simpson's Island*; to the other, which

which is lofty, and has a stately appearance, we gave the
name of *Carteret's Island.* The east end of it bears about
south from Gower's island, and the distance between them
is about ten or eleven leagues. Carteret's Island lies in
about the latitude of 8° 26' S. longitude 159° 14 E. and its
length from east to west is about six leagues. We found
the variation here 8° 30' E. Both these islands were right
to windward of us, and we bore down to Gower's Island.
It is about two leagues and a half long on the western side,
which makes in bays: The whole is well wooded, and many
of the trees are cocoa-nut. We found here a considerable
number of the Indians, with two boats or canoes, which we
supposed to belong to Carteret's Island, and to have brought
the people hither only to fish. We sent the boat on shore,
which the natives endeavoured to cut off; and hostilities
being thus commenced, we seized their canoe, in which we
found about an hundred cocoa-nuts, which were very acceptable. We saw some turtle near the beach, but were
not fortunate enough to take any of them. The canoe, or
boat, was large enough to carry eight or ten men, and was
very neatly built, with planks well jointed; it was adorned
with shell-work, and figures rudely painted, and the seams
were covered with a substance somewhat like our black
putty, but it appeared to me to be of a better consistence.
The people were armed with bows, arrows, and spears; the
spears and arrows were pointed with flint. By some signs
which they made, pointing to our muskets, we imagined
they were not wholly unacquainted with fire-arms. They
are much the same kind of people as we had seen at Egmont island, and, like them, were quite naked; but their
canoes were of a very different structure, and a much larger
size, though we did not discover that any of them had sails.
The cocoa-nuts which we got here, and at Egmont island,
were of infinite advantage to the sick.

From the time of our leaving Egmont island, we had observed a current setting strongly to the southward, and in
the neighbourhood of these islands we found its force greatly increased: This determined me, when I sailed from
Gower's island, to steer N.W. fearing we might otherwise
fall in with the main land too far to the southward; for if
we had got into any gulph or deep bay, our crew was so
sickly, and our ship so bad, that it would have been impossible for us to have got out again.

About

About eight o'clock in the morning of the 22d, as we were continuing our course with a fine fresh gale, Patrick Dwyer, one of the marines, who was doing something over the ship's quarter, by some accident missed his hold and fell into the sea; we instantly threw overboard the canoe which we had seized at Gower's island, brought the ship to, and hoisted out the cutter with all possible expedition; but the poor fellow, though remarkably strong and healthy, sunk at once, and we saw him no more. We took the canoe on board again; but she had received so much damage by striking against one of the guns, as the people were hoisting her overboard, that we were obliged to cut her up.

In the night of Monday the 24th, we fell in with nine islands. They stretch nearly N.W. by W. and S.E. by E. about fifteen leagues, and lie in latitude 4° 36' S. longitude 154° 17' E. according to the ship's account. I imagine these to be the islands which are called Ohang Java, and were discovered by Tasman; for the situation answers very nearly to their place in the French chart, which in the year 1756 was corrected for the king's ships. The other islands, Carteret's, Gower's, and Simpson's, I believe had never been seen by an European navigator before. There is certainly much land in this part of the ocean not yet known.

One of these islands is of considerable extent, the other eight are scarcely better than large rocks; but though they are low and flat, they are well covered with wood, and abound with inhabitants. The people are black, and woolly-headed, like the negroes of Africa: Their weapons are bows and arrows; and they have large canoes which they navigate with a sail, one of which came near us, but would not venture on board.

We went to the northward of these islands, and steered W. by S. with a strong south-westerly current. At eleven o'clock at night, we fell in with another island of a considerable extent, flat, green, and of a pleasant appearance. We saw none of its inhabitants; but it appeared by the many fires which we saw in the night to be well peopled. It lies in latitude 4° 50' S. and bears west fifteen leagues from the northermost of the Nine Islands, and we called it *Sir Charles Hardy's Island.*

At day-break the next morning, we discovered another large high island, which, rising in three considerable hills, had, at a distance, the appearance of three islands. We

gave

gave it the name of *Winchelsea's Island;* it is distant from
Sir Charles Hardy's island about ten leagues, in the direction of S. by E. We had here the wind squally, with unsettled weather, and a very strong westerly current

About ten o'clock in the morning of the 26th, we saw
another large island to the northward, which I supposed to
be the same that was dicovered by Schouten, and called
the island of Saint John.   Soon after we saw high land to
the westward, which proved to be Nova Britannia; and as
we approached it we found a very strong S.S. westerly current, setting at the rate of no less than thirty-two miles a-
day. The next day, having only light winds, a north-westerly current set us into a deep bay or gulph, which proved
to be that which Dampier has distinguished by the name
of Saint George's Bay.

On the 28th, we anchored in a bay near a little island at
the distance of about three leagues to the N.W. of Cape
Saint George, which was called *Wallis's Island.* I found the
latitude of this Cape to be about 5° S. and its longitude
by account 152° 19' E. which is about two thousand five
hundred leagues due west from the continent of America,
and about one degree and a half more to the eastward
than its place in the French chart which has been just mentioned.   In the afternoon I sent the cutter to examine the
coast, and the other boat to get some cocoa-nuts, and haul
the seine.   The people in this boat caught no fish, but they
brought on board about an hundred and fifty cocoa-nuts,
which were distributed to the men at the surgeon's discretion. We had seen some turtle as we were coming into the
bay, and hoping that some of them might repair to the
island in the night, especially as it was sandy, barren, and
uninhabited, like the places these animals most frequent, I
sent a few men on shore to watch for them, but they returned in the morning without success.

We anchored here only to wait till the boats could find
a fit place for our purpose; and several very good harbours
being discovered not far distant, we now endeavoured to
weigh anchor, but, with the united strength of our whole
company, were not able: This was an alarming proof of our
debility, and with heavy hearts we had recourse to an additional purchase; with this assistance, and our utmost efforts, we got the anchor just clear of the bottom, but the
ship casting in shore, it almost immediately hooked again

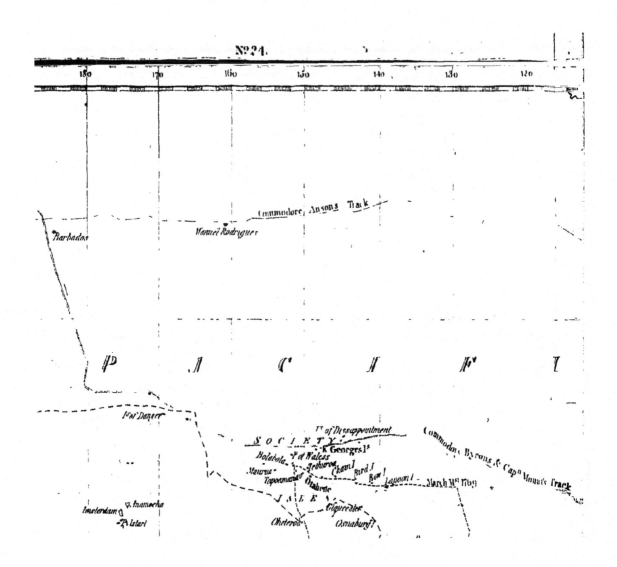

180   170   160   150   140   130   120

Commodore Ansons Track

Barbados

Manuel Rodriguez

P   A   C   H   I   F   I

Isᵈ of Danger

Iˢ of Dissapointment

SOCIETY

K Georges Iˢ

Commodore Byrons & Capⁿ Mouat's Track

Bolabola   Pˢ of Waless

Maurua   Jerburoa   Chain I   Bird I

Tapoamanao   Olaheile   Bow I   Lagoon I   March 14ᵗʰ 1769

Amsterdam   Anamocha   J   S   E   E   Gloucester

Isʰ Islaⁿᵈ   Oheteroa   Osnaburgᶠ

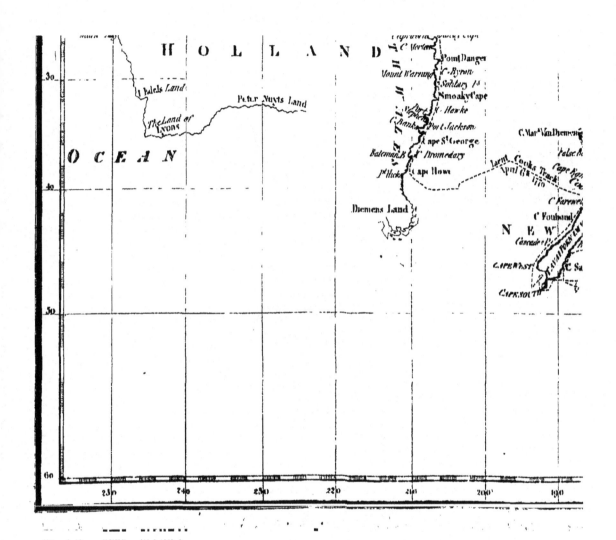

H O L L A N D

30

I Falels Land

Peter Nuyts Land

The Land of Lyons

O C E A N

40

Diemens Land

50

60

230   240   230   220   210   200   190

C. Morton
Point Danger
Mount Warning
C. Byron
Solitary I⁵
Smoaky Cape
Port N. Hawke
C. Banks
Port Jackson
Cape S⁺ George
Bateman B.
C⁺ Dromedary
J⁺ Hicks
Cape Howe
Begin. Cooks Track
April 6⁺ 1770

C. Mar⁴ Van Diemens
False B.
Cape Ag.
C⁺ Farewell
C⁺ Foulwind
N E W
Cascade r.
CAPE WEST
CAVALION BAY
C⁺ Sa
CAPE SOUTH

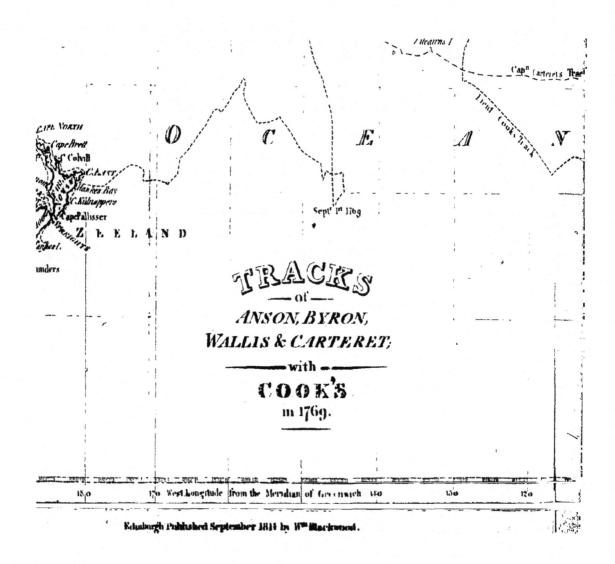

TRACKS
— of —
ANSON, BYRON,
WALLIS & CARTERET;
— with —
COOK'S
in 1769.

Septr 1st 1769

Cape North
Cape Brett
C. Colvill
C. East
Hawkes Bay
C. Kidnappers
Cape Palliser

ZEELAND

O C E A N

Pitcairns I.

Cap.ⁿ Carteret's Track

Lieut. Cook's Track

180   170 West Longitude from the Meridian of Greenwich   140   130   120

Edinburgh Published September 1811 by Wm Blackwood.

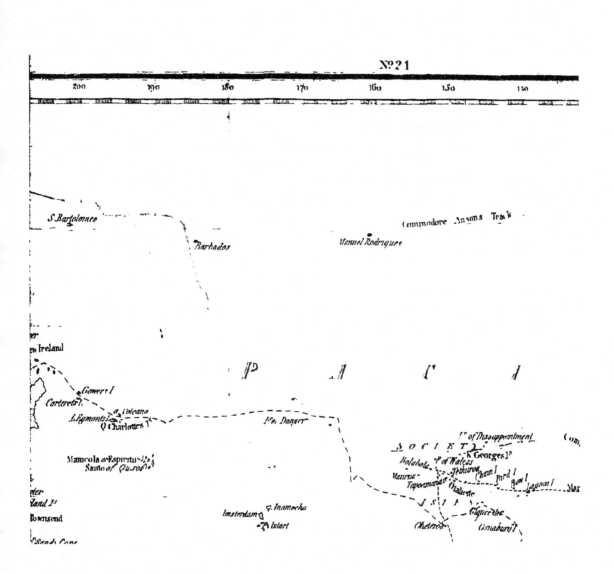

200 190 180 170 160 150 140

S. Bartolomeo

Barbados

Commodore Ansons Track

Manuel Rodriguez

PACIFIC

New Ireland

Gomers I

Carteret I

Volcano

L. Egmonts I

Q Charlottes I

I. of Danger

SOCIETY

I. of Disappointment

Com

Maincola or Espiritu
Santo of Quiros

Bolabola I. d' Wales S. Georges Is

Maurua Otahenroa Chain I

Tapoamanao Huahene Bird I

Otaheite

Bow I

Lagoon I Mar

der

land Is

Townsend

ISLES

Amsterdam I. Anamocha

I. Start

Cheteroa Cigree Iles

Osnaburg I

Sandy Cape

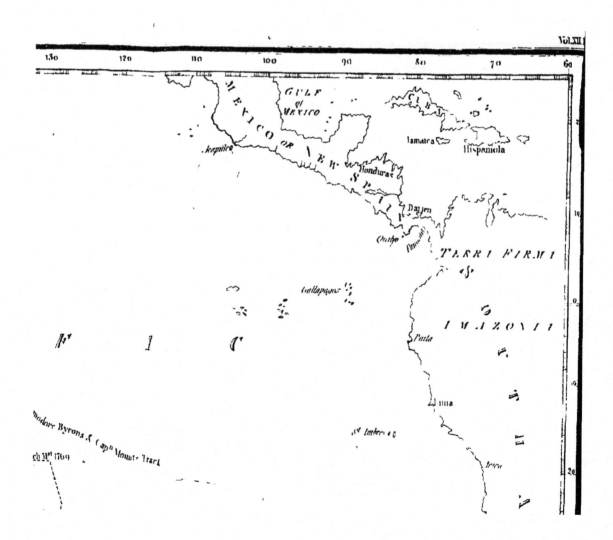

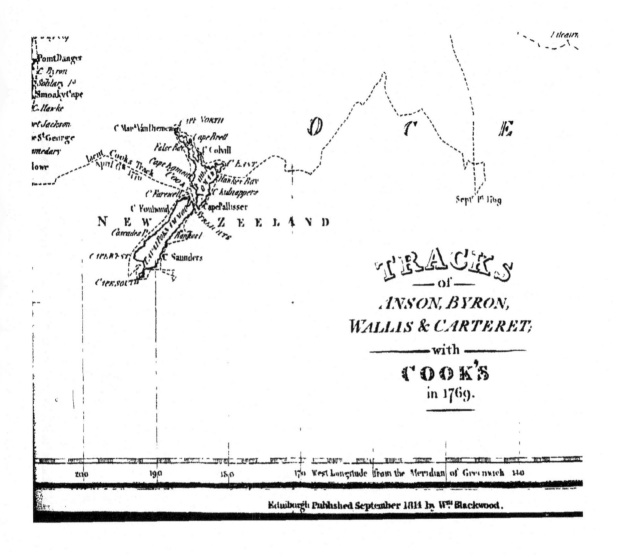

PomtDanger
C. Byron
Sohlars Id
Smoaky Cape
C. Harke
rt Jackson
rt St George
mredary
lowr

Lient Cooks Track
April 6th 1770

C. Mar VanDiemens   IPt NORTH
Cape Brett
False Bay   C. Colvill
Cape Egmont
COOK   C. East
C. Farewell   Hankes Bay
C. Kidnappers

NEW   ZEELAND
C. Youhand   CapePallisser

Cascades P.   Hankes I.
C. PERPST   C. Saunders
C. EESOUTH

O   C   E

Sept 1st 1769

TRACKS
— of —
ANSON, BYRON,
WALLIS & CARTERET;
— with —
COOK'S
in 1769.

200   190   180   170 West Longitude from the Meridian of Greenwich 140

Edinburgh Published September 1814 by Wm Blackwood.

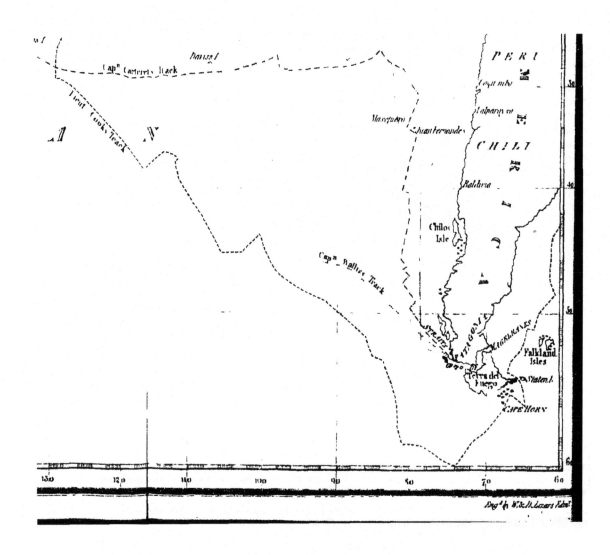

in foul ground. Our task was now to begin again; and though all hands that were able to move applied their utmost force, the whole remaining part of the day, with the greatest purchase we could make, we were not able to stir it: We were very unwilling to cut the cable, for though it was much worn, we could at this time ill sustain the loss of it, as we intended to make small cord, which we much wanted, of the best part of it. We therefore, with whatever reluctance, desisted for the night; and the next day, having a little recruited our strength, we were more successful. We got the anchor up; but we found it so much injured as to be wholly unserviceable, the palm being broken.

From this place we sailed to a little cove about three or four miles distant, to which we gave the name of *English Cove.* Here we anchored, and immediately began to get wood and water, which we found in great plenty, besides ballast. I also sent the boat out every day to different places with the seine, but though there was plenty of fish, we were able to catch very little,—a misfortune which was probably owing in part to the clearness of the water, in part to the rockiness of the beach, and perhaps in some degree also to our want of skill. We plied this labour day and night, notwithstanding the want of success, and at the same time had recourse to the hook and line, but, to our great mortification, not a single fish would take the bait. We saw a few turtle, but they were so shy that we could not catch one of them: Here, therefore, we were condemned to the curse of Tantalus, perpetually in sight of what our appetites most importunately craved, and perpetually disappointed in our attempts to reach it. We got, however, from the rocks, at low water, a few rock-oysters, and cockles of a very large size; and from the shore some cocoa-nuts, and the upper part of the tree that bears them, which is called the cabbage: This cabbage is a white, crisp, juicy substance, which, eaten raw, tastes somewhat like a chesnut, but when boiled is superior to the best parsnip, we cut it small into the broth that we made of our portable soup, which was afterwards thickened with oatmeal, and made a most comfortable mess: For each of these cabbages, however, we were forced to cut down a tree; and it was with great regret that we destroyed, in the parent stock, so much fruit, which perhaps is the most powerful

antiscorbutic in the world ; but necessity has no law. This
supply of fresh vegetable, and especially the milk, or rather the water of the nut, recovered our sick very fast.
They also received great benefit and pleasure from the fruit
of a tall tree, that resembles a plum, and particularly that
which in the West Indies is called the Jamaica Plum. Our
men gave it the same name ; it has a pleasant tartish taste,
but is a little woody, probably only for want of culture :
These plums were not plenty ; so that having the two qualities of a dainty, scarcity and excellence, it is no wonder
that they were held in the highest estimation.

The shore about this place is rocky, and the country
high and mountainous, but covered with trees of various
kinds, some of which are of an enormous growth, and probably would be useful for many purposes. Among others,
we found the nutmeg tree in great plenty ; and I gathered
a few of the nuts, but they were not ripe : They did not indeed appear to be the best sort, but perhaps that is owing partly to their growing wild, and partly to their being
too much in the shade of taller trees. The cocoa-nut tree
is in great perfection, but does not abound. Here are, I believe, all the different kinds of palm, with the beetle-nut
tree, various species of the aloe, canes, bamboos, and rattans, with many trees, shrubs, and plants, altogether unknown to me ; but no esculent vegetable of any kind. The
woods abound with pigeons, doves, rooks, parrots, and a
large bird with black plumage, that makes a noise somewhat like the barking of a dog ; with many others which I
can neither name nor describe. Our people saw no quadruped but two of a small size that they took for dogs ; the
carpenter and another man got a transient glimpse of them
in the woods as they were cutting spars for the ship's use,
and said they were very wild, and ran away the moment
they saw them with great swiftness. We saw centipieds,
scorpions, and a few serpents of different kinds, but no inhabitants. We fell in, however, with several deserted habitations ; and by the shells that were scattered about them,
and seemed not long to have been taken out of the water,
and some sticks half burnt, the remains of a fire, there is
reason to conclude that the people had but just left the
place when we arrived. If we may judge of the people by
that which had been their dwelling, they must stand low

even

even in the scale of savage life : For it was the most miserable hovel we had ever seen.

While we lay here, having cleared and lightened the ship, we heeled her so as to come at her leak, which the carpenter stopped as well as he could; we found the sheathing greatly decayed, and the bottom much eaten by the worms, but we payed it as far as we could get at it with a mixture of hot pitch and tar boiled together. The carpenter also cut down many spars, for studding-sail booms, having but few left of those which he had brought from England.

English Cove lies N. E. ½ N. three or four miles from Wallis's Island; there is a small shoal on the starboard hand going in, which will be easily seen by the seas breaking upon it. The water ebbs and flows once in four-and-twenty hours; the flood came in about nine or ten o'clock, and it was high water between three and four in the afternoon, after which it ebbed all night, and was low water about six in the morning. The water rises and falls between eight and nine feet, sometimes more, sometimes less; but I doubt whether this fluctuation is not rather the effect of the sea and land-breeze, than of a regular tide. We anchored here with our best bower in twenty-seven fathom water, with a bottom of sand and mud; we veered into the cove a cable and a half from the anchor, moored head and stern with the stream anchor, and steadied with hawsers on each bow; the ship then lay in ten fathom, at the distance of a cable's length from the shore at the bottom of the cove, Wallis's point bearing S. W. ½ S., distant about three or four miles. At this place there is plenty of excellent wood and water, and good shingle ballast. The variation was 6° ½ E.

On Monday the 7th of September, I weighed anchor, but before I sailed, I took possession of this country, with all its islands, bays, ports, and harbours, for his majesty George the Third, king of Great Britain; and we nailed upon a high tree a piece of board, faced with lead, on which was engraved the English union, with the name of the ship, and her commander, the name of the cove, and the time of her coming in and sailing out of it. While we

The following quotation from the account of Bougainville's voyage may interest the reader :—" A sailor, belonging to my barge, being in

we lay here, I sent the boat out to examine the harbours upon the coast, from one of which expeditions she return-ed with a load of cocoa-nuts, which she procured in a fine little harbour, about four leagues W.N.W. from the sta-tion we were in. The officer on board reported that the trees grew where he had gathered the fruit in great plenty; but as he had observed that several of them were marked, and that there were many huts of the natives near them, I did not think it proper that the boat should return: But the refreshment which now offered was of such importance to the sick, that I determined to go into the harbour with the ship, and place her so as to protect the men who should be employed to fell the trees, and cut off the cabbages and the fruit. We sailed from English Cove with the land-breeze early in the morning, and in the evening secured the ship a-breast of the grove, where the cocoa-nuts had been ga-thered, and at very little distance from the shore. Here we procured above a thousand cocoa-nuts, and as many of the cabbages

search of shells, found buried in the sand, a piece of a plate of lead, on which we read these remains of English words, HOR'D HERE ICK MAJESTY. There yet remained the mark of the nails, with which they had fastened this inscription, that did not seem to be of any ancient date. The savages had, doubtless, torn off the plate, and broken it in pieces. This adventure engaged us carefully to examine all the neighbourhood of our anchorage. We therefore ran along the coast within the isle which covers the bay; we followed it for about two leagues, and came to a deep bay of very little breadth, open to the S.W. at the bottom of which we landed, near a fine river. Some trees sawed in pieces, or cut down with hatchets, immediately struck our eyes, and shewed us that this was the place where the English put in at. We now had little trouble to find the spot where the inscription had been placed. It was a very large and very apparent tree, on the right-hand shore of the river, in the middle of a great place, where we concluded that the English had pitched their tents; for we still saw several ends of ropes fastened to the trees, the nails stuck in the tree; and the plate had been torn off but a few days before; for the marks of it appeared quite fresh. In the tree itself, there were notches cut, either by the English or the islanders. Some fresh shoots coming up from one of the trees which was cut down, gave us an opportunity of concluding, that the English had anchored in this bay but about four months ago. The rope which we found, likewise sufficiently indicated it, for though it lay in a very wet place, it was not rotten. I make no doubt but that the ship which touched here was the Swallow, a vessel of 14 guns, commanded by Captain Carteret, and which sailed from Europe in August 1766, with the Dolphin, Captain Wallis. This is a very strange chance, by which we, among so many lands, come to the very spot where this rival nation had left a monument of an enterprize similar to ours." The name which B. gave to this harbour was Port Praslin.—E.

cabbages as we could use while they were good, and I would have staid long enough to have given my people all the refreshments they wanted, but the season of the year made the shortest delay dangerous. There was too much reason to suppose that the lives of all on board depended upon our getting to Batavia while the monsoon continued to blow from the eastward ; there was indeed time enough for any other ship to have gone three times the distance, but I knew it was scarcely sufficient for the Swallow in her present condition : And that if we should be obliged to continue here another season, it would probably become impossible to navigate her at all, especially as she had but a single sheathing, and her bottom was not filled with nails, so that the worms would have eaten through it ; besides that our provision would long before that time have been totally exhausted. I therefore weighed anchor and quitted this station, which was much the best that had been our lot during the whole run from the Strait of Magellan, on the 9th in the morning, at break of day, with a light breeze from the land.

To this place we gave the name of *Carteret's Harbour;* It is about W.N.W. four leagues from English Cove, and formed by two islands and the main ; the largest, which is to the N.W. we called *Cocoa-nut Island,* and the other, which is to the S.E. we called *Leigh's Island.* Between these two islands there is shoal water, and each of them forms an entrance into the harbour ; the south-east or weather entrance is formed by Leigh's Island, and in this there is a rock that appears above water, to which we gave the name of *Booby Rock;* the passage is between the rock and the island, nor is the rock dangerous, there being deep water close to it. The north-west, or lee entrance, is formed by Cocoa-nut Island, and this is the best, because there is good anchorage in it, the water in the other being too deep : We entered the harbour by the south-east passage, and went out of it by the north-west. At the south-east end of the harbour there is a large cove, which is secure from all winds, and fit to haul a ship into. Into this cove a river seemed to empty itself, but our boats did not examine it. In the north-west part of the harbour there is another cove, which our boat did examine, and from which she brought us very good water ; this also is fit for a ship to haul into, and very convenient for wooding and watering ;

ing: She may lie in any depth from thirty to five fathom, and at any distance from the shore, with a bottom of soft mud. The harbour runs about S.E. by S. and N.W. by N. and is about three miles long, and four cables' length broad. We anchored in thirty fathom, near the north-west entrance, and a-breast of the trees on Cocoa-nut Island.

Section VI.

Discovery of a Strait dividing the Land called Nova Britannia into two Islands, with a Description of several small Islands that lie in the Passage, and the Land on each Side, with the Inhabitants.

WHEN we got about four leagues off the land, after leaving this harbour, we met with a strong gale at E.S.E. a direction just contrary to that which would have favoured our getting round the land, and doubling Cape Saint Maria. We found at the same time a strong current, setting us to the N.W. into a deep bay or gulph, which Dampier calls St George's Bay, and which lies between Cape St George and Cape Orford. As it was impossible to get round the land, against both the wind and current, and follow the track of Dampier, I was under the necessity of attempting a passage to the westward by this gulph, and the current gave me hopes that I should succeed. When I had got, therefore, about five miles to the south-west of Cocoa-nut Island, I steered to the N.W. and the N.N.W. as the land trends, and had soon good reason to believe that what has been called St George's Bay, and thought to be formed by two points of the same island, was indeed a channel between two islands, and so the event proved it to be.

Before it was dark, we found this channel divided by a pretty large island which I called the *Duke of York's Island*, and some smaller islands that were scattered about it. On the southermost side of the main, or the largest of the two islands that are divided by the channel or strait, which I left in possession of its ancient name, New Britain, there is some high land, and three remarkable hills close to each other, which I called the *Mother and Daughters.* The Mother is the middlemost and largest, and behind them we saw a vast column of smoke, so that probably one of them

is

is a volcano : They are easily seen in clear weather at the distance of twenty leagues, and will then, by those who do not know them, be taken for islands ; they seem to lie far inland, and the Mother bears about west from the Duke of York's Island. To the east of these hills there is a point making like a cape land, which I called *Cape Palliser*; and another to the westward, which I called *Cape Stephens.* Cape Stephens is the northermost part of New Britain. North of this Cape is an island, which I called the *Isle of Man.* Cape Palliser and Cape Stephens bear about N.W. and S.E. of each other ; and between them is a bay, the land of which near the water-side is low, pleasant, and level, and gradually rises, as it retires towards the Mother and Daughters, into very lofty hills, in general covered with vast woods, but having many clear spots like plantations intermixed. Upon this part of the country we saw many fires in the night, and have therefore reason to suppose that it is well inhabited. The Duke of York's Island lies between the two points, Cape Palliser and Cape Stephens. As it was not safe to attempt either of the passages into which the strait was divided by this island in the dark, we brought to for the night, and kept sounding, but had no ground with one hundred and forty fathom. The strait here, including the two passages, is about fifteen leagues broad. The land of the Duke of York's Island is level, and has a delightful appearance: Inland it is covered with lofty woods, and near the water-side are the houses of the natives, which stand not far from each other, among groves of cocoa-nut trees, so that the whole forms a prospect the most beautiful and romantic that can be imagined. We saw many of their canoes, which are very neatly made, and in the morning, soon after I made sail, some of them came off towards the ship ; but as we had a fresh gale at that time, we could not stay for them. The latitude of this island is 4° 9′ S., longitude 151° 20′ E.; and it is five-and-twenty leagues distant from Cape George. As I coasted not New Britain, but the northermost coast of the strait, I passed through the passage that is formed by that coast, and the corresponding side of the Duke of York's Island, which is about eight leagues broad, and may be considered as the first narrow of the strait, and then steering N.W. by W. all night, we found at day-break that we had lost sight of the southermost island, or New Britain, and having now ascertained
the

the supposed bay to be a strait, I called it *St George's Channel*, and to the northern island I gave the name of *Nova Hibernia*, or *New Ireland*. The weather being hazy, with a strong gale and sudden gusts, I continued to steer along the coast of New Ireland at about the distance of six leagues from the shore, till I came off the west end of it, and then, altering our course, I steered W.N.W. I could plainly perceive, that we were set along the shore by a strong westerly current. At noon, we found, by observation, that we were much to the northward of the log; but as it was impossible the current could set due north, as that would be right against the land, I was obliged, for the correction of my account, to allow no less than four-and-twenty miles W.N.W. which is nearly as the land lies along the shore. At this time we had about half a point east variation; and at night we discovered a fine large island, forming a strait or passage with New Ireland. As it was very dark and squally, with rain, we brought-to, not knowing to what danger the navigation of this strait might expose us. The night was tempestuous, with much thunder and lightning, but about two in the morning the weather cleared; the gusts settled into a little breeze, and the moon shone very bright. At this time therefore we made sail again, and found a strong current setting us to the westward, through the passage of the second narrow, which is about five leagues wide. The island, which has a pleasant appearance, and is very populous, I called *Sandwich Island*, in honour of the earl, then first lord of the admiralty: It is larger than the Duke of York's Island, and there seems to be some good bays and harbours upon the coast. On the north part of it there is a remarkable peak, like a sugar-loaf; and opposite to it, upon the coast of New Ireland, there is just such another: They are distant about five leagues, in the direction of S. by E. $\frac{1}{4}$ E. and N. by W. $\frac{1}{2}$ W. All the while we lay-to off this island, we heard an incessant noise in the night, like the beating of a drum: And being becalmed just as we got through the strait, ten canoes put off from New Ireland, with about one hundred and fifty men on board, and rowed towards the ship; they came near enough to exchange some trifles with us, which were conveyed at the end of a long stick, but none of them would venture on board. They seemed to prefer such iron as we gave them to every thing else, though none of it was

manufactured

manufactured except nails; for, as I observed before, we had no cutlery ware on board. The canoes were very long and very narrow, with an outrigger, and some of them were very neatly made: One of them could not be less than ninety feet long, for it was very little shorter than the ship; it was, notwithstanding, formed of a single tree; it had some carved ornaments about it, and was rowed or paddled by three-and-thirty men: We saw no appearance of sails. The people are black, and woolly-headed, like Negroes, but have not the flat nose and thick lips; and we thought them much the same people as the inhabitants of Egmont's Island : Like them, they were all stark naked, except a few ornaments made of shells upon their arms and legs. They had, however, adopted a practice without which none of our belles and beaux are supposed to be completely drest, for the hair, or rather the wool, upon their heads, was very abundantly powdered with white powder; the fashion of wearing powder, therefore, is probably of higher antiquity than it is generally supposed to be, as well as of more extensive influence; it is indeed carried farther among these people than among any of the inhabitants of Europe, for they powder not only their heads but their beards too. Their heads however were decorated with more showy ornaments, for I observed that most of them had, just above one ear, stuck a feather, which appeared to have been taken from the tail of the common dunghill cock; so that these gentlemen are not without poultry for their table. They were armed with spears, and long sticks or poles, like the quarter-staff; but we did not see any bows and arrows among them: Possibly they might have them on board, and think proper to keep them out of sight. On my part, I kept every body at their quarters while they were hovering about the ship, and I observed that they had a very watchful eye upon our guns, as if they apprehended danger from them; so that possibly they are not wholly unacquainted with the effect of firearms. They had fishing nets with them, which, as well as their cordage, seemed to be very well made. After they had been some time with us, a breeze sprung up, and they returned to the shore.

The peak upon Sandwich Island lies in latitude $2° 53'$ S., longitude $149° 17'$ E. After the Indians had left us, we steered nearly west, and soon after saw a point of land, which proved to be the south-west extremity of New Ireland,

land, to which I gave the name of *Cape Byron :* It lies in latitude 2° 30′ S., longitude 149° 2′ E. Over-against the coast of New Ireland, to the westward of Cape Byron, lies a fine large island, to which I gave the name of *New Hanover.* Between this island and New Ireland, there is a strait or passage, which turns away to the N.E. In this passage lie several small islands, upon one of which there is a remarkable peak : This island I called *Byron's Island,* and the passage, or strait, I called *Byron's Strait.* The land of New Hanover is high; it is finely covered with trees, among which are many plantations, and the whole has a most beautiful appearance. The south-west point of it, which is a high bluff point, I called *Queen Charlotte's Foreland,* in honour of her majesty. This foreland, and the land about it, is remarkable for a great number of little hummocks or hills, but night coming on, with thick weather, hard squalls, and much rain, we could not see more of it distinctly enough to describe its appearance.

We steered westward all night, and in the morning, the weather being still thick, our view of New Hanover was very imperfect; but we saw, about eight leagues to the westward of it, six or seven small islands, which I called the *Duke of Portland's Islands,* two of which are pretty large. I now perceived by the swell of the sea that we were clear of all the land, and I found Saint George's Channel to be a much better and shorter passage, whether from the eastward or the westward, than round all the land and islands to the northward; the distress, therefore, which pushed me upon this discovery, may probably be, in its consequences, of great advantage to future navigators, especially as there can be no doubt but that refreshments of every kind may easily be procured from the natives who inhabit either of the coasts of the channel, or the islands that lie near them, for beads, ribbands, looking-glasses, and especially iron tools and cutlery-ware, of which they are immoderately fond, and with which, to our great misfortune, we were not furnished.

Queen Charlotte's Foreland, the south-west part of New Hanover, lies in latitude 2° 29′ S., longitude 148° 27′ E.; and the middle of Portland's Islands in latitude 2° 27′ S., longitude 148° 3′ E. The length of this streight or channel, from Cape Saint George to Cape Byron, the south-west extremity of New Ireland, is above eighty leagues; the

distance

distance from Cape Byron to Queen Charlotte's Foreland is about twelve leagues, and from the foreland to Portland's Islands about eight leagues; so that the whole length of Saint George's Channel is about one hundred leagues, or three hundred miles.

Though we cleared the streight in the morning of Sunday the 13th of September, we had no observation of the sun till the 15th, which I could not but greatly regret, as it prevented my being so exact in my latitude and longitude as might be expected. The description also of the country, its productions and people, would have been much more full and circumstantial, if I had not been so much enfeebled and dispirited by sickness, as almost to sink under the duty that for want of officers devolved upon me, being obliged, when I was scarcely able to crawl, to keep watch and watch, and share other duties with my lieutenant, whose health also was greatly impaired.

SECTION VII.

The Passage from Saint George's Channel to the Island of Mindanao, with an Account of many Islands that were seen, and Incidents that happened by the Way.

As soon as we had cleared Saint George's Channel, we steered westward, and the next day we discovered land bearing W.N.W. and hauled up for it; it proved to be an island of considerable extent, and soon afterwards we saw another to the north-east of it, but this appeared to be little more than a large rock above water. As I had here strong currents, and for several days had not been able to get an observation of the sun, I cannot so exactly ascertain the situation of these islands as I might otherwise have done. As we proceeded to the westward, we discovered more land, consisting of many islands lying to the southward of the large one which we had first discovered. As the nights were now moonlight, we kept on till eleven o'clock, and the lieutenant, who was then officer of the watch, finding that the course we were steering would carry us among them, and not being willing to awaken me till it was my turn to watch, hauled off S. by E. and S.S.E. I came upon deck about midnight, and at one in the morning, perceiving

that

that we were clear of them, I bore away again to the westward with an easy sail: The islands, however, were not far
distant, and about six o'clock, a considerable number of canoes, with several hundred people on board, came off, and
paddled toward the ship: One of them, with seven men on
board, came near enough to hail us, and made us several
signs which we could not perfectly understand, but repeated, as near as we could, to shew that whatever they meant
to us we meant to them; however, the better to bespeak
their good-will, and invite them on board, we held up to
them several of the few trifles we had: Upon this they drew
nearer to the ship, and I flattered myself that they were coming on board; but on the contrary, as soon as they came
within reach of us they threw their lances, with great force,
where we stood thickest upon the deck. As I thought it
better to prevent than to repress a general attack, in which
as the number would be more, the mischief would be greater, and having now no doubt of their hostile intentions, I
fired some muskets, and one of the swivel guns, upon which
some of them being killed or wounded, they rowed off and
joined the other canoes, of which there were twelve or fourteen, with several hundred men on board. I then brought-
to, waiting for the issue, and had the satisfaction to see,
that, after having long consulted together, they made for
the shore: That I might still farther intimidate them, and
more effectually prevent their return, I fired a round shot
from one of my six-pounders, so as to fall into the water beyond them: This seemed to have a good effect, for they not
only used their paddles more nimbly, but hoisted sail, still
standing towards the shore. Soon after, however, several
more canoes put off from another part of the island, and
came towards us very fast: They stopped at about the same
distance as the other had done, and one of them also in
the same manner came forward: To the people on board
this vessel we made all the signs of friendship we could devise, shewing them every thing we had which we thought
would please them, opening our arms, and inviting them on
board: But our rhetoric was to no effect, for as soon as they
came within a cast of the ship, they poured in a shower of
darts and lances, which, however, did us no harm. We returned the assault by firing some muskets, and one man being killed, the rest precipitately leaped into the sea, and
swimming to the others, who waited at a distance, all returned

turned together from whence they came. As soon as the
canoe was deserted, we got out our boat and brought it on
board : It was full fifty feet long, though one of the smallest
that came against us ; it was very rudely made out of one
tree, but had an out-rigger. We found in it six fine fish,
and a turtle, some yams, one cocoa-nut, and a bag full of a
small kind of apple or plum, of a sweetish taste and farina-
ceous substance ; it had a flattish kernel, and was wholly
different from every thing we have seen either before or
since ; it was eatable raw, but much better boiled, or roasted in the embers : We found also two large earthen pots,
shaped somewhat like a jug, with a wide mouth, but without handles, and a considerable quantity of matting, which
these people use both for sails and awning, spreading it over
bent sticks, much in the same manner as the tilts of the
London wherries. From the contents of this vessel we judged that it had been fishing, and we observed that the people had a fire on board, with one of their pots on it, in which
they were boiling their provision. When we had satisfied
our curiosity by examining it, we cut it up for fire-wood.

These Indians were the same kind of people that we had
seen before on the coast of New Ireland, and at Egmont
Island : They were of a very dark copper colour, nearly
black, with woolly heads. They chew beetle-nut, and go
quite naked, except the rude ornaments of shells strung together, which they wear round their legs and arms : They
were also powdered like our last visitors, and had, besides,
their faces painted with white streaks : But I did not observe that they had any beards. Their lances were pointed
with a kind of bluish flint.

Having disengaged ourselves from this fierce and unfriendly people, we pursued our course along the other islands,
which are between twenty and thirty in number, and of considerable extent ; one in particular would alone make a
large kingdom. I called them the *Admiralty Islands,* and
should have been glad to have examined them, if my ship
had been in a better condition, and I had been provided
with such articles as are proper for an Indian trade, especially as their appearance is very inviting : They are clothed with the most beautiful verdure ; the woods are lofty and
luxuriant, interspersed with spots that have been cleared
for plantations, groves of cocoa-nut trees, and houses of the
natives, who seem to be very numerous. Nothing would be
more

more easy than to establish an amicable intercourse with them, as they would soon be sensible that our superiority would render contest vain, and traffic advantageous. I judge the middle of the largest to lie in latitude 2° 18′ S., longitude 146° 44′ E. and at the distance of five-and-thirty leagues from Queen Charlotte's Foreland in New Hanover, in the direction of W.¼N. On the south side of this island, there is a small one, which rises conically in a high peak. The latitude of this peak is 2° 27′ S., and it lies five degrees and a half westward of Cape Saint George in New Ireland. As we ran along the south side of the large island, we found it to be eighteen leagues long, in the direction of east and west; how far it runs to the northward, I do not know, but by its appearance there is reason to suppose a very considerable distance. I think it probable, in the highest degree, that these islands produce many valuable articles of trade, particularly spices, especially as they lie in the same climate and latitude as the Malaccas, and as I found the nutmeg-tree in a soil comparatively rocky and barren upon the coast of New Ireland.

Having passed these islands, we continued our course W. by N. with a fine eastern breeze, and smooth water. On the 16th in the morning, we found the variation, by a medium of several azimuths, to be 6° 30′ E., our latitude being 2° 19′ S., and our longitude 145° 40′ E. by observation. I was surprised to find the variation on this side the land of New Britain and New Ireland so much, as we had found it gradually decreasing during our progress to the N.W., but I recollected that about two years before I had found nearly the same variation in this meridian, about the island of Tinian.

On Saturday evening the 19th, we discovered two small islands, both low land, level, and green: One of them we saw only from the main-top-gallant-mast head; this I called *Durour's Island.* Its latitude is about 1° 14′ or 16′ S., its longitude 145° 21′ E. The other island, which I called *Maty's Island,* we coasted during the night, and saw the inhabitants, in great numbers, run along the beach, a-breast of the ship, with lights: The side along which we sailed seemed to be about six miles in length, E. by N. and W. by S. As it was dark we could see no more of it, and having a fine breeze, which we could not afford to lose, we kept on. Its latitude is about 1° 45′ S., and its longitude about 143°

2′ E.;

2' E. ; the variation here was 4° 4′ E. and we found a strong north-westerly current. We had now fresh gales and squalls, with rain, the wind blowing very unsteadily from E.S.E. to E.N.E. till the 22d, when it became variable. Our latitude was then 53′ S., longitude 140° 5′ E.; the variation was 4° 40′ E.

On the 24th, we saw two small islands to the south-west, but it being calm, with light airs, and a strong westerly current, we could not get nearer to them than four or five leagues : They had a green, pleasant appearance, and were well covered with trees ; but whether they are inhabited I do not know. They run about N.W. by W. S.E. by E. One is about three miles long, and the other about six : The passage between them appeared to be about two miles broad. They lie in latitude 22′ S., longitude 138° 39 E. and I gave them the name of *Stephens's Islands.* We kept steering N. W. by W. with a light variable wind, and a strong north-west current.

On the 25th, we saw land a-head, which proved to be three small islands ; and before it was dark we got pretty near them. Several canoes soon came off, filled with the natives, who, after making signs of peace, came on board without the least appearance of fear or distrust: They had nothing with them but a few cocoa-nuts, which they sold with great joy for a few pieces of an iron hoop. We soon found that they were not unacquainted with that metal, which they called *parram;* and they made us understand, by signs, that a ship like ours sometimes touched at their islands for refreshment. I gave one of them three pieces of an old iron hoop, each about four inches long, which threw him into an extacy little short of distraction. I could not but sympathise in his joy, nor observe, without great pleasure, the changes of countenance, and extravagance of gesture, by which it was expressed. All these people, indeed, appeared to be more fond of iron than any we had seen before ; and I am sure, that for iron tools we might have purchased every thing upon the islands which we could have brought away. They are of the Indian copper colour ; the first of that complexion that we had seen in these parts, with fine long black hair, and little beards, for we observed that they were continually plucking the hair from their chin and upper-lip by the roots. Their features are pleasing, and their teeth remarkably white and
even :

even : They were of the common stature, but nimble, vigorous, and active, in a surprising degree, running up to the mast-head much faster than our own people. Their disposition was free and open ; they eat and drank whatever was given them ; went without hesitation into every part of the ship, and were as familiar and merry with the crew as if they had been of long and intimate acquaintance. They were not, like the people on all the other islands that we had visited, quite naked, though they had only a slight covering for the waist, which consisted of a narrow piece of fine matting. Their canoes were very well and neatly made, having a hollow tree for the bottom, and planks for the sides, with a sail of fine matting, and an outrigger; their ropes and netting were also very good. They urged us strongly to go on shore, offering to leave an equal number of their own people behind, as a pledge of their safe return ; and indeed I would gladly have consented if it had been in my power; but a strong westerly current hurried me to so great a distance, that I had no opportunity to seek for anchorage, and night coming on we pursued our course. When our visitors perceived this, one of them insisted upon going with us, and, notwithstanding all that I and his companions could say or do, obstinately refused to go on shore. As I thought it possible that this man might be the means of our making some useful discovery, I did not put him ashore by force, but indulged him in his desire. We learned from him that there were other islands to the northward, the inhabitants of which, he said, had iron, and always killed his countrymen when they could catch them out at sea. It was with great concern that I perceived this poor fellow, whom I called Joseph Freewill, from his readiness to go with us, become gradually sickly after he had been some time at sea. He lived till I got to the island of Celebes, and there died. As the islands from which I had taken him were very small and low, the largest being not more than five miles in compass, I was surprised to see with how many of the productions of Celebes he was acquainted ; beside the cocoa-nut and palm, he knew the beetle-nut and the lime, and the moment he got a bread-fruit, he went to the fire and roasted it in the embers. He made us understand also, that in his country they had plenty of fish, and turtle in their season. It is, however, very probable, notwithstanding the number of people who subsist upon
these

these islands, that they have no fresh water but what falls in rain : How they catch and preserve it, I had no opportunity to learn, but I never met with a spring in a spot so small and low, and in such a spot I believe no spring was ever found. The largest of these islands, which the natives call Pegan, and to which I gave the name of *Freewill Island*, lies fifty minutes north of the Line, and in 137° 51' east longitude. They are all surrounded by a reef of rocks. The chart of these islands I drew from the Indian's description, who delineated them with chalk upon the deck, and ascertained the depth of water by stretching his arms as a fathom.

I now steered N.W. by N. to get from under the sun, and had light winds at E S.E. with which almost any ship but the Swallow would have made good way, but with every possible advantage she went at a heavy rate. We now found our variation begin again to decrease, as will appear by the following table :

Latitude.	Longitude from Queen Charlotte's Foreland.	Variation.
40' S.	8° 36' W.	4° 40' E.
Upon the Line.	9 40 W.	4 17 E.
30' N.	10 30 W.	3 10 E.
2° N.	11 40 W.	2 30 E.
2° 50' N.	12 10 W.	2 E.

On the 28th, being in latitude 2° 53' N. longitude 136° 10' E. we fell in with a very dangerous shoal, which is about eleven or twelve miles in circuit, and surrounded with small stones that just shew themselves above water. We found here a strong northerly current, but could not determine whether it inclined to the east or west.

In the evening, we discovered from the mast-head another island to the southward of us ; the east end of it seemed to rise in a peak, and had the appearance of a sail, but we did not go near enough to see any thing of it from the deck. I suppose its latitude to be about 2° 50' N. and its longitude east of London about 136° 10' E.

We continued to have a current to the northward till Monday the 5th of October, when, being in latitude 4° 30' N. I found it southerly, and very strong. I had, among other deficiencies and misfortunes, no small boat on board, so that I could not try these currents, which I had a great desire to do ; but I am of opinion, that when the current set southward, it inclined to the east; and that when it set northward, it inclined to the west.

On Monday the 12th, we discovered a small island, with trees upon it, though scarcely bigger than a rock, and I called it *Current Island*. It lies in latitude 4° 40' N. longitude 14° 24' W. of Queen Charlotte's Foreland. The next day, we discovered two other small islands, which I called *Saint Andrew's Islands*. They lie in latitude 5° 18' N. longitude 14° 47' W. of Queen Charlotte's Foreland. I called the small island Current Island, because we had here a southerly current so strong that it set us from twenty-four to thirty miles southward every day, besides the difference it might make in our longitude. The wind was now variable, blowing by turns from every point in the compass, with much rain and hard squalls. On Tuesday the 20th, being in latitude 8° N. it blew with such violence that we were obliged to lie-to sixty-four hours. This gale, which made a very great sea, I supposed to be the shifting of the monsoon ; and, notwithstanding the southerly current, it drove us, while we lay-to, as far as nine degrees northward.

Section VIII.

Some Account of the Coast of Mindanao, and the Islands near it, in which some Mistakes of Dampier are corrected.

On the 26th, we discovered land again, but not being able to make an observation, we could ascertain our latitude and longitude only by our dead reckoning; the next day, however, was more favourable, and I then found the effect of the current had been so great, that I was obliged to add to the log S.W. by S. no less than sixty-four miles for the last two days. We now knew that the land we had seen was the north-east part of the island of Mindanao.[1] As I had many sick people on board, and was in the most pressing need of refreshments, I determined to try what could

[1] For some particulars respecting this island, see vol. X. p. 275, &c. Playfair's and Pinkerton's Geography also may be advantageously consulted as to Mindanao and the other eastern islands spoken of in this voyage. Some account will be given of them when we come to treat of Cook's discoveries.

could be procured in a bay which Dampier has described as lying on the south-east part of the island, and which, he says, furnished him with great plenty of deer from a savannah. I therefore coasted that side of the island, and that I might be sure not to miss the bay, I sent out the lieutenant with the boat and a proper number of hands, to keep in-shore a-head of the ship. No such bay, however, was to be found; but, at the very southermost extremity of the island, they opened a little nook, at the bottom of which was a town and a fort. As soon as our boat was discovered by the people on shore, they fired a great gun, and sent off three boats or canoes full of people. As the lieutenant had not a sufficient force to oppose them, he immediately made towards the ship, and the canoes chaced him till they came within sight of her, and being then overmatched in their turn, they thought fit to go back. Being thus disappointed in my search of Dampier's Bay and Savannah, I would have anchored off this town, notwithstanding these hostile appearances, if it had not been necessary first to get up some guns from the hold, and make a few necessary repairs in the rigging; this however being the case, I ran a little to the eastward, where, on the 2d of November, I came to an anchor in a little bay, having a bottom of soft mud, and seven fathom of water, at the distance of a cable's length from the shore. The westermost point of the bay bore W.S.W. distant about three miles; the eastermost point E. by S. distant about one mile; a river, which empties itself into the bay, about N.W. and the peak of an island, called Hummock Island, S. 7° E. distant about five leagues. Before it was dark the same day, our two boats went to the river, and brought off their loads of water: They saw no signs of inhabitants where they were on shore, but we observed a canoe come round the westermost point of the bay, which we supposed had been dispatched from the town, to learn what we were, or at least to see what we were doing. As soon as I discovered this canoe, I hoisted English colours, and was not without hope that she would come on board: but after viewing us some time, she returned. As we had seen no inhabitants, nor any signs of inhabitants where we got our water, I intended to procure a further supply the next day from the same place, and endeavour also to recruit our wood; but about nine o'clock at night, we were suddenly surprised by a loud noise on that part of the shore which was a-breast of the ship : It was made by a great number of human voices, and very much resembled the war-whoop of the American savages; a hideous shout which they give at the moment of their attack, and in which all who have heard it agree there is something inexpressibly terrifying and horrid.

As I was now farther convinced that it was necessary to dispose of our little force to the greatest advantage, we began the next day by getting the guns up from the hold, and making the necessary repairs to our rigging. At eleven o'clock, not having seen any thing of the people, who had endeavoured to terrify us by their yells in the night, I sent the long-boat on shore for more water; but as I thought it probable that they might have concealed themselves in the woods, I kept the cutter manned and armed, with the lieutenant on board, that immediate succour might be sent to the waterers, if any danger should threaten them. It soon appeared that my conjectures were well-founded, for our people had no sooner left their boat, than a number of armed men rushed out of the woods, one of whom held up somewhat white, which I took to be a signal of peace. Upon this occasion I was again sensible of the mortifying deficiency in the ship's equipment, which I had so often experienced before. I had no white flag on board, and therefore, as the best expedient in my power, I ordered the lieutenant, whom I sent on shore in the cutter, to display one of my table-cloths: As soon as the officer landed, the standard-bearer and another came down to him unarmed, and received him with great appearance of friendship. One of them addressed him in Dutch, which none of our people understood; he then spoke a few words in Spanish, in which one of the persons of the cutter was a considerable proficient: The Indian however spoke it so very imperfectly, that it was with great difficulty, and by the help of many signs, he made himself understood; possibly if any of our people had spoken Dutch, he might have been found equally deficient in that language. He asked for the captain however by the name of the skipper, and enquired whether we were Hollanders; whether our ship was intended for merchandize or for war; how many guns and men she carried; and whether she had been, or was going to Batavia. When we had satisfied him in all these particulars, he said that we should go to the town, and that he would introduce us to the

the governor, whom he distinguished by the title of Raja.
The lieutenant then told him, that we intended to go to the
town, but that we were in immediate want of water, and
therefore desired permission to fill some casks; he also requested that the people who were armed with bows and arrows, might be ordered to a greater distance. With both
these requisitions the Indian, who seemed to be invested
with considerable authority, complied; and as he seemed
to take particular notice of a silk handkerchief which the
lieutenant had tied round his neck, it was immediately presented to him; in return for which he desired him to accept a kind of cravat, made of coarse calico, which was tied
round his own, his dress being somewhat after the Dutch
fashion. After this interchange of cravats, he enquired of
the officer whether the ship was furnished with any articles
for trade; to which he answered that she was sufficiently
furnished to trade for provisions, but nothing more: The
chief replied, that whatever we wanted we should have.
After this conference, which I considered as an earnest of
every advantage which this place could afford us, the boats
returned on board laden with water, and we went cheerfully
on with our business on board the ship. In about two hours,
however, we saw with equal surprise and concern, many
hundreds of armed men, posting themselves in parties at
different places, among the trees, upon the beach, a-breast
of the ship; their weapons were muskets, bows and arrows,
long pikes or spears, broad-swords, a kind of hanger called
a cress, and targets: We observed also, that they hauled
a canoe, which lay under a shed upon the beach, up into
the woods. These were not friendly appearances, and they
were succeeded by others that were still more hostile; for
these people spent all the remainder of the day in entering
and rushing out of the woods, as if they had been making
sallies to attack an enemy; sometimes shooting their arrows, and throwing their lances into the water towards the
ship; and sometimes lifting their targets, and brandishing
their swords at us in a menacing manner. In the mean time
we were not idle on board: We got up our guns, repaired
our rigging, and put every thing in order before evening,
and then, being ready to sail, I determined, if possible, to
get another conference with the people on shore, and learn
the reason of so sudden and unaccountable a change of behaviour. The lieutenant therefore was again dispatched,

and

and as a testimony that our disposition was still peaceable, the table-cloth was again displayed as a flag of truce. I had the precaution, however, to order the boat to a part of the beach which was clear of wood, that the people on board might not be liable to mischief from enemies whom they could not see; I also ordered that nobody should go on shore. When the Indians saw the boat came to the beach, and observed that nobody landed, one of them came out of the wood, with a bow and arrows in his hand, and made signs for the boat to come to the place where he stood. This the officer very prudently declined, as he would then have been within bow-shot of an ambuscade, and after waiting some time, and finding that a conference could be procured upon no other terms, he returned back to the ship. It was certainly in my power to have destroyed many of these unfriendly people, by firing my great guns into the wood, but it would have answered no good purpose: We could not afterwards have procured wood and water here without risking the loss of our own people, and I still hoped that refreshment might be procured upon friendly terms at the town, which, now I was in a condition to defend myself against a sudden assault, I resolved to visit.

The next morning, therefore, as soon as it was light, I sailed from this place, which I called *Deceitful Bay*, with a light land-breeze, and between ten and eleven o'clock we got off the bay or nook, at the bottom of which our boats had discovered the town and fort. It happened however that just at this time the weather became thick, with heavy rain, and it began to blow hard from a quarter which made the land here a lee-shore; this obliged me to stand off, and having no time to lose, I stood away to the westward, that I might reach Batavia before the season was past.

I shall now give a more particular account of our navigating the sea that washes the coasts of this island, the rather as Dampier's description is in several particulars erroneous.

Having seen the north-east part of the island on the twenty-sixth of October, without certainly knowing whether it was Mindanoa or Saint John's, we got nearer to it the next day, and made what we knew to be Saint Augustina, the south-eastermost part of the island, which rises in little hummocks, that run down to a low point at the water's edge; it bears N. 40 E. at the distance of two-and-twenty leagues from a little island, which is distinguished from the other

islands

islands that lie off the southermost point of Mindanao by a hill or hummock, and which for that reason I called *Hummock Island.* All this land is very high, one ridge of mountains rising behind another, so that at a great distance it appears not like one island but several. After our first discovery of the island, we kept turning along the east side from the northward to Cape Saint Augustina, nearly S. by W. ½ W. and N. by E. ½ E. for about twenty leagues. The wind was to the southward along the shore, and as we approached the land, we stood in for an opening, which had the appearance of a good bay, where we intended to anchor; but we found that it was too deep for our purpose, and that some shoals rendered the entrance of it dangerous. To this bay, which lies about eight or ten leagues N. by E. from Cape Saint Augustina, the south-east extremity of the island, I gave the name of *Disappointment Bay.* When we were in the offing standing in for this bay, we observed a large hummock, which had the appearance of an island, but which I believe to be a peninsula, joined by a low isthmus to the main; this hummock formed the northermost part of the entrance, and another high bluff point opposite to it formed the southermost part; between these two points are the shoals that have been mentioned; and several small islands, only one of which can be seen till they are approached very near. On this part of the coast we saw no signs of inhabitants; the land is of a stupendous height, with mountains piled upon mountains till the summits are hidden in the clouds: In the offing therefore it is almost impossible to estimate its distance, for what appear then to be small hillocks, just emerging from the water, in comparison of the mountains that are seen over them, swell into high hills as they are approached, and the distance is found to be thrice as much as it was imagined; perhaps this will account for the land here being so ill laid down, and in situations so very different, as it appears to be in all our English charts. We found here a strong current setting to the southward along the shore, as the land trended. The high land that is to the north of Saint Augustina, becomes gradually lower towards the Cape, a low flat point in which it terminates, and off which, at a very little distance, lie two large rocks. Its latitude is 6° 15′ N. and the longitude, by account, 127° 20′ E.

From this Cape the land trends away W. and W. by S.
for

for six or seven leagues, and then turns up to the N.W. making a very deep bay, the bottom of which, as we crossed it from Saint Augustina to the high land on the other side, which is not less than twelve leagues, we could not see. The coast on the farther side of it, coming up from the bottom, trends first to the S. and S.S.W. and then to the S.W. by W. towards the south extremity of the island.

Off this southern extremity, which Dampier calls the south-east by mistake, the south-east being Saint Augustina, at the distance of five, six, and seven leagues, lie ten or twelve islands, though Dampier says there are only two, and that together they are about five leagues round. The islands that I saw could not be contained in a circuit of less than fifteen leagues, and from the number of boats that I saw among them I imagine they are well inhabited. The largest of these lies to the S W. of the others, and makes in a remarkable peak, so that it is first seen in coming in with the land, and is indeed visible at a very great distance. Its latitude I make 5° 24′ N., and its longitude, by account, 126° 37′ E. This island, which I called *Hummock Island,* bears from Saint Augustina, S. 40 W. at the distance of between twenty and two-and-twenty leagues; and from the same Cape, the southermost part of the island Mindanao bears S.W. ¾ W. at the distance of between twenty-one and twenty-three leagues. This southermost extremity consists of three or four points, which bear east and west of each other for about seven miles. They lie in latitude 5° 34′ N., longitude 126° 25′ E. according to my account. The variation here was one point east.

I passed between these islands and the main, and found the passage good, the current setting to the westward. Dampier has placed his bay and savannah four leagues N.W. from the eastermost island, and there I sought it, as indeed I did on all the S.E. part of the island till we came to the little creek which ran up to the town.

All the southern part of Mindanao is extremely pleasant, with many spots where the woods had been cleared for plantations, and fine lawns of a beautiful verdure: This part also is well inhabited, as well as the neighbouring islands. Of the town I can give no account, as the weather was so thick that I could not see it; neither could I sufficiently distinguish the land to set off the points, at which I was not a little mortified.

When

When I came to open the land to the westward of the southermost point, I found it trend from that point W.N.W. and N.W. by W. forming first a point at the distance of about seven or eight leagues, and then a very deep bay running so far into the N. and N.E. that I could not see the bottom of it. The westermost point of this bay is low, but the land soon rises again, and runs along to the N.W. by W., which seems to be the direction of this coast, from the southermost point of the island towards the city of Mindanao.

To the westward of this deep bay, the land is all flat, and in comparison of the other parts of the island, but thinly wooded. Over this flat appears a peak of stupendous height, which rises into the clouds like a tower. Between the entrance of this bay and the south point of the island there is another very high hill, the top of which has the funnel shape of a volcano, but I did not perceive that it emitted either fire or smoke. It is possible that this deep bay is that which Dampier mentions, and that is misplaced by an error of the press; for, if, instead of saying it bore N.W. *four* leagues from the *eastermost* of the islands, he had said it bore N.W. *fourteen* leagues from the *westermost* of the islands, it would correspond well with his description, the bearings being the same, and the land on the east side of it high, and low on the west: He is also nearly right in the latitude of his islands, which he makes 5° 10′ N.; for probably some parts of the southermost of them may lie in that latitude; but as I did not go to the southward of them, this is only conjecture.

Between Hummock Island, which is the largest and westermost of them, and the islands to the eastward of it, which are all flat and even, is a passage running north and south, which appears to be clear. The north-eastermost of these islands is small, low, and flat, with a white sandy beach all round it, and a great many trees in the middle. East, or north-east of this island, there are shoals and breakers; and I saw no other appearance of danger in these parts. Neither did I see any of the islands which are mentioned by Dampier, and laid down in all the charts, near Mindanao in the offing: Perhaps they are at a more remote distance than is commonly supposed; for without great attention, navigators will be much deceived in this particular by the height of the land, as I have observed already. As I coast-

ed

ed this island, I found the current set very strong to the southward along the shore, till I came to the south end of it, where I found it run N.W. and N.W. by W. which is nearly as the land trends. We had the winds commonly from S.W. to N.W. with light airs, frequent rain, and un-settled weather.

We now bid farewell to Mindanao, greatly disappointed in our hope of obtaining refreshments, which at first the in-habitants so readily promised to furnish. We suspected that there were Dutchmen, or at least Dutch partisans in the town; and that, having discovered us to be English, they had dispatched an armed party to prevent our having any intercourse with the natives, who arrived about two hours after our friendly conference, and were the people that defied us from the shore.

SECTION IX.

The Passage from Mindanao to the Island of Celebes, with a particular Account of the Streight of Macassar, in which many Errors are corrected.

AFTER leaving Mindanao, I stood to the westward for the passage between the islands of Borneo and Celebes, call-ed the Streight of Macassar, and made it on Saturday the 14th. I observed, that during the whole of this run we had a strong north-westerly current; but that while we were nearer to Mindanao than Celebes, it ran rather towards the north than the west; and that when we came nearer to Celebes than we were to Mindanao, it ran rather towards the west than the north. The land of Celebes on the north end runs along to the entrance of the passage, is very lofty, and seems to trend away about W. by S. to a remarkable point in the passage, which makes in a hummock, and which at first we took for an island. I believe it to be the same which in the French charts is called Stroomen Point, but I gave it the name of *Hummock Point.* Its latitude, accord-ing to my account, is 1° 20′ N., longitude 121° 39′ E.; and it is a good mark for those to know the passage that fall in with the land coming from the eastward, who, if possible, should always make this side of the passage. From Hum-mock Point the land trends more away to the southward,

about

about S.W. by W. and to the southward of it there is a deep
bay, full of islands and rocks, which appeared to me to be
very dangerous. Just off the point there are two rocks,
which, though they are above water, cannot be seen from
a ship till she is close to the land. To the eastward of this
point, close to the shore, are two islands, one of them very
flat, long, and even, and the other swelling into a hill; both
these islands, as well as the adjacent country, are well covered with trees : I stood close in a little to the eastward of
them, and had no ground with an hundred fathom, within
half a mile of the shore, which seemed to be rocky. A little to the westward of these islands, we saw no less than sixty boats, which were fishing on some shoals that lie between
them and Hummock Point. This part of the shore appeared to be foul, and I think should not be approached without
great caution. In this place I found the currents various
and uncertain, sometimes setting to the southward, and
sometimes to the northward, and sometimes there was no
current at all ; the weather also was very unsettled, and so
was the wind ; it blew, however, chiefly to the south and
south-west quarter, but we had sometimes sudden and violent gusts, and tornadoes from the N.W. with thunder,
lightning, and rain : These generally lasted about an hour,
when they were succeeded by a dead calm, and the wind
would afterwards spring up fresh from the S. W. or S.S.W.
which was right against us, and blow strong. From these
appearances I conjectured that the shifting season had commenced, and that the west monsoon would soon set in. The
ship sailed so ill that we made very little way ; we frequently sounded in this passage, but could get no ground.

On the 21st of November, as we were standing towards
Borneo, we made two small islands, which I judged to be
the same that in the French chart are called Taba Islands :
They are very small, and covered with trees. By my account, they lie in latitude 1° 44' N., longitude 7° 32 W. off
the south end of Mindanao, and are distant from Hummock,
or Stroomen Point, about fifty-eight leagues. The weather
was now hazy, but happening suddenly to clear up, we saw
a shoal, with breakers, at the distance of about five or six
miles, from the south to the north-west. Off the north end
of this shoal we saw four hummocks close together, which
we took for small islands, and seven more from the S.½ W.
to the W.½ S. : Whether these are really islands, or some

hills

hills on the island of Borneo, I could not determine. This
shoal is certainly very dangerous, but may be avoided by
going to the westward of Taba Islands, where the passage
is clear and broad. In the French chart of Monsieur D'Apres
de Mandevillette, published in 1745, two shoals are laid
down, to the eastward, and a little to the north of these
islands : One of them is called Vanloorif, and the other, on
which are placed two islands, Harigs ; but these shoals and
islands have certainly no existence, as I turned through this
part of the passage from side to side, and sailed over the
very spot where they are supposed to lie. In the same chart
seven small islands are also laid down within half a degree
to the northward of the Line, and exactly in the middle of
the narrowest part of this passage ; but neither have these
islands any existence, except upon paper, though I believe
there may be some small islands close to the main land of
Borneo : We thought we had seen two, which we took to
be those that are laid down in the charts off *Porto Tubo*,
but of this I am not certain. The southermost and narrowest part of this passage is about eighteen or twenty leagues
broad, with high lands on each side. We continued labouring in it till the 27th, before we crossed the Line, so that we
were a fortnight in sailing eight-and twenty leagues, the
distance from the north entrance of the streight, which we
made on the 14th   After we got to the southward of the
Line, we found a slight current cutting against us to the
northward, which daily increased : The weather was still
unsettled, with much wet : The winds were chiefly S.W.
and W.S.W. and very seldom farther to the northward than
W.N.W. except in the tornadoes, which grew more frequent and violent ; and by them we got nothing but hard
labour, as they obliged us to hand all our sails, which indeed with our utmost effort we were scarcely able to do,
our debility daily increasing by the falling sick of the few
that were well, or the death of some among the many that
were sick.   Under these circumstances we used our utmost
endeavours to get hold of the land on the Borneo side, but
were not able, and continued to struggle with our misfortunes till the 3d of December, when we fell in with the small
islands and shoals called the Little Pater-nosters, the southermost of which, according to my account, lies in latitude
2° 31' S. and the northermost in 2° 15' S. the longitude of
the northermost I made 117° 12' E. : They bear about S.E.
¾ S.

¼S. and N.W.¼N. of each other, distant eight leagues, and between them are the others; the number of the whole is eight. They lie very near the Celebes side of the streight, and being unable either to weather them, or get to the westward of them, we were obliged to go between them and the island. We had here tempestuous weather and contrary winds, with sudden and impetuous gusts, which, as we had not a number of hands sufficient to bend the sails, often endangered our masts and yards, and did great damage to our sails and rigging, especially at this time, as we were obliged to carry all the sail we could to prevent our falling into a deep bight, on the Celebes shore. The ravages of the scurvy were now universal, there not being one individual among us that was free, and the winds and currents being so hard against us, that we could neither get westing nor southing to reach any place of refreshment; the mind participated in the sufferings of the body, and a universal despondency was reflected from one countenance to another, especially among those who were not able to come upon the deck. In this deplorable situation we continued till the 10th, and it is not perhaps very easy for the most fertile imagination to conceive by what our danger and distress could possibly be increased; yet debilitated, sick, and dying as we were, in sight of land that we could not reach, and exposed to tempests which we could not resist, we had the additional misfortune to be attacked by a pirate: That this unexpected mischief might lose none of its force, it happened at midnight, when the darkness that might almost be felt, could not fail to co-operate with whatever tended to produce confusion and terror. This sudden attack, however, rather roused than depressed us, and though our enemy attempted to board us, before we could have the least apprehension that an enemy was near, we defeated his purpose: He then plied us with what we supposed to be swivel guns, and small arms, very briskly; but though he had the start of us, we soon returned his salute with such effect, that shortly after he sunk, and all the unhappy wretches on board perished. It was a small vessel, but of what country, or how manned, it was impossible for us to know. The lieutenant, and one of the men, were wounded, though not dangerously; part of our running rigging was cut, and we received some other slight damage. We knew this pirate to be a vessel which we had seen in the dusk of
the

the evening, and we afterwards learned that she belonged
to a freebooter, who had more than thirty such vessels under his command. The smallness of our vessel encouraged
the attack, and her strength being so much more than in
proportion to her size, supposing her a merchantman, rendered it fatal.

On Saturday the 12th, we fell in with the dangerous
shoals called the Spera Mondes, and had the mortification
to find that the westerly monsoon was now set in, against
which, and the current, it was impossible for any ship to
get as far westward as Batavia. As it was now necessary to
wait till the return of the eastern monsoon, and the shifting
of the current; as we had buried thirteen of our crew, and
no less than thirty more were at the point of death; as all
the petty officers were among the sick, and the lieutenant
and myself, who did all duties, in a feeble condition; it was
impossible that we should keep the sea, and we had no
chance of preserving those who were still alive, but by getting on shore at some place, where rest and refreshment
might be procured; I therefore determined that I would
take advantage of our being so far to the southward, and
endeavour to reach Macassar, the principal settlement of
the Dutch upon the island of Celebes.

The next day, we made some islands which lie not far
from that place, and saw, what sometimes we took for shoals,
and sometimes for boats with men on board, but what afterwards appeared to be trees, and other drift, floating about,
with birds sitting upon them; we suddenly found ourselves
twenty miles farther to the southward than we expected,
for the current, which had for some time set us to the northward, had set us to the southward during the night. We
now hauled up east, and E.$\frac{1}{4}$N. intending to have gone to
the northward of a shoal, which has no name in our East
India Pilot, but which the Dutch call the Thumb: By noon,
however, we found ourselves upon it, our water shallowing
at once to four fathom, with rocky ground. We now hauled off to the south-west, and keeping the boat a-head to
sound, ran round the west side of the shoal in ten and twelve
fathom; our water deepening when we hauled off to the
west, and shallowing when we hauled off east. Our latitude, by observation, when we were upon the shoal, was 5°
20′ S. and the northermost of the islands, called the Three
Brothers, then bore S. 81 E. at the distance of five or six

leagues.

leagues. This island is, in the English Pilot, called Don Di-
nanga, but by the Dutch the North Brother.

Between the Three Brothers, and the main of Celebes,
there is another island, much larger than either of them,
called the island of Tonikiky; but none of them are inhabited, though there are a few huts belonging to fishermen
upon them all. The passage between the shoal and this
island is clear and good, with from ten to thirteen fathom
and a sandy bottom; but the soundings are to be kept on
the side of the island in twelve fathom, and never under
ten: It is, however, very difficult and dangerous for ships
to fall in with the land this way without a pilot on board,
for there are many shoals and rocks under water. I ran
in by a chart in the English East India Pilot, which upon
the whole I found a good one, though the names of the
islands, points, and bays, differ very much from those by
which they are now known. When we got near to the Celebes shore, we had land and sea-breezes, which obliged us
to edge along the coast, though our strength was so much
reduced, that it was with the utmost difficulty we could
work the stream anchor.

In the evening of Tuesday the 15th, we anchored at about
the distance of four miles from the town of Macassar, which,
according to my account, lies in latitude 5° 10' or 5° 12' S.,
longitude 117° 28' E. having spent no less than five and
thirty weeks in our passage from the Streight of Magellan.

I have been the more particular in my description of as
much as I saw of this streight, because all the charts, both
English and French, that I consulted, are extremely deficient and erroneous, and because an exact knowledge of it
may be of great service to our China trade: The ships by
which that trade is carried on, may pass this way with as
little danger as by the common one, which lies along the
Prassel shoals; and when they miss their passage to China,
in the south-east monsoon, and lose the season, they may
be sure of a clear channel here, and fair winds at W.S.W.,
W. and round to W.N.W., in November, December, and
the four following months: I am also of opinion, that it is
a better and shorter way to go to the N.E. and eastward of
the Philippine Islands, than to thread the Moluccas, or
coast New Guinea, where there are shoals, currents, and
innumerable other dangers, as they were forced to do when
the

the French were cruising for them in the common passage during the last war.

Section X.

Transactions off Macassar, and the Passage thence to Bonthain.

THE same night that we came to an anchor, at about eleven o'clock, a Dutchman came on board, who had been dispatched by the governor, to learn who we were. When I made him understand that the ship was an English man-of-war, he seemed to be greatly alarmed, no man-of-war belonging to the King of Great Britain having ever been there before, and I could not by any means persuade him to leave the deck, and go down into the cabin; we parted, however, to all appearance, good friends.

The next morning, at break of day, I sent the lieutenant to the town, with a letter to the governor, in which I acquainted him with the reason of my coming thither, and requested the liberty of the port to procure refreshments for my ship's company, who were in a dying condition, and shelter for the vessel against the approaching storms, till the return of a fit season for sailing to the westward. I ordered that this letter should, without good reason to the contrary, be delivered into the governor's own hand; but when my officer got to the wharf of the town, neither he nor any other person in the boat was suffered to land. Upon his refusal to deliver the letter to a messenger, the governor was made acquainted with it, and two officers, called the shebander and the fiscal, were sent down to him, who, as a reason why he could not deliver the letter to the governor himself, pretended that he was sick, and said, that they came by his express order to fetch it; upon this the letter was at length delivered to them, and they went away. While they were gone, the officer and men were kept on board their boat, exposed to the burning heat of the sun, which was almost vertical at noon, and none of the country boats were suffered to come near enough to sell them any refreshment. In the mean time, our people observed a great hurry and bustle on shore, and all the sloops and vessels that were proper for war were fitted out with the utmost expedition:

1

expedition : We should, however, I believe, have been an overmatch for their whole sea force, if all our people had been well.   In the mean time I intended to have gone and anchored close to the town; but now the boat was absent, our united strength was not sufficient to weigh the anchor though a small one.   After waiting five hours in the boat, the lieutenant was told that the governor had ordered two gentlemen to wait upon me with an answer to my letter. Soon after he had returned, and made this report, the two gentlemen came on board, and we afterwards learned that one of them was an ensign of the garrison, named Le Cerf, and the other Mr Douglas, a writer of the Dutch East India company : They delivered me the governor's letter, but it proved to be written in Dutch, a language which not a single person on board could understand : The two gentlemen who brought it, however, both spoke French, and one of them interpreted the contents to me in that language. The purport of it was, " that I should instantly depart from the port, without coming any nearer to the town ; that I should not anchor on any part of the coast, or permit any of my people to land in any place that was under his jurisdiction."   Before I made any reply to this letter, I shewed the gentlemen who brought it the number of my sick : At the sight of so many unhappy wretches, who were dying of languor and disease, they seemed to be much affected ; and I then urged again the pressing necessity I was under of procuring refreshment, to which they had been witnesses, the cruelty and injustice of refusing to supply me, which was not only contrary to treaty, as we were in a king's ship, but to the laws of nature, as we were human beings: They seemed to admit the force of this reasoning, but they had a short and final answer ready, " that they had absolute and indispensable orders from their masters, not to suffer any ship, of whatever nation, to stay at this port, and that these orders they must implicitly obey."   To this I replied, that persons in our situation had nothing worse to fear than what they suffered, and that therefore, if they did not immediately allow me the liberty of the port, to purchase refreshments, and procure shelter, I would, as soon as the wind would permit, in defiance of all their menaces, and all their force, go and anchor close to the town ; that if at last I should find myself unable to compel them to comply with requisitions, the reasonableness of which could not be controverted, I would run the ship a-ground under their walls, and, after selling our lives as dearly as we could, bring upon them the disgrace of having reduced a friend and ally to so dreadful an extremity. At this they seemed to be alarmed, as our situation alone was sufficient to convince them that I was in earnest, and urged me with great emotion to remain where I was, at least till I had heard again from the governor: To this, after some altercation, I consented, upon condition that I heard from the governor before the sea-breeze set in the next day.

We passed all the remainder of this day, and all the night, in a state of anxiety, not unmixed with indignation, that greatly aggravated our distress; and very early the next morning, we had the mortification to see a sloop that mounted eight carriage guns, and one of the vessels of the country, fitted out for war, with a great number of soldiers on board, come from the town, and anchor under each of our bows. I immediately sent my boat to speak with them, but they would make no reply to any thing that was said. About noon, the sea-breeze set in, and not having then heard again from the governor, I got under sail, and proceeded towards the town, according to my declaration, resolving, if the vessels that had anchored under our bows should oppose us, to repress force with force as far as we were able: These two vessels, however, happily both for us and for them, contented themselves with weighing anchor, and attending our motions.

Very soon after we had got under sail, a handsome vessel, with a band of music, and several gentlemen on board, made up to us, and told us that they were sent by the governor, but could not come on board if we did not drop our anchor again; our anchor therefore was immediately dropped, and the gentlemen came on board: They proved to be Mr Blydenbourg the fiscal, Mr Voll the shebander, an officer called the licence-master, or master of the port, and Mr Douglas the writer, who has been mentioned already. They expressed some surprise at my having got under sail, and asked me what I intended to have done; I told them that I intended neither more nor less than to fulfil the declarations I had made the day before; that, justified by the common rights of mankind, which were superior to every other law, I would, rather than have put again to sea, where our destruction, either by shipwreck, sickness, or famine, was inevitable

evitable, have come up to their walls, and either have compelled them to furnish the necessaries we wanted, or have run the ship on shore, since it was better to perish at once in a just contest, than to suffer the lingering misery of anticipating the perdition that we could not avoid. I observed also, that no civilized people had ever suffered even the captives of war to perish for want of the necessaries of life, much less the subjects of an ally, who asked nothing but permission to purchase food with their money. They readily allowed the truth of all I had said, but seemed to think I had been too hasty: I then observed that I had waited the full time of my stipulation, and they in return made some excuse for their not having come sooner, telling me, that as a proof of their having admitted my claim, they had brought me such provisions as their country would afford. These were immediately taken on board, and consisted of two sheep, an elk ready killed, and a few fowls, with some vegetables and fruit. This most welcome supply was divided among the people; and that most salutary, and to us exquisite dainty, broth, made for the sick. Another letter from the governor was then produced, in which, to my great disappointment, I was again ordered to leave the port, and to justify the order, it was alleged, that to suffer a ship of any nation to stay and trade, either at this port, or any other part of the island, was contrary to the agreement which had been made by the East India Company with the native kings and governors of the country, who had already expressed some displeasure on our account; and for farther particulars I was referred to the gentlemen that brought the letter, whom the governor styled his commissaries. To these gentlemen I immediately observed, that no stipulation concerning trade could affect us, as we were a king's ship; at the same time I produced my commission, it not being possible to bring under the article of trade the selling us food and refreshments for our money, without the utmost violence to language and common sense. After this they made me several propositions, which I rejected, because my departure from this place, before the return of the season, was included in them all. I then recurred to my former declaration, and to enforce it, shewed them the corpse of a man who had died that morning, and whose life would probably have been saved, if they had afforded us refreshments when we first came to an anchor upon their

coast

coast. This put them to a stand, but, after a short pause, they enquired very particularly whether I had been among the spice islands; I answered them in the negative, and they appeared to be convinced that I spoke truth. After this, we came to a better understanding, and they told me, that though they could not, without disobedience to the most direct and positive orders of the Company, suffer us to remain here, yet that I was welcome to go to a little bay not far distant, where I should find effectual shelter from the bad monsoon, and might erect an hospital for my sick, assuring me at the same time that provision and refreshments were more plenty there than at Macassar, from whence, whatever else I wanted should be sent me, and offering me a good pilot to carry me to my station. To this I gladly consented, upon condition that what they had offered should be confirmed to me by the governor and council of Macassar, that I might be considered as under the protection of the Dutch nation, and that no violence should be offered to my people : For all this they engaged their honour on behalf of the governor and council, promising me the assurance I had required on the next day, and requesting that in the mean time I would remain where I was. I then enquired why the two vessels which were at anchor under our bows were allotted to that station; and they told me, for no other reason than to prevent the people of the country from offering us any violence. When matters were thus far settled between us, I expressed my concern that, except a glass of wine, I could present them with nothing better than bad salt meat, and bread full of weevils; upon which they very politely desired that I would permit their servants to bring in the victuals which had been dressing in their own vessel; I readily consented, and a very genteel dinner was soon served up, consisting of fish, flesh, vegetables, and fruit. It is with the greatest pleasure that I take this opportunity of acknowledging my obligations to these gentlemen for the politeness and humanity of their behaviour in their private capacity, and particularly to Mr Douglas, who, being qualified by his knowledge of the French language to interpret between us, undertook that office, with a courtesy and politeness which very much increased the value of the favour. After this we parted, and at their leaving the ship, I saluted them with nine guns.

The next morning the shebander was sent to acquaint me,
that

that the governor and council had confirmed the engagement which had been made with me on their behalf. Every thing was now settled much to my satisfaction, except the procuring money for my bills upon the government of Great Britain, which the shebander said he would solicit. At eight o'clock in the evening, he came on board again, to let me know that there was not any person in the town who had money to remit to Europe, and that there was not a dollar in the Company's chest. I answered, that as I was not permitted to go on shore to negociate my bills myself, I hoped they would give me credit, offering him bills for any debt I should contract, or to pay it at Batavia. To this the shebander replied, that the resident at Bouthain, the place to which I was going, would receive orders to supply me with whatever I should want, and would be glad to take my bills in return, as he had money to remit, and was himself to go to Europe the next season. He told me also, that he had considerable property in England, being a denizen of that country; "and," said the shebander, "he has also money in my hands, with which I will purchase such things as you want from Macassar, and see that they are sent after you." Having specified what these articles were to be, and agreed with him for the quantity and the price, we parted.

The next day, in the afternoon, I received a letter, signed by the governor and council of Macassar, containing the reasons why I was sent to Bonthain, and confirming the verbal agreement which subsisted between us.

Soon after, the ensign M. le Cerf, the secretary of the council, and a pilot, came on board to attend us to Bonthain. Le Cerf was to command the soldiers who were on board the guard boats; and the secretary, as we afterwards discovered, was to be a check upon the resident whose name was Swellingrabel. This gentleman's father died second governor at the Cape of Good Hope, where he married an English lady of the name of Fothergill. Mr Swellingrabel, the resident here, married the daughter of Cornelius Sinklaar, who had been governor of Macassar, and died some time ago in England, having come hither to see some of his mother's relations.

Section XI.

Transactions at Bonthain, while the Vessel was waiting for a Wind to carry her to Batavia, with some Account of the Place, the Town of Macassar, and the adjacent Country.

THE next morning at day-break we sailed, and the day following in the afternoon we anchored in Bonthain road with our two guard-boats, which were immediately moored close in to the shore, to prevent the country boats from coming near us, and our boats from going near them. As soon as I arrived at this place, I altered our reckoning. I had lost about eighteen hours, in coming by the west, and the Europeans that we found here having come by the east had gained about six, so that the difference was just a day.

I immediately waited upon the resident, Mr Swellingrabel, who spoke English but very imperfectly, and having settled with him all matters relating to money and provisions, a house was allotted me near the sea-side, and close to a little pallisadoed fort of eight guns, the only one in this place, which I converted into an hospital, under the direction of the surgeon; to this place I immediately sent all the people who were thought incapable of recovering on board, and reserved the rest as a security against accidents. As soon as our people were on shore, a guard of thirty-six private men, two serjeants, and two corporals, all under the command of Ensign Le Ceif, was set over them; and none of them were suffered to go more than thirty yards from the hospital, nor were any of the country people allowed to come near enough to sell them any thing; so that our men got nothing of them, but through the hands of the Dutch soldiers, who abused their power very shamefully. When they saw any of the country people carrying what they thought our invalids would purchase, they first took it away, and then asked the price: What was demanded signified little, the soldier gave what he thought proper, which was seldom one-fourth of the value; and if the countryman ventured to express any discontent, he gave him immediately an earnest of perfect satisfaction, by flourishing his broad-sword over his head: This was always sufficient to

silence

silence complaint, and send the sufferer quietly away; after which the soldier sold what he had thus acquired for profit of sometimes more than a thousand per cent. This behaviour was so cruel to the natives, and so injurious to us, that I ventured to complain of it to the resident, and the other two gentlemen, Le Cerf and the secretary. The resident, with becoming spirit, reprimanded the soldiers; but it produced so little effect that I could not help entertaining suspicions that Le Cerf connived at these practices, and shared the advantages which they produced. I suspected him also of selling arrack to my people, of which I complained, but without redress; and I know that his slaves were employed to buy things at the market which his wife afterwards sold to us for more than twice as much as they cost. The soldiers were indeed guilty of many other irregularities: It was the duty of one of them by rotation to procure the day's provision for the whole guard, a service which he constantly performed by going into the country with his musket and a bag; nor was the honest proveditor always content with what the bag would contain; for one of them, without any ceremony, drove down a young buffalo that belonged to some of the country people, and his comrades not having wood at hand to dress it when it was killed, supplied themselves by pulling down some of the pallisadoes of the fort. When this was reported to me, I thought it so extraordinary that I went on shore to see the breach, and found the poor black people repairing it.

On the 26th, a sloop laden with rice was sent out from this place in order to land her cargo at Macassar; but after having attempted it three days she was forced to return. The weather was now exceedingly tempestuous, and all navigation at an end from east to west till the return of the eastern monsoon. On the same day two large sloops that were bound to the eastward anchored here, and the next morning also a large ship from Batavia, with troops on board for the Banda Islands; but none of the crew of any of these vessels were suffered to speak to any of our people, our boats being restrained from going on board them, and theirs from coming on board us. As this was a mortifying restriction, we requested Mr Swellingrabel to buy us some salt meat from the large ship; and he was so obliging as to procure us four casks of very good European meat, two of pork, and two of beef.

On

On the 28th a fleet of more than an hundred sail of the small country vessels, called pioas, anchored here; their burden is from twelve to eighteen and twenty tons, and they carry from sixteen to twenty men. I was told that they carried on a fishery round the island, going out with one monsoon, and coming back with the other, so as always to keep under the lee of the land: The fish was sent to the China market, and I observed that all these vessels carried Dutch colours.

No event worthy of notice happened till the 18th of January, and then I learnt by a letter from Macassar that the Dolphin had been at Batavia. On the 28th, the secretary of the council, who had been sent hither with Le Cerf, as we supposed to be a check upon the resident, was called to Macassar. By this time our carpenter, having in a great degree recovered his health, examined the state of our vessel, and to our great regret she appeared to be very leaky: Our main yard also was found not only to be sprung, but to be rotten and unserviceable. We got it down and patched it up as well as we could, without either iron or a forge, so that we hoped it would serve us till we got to Batavia, for no wood was to be procured here of which a new one could be made. To our leaks very little could be done, and we were therefore reduced to an entire dependence upon our pumps.

On Friday the 19th of February, Le Cerf, the military officer who commanded the soldiers on shore, was recalled, as it was said, to fit out an expedition for the island of Bally; on the 7th of March, the largest of our guard-boats, a sloop about forty-five tons, was ordered back to Macassar with part of the soldiers; and on the 9th, the resident, Mr Swellingrabel, received a letter from the governor of that place, enquiring when I should sail for Batavia. I must confess, that I was surprised at the recal of the officer, and the guard boat; but I was much more surprised at the contents of the governor's letter, because he knew that it was impossible I should sail till May, as the eastern monsoon would not sooner set in. All matters, however, remained in the same situation till near the end of the month, when some of my people took notice, that for a short time past a small canoe had gone round us several times at different hours of the night, and had disappeared as soon as those on board perceived any body stirring in the ship. On the 29th,

29th, while these things were the subjects of speculation, one of my officers who came from the shore brought me a letter, which he said had been delivered to him by a black man: It was directed, " To the Commander of the English ship at Bonthyn." That the reader may understand this letter, it is necessary to acquaint him, that the island of Celebes is divided into several districts, which are distinct sovereignties of the native princes. The town of Macassar is in a district called also Macassar, or Bony, the king of which is in alliance with the Dutch, who have been many times repulsed in an attempt to reduce other parts of the island, one of which is inhabited by a people called Buggueses, and another is called Waggs or Tosora. The town of Tosora is fortified with cannon, for the natives had been long furnished with fire-arms from Europe, before the Dutch settled themselves at Macassar in the room of the Portuguese.

The letter acquainted me, that a design had been formed by the Dutch, in conjunction with the king of Bony, to cut us off: That the Dutch, however, were not to appear in it: That the business was to be done by a son of the king of Bony, who was, besides a gratuity from the Dutch, to receive the plunder of the vessel for his reward, and who, with eight hundred men, was then at Bonthain for that purpose: That the motive was jealousy of our forming a connection with the Buggueses, and other people of the country, who were at enmity with the Dutch and their allies, and driving them out of the island; or at least a suspicion that, if we got back to England, some project of that kind might be founded upon the intelligence we should give, no English man-of-war, as I have already observed, having ever been known to have visited the island before.

This letter was a new subject of surprise and speculation. It was extremely ill written with respect to the style and manner, yet it did not therefore the less deserve notice. How far the intelligence which it contained was true or false, I was utterly unable to determine: It was possible that the writer might be deceived himself; it was also possible that he might have some view in wilfully deceiving me: The falsehood might procure some little reward for the kindness and zeal which it placed to his account, or it might give him an importance which would at least be a gratification to his vanity. It behoved me, however, to take
the

the same measures as if I had known it to be true; and I must confess, that I was not perfectly at ease when I recollected the recal of the Secretary and Le Cerf, with the large sloop, and part of the soldiers, who were said to have been sent hither for no other reason than to guard us against the insults of the country people; the assembling an armed force at Macassar, as it was said, for an expedition to Bally; and the little canoe that we had seen rowing round us in the night, not to mention the governor's enquiry by letter, when we intended to leave the island. However, whether either our intelligence or conjectures were true or false, we immediately went to work: We rigged the ship, bent the sails, unmoored, got springs upon our cables, loaded all our guns, and barricadoed the deck. At night every body slept under arms, and the next day we warped the vessel farther off from the bottom of the bay, towards the eastern shore, that we might have more room, fixed four swivel guns on the forepart of the quarter-deck, and took every other measure that appeared to be necessary for our defence.

The resident, Mr Swellingrabel, was at this time absent twenty miles up the country upon the Company's business, but had told me, that he should certainly return on the 1st of April, a day which I now expected with great impatience, especially as an old drunken serjeant was the most respectable person at the fort. In the evening of the 31st, a packet of letters for him arrived here from Macassar, which I considered as a good omen, and a pledge of his return at the time appointed; but I conceived very different sentiments when I learnt that they were sent to him. I did not suspect that he was privy to any such design as had been intimated to me by the letter; but I could not help doubting, whether he was not kept in the country that he might be out of the way when it should be executed. In this state of anxiety and suspense, I sent a message to the fort, desiring that an express might be dispatched to him, to acquaint him that I wished to see him immediately upon business of great importance, which would admit of no delay. Whether my message was forwarded to him or not, I cannot tell; but having waited till the 4th of April, without having seen him or received any answer, I wrote him a letter, requesting to speak with him, in the most pressing terms, and the next day he came on board. A few minutes

convinced

convinced me that he was wholly a stranger to any such design as I had been made to apprehend; and he was clearly of opinion that no such design had been formed. He said, indeed, that one Tomilaly, a counsellor or minister of the king of Bony, had lately paid him a visit, and had not well accounted for his being in this part of the country; and, at my request, he very readily undertook to make further enquiries concerning him and his people. The resident and his attendants took notice that the ship was put into a state of defence, and that every thing was ready for immediate action; and he told us, that the people on shore had acquainted him, before he came on board, with our vigilance and activity, and in particular, with our having exercised the ship's company at small arms every day. I informed him, that we should, at all events, continue upon our guard, which he seemed to approve, and we parted with mutual protestations of friendship and good faith. After a few days, he sent me word that having made a very strict enquiry, whether any other persons belonging to the king of Bony had been at Bonthain, he had been credibly informed that one of the princes of that kingdom had been there in disguise; but that of the eight hundred men who were said in my intelligence to be with him, he could find no traces; so that, except they too, like the troops of the king of Brentford, were an army in disguise, I knew that no such people could be in that country.

On the 16th, in the morning, the resident sent me word, that M. Le Cerf was returned from Macassar with another officer, and that they would come on board and dine with me. When dinner was over, I asked Le Cerf, among other conversation, while we were taking our wine, what was become of his expedition to Bally; to which he answered dryly, that it was laid aside, without saying any thing more upon the subject. On the 23d, he returned to Macassar by sea, and the other officer, who was also an ensign, remained to take the command of the soldiers that were still left at this place.

The season now approached in which navigation to the westward would be again practicable, which gave us all great pleasure; especially as putrid diseases had begun to make their appearance among us, and a putrid fever had carried off one of our people.

On the 7th of May, the resident gave me a long letter
from

from the governor of Macassar, which was written in Dutch, and of which he gave me the best interpretation he was able. The general purport of it was, that he had heard a letter had been sent to me, charging him, in conjunction with the king of Bony, with a design to cut us off: That the letter was altogether false, exculpating himself with the most solemn protestations, and requiring the letter to be delivered up, that the writer might be brought to such punishment as he deserved. It is scarcely necessary to say, that I did not deliver up the letter, because the writer would certainly have been punished with equal severity whether it was true or false; but I returned the governor a polite answer, in which I justified the measures I had taken, without imputing any evil design to him or his allies; and indeed there is the greatest reason to believe, that there was not sufficient ground for the charge contained in the letter, though it is not equally probable that the writer believed it to be false.

At day-break on Sunday the 22d of May, we sailed from this place, of which, and of the town of Macassar, and the adjacent country, I shall say but little, there being many accounts of the island of Celebes and its inhabitants already extant. The town is built upon a kind of point or neck of land, and is watered by a river or two, which either run through, or very near it. It seems to be large, and there is water for a ship to come within half cannon-shot of the walls: The country about it is level, and has a most beautiful appearance; it abounds with plantations, and groves of cocoa-nut trees, with a great number of houses interspersed, by which it appears to abound with people. At a distance inland, the country rises into hills of a great height, and becomes rude and mountainous. The town lies in latitude 5° 10' or 5° 12' S. and longitude, by account, 117° 28' E. of London.

Bonthain is a large bay, where ships may lie in perfect security during both the monsoons: The soundings are good and regular, and the bottom soft mud; nor is there any danger coming in, but a ledge of rocks which are above water, and are a good mark for anchoring. The highest land in sight here is called Bonthain hill, and when a ship is in the offing at the distance of two or three miles from the land, she should bring this hill north, or N. ½ W., and then run in with it and anchor. We lay right under it, at

the

3

the distance of about a mile from the shore. In this bay there are several small towns; that which is called Bonthain lies in the north-east part of the bay, and here is the small pallisadoed fort that has been mentioned already, on which there are mounted eight guns that carry a ball of about eight pounds weight: It is just sufficient to keep the country people in subjection, and is intended for no other purpose: It lies on the south side of a small river, and there is water for a ship to come close to it. The Dutch resident has the command of the place, and of Bullocomba, another town which lies about twenty miles farther to the eastward, where there is such another fort, and a few soldiers, who at the proper season are employed in gathering the rice, which the people pay as a tax to the Dutch.

Wood and water are to be procured here in great plenty; we cut our wood near the river, under Bonthain hill: Our water was procured partly from that river, and partly from another; when from the other, our boat went above the fort with the casks that were to be filled, where there is a good rolling way; but as the river is small, and has a bar, the boat, after it is loaded, can come out only at high water. There are several other small rivers in the bay, from which water may be got upon occasion.

We procured plenty of fresh provisions all the while we lay here at a reasonable rate: The beef is excellent; but it would be difficult to procure enough of it for a squadron. Rice may be had in any quantity, so may fowls and fruit: There are also abundance of wild hogs in the woods, which may be purchased at a low price, as the natives being Mahometans, never eat them. Fish may be caught with the seine, and the natives, at times, supplied us with turtle; for this, like pork, is a dainty which they never touch.

Celebes is the key of the Molucca, or Spice Islands, which, whoever is in possession of it must necessarily command: Most of the ships that are bound to them, or to Banda, touch here, and always go between this island and that of Solayer. The bullocks here are the breed that have the bunch on the back, besides which the island produces horses, buffaloes, goats, sheep, and deer. The arrack and sugar that are consumed here are brought from Batavia.

The latitude of Bonthain hill is 5° 30′ S., longitude, by account, 117° 53′ E. The variation of the compass while

we

we were here was 1° 16′ W. The tides are very irregular; commonly it is but once high water and once low water in four-and-twenty hours, and there is seldom six feet difference between them.

Section XII.

Passage from Bonthain Bay, in the Island of Celebes, to Batavia: Transactions there, and the Voyage round the Cape of Good Hope to England.

When we left Bonthain Bay, we kept along the shore, at the distance of two or three miles, till evening, and then anchored for the night, in the passage between the two islands of Celebes and Tonikaky, in seven fathom and a half, with a bottom of soft mud. The next morning, we got again under sail, and took our departure from Tonikaky, which, according to my account, lies in latitude 5° 31′ S., longitude 117° 17′ E.; the variation here was 1° W. We went to the southward of Tonikaky, and stood to the westward. About three o'clock in the afternoon, we were abreast of the easternmost of the islands which in the Dutch charts are called Tonyn's Islands. This island bore from us about N. by W. at the distance of four miles, and the two westernmost were in sight. These three islands make a kind of right-angled triangle with each other, the distance between the easternmost and westernmost is about eleven miles, and their relative bearings are very nearly east and west. The distance between the two westernmost is nearly the same, and they bear to each other S. by E. and N. by W. About six o'clock, having just sounded, and got no ground, we suddenly found ourselves upon a shoal, with not three fathom, and the water being smooth and clear, we could see great crags of coral rocks under our bottom: We immediately threw all the sails aback, and happily got off without damage: We had just passed over the eastermost edge of it, which is as steep as a wall, for we had not gone back two cables' length before we were out of soundings again. At this time, we had the two westernmost of the Tonyn Islands in one, bearing N. by W. at the distance of somewhat more than four miles from the nearest. This is a very dangerous shoal, and is not laid down in any chart
that

that I have seen : It seemed to extend itself to the southward and westward, all round the two westermost of these
three islands, for near six miles, but about the eastermost
island there seemed to be no danger; there was also a clear
passage between this island and the other two. The latitude of the eastermost and westermost of these islands is 5°
31′ S. The eastermost is distant thirty-four miles due west
from Tonikaky, and the westermost lies ten miles farther.

In the afternoon of the 25th, we found the water much
discoloured; upon which we sounded, and had five-and-
thirty fathom, with soft mud. Soon after we went over to
the northermost part of a shoal, and had no more than ten
fathom, with soft mud. In this place, where we found the
water shallowest, it was very foul; it seemed to be still
shallower to the southward, but to the northward of us it
appeared to be clear. We had no observation this day, by
which I could ascertain the latitude; but I believe this to
be the northermost part of the shoals that lie to the eastward of the island Madura, and in the English East-India
Pilot are called Bralleron's Shoals, the same which in the
Dutch charts are called Kalcain's Eylandens. By my reckoning, the part that we went over lies in 5° 50′ or 5° 52′ S.
and 3° 36′ to the westward of the island Tonikaky, or S.
84° 27′ W. distance sixty-nine leagues. At eleven o'clock
the same night, we saw, to the northward of us, the southermost of the islands Salombo. I make its latitude to be
5° 33′ S. and its longitude west of Tonikaky 4° 4′, at the
distance of about eighty-two or eighty-three leagues. It
bears from the last shoal N.W. by W. ¼ W. at the distance
of about fourteen leagues. It is to be remarked, that here-
about, off the island of Madura, the winds of the monsoons are commonly a month later in settling than at Celebes. The variation here was not more than half a degree
west; and we found the current, which before set to the
southward, now setting to the N.W.

In the afternoon of the 26th, we saw from the mast-head
the island of Luback, and had soundings from thirty-five to
forty fathom, with a bottom of bluish clay. The latitude
of this island is 5° 43′ S. and its longitude 5° 36′ west of
Tonikaky, from which it is distant about one hundred and
twelve leagues. Its distance west from the islands of Salombo is thirty-one leagues. We went to the northward of
this island, and found a current setting to the W.N W.

In

In the evening of Sunday the 29th, we saw the cluster of small islands called Carimon-Java. The latitude of the eastermost, which is also the largest, is 5° 48′ S. and its longitude, west of Tonikaky, 7° 52′. From this island it is distant about one hundred and fifty-eight leagues, and forty-five leagues from Luback.

On Thursday the 2d of June, we hauled in and made the land of Java, which proved to be that part of the island which makes the eastermost point of the Bay of Batavia, called Carawawang Point. When we first got sight of the land, we had gradually decreased our soundings from forty to eight-and-twenty fathom, with a bottom of bluish mud. As we steered along the shore for Batavia, we decreased them gradually, still farther, to thirteen fathom, the depth in which, night coming on, we anchored near the two small islands called Leyden and Alkmar, in sight of Batavia; and in the afternoon of the next day, we anchored in the road, which is so good that it may well be considered as an harbour. We had now great reason to congratulate ourselves upon our situation; for during the whole of our passage from Celebes, the ship admitted so much water by her leaks, that it was all we could do to keep her from sinking, with two pumps constantly going.

We found here eleven large Dutch ships, besides several that were less; one Spanish ship, a Portuguese snow, and several Chinese junks. The next morning we saluted the town with eleven guns, and the same number was returned. As this was the birth-day of his Britannic majesty, our sovereign, we afterwards fired one-and-twenty guns more on that occasion. We found the variation here to be less than half a degree to the westward.

In the afternoon, I waited upon the governor, and acquainted him with the condition of the ship, desiring liberty to repair her defects; to which he replied, that I must petition the council.

On the 6th, therefore, which was council day, I addressed a letter to the governor and council, setting forth, more particularly, the condition of the ship; and, after requesting leave to repair her, I added, that I *hoped* they would allow me the use of such wharfs and storehouses as should be necessary. In the afternoon of the next day, the shebander, with Mr Garrison, a merchant of the place, as interpreter, and another person, came to me. After the first
compliments,

compliments, the shebander said, that he was sent by the governor and council for a letter, which they had heard I had received when I was at Bonthain, acquainting me, that a design had been formed to cut off my ship, that the author of it, who had injured both me and their nation in the person of the governor of that place, might be punished. I readily acknowledged that I had received such information, but said, that I had never told any body it was by letter. The shebander then asked me, if I would take an oath that I had received no such letter as he had been directed to demand, to which I answered, that I was surprised at the question; and desired, that if the council had any such uncommon requisition to make of me, it might be in writing; and I would give such reply, as, upon mature consideration, I should think proper. I then desired to know what answer he had been instructed to give to my letter concerning the refitting of the ship? Upon which he told me, that the council had taken offence at my having used the word *hope,* and not written in the style of request, which had been invariably adopted by all merchants upon the like occasion. I replied, that no offence was intended on my part; and that I had used the first words which occurred to me as proper to express my meaning. Thus we parted; and I heard nothing more of them till the afternoon of the 9th, when the shebander, and the same two gentlemen, came to me a second time. The shebander said, that he was then commissioned from the council, to require a writing under my hand, signifying, that I believed the report of an intention formed at the island of Celebes to cut off my ship, was false and malicious; saying, that he hoped I had a better opinion of the Dutch nation than to suppose them capable of suffering so execrable a fact to be perpetrated under their government. Mr Garrison then read me a certificate, which, by order of the council, had been drawn up for me to sign: As, whatever was my opinion, I did not think it advisable to sign such a certificate, especially as it appeared to be made a condition of complying with my request by the delay of an answer during this solicitation, I desired the shebander to shew me his authority for the requisition he had made. He replied, that he had no testimony of authority but the notoriety of his being a public officer, and the evidence of the gentlemen that were with him, confirming his own declaration, that

he acted in this particular by the express order of council.
I then repeated my request, that whatever the council required of me might be given me in writing, that the sense
of it might be fixed and certain, and that I might have
time to consider of my reply; but he gave me to understand, that he could not do this without an order from the
council, and I then absolutely refused to sign the paper, at
the same time desiring an answer to my letter, which they
not being prepared to give, we parted, not in very good
humour with each other.

After this, I waited in a fruitless expectation till the 15th,
when the same three gentlemen came to me the third time,
and said, they had been sent to tell me that the council
had protested against my behaviour at Macassar, and my
having refused to sign the certificate which had been required of me, as an insult upon them, and an act of injustice to their nation. I replied, that I was not conscious of
having in any instance acted contrary to the treaties sub-
sisting between the two kingdoms, unworthy of my character as an officer, honoured with a commission of his Britannic majesty, or unsuitable to the trust reposed in me,
though I did not think I had been used by the governor of
Macassar as the subject of a friend and ally; desiring, that
if they had any thing to allege against me, it might be reduced to writing, and laid before the king my master, to
whom alone I thought myself amenable. With this answer
they again departed; and the next day, having not yet received any answer to my letter, I wrote a second, directed
like the first, in which I represented that the ship's leaks
were every day increasing, and urged, in more pressing
terms, my request that she might be repaired, and that the
use of wharfs and store-houses might be afforded me.

On the 18th, the shebander came again to me, and acquainted me, that the council had given orders for the repair of the ship at Onrust; and as there was no store-house
empty, had appointed one of the company's vessels to attend me, and take in my stores. I enquired whether there
was not an answer to my letter in writing; to which he answered in the negative, adding, that it was not usual, a message by him, or some other officer, having been always
thought sufficient.

After this I was supplied, for my money, with every
thing

thing I could desire from the company's stores, without any further difficulty.

A pilot was ordered to attend me, and on the 22d we anchored at Onrust, where, having cleared the ship, and put her stores on board the company's vessel, we found the bowsprit and cap, as well as the main-yard, rotten, and altogether unserviceable, the sheathing every where eaten off by the worms, and the main planks of the ship's bottom so much damaged and decayed, that it was absolutely necessary to heave her down, before she could be sufficiently repaired to sail for Europe; but as other ships were already heaved down, and consequently the wharfs at this time preoccupied, the carpenters could not begin their work till the 24th of July.

Under the hands of these people the ship continued till Tuesday the 16th of August. When they came to examine her bottom, they found it so bad, that they were unanimously of opinion it should be shifted: This, however, I strenuously opposed. I knew she was an old ship; and I was afraid that if her bottom was opened, it might be found still worse than it was thought; and possibly so bad, as that, like the Falmouth, she might be condemned; I therefore desired that a good sheathing only might be put over all; but the *bawse*, or master-carpenter, would not consent, except I would certify, under my hand, that what should be done to the ship was not according to his judgment but my own, which, he said, was necessary for his justification, if, after such repairs only as I thought fit to direct had been made, the ship should come short of her port. As I thought this a reasonable proposition, I readily complied; but as I was now become answerable for the fate of the ship, I had her carefully examined by my own carpenter and his mate, myself and officers always attending. The but-ends of the planks that joined to the stern were so open, that a man's hand might be thrust in between; seven chain-plates were broken and decayed; the iron work, in general, was in a very bad state; several of the knees were loose, and some of them were broken.

While I remained here, two ships belonging to our India Company put into this port; and we found, among other private ships from India, one called the Dudly, from Bengal, which had proved so leaky that it was impossible to carry her back. Application had been made to the governor

vernor and council for leave to careen her, which had been granted; but as the wharfs had been kept in continual use, she had been put off above four months. The captain, not without reason, was apprehensive that he might be kept here till the worms had eaten through the bottom of his vessel, and knowing that I had received particular civilities from Admiral Houting, applied to me to intercede for him, which I was very happy to do with such success, that a wharf was immediately allotted her. Mr Houting was an old man, and an admiral in the service of the States, with the rank of commander-in-chief of their marine, and the ships belonging to the company in India. He received his first maritime knowledge on board an English man-of-war, speaks English and French extremely well, and did honour to the service both by his abilities and politeness: He was so obliging as to give me a general invitation to his table, in consequence of which I was often with him; and it is with pleasure that I take this opportunity of making a public acknowledgment of the favours I received from him, and bearing this testimony to his public and private merit. He was indeed the only officer belonging to the company from whom I received any civility, or with whom I had the least communication; for I found them, in general, a reserved and supercilious set of people. The governor, although the servant of a republic, takes upon himself more state, in some particulars, than any sovereign prince in Europe. Whenever he goes abroad, he is attended by a party of horse-guards, and two black men go before his coach in the manner of running-footmen; each having a large cane in his hand, with which they not only clear the way, but severely chastise all who do not pay the homage that is expected from people of all ranks, as well those belonging to the country as strangers. Almost every body in this place keeps a carriage, which is drawn by two horses, and driven by a man upon a box, like our chariots, but is open in front: Whoever, in such a carriage, meets the governor, either in the town or upon the road, is expected not only to draw it on one side, but to get out of it, and make a most respectful obeisance while his excellency's coach goes by; nor must any carriage that follows him drive past on any account, but keep behind him, however pressing be the necessity for haste. A very mortifying homage of the same kind is also exacted by the members of the council, called

Edele

Edele Heeren; for whoever meets them is obliged to stop
his coach, and, though not to get out, to stand up in it,
and make his reverence. These Édele Heeren are preceded
by one black man with a stick; nor must any person presume to pass their carriage any more than that of the governor. These ceremonies are generally complied with by
the captains of Indiamen and other trading ships; but,
having the honour to bear his majesty's commission, I did
not think myself at liberty to pay to a Dutch governor any
homage which is not paid to my own sovereign: It is, however, constantly required of the King's officers; and two
or three days after I came hither, the landlord of the hotel
where I lodged told me, he had been ordered by the shebander to let me know, that my carriage, as well as others,
must stop, if I should meet the governor or any of the council; but I desired him to acquaint the shebander, that I
could not consent to perform any such ceremony; and upon his intimating somewhat about the black men with sticks,
I told him, that if any insult should be offered me, I knew
how to defend myself, and would take care to be upon my
guard; at the same time pointing to my pistols, which then
happened to lie upon the table. Upon this he went away,
and about three hours afterwards he returned, and told me
he had orders from the governor to acquaint me that I
might do as I pleased. The hotel at which I resided is licensed by the governor and council, and all strangers are
obliged to take up their abode there, except officers in his
majesty's service, who are allowed private lodgings, which,
however, I did not chuse.

At this place I continued between three and four months,
and during all that time I had the honour to see the governor but twice. The first time was at my arrival, when I
waited upon him at one of his houses, a little way in the
country; the next was in town, as he was walking before
his house there, when I addressed him upon a particular
occasion. Soon after the news of the Prince of Orange's
marriage arrived here, he gave a public entertainment, to
which I had the honour of being invited; but having heard
that Commodore Tinker, upon a like occasion, finding that
he was to be placed below the gentlemen of the Dutch
council, had abruptly left the room, and was followed by
all the captains of his squadron; and being willing to avoid
the disagreeable dilemma of either sitting below the council,

cil, or following the commodore's example, I applied to the governor to know the station that would be allotted me before I accepted his invitation; and finding that I could not be permitted to take place of the council, I declined it. On both these occasions I spoke to his excellency by an English merchant, who acted as an interpreter. The first time he had not the civility to offer me the least refreshment, nor did he the last time so much as ask me to go into the house.

The defects of the ship were at length repaired, much to my satisfaction, and I thought she might then safely proceed to Europe, though the Dutch carpenters were of a different opinion. The proper season for sailing was not yet arrived, and my worthy friend, Admiral Houting, represented, that if I went to sea before the proper time, I should meet with such weather off the Cape of Good Hope as would make me repent it; but being very ill myself, and the people being sickly, I thought it better to run the risk of a few hard gales off the Cape, than remain longer in this unhealthy place, especially as the west monsoon was setting in, during which the mortality here is yet greater than at other times.

On Wednesday the 15th of September, therefore, we set sail from Onrust, where the ship had been refitted, without returning, as is usual, into Batavia Road; and as I was not well, I sent my lieutenant to take leave of the governor on my behalf, and offer my service, if he had any dispatches for Europe. It was happy for me that I was able to procure a supply of English seamen here, otherwise I should not at last have been able to bring the ship home; for I had now lost no less than four-and-twenty of the hands I had brought out of Europe, and had four-and-twenty more so ill, that seven of them died in our passage to the Cape.

On the 20th, we anchored on the south-east side of Prince's Island, in the Streight of Sunda, and the next morning, I sent out the boats for wood and water: Of water, however, we could not get a sufficient quantity to complete our stock, for there had not yet been rain enough to supply the springs, the wet monsoon having but just set in. At this time we had the wind so fresh from the south-east, which made this part of the island a lee-shore, that I could not get under sail till the 25th, when, it being more moderate, we weighed and worked over to the Java shore. In the evening
ing

ing, we anchored in a bay called by some New Bay, and by
others Canty Bay, which is formed by an island of the same
name. We had fourteen fathoms water, with a fine sandy
bottom. The peak of Prince's Island bore N. 13 W. the
westermost point of New Island S. 82 W. and the eastermost point of Java that was in sight, N.E. Our distance
from the Java shore was about a mile and a quarter, and
from the watering-place a mile and a half. New Bay is the
best place for wooding and watering of any in these parts:
The water is extremely clear, and so good that I made my
people stave all that we had taken in at Batavia and Prince's
Island, and supply it from this place. It is procured from
a fine strong run on the Java shore, which falls down from
the land into the sea, and by means of a hoase it may be
laded into the boats, and the casks filled without putting
them on shore, which renders the work very easy and ex-
peditious. There is a little reef of rocks within which the
boats go, and lie in as smooth water, and as effectually sheltered from any swell, as if they were in a mill-pond; nor
does the reef run out so far as to be dangerous to shipping, though the contrary is asserted in Herbert's Directo-
ry; and if a ship, when lying there, should be driven from
her anchors by a wind that blows upon the shore, she may,
with the greatest ease, run up the passage between New
Island and Java, where there is a sufficient depth of water
for the largest vessel, and a harbour, in which, being land-
locked, she will find perfect security. Wood may be had
any where either upon Java or New Island, neither of which,
in this part, are inhabited.

Having in a few days completed our wood and water, we
weighed and stood out of the Streight of Sunda, with a fine
fresh gale at south-east, which did not leave us till the island
of Java was seven hundred leagues behind us.

On Monday the 23d of November, we discovered the
coast of Africa; at day-break on the 28th we made the Table
Land of the Cape of Good Hope, and the same evening anchored in the bay. We found here only a Dutch ship from
Europe, and a snow belonging to the place, which however
was in the Company's service, for the inhabitants are not
permitted to have any shipping.

Table Bay is a good harbour in summer, but not in winter; so that the Dutch will not permit any of their vessels

to lie here longer than the 15th of May, which answers to our November. After that time, all ships go to False Bay, which is well sheltered from the north-west winds, which blow here with great violence.

At this place we breathed a pure air, had wholesome food, and went freely about the country, which is extremely pleasant, so that I began to think myself already in Europe. We found the inhabitants open, hospitable, and polite, there being scarcely a gentleman in the place, either in a public or private station, from whom I did not receive some civility; and I should very ill deserve the favours they bestowed, if I did not particularly mention the first and second governor, and the fiscal.

The recovery of my people made it necessary to continue here till the 6th of January, 1769; in the evening of this day I set sail, and before it was dark cleared the land.

On the 20th, after a fine and pleasant passage, we made the island of St Helena; and set sail again on the morning of the 24th. At midnight on the 30th, we made the north-east part of the Island of Ascension, and brought-to till daylight, when we ran in close to it. I sent a boat out to discover the anchoring-place, which is called Cross-hill bay, while we kept running along the north-east and north side of the island, till we came to the north-west extremity of it, and in the afternoon anchored in the bay we sought. The way to find this place at once, is to bring the largest and most conspicuous hill upon the island to bear S.E.; when the ship is in this position, the bay will be open, right in the middle, between two other hills, the westermost of which is called Cross-hill, and gives name to the bay. Upon this hill there is a flag-staff, which if a ship brings to bear S.S.E. ½ E. or S.E. by E. and runs in, keeping it so till she is in ten fathom water, she will be in the best part of the bay. In our run along the north-east side of the island, I observed several other small sandy bays, in some of which my boat found good anchorage, and saw plenty of turtle, though they are not so convenient as this, where we had plenty of turtle too. The beach here is a fine white sand; the landing-place is at some rocks, which lie about the middle of the bay, and may be known by a ladder of ropes which hangs from the top to mount them by. In the evening I landed a few men to turn the turtle that should come on shore during the night, and in the morning I found that they had

thus

thus secured no less than eighteen, from four hundred to six hundred weight each, and these were as many as we could well stow on the deck. As there are no inhabitants upon this island, it is a custom for the ships that touch at it to leave a letter in a bottle, with their names and destination, the date, and a few other particulars. We complied with this custom, and in the evening of Monday the 1st of February, we weighed anchor and set sail.

On Friday the 19th, we discovered a ship at a considerable distance to leeward in the south-west quarter, which hoisted French colours; she continued in sight all day, and the next morning we perceived that she had greatly out-sailed us during the night; she made a tack, however, in order to get farther to windward, and as it is not usual for ships to turn to windward in these parts, it was evident that she had tacked in order to speak with us. By noon she was near enough to hail us, and, to my great surprise, made use both of my name and that of the ship, enquiring after my health, and telling me, that after the return of the Dolphin to Europe, it was believed we had suffered shipwreck in the Streight of Magellan, and that two ships had been sent out in quest of us. I asked, in my turn, who it was that was so well acquainted with me and my ship, and with the opinions that had been formed of us in Europe after the return of our companion, and how this knowledge had been acquired. I was answered, that the ship which hailed us was in the service of the French East India Company, commanded by M. Bougainville; that she was returning to England from the Isle of France; that what was thought of the Swallow in England, had been learnt from the French Gazette at the Cape of Good Hope; and that we were known to be that vessel by the letter which had been found in the bottle at the Island of Ascension, a few days after we had left that place. An offer was then made of supplying me with refreshments, if I wanted any, and I was asked if I had any letters to send to France. I returned thanks for the offer of refreshments, which however was a mere verbal civility, as it was known that I had lately sailed from the places where M. Bougainville himself had been supplied; but I said that I had received letters for France from some gentlemen of that country at the Cape, and if he would send his boat on board, they should be delivered to his messenger. Thus was an occasion furnished for what I have reason to believe

was

was the principal object of M. Bougainville in speaking with us : A boat was immediately sent on board, and in her a young officer, dressed in a waistcoat and trowsers; whether he was thus dressed by design I shall not determine, but I soon perceived that his rank was much superior to his appearance. He came down to me in my cabin, and after the usual compliments had passed, I asked him how he came to go home so soon in the season ; to which he replied, that there had been some disagreement between the governor and inhabitants of the Isle of France, and that he had been sent home in haste with dispatches : This story was the more plausible, as I had heard of the dispute between the governor and inhabitants of the Isle of France, from a French gentleman who came from thence, at the Cape of Good Hope; yet I was not perfectly satisfied : For, supposing M. Bougainville to have been sent in haste to Europe with dispatches, I could not account for his losing the time which it cost him to speak with me; I therefore observed to this gentleman, that although he had accounted for his coming before the usual time from the Isle of France, he had not accounted for his coming at an unusual time from India, which must have been the case. To this, however, he readily replied, that they had made only a short trading voyage on the western coast of Sumatra. I then enquired, what commodities he had brought from thence; and he answered, cocoa-nut oil, and rattans : But, said I, these are commodities which it is not usual to bring into Europe : It is true, said he, but these commodities we left at the Isle of France, the oil for the use of the island, and the rattans for ships which were to touch there in their way to China, and in exchange we took in another freight for Europe; this freight I think he said was pepper, and his whole tale being at least possible, I asked him no more questions. He then told me, he had heard at the Cape, that I had been with Commodore Byron at Falkland's Islands; and, said he, I was on board the French ship that met you in the Streight of Magellan, which must have been true, for he mentioned several incidents that it was otherwise highly improbable he should know, particularly the store-ship's running a-ground, and many of the difficulties that occurred in that part of the Streight which we passed together : By this conversation he contrived to introduce several enquiries, concerning the western part of the Streight, the time it cost me to get through, and the

difficulties

difficulties of the navigation ; but perceiving that I declined giving any account of these particulars, he changed his subject. He said, he had heard that we lost an officer and some men in an engagement with the Indians; and taking notice that my ship was small, and a bad sailer, he insinuated that we must have suffered great hardship in so long a voyage; but, said he, it is thought to be safer and pleasanter sailing in the South Sea than any where else. As I perceived that he waited for a reply, I said, that the great ocean, called the South Sea, extended almost from one pole to the other; and therefore, although that part of it which lay between the tropics might justly be called the Pacific, on account of the trade-winds that blow there all the year, yet without the tropics, on either side, the winds were variable, and the seas turbulent. In all this he readily acquiesced, and finding that he could not draw from me any thing to satisfy his curiosity, by starting leading subjects of conversation, he began to propose his questions in direct terms, and desired to know on which side the equator I had crossed the South Seas. As I did not think proper to answer this question, and wished to prevent others of the same kind, I rose up somewhat abruptly, and I believe with some marks of displeasure: At this he seemed to be a little disconcerted, and I believe was about to make an apology for his curiosity, but I prevented him, by desiring that he would make my compliments to his captain, and in return for his obliging civilities presented him with one of the arrows that had wounded my men, which I immediately went into my bed-room to fetch: He followed me, looking about him with great curiosity, as indeed he had done from the time of his first coming on board, and having received the arrow, he took his leave.

After he was gone, and we had made sail, I went upon the deck, where my lieutenant asked me, if my visitor had entertained me with an account of his voyage. This led me to tell him the general purport of our conversation, upon which he assured me that the tale I had heard was a fiction, for, says he, the boat's crew could not keep their secret so well as their officer, but after a little conversation told one of our people who was born at Quebec, and spoke French, that they had been round the globe as well as we. This naturally excited a general curiosity, and with a very little difficulty we learnt that they had sailed from Europe in

company

company with another ship, which, wanting some repair, had been left at the Isle of France; that they had attempted to pass the Streight of Magellan the first summer, but not being able, had gone back, and wintered in the river de la Plata; that the summer afterwards they had been more successful, and having passed the Streight, spent two months at the island of Juan Fernandes. My lieutenant told me also, that a boy in the French boat said he had been upon that island two years, and that while he was there, an English frigate put into the road, but did not anchor, mentioning the time as well as he could recollect, by which it appeared that the frigate he had seen was the Swallow. On the boy's being asked how he came to be so long upon the island of Juan Fernandes, he said that he had been taken upon the Spanish coast in the West Indies in a smuggling party, and sent thither by the Spaniards; but that by the French ship, in whose boat he came on board us, having touched there, he had regained his liberty. After having received this information from my lieutenant, I could easily account for M. Bougainville's having made a tack to speak to me, and for the conversation and behaviour of my visitor; but I was now more displeased at the questions he had asked me than before, for if it was improper for him to communicate an account of his voyage to me, it was equally improper for me to communicate an account of my voyage to him: And I thought an artful attempt to draw me into a breach of my obligation to secrecy, while he imposed upon me by a fiction that he might not violate his own, was neither liberal nor just. As what the boat's crew told my people, differs in several particulars from the account printed by M. Bougainville, I shall not pretend to determine how much of it is true; but I was then very sorry that the lieutenant had not communicated to me the intelligence he received, such as it was, before my guest left me, and I was now very desirous to speak with him again, but this was impossible; for though the French ship was foul from a long voyage, and we had just been cleaned, she shot by us as if we had been at anchor, notwithstanding we had a fine fresh gale, and all our sails set.[6]

On

[6] Bougainville passes over the circumstance of meeting with the Swallow in a very cursory manner: " The 28th we perceived a ship to windward, and a-head of us; we kept sight of her during the night, and joined

On the 7th of March we made the Western Islands, and went between St Michael and Tercera ; in this situation we found the variation 13° 36′ W., and the winds began to blow from the S.W. The gale, as we got farther to the westward, increased, and on the 11th, having got to W.N.W. it blew very hard, with a great sea ; we scudded before it with the foresail only, the foot-rope of which suddenly breaking, the sail blew all to pieces, before we could get the yard down, though it was done instantly. This obliged us to bring the ship to, but having, with all possible expedition, bent a new foresail, and got the yard up, we bore away again ; this was the last accident that happened to us during the voyage. On the 16th, being in latitude 49° 15′ N. we got soundings. On the 18th, I knew by the depth of water that we were in the Channel, but the wind being to the northward, we could not make land till the next day, when we saw the Star Point ; and on the 20th, to our great joy, we anchored at Spithead, after a very fine passage, and a fair wind all the way from the Cape of Good Hope.

her the next morning, it was the Swallow. I offered Capt. C. all the services that one may render to another at sea. He wanted nothing ; but upon his telling me that they had given him letters for France at the Cape, I sent on board for them. He presented me with an arrow which he had got in one of the isles he had found in his voyage round the world, *a voyage that he was far from suspecting we had likewise made.* His ship was very small, went very ill, and when we took leave of him, he remained as it were at anchor. How much he must have suffered in so bad a vessel, may well be conceived. There were eight leagues difference between his estimated longitude and ours ; he reckoned himself so much more to the westward.” A little before, he had spoken of his wishing to join Carteret, over whom he knew he had great advantage in sailing. This was in leaving the Cape of Good Hope, at which time Carteret was eleven days gone before him.—E.

A Table

A Table of the Variation of the Compass, as observed on board the Swallow, in her Voyage round the Globe, in the Years 1766, 1767, 1768, and 1769.

N.B. The days of the month in this Table are not by the nautical account, as is the custom, but, for the convenience of those that are not used to that way of reckoning, are reduced to the civil account. A.M. denotes that the observation was made in the forenoon, and P.M. in the afternoon of that day on the noon of which the latitude and longitude of the ship were taken.

TIME.	Lat. in at Noon	Long in at Noon from London.	Varia-tion.	REMARKS.
	North.	West.	West.	
1766, August.	English	Channel	22° 30′	
30, P.M.	45° 22	13° 17	20 25	From the Downs to the Island
Sept. 3, P.M.	38 36	13 40	19 04	of Madeira.
4, A.M.	37 27	14 12	20 17	
Island Madeira.	32 34	16 35	16 00	
17, A.M.	24 33	19 22	13 00	
21, A.M.	17 19	22 19	11 14	The island of Sall in sight, S. by W ten leagues.
22, P.M.	16 34	22 29	8 20	Was then between the island of Sall and the island of May.
Porto Praya	15 00	23 00	8 00	Island of St Jago.
Oct. 10, P.M.	6 34	21 41	5 36	
11, P.M.	6 40	21 35	6 00	
	South			
22, A.M.	0 06	25 03	6 23	On the passage from the island
25, P.M.	4 14	27 23	4 30	of St Jago to the Streights
27, A.M.	7 03	28 49	3 52	of Magellan.
28, P.M.	8 46	29 14	1 50	
30, P.M.	10 57	30 09	0 30	
31, A.M.	12 30	30 30	Novar.	
			East.	
Oct. 31, P.M.	12 56	30 46	1 24	
Nov. 2, P.M.	17 22	32 09	1 40	
7, A.M.	23 54	38 10	4 56	
P.M.	- -	- -	5 56	
8, P.M.	25 49	39 21	6 45	Coast of Patagonia.
11, A.M.	29 57	42 27	8 50	
15, A.M.	34 12	46 41	12 00	
16, A.M.	34 38	47 58	12 36	
17, A.M.	34 46	48 28	13 03	
P.M.	- -	- -	14 20	

				A Table of the Variation of the Compass, &c. continued.

TIME.	Lat. in at Noon.	Long. in at Noon from London.	Varia-tion	REMARKS.
1766.	South.	West.	West.	
Nov. 18, A.M.	35° 37′	49° 49′	0 30′	Soundings 54 fathoms of wa-ter, with a bottom of fine black sand, rather muddy.
P.M.	- -	- -	15 45	Ditto depth and bottom.
20, P.M.	36 57	51 48	15 33	Ditto depth, fine sand, but not so black, with small shells.
21, A.M.	37 40	51 05	15 52	Had no bottom with 80 fa-thoms of line.
	38 53	53 12	- -	Had soundings at 70 fathoms water.
	40 34	53 47	- -	No bottom with 90 fathoms of line.
	41 34	55 39	- -	45 fathoms, dark brown sandy bottom.
	41 57	56 06	- -	42 fathoms, fine grey sand.
	41 06	57 18	- -	46 fathoms, fine dark brown sand.
28, A.M.	41 14	56 48	19 00	39 fathoms ditto bottom. Here we caught very good fish with hooks and lines.
29, A.M.	42 08	58 41	19 02	32 fathoms of water, with dit-to bottom.
P.M.	- -	- -	19 45	33 fathoms depth.
	43 18	58 56	- -	Depth 45 fathoms, the same bottom; we had here a calm, and we caught good fish.
	44 04	58 53	- -	52 fathoms water, the same bottom.
	45 00	59 34	- -	53 fathoms, fine light brown sand.
Dec. 4, P.M.	47 00	60 51	20 20	
	47 15	61 10	- -	60 fathoms, fine dark sand.
5, A.M.	48 01	61 28	20 40	56 fathoms, with ditto bottom, and grains of sparkling sand mixed with it.
6, A.M.	47 35	62 50	20 34	
	47 30	63 08	- -	45 fathoms of water, dark sand, with small stones, and in go-ing west about 10 miles, we had 52 fathoms, a bottom of soft mud.
7, A.M.	47 14	63 37	19 40	54 fathoms, soft mud, with small stones; at this time the Land was seen from the mast-heads, somewhere about Cape Blanco.
8, P.M	48 54	64 14	20 40	
9, A.M	49 12	65 31	20 35	

A Table of the Variation of the Compass, &c. continued.				
TIME.	Lat. in at Noon.	Long. in at Noon from London.	Varia-tion.	REMARKS.
1766.	South.	West.	East.	
Dec. 9, A.M.	51°15'	66°02'	- -	53 fathoms, dark grey sand, with small stones.
17,	Cape Virgin Mary, eastermost entrance of the Streight.			
Magellan -	52 29	68 02'	22 50	
	Elizabeth Island		22 36	
	Port Famine -		22 22	
	Off C. Forward		22 10	
	York Road -		Ditto	In the Streights of Magellan.
	Swallow Har.			
	Off C. Notch		22 00	
1767,	Off C. Upr.			
Off C. Pillar -	52 45	75 10	21 50	Westermost entrance of the Streights.
April 18, P.M.	49 18	79 06	17 36	
20, A.M.	48 04	80 56	17 20	Coast of Chili, in the South Sea.
26, P.M.	45 57	81 22	16 17	
28, P.M.	44 27	81 24	15 10	
May -	33 40	78 52	11 00	E. end of the island Juan Fernandes.
	33 45	80 46	10 24	Island of Massafuero.
28, P.M.	29 45	79 50	9 40	
31, P M.	26 26	82 15	8 10	
June 1, P.M.	25 51	84 23	8 8	
7, P.M.	27 23	97 16	5 45	
8, A.M.	27 20	97 51	5 45	
10, A.M.	26 30	98 25	5 40	In crossing the South Sea.
12, P.M.	26 53	100 21	4 13	
16, P.M.	28 11	111 15	2 00	
17, A.M.	28 04	112 37	1 51	
18, P.M.	28 07	113 55	2 00	
20, A.M.	28 04	116 29	2 09	
30, P.M.	26 00	130 55	2 32	
July 2, P.M.	25 02	133 38	2 46	Off Pitcairn's Island.
3,	25 00	136 16'	2 30	
4, A.M.	25 24	137 18	3 43	
5, A.M.	24 56	137 23	5 24	
6, A.M.	24 32	138 31	4 16	
7, A.M.	24 10	139 55	5 12	
P.M.	- -	- -	4 02	
8, A.M.	23 46	139 55	5 56	
10, P.M.	21 38	141 36	4 20	Crossing the South Sea.
12, A.M.	20 36	145 39	4 40	
	20 38	146 00	5 00	
13 P.M.	21 07	147 44	5 46	
15, A.M.	21 46	150 50	6 23	
16, P.M.	22 02	151 09	6 34	
19, P.M.	19 50	153 59	6 08	
20, P.M.	19 08	156 15	7 09	
21, P.M.	18 43	158 27	7 38	

A Table of the Variation of the Compass, &c. continued.

TIME.	Lat. in at Noon.	Long. in at Noon from London.	Variation.	REMARKS.
1767.	South.	West.	East.	
July 23, P.M.	16°22'	162 32'	6 05'	
24, P.M.	14 19	163 34	6 29	
25, A.M.	12 13	164 50	9 30	
P.M.	- -	- -	9 40	
26, A.M.	10 01	166 52	9 00	
28, A.M.	9 50	171 26	9 04	
30, A.M.	9 50	175 38	9 32	
P.M.	- -	- -	9 00	Crossing the South Sea.
Aug. 1, A.M.	9 53	179 33	10 04	
		East.		
2, A.M.	10 09	178 58	10 30	
4, A.M.	10 22	177 10	10 54	
5, A.M.	10 35	175 50	11 14	
P.M.	- -	- -	10 52	
7, P.M.	10 52	172 23	11 17	
8, P.M.	11 02	171 15	10 27	
9, A.M.	10 50	171 00	10 02	
11, P.M.	10 49	167 00	10 38	
Cape Byron -	10 40	164 49	11 00	N.E. end of Egmont, one of the Charlotte Islands.
18, P.M.	9 58	162 57	8 30	
19, P.M.	8 52	160 41	8 30	
20, A.M.	7 53	158 56	8 31	
	7 56	158 56	8 20	Off Carteret's and Gower's Isl.
22, P.M.	6 24	157 32	7 42	
24, P.M.	5 07	155 08	6 25	
26, P.M.	4 46	153 17	7 14	
In sight and on the west side of Nova Britannia.			6 30	
C. Saint George.	5 00	152 19	5 20	Nova Hibernia.
In St George s Channel			4 40	Nova Britannia. Here the land seemed to have an effect on the needle.
Sept. 16, A.M.	2 19	145 31	6 30	Off the Admiralty Islands.
19, A.M.	1 57	143 28	5 26	
	1 45	143 02	4 40	
20, P.M.	1 33	142 22	4 40	
21, A.M.	1 20	141 29	4 54	
22, P.M.	0 52	139 56	4 30	
23, P.M.	0 05	138 56	4 17	
	North.	- -		
24, P.M.	0 05	138 41	3 09	From the Admiralty Islands to the island of Mindanao.
27, A.M.	2 13	136 41	2 30	
P.M.	- -	- -	2 09	
	2 50	136 17	2 00	
30, A.M.	4 25	134 37	1 41	
Oct. 3, A.M.	4 41	132 51	3 09	
P.M.	- -	- -	3 14	
5, P.M.	4 31	132 39	3 10	

A Table of the Variation of the Compass, &c continued

TIME.	Lat. in at Noon.	Long. in at Noon from London.	Varia- tion.	REMARKS.
1767.	North.	West.	West.	
Oct. 6, A.M.	4°21′	132°45′	3°33	
8, A.M.	3 53	134 13	3 38	
9, A.M.	4 03	134 04	3 11	
12, P.M.	4 49	133 42	2 19	From the Admiralty Islands to
13, P.M.	5 12	133 27	2 20	the island of Mindanao.
16, A.M.	5 54	133 10	2 34	
27, P.M.	6 35	127 56	2 10	
Cape St Aug.	6 15	127 20	1 45	Island of Mindanao.
South End -	5 34	126 25	1 20	Off the island Mindanao.
Nov. 6, A.M.	5 34	125 40	0 48	
P.M.	- -	- -	0 49	
7, P.M.	5 37	125 23	0 39	
8, P.M.	5 30	124 41	0 50	
14, A.M.	1 57	122 04	0 06	From the island of Mindanao
26, P.M.	0 04	118 15	0 19	to the Streights of Macassar.
	South.			
27, A.M.	0 14	117 45	0 12	
Dec. 7.	3 26	116 45	0 27	
Bontham	5 30	117 53	1 16	At the island of Celebes.
Island Tonikaky	5 31	117 17	1 00	Off the S.E. end of the island
1768.				Celebes.
May 29, P.M.	5 29	110 23	0 56	
	Off Madura -		0 30	On the N.E. part of the island
	Batavia - -		0 25	of Java.
Sept. 30, P.M.	7 41	101 36	0 51	
Oct. 2, P.M.	10 37	97 19	2 06	
4, P.M.	12 13	93 56	3 13	
12, P.M.	19 50	76 40	3 30	
14, P.M.	21 47	72 47	6 26	
15, P.M.	22 53	70 47	8 09	
17, A.M.	24 23	68 02	9 36	
P.M.	- -	- -	11 20	
18, P.M.	25 08	67 21	11 50	
19, P.M.	25 08	67 08	12 49	
20, A.M.	24 59	66 35	12 54	
P.M.	- -	- -	11 48	From the Streights of Sunda to
24, A.M.	23 21	64 51	12 54	the Cape of Good Hope.
25, P.M.	23 23	63 35	12 39	
26, A.M.	23 32	62 43	13 42	
28, P.M.	24 52	60 14	16 10	
30, P.M.	25 40	56 50	18 18	
31, P.M.	26 31	54 49	18 24	
Nov. 1, A.M.	27 05	52 57	20 12	
P.M.	- -	- -	20 20	
3, A.M.	27 40	50 55	20 58	
P.M.	- -	- -	21 23	
4, P.M.	27 42	50 10	21 15	
5, P.M	27 44	49 01	21 09	
6, P.M.	28 58	46 23	22 38	

TIME.	' at. in at Noon.	Long. in at Noon from London.	Varia- tion.	REMARKS.
1768.	South.	East.	West.	
Nov. 7, A.M.	29°59′	43 ′55	24°40′	
P.M.	- -	- -	24 55	
8, P.M.	30 12	42 51	25 39	
9, A.M.	30 19	41 37	25 50	
10, P.M.	30 37	40 48	25 32	
11, A.M.	32 02	38 47	25 08	
12, P.M.	32 39	37 17	25 02	From the Streights of Sunda to
13, P.M.	33 21	35 27	25 05	the Cape of Good Hope.
19, P.M.	35 17	28 38	22 32	
20, P.M.	35 42	27 22	22 46	
21, P.M.	35 46	27 00	22 18	
22, P.M.	35 04	26 29	22 50	
23, P.M.	34 57	25 46	21 39	
24, P.M.	34 52	25 28	21 44	
C. Good Hope.	34 24	18 30	19 30	
1769.				
Jan. 9, P.M.	30 37	13 08	19 20	
14, P.M.	22 16	4 52	16 39	
15, P.M.	21 04	3 54	16 31	From the Cape to the island of
18, P.M.	17 05	0 10	14 38	Saint Helena.
		West.		
19, P.M.	16 06	1 38	13 46	
25, P.M.	14 22	7 04	12 30	From the island of Saint He-
26, P.M.	12 54	8 05	11 47	lena to the island of Ascen-
27, P.M.	11 36	9 25	11 40	sion.
28, P.M.	10 26	10 36	10 46	
Feb. 2, P.M.	6 45	14 42	9 34	
3, P.M.	5 04	15 45	9 04	
4, A.M.	3 26	16 49	9 10	
5, P.M.	2 01	17 34	8 58	
6, P.M.	0 20	18 27	8 32	
	North.			
7, P.M.	0 58	19 24	8 37	
8, A.M.	1 56	20 16	8 25	
10, P.M.	2 39	28 58	7 21	
15, P.M.	6 38	32 40	4 35	From the island of Ascension
16, P M.	8 03	24 18	6 09	to England.
19, P.M.	12 06	24 34	6 48	
21, P.M.	14 39	27 15	6 12	
26, A.M.	23 54	28 15	6 00	
March 3, P.M.	32 33	23 35	13 26	
4, A.M.	34 02	22 32	13 43	
5, P.M.	35 30	21 56	14 53	
6, A.M.	36 46	21 23	15 15	
P.M.	- -	- -	14 58	
Between the islands of Tercera and Saint Michael.			13 36	

A Table of the Variation of the Compass, &c. continued

A Table of the Variation of the Compass, &c concluded.				
TIME.	Lat. in atNoon.	Long.in at Noon from London.	Varia-tion.	REMARKS.
1769.	North.	West.	West.	From this day till my arrival in England, the weather was so bad that we had no opportunity of making any observation of the variation.
Mar. 28, P.M.	39°09'	19°02'	16°46'	

N.B. The ill sailing of the Swallow prevented me from getting a sufficient number of soundings to make a separate Table.

CHAPTER IV.

AN ACCOUNT OF A VOYAGE ROUND THE WORLD, IN THE
YEARS 1768, 1769, 1770, AND 1771, BY LIEUTENANT
JAMES COOK, COMMANDER OF HIS MAJESTY'S BARK
THE ENDEAVOUR.

[In addition to Cook's papers, Dr Hawkesworth had the use
of a journal kept by Sir Joseph Banks, in drawing up the
account of this voyage; a favour which he has not neglected to specify in his introduction. That introduction,
however, and several references to plates, with some other
matters deemed of little or no import, or elsewhere given,
are now omitted.]

SECTION I.

*The Passage from Plymouth to Madeira, with some Account
of that Island.*

HAVING received my commission, which was dated
the 25th of May 1768, I went on board on the 27th,
hoisted the pennant, and took charge of the ship, which
then lay in the bason in Deptford yard. She was fitted
for sea with all expedition; and stores and provisions being
taken on board, sailed down the river on the 30th of July,
and on the 13th of August anchored in Plymouth Sound.

While we lay here waiting for a wind, the articles of war
and the act of parliament were read to the ship's company,
who were paid two months' wages in advance, and told that
they were to expect no additional pay for the performance
of the voyage.

On Friday the 26th of August, the wind becoming fair,
we got under sail, and put to sea. On the 31st, we saw several

veral of the birds which the sailors call Mother Carey's Chickens, and which they suppose to be the forerunners of a storm; and on the next day we had a very hard gale, which brought us under our courses, washed overboard a small boat belonging to the boatswain, and drowned three or four dozen of our poultry, which we regretted still more.

On Friday the 2d of September we saw land between Cape Finisterre and Cape Ortegal, on the coast of Gallicia, in Spain; and on the 5th, by an observation of the sun and moon, we found the latitude of Cape Finisterre to be 42° 53′ north, and its longitude 8° 46′ west, our first meridian being always supposed to pass through Greenwich; variation of the needle 21° 4′ west.

During this course, Mr Banks and Dr Solander had an opportunity of observing many marine animals, of which no naturalist has hitherto taken notice; particularly a new species of the *oniscus*, which was found adhering to the *medusa pelagica*; and an animal of an angular figure, about three inches long, and one thick, with a hollow passing quite through it, and a brown spot on one end, which they conjectured might be its stomach; four of these adhered together by their sides when they were taken, so that at first they were thought to be one animal; but upon being put into a glass of water they soon separated, and swam about very briskly. These animals are of a new genus, to which Mr Banks and Dr Solander gave the name of *Dagysa*, from the likeness of one species of them to a gem. Several specimens of them were taken adhering together sometimes to the length of a yard or more, and shining in the water with very beautiful colours. Another animal of a new genus they also discovered, which shone in the water with colours still more beautiful and vivid, and which indeed exceeded in variety and brightness any thing that we had ever seen: The colouring and splendour of these animals were equal to those of an opal, and from their resemblance to that gem, the genus was called *Carcinium Opalinum*. One of them lived several hours in a glass of salt water, swimming about with great agility, and at every motion displaying a change of colours almost infinitely various. We caught also among the rigging of the ship, when we were at the distance of about ten leagues from Cape Finisterre, several birds which have not been described by Linnæus; they were supposed to have come from Spain, and our gentlemen

tlemen called the species *Motacilla velificans*, as they said none but sailors would venture themselves on board a ship that was going round the world. One of them was so exhausted that it died in Mr Banks's hand, almost as soon as it was brought to him.

It was thought extraordinary that no naturalist had hitherto taken notice of the Dagysa, as the sea abounds with them not twenty leagues from the coast of Spain; but, unfortunately for the cause of science, there are but very few of those who traverse the sea, that are either disposed or qualified to remark the curiosities of which nature has made it the repository.

On the 12th we discovered the islands of Porto Santo and Madeira, and on the next day anchored in Funchiale road, and moored with stream-anchor: But, in the night, the bend of the hawser of the stream-anchor slipped, owing to the negligence of the person who had been employed to make it fast. In the morning the anchor was heaved up into the boat, and carried out to the southward; but in heaving it again, Mr Weir, the master's mate, was carried overboard by the buoy-rope, and went to the bottom with the anchor; the people in the ship saw the accident, and got the anchor up with all possible expedition; it was however too late, the body came up entangled in the buoy-rope, but it was dead.

When the island of Madeira is first approached from the sea, it has a very beautiful appearance; the sides of the hills being entirely covered with vines almost as high as the eye can distinguish; and the vines are green when every kind of herbage, except where they shade the ground, and here and there by the sides of a rill, is entirely burnt up, which was the case at this time.

On the 13th, about eleven o'clock in the forenoon, a boat, which our sailors call the product boat, came on board from the officers of health, without whose permission no person is suffered to land from on board a ship. As soon as this permission was obtained, we went on shore at Funchiale, the capital of the island, and proceeded directly to the house of Mr Cheap, the English consul there, and one of the most considerable merchants of the place. This gentleman received us with the kindness of a brother, and the liberality of a prince; he insisted upon

our

our taking possession of his house, in which he furnished us with every possible accommodation during our stay upon the island : He procured leave for Mr Banks and Dr Solander to search the island for such natural curiosities as they should think worth their notice ; employed persons to take fish and gather shells, which time would not have permitted them to collect for themselves ; and he provided horses and guides to take them to any part of the country which they should chuse to visit.   With all these advantages, however, their excursions were seldom pushed farther than three miles from the town, as they were only five days on shore ; one of which they spent at home, in receiving the honour of a visit from the governor.   The season was the worst in the year for their purpose, as it was neither that of plants nor insects ; a few of the plants, however, were procured in flower, by the kind attention of Dr Heberden, the chief physician of the island, and brother to Dr Heberden of London, who also gave them such specimens as he had in his possession, and a copy of his Botanical Observations ; containing, among other things, a particular description of the trees of the island.   Mr Banks enquired after the wood which has been imported into England for cabinet-work, and is here called Madeira mahogany :   He learnt that no wood was exported from the island under that name, but he found a tree called by the natives Vigniatico, the *Laurus indicus* of Linnæus, the wood of which cannot easily be distinguished from mahogany.   Dr Heberden had a book-case in which the vigniatico and mahogany were mixed, and they were no otherwise to be known from each other than by the colour, which, upon a nice examination, appears to be somewhat less brown in the vigniatico than the mahogany ; it is therefore in the highest degree probable, that the wood known in England by the name of Madeira mahogany, is the vigniatico.

There is great reason to suppose that this whole island was, at some remote period, thrown up by the explosion of subterraneous fire, as every stone, whether whole or in fragments, that we saw upon it, appeared to have been burnt, and even the sand itself to be nothing more than ashes : We did not, indeed, see much of the country, but the

the people informed us that what we did see was a very exact specimen of the rest.[1]

The only article of trade in this island is wine, and the manner in which it is made is so simple, that it might have been used by Noah, who is said to have planted the first vineyard after the flood : The grapes are put into a square wooden vessel, the dimensions of which are proportioned to the size of the vineyard to which it belongs ; the servants then, having taken off their stockings and jackets, get into it, and with their feet and elbows, press out as much of the juice as they can : The stalks are afterwards collected, and being tied together with a rope, are put under a square piece of wood, which is pressed down upon them by a lever with a stone tied to the end of it.

It was with great difficulty that the people of Madeira were persuaded to engraft their vines, and some of them still obstinately refused to adopt the practice, though a whole vintage is very often spoiled by the number of bad grapes which are mixed in the vat, and which they will not throw out, because they increase the quantity of the wine : An instance of the force of habit, which is the more extraordinary, as they have adopted the practice of engrafting with respect to their chesnut-trees, an object of much less importance, which, however, are thus brought to bear sooner than they would otherwise have done.[2]

We

---

[1] This opinion about the volcanic origin of the island of Madeira, has found several advocates since the publication of this work. The following quotation from a paper by the Hon. H. G. Bennet, contained in the first volume of the Geological Society Transactions, may furnish the inquisitive reader with a short summary of the principal appearances on which this opinion rests. " To my mind, the most interesting geological facts, are, 1. The intersection of the lava, by dikes at right angles with the strata.—2. The rapid dips which the strata make, particularly the overlaying of that of the Brazen Head to the eastward of Funchial, where the blue, grey, and red lavas are rolled up in one mass, as if they had slipped together from an upper stratum.—3. The columnar form of the lava itself, reposing on, and covered by beds of scoria, ashes, and pumice, which affords a strong argument for the volcanic origin of the columns themselves. And, 4. The veins of carbonate of lime and zeolite, which are not found here in solitary pieces, as in the vicinity of Ætna and Vesuvius, but are amid the lavas and in the strata of pumice and tufa, and are diffused on the lava itself, and occasionally crystallized in its cavities."—E.

[2] The censure passed on the carelessness of the people of Madeira as

We saw no wheel-carriages of any sort in the place, which perhaps was not more owing to the want of ingenuity to invent them, than to the want of industry to mend the roads, which, at that time, it was impossible that any wheel-carriage should pass: The inhabitants had horses and mules indeed, excellently adapted to such ways; but their wine, notwithstanding, was brought to town from the vineyards where it was made, in vessels of goat-skins, which were carried by men upon their heads. The only imitation of a carriage among these people was a board, made somewhat hollow in the middle, to one end of which a pole was tied, by a strap of whit-leather: This wretched sledge approached about as near to an English cart, as an Indian canoe to a ship's long-boat; and even this would probably never have been thought of, if the English had not introduced wine vessels, which are too big to be carried by hand, and which, therefore, were dragged about the town upon these machines.

One reason, perhaps, why art and industry have done so little for Madeira is, nature's having done so much. The soil is very rich, and there is such a difference of climate between the plains and the hills, that there is scarcely a single object of luxury that grows either in Europe or the Indies, that might not be produced here. When we went to visit Dr Heberden, who lived upon a considerable ascent, about two miles from town, we left the thermometer at 74, and when we arrived at his house, we found it at 66. The hills produce, almost spontaneously, walnuts, chesnuts, and apples in great abundance; and in the town there are many plants which are the natives both of the East and West Indies, particularly the banana, the guava, the pine-apple or anana, and the mango, which flourish almost without culture. The corn of this country is of a most excellent quality, large-grained and very fine, and the island would produce it in great plenty, yet most of what is consumed by the inhabitants is imported. The mutton, pork, and beef are also very good; the beef in particular, which

to the manufacture of their wine, does not now apply; for, according to Mr Barrow, who touched here in his voyage to Cochin China, (an account of which appeared in 1806) the care and pains used in choosing the freshest and ripest grapes only for the wine-press, are almost incredible. Madeira exports about 1 ,000 pipes of wine yearly, of which not one-third part comes to England—about 5500 pipes are taken out to India.—E.

we took on board here, was universally allowed to be
scarcely inferior to our own; the lean part was very like
it, both in colour and grain, though the beasts are much
smaller, but the fat is as white as the fat of mutton.

The town of Funchiale derives its name from *Funcho,*
the Portuguese name for fennel, which grows in great
plenty upon the neighbouring rocks; by the observation
of Dr Heberden, it lies in the latitude of 32° 33' 33" N.
and longitude 16° 49' W. It is situated in the bottom of
a bay, and though larger than the extent of the island
seems to deserve, is very ill built; the houses of the principal inhabitants are large, those of the common people
are small, the streets are narrow, and worse paved than
any I ever saw. The churches are loaded with ornaments,
among which are many pictures, and images of favourite
saints, but the pictures are in general wretchedly painted,
and the saints are dressed in laced clothes. Some of the
convents are in a better taste, especially that of the Fran-
ciscans, which is plain, simple, and neat in the highest degree. The infirmary in particular drew our attention as a
model which might be adopted in other countries with
great advantage. It consists of a long room, on one side
of which are the windows, and an altar for the convenience of administering the sacrament to the sick: The
other side is divided into wards, each of which is just big
enough to contain a bed, and neatly lined with gally-tiles;
behind these wards, and parallel to the room in which they
stand, there runs a long gallery, with which each ward
communicates by a door, so that the sick may be separately supplied with whatever they want without disturbing
their neighbours. In this convent there is also a singular
curiosity of another kind; a small chapel, the whole lining of which, both sides and cieling, is composed of human
sculls and thigh-bones; the thigh-bones are laid across
each other, and a scull is placed in each of the four angles.
Among the sculls one is very remarkable; the upper and
the lower jaw, on one side, perfectly and firmly cohere;
how the ossification which unites them was formed, it is
not perhaps very easy to conceive, but it is certain that
the patient must have lived some time without opening his
mouth: What nourishment he received was conveyed
through a hole which we discovered to have been made

on

on the other side, by forcing out some of the teeth, in doing which the jaw also seems to have been injured.

We visited the good fathers of this convent on a Thursday evening, just before supper-time, and they received us with great politeness: " We will not ask you, said they, to sup with us, because we are not prepared, but if you will come to-morrow, though it is a fast with us, we will have a turkey roasted for you." This invitation, which shewed a liberality of sentiment not to have been expected in a convent of Portuguese friars at this place, gratified us much, though it was not in our power to accept it.[3]

We visited also a convent of nuns, dedicated to *Santa Clara,* and the ladies did us the honour to express a particular pleasure in seeing us there : They had heard that there were great philosophers among us, and not at all knowing what were the objects of philosophical knowledge, they asked us several questions that were absurd and extravagant in the highest degree; one was, when it would thunder; and another, whether a spring of fresh water was to be found any where within the walls of their convent, of which it seems they were in great want. It will naturally be supposed that our answers to such questions were neither satisfactory to the ladies, nor, in their estimation, honourable to us; yet their disappointment did not in the least lessen their civility, and they talked, without ceasing, during the whole of our visit, which lasted about half an hour.[4]

The hills of this country are very high; the highest, Pico Ruivo, rises 5,068 feet, near an English mile, perpendicularly from its base, which is much higher than any land that has been measured in Great Britain.[5] The sides of these hills are covered with vines to a certain height, above which there are woods of chesnut and pine of immense

[3] Mr Barrow is no admirer of the monks that swarm in Madeira—he represents them as a very worthless, and a very ignorant race of beings. —E.

[4] According to Mr Barrow's account, it should seem, that though there are several nunneries in this island, " not a single instance of the veil being taken has occurred for many years past."—E.

[5] In Mr Leslie's table of the heights of mountains appended to the second edition of his Elements of Geometry, the altitude of this remarkable peak is stated to be 5162 English feet, but on what authority is not mentioned. That of Ben Nevis, in Inverness-shire, as ascertained by the barometer, is 4980.—E.

mense extent, and above them forests of wild timber of various kinds not known in Europe; particularly two, called by the Portuguese *Mirmulano* and *Paobranco*, the leaves of both which, particularly the *Paobranco*, are so beautiful, that these trees would be a great ornament to the gardens of Europe.

The number of inhabitants in this island is supposed to be about 80,000, and the custom-house duties produce a revenue to the king of Portugal of 20,000l. a-year, clear of all expences, which might easily be doubled by the product of the island, exclusive of the vines, if advantage were taken of the excellence of the climate, and the amazing fertility of the soil; but this object is utterly neglected by the Portugueze. In the trade of the inhabitants of Madeira with Lisbon the balance is against them, so that all the Portugueze money naturally going thither, the currency of the island is Spanish; there are indeed a few Portugueze pieces of copper, but they are so scarce that we did not see one of them: The Spanish coin is of three denominations; Pistereens, worth about a shilling; Bitts, worth about sixpence; and Half bitts, threepence.[6]

The tides at this place flow at the full and change of the moon, north and south; the spring-tides rise seven feet perpendicular, and the neap-tides four. By Dr Heberden's observation, the variation of the compass here is now 15° 30' west, and decreasing; but I have some doubt whether he is not mistaken with respect to its decrease: We found that the north point of the dipping needle belonging to the Royal Society dipped 77° 18".

The refreshments to be had here, are water, wine, fruit of several sorts, onions in plenty, and some sweetmeats; fresh meat and poultry are not to be had without leave from the governor, and the payment of a very high price.

We took in 270 lib. of fresh beef, and a live bullock, charged at 613 lib. 3,032 gallons of water, and ten tons of wine; and in the night, between Sunday the 18th and Monday the 19th of September, we set sail in prosecution of our voyage.

When Funchiale bore north, 13 east, at the distance of
                                                    seventy-six

___

[6] The reader need scarcely be apprized of the necessity of verifying or modifying the account of some of the particulars now given respecting Madeira, by an appeal to more recent authorities. A hint to this effect is sufficient, without further occupying his attention on the subject.—E.

seventy-six miles, the variation appeared by several azimuths to be 16° 30' West.

Section II.

The Passage from Madeira to Rio de Janeiro, with some Account of the Country, and the Incidents that happened there.

On the 21st of September we saw the islands called the Salvages, to the north of the Canaries; when the principal of these bore S ¼ W. at the distance of about five leagues, we found the variation of the compass by an azimuth to be 17° 50. I make these islands to lie in latitude 30° 11' north, and distant fifty-eight leagues from Funchiale in Madeira, in the direction of S. 16° E.

On Friday the 23d we saw the Peak of Teneriffe bearing W. by S. ¼ S. and found the variation of the compass to be from 17° 22' to 16° 30'. The height of this mountain, from which I took a new departure, was determined by Dr Heberden, who has been upon it, to be 15,396 feet, which is but 148 yards less than three miles, reckoning the mile at 1760 yards.[1] Its appearance at sunset was very striking, when

---

[1] It is not said by what means Dr H. ascertained the height of this peak, and one may safely call in question his accuracy. In the table referred to in a former note, its height, as measured by the barometer, is stated to be 12,358 English feet, being nearly 10,000 feet lower than that of Chimborazo, the highest summit of the Andes, which is estimated at 21,440. But there is a good deal of contrariety in the statements of the heights of mountains. The following quotations from Krusenstern's account of his voyage will both prove this, and at the same time give the reader some lively conception of the magnificent effect of the Peak " At half past six in the morning, we distinctly saw the island of Teneriffe, and at seven the pic cleared itself of the clouds in which it had been enveloped until then, and appeared to us in all its majestic grandeur. As its summit was covered with snow, and was extremely brilliant from the reflection of the sun, this contributed very much to the beauty of the scene. On either side, to the east and west, the mountains, which nature seems to have destined to sustain this enormous mass, appeared gradually to decline. Every one of the mountains which surround the pic, would be considerable in itself; but their height scarcely attracts the attention of the beholder, although they contribute to diminish the apparent size of the pic, which, if it stood alone, would be much more striking," " At six the next morning, (this was the second morning after leaving Teneriffe) we still saw the pic from the deck; it bore by compass, N.E. 15° 30', that is, allowing for the variation, which is here 16° W.; N.W. 0° 30. At

when the sun was below the horizon, and the rest of the island appeared of a deep black, the mountain still reflected his rays, and glowed with a warmth of colour which no painting can express. There is no eruption of visible fire from it, but a heat issues from the chinks near the top, too strong to be borne by the hand when it is held near them. We had received from Dr Heberden, among other favours, some salt which he collected on the top of the mountain, where it is found in large quantities, and which he supposed to be the true *natrum* or *nitrum* of the ancients : He gave us also some native sulphur exceedingly pure, which he had likewise found upon the surface in great plenty.

On the next day, Saturday the 24th, we came into the north-east trade-wind, and on Friday the 30th saw Bona Vista, one of the Cape de Verd Islands ; we ranged the east side of it, at the distance of three or four miles from the shore, till we were obliged to haul off to avoid a ledge of rocks which stretch out S.W. by W. from the body, or S E point of the island, to the extent of a league and a half. Bona Vista by our observation lies in latitude 16° N. and longitude 21° 51′ west.

On the 1st of October, in latitude 14° 6′ N. and longitude 22° 10′ W. we found the variation by a very good azimuth to be 10° 37′ W. and the next morning it appeared to be 10°. This day we found the ship five miles a-head of the log, and the next day seven. On the 3d, hoisted out the boat to discover whether there was a current, and found

noon, we had an observation in 26° 13′ 51″ latitude, and 16° 58 25 longitude. Between six in the morning and noon we had lessened our latitude 21′ 5″, and increased our longitude 19 15″. The ship was consequently, at the time we saw the pic, in 26° 35′ 45′ lat. and 16° 59 10 long and as, according to Borda and Pingre, the pic lies in 28° 17′ N. lat. and 19° 00′ W. long. of Paris, or 16° 40′ of Greenwich, we must have seen it at six o'clock at the distance of 101 miles, and due north of us, in which direction it in fact bore. In very clear weather the pic may be seen 25 miles farther off from the mast-head ; but this is the greatest distance which it is visible even from that height, and under the most favourable circumstances. The elevation of the pic has been determined by several observations. Borda's calculation, which is founded on a geometrical admeasurement, and is conceived to be the most correct, makes it 1905 toises, or 11,430 feet." The relations which some authors have given of the height of this famous pic or peak, are extravagant beyond all credibility. The reader will meet with some of them in Crutwell's Gazetteer.—Γ.

found one to the eastward, at the rate of three quarters of a mile an hour.

During our course from Teneriffe to Bona Vista we saw great numbers of flying fish, which from the cabin-windows appear beautiful beyond imagination, their sides having the colour and brightness of burnished silver; when they are seen from the deck they do not appear to so much advantage, because their backs are of a dark colour. We also took a shark, which proved to be the *Squalus Carcharias* of Linnæus.

Having lost the trade-wind on the 3d, in latitude 12° 14', and longitude 22° 10', the wind became somewhat variable, and we had light airs and calms by turns.

On the 7th, Mr Banks went out in the boat, and took what the seamen call a Portuguese man of war; it is the *Holuthuria Physalis* of Linnæus, and a species of the *Mollusca*. It consisted of a small bladder about seven inches long, very much resembling the air-bladder of fishes, from the bottom of which descended a number of strings of a bright blue and red, some of them three or four feet in length, which upon being touched sting like a nettle, but with much more force. On the top of the bladder is a membrane which is used as a sail, and turned so as to receive the wind which way soever it blows: This membrane is marked in fine pink-coloured veins, and the animal is in every respect an object exquisitely curious and beautiful.

We also took several of the shell-fishes, or testaceous animals, which are always found floating upon the water, particularly the *Helix Janthina* and *Violacea*; they are about the size of a snail, and are supported upon the surface of the water by a small cluster of bubbles, which are filled with air, and consist of a tenacious slimy substance that will not easily part with its contents; the animal is oviparous, and these bubbles serve also as a *nidus* for its eggs. It is probable that it never goes down to the bottom, nor willingly approaches any shore; for the shell is exceedingly brittle, and that of few fresh-water snails is so thin: Every shell contains about a tea-spoonful of liquor, which it easily discharges upon being touched, and which is of the most beautiful red-purple that can be conceived. It dies linen cloth, and it may perhaps be worth enquiry, as the shell is certainly found in the Mediterranean, whether it be not the *Purpura* of the ancients.[2]

On the 8th, in latitude 8° 25 north, longitude 22° 4' west, we found a current setting to the southward, which the next day in latitude 7° 58', longitude 22° 13, shifted to the N.N.W.¼W. at the rate of one mile and a furlong an hour. The variation here, by the mean of several azimuths, appeared to be 8 39 W.

On the 10th, Mr Banks shot the black-toed gull, not yet described according to Linnæus's system; he gave it the name of *Larus crepidatus:* It is remarkable that the dung of this bird is of a lively red, somewhat like that of the liquor procured from the shells, only not so full; its principal food therefore is probably the *Helix* just mentioned. A current to the N.W. prevailed more or less till Monday the 24th, when we were in latitude 1° 7' N. and longitude 28° 50'.

On the 25th we crossed the Line with the usual ceremonies, in longitude 29° 30', when, by the result of several very good azimuths, the variation was 2° 24.

On the 28th, at noon, being in the latitude of Ferdinand Noronha, and, by the mean of several observations by Mr Green and myself, in longitude 32° 5 16" W. which is to the westward of it by some charts, and to the eastward by others, we expected to see the island, or some of the shoals that

---

[2] It is quite impossible to discuss this subject here. But it may be worth while to refer the learned reader for some curious information about it, to the illustrious Bochart's work entitled Hierozoicon, Part II. Book V. Ch. II. There are several sorts of sea shells, that yield the purple-dye so much esteemed among the ancients. Pliny, who has written on the subject, divides them into two classes, the *buccinum* and *purpura,* of which the latter was most in request. According to him, the best kinds were found in the vicinity of Tyre. That city was famous for the manufacture of purple. To be *Tyrio conspectus in ostro,* seemed, in the estimation of the Mantuan poet, essential to his due appearance in honour of Augustus, Geor. 3—17. But several other places in the Mediterranean afforded this precious article. Thus Horace speaks of Spartan purple,

Nec *Laconicas* mihi
Trabunt honestæ *purpuras* clientæ.
          Od. Lib. 2. 18.

The English reader will be much pleased with several interesting remarks as to the purple and other colours known to the ancients, given in President Goguet's valuable work on the origin of laws, arts. &c. &c. of which a translation by Dr Henry was published at Edinburgh 1761.—E.

that are laid down in the charts between it and the main, but we saw neither one nor the other.

In the evening of the 29th, we observed that luminous appearance of the sea which has been so often mentioned by navigators, and of which such various causes have been assigned ; some supposing it to be occasioned by fish, which agitated the water by darting at their prey, some by the putrefaction of fish and other marine animals, some by electricity, and others referring it to a great variety of different causes. It appeared to emit flashes of light exactly resembling those of lightning, only not so considerable, but they were so frequent that sometimes eight or ten were visible almost at the same moment. We were of opinion that they proceeded from some luminous animal, and upon throwing out the casting-net our opinion was confirmed : It brought up a species of the *Medusa*, which when it came on board had the appearance of metal violently heated, and emitted a white light: With these animals were taken some very small crabs, of three different species, each of which gave as much light as a glow-worm, though the creature was not so large by nine-tenths : Upon examination of these animals, Mr Banks had the satisfaction to find that they were all entirely new.[3]

On Wednesday the 2d of November, about noon, being in the latitude of 10° 38' S. and longitude 32° 13' 43" W. we passed the Line, in which the needle at this time would have pointed due north and south, without any variation : For in the morning, having decreased gradually in its deviation for some days, it was no more than 18' W. and in the afternoon it was 34' east.

On the 6th, being in latitude 19° 3' south, longitude 35° 50' west, the colour of the water was observed to change, upon which we sounded, and found ground at the depth of thirty-two fathoms ; the lead was cast three times within about four hours, without a foot difference in the depth or quality of the bottom, which was coral rock, fine sand, and shells; we therefore supposed that we had passed over the tail of the great shoal which is laid down in all

our

[3] The reader is referred to the account of Captain Krusenstern's circumnavigation, for a very satisfactory relation of an experiment on this subject, which clearly proves the truth of the opinion above stated, as to the cause of the shining appearance so often noticed at sea. It is too long for quotation in this place.—E.

our charts by the name of Abrothos, on which Lord Anson struck soundings in his passage outwards : At four the next morning we had no ground with 100 fathom.

As several articles of our stock and provisions now began to fall short, I determined to put into Rio de Janeiro, rather than at any port in Brazil or Falkland's Islands, knowing that it could better supply us with what we wanted, and making no doubt but that we should be well received.

On the 8th, at day-break, we saw the coast of Brazil, and about ten o'clock we brought-to, and spoke with a fishing-boat ; the people on board told us that the land which we saw, lay to the southward of Santo Espirito, but belonged to the captainship of that place.

Mr Banks and Dr Solander went on board this vessel, in which they found eleven men, nine of whom were blacks : they all fished with lines, and their fresh cargo, the chief part of which Mr Banks bought, consisted of dolphins, large pelagic scombers of two kinds, sea-bream, and some of the fish which in the West Indies are called Welshmen. Mr Banks had taken Spanish silver with him, which he imagined to be the currency of the continent, but to his great surprise the people asked him for English shillings ; he gave them two, which he happened to have about him, and it was not without some dispute that they took the rest of the money in pistereens. Their business seemed to be to catch large fish at a good distance from the shore, which they salted in bulk, in a place made for that purpose in the middle of their boat : Of this merchandise they had about two quintals on board, which they offered for about fifteen shillings, and would probably have sold for half the money. The fresh fish, which was bought for about nineteen shillings and sixpence, served the whole ship's company ; the salt was not wanted.

The sea-provision of these fishermen consisted of nothing more than a cask of water, and a bag of Cassada flour, which they called Farinha de Pao, or wooden flour, which indeed is a name which very well suits its taste and appearance. Their water-cask was large, as wide as their boat, and exactly fitted a place that was made for it in the ballast ; it was impossible therefore to draw out any of its contents by a tap, the sides being, from the bottom to the top, wholly inaccessible ; neither could any be taken out

by

by dipping a vessel in at the head, for an opening sufficiently wide for that purppse would have endangered the
loss of great part of it by the rolling of the vessel : Their
expedient to get at their water, so situated, was curious ;
when one of them wanted to drink, he applied to his neigh-
bour, who accompanied him to the water-cask with a hollow cane about three feet long, which was open at both
ends ; this he thrust into the cask through a small hole in
the top, and then, stopping the upper end with the palm
of his hand, drew it out ; the pressure of the air against
the other end keeping in the water which it contained ;
to this end the person who wanted to drink applied his
mouth, and the assistant then taking his hand from the
other, and admitting the air above, the cane immediately
parted with its contents, which the drinker drew off till he
was satisfied.[*]

We stood off and on along the shore till the 12th, and
successively saw a remarkable hill near Santo Espirito,
then Cape St Thomas, and then an island just without Cape
Frio, which in some maps is called the island of Frio, and
which being high, with a hollow in the middle, has the appearance of two islands when seen at a distance. On this
day we stood along the shore for Rio de Janeiro, and at
nine the next morning made sail for the harbour. I then
sent Mr Hicks, my first lieutenant, before us in the pinnace, up to the city, to acquaint the governor, that we put
in there to procure water and refreshments ; and to desire
the assistance of a pilot to bring us into proper anchoring-
ground. I continued to stand up the river, trusting to Mr
Bellisle's draught, published in the *Petit Atlas Maritime,*
vol. ii. N°. 54, which we found very good, till five o'clock
in the evening, expecting the return of my lieutenant; and
just

[*] It seems pretty obvious that the form and position of the water-cask,
were accommodated to this known practicability of getting conveniently
at its contents. But how such a method should have become familiar to
these fishermen, it is difficult to conjecture. Some accidental observation
of a reed or similar body containing water when one of its ends was pressed close, had, in all probability, furnished them or their ancestors with
the hint. Man, when necessitated to exertion, is essentially a philosopher ;
but when his natural wants are by any means supplied, he dwindles into a
fool. Hence his discoveries are often invaluable in their consequences,
whilst his reasonings in explanation of them are absurd and childish. A
contrasted collection of both would be a most amusing, and at the same
time a humiliating picture of the inconsistency of human nature.—E.

just as I was about to anchor, above the island of Cobras, which lies before the city, the pinnace came back without him, having on board a Portuguese officer, but no pilot. The people in the boat told me, that my lieutenant was detained by the viceroy till I should go on shore.[5] We came immediately to an anchor; and, almost at the same time, a ten-oared boat, full of soldiers, came up, and kept rowing round the ship, without exchanging a word: In less than a quarter of an hour, another boat came on board with several of the viceroy's officers, who asked, whence we came; what was our cargo; the number of men and guns on board; the object of our voyage, and several other questions, which we directly and truly answered: They then told me, as a kind of apology for detaining my lieutenant, and putting an officer on board my pinnace, that it was the invariable custom of the place, to detain the first officer who came on shore from any ship on her arrival, till a boat from the viceroy had visited her, and to suffer no boat to go either from or to a ship, while she lay there, without having a soldier on board. They said that I might go on shore when I pleased; but wished that every other person might remain on board till the paper which they should

draw

---

[5] There is no reason for supposing that this viceroy had any greater dislike to our countrymen than to any other, or that he acted otherwise towards them than he was accustomed to do in similar cases. Bougainville complains of him much, and represents him as a turbulent ill-mannered fellow. "Having," says he, "on one occasion, upon the repeated leave of the viceroy, concluded a bargain for buying a snow, his excellency forbad the seller to deliver it to me. He likewise gave orders, that we should not be allowed the necessary timber out of the royal dock-yards, for which we had already agreed; he then refused me the permission of lodging with my officers (during the time that the frigate underwent some essential repairs) in a house near the town, offered me by its proprietor, and which Commodore Byron had occupied in 1765, when he touched at this port. On this account, and likewise on his refusing me the snow and the timber, I wanted to make some remonstrances to him. He did not give me time to do it: And at the first words I uttered, he rose in a furious passion, and ordered me to go out; and being certainly piqued, that in spite of his anger, I remained sitting with two officers who accompanied me, he called his guards; but they, wiser than himself, did not come, and we retired, so that nobody seemed to have been disturbed. We were hardly gone, when the guards of his palace were doubled, and orders given to arrest all the French that should be found in the streets after sunsetting." According to this writer, it appears that neither the laws of nations, nor the rules of good breeding, were respected by this very important being, "vain of his authority."—E.

draw up had been delivered to the viceroy, promising that, immediately upon their return, the lieutenant should be sent on board.

This promise was performed, and on the next morning, the 14th, I went on shore, and obtained leave of the viceroy to purchase provisions and refreshments for the ship, provided I would employ one of their own people as a factor, but not otherwise. I made some objections to this, but he insisted upon it as the custom of the place. I objected also against the putting a soldier into the boat every time she went between the ship and the shore; but he told me, that this was done by the express orders of his court, with which he could in no case dispense. I then requested, that the gentlemen whom I had on board might reside on shore during our stay, and that Mr Banks might go up the country to gather plants; but this he absolutely refused. I judged from his extreme caution, and the severity of these restrictions, that he suspected we were come to trade; I therefore took some pains to convince him of the contrary. I told him, that we were bound to the southward, by the order of his Britannic majesty, to observe a transit of the planet Venus over the sun, an astronomical phenomenon of great importance to navigation. Of the transit of Venus, however, he could form no other conception, than that it was the passing of the north star through the south pole; for these are the very words of his interpreter, who was a Swede, and spoke English very well. I did not think it necessary to ask permission for the gentlemen to come on shore during the day, or that, when I was on shore myself, I might be at liberty, taking for granted that nothing was intended to the contrary; but in this I was unfortunately mistaken. As soon as I took leave of his excellency, I found an officer who had orders to attend me wherever I went: Of this I desired an explanation, and was told that it was meant as a compliment; I earnestly desired to be excused from accepting such an honour, but the good viceroy would by no means suffer it to be dispensed with.[6]

With

---

[6] Mr Barrow notices the extreme jealousy and circumspection of the government, as to strangers. None, he says, is permitted to walk the streets in the day time, unless a soldier attend him. Bad governments are usually fearful, and often expose their weakness by the very means they employ to conceal it. On this principle, admitting its truth, the policy of the Portuguese in general forfeits all claim to admiration. What changes have

With this officer, therefore, I returned on board, about twelve o'clock, where I was impatiently expected by Mr Banks and Dr Solander, who made no doubt but that a fair account of us having been given by the officers who had been on board the evening before in their paper called a Practica, and every scruple of the viceroy removed in my conference with his excellency, they should immediately be at liberty to go on shore, and dispose of themselves as they pleased. Their disappointment at receiving my report may easily be conceived ; and it was still increased by an account, that it had been resolved, not only to prevent them residing on shore, and going up the country, but even their leaving the ship; orders having been given, that no person except the captain, and such common sailors as were required to be upon duty, should be permitted to land ; and that probably there was a particular view to the passengers in this prohibition, as they were reported to be gentlemen sent abroad to make observations and discoveries, and were uncommonly qualified for that purpose. In the evening, however, Mr Banks and Dr Solander dressed themselves, and attempted to go on shore, in order to make a visit to the viceroy; but they were stopped by the guard-boat which had come off with our pinnace, and which kept hovering round the ship all the while she lay here, for that purpose; the officer on board saying, that he had particular orders, which he could not disobey, to suffer no passenger, nor any officer, except the captain, to pass the boat. After much expostulation to no purpose, they were obliged, with whatever reluctance and mortification, to return on board. I then went on shore myself, but found the viceroy inflexible ; he had one answer ready for every thing I could say, That the restrictions under which he had laid us, were in obedience to the king of Portugal's commands, and therefore indispensable.

. In this situation I determined, rather than be made a prisoner in my own boat, to go on shore no more; for the officer who, under pretence of a compliment, attended me when I was ashore, insisted also upon going with me to and from the ship: But still imagining, that the scrupulous vigilance of the viceroy must proceed from some mistaken
notion

been wrought in it, since the transatlantic emigration of the royal family remain to be elucidated.—E.

notion about us, which might more easily be removed by writing than in conversation, I drew up a memorial, and Mr Banks drew up another, which we sent on shore. These memorials were both answered, but by no means to our satisfaction; we therefore replied: In consequence of which, several other papers were interchanged between us and the viceroy, but still without effect. However, as I thought some degree of force, on the part of the viceroy, to enforce these restrictions, necessary to justify my acquiescence in them to the Admiralty, I gave orders to my lieutenant, Mr Hicks, when I sent him with our last reply on Sunday the 20th, in the evening, not to suffer a guard to be put into his boat. When the officer on board the guard-boat found that Mr Hicks was determined to obey my orders, he did not proceed to force, but attended him to the landing-place, and reported the matter to the viceroy. Upon this his excellency refused to receive the memorial, and ordered Mr Hicks to return to the ship; when he came back to the boat, he found that a guard had been put on board in his absence, but he absolutely refused to return till the soldier was removed: The officer then proceeded to enforce the viceroy's orders; he seized all the boat's crew, and sent them under an armed force to prison, putting Mr Hicks at the same time into one of their own boats, and sending him under a guard back to the ship. As soon as he had reported these particulars, I wrote again to the viceroy, demanding my boat and crew, and in my letter inclosed the memorial which he had refused to receive from Mr Hicks: These papers I sent by a petty officer, that I might wave the dispute about a guard, against which I had never objected except when there was a commissioned officer on board the boat. The petty officer was permitted to go on shore with his guard, and, having delivered his letter, was told that an answer would be sent the next day.

About eight o'clock this evening it began to blow very hard in sudden gusts from the south, and our long-boat coming on board just at this time with four pipes of rum, the rope which was thrown to her from the ship, and which was taken hold of by the people on board, unfortunately broke, and the boat, which had come to the ship before the wind, went adrift to windward of her, with a small skiff of Mr Banks's that was fastened to her stern. This was a great misfortune, as, the pinnace being detained on shore,

we had no boat on board but a four-oared yawl: The yawl,
however, was immediately manned and sent to her assistance; but, notwithstanding the utmost effort of the people
in both boats, they were very soon out of sight: Far indeed
we could not see at that time in the evening, but the distance was enough to convince us that they were not under
command, which gave us great uneasiness, as we knew they
must drive directly upon a reef of rocks which ran out just
to leeward of where we lay: After waiting some hours in
the utmost anxiety, we gave them over for lost, but about
three o'clock the next morning had the satisfaction to see
all the people come on board in the yawl. From them we
learnt, that the long-boat having filled with water, they had
brought her to a grappling and left her; and that, having
fallen in with the reef of rocks in their return to the ship,
they had been obliged to cut Mr Banks's little boat adrift.
As the loss of our long-boat, which we had now too much
reason to apprehend, would have been an unspeakable disadvantage to us, considering the nature of our expedition,
I sent another letter to the viceroy, as soon as I thought he
could be seen, acquainting him with our misfortune, and
requesting the assistance of a boat from the shore for the
recovery of our own; I also renewed my demand that the
pinnace and her crew should be no longer detained: After
some delay, his excellency thought fit to comply both with
my request and demand; and the same day we happily recovered both the long-boat and the skiff, with the rum, but
every thing else that was on board was lost. On the 23d,
the viceroy, in his answer to my remonstrance against
seizing my men and detaining the boat, acknowledged that
I had been treated with some incivility, but said that the
resistance of my officers, to what he had declared to be the
king's orders, made it absolutely necessary; he also expressed some doubts whether the Endeavour, considering her
structure and other circumstances, was in the service of his
majesty, though I had before shewed him my commission:
To this I answered in writing, That to remove all scruples,
I was ready to produce my commission again. His excellency's scruples however still remained, and in his reply to
my letter he not only expressed them in still plainer terms,
but accused my people of smuggling. This charge, I am
confident, was without the least foundation in truth. Mr
Banks's servants had indeed found means to go on shore on
the

the 22d at day-break, and stay till it was dark in the evening, but they brought on board only plants and insects, having been sent for no other purpose. And I had the greatest reason to believe that not a single article was smuggled by any of our people who were admitted on shore, though many artful means were used to tempt them, even by the very officers that were under his excellency's roof, which made the charge still more injurious and provoking. I have indeed some reason to suspect that one poor fellow bought a single bottle of rum with some of the clothes upon his back; and in my answer I requested of his excellency, that, if such an attempt at illicit trade should be repeated, he would without scruple order the offender to be taken into custody. And thus ended our altercation, both by conference and writing, with the viceroy of Rio de Janeiro.

A friar in the town having requested the assistance of our surgeon, Dr Solander easily got admittance in that character on the 25th, and received many marks of civility from the people. On the 26th, before day-break, Mr Banks also found means to elude the vigilance of the people in the guard-boat, and got on shore; he did not however go into the town, for the principal objects of his curiosity were to be found in the fields: to him also the people behaved with great civility, many of them invited him to their houses, and he bought a porker and some other things of them for the ship's company; the porker, which was by no means lean, cost him eleven shillings, and he paid something less than two for a Muscovy duck.

On the 27th, when the boats returned from watering, the people told us there was a report in town, that search was making after some persons who had been on shore from the ship without the viceroy's permission; these persons we conjectured to be Dr Solander and Mr Banks, and therefore they determined to go on shore no more.

On the first of December, having got our water and other necessaries on board, I sent to the viceroy for a pilot to carry us to sea, who came off to us; but the wind preventing us from getting out, we took on board a plentiful supply of fresh beef, yams, and greens for the ship's company. On the 2d, a Spanish packet arrived, with letters from Buenos Ayres for Spain, commanded by Don Antonio de Monte Negro y Velasco, who with great politeness offered

to

to take our letters to Europe: I accepted the favour, and gave him a packet for the secretary of the Admiralty, containing copies of all the papers that had passed between me and the viceroy; leaving also duplicates with the viceroy, to be by him forwarded to Lisbon.

On Monday the 5th, it being a dead calm, we weighed anchor and towed down the bay; but, to our great astonishment, when we got abreast of Santa Cruz, the principal fortification, two shot were fired at us. We immediately cast anchor, and sent to the fort to enquire the reason of what had happened: Our people brought us word, That the commandant had received no order from the viceroy to let us pass; and that, without such an order, no vessel was ever suffered to go below the fort. It was now, therefore, become necessary, that we should send to the viceroy, to enquire why the necessary order had not been given, as he had notice of our departure, and had thought fit to write me a polite letter, wishing me a good voyage. Our messenger soon returned with an account, that the order had been written some days, but by an unaccountable negligence not sent.

We did not get under sail till the 7th; and when we had passed the fort, the pilot desired to be discharged. As soon as he was dismissed, we were left by our guard-boat, which had hovered about us from the first hour of our being in this place to the last: And Mr Banks, having been prevented from going ashore at Rio de Janeiro, availed himself of her departure to examine the neighbouring islands, where, particularly on one in the mouth of the harbour called Raza, he gathered many species of plants, and caught a variety of insects.

It is remarkable, that, during the last three or four days of our staying in this harbour, the air was loaded with butterflies: They were chiefly of one sort, but in such numbers that thousands were in view in every direction, and the greatest part of them above our mast-head.

We lay here from the 14th of November to the 7th of December, something more than three weeks, during which time Mr Monkhouse, our surgeon, was on shore every day to buy our provisions; Dr Solander was on shore once; I was several times on shore myself, and Mr Banks also found means to get into the country, notwithstanding the watch that was set over us. I shall, therefore, with the in-

telligence

telligence obtained from these gentlemen, and my own observations, give some account of the town, and the country adjacent.

Rio de Janeiro, or the river of Januarius, was probably so called from its having been discovered on the feast-day of that saint; and the town, which is the capital of the Portuguese dominions in America, derives its name from the river, which indeed is rather an arm of the sea, for it did not appear to receive any considerable stream of fresh water: It stands on a plain, close to the shore, on the west side of the bay, at the foot of several high mountains which rise behind it. It is neither ill designed nor ill built; the houses, in general, are of stone, and two stories high; every house having, after the manner of the Portuguese, a little balcony before its windows, and a lattice of wood before the balcony. I computed its circuit to be about three miles; for it appears to be equal in size to the largest country towns in England, Bristol and Liverpool not excepted; the streets are straight, and of a convenient breadth, intersecting each other at right angles; the greater part, however, lie in a line with the citadel called St Sebastian, which stands on the top of a hill which commands the town.

It is supplied with water from the neighbouring hills, by an aqueduct, which is raised upon two stories of arches, and is said at some places to be at a great height from the ground, from which the water is conveyed by pipes into a fountain in the great square that exactly fronts the viceroy's palace. At this fountain great numbers of people are continually waiting for their turn to draw water; and the soldiers, who are posted at the governor's door, find it very difficult to maintain any regularity among them. The water at this fountain however is so bad, that we, who had been two months at sea, confined to that in our casks, which was almost always foul, could not drink it with pleasure. Water of a better quality is led into some other part of the town, but I could not learn by what means.

The churches are very fine, and there is more religious parade in this place than in any of the popish countries in Europe; there is a procession of some parish every day, with various insignia, all splendid and costly in the highest degree: They beg money, and say prayers in great form, at the corner of every street.

While we lay here, one of the churches was rebuilding; and

and to defray the expence, the parish to which it belonged had leave to beg in procession through the whole city once a week, by which very considerable sums were collected. At this ceremony, which was performed by night, all the boys of a certain age were obliged to assist, the sons of gentlemen not being excused. Each of these boys was dressed in a black cassock, with a short red cloak, hanging about as low as the waist, and carried in his hand a pole about six or seven feet long, at the end of which was tied a lantern : the number of lanterns was generally above two hundred, and the light they gave was so great, that the people who saw it from the cabin windows thought the town had been on fire.

The inhabitants, however, may pay their devotions at the shrine of any saint in the calendar, without waiting till there is a procession; for before almost every house there is a little cupboard, furnished with a glass window, in which one of these tutelary powers is waiting to be gracious; and to prevent his being out of mind, by being out of sight, a lamp is kept constantly burning before the window of his tabernacle in the night. The people indeed are by no means remiss in their devotions, for before these saints they pray and sing hymns with such vehemence, that in the night they were very distinctly heard on board the ship, though she lay at the distance of at least half a mile from the town.

The government here, as to its form, is mixed; it is notwithstanding very despotic in fact. It consists of the viceroy, the governor of the town, and a council, the number of which I could not learn : Without the consent of this council, in which the viceroy has a casting vote, no judicial act should be performed; yet both the viceroy and governor frequently commit persons to prison at their own pleasure, and sometimes send them to Lisbon, without acquainting their friends or family with what is laid to their charge, or where they may be found.

To restrain the people from travelling into the country, and getting into any district where gold or diamonds may be found, of both which there is much more than the government can otherwise secure, certain bounds are prescribed them, at the discretion of the viceroy, sometimes at a few, and sometimes at many miles distance from the city. On the verge of these limits a guard constantly patroles,

and

and whoever is found beyond it, is immediately seized and thrown into prison: And if a man is, upon any pretence, taken up by the guard without the limits, he will be sent to prison, though it should appear that he did not know their extent.

The inhabitants, which are very numerous, consist of Portuguese, negroes, and Indians, the original natives of the country. The township of Rio, which, as I was told, is but a small part of the capitanea, or province, is said to contain 37,000 white persons, and 629,000 blacks, many of whom are free; making together 666,000, in the proportion of seventeen to one. The Indians, who are employed to do the king's work in this neighbourhood, can scarcely be considered as inhabitants; their residence is at a distance, from whence they come by turns to their task, which they are obliged to perform for a small pay. The guard-boat was constantly rowed by these people, who are of a light copper colour, and have long black hair.[7]

The military establishment here consists of twelve regiments of regular troops, six of which are Portuguese, and six creoles; and twelve other regiments of provincial militia. To the regulars the inhabitants behave with the utmost humility and submission; and I was told, that if any of them should neglect to take off his hat upon meeting an officer,

---

[7] Mr Barrow says, that it is with some difficulty so many as twelve Brazilians can be obtained to row the governor's barge on certain solemn occasions. The Portuguese apostles who went over to this country in order to convert the inhabitants to their faith, commenced their labours by endeavouring to reduce them as fast as possible to the condition of slaves, as if no other promised a suitable foundation for the fabric of superstition. These incorrigible and misguided pagans, it should seem however, disliked the process, preferring liberty and error, darkness and death, to the whips, the chains, and torches, so kindly held out to them by their zealous visitants. The consequence was plain and summary: These wretched creatures were soon almost totally extirpated, so that it became necessary to procure other beings to cultivate the soil: And who so proper a substitute, as the black crispy-haired animals of the opposite continent? These, according to Mr Barrow, have been comparatively well treated; but, notwithstanding, he says, it requires an importation of no less than 20,000 negroes annually, to supply the loss of those who are worked out in the service of the very devout Portuguese! In Cook's time, it is likely, from what he mentions afterwards as to the number of negroes imported, that things were even worse then than they are now. It is scarcely conceivable indeed, that any people so closely connected with Europe as the lords of Brazil, should not have acquired humanity, or at least improved in its notions of good policy, in half a century.—E.

officer, he would immediately be knocked down.   These
haughty severities render the people extremely civil to any
stranger who has the appearance of a gentleman.   But the
subordination of the officers themselves to the viceroy is en-
forced with circumstances equally mortifying, for they are
obliged to attend in his hall three times every day to ask
his commands; the answer constantly is, " There is nothing
new."   I have been told, that this servile attendance is exacted to prevent their going into the country; and if so, it
effectually answers the purpose.

It is, I believe, universally allowed, that the women, both
of the Spanish and Portuguese settlements in South America, make less difficulty of granting personal favours, than
those of any other civilized country in the world.   Of the
ladies of this town, some have formed so unfavourable an
opinion as to declare, that they did not believe there was a
modest one among them.   This censure is certainly too general; but what Dr Solander saw of them when he was on
shore, gave him no very exalted idea of their chastity: He
told me, that as soon as it was dark, one or more of them
appeared in every window, and distinguished those whom
they liked, among the gentlemen that walked past them,
by giving them nosegays; that he, and two gentlemen who
were with him, received so many of these favours, that, at
the end of their walk, which was not a long one, they threw
whole hatfuls of them away.   Great allowance must certainly be made for local customs; that which in one country would be an indecent familiarity, is a mere act of general courtesy in another; of the fact, therefore, which I have
related, I shall say nothing, but that I am confident it is
true.[8]

Neither

[8] Mr Barrow allows the existence of the fact here stated, but is decided-
ly of opinion in favour of the sex implicated by it.   In his judgment, it is
merely a harmless remnant of their earlier days.   If so, and far be it from
the writer to think otherwise, it betokens the innocency of fancy much more
than the effrontery of licentiousness.   Besides, there is reason to think,
that dissoluteness in the particular now alluded to, among a civilized and
luxurious people, seeks concealment in its gratification, as congenial to its
excessive and morbid sensibility.   The opposite to this condition is to be
found in some of the earlier stages of society, where the climate and fertility of the soil are naturally suitable,—as at Otaheite, when first known
to Europeans.   If, however, the terrifying pages of Juvenal may be allowed authority, there is too much ground for apprehension, that the extremity of animal indulgence is also one of the fearful symptoms of national

Neither will I take upon me to affirm, that murders are frequently committed here; but the churches afford an asylum to the criminal: And as our cockswain was one day looking at two men, who appeared to be talking together in a friendly manner, one of them suddenly drew a knife and stabbed the other; who not instantly falling, the murderer withdrew the weapon, and stabbed him a second time. He then ran away, and was pursued by some negroes, who were also witnesses of the fact; but whether he escaped or was taken I never heard.

The country, at a small distance round the town, which is all that any of us saw, is beautiful in the highest degree; the wildest spots being varied with a greater luxuriance of flowers, both as to number and beauty, than the best gardens in England.

Upon the trees and bushes sat an almost endless variety of birds, especially small ones, many of them covered with the most elegant plumage; among which were the humming-bird. Of insects too there was a great variety, and some of them very beautiful; but they were much more nimble than those of Europe, especially the butterflies, most of which flew near the tops of the trees, and were therefore very difficult to be caught, except when the sea-breeze blew fresh, which kept them nearer to the ground.

The banks of the sea, and of the small brooks which water this part of the country, are almost covered with the small crabs, called *cancer vocans;* some of these had one of the claws, called by naturalists the hand, very large; others had them both remarkably small, and of equal size, a difference which is said to distinguish the sexes, that with the large claw being the male.

There is the appearance of but little cultivation; the greater part of the land is wholly uncultivated, and very little care and labour seem to have been bestowed upon the rest; there are indeed little patches or gardens, in which many kinds of European garden stuff are produced, particularly cabbages, pease, beans, kidney-beans, turnips, and white-

corruption in its lethalic stage. But even this indignant and most exaltedly moral poet, in his relation of the infamous actions of noble and royal prostitutes, does not fail to imply the advantages they sought in deception and secrecy—the night-hood, the yellow veil, and the cunning artifices of proficient mothers.—E.

white radishes, but all much inferior to our own: Water-melons and pine-apples are also produced in these spots, and they are the only fruits that we saw cultivated, though the country produces musk, melons, oranges, limes, lemons, sweet lemons, citrons, plantains, bananas, mangos, mamane-apples, acajou or cashou apples and nuts; jamboira of two kinds, one of which bears a small black fruit; cocoa-nuts, mangos, palm nuts of two kinds, one long, the other round ; and palm berries, all which were in season while we were there.

Of these fruits the water-melons and oranges are the best in their kind, the pine-apples are much inferior to those that I have eaten in England; they are indeed more juicy and sweet, but have no flavour; I believe them to be natives of this country, though we heard of none that at this time grow wild; they have, however, very little care bestowed upon them, the plants being set between beds of any kind of garden-stuff, and suffered to take the chance of the season. The melons are still worse, at least those that we tasted, which were mealy and insipid; but the water-melons are excellent; they have a flavour, at least a degree of acidity, which ours have not. We saw also several species of the prickle-pear, and some European fruits, particularly the apple and peach, both which were very mealy and insipid. In these gardens also grow yams, and mandihoca, which in the West Indies is called cassada or cassava, and to the flower of which the people here, as I have before observed, give the name of *farinha de pao,* which may not improperly be translated, powder of post. The soil, though it produces tobacco and sugar, will not produce bread-corn ; so that the people here have no wheat-flour, but what is brought from Portugal, and sold at the rate of a shilling a pound, though it is generally spoiled by being heated in its passage. Mr Banks is of opinion, that all the products of our West In-dian islands would grow here; notwithstanding which, the inhabitants import their coffee and chocolate from Lisbon.[4]

Most

---

[4] The Portuguese government, it appears, from Mr Barrow's represen-tation, have taken effectual measures to preserve this colony in a state of dependance on the mother country: " It no sooner discovered," says that gentleman, " that sugar could be raised in any quantity, and afforded, in the markets of Europe, at reasonable prices, than it thought proper to impose on them an export duty of 20 *per cent* which operated as an immediate check on the growth of this article When the cultivation of the indigo

Most of the land, as far as we saw of the country, is laid down in grass, upon which cattle are pastured in great plenty; but they are so lean, that an Englishman will scarcely eat of their flesh : The herbage of these pastures consists principally of cresses, and consequently is so short, that though it may afford a bite for horses and sheep, it can scarcely be grazed by horned cattle in a sufficient quantity to keep them alive.

This country may possibly produce many valuable drugs; but we could not find any in the apothecaries shops, except pariera brava, and balsam capivi; both of which were excellent in their kind, and sold at a very low price. The drug trade is probably carried on to the northward, as well as that of the dying woods, for we could get no intelligence of either of them here.

As to manufactures, we neither saw nor heard of any except that of cotton hammocks, in which people are carried about here, as they are with us in sedan chairs; and these are principally, if not wholly, fabricated by the Indians.

The riches of the place consist chiefly in the mines which we supposed to lie far up the country, though we could never learn where, or at what distance; for the situation is concealed as much as possible, and troops are continually employed in guarding the roads that lead to them : It is almost impossible for any man to get a sight of them, except those who are employed there, and indeed the strongest curiosity would scarcely induce any man to attempt it, for whoever is found upon the road to them, if he cannot give undeniable evidence of his having business there, is immediately hanged up upon the next tree.

Much gold is certainly brought from these mines, but at an expence of life that must strike every man, to whom custom has not made it familiar, with horror. No less than forty thousand negroes are annually imported, on the king's account, to dig the mines; and we were credibly informed, that,

plant had been considerably extended, and the preparation sufficiently understood, so as to enable the colonists to meet their competitors in the markets of Europe, this article was assumed as a royal monopoly." Salt, he says, is another royal monopoly, and yields the sum of L.15,000 annually : But one of the immediate effects of its being so, is the entire destruction of the valuable fisheries. Does the reader remember the fable of the hen that laid golden eggs? Would not certain governments do well to study the moral of it?—E.

that, the last year but one before we arrived here, this number fell so short, probably from some epidemic disease, that twenty thousand more were draughted from the town of Rio.

Precious stones are also found here in such plenty, that a certain quantity only is allowed to be collected in a year; to collect this quantity, a number of people are sent into the country where they are found, and when it is got together, which sometimes happens in a month, sometimes in less and sometimes in more, they return; and after that, whoever is found in these precious districts, on any pretence, before the next year, is immediately put to death.

The jewels found here, are diamonds, topazes of several kinds, and amethysts. We did not see any of the diamonds, but were informed that the viceroy had a large quantity by him, which he would sell on the king of Portugal's account, but not at a less price than they are sold for in Europe. Mr Banks bought a few topazes and amethysts as specimens: Of the topazes there are three sorts, of very different value, which are distinguished by the names of pinga d'agua qualidade primeiro, pinga d'agua qualidade secundo, and chrystallos armerillos: They are sold, large and small, good and bad together, by octavos, or the eighth part of an ounce; the best at 4s. 9d. All dealing, however, in these stones, is prohibited to the subject under the severest penalties: There were jewellers here formerly, who purchased and worked them on their own account; but about fourteen months before our arrival, orders came from the court of Portugal, that no more stones should be wrought here, except on the king's account: The jewellers were ordered to bring all their tools to the viceroy, and left without any means of subsistence. The persons employed here to work stones for the king are slaves.

The coin that is current here, is either that of Portugal, consisting chiefly of thirty-six shillings pieces; or pieces both of gold and silver, which are struck at this place: The pieces of silver, which are very much debased, are called petacks, and are of different value, and easily distinguished by the number of rees that is marked on the outside. Here is also a copper coin, like that in Portugal, of five and ten ree pieces. A ree is a nominal coin of Portugal, ten of which are equal in value to about three farthings sterling.

The harbour of Rio de Janeiro is situated W. by N. 18

leagues

leagues from Cape Frio, and may be known by a remarkable hill, in the form of a sugar-loaf, at the west point of the bay;[5] but as all the coast is very high, and rises in many peaks, the entrance of this harbour may be more certainly distinguished by the islands that lie before it; one of which, called Rodonda, is high and round like a hay-stack, and lies at the distance of two leagues and a half from the entrance of the bay, in the direction of S. by W.; but the first islands which are met with, coming from the east, or Cape Frio, are two that have a rocky appearance, lying near to each other, and at the distance of about four miles from the shore: There are also, at the distance of three leagues to the westward of these, two other islands which lie near to each other, a little without the bay on the east side, and very near the shore. This harbour is certainly a good one; the entrance indeed is not wide, but the sea-breeze, which blows every day from ten or twelve o'clock till sunset, makes it easy for any ship to go in before the wind; and it grows wider as the town is approached, so that a-breast of it there is room for the largest fleet, in five or six fathom water, with an oozy bottom. At the narrow part, the entrance is defended by two forts. The principal is Santa Cruz, which stands on the east point of the bay, and has been mentioned before; that on the west side is called Fort Lozia, and is built upon a rock that lies close to the main; the distance between them is about three quarters of a mile, but the channel is not quite so broad, because there are sunken rocks which lie off each fort, and in this part alone there is danger: The narrowness of the channel causes the tides, both flood and ebb, to run with considerable strength, so that they cannot be stemmed without a fresh breeze. The rockiness of the bottom makes it also unsafe to anchor here: But all danger may be avoided by keeping in the middle of the

[5] Mr Barrow, during his stay at Rio de Janeiro, had an opportunity of ascertaining the height of the Sugar-loaf, as it is called from its conical appearance. It is, he says, 680 feet high, above the surface out of which it rises, and is a solid mass of hard sparkling granite. On the eastern side of the chasm which forms the entrance into the bay, there is a mountain of the same material, but so far different in form, that it slopes easily and gradually from the water's edge to the summit, which however is about as high as the cone. This side is well defended by forts and batteries. Mr Barrow's description of the magnificent scenery of this harbour, is perhaps somewhat poetically conceived, but may be advantageously consulted by the reader.—E.

the channel. Within the entrance, the course up the bay is first N. by W. $\frac{1}{2}$ W. and N.N.W. something more than a league; this will bring the vessel the length of the great road; and N.W. and W.N.W. one league more will carry her to the isle dos Cobras, which lies before the city: She should then keep the north side of this island close on board, and anchor above it, before a monastery of Benedictines which stands upon a hill at the N.W. end of the city.

The river, and indeed the whole coast, abounds with a greater variety of fish than we had ever seen; a day seldom passed in which one or more of a new species were not brought to Mr Banks: The bay also is as well adapted for catching these fish as can be conceived; for it is full of small islands, between which there is shallow water, and proper beaches for drawing the seine. The sea, without the bay, abounds with dolphins, and large mackerel of different kinds, which readily bite at a hook, and the inhabitants always tow one after their boats for that purpose.

Though the climate is hot, the situation of this place is certainly wholesome;[6] while we stayed here the thermometer never rose higher than 83 degrees. We had frequent rains, and once a very hard gale of wind.

Ships water here at the fountain in the great square, though, as I have observed, the water is not good; they land their casks upon a smooth sandy beach, which is not more than a hundred yards distant from the fountain, and upon application to the viceroy, a centinel will be appointed to look after them, and clear the way to the fountain where they are to be filled.

Upon the whole, Rio de Janeiro is a very good place for ships to put in at that want refreshment · The harbour is safe and commodious; and provisions, except wheaten-bread and flour, may be easily procured: As a succedaneum for bread, there are yams and cassada in plenty; beef, both fresh and jerked, may be bought at about two-pence
farthing

---

[6] Mr Barrow seems to think otherwise; according to him, it is by no means healthy, and the interminable annoyance of the musquitoes renders it as injurious to intellectual, as it is on other accounts to bodily welfare. Perhaps, however, he assigns too much agency to these very vexatious insects, when he says it is impossible for any man to think at all profitably in their company. His description then, it may be inferred, was written at a very respectful distance from the din and venom of the noisome pest.—E.

farthing a pound; though, as I have before remarked, it is very lean. The people here jerk their beef by taking out the bones, cutting it into large but thin slices, then curing it with salt, and drying it in the shade: It eats very well, and, if kept dry, will remain good a long time at sea. Mutton is scarcely to be procured, and hogs and poultry are dear; of garden-stuff and fruit-trees there is abundance, of which, however, none can be preserved at sea but the pumpkin; rum, sugar, and molasses, all excellent in their kind, may be had at a reasonable price; tobacco also is cheap, but it is not good. Here is a yard for building shipping, and a small hulk to heave down by; for, as the tide never rises above six or seven feet, there is no other way of coming at a ship's bottom.

When the boat which had been sent on shore returned, we hoisted her on board, and stood out to sea.

SECTION III.

The Passage from Rio de Janeiro to the entrance of the Streight of Le Maire, with a Description of some of the Inhabitants of Terra del Fuego.

ON the 9th of December, we observed the sea to be covered with broad streaks of a yellowish colour, several of them a mile long, and three or four hundred yards wide: Some of the water thus coloured was taken up, and found to be full of innumerable atoms pointed at the end, of a yellowish colour, and none more than a quarter of a line, or the fortieth part of an inch long: In the microscope they appeared to be *fasciculi* of small fibres interwoven with each other, not unlike the nidus of some of the *phyganeus,* called caddices; but whether they were animal or vegetable substances, whence they came, or for what they were designed, neither Mr Banks nor Dr Solander could guess. The same appearance had been observed before, when we first discovered the continent of South America.[1]

On

[1] The Portuguese have a name for what is here spoken of. They call it the grassy sea. There is reason to think that it is a vegetable, and not an animal production. But, on the whole, the subject has been little investigated.—E.

On the 11th we hooked a shark, and while we were playing it under the cabin window, it threw out, and drew in again several times what appeared to be its stomach: It proved to be a female, and upon being opened six young ones were taken out of it; five of them were alive, and swam briskly in a tub of water, but the sixth appeared to have been dead some time.

Nothing remarkable happened till the 30th, except that we prepared for the bad weather, which we were shortly to expect, by bending a new suit of sails; but on this day we ran a course of one hundred and sixty miles by the log, through innumerable land insects of various kinds, some upon the wing, and more upon the water, many of which were alive; they appeared to be exactly the same with the *carabi*, the *grylli*, the *phalanae, aranea*, and other flies that are seen in England, though at this time we could not be less than thirty leagues from land; and some of these insects, particularly the *grylli aranea*, never voluntarily leave it at a greater distance than twenty yards. We judged ourselves to be now nearly opposite to *Baye sans fond*, where Mr Dalrymple supposes there is a passage quite through the continent of America; and we thought from the insects that there might be at least a very large river, and that it had overflowed its banks.[2]

On the 3d of January, 1769, being in latitude 47° 17' S. and longitude 61° 29' 45" W. we were all looking out for Pepy's island, and for some time an appearance was seen in the east which so much resembled land, that we bore away for it; and it was more than two hours and a half before we were convinced that it was nothing but what sailors call a fog-bank.

The people now beginning to complain of cold, each of them received what is called a Magellanic jacket, and a pair of trowsers. The jacket is made of a thick woollen
stuff

[2] The place alluded to is denominated Sin-fondo bay in Jeffrey's map, which, however imperfect as to actual geography, is perhaps the best companion to the account of the voyages published about the same period. Mr Dalrymple is an example of those warm-fancied men that make discoveries with the celerity of mushroom beds, and from as unimportant materials too. Some Spanish charts, often the very worst authority in the world, had drawn a connection betwixt the branches of two rivers, on opposite sides of the continent, and hence was deduced, in his lively imagination, a passage from sea to sea. See Jeffrey's American Atlas, where the imaginary communication is represented by dotted lines.—E.

stuff, called *Fearnought*, which is provided by the government. We saw, from time to time, a great number of penguins, albatrosses, and sheer-waters, seals, whales, and porpoises: And on the 11th, having passed Falkland's islands, we discovered the coast of Terra del Fuego, at the distance of about four leagues, extending from the W. to S. E. by S. We had here five-and-thirty fathom, the ground soft, small slate stones. As we ranged along the shore to the S. E. at the distance of two or three leagues, we perceived smoke in several places, which was made by the natives, probably as a signal, for they did not continue it after we had passed by. This day we discovered that the ship had got near a degree of longitude to the westward of the log, which, in this latitude, is thirty-five minutes of a degree on the equator: Probably there is a small current setting westward, which may be caused by the westerly current coming round Cape Horn, and through the Streight of Le Maire, and the indraught of the Streight of Magellan.

Having continued to range the coast on the 14th, we entered the Streight of Le Maire; but the tide turning against us, drove us out with great violence, and raised such a sea off Cape St Diego, that the waves had exactly the same appearance as they would have had if they had broke over a ledge of rocks; and when the ship was in this torrent, she frequently pitched, so that the bowsprit was under water. About noon, we got under the land between Cape St Diego and Cape St Vincent, where I intended to have anchored; but finding the ground every where hard and rocky, and shallowing from thirty to twelve fathoms, I sent the master to examine a little cove, which lay at a small distance to the eastward of Cape St Vincent. When he returned, he reported, that there was anchorage in four fathom, and a good bottom, close to the eastward of the first bluff point, on the east of Cape St Vincent, at the very entrance of the cove, to which I gave the name of VINCENT's BAY: Before this anchoring ground, however, lay several rocky ledges, that were covered with sea-weed; but I was told that there was not less than eight and nine fathom over all of them. It will probably be thought strange, that where weeds, which grow at the bottom, appear above the surface, there should be this depth of water; but the weeds which grow upon rocky ground in these countries, and which always distinguish it from sand and ooze, are of an

enormous

enormous size. The leaves are four feet long, and some of
the stalks, though not thicker than a man's thumb, above
one hundred and twenty: Mr Banks and Dr Solander examined some of them, over which we sounded and had fourteen fathom, which is eighty four feet; and as they made a
very acute angle with the bottom, they were thought to be
at least one-half longer: The foot-stalks were swelled into
an air vessel, and Mr Banks and Dr Solander called this
plant *Fucus giganteus.* Upon the report of the master, I
stood in with the ship; but not trusting implicitly to his
intelligence, I continued to sound, and found but four fathom upon the first ledge that I went over; concluding,
therefore, that I could not anchor here without risk, I determined to seek some port in the Streight, where I might
get on board such wood and water as we wanted.

Mr Banks and Dr Solander, however, being very desirous
to go on shore, I sent a boat with them and their people,
while I kept plying as near as possible with the ship.

Having been on shore four hours, they returned about
nine in the evening, with above an hundred different plants
and flowers, all of them wholly unknown to the botanists of
Europe. They found the country about the bay to be in
general flat, the bottom of it in particular was a plain, covered with grass, which might easily have been made into a
large quantity of hay; they found also abundance of good
wood and water, and fowls in great plenty. Among other
things, of which nature has been liberal in this place, is
Winter's bark, *Winteranea aromatica;* which may easily be
known by its broad leaf, shaped like the laurel, of a light
green colour without, and inclining to blue within; the
bark is easily stripped with a bone or a stick, and its vir-
tues are well known: It may be used for culinary purposes
as a spice, and is not less pleasant than wholesome: Here
is also plenty of wild celery and scurvy-grass. The trees
are chiefly of one kind, a species of the birch, called *Betula
antarctica;* the stem is from thirty to forty feet long, and
from two to three feet in diameter, so that in a case of necessity they might possibly supply a ship with top-masts:
They are a light white wood, bear a small leaf, and cleave
very straight. Cranberries were also found here in great
plenty, both white and red.

The persons who landed saw none of the inhabitants, but

fell

fell in with two of their deserted huts, one in a thick wood, and the other close by the beach.

Having taken the boat on board, I made sail into the Streight, and at three in the morning of the 15th, I anchored in twelve fathom and a half, upon coral rocks, before a small cove, which we took for Port Maurice, at the distance of about half a mile from the shore. Two of the natives came down to the beach, expecting us to land; but this spot afforded so little shelter, that I at length determined not to examine it: I therefore got under sail again about ten o'clock, and the savages retired into the woods.

At two o'clock, we anchored in the bay of Good Success; and after dinner I went on shore, accompanied by Mr Banks and Dr Solander, to look for a watering-place. and speak to the Indians, several of whom had come in sight. We landed on the starboard side of the bay near some rocks, which made smooth water and good landing, thirty or forty of the Indians soon made their appearance at the end of a sandy beach on the other side of the bay, but seeing our number, which was ten or twelve, they retreated. Mr Banks and Dr Solander then advanced about one hundred yards before us, upon which two of the Indians returned, and, having advanced some paces towards them, sat down; as soon as they came up, the Indians rose. and each of them having a small stick in his hand threw it away, in a direction both from themselves and the strangers, which was considered as the renunciation of weapons in token of peace: They then walked briskly towards their companions, who had halted at about fifty yards behind them, and beckoned the gentlemen to follow, which they did. They were received with many uncouth signs of friendship; and, in return, they distributed among them some beads and ribbons, which had been brought on shore for that purpose, and with which they were greatly delighted. A mutual confidence and good-will being thus produced, our parties joined; the conversation, such as it was, became general; and three of them accompanied us back to the ship. When they came on board, one of them, whom we took to be a priest, performed much the same ceremonies which M. Bougainville describes, and supposes to be an exorcism. When he was introduced into a new part of the ship, or when any thing that he had not seen before caught

caught his attention, he shouted with all his force for some
minutes, without directing his voice either to us or his companions.[3]

They ate some bread and some beef, but not apparently
with much pleasure, though such part of what was given
them as they did not eat, they took away with them; but
they would not swallow a drop either of wine or spirits:
They put the glass to their lips, but, having tasted the liquor, they returned it with strong expressions of disgust.
Curiosity seems to be one of the few passions which distinguish men from brutes; and of this our guests appeared to
have very little. They went from one part of the ship to
another,

[3] The incident related by Bougainville, to which the allusion is made, is
somewhat affecting. An interesting boy, one of the savages' children, had
unwarily, and from ignorance of its dangerous nature, put some bits of
glass into his mouth which the sailors gave him. His lips and palate, &c.
were cut in several places, and he soon began to spit blood, and to be violently convulsed. This excited the most distressing alarm and suspicion
among the savages. One of them, whom Bougainville denominates a juggler, immediately had recourse to very strange and unlikely means in order to relieve the poor child. He first laid him on his back, then kneeling
down between his legs, and bending himself, he pressed the child's belly
as much as he could with his head and hands, crying out continually, but
with inarticulate sounds. From time to time he raised himself, and seeming to hold the disease in his joined hands, opened them at once into the
air, blowing, as if he drove away some evil spirit. During those rites, an
old woman in tears howled with great violence in the child's ears. These
ceremonies, however, not proving effectual, but rather, indeed, as might
have been expected, doing mischief, the juggler disappeared for a little, in
order, as should seem, to procure a peculiar dress, in which he might practise his exorcism with greater confidence of success, and to bring a brother
in the trade, similarly apparelled, to aid him in his labours. But so much
the worse for the wretched patient, who was now pummelled and squeez-
ed all over, till his body was completely bruised. Such treatment, it is almost unnecessary to say, aggravated his sufferings, but accomplished no cure.
The jugglers at last consented to allow the interference of the French surgeon, but appeared to be very jealous of his skill. The child became somewhat easier towards night; however, from his continual sickness, there was
much room to apprehend that he had swallowed some of the glass, and
died in consequence; for " about two o'clock in the morning," says Bougainville, " we on board heard repeated howls, and at break of day, though
the weather was very dreadful, the savages went off. They doubtless fled
from a place defiled by death, and by unlucky strangers, who, they thought,
were come merely to destroy them." It is very probable that the person
whom Cook supposed a priest, practised the charms spoken of, in order to
destroy any ill luck, and to prevent the occurrence of such like misfortunes in his intercourse with the wonderful strangers. There is an allusion
to this incident in a following section.—F.

another, and looked at the vast variety of new objects that every moment presented themselves, without any expression either of wonder or pleasure, for the vociferation of our exorcist seemed to be neither.

After having been on board about two hours, they expressed a desire to go ashore. A boat was immediately ordered, and Mr Banks thought fit to accompany them : He landed them in safety, and conducted them to their companions, among whom he remarked the same vacant indifference, as in those who had been on board; for as on one side there appeared no eagerness to relate, so on the other there seemed to be no curiosity to hear, how they had been received, or what they had seen. In about half an hour Mr Banks returned to the ship, and the Indians retired from the shore.

SECTION IV.

An Account of what happened in ascending a Mountain to search for Plants.

ON the 16th, early in the morning, Mr Banks and Dr Solander, with their attendants and servants, and two seamen to assist in carrying the baggage, accompanied by Mr Monkhouse the surgeon, and Mr Green the astronomer, set out from the ship with a view to penetrate as far as they could into the country, and return at night. The hills, when viewed at a distance, seemed to be partly a wood, partly a plain, and above them a bare rock. Mr Banks hoped to get through the wood, and made no doubt, but that, beyond it, he should, in a country which no botanist had ever yet visited, find alpine plants which would abundantly compensate his labour. They entered the wood at a small sandy beach, a little to the westward of the watering-place, and continued to ascend the hill, through the pathless wilderness, till three o'clock, before they got a near view of the places which they intended to visit. Soon after they reached what they had taken for a plain ; but, to their great disappointment, found it a swamp, covered with low bushes of birch, about three feet high, interwoven with each other, and so stubborn that they could not be bent out

of

of the way; it was therefore necessary to lift the leg over them, which at every step was buried, ancle deep, in the soil. To aggravate the pain and difficulty of such travelling, the weather, which had hitherto been very fine, much like one of our bright days in May, became gloomy and cold, with sudden blasts of a most piercing wind, accompanied with snow. They pushed forward, however, in good spirits, notwithstanding their fatigue, hoping the worst of the way was past, and that the bare rock which they had seen from the tops of the lower hills was not more than a mile before them; but when they had got about two-thirds over this woody swamp, Mr Buchan, one of Mr Banks's draughtsmen, was unhappily seized with a fit. This made it necessary for the whole company to halt, and as it was impossible that he should go any farther, a fire was kindled, and those who were most fatigued were left behind to take care of him. Mr Banks, Dr Solander, Mr Green, and Mr Monkhouse, went on, and in a short time reached the summit. As botanists, their expectations were here abundantly gratified; for they found a great variety of plants, which, with respect to the alpine plants in Europe, are exactly what those plants are with respect to such as grow in the plain.

The cold was now become more severe, and the snow-blasts more frequent; the day also was so far spent, that it was found impossible to get back to the ship, before the next morning: To pass the night upon such a mountain, in such a climate, was not only comfortless but dreadful; it was impossible, however, to be avoided, and they were to provide for it as well as they could.

Mr Banks and Dr Solander, while they were improving an opportunity which they had, with so much danger and difficulty, procured, by gathering the plants which they found upon the mountain, sent Mr Green and Mr Monkhouse back to Mr Buchan and the people that were with him, with directions to bring them to a hill, which they thought lay in a better route for returning to the wood, and which was therefore appointed as a general rendezvous. It was proposed, that from this hill they should push through the swamp, which seemed by the new route not to be more than half a mile over, into the shelter of the wood, and there build their wigwam, and make a fire: This, as their way was all down hill, it seemed easy to accomplish. Their whole company assembled at the rendezvous, and, though

2

though pinched with the cold, were in health and spirits, Mr Buchan himself having recovered his strength in a much greater degree than could have been expected. It was now near eight o'clock in the evening, but still good day-light, and they set forward for the nearest valley, Mr Banks himself undertaking to bring up the rear, and see that no straggler was left behind : This may perhaps be thought a superfluous caution, but it will soon appear to be otherwise. Dr Solander, who had more than once crossed the mountains which divide Sweden from Norway, well knew that extreme cold, especially when joined with fatigue, produces a torpor and sleepiness that are almost irresistible. He therefore conjured the company to keep moving, whatever pain it might cost them, and whatever relief they might be promised by an inclination to rest : Whoever sits down, says he, will sleep; and whoever sleeps, will wake no more. Thus, at once admonished and alarmed, they set forward; but while they were still upon the naked rock, and before they had got among the bushes, the cold became suddenly so intense, as to produce the effects that had been most dreaded. Dr Solander himself was the first who found the inclination, against which he had warned others, irresistible; and insisted upon being suffered to lie down. Mr Banks entreated and remonstrated in vain, down he lay upon the ground, though it was covered with snow; and it was with great difficulty that his friend kept him from sleeping. Richmond also, one of the black servants, began to linger, having suffered from the cold in the same manner as the doctor. Mr Banks, therefore, sent five of the company, among whom was Mr Buchan, forward to get a fire ready at the first convenient place they could find; and himself, with four others, remained with the doctor and Richmond, whom, partly by persuasion and entreaty, and partly by force, they brought on ; but when they had got through the greatest part of the birch and swamp, they both declared they could go no farther. Mr Banks had recourse again to entreaty and expostulation, but they produced no effect : When Richmond was told, that if he did not go on he would in a short time be frozen to death, he answered, that he desired nothing but to lie down and die : The doctor did not so explicitly renounce his life ; he said he was willing to go on, but that he must first take some sleep, though he had before told the company that to

sleep

sleep was to perish. Mr Banks and the rest found it impossible to carry them, and there being no remedy they were both suffered to sit down, being partly supported by the bushes, and in a few minutes they fell into a profound sleep: Soon after, some of the people who had been sent forward returned, with the welcome news that a fire was kindled about a quarter of a mile farther on the way. Mr Banks then endeavoured to wake Dr Solander, and happily succeeded: But, though he had not slept five minutes, he had almost lost the use of his limbs, and the muscles were so shrunk that his shoes fell from his feet; he consented to go forward with such assistance as could be given him, but no attempts to relieve poor Richmond were successful. It being found impossible to make him stir, after some time had been lost in the attempt, Mr Banks left his other black servant and a seaman, who seemed to have suffered least by the cold, to look after him; promising, that as soon as two others should be sufficiently warmed, they should be relieved. Mr Banks, with much difficulty, at length got the doctor to the fire; and soon after sent two of the people who had been refreshed, in hopes that, with the assistance of those who had been left behind, they would be able to bring Richmond, even though it should still be found impossible to wake him. In about half an hour, however, they had the mortification to see these two men return alone: they said, that they had been all round the place to which they had been directed, but could neither find Richmond nor those who had been left with him, and that though they had shouted many times, no voice had replied. This was matter of equal surprise and concern, particularly to Mr Banks, who, while he was wondering how it could happen, missed a bottle of rum, the company's whole stock, which they now concluded to be in the knapsack of one of the absentees. It was conjectured, that with this Richmond had been roused by the two persons who had been left with him, and that, having perhaps drank too freely of it themselves, they had all rambled from the place where they had been left, in search of the fire, instead of waiting for those who should have been their assistants and guides. Another fall of snow now came on, and continued incessantly for two hours, so that all hope of seeing them again, at least alive, were given up; but about twelve o'clock, to the great joy of those at the fire, a shouting was heard at

some

some distance. Mr Banks, with four more, immediately went out, and found the seaman with just strength enough left to stagger along, and call out for assistance: Mr Banks sent him immediately to the fire, and, by his direction, proceeded in search of the other two, whom he soon after found. Richmond was upon his legs, but not able to put one before the other; his companion was lying upon the ground, as insensible as a stone. All hands were now called from the fire, and an attempt was made to carry them to it; but this, notwithstanding the united efforts of the whole company, was found to be impossible. The night was extremely dark, the snow was now very deep, and, under these additional disadvantages, they found it very difficult to make way through the bushes and the bog for themselves, all of them getting many falls in the attempt. The only alternative was to make a fire upon the spot; but the snow which had fallen, and was still falling, besides what was every moment shaken in flakes from the trees, rendered it equally impracticable to kindle one there, and to bring any part of that which had been kindled in the wood thither: They were, therefore, reduced to the sad necessity of leaving the unhappy wretches to their fate; having first made them a bed of boughs from the trees, and spread a covering of the same kind over them to a considerable height.

Having now been exposed to the cold and the snow near an hour and a half, some of the rest began to lose their sensibility; and one Briscoe, another of Mr Banks's servants, was so ill, that it was thought he must die before he could be got to the fire.

At the fire, however, at length they arrived; and passed the night in a situation, which, however dreadful in itself, was rendered more afflicting by the remembrance of what was past, and the uncertainty of what was to come. Of twelve, the number that set out together in health and spirits, two were supposed to be already dead; a third was so ill, that it was very doubtful whether he would be able to go forward in the morning; and a fourth, Mr Buchan, was in danger of a return of his fits, by fresh fatigue, after so uncomfortable a night: They were distant from the ship a long day's journey, through pathless woods, in which it was too probable they might be bewildered till they were overtaken by the next night; and, not having prepared for a journey of more than eight or ten hours, they were wholly
destitute

destitute of provisions, except a vulture, which they happened to shoot while they were out, and which, if equally
divided, would not afford each of them half a meal; and
they knew not how much more they might suffer from the
cold, as the snow still continued to fall. A dreadful testimony of the severity of the climate, as it was now the
midst of summer in this part of the world, the 21st of December being here the longest day; and every thing might
justly be dreaded from a phænomenon which, in the corresponding season, is unknown even in Norway and Lap-
land.

When the morning dawned, they saw nothing round
them, as far as the eye could reach, but snow, which seemed
to lie as thick upon the trees as upon the ground; and the
blasts returned so frequently, and with such violence, that
they found it impossible for them to set out: How long
this might last they knew not, and they had but too much
reason to apprehend that it would confine them in that desolate forest till they perished with hunger and cold.

After having suffered the misery and terror of this situation till six o'clock in the morning, they conceived some
hope of deliverance by discovering the place of the sun
through the clouds, which were become thinner, and began to break away. Their first care was to see whether the
poor wretches whom they had been obliged to leave among
the bushes were yet alive; three of the company were dispatched for that purpose, and very soon afterwards returned with the melancholy news, that they were dead.

Notwithstanding the flattering appearance of the sky, the
snow still continued to fall so thick that they could not venture out on their journey to the ship; but about eight
o'clock a small regular breeze sprung up, which, with the
prevailing influence of the sun, at length cleared the air;
and they soon after, with great joy, saw the snow fall in
large flakes from the trees, a certain sign of an approaching thaw: They now examined more critically the state of
their invalids; Briscoe was still very ill, but said, that he
thought himself able to walk; and Mr Buchan was much
better than either he or his friends had any reason to expect. They were now, however, pressed by the calls of hunger, to which, after long fasting, every consideration of future good or evil immediately gives way. Before they set
forward, therefore, it was unanimously agreed that they

should

should eat their vulture ; the bird was accordingly skinned, and, it being thought best to divide it before it was fit to be eaten, it was cut into ten portions, and every man cooked his own as he thought fit. After this repast, which furnished each of them with about three mouthfuls, they prepared to set out; but it was ten o'clock before the snow was sufficiently gone off, to render a march practicable. After a walk of about three hours, they were very agreeably surprised to find themselves upon the beach, and much nearer to the ship than they had any reason to expect. Upon reviewing their track from the vessel, they perceived, that, instead of ascending the hill in a line, so as to penetrate into the country, they had made almost a circle round it. When they came on board, they congratulated each other upon their safety, with a joy that no man can feel who has not been exposed to equal danger ; and as I had suffered great anxiety at their not returning in the evening of the day on which they set out, I was not wholly without my share.

Section V.

The Passage through the Streight of Le Maire, and a further Description of the Inhabitants of Terra del Fuego and its Productions.

On the 18th and 19th, we were delayed in getting on board our wood and water by a swell: But on the 20th, the weather being more moderate, we again sent the boat on shore, and Mr Banks and Dr Solander went in it. They landed in the bottom of the bay, and while my people were employed in cutting brooms, they pursued their great object, the improvement of natural knowledge, with success, collecting many shells and plants which hitherto have been altogether unknown: They came on board to dinner, and afterwards went again on shore to visit an Indian town, which some of the people had reported to lie about two miles up the country. They found the distance not more than by the account, and they approached it by what appeared to be the common road, yet they were above an hour in getting thither, for they were frequently up to their knees in mud; when they got within a small distance, two of the people came out to meet them, with such state as they could as-

sume;

sume; when they joined them, they began to halloo as they had done on board the ship, without addressing themselves either to the strangers or their companions; and having continued this strange vociferation some time, they conducted them to the town. It was situated on a dry knoll, or small hill, covered with wood, none of which seemed to have been cleared away, and consisted of about twelve or fourteen hovels, of the most rude and inartificial structure that can be imagined. They were nothing more than a few poles set up so as to incline towards each other, and meet at the top, forming a kind of a cone, like some of our bee-hives: On the weather-side they were covered with a few boughs, and a little grass; and on the lee-side about one-eighth of the circle was left open, both for a door and a fire-place; and of this kind were the huts that had been seen in St Vincent's bay, in one of which the embers of a fire were still remaining. Furniture they had none; a little grass, which lay round the inside of the hovel, served both for chairs and beds; and of all the utensils which necessity and ingenuity have concurred to produce among other savage nations, they saw only a basket to carry in the hand, a satchel to hang at the back, and the bladder of some beast to hold water, which the natives drink through a hole that is made near the top for that purpose.

The inhabitants of this town were a small tribe, not more than fifty in number, of both sexes and of every age. Their colour resembles that of the rust of iron mixed with oil, and they have long black hair: The men are large, but clumsily built; their stature is from five feet eight to five feet ten; the women are much less, few of them being more than five feet high. Their whole apparel consists of the skin of a guanicoe, or seal, which is thrown over their shoulders, exactly in the state in which it came from the animal's back; a piece of the same skin, which is drawn over their feet, and gathered about the ancles like a purse, and a small flap, which is worn by the women as a succedaneum for a fig-leaf. The men wear their cloak open, the women tie it about their waist with a thong. But although they are content to be naked, they are very ambitious to be fine. Their faces were painted in various forms: The region of the eye was in general white, and the rest of the face adorned with horizontal streaks of red and black; yet scarcely any two were exactly alike. This decoration seems to be more pro-

fuse and elaborate upon particular occasions, for the two
gentlemen who introduced Mr Banks and the doctor into
the town, were almost covered with streaks of black in all
directions, so as to make a very striking appearance. Both
men and women wore bracelets of such beads as they could
make themselves of small shells or bones; the women both
upon their wrists and ancles, the men upon their wrists only; but to compensate for the want of bracelets on their
legs, they wore a kind of fillet of brown worsted round their
heads. They seemed to set a particular value upon any
thing that was red, and preferred beads even to a knife or
a hatchet.

Their language in general is guttural, and they express
some of their words by a sound exactly like that which we
make to clear the throat when any thing happens to ob-
struct it; yet they have words that would be deemed soft
in the better languages of Europe. Mr Banks learned what
he supposes to be their name for beads and water. When
they wanted beads, instead of ribbons or other trifles, they
said *halleca*; and when they were taken on shore from the
ship, and by signs asked where water might be found, they
made the sign of drinking, and pointing as well to the casks
as the watering-place, cried *Oodâ*.

We saw no appearance of their having any food but shell-
fish; for though seals were frequently seen near the shore,
they seemed to have no implements for taking them. The
shell-fish are collected by the women, whose business it seems
to be to attend at low water, with a basket in one hand, and
a stick, pointed and barbed, in the other, and a satchel at
their backs: They loosen the limpets, and other fish that
adhere to the rocks, with the stick, and put them into the
basket; which, when full, they empty into the satchel.

The only things that we found among them in which there
was the least appearance of neatness or ingenuity, were their
weapons, which consisted of a bow and arrows. The bow
was not inelegantly made, and the arrows were the neatest
that we had ever seen: They were of wood, polished to the
highest degree; and the point, which was of glass or flint,
and barbed, was formed and fitted with wonderful dexterity.
We saw also some pieces of glass and flint among them un-
wrought,-besides rings, buttons, cloth, and canvas, with
other European commodities; they must, therefore, sometimes travel to the northward, for it was many years since
                                                    any

any ship had been so far south as this part of Terra del Fuego. We observed also, that they shewed no surprise at our fire-arms, with the use of which they appeared to be well acquainted; for they made signs to Mr Banks to shoot a seal which followed the boat, as they were going on shore from the ship.

M. de Bougainville, who, in January 1768, just one year before us, had been on shore upon this coast in latitude 53° 40′ 41″, had, among other things, given glass to the people whom he found here; for he says, that a boy about twelve years old took it into his head to eat some of it, by which unhappy accident he died in great misery. These people might probably have some of the very glass which Bougainville left behind him, either from other natives, or perhaps from himself; for they appeared rather to be a travelling horde, than to have any fixed habitation. Their houses were built to stand but for a short time; they had no utensil or furniture but the basket and satchel, which have been mentioned before, and which had handles adapted to the carrying them about, in the hand and upon the back; the only clothing they had here was scarcely sufficient to prevent their perishing with cold in the summer of this country, much less in the extreme severity of winter; the shell-fish, which seemed to be their only food, would soon be exhausted at any one place; and we had seen houses upon what appeared to be a deserted station in St Vincent's bay.

It is also probable that the place where we found them was only a temporary residence, from their having here nothing like a boat or canoe, of which it can scarcely be supposed that they were wholly destitute, especially as they were not sea-sick, or particularly affected, either in our boat or on board the ship. We conjectured that there might be a streight or inlet, running from the sea through great part of this island, from the Streight of Magellan, whence these people might come, leaving their canoes where such inlet terminated.

They did not appear to have among them any government or subordination: None was more respected than another; yet they seemed to live together in the utmost harmony and good fellowship. Neither did we discover any appearance of religion among them, except the noises which have been mentioned, and which we supposed to be a superstitious ceremony, merely because we could refer them

to

1

to nothing else: They were used only by one of those who came on board the ship, and the two who conducted Mr Banks and Dr Solander to the town, whom we therefore conjectured to be priests.   Upon the whole, these people appeared to be the most destitute and forlorn, as well as the most stupid of all human beings; the outcasts of Nature, who spent their lives in wandering about the dreary wastes, where two of our people perished with cold in the midst of summer; with no dwelling but a wretched hovel of sticks and grass, which would not only admit the wind, but the snow and the rain: almost naked, and destitute of every convenience that is furnished by the rudest art, having no implement even to dress their food : Yet they were content. They seemed to have no wish for any thing more than they possessed, nor did any thing that we offered them appear acceptable but beads.

In this place we saw no quadruped except seals, sea-lions, and dogs; of the dogs it is remarkable that they bark, which those that are originally bred in America do not.   And this is a further proof, that the people we saw here had, either immediately or remotely, communicated with the inhabitants of Europe   There are, however, other quadrupeds in this part of the country; for when Mr Banks was at the top of the highest hill that he ascended in his expedition through the woods, he saw the footsteps of a large beast imprinted upon the surface of a bog, though he could not with any probability guess of what kind it might be.

Of land-birds there are but few; Mr Banks saw none larger than an English blackbird, except some hawks and a vulture; but of water-fowl there is great plenty, particularly ducks.   Of fish we saw scarce any, and with our hooks could catch none that was fit to eat; but shell-fish, limpets, clams, and mussels were to be found in abundance.

Among the insects, which were not numerous, there was neither gnat nor musquito, nor any other species that was either hurtful or troublesome, which perhaps is more than can be said of any other uncleared country.   During the snow-blasts which happened every day while we were here, they hide themselves; and the moment it is fair they appear again, as nimble and vigorous as the warmest weather could make them.

Of plants, Mr Banks and Dr Solander found a vast variety; the far greater part wholly different from any that have

been

been hitherto described.   Besides the birch and winter's bark, which have been mentioned already, there is the beech, *Fagus antarcticus*, which, as well as the birch, may be used for timber.   The plants cannot be enumerated here ; but as the scurvy-grass, *Cardamine antiscorbutica*, and the wild celery, *Apium antarcticum*, probably contain antiscorbutic qualities, which may be of great benefit to the crews of such ships as shall hereafter touch at this place, the following short description is inserted :

The scurvy-grass will be found in plenty in damp places, near springs of water, and in general in all places that lie near the beach, especially at the watering-place in the Bay of Good Success : When it is young, the state of its greatest perfection, it lies flat upon the ground, having many leaves of a bright green, standing in pairs opposite to each other, with a single one at the end, which generally makes the fifth upon a foot-stalk : The plant, passing from this state, shoots up in stalks that are sometimes two feet high, at the top of which are small white blossoms, and these are succeeded by long pods : The whole plant greatly resembles that which in England is called Lady's Smock, or Cuckow-flower.   The wild celery is very like the celery in our gardens, the flowers are white, and stand in the same manner, in small tufts at the top of the branches, but the leaves are of a deeper green.   It grows in great abundance near the beach, and generally upon the soil that lies next above the spring tides.   It may indeed easily be known by the taste, which is between that of celery and parsley.   We used the celery in large quantities, particularly in our soup, which, thus medicated, produced the same good effects which seamen generally derive from a vegetable diet, after having been long confined to salt provisions.

On Sunday the 22d of January, about two o'clock in the morning, having got our wood and water on board, we sailed out of the bay, and continued our course through the streight.

SECTION

SECTION VI.

*A general Description of the S. E. Part of Terra del Fuego,
and the Streight of Le Maire ; with some Remarks on Lord
Anson's Account of them, and Directions for the Passage
Westward, round this Part of America, into the South Seas.*

ALMOST all writers who have mentioned the island of
Terra del Fuego, describe it as destitute of wood, and covered with snow. In the winter it may possibly be covered with snow, and those who saw it at that season might
perhaps be easily deceived, by its appearance, into an opinion that it was destitute of wood. Lord Anson was there
in the beginning of March, which answers to our September ; and we were there the beginning of January, which
answers to our July, which may account for the difference
of his description of it from ours. We fell in with it about
twenty-one leagues to the westward of the streight of Le
Maire, and from the time that we first saw it, trees were
plainly to be distinguished with our glasses ; and as we came
nearer, though here and there we discovered patches of
snow, the sides of the hills and the sea-coast appeared to be
covered with a beautiful verdure. The hills are lofty, but
not mountainous, though the summits of them are quite naked. The soil in the valleys is rich, and of a considerable
depth ; and at the foot of almost every hill there is a brook,
the water of which has a reddish hue, like that which runs
through our turf bogs in England, but it is by no means ill
tasted, and upon the whole proved to be the best that we
took in during our voyage. We ranged the coast to the
streight, and had soundings all the way from 40 to 20 fathom, upon a gravelly and sandy bottom. The most remarkable land on Terra del Fuego is a hill, in the form of a
sugar-loaf, which stands on the west side not far from the
sea ; and the three hills, called the Three Brothers, about
nine miles to the westward of Cape St Diego, the low point
that forms the north entrance of the streight of Le Maire.

It is said in the account of Lord Anson's voyage, that it
is difficult to determine exactly where the streight lies,
though the appearance of Terra del Fuego be well known,
without knowing also the appearance of Staten Land ; and
that

that some navigators have been deceived by three hills on
Staten Land, which have been mistaken for the Three Brothers on Terra del Fuego, and so overshot the streight.
But no ship can possibly miss the streight that coasts Terra
del Fuego within sight of land, for it will then, of itself, be
sufficiently conspicuous ; and Staten Land, which forms the
east side, will be still more manifestly distinguished, for
there is no land on Terra del Fuego like it.   The streight
of Le Maire can be missed only by standing too far to the
eastward, without keeping the land of Terra del Fuego in
sight : If this is done, it may be missed, however accurately the appearance of the coast of Staten Land may have
been exhibited ; and if this is not done, it cannot be missed, though the appearance of that coast be not known.   The
entrance of the streight should not be attempted but with
a fair wind and moderate weather, and upon the very beginning of the tide of flood, which happens here, at the full
and change of the moon, about one or two o'clock ; it is also best to keep as near to the Terra del Fuego shore as the
winds will admit.   By attending to these particulars, a ship
may be got quite through the streight in one tide ; or, at
least, to the southward of Success Bay, into which it will
be more prudent to put, if the wind should be southerly,
than to attempt the weathering of Staten Land with a lee
wind and a current, which may endanger her being driven
on that island.

The streight itself, which is bounded on the west by Terra del Fuego, and on the east by the west end of Staten
Land, is about five leagues long, and as many broad. The
Bay of Good Success lies about the middle of it, on the
Terra del Fuego side, and is discovered immediately upon
entering the streight from the northward ; and the south
head of it may be distinguished by a mark on the land, that
has the appearance of a broad road, leading up from the
sea into the country : At the entrance it is half a league
wide, and runs in westward about two miles and a half.
There is good anchorage in every part of it, in from ten to
seven fathom, clear ground ; and it affords plenty of exceeding good wood and water.   The tides flow in the bay,
at the full and change of the moon, about four or five o'clock,
and rise about five or six feet perpendicular.   But the flood
runs two or three hours longer in the streight than in the
bay ;

bay; and the ebb, or northerly current, runs with near double the strength of the flood.

In the appearance of Staten Land, we did not discover the wildness and horror that is ascribed to it in the account of Lord Anson's voyage. On the north side are the appearances of bays or harbours; and the land when we saw it, was neither destitute of wood nor verdure, nor covered with snow. The island seems to be about twelve leagues in length and five broad.

On the west side of the Cape of Good Success, which forms the S.W. entrance of the streight, lies Valentine's Bay, of which we only saw the entrance; from this bay the land trends away to the W.S.W. for twenty or thirty leagues; it appears to be high and mountainous, and forms several bays and inlets.

At the distance of fourteen leagues from the Bay of Good Success, in the direction of S.W.½W. and between two and three leagues from the shore, lies New Island. It is about two leagues in length from N.E. to S.W. and terminates to the N.E. in a remarkable hillock. At the distance of seven leagues from New Island, in the direction of S.W. lies the isle *Evouts;* and a little to the west of the south of this island lie Barnevelt's two small flat islands, close to each other; they are partly surrounded with rocks, which rise to different heights above the water, and lie twenty-four leagues from the streight of Le Maire. At the distance of three leagues from Barnevelt's islands, in the direction of S.W. by S. lies the S.E. point of Hermit's islands: These islands lie S.E. and N.W. and are pretty high: From most points of view they will be taken for one island, or a part of the main.

From the S.E. point of Hermit's islands to Cape Horn the course is S.W. by S. distance three leagues.

In the chart I drew of this coast, from our first making land to the cape, which includes the Streight of Le Maire, and part of Staten Land, I have laid down no land, nor traced out any shore, but what I saw myself, and thus far it may be depended upon: The bays and inlets, of which we saw only the openings, are not traced; it can, however, scarcely be doubted but that most, if not all of them, afford anchorage, wood and water. The Dutch squadron, commanded by Hermit, certainly put into some of them in the year 1624: And it was Chapenham, the vice-admiral of this
squadron,

squadron, who first discovered that the land of Cape Horn consisted of a number of islands. The account, however, which those who sailed in Hermit's fleet have given of these parts, is extremely defective; and those of Schouton and Le Maire are still worse: It is therefore no wonder that the charts hitherto published should be erroneous, not only in laying down the land, but in the latitude and longitude of the places they contain. I will, however, venture to assert, that the longitude of few parts of the world is better ascertained than that of the Streight of Le Maire, and Cape Horn, in the chart now alluded to, as it was laid down by several observations of the sun and moon that were made both by myself and Mr Green.[1]

The variation of the compass on this coast I found to be from 23° to 25° E. except near Barnevelt's islands and Cape Horn, where we found it less, and unsettled: Probably it is disturbed here by the land, as Hermit's squadron, in this very place, found all their compasses differ from each other. The declination of the dipping-needle, when set upon shore in Success Bay, was 68° 15' below the horizon.

Between Streight Le Maire and Cape Horn we found a current setting, generally very strong, to the N.E. when we were in with the shore; but lost it when we were at the distance of fifteen or twenty leagues.

On the 26th of January, we took our departure from Cape Horn, which lies in latitude 55° 53' S. longitude 68° 13' W. The farthest southern latitude that we made was 60° 10', our longitude was then 74° 30' W.; and we found the variation of the compass, by the mean of eighteen azimuths, to be 27° 9' E. As the weather was frequently calm, Mr Banks went out in a small boat to shoot birds, among which were some albatrosses and sheer-waters. The albatrosses were observed to be larger than those which had been taken northward of the streight; one of them measured ten feet two inches from the tip of one wing to that of the other, when they were extended: The sheer-water, on the contrary,

---

[1] This chart is necessarily omitted. Krusenstern, speaking of the observations respecting the position of Cape St John, says, " There are few cities in Europe, the geographical longitude of which is determined with the same degree of accuracy as that of this barren rock, in one of the roughest and most inhospitable islands of the globe. But how infinitely important is this accuracy to the safety of shipping!" He verified Cook's determination of the longitude of this cape.—E.

contrary, is less, and darker coloured on the back. The albatrosses we skinned, and having soaked them in salt water till the morning, we parboiled them, then throwing away the liquor, stewed them in a very little fresh water till they were tender, and had them served up with savoury sauce; thus dressed, the dish was universally commended, and we eat of it very heartily even when there was fresh pork upon the table.

From a variety of observations which were made with great care, it appeared probable in the highest degree, that, from the time of our leaving the land to the 13th of February, when we were in latitude 49° 32, and longitude 90° 37', we had no current to the west.

At this time we had advanced about 12° to the westward, and 3 and ½ to the northward of the Streight of Magellan: Having been just three and thirty days in coming round the land of Terra del Fuego, or Cape Horn, from the east entrance of the streight to this situation. And though the doubling of Cape Horn is so much dreaded, that, in the general opinion, it is more eligible to pass through the Streight of Magellan, we were not once brought under our close reef ed top sails after we left the Streight of Le Maire. The Dolphin in her last voyage, which she performed at the same season of the year with ours, was three months in getting through the Streight of Magellan, exclusive of the time that she lay in Port Famine; and I am persuaded, from the winds we had, that if we had come by that passage, we should not at this time have been in these seas; that our people would have been fatigued, and our anchors, cables, sails, and rigging much damaged, neither of which inconveniences we had now suffered. But supposing it more eligible to go round the cape, than through the Streight of Magellan, it may still be questioned, whether it is better to go through the Streight of Le Maire, or stand to the eastward, and go round to Staten Land. The advice given in the account of Lord Anson's voyage is, " That all ships bound to the South Seas, instead of passing through the Streight of Le Maire, should constantly pass to the eastward of Staten Land, and should be invariably bent on running to the southward as far as the latitude of 61 or 62 degrees, before they endeavour to stand to the westward." But, in my opinion, different circumstances may at one time render it eligible to pass through the streight, and to keep

to

to the eastward of Staten Land at another. If the land is fallen in with to the westward of the streight, and the wind is favourable for going through, I think it would be very injudicious to lose time by going round Staten Land, as I am confident that, by attending to the directions which I have given, the streight may be passed with the utmost safety and convenience: But if, on the contrary, the land is fallen in with to the eastward of the streight, and the wind should prove tempestuous or unfavourable, I think it would be best to go round Staten Land. But I cannot in any case concur in recommending the running into the latitude of 61 or 62, before any endeavour is made to stand to the westward. We found neither the current nor the storms which the running so far to the southward is supposed necessary to avoid, and indeed, as the winds almost constantly blow from that quarter, it is scarcely possible to pursue the advice. The navigator has no choice but to stand to the southward, close upon a wind, and by keeping upon that tack, he will not only make southing, but westing; and, if the wind varies towards the north of the west, his westing will be considerable. It will indeed be highly proper to make sure of a westing sufficient to double all the lands, before an attempt is made to stand to the northward, and to this every man's own prudence will of necessity direct him.[2]

We now began to have strong gales and heavy seas, with irregular intervals of calm and fine weather.

SECTION

---

[2] Captain Krusenstern gave the preference to weathering the island: " Although," says he, " the wind was very favourable for us to have passed through Streight Le Maire, I thought it better to sail round Staten Land, the violent currents in the streight being often very dangerous to shipping, as the experience of many navigators has shewn; and the advantages, on the contrary, but very trifling, since, the only wind which will carry you through it, soon brings you back the short distance to the westward, which you lose by steering an easterly course round Cape John."—E.

Section VII.

The Sequel of the Passage from Cape Horn to the newly discovered Islands in the South Seas, with a Description of their Figure and Appearance; some Account of the Inhabitants, and several Incidents that happened during the Course, and at the Ship's Arrival among them.

On the 1st of March, we were in latitude 38° 44' S. and longitude 110° 33' W. both by observation and by the log. This agreement, after a run of 660 leagues, was thought to be very extraordinary; and is a demonstration, that after we left the land of Cape Horn we had no current that affected the ship. It renders it also highly probable, that we had been near no land of any considerable extent; for currents are always found when land is not remote, and sometimes, particularly on the east side of the continent in the North Sea, when land has been distant one hundred leagues.

Many birds, as usual, were constantly about the ship, so that Mr Banks killed no less than sixty-two in one day; and what is more remarkable, he caught two forest flies, both of them of the same species, but different from any that have hitherto been described; these probably belonged to the birds, and came with them from the land, which we judged to be at a great distance. Mr Banks also, about this time, found a large cuttle-fish, which had just been killed by the birds, floating in a mangled condition upon the water; it is very different from the cuttle-fishes that are found in the European seas; for its arms, instead of suckers, were furnished with a double row of very sharp talons, which resemble those of a cat, and, like them, were retractable into a sheath of skin, from which they might be thrust at pleasure. Of this cuttle-fish we made one of the best soups we had ever tasted

The albatrosses now began to leave us, and after the 8th there was not one to be seen. We continued our course without any memorable event till the 24th, when some of the people who were upon the watch in the night reported that they saw a log of wood pass by the ship; and that the sea, which was rather rough, became suddenly as smooth as a mill-pond. It was a general opinion, that there was land to windward; but I did not think myself at liberty to

search

search for what I was not sure to find; though I judged
we were not far from the islands that were discovered by
Quiros in 1606.   Our latitude was 22° 11′ S. and longitude
127° 55′ W.[1]

On the 25th, about noon, one of the marines, a young
fellow about twenty, was placed as sentry at the cabin-
door; while he was upon this duty, one of my servants was
at the same place preparing to cut a piece of seal-skin into
tobacco-pouches: He had promised one to several of the
men, but had refused one to this young fellow, though he
had asked him several times; upon which he jocularly
threatened to steal one, it it should be in his power.   It
happened that the servant, being called hastily away, gave
the skin in charge to the centinel, without regarding what
had passed between them.   The centinel immediately secured a piece of the skin, which the other missing at his return, grew angry; but, after some altercation, contented
himself with taking it away, declaring, that, for so trifling
an affair, he would not complain of him to the officers.
But it happened that one of his fellow-soldiers, overhear-
ing the dispute, came to the knowledge of what had happened, and told it to the rest; who, taking it into their heads
to stand up for the honour of their corps, reproached the
offender with great bitterness, and reviled him in the most
opprobrious terms; they exaggerated his offence into a
crime of the deepest dye; they said it was a theft by a centry when he was upon duty, and of a thing that had been
committed to his trust; they declared it a disgrace to associate with him; and the serjeant, in particular, said, that,
if the person from whom the skin had been stolen would
not complain, he would complain himself; for that his honour would suffer if the offender was not punished.   From
the scoffs and reproaches of these men of honour, the poor
young fellow retired to his hammock in an agony of confusion and shame.   The serjeant soon after went to him,
and ordered him to follow him to the deck.   He obeyed
without reply; but it being in the dusk of the evening, he
slipped from the serjeant and went forward.   He was seen
by some of the people, who thought he was gone to the
head; but a search being made for him afterwards, it was
found

---

[1] Arrowsmith has laid down Ducies Island very near to this position
See his map of America

found that he had thrown himself overboard ; and I was then first made acquainted with the theft and its circumstances. The loss of this man was the more regretted, as he was remarkably quiet and industrious.

On Tuesday the 4th of April, about ten o'clock in the morning, Mr Banks's servant, Peter Briscoe, discovered land, bearing south, at the distance of about three or four leagues. I immediately hauled up for it, and found it to be an island of an oval form, with a lagoon in the middle, which occupied much the larger part of it ; the border of land which circumscribes the lagoon is in many places very low and narrow, particularly on the south side, where it consists principally of a beach or reef of rocks : It has the same appearance also in three places on the north side ; so that the firm land being disjoined, the whole looks like many islands covered with wood. On the west end of the island is a large tree, or clump of trees, that in appearance resembles a tower ; and about the middle are two cocoa-nut trees, which rise above all the rest, and, as we came near to the island, appeared like a flag. We approached it on the north side, and though we came within a mile, we found no bottom with one hundred and thirty fathom of line, nor did there appear to be any anchorage about it. The whole is covered with trees of different verdure, but we could distinguish none, even with our glasses, except cocoa-nuts and palm-nuts. We saw several of the natives upon the shore, and counted four-and-twenty. They appeared to be tall, and to have heads remarkably large ; perhaps they had something wound round them, which we could not distinguish ; they were of a copper colour, and had long black hair. Eleven of them walked along the beach abreast of the ship, with poles or pikes in their hands, which reached twice as high as themselves. While they walked on the beach they seemed to be naked ; but soon after they retired, which they did as soon as the ship had passed the island, they covered themselves with something that made them appear of a light colour. Their habitations were under some clumps of palm-nut trees, which at a distance appeared like high ground ; and to us, who for a long time had seen nothing but water and sky, except the dreary hills of Terra del Fuego, these groves seemed a terrestrial paradise. To this spot, which lies in latitude 18 47"

S

S. and longitude 139° 28′ W. we gave the name of *Lagoon Island*. The variation of the needle here is 2° 54′ E.

About one o'clock we made sail to the westward, and about half an hour after three we saw land again to the N. W. We got up with it at sun-set; and it proved to be a low woody island, of a circular form, and not much above a mile in compass. We discovered no inhabitants, nor could we distinguish any cocoa-nut trees, though we were within half a mile of the shore. The land, however, was covered with verdure of many hues. It lies in latitude 18° 35′ S. and longitude 139° 48′ W. and is distant from Lagoon Island, in the direction of N. 62 W. about seven leagues. We called it *Thrumb-Cap*. I discovered, by the appearance of the shore, that at this place it was low water; and I had observed at Lagoon Island, that it was either high-water, or that the sea neither ebbed nor flowed. I infer, therefore, that a S. by E. or S. moon makes high water.

We went on with a fine trade-wind and pleasant weather; and on the 5th, about three in the afternoon, we discovered land to the westward. It proved to be a low island, of much greater extent than either of those that we had seen before, being about ten or twelve leagues in compass. Several of us remained at the mast-head the whole evening, admiring its extraordinary figure. It was shaped exactly like a bow; the arch and cord of which were land, and the space between them water; the cord was a flat beach, without any signs of vegetation, having nothing upon it but heaps of sea-weed, which lay in different ridges, as higher or lower tides had left them. It appeared to be about three or four leagues long, and not more than two hundred yards wide: but as a horizontal plane is always seen in perspective, and greatly foreshortened, it is certainly much wider than it appeared: The horns, or extremities of the bow, were two large tufts of cocoa-nut trees; and much the greater part of the arch was covered with trees of different height, figure, and hue; in some parts, however, it was naked and low like the cord. Some of us thought they discovered openings through the cord into the pool or lake, that was included between that and the bow; but whether there were or were not such openings is uncertain. We sailed abreast of the low beach or bow-string, within less than a league of the shore, till sun-set,

and we then judged ourselves to be about half-way between the two horns. Here we brought-to, and sounded,
but found no bottom with one hundred and thirty fathom;
and as it is dark almost instantly after sun set in these latitudes, we suddenly lost sight of the land; and making sail
again, before the line was well hauled in, we steered by the
sound of the breakers, which were distinctly heard till we
got clear of the coast.

We knew this island to be inhabited, by smoke which
we saw in different parts of it, and we gave it the name of
Bow Island. Mr Gore, my second lieutenant, said, after
we had sailed by the island, that he had seen several of the
natives, under the first clump of trees, from the deck; that
he had distinguished their houses, and seen several canoes
hauled up under the shade; but in this he was more fortunate than any other person on board. The east end of this
island, which, from its figure, we called the Bow, lies in latitude 18° 23′ S. and longitude 141° 12′ W. We observed
the variation of the compass to be 5° 38′ E.

On the next day, Thursday the 6th, about noon, we saw
land again to the westward, and came up with it about
three. It appeared to be two islands, or rather groups of
islands, extending from N.W. by N. to S.E. by S. about
nine leagues. Of these, the two largest were separated from
each other by a channel of about half-a-mile broad, and
were severally surrounded by smaller islands, to which they
were joined by reefs that lay under water.

These islands were long narrow strips of land, ranging
in all directions, some of them ten miles or upwards in
length, but none more than a quarter of a mile broad, and
upon all of them there were trees of various kinds, particularly the cocoa-nut. The south-eastermost of them lies
in the latitude of 18° 12′ S. and longitude 142° 42′ W. and
at the distance of twenty-five leagues in the direction of
W. ½ N. from the west end of Bow Island. We ranged
along the S.W. side of this island, and hauled into a bay
which lies to the N.W. of the southermost point of the
Group, where there was a smooth sea, and the appearance of
anchorage, without much surf on the shore. We sounded,
but we found no bottom with one hundred fathom, at the
distance of no more than three quarters of a mile from the
beach, and I did not think it prudent to go nearer.

While this was doing, several of the inhabitants assembled

bled upon the shore, and some came out in their canoes
as far as the reefs, but would not pass them : When we saw
this, we ranged, with an easy sail, along the shore ; but just
as we were passing the end of the island, six men, who had
for some time kept abreast of the ship, suddenly launched
two canoes with great quickness and dexterity, and three
of them getting into each, they put off, as we imagined,
with a design to come on board us ; the ship was therefore
brought-to, but they, like their fellows, stopped at the reef ;
we did not however immediately make sail, as we observed
two messengers dispatched to them from the other canoes,
which were of a much larger size : We perceived that
these messengers made great expedition, wading and swimming along the reef; at length they met, and the men on
board the canoes making no dispositions to pass the reef,
after having received the message, we judged that they had
resolved to come no farther. After waiting, therefore, some
little time longer, we stood off; but when we were got
about two or three miles from the shore, we perceived
some of the natives following us in a canoe with a sail; we
did not, however, think it worth while to wait for her, and
though she had passed the reef, she soon after gave over
the chace.

According to the best judgment that we could form of
the people, when we were nearest the shore, they were
about our size, and well-made. They were of a brown
complexion, and appeared to be naked ; their hair, which
was black, was confined by a fillet that went round the
head, and stuck out behind like a bush. The greater part
of them carried in their hands two weapons ; one of them
was a slender pole, from ten to fourteen feet long, on one
end of which was a small knob, not unlike the point of a
spear; the other was about four feet long, and shaped like
a paddle, and possibly might be so, for some of their canoes were very small: Those which we saw them launch
seemed not intended to carry more than the three men
that got into them. We saw others that had on board six
or seven men, and one of them hoisted a sail, which did
not seem to reach more than six feet above the gunwale of
the boat, and which, upon the falling of a slight shower,
was taken down and converted into an awning or tilt. The
canoe which followed us to sea hoisted a sail not unlike an
Eng'ish

English lug-sail, and almost as lofty as an English boat of the same size would have carried.

The people, who kept abreast of the ship on the beach, made many signals; but whether they were intended to frighten us away, or invite us on shore, it is not easy to determine. We returned them by waving our hats and shouting, and they replied by shouting again. We did not put their disposition to the test by attempting to land; because, as the island was inconsiderable, and as we wanted nothing that it could afford, we thought it imprudent as well as cruel to risk a contest, in which the natives must have suffered by our superiority, merely to gratify an idle curiosity; especially as we expected soon to fall in with the island where we had been directed to make our astronomical observation, the inhabitants of which would probably admit us without opposition, as they were already acquainted with our strength, and might also procure us a ready and peaceable reception among the neighbouring people, if we should desire it.

To these islands we gave the name of *The Groups.*

On the 7th, about half an hour after six in the morning, being just at day-break, we discovered another island to the northward, which we judged to be about four miles in circumference. The land lay very low, and there was a piece of water in the middle of it; there seemed to be some wood upon it, and it looked green and pleasant; but we saw neither cocoa-trees nor inhabitants: It abounded, however, with birds, and we therefore gave it the name of *Bird-Island.*

It lies in latitude 17° 48′ S. and longitude 148° 35′ W. at the distance of ten leagues, in the direction W. ¼ N. from the west end of the Groups. The variation here was 6° 32′ E.

On the 8th, about two o'clock in the afternoon, we saw land to the northward, and about sun-set came abreast of it, at about the distance of two leagues. It appeared to be a double range of low woody islands joined together by reefs, so as to form one island, in the form of an ellipsis or oval, with a lake in the middle of it. The small islands and reefs that circumscribe the lake have the appearance of a chain, and we therefore gave it the name of *Chain Island.* Its length seemed to be about five leagues, in the direction of N.W. and S.E. and its breadth about five miles. The

trees

trees upon it appeared to be large, and we saw smoke rising in different parts of it from among them, a certain sign that it was inhabited. The middle of it lies in latitude 17° 23' S. and longitude 145° 54' W. and is distant from Bird Island forty-five leagues, in the direction of W. by N. The variation here was, by several azimuths, found to be 4° 54' E.

On the 10th, having had a tempestuous night, with thunder and rain, the weather was hazy till about nine o'clock in the morning, when it cleared up, and we saw the island to which Captain Wallis, who first discovered it, gave the name of Osnaburgh Island, called by the natives *Maitea*, bearing N.W. by W. distant about five leagues. It is a high round island, not above a league in circuit; in some parts it is covered with trees, and in others a naked rock. In this direction it looked like a high-crowned hat; but when it bears north, the top of it has more the appearance of the roof of a house. We made its latitude to be 17° 48' S. its longitude 148° 10' W. and its distance from Chain Island 44 leagues, in the direction of W. by S.[2]

Section VIII.

The Arrival of the Endeavour at Otaheite, called by Captain Wallis, King George the Third's Island. Rules established for Traffic with the Natives, and an Account of several Incidents which happened in a Visit to Tootahah and Toubourai Tamaida, two Chiefs.[3]

ABOUT one o'clock, on Monday the 10th of April, some of the people who were looking out for the island to which we were bound, said they saw land ahead, in that part of the

---

[2] The islands mentioned in this section, with some others since discovered, constitute what has been called Dangerous Archipelago. This is the name which Bougainville gave to this cluster. E.

[3] It would have been easy to have contributed largely to the information respecting Otaheite, contained in this section and several of the succeeding ones; but, on the whole, it did not seem eligible to anticipate the events and incidents which fall to be elsewhere related. Notes are therefore very sparingly given, and only for specific purposes. Some modifications also, and some omissions of the text, have been made, in order to correspond with what has been already narrated, or what will be afterwards given in a better manner.—E.

the horizon where it was expected to appear; but it was so faint, that, whether there was land in sight or not, remained a matter of dispute till sun-set. The next morning, however, at six o'clock, we were convinced that those who said they had discovered land were not mistaken; it appeared to be very high and mountainous, extending from W. by S. ½ S. to W. by N. ½ N. and we knew it to be the same that Captain Wallis had called King George the Third's Island. We were delayed in our approach to it by light airs and calms, so that in the morning of the 12th we were but little nearer than we had been the night before; but about seven a breeze sprung up, and before eleven several canoes were seen making towards the ship. There were but few of them, however, that would come near; and the people in those that did, could not be persuaded to come on board. In every canoe there were young plantains, and branches of a tree which the Indians call *E'Midho;* these, as we afterwards learnt, were brought as tokens of peace and amity; and the people in one of the canoes handed them up the ship's side, making signals at the same time with great earnestness, which we did not immediately understand; at length we guessed that they wished these symbols should be placed in some conspicuous part of the ship; we, therefore, immediately stuck them among the rigging, at which they expressed the greatest satisfaction. We then purchased their cargoes, consisting of cocoa-nuts, and various kinds of fruit, which, after our long voyage, were very acceptable.

We stood on with an easy sail all night, with soundings from twenty-two fathom to twelve; and about seven o'clock in the morning we came to an anchor in thirteen fathom in Port-Royal Bay, called by the natives Matavai. We were immediately surrounded by the natives in their canoes, who gave us cocoa-nuts, fruit resembling apples, bread-fruit, and some small fishes, in exchange for beads and other trifles. They had with them a pig, which they would not part with for any thing but a hatchet, and therefore we refused to purchase it; because, if we gave them a hatchet for a pig now, we knew they would never afterwards sell one for less, and we could not afford to buy as many as it was probable we should want at that price. The bread-fruit grows on a tree that is about the size of a middling oak: Its leaves are frequently a foot and an half long, of an ob-

                                                                long

long shape, deeply sinuated like those of the fig-tree, which they resemble in consistence and colour, and in the exuding of a white milky juice upon being broken. The fruit is about the size and shape of a child's head, and the surface is reticulated not much unlike a truffle: It is covered with a thin skin, and has a core about as big as the handle of a small knife: The eatable part lies between the skin and the core; it is as white as snow, and somewhat of the consistence of new bread. It must be roasted before it is eaten, being first divided into three or four parts. Its taste is insipid, with a slight sweetness somewhat resembling that of the crumb of wheaten-bread mixed with a Jerusalem artichoke.[4]

Among others who came off to the ship was an elderly man, whose name, as we learnt afterwards, was *Owhaw*, and who was immediately known to Mr Gore, and several others who had been here with Captain Wallis; as I was informed that he had been very useful to them, I took him on board the ship with some others, and was particularly attentive to gratify him, as I hoped he might also be useful to us.

As our stay here was not likely to be very short, and as it was necessary that the merchandise which we had brought for

---

[4] "Among all the labours of life," says Mr Bryan Edwards, in his History of the West Indies, "if there is one pursuit more replete than any other with benevolence, more likely to add comforts to existing people, and even to augment their numbers by augmenting their means of subsistence, it is certainly that of spreading abroad the bounties of creation, by transplanting from one part of the globe to another such natural productions as are likely to prove beneficial to the interests of humanity. In this generous effort, Sir Joseph Banks has employed a considerable part of his time, attention, and fortune; and the success which, in many cases, has crowned his endeavours, will be felt in the enjoyments, and rewarded by the blessings of posterity." The reader will at once acknowledge the justice of this eulogium, when he is informed, that, to the beneficent president of the Royal Society, the inhabitants of the West Indies are most materially indebted for the introduction among them, of that invaluable production the bread-fruit tree here described. It was principally by his warm and unwearied exertions that this at last was accomplished in January 1793, by the arrival at St Vincent of his majesty's ship Providence, Captain Bligh, and the Assistant brig, Captain Portlocke, from the South Seas, having on board many hundreds of those trees, and a vast number of other plants, likely to augment the comforts and supply the wants of the colonies. How pleasing would be the records of discoveries, and how animating to every humane sentiment, if they presented us with no other pictures than of such like labours in the cause of our common nature!—E.

for traffic with the natives should not diminish in its value, which it would certainly have done, if every person had been left at liberty to give what he pleased for such things as he should purchase; at the same time that confusion and quarrels must necessarily have arisen from there being no standard at market; I drew up the following rules, and ordered that they should be punctually observed.

Rules to be observed by every person in or belonging to his Majesty's bark the Endeavour, for the better establishing a regular and uniform trade for provision, &c. with the inhabitants of King George's Island.

I. To endeavour, by every fair means, to cultivate a friendship with the natives; and to treat them with all imaginable humanity.

II. A proper person or persons will be appointed to trade with the natives for all manner of provisions, fruit, and other productions of the earth; and no officer or seaman, or other person belonging to the ship, excepting such as are so appointed, shall trade or offer to trade for any sort of provision, fruit, or other production of the earth, unless they have leave so to do.

III. Every person employed on shore, on any duty whatsoever, is strictly to attend to the same; and if by any neglect he loseth any of his arms, or working tools, or suffers them to be stolen, the full value thereof will be charged against his pay, according to the custom of the navy in such cases, and he shall receive such farther punishment as the nature of the offence may deserve.

IV. The same penalty will be inflicted on every person who is found to embezzle, trade, or offer to trade, with any part of the ship's stores of what nature soever.

V. No sort of iron, or any thing that is made of iron, or any sort of cloth, or other useful or necessary articles, are to be given in exchange for any thing but provision.

J. COOK.

As soon as the ship was properly secured, I went on shore with Mr Banks and Dr Solander, a party of men under arms, and our friend Owhaw. We were received from the boat by some hundreds of the inhabitants, whose looks at least gave us welcome, though they were struck with such awe,

awe, that the first who approached us crouched so low that he almost crept upon his hands and knees. It is remarkable, that he, like the people in the canoes, presented to us the same symbol of peace that is known to have been in use among the ancient and mighty nations of the northern hemisphere,—the green branch of a tree. We received it with looks and gestures of kindness and satisfaction; and observing that each of them held one in his hand, we immediately gathered every one a bough, and carried it in our hands in the same manner.

They marched with us about half a mile towards the place where the Dolphin had watered, conducted by Owhaw; they then made a full stop, and having laid the ground bare, by clearing away all the plants that grew upon it, the principal persons among them threw their green branches upon the naked spot, and made signs that we should do the same; we immediately showed our readiness to comply, and to give a greater solemnity to the rite, the marines were drawn up, and marching in order, each dropped his bough upon those of the Indians, and we followed their example. We then proceeded, and when we came to the watering-place it was intimated to us by signs, that we might occupy that ground, but it happened not to be fit for our purpose. During our walk they had shaken off their first timid sense of our superiority, and were become familiar: they went with us from the watering-place and took a circuit through the woods; as we went along, we distributed beads and other small presents among them, and had the satisfaction to see that they were much gratified. Our circuit was not less than four or five miles, through groves of trees, which were loaded with cocoa-nuts and bread-fruit, and afforded the most grateful shade. Under these trees were the habitations of the people, most of them being only a roof without walls, and the whole scene realized the poetical fables of Arcadia. We remarked, however, not without some regret, that in all our walk we had seen only two hogs, and not a single fowl. Those of our company who had been here with the Dolphin told us, that none of the people whom we had yet seen were of the first class; they suspected that the chiefs had removed, and upon carrying us to the place where what they called the Queen's Palace had stood, we found that no traces of it were left. We determined therefore to return in the morning,

morning, and endeavour to find out the *Noblesse* in their retreats.

In the morning, however, before we could leave the ship, several canoes came about us, most of them from the westward, and two of them were filled with people, who by their dress and deportment appeared to be of a superior rank : two of these came on board, and each singled out his friend ; one of them, whose name we found to be *Matahah,* fixed upon Mr Banks, and the other upon me : this ceremony consisted in taking off great part of their clothes and putting them upon us. In return for this, we presented each of them with a hatchet and some beads. Soon after they made signs for us to go with them to the places where they lived, pointing to the S.W.; and as I was desirous of finding a more commodious harbour, and making farther trial of the disposition of the people, I consented.

I ordered out two boats, and with Mr Banks and Dr Solander, the other gentlemen, and our two Indian friends, we embarked for our expedition. After rowing about a league, they made signs that we should go on shore, and gave us to understand that this was the place of their residence. We accordingly landed, among several hundreds of the natives, who conducted us into a house of much greater length than any we had seen. When we entered, we saw a middle-aged man, whose name was afterwards discovered to be *Tootahah;* mats were immediately spread, and we were desired to sit down over against him. Soon after we were seated, he ordered a cock and hen to be brought out, which he presented to Mr Banks and me; we accepted the present, and in a short time each of us received a piece of cloth, perfumed after their manner, by no means disagreeably, which they took great pains to make us remark. The piece presented to Mr Banks was eleven yards long and two wide; in return for which, he gave a laced silk neckcloth, which he happened to have on, and a linen pocket handkerchief: Tootahah immediately dressed himself in this new finery, with an air of perfect complacency and satisfaction. But it is now time that I should take some notice of the ladies.

Soon after the interchanging of our presents with Tootahah, they attended us to several large houses, in which we walked about with great freedom: they shewed us all the civility of which, in our situation, we could accept;

                                                              and,

and, on their part, seemed to have no scruple that would have prevented its being carried farther. The houses, which as I have observed before, are all open, except a roof, afforded no place of retirement; but the ladies, by frequently pointing to the mats upon the ground, and sometimes seating themselves and drawing us down upon them, left us no room to doubt of their being much less jealous of observation than we were.

We now took leave of our friendly chief, and directed our course along the shore; when we had walked about a mile, we met, at the head of a great number of people, another chief, whose name was *Toubourai Tamaide*, with whom we were also to ratify a treaty of peace, with the ceremony of which we were now become better acquainted. Having received the branch which he presented to us, and given another in return, we laid our hands upon our left breasts, and pronounced the word *Taio*, which we supposed to signify friend; the chief then gave us to understand, that if we chose to eat, he had victuals ready for us. We accepted his offer, and dined very heartily upon fish, bread-fruit, cocoa-nuts and plantains, dressed after their manner; they eat some of their fish raw, and raw fish was offered to us, but we declined that part of the entertainment.

During this visit a wife of our noble host, whose name was *Tomio*, did Mr Banks the honour to place herself upon the same matt, close by him. Tomio was not in the first bloom of her youth, nor did she appear to have been ever remarkable for her beauty: he did not therefore, I believe, pay her the most flattering attention: it happened too, as a farther mortification to this lady, that seeing a very pretty girl among the crowd, he, not adverting to the dignity of his companion, beckoned her to come to him: the girl, after some entreaty, complied, and sat down on the other side of him; he loaded her with beads, and every showy trifle that would please her: his princess, though she was somewhat mortified at the preference that was given to her rival, did not discontinue her civilities, but still assiduously supplied him with the milk of the cocoa-nut, and such other dainties as were in her reach. This scene might possibly have become more curious and interesting, if it had not been suddenly interrupted by an interlude of a more serious kind. Just at this time, Dr Solander and Mr Monkhouse complained that their pockets had been picked. Dr Solander

lander had lost an opera glass in a shagreen case, and Mr Monkhouse his snuff box. This incident unfortunately put an end to the good-humour of the company. Complaint of the injury was made to the chief; and, to give it weight, Mr Banks started up, and hastily struck the butt end of his firelock upon the ground: this action, and the noise that accompanied it, struck the whole assembly with a panic, and every one of the natives ran out of the house with the utmost precipitation, except the chief, three women, and two or three others, who appeared by their dress to be of a superior rank.

The chief, with a mixture of confusion and concern, took Mr Banks by the hand, and led him to a large quantity of cloth, which lay at the other end of the house: this he offered to him piece by piece, intimating by signs, that if that would atone for the wrong which had been done, he might take any part of it, or, if he pleased, the whole. Mr Banks put it by, and gave him to understand that he wanted nothing but what had been dishonestly taken away. Toubourai Tamaide then went hastily out, leaving Mr Banks with his wife Tomio, who during the whole scene of terror and confusion had kept constantly at his side, and intimating his desire that he should wait there till his return. Mr Banks accordingly sat down, and conversed with her, as well as he could by signs, about half an hour. The chief then came back with the snuff-box and the case of the opera glass in his hand, and, with a joy in his countenance that was painted with a strength of expression which distinguishes these people from all others, delivered them to the owners. The case of the opera glass, however, upon being opened, was found to be empty; upon this discovery, his countenance changed in a moment; and catching Mr Banks again by the hand, he rushed out of the house, without uttering any sound, and led him along the shore, walking with great rapidity: when they had got about a mile from the house, a woman met him and gave him a piece of cloth, which he hastily took from her, and continued to press forward with it in his hand. Dr Solander and Mr Monkhouse had followed them, and they came at length to a house where they were received by a woman, to whom he gave the cloth, and intimated to the gentlemen that they should give her some beads. They immediately complied; and the beads and cloth being deposited upon the

floor,

floor, the woman went out, and in about half an hour returned with the opera-glass, expressing the same joy upon the occasion that had before been expressed by the chief. The beads were now returned, with an inflexible resolution not to accept them; and the cloth was, with the same pertinacity, forced upon Dr Solander, as a recompence for the injury that had been done him. He could not avoid accepting the cloth, but insisted in his turn upon giving a new present of beads to the woman. It will not perhaps be easy to account for all the steps that were taken in the recovery of this glass and snuff-box; but this cannot be thought strange, considering that the scene of action was among a people whose language, policy, and connections are even now but imperfectly known; upon the whole, however, they show an intelligence and influence which would do honour to any system of government, however regular and improved. In the evening, about six o'clock, we returned to the ship.

Section IX.

A place fixed upon for an Observatory and Fort: an Excursion into the Woods, and its Consequences. The Fort erected. a Visit from several Chiefs on board and at the Fort, with some Account of the Music of the Natives, and the Manner in which they dispose of their Dead.

On the next morning, Saturday the 15th, several of the chiefs whom we had seen the day before came on board, and brought with them, hogs, bread-fruit, and other refreshments, for which we gave them hatchets and linen, and such things as seemed to be most acceptable.

As in my excursion to the westward, I had not found any more convenient harbour than that in which we lay, I determined to go on shore and fix upon some spot, commanded by the ship's guns, where I might throw up a small fort for our defence, and prepare for making our astronomical observation.

I therefore took a party of men, and landed without delay, accompanied by Mr Banks, Dr Solander, and the astronomer, Mr Green. We soon fixed upon a part of the sandy beach, on the N.E. point of the bay, which was in every respect convenient for our purpose, and not near any habitation of the natives. Having marked out the ground that we intended to occupy, a small tent belonging to Mr Banks was set up, which had been brought on shore for that purpose: by this time a great number of the people had gathered about us; but, as it appeared, only to look on, there not being a single weapon of any kind among them. I intimated, however, that none of them were to come within the line I had drawn, except one who appeared to be a chief, and Owhaw. To these two persons I addressed myself by signs, and endeavoured to make them understand, that we wanted the ground which we had marked out to sleep upon for a certain number of nights, and that then we should go away. Whether I was understood I cannot certainly determine; but the people behaved with a deference and respect that at once pleased and surprised us; they sat down peaceably without the circle, and looked on, without giving us any interruption, till we had done, which was upwards of two hours. As we had seen no poultry, and but two hogs, in our walk when we were last on shore at this place, we suspected that, upon our arrival, they had been driven farther up the country; and the rather, as Owhaw was very importunate with us, by signs, not to go into the woods, which, however, and partly for these reasons, we were determined to do. Having therefore appointed the thirteen marines and a petty officer to guard the tent, we set out, and a great number of the natives joined our party. As we were crossing a little river that lay in our way we saw some ducks, and Mr Banks, as soon as he had got over, fired at them, and happened to kill three at one shot: this struck them with the utmost terror, so that most of them fell suddenly to the ground, as if they also had been shot at the same discharge: it was not long, however, before they recovered from their fright, and we continued our route; but we had not gone far before we were alarmed by the report of two pieces, which were fired by the guard at the tent. We had then straggled a little distance from each other, but Owhaw immediately called us together, and by waving his hand, sent away every Indian who followed us except three, each of whom, as a pledge of peace on their part, and an entreaty that there might be peace on ours, hastily broke a branch from the trees, and came to us with it in their hands. As we had too much reason to fear that some

mischief

mischief had happened, we hasted back to the tent, which was not distant above half a mile, and when we came up, we found it entirely deserted, except by our own people.

It appeared, that one of the Indians who remained about the tent after we left it, had watched his opportunity, and, taking the centry unawares, had snatched away his musquet. Upon this, the petty officer, a midshipman, who commanded the party, perhaps from a sudden fear of farther violence, perhaps from the natural petulance of power newly acquired, and perhaps from a brutality in his nature, ordered the marines to fire: the men, with as little consideration or humanity as the officer, immediately discharged their pieces among the thickest of the flying crowd, consisting of more than a hundred; and observing that the thief did not fall, pursued him, and shot him dead. We afterwards learnt, that none of the others were either killed or wounded.

Owhaw, who had never left us, observing that we were now totally deserted, got together a few of those who had fled, though not without some difficulty, and ranged them about us; we endeavoured to justify our people as well as we could, and to convince the Indians that if they did no wrong to us, we should do no wrong to them: they went away without any appearance of distrust or resentment; and having struck our tent, we returned to the ship, but by no means satisfied with the transactions of the day.

Upon questioning our people more particularly, whose conduct they soon perceived we could not approve, they alleged that the centinel whose musket was taken away, was violently assaulted and thrown down, and that a push was afterwards made at him by the man who took the musket, before any command was given to fire. It was also suggested, that Owhaw had suspicions, at least, if not certain knowledge, that something would be attempted against our people at the tent, which made him so very earnest in his endeavours to prevent our leaving it; others imputed his importunity to his desire that we should confine ourselves to the beach: and it was remarked that neither Owhaw, nor the chiefs who remained with us after he had sent the rest of the people away, would have inferred the breach of peace from the firing at the tent, if they had had no reason to suspect that some injury had been offered by their countrymen; especially
cially

cially as Mr Banks had just fired at the ducks: And yet that they did infer a breach of peace from that incident, was manifest from their waving their hands for the people to disperse, and instantly pulling green branches from the trees. But what were the real circumstances of this unhappy affair, and whether either, and which of these conjectures were true, could never certainly be known.

The next morning but few of the natives were seen upon the beach, and not one of them came off to the ship. This convinced us that our endeavours to quiet their apprehensions had not been effectual; and we remarked with particular regret, that we were deserted even by Owhaw, who had hitherto been so constant in his attachment, and so active in renewing the peace that had been broken.

Appearances being thus unfavourable, I warped the ship nearer to the shore, and moored her in such a manner as to command all the N. E. part of the bay, particularly the place which I had marked out for the building a fort. In the evening, however, I went on shore with only a boat's crew, and some of the gentlemen: The natives gathered about us, but not in the same number as before; there were I believe between thirty and forty, and they trafficked with us for cocoa-nuts and other fruit, to all appearance as friendly as ever.

On the 17th, early in the morning, we had the misfortune to lose Mr Buchan, the person whom Mr Banks had brought out as a painter of landscapes and figures. He was a sober, diligent, and ingenious young man, and greatly regretted by Mr Banks; who hoped, by his means, to have gratified his friends in England with representations of this country and its inhabitants, which no other person on board could delineate with the same accuracy and elegance. He had always been subject to epileptic fits, one of which seized him on the mountains of Terra del Fuego, and this disorder being aggravated by a bilious complaint which he contracted on board the ship, at length put an end to his life. It was at first proposed to bury him on shore, but Mr Banks thinking that it might perhaps give offence to the natives, with whose customs we were then wholly unacquainted, we committed his body to the sea, with as much decency and solemnity as our circumstances and situation would admit.

In the forenoon of this day we received a visit from Tu-
boumai

bourai Tamaide, and Tootahah, our chiefs, from the west:
They brought with them, as emblems of peace, not branches
of plantain, but two young trees, and would not venture
on board till these had been received, having probably been
alarmed by the mischief which had been done at the tent.
Each of them also brought, as propitiatory gifts, some
bread-fruit, and a hog ready dressed: This was a most acceptable present, as we perceived that hogs were not always
to be got; and in return we gave to each of our noble be-
nefactors a hatchet and a nail. In the evening we went on
shore and set up a tent, in which Mr Green and myself
spent the night, in order to observe an eclipse of the first
satellite of Jupiter; but the weather becoming cloudy, we
were disappointed.

On the 18th, at day-break, I went on shore, with as many
people as could possibly be spared from the ship, and began to erect our fort. While some were employed in throwing up intrenchments, others were busy in cutting pickets
and fascines, which the natives, who soon gathered round
us as they had been used to do, were so far from hindering,
that many of them voluntarily assisted us, bringing the
pickets and fascines from the wood where they had been
cut, with great alacrity: We had indeed been so scrupulous of invading their property, that we purchased every
stake which was used upon this occasion, and cut down no
tree till we had first obtained their consent. The soil where
we constructed our fort was sandy, and this made it necessary to strengthen the entrenchments with wood; three
sides were to be fortified in this manner; the fourth was
bounded by a river, upon the banks of which I proposed to
place a proper number of water-casks. This day we served
pork to the ship's company for the first time, and the Indians brought down so much bread-fruit and cocoa-nuts,
that we found it necessary to send away part of them un-
bought, and to acquaint them, by signs, that we should
want no more for two days to come. Every thing was purchased this day with beads: A single bead, as big as a pea,
being the purchase of five or six cocoa-nuts, and as many
of the bread-fruit. Mr Banks's tent was got up before night
within the works, and he slept on shore for the first time.
Proper centries were placed round it, but no Indian attempted to approach it the whole night.

The next morning, our friend Tubourai Tamaide made Mr Banks a visit, at the tent, and brought with him not only his wife and family, but the roof of a house, and several materials for setting it up, with furniture and implements of various kinds, intending, as we understood him, to take up his residence in our neighbourhood : This instance of his confidence and good-will gave us great pleasure, and we determined to strengthen his attachment to us by every means in our power. Soon after his arrival he took Mr Banks by the hand, and leading him out of the line, signified that he should accompany him into the woods. Mr Banks readily consented, and having walked with him about a quarter of a mile, they arrived at a kind of awning which he had already set up, and which seemed to be his occasional habitation. Here he unfolded a bundle of his country cloth, and taking out two garments, one of red cloth, and the other of very neat matting, he clothed Mr Banks in them, and without any other ceremony immediately conducted him back to the tent. His attendants soon after brought him some pork and bread-fruit, which he eat, dipping his meat into salt water instead of sauce: After his meal he retired to Mr Banks's bed, and slept about an hour. In the afternoon, his wife Tomio brought to the tent a young man about two-and-twenty years of age, of a very comely appearance, whom they both seemed to acknowledge as their son, though we afterwards discovered that he was not so. In the evening, this young man and another chief, who had also paid us a visit, went away to the westward, but Tubourai Tamaide and his wife returned to the awning in the skirts of the wood.

Our surgeon, Mr Monkhouse, having walked out this evening, reported that he had seen the body of the man who had been shot at the tents, which he said was wrapped in cloth, and placed on a kind of bier, supported by stakes, under a roof that seemed to have been set up for the purpose: That near it were deposited some instruments of war, and other things, which he would particularly have examined but for the stench of the body, which was intolerable. He said, that he saw also two more sheds of the same kind, in one of which were the bones of a human body that had lain till they were quite dry. We discovered afterwards, that this was the way in which they usually disposed of their dead.

A kind

A kind of market now began to be kept just without the lines, and was plentifully supplied with every thing but pork. Tubourai Tamaide was our constant guest, imitating our manners, even to the using of a knife and fork, which he did very handily.

As my curiosity was excited by Mr Monkhouse's account of the situation of the man who had been shot, I took an opportunity to go with some others to see it. I found the shed under which his body lay, close by the house in which he resided when he was alive, some others being not more than ten yards distant; it was about fifteen feet long, and eleven broad, and of a proportionable height: One end was wholly open, and the other end, and the two sides, were partly inclosed with a kind of wicker work. The bier on which the corpse was deposited, was a frame of wood like that in which the sea-beds, called cotts, are placed, with a matted bottom, and supported by four posts, at the height of about five feet from the ground. The body was covered first with a matt, and then with white cloth; by the side of it lay a wooden mace, one of their weapons of war, and near the head of it, which lay next to the close end of the shed, lay two cocoa-nut shells, such as are sometimes used to carry water in; at the other end a bunch of green leaves, with some dried twigs, all tied together, were stuck in the ground, by which lay a stone about as big as a cocoa-nut: Near these lay one of the young plantain trees, which are used for emblems of peace, and close by it a stone axe. At the open end of the shed also hung, in several strings, a great number of palm-nuts, and without the shed, was stuck upright in the ground, the stem of a plantain tree about five feet high, upon the top of which was placed a cocoa-nut shell full of fresh water: Against the side of one of the posts hung a small bag, containing a few pieces of bread-fruit ready roasted, which were not all put in at the same time, for some of them were fresh, and others stale. I took notice that several of the natives observed us with a mixture of solicitude and jealousy in their countenances, and by their gestures, expressed uneasiness when we went near the body, standing themselves at a little distance while we were making our examination, and appearing to be pleased when we came away.

Our residence on shore would by no means have been disagreeable if we had not been incessantly tormented by

the

the flies, which, among other mischief, made it almost impossible for Mr Parkinson, Mr Banks's natural history painter, to work; for they not only covered his subject so as that no part of its surface could be seen, but even eat the colour off the paper as fast as he could lay it on.' We had recourse to musquito-nets and fly-traps, which, though they made the inconvenience tolerable, were very far from removing it.

On the 22d, Tootahah gave us a specimen of the music of this country; four persons performed upon flutes, which had only two stops, and therefore could not sound more than four notes, by half tones: They were sounded like our German flutes, except that the performer, instead of applying it to his mouth, blew into it with one nostril, while he stopped the other with his thumb: To these instruments four other persons sung, and kept very good time; but only one tune was played during the whole concert.

Several of the natives brought us axes, which they had received from on board the Dolphin, to grind and repair; but among others there was one which became the subject of much speculation, as it appeared to be French: After much enquiry, we learnt that a ship had been here between our arrival and the departure of the Dolphin, which we then conjectured to have been a Spaniard, but afterwards knew to have been the Boudeuse, commanded by M. Bougainville.

SECTION X.

An Excursion to the Eastward, an Account of several Incidents that happened both on board and on shore, and of the first Interview with Oberea, the Person who, when the Dolphin was here, was supposed to be Queen of the Island, with a Description of the Fort.

On the 24th, Mr Banks and Dr Solander examined the country for several miles along the shore to the eastward:
For

' Mr Sydney Parkinson, the person here mentioned, published a journal of this voyage at London, 1775, in 4to. Another edition of it, with the remarks of John Fothergill, appeared in 1784; and a French translation of it, with additional matter, was printed at Paris in 1767. " Il est recom-

For about two miles it was flat and fertile; after that the hills stretched quite to the water's edge, and a little farther ran out into the sea, so that they were obliged to climb over them. These hills, which were barren, continued for about three miles more, and then terminated in a large plain, which was full of good houses, and people who appeared to live in great affluence. In this place there was a river, much more considerable than that at our fort, which issued from a deep and beautiful valley, and, where our travellers crossed it, though at some distance from the sea, was near one hundred yards wide. About a mile beyond this river the country became again barren, the rocks every where projecting into the sea, for which reason they resolved to return. Just as they had formed this resolution, one of the natives offered them refreshment, which they accepted. They found this man to be of a kind that has been described by various authors, as mixed with many nations, but distinct from them all. His skin was of a dead white, without the least appearance of what is called complexion, though some parts of his body were in a small degree less white than others: His hair, eye-brows, and beard, were as white as his skin; his eyes appeared as if they were bloodshot, and he seemed to be very short-sighted.[2]

At

mandable surtout, (says the Bibl. Univ. des voyages) par des details sur l'histoire naturelle, et par des vocabulaires plus etendus que ceux qui se trouvent dans le Premier Voyage de Cook." How far it is entitled to this, or to any praise, the editor is unable to say, having never been favoured with a sight of it.—E.

[2] Several authors have collected facts, and reasoned on the subject of that remarkable race of beings, denominated, from their colour, Albinos. Mention is made of some of them in the article Complexion, in the Edinburgh Encyclopædia, to which the reader is referred. After all, however, it remains very doubtful whether the peculiarity of the beings in question is to be attributed to disease, or to some distinct constitution of animal economy, which may be considered as sufficient to characterize a species of our nature. The writer of this note inclines to the former opinion This place, however, is improper for the discussion of arguments for or against that opinion. It may be more satisfactory to the general reader to be informed, that individuals answering the usual description of the Albinos, have been found in all the quarters of the earth, and that some families are so peculiarly constituted as to produce them very frequently, so that the affection is, properly speaking, hereditary in them. Few persons any way curiously disposed have not had it in their power to see specimens of Albinos, as exhibited for emolument in travelling shows. But, notwithstanding, such opportunities have not been much improved by philosophical minds, so that the history of Albinos is still involved in considerable mystery.—E.

At their return they were met by Tubourai Tamaide, and his women, who, at seeing them, felt a joy which not being able to express, they burst into tears, and wept some time before their passion could be restrained.

This evening Dr Solander lent his knife to one of these women, who neglected to return it, and the next morning Mr Banks's also was missing; upon this occasion I must bear my testimony, that the people of this country, of all ranks, men and women, are the arrantest thieves upon the face of the earth: The very day after we arrived here, when they came on board us, the chiefs were employed in stealing what they could in the cabin, and their dependants were no less industrious in other parts of the ship; they snatched up every thing that it was possible for them to secrete, till they got on shore, even to the glass ports, two of which they carried off undetected. Tubourai Tamaide was the only one except Tootahah who had not been found guilty, and the presumption, arising from this circumstance, that he was exempt from a vice, of which the whole nation besides were guilty, could not be supposed to outweigh strong appearances to the contrary. Mr Banks therefore, though not without some reluctance, accused him of having stolen his knife: He solemnly and steadily denied that he knew any thing of it; upon which Mr Banks made him understand, that whoever had taken it, he was determined to have it returned: Upon this resolute declaration, one of the natives who was present produced a rag in which three knives were very carefully tied up. One was that which Dr Solander had lent to the woman, another was a table knife belonging to me, and the owner of the third was not known. With these the chief immediately set out in order to make restitution of them to their owners at the tents. Mr Banks remained with the women, who expressed great apprehensions that some mischief was designed against their lord. When he came to the tents he restored one of the knives to Dr Solander and another to me, the third not being owned, and then began to search for Mr Banks's in all the places where he had ever seen it. After some time, one of Mr Banks's servants, understanding what he was about, immediately fetched his master's knife, which it seems he had laid by the day before, and till now knew nothing of its having been missed. Tubourai Tamaide, upon this demonstration of his innocence, expressed the strongest emotions

of

of mind, both in his looks and gestures; the tears started from his eyes, and he made signs with the knife, that, if he was ever guilty of such an action as had been imputed to him, he would submit to have his throat cut. He then rushed out of the lines, and returned hastily to Mr Banks, with a countenance that severely reproached him with his suspicions. Mr Banks soon understood that the knife had been received from his servant, and was scarcely less affected at what had happened than the chief; he felt himself to be the guilty person, and was very desirous to atone for his fault. The poor Indian, however violent his passions, was a stranger to sullen resentment; and upon Mr Banks's spending a little time familiarly with him, and making him a few trifling presents, he forgot the wrong that had been done him, and was perfectly reconciled.

Upon this occasion it may be observed, that these people have a knowledge of right and wrong from the mere dictates of natural conscience; and involuntarily condemn themselves when they do that to others, which they would condemn others for doing to them. That Tubourai Tamaide felt the force of moral obligation is certain; for the imputation of an action which he considered as indifferent, would not, when it appeared to be groundless, have moved him with such excess of passion. We must indeed estimate the virtue of these people, by the conformity of their conduct to what in their opinion is right; but we must not hastily conclude that theft is a testimony of the same depravity in them that it is in us, in the instances in which our people were sufferers by their dishonesty; for their temptation was such, as to surmount would be considered as a proof of uncommon integrity among those who have more knowledge, better principles, and stronger motives to resist the temptations of illicit advantage: An Indian among penny knives, and beads, or even nails and broken glass, is in the same state of trial with the meanest servant in Europe among unlocked coffers of jewels and gold.

On the 26th, I mounted six swivel guns upon the fort, which I was sorry to see struck the natives with dread: Some fishermen who lived upon the point removed farther off, and Owhaw told us, by signs, that in four days we should fire great guns.

On the 27th, Tubourai Tamaide, with a friend, who eat with a voracity that I never saw before, and the three wo-

men

men that usually attended him, whose names were TERAPO, TIRAO, and OMIE, dined at the fort: In the evening they took their leave, and set out for the house which Tubourai Tamaide had set up in the skirts of the wood; but in less than a quarter of an hour, he returned in great emotion, and hastily seizing Mr Banks's arm, made signs that he should follow him. Mr Banks immediately complied, and they soon came up to a place where they found the ship's butcher, with a reaping-hook in his hand: Here the chief stopped, and, in a transport of rage which rendered his signs searcely intelligible, intimated that the butcher had threatened, or attempted, to cut his wife's throat with the reaping-hook. Mr Banks then signified to him, that if he could fully explain the offence, the man should be punished. Upon this he became more calm, and made Mr Banks understand that the offender, having taken a fancy to a stone hatchet which lay in his house, had offered to purchase it of his wife for a nail: That she having refused to part with it upon any terms, he had catched it up, and throwing down the nail, threatened to cut her throat if she made any resistance: To prove this charge the hatchet and the nail were produced, and the butcher had so little to say in his defence that there was not the least reason to doubt of its truth.

Mr Banks having reported this matter to me, I took an opportunity, when the chief and his women, with other Indians, were on board the ship, to call up the butcher, and after a recapitulation of the charge and the proof, I gave orders that he should be punished, as well to prevent other offences of the same kind, as to acquit Mr Banks of his promise; the Indians saw him stripped and tied up to the rigging with a fixed attention, waiting in silent suspense for the event; but as soon as the first stroke was given, they interfered with great agitation, earnestly entreating that the rest of the punishment might be remitted: To this, however, for many reasons, I could not consent, and when they found that they could not prevail by their intercession, they gave vent to their pity by tears.

Their tears, indeed, like those of children, were always ready to express any passion that was strongly excited, and, like those of children, they also appeared to be forgotten as soon as shed; of which the following, among many others, is a remarkable instance. Very early in the morning of the 28th,

28th, even before it was day, a great number of them came
down to the fort, and Terapo being observed among the
women on the outside of the gate, Mr Banks went out and
brought her in; he saw that the tears then stood in her
eyes, and as soon as she entered they began to flow in great
abundance: He enquired earnestly the cause, but instead
of answering, she took from under her garment a shark's
tooth, and struck it six or seven times into her head with
great force; a profusion of blood followed, and she talked
loud, but in a most melancholy tone, for some minutes,
without at all regarding his enquiries, which he repeated
with still more impatience and concern, while the other Indians, to his great surprise, talked and laughed, without taking the least notice of her distress. But her own behaviour was still more extraordinary. As soon as the bleeding
was over, she looked up with a smile, and began to collect
some small pieces of cloth, which during her bleeding she
had thrown down to catch the blood; as soon as she had
picked them all up, she carried them out of the tent, and
threw them into the sea, carefully dispersing them abroad,
as if she wished to prevent the sight of them from reviving
the remembrance of what she had done. She then plunged
into the river, and after having washed her whole body, returned to the tents with the same gaiety and cheerfulness as
if nothing had happened.

It is not indeed strange that the sorrows of these artless
people should be transient, any more than that their passions should be suddenly and strongly expressed: What
they feel they have never been taught either to disguise or
suppress, and having no habits of thinking which perpetually recal the past, and anticipate the future, they are affected by all the changes of the passing hour, and reflect
the colour of the time, however frequently it may vary:
They have no project which is to be pursued from day to
day, the subject of unremitted anxiety and solicitude, that
first rushes into the mind when they awake in the morning,
and is last dismissed when they sleep at night. Yet if we
admit that they are upon the whole happier than we, we
must admit that the child is happier than the man, and that
we are losers by the perfection of our nature, the increase
of our knowledge, and the enlargement of our views.

Canoes were continually coming in during all this forenoon,

noon, and the tents at the fort were crowded with people of both sexes from different parts of the island. I was myself busy on board the ship, but Mr Mollineux, our master, who was one of those that made the last voyage in the Dolphin, went on shore. As soon as he entered Mr Banks's tent he fixed his eyes upon one of the women, who was sitting there with great composure among the rest, and immediately declared her to be the person who at that time was supposed to be the queen of the island; she also, at the same time, acknowledging him to be one of the strangers whom she had seen before. The attention of all present was now diverted from every other object, and wholly engaged in considering a person who had made so distinguished a figure in the accounts that had been given of this island by its first discoverers; and we soon learnt that her name was OBEREA. She seemed to be about forty years of age, and was not only tall, but of a large make; her skin was white, and there was an uncommon intelligence and sensibility in her eyes: She appeared to have been handsome when she was young, but at this time little more than memorials of her beauty were left.

As soon as her quality was known, an offer was made to conduct her to the ship. Of this she readily accepted, and came on board with two men and several women, who seemed to be all of her family: I received her with such marks of distinction as I thought would gratify her most, and was not sparing of my presents, among which this august personage seemed particularly delighted with a child's doll. After some time spent on board, I attended her back to the shore; and as soon as we landed, she presented me with a hog, and several bunches of plantains, which she caused to be carried from her canoes up to the fort in a kind of procession, of which she and myself brought up the rear. In our way to the fort we met Tootahah, who, though not king, appeared to be at this time invested with the sovereign authority; he seemed not to be well pleased with the distinction that was shewed to the lady, and became so jealous when she produced her doll, that to propitiate him it was thought proper to compliment him with another. At this time, he thought fit to prefer a doll to a hatchet; but this preference arose only from a childish jealousy, which could not be soothed but by a gift of exactly the same kind

with

'with that which had been presented to Oberea; for dolls in a very short time were universally considered as trifles of no value.

The men who had visited us from time to time had, without scruple, eaten of our provisions; but the women had never yet been prevailed upon to taste a morsel. To-day, however, though they refused the most pressing solicitations to dine with the gentlemen, they afterwards retired to the servants' apartment, and eat of plantains very heartily; a mystery of female œconomy here, which none of us could explain.

On the 29th, not very early in the forenoon, Mr Banks went to pay his court to Oberea, and was told that she was still asleep under the awning of her canoe: Thither therefore he went, intending to call her up, a liberty which he thought he might take, without any danger of giving offence: But, upon looking into her chamber, to his great astonishment, he found her in bed with a handsome young fellow about five-and-twenty, whose name was OBADEE: He retreated with some haste and confusion, but was soon made to understand, that such amours gave no occasion to scandal, and that Obadée was universally known to have been selected by her as the object of her private favours. The lady being too polite to suffer Mr Banks to wait long in her anti-chamber, dressed herself with more than usual expedition, and, as a token of special grace, clothed him in a suit of fine cloth and proceeded with him to the tents. In the evening Mr Banks paid a visit to Tubourai Tamaide, as he had often done before, by candle light, and was equally grieved and surprised to find him and his family in a melancholy mood, and most of them in tears: He endeavoured in vain to discover the cause, and therefore his stay among them was but short. When he reported this circumstance to the officers at the fort, they recollected that Owhaw had foretold, that in four days we should fire our great guns; and as this was the eve of the third day, the situation in which Tubourai Tamaide and his family had been found, alarmed them. The centries therefore were doubled at the fort, and the gentlemen slept under arms; at two in the morning, Mr Banks himself went round the point, but found every thing so quiet, that he gave up all suspicions of mischief intended by the natives as groundless. We had, however, another source of security; our little fortification

was

was now complete. The north and south sides consisted of a bank of earth four feet and a half high on the inside, and a ditch without ten feet broad and six deep; on the west side, facing the bay, there was a bank of earth four feet high, and pallisadoes upon that, but no ditch, the works here being at high-water mark; on the east side, upon the bank of the river, was placed a double row of water casks, filled with water; and as this was the weakest side, the two four-pounders were planted there, and six swivel guns were mounted so as to command the only two avenues from the woods. Our garrison consisted of about five-and-forty men with small arms, including the officers, and the gentlemen who resided on shore; and our centries were as well relieved as on the best regulated frontier in Europe.

We continued our vigilance the next day, though we had no particular reason to think it necessary; but about ten o'clock in the morning, Tomio came running to the tents, with a mixture of grief and fear in her countenance, and taking Mr Banks, to whom they applied in every emergency and distress, by the arm, intimated that Tubourai Tamaide was dying, in consequence of something which our people had given him to eat, and that he must instantly go with her to his house. Mr Banks set out without delay, and found his Indian friend leaning his head against a post, in an attitude of the utmost languor and despondency; the people about him intimated that he had been vomitting, and brought out a leaf folded up with great care, which they said contained some of the poison, by the deleterious effects of which he was now dying. Mr Banks hastily opened the leaf, and upon examining its contents found them to be no other than a chew of tobacco, which the chief had begged of some of our people, and which they had indiscreetly given him: He had observed that they kept it long in the mouth, and being desirous of doing the same, he had chewed it to powder, and swallowed the spittle. During the examination of the leaf and its contents, he looked up at Mr Banks with the most piteous aspect, and intimated that he had but a very short time to live. Mr Banks, however, being now master of his disease, directed him to drink plentifully of cocoa-nut milk, which in a short time put an end to his sickness and apprehensions, and he spent the day at the fort with that uncommon flow of cheerfulness and good-humour, which is always produced by a
sudden

sudden and unexpected relief from pain either of body or mind.

Captain Wallis having brought home one of the adzes, which these people, having no metal of any kind, make of stone, Mr Stevens, the secretary to the Admiralty, procured one to be made of iron in imitation of it, which I brought out with me, to shew how much we excelled in making tools after their own fashion: This I had not yet produced, as it never happened to come into my mind. But on the 1st of May, Tootahah coming on board about ten o'clock in the forenoon, expressed a great curiosity to see the contents of every chest and drawer that was in my cabin; as I always made a point of gratifying him, I opened them immediately, and having taken a fancy to many things that he saw, and collected them together, he at last happened to cast his eye upon this adze; he instantly snatched it up with the greatest eagerness, and putting away every thing which he had before selected, he asked me whether I would let him have that: I readily consented; and, as if he was afraid I should repent, he carried it off immediately in a transport of joy, without making any other request, which, whatever had been our liberality, was seldom the case.

About noon, a chief, who had dined with me a few days before, accompanied by some of his women, came on board alone: I had observed that he was fed by his women, but I made no doubt, that upon occasion he would condescend to feed himself: In this, however, I found myself mistaken. When my noble guest was seated, and the dinner upon the table, I helped him to some victuals: As I observed that he did not immediately begin his meal, I pressed him to eat: But he still continued to sit motionless like a statue, without attempting to put a single morsel into his mouth, and would certainly have gone without his dinner, if one of the servants had not fed him.[3]

SECTION

[3] The great people of Otaheite, whether men or women, seem to think that the labour of eating is sufficient employment, without the additional task of feeding, which in all probability they find can be done more expeditiously by proxy. Nor is such a consideration entirely unworthy of nobility, where the power of consuming food is so exorbitant as among those islanders. It might be convenient, one should think, for any man of rank who was capable of swallowing enormous quantities of food every hour or two, to have an attendant properly instructed in the art of stowing the

Section XI.

The Observatory set up ; the Quadrant stolen, and Consequences of the Theft : A Visit to Tootahah : Description of a Wrestling-match : European Seeds sown : Names given to our People by the Indians.

In the afternoon of Monday the 1st of May, we set up the observatory, and took the astronomical quadrant, with some other instruments, on shore, for the first time.

The next morning, about nine o'clock, I went on shore with Mr Green to fix the quadrant in a situation for use, when, to our inexpressible surprise and concern, it was not to be found. It had been deposited in the tent which was reserved for my use, where, as I passed the night on board, nobody slept : It had never been taken out of the packing-case ; which was eighteen inches square, and the whole was of considerable weight ; a centinel had been posted the whole night within five yards of the tent door, and none of the

---

belly-timber, as honest Sancho, of eating notoriety, calls it. " Tinah," says Captain Bligh, in the account of his voyage to this island, &c. " was fed by one of his attendants, who sat by him for that purpose, this being a particular custom among some of the superior chiefs ; and I must do him the justice to say, he kept his attendant constantly employed : There was indeed little reason to complain of want of appetite in any of my guests. As the women are not allowed to eat in presence of the men, Iddeah dined with some of her companions about an hour afterwards, in private, except her husband, Tinah, favoured them with his company, and seemed to have entirely forgotten that he had dined already." The capabilities of Tinah's stomach, it seems, were of very common acquirement at Otaheite. " They have not always regular meals," says the account of the Mis. Voy., " but usually eat as soon as they rise at day-break. Some are very voracious, especially the chiefs. Pomarae hath eaten a couple of fowls and two pounds at least of pork, besides other things, at a meal with us on board." Some persons may imagine this impossible ; but the fact is, the stomach, like every other member, acquires strength by exercise, and can, by due care, if there be no disease, be made to digest quantities of food as great as its distended limits are capable of receiving. There cannot be a more erroneous, or a more pernicious opinion, than what is commonly entertained, that the keenness of the appetite, and the energy of the digestion, are never above what the necessities of the system require. They are often enormously greater, and sometimes actually constitute most troublesome and highly formidable symptoms in certain diseases.—E.

the other instruments were missing. We at first suspected
that it might have been stolen by some of our own people,
who seeing a deal box, and not knowing the contents, might
think it contained nails, or some other subjects of traffic
with the natives. A large reward was therefore offered to
any one who could find it, as, without this, we could not
perform the service for which our voyage was principally
undertaken. Our search in the mean time was not confined
to the fort and places adjacent, but as the case might possibly
have been carried back to the ship, if any of our own people
had been the thieves, the most diligent search was made for
it on board: All the parties however returned without any
news of the quadrant. Mr Banks, therefore, who upon
such occasions declined neither labour nor risk, and who
had more influence over the Indians than any of us, determined to go in search of it into the woods; he hoped, that
if it had been stolen by the natives, he should find it where-
ever they had opened the box, as they would immediately
discover that to them it would be wholly useless; or, if in
this expectation he should be disappointed, that he might
recover it by the ascendancy he had acquired over the
chiefs. He set out, accompanied by a midshipman and
Mr Green, and as he was crossing the river he was met by
Tubourai Tamaide, who immediately made the figure of a
triangle with three bits of straw upon his hand. By this
Mr Banks knew that the Indians were the thieves; and that,
although they had opened the case, they were not disposed
to part with the contents. No time was therefore to be
lost, and Mr Banks made Tubourai Tamaide understand,
that he must instantly go with him to the place whither
the quadrant had been carried; he consented, and they set
out together to the eastward, the chief enquiring at every
house which they passed after the thief by name: The
people readily told him which way he was gone, and how
long it was since he had been there: The hope which this
gave them that they should overtake him, supported them
under their fatigue, and they pressed forward, sometimes
walking, sometimes running, though the weather was intolerably hot; when they had climbed a hill at the distance
of about four miles, their conductor shewed them a point
full three miles farther, and gave them to understand that
they were not to expect the instrument till they had got
thither. H   they paused; they had no arms, except a
pair

pair of pistols, which Mr Banks always carried in his pocket; they were going to a place that was at least seven miles distant from the fort, where the Indians might be less submissive than at home, and to take from them what they had ventured their lives to get; and what, notwithstanding our conjectures, they appeared desirous to keep: These were discouraging circumstances, and their situation would become more critical at every step. They determined, however, not to relinquish their enterprise, nor to pursue it without taking the best measures for their security that were in their power. It was therefore determined, that Mr Banks and Mr Green should go on, and that the midshipman should return to me, and desire that I would send a party of men after them, acquainting me at the same time, that it was impossible they should return till it was dark. Upon receiving this message I set out, with such a party as I thought sufficient for the occasion; leaving orders, both at the ship and at the fort, that no canoe should be suffered to go out of the bay, but that none of the natives should be seized or detained.

In the mean time, Mr Banks and Mr Green pursued their journey, under the auspices of Tubourai Tamaide, and in the very spot which he had specified, they met one of his own people, with part of the quadrant in his hand. At this most welcome sight they stopped; and a great number of Indians immediately came up, some of whom pressing rather rudely upon them, Mr Banks thought it necessary to shew one of his pistols, the sight of which reduced them instantly to order: As the crowd that gathered round them was every moment increasing, he marked out a circle in the grass, and they ranged themselves on the outside of it, to the number of several hundreds, with great quietness and decorum. Into the middle of this circle, the box, which was now arrived, was ordered to be brought, with several reading glasses, and other small matters, which in their hurry they had put into a pistol-case, that Mr Banks knew to be his property, it having been some time before stolen from the tents, with a horse-pistol in it, which he immediately demanded, and which was all restored.

Mr Green was impatient to see whether all that had been taken away was returned, and upon examining the box found the stand, and a few small things of less consequence wanting; several persons were sent in search of these, and

most

most of the small things were returned: But it was signified that the thief had not brought the stand so far, and
that it would be delivered to our friends as they went back;
this being confirmed by Tubourai Tamaide they prepared
to return, as nothing would then be wanting but what might
easily be supplied; and after they had advanced about two
miles, I met them with my party, to our mutual satisfaction,
congratulating each other upon the recovery of the quadrant, with a pleasure proportioned to the importance of
the event.

About eight o'clock, Mr Banks, with Tubourai Tamaide,
got back to the fort; when, to his great surprise, he found
Tootahah in custody, and many of the natives in the utmost
terror and distress, crowding about the gate. He went hastily in, some of the Indians were suffered to follow him, and
the scene was extremely affecting. Tubourai Tamaide
pressing forward, ran up to Tootahah, and catching him in
his arms, they both burst into tears, and wept over each
other, without being able to speak: The other Indians
were also in tears for their chief, both he and they being
strongly possessed with the notion that he was to be put to
death. In this situation they continued till I entered the
fort, which was about a quarter of an hour afterwards. I
was equally surprised and concerned at what had happened,
the confining Tootahah being contrary to my orders, and
therefore instantly set him at liberty. Upon enquiring into
the affair, I was told, that my going into the woods with a
party of men under arms, at a time when a robbery had
been committed, which it was supposed I should resent, in
proportion to our apparent injury by the loss, had so alarmed the natives, that in the evening they began to leave the
neighbourhood of the fort, with their effects: That a
double canoe having been seen to put off from the bottom
of the bay by Mr Gore, the second lieutenant, who was left
in command on board the ship, and who had received orders not to suffer any canoe to go out, he sent the boatswain with a boat after her to bring her back: That as soon
as the boat came up, the Indians being alarmed, leaped into
the sea; and that Tootahah, being unfortunately one of the
number, the boatswain took him up, and brought him to
the ship, suffering the rest of the people to swim on shore:
That Mr Gore, not sufficiently attending to the order that
none of the people should be confined, had sent him to the

fort, and Mr Hicks, the first lieutenant, who commanded there, receiving him in charge from Mr Gore, did not think himself at liberty to dismiss him.

The notion that we intended to put him to death had possessed him so strongly, that he could not be persuaded to the contrary till by my orders he was led out of the fort. The people received him as they would have done a father in the same circumstances, and every one pressed forward to embrace him. Sudden joy is commonly liberal, without a scrupulous regard to merit; and Tootahah, in the first expansion of his heart, upon being unexpectedly restored to liberty and life, insisted upon our receiving a present of two hogs; though, being conscious that upon this occasion we had no claim to favours, we refused them many times.

Mr Banks and Dr Solander attended the next morning in their usual capacity of market-men, but very few Indians appeared, and those who came brought no provisions. Tootahah, however, sent some of his people for the canoe that had been detained, which they took away. A canoe having also been detained that belonged to Oberea, Tupia, the person who managed her affairs when the Dolphin was here, was sent to examine whether any thing on board had been taken away: And he was so well satisfied of the contrary, that he left the canoe where he found it, and joined us at the fort, where he spent the day, and slept on board the canoe at night. About noon, some fishing-boats came a-breast of the tents, but would part with very little of what they had on board; and we felt the want of cocoa-nuts and bread-fruit very severely. In the course of the day, Mr Banks walked out into the woods, that by conversing with the people he might recover their confidence and good-will: He found them civil, but they all complained of the ill-treatment of their chief; who, they said, had been beaten and pulled by the hair. Mr Banks endeavoured to convince them, that he had suffered no personal violence, which, to the best of our knowledge, was true; yet, perhaps, the boatswain had behaved with a brutality which he was afraid or ashamed to acknowledge. The chief himself being probably, upon recollection, of opinion that we had ill-deserved the hogs, which he had left with us as a present, sent a messenger in the afternoon to demand an axe, and a shirt, in return; but as I was told that he did not intend to come down to the fort for ten days, I excused myself from giving

them

them till I should see him, hoping that his impatience might induce him to fetch them, and knowing that absence would probably continue the coolness between us, to which the first interview might put an end.

The next day we were still more sensible of the inconvenience we had incurred by giving offence to the people in the person of their chief, for the market was so ill supplied that we were in want of necessaries. Mr Banks therefore went into the woods to Tuboural Tamaide, and with some difficulty persuaded him to let us have five baskets of breadfruit; a very seasonable supply, as they contained above one hundred and twenty. In the afternoon another messenger arrived from Tootahah for the axe and shirt; as it was now become absolutely necessary to recover the friendship of this man, without which it would be scarcely possible to procure provisions, I sent word that Mr Banks and myself would visit him on the morrow, and bring what he wanted with us.

Early the next morning he sent again to remind me of my promise, and his people seemed to wait till we should set out with great impatience: I therefore ordered the pinnace, in which I embarked with Mr Banks and Dr Solander about ten o'clock: We took one of Tootahah's people in the boat with us, and in about an hour we arrived at his place of residence, which is called Eparre, and is about four miles to the westward of the tents.

We found the people waiting for us in great numbers upon the shore, so that it would have been impossible for us to have proceeded, if way had not been made for us by a tall well-looking man, who had something like a turban about his head, and a long white stick in his hand, with which he laid about him at an unmerciful rate. This man conducted us to the chief, while the people shouted round us, *Taio Tootahah,* "Tootahah is your friend." We found him, like an ancient patriarch, sitting under a tree, with a number of venerable old men standing round him; he made a sign to us to sit down, and immediately asked for his axe: This I presented to him, with an upper garment of broad cloth, made after the country fashion, and trimmed with tape, to which I also added a shirt: He received them with great satisfaction, and immediately put on the garment; but the shirt he gave to the person who had cleared the way for us upon our landing, who was now seated by us, and

of

of whom he seemed desirous that we should take particular notice. In a short time, Oberea, and several other women whom we knew, came and sat down among us: Tootahah left us several times, but after a short absence returned; we thought it had been to shew himself in his new finery to the people, but we wronged him, for it was to give directions for our refreshment and entertainment. While we were waiting for his return the last time he left us, very impatient to be dismissed, as we were almost suffocated in the crowd, word was brought us, that he expected us elsewhere: We found him sitting under the awning of our own boat, and making signs that we should come to him: As many of us therefore went on board as the boat would hold, and he then ordered bread-fruit and cocoa-nuts to be brought, of both which we tasted, rather to gratify him than because we had a desire to eat. A message was soon after brought him, upon which he went out of the boat, and we were in a short time desired to follow. We were conducted to a large area or court-yard, which was railed round with bamboos about three feet high, on one side of his house, where an entertainment was provided for us, entirely new: This was a wrestling-match. At the upper end of the area sat the chief, and several of his principal men were ranged on each side of him, so as to form a semicircle; these were the judges, by whom the victor was to be applauded; seats were also left for us at each end of the line; but we chose rather to be at liberty among the rest of the spectators.

When all was ready, ten or twelve persons, whom we understood to be the combatants, and who were naked, except a cloth that was fastened about the waist, entered the area, and walked slowly round it, in a stooping posture, with their left hands on their right breasts, and their right hands open, with which they frequently struck the left fore-arm so as to produce a quick smart sound: This was a general challenge to the combatants whom they were to engage, or any other person present: After these followed others in the same manner, and then a particular challenge was given, by which each man singled out his antagonist: This was done by joining the finger ends of both hands, and bringing them to the breast, at the same time moving the elbows up and down with a quick motion: If the person to whom this was addressed accepted the challenge, he repeated the signs, and immediately each put himself into an attitude to engage:

The

The next minute they closed; but, except in first seizing each other, it was a mere contest of strength: Each endeavoured to lay hold of the other, first by the thigh, and if that failed by the hand, the hair, the cloth, or elsewhere as he could: When this was done they grappled, without the least dexterity or skill, till one of them, by having a more advantageous hold, or greater muscular force, threw the other on his back. When the contest was over, the old men gave their plaudit to the victor in a few words, which they repeated together in a kind of tune: His conquest was also generally celebrated by three huzzas. The entertainment was then suspended for a few minutes, after which another couple of wrestlers came forward and engaged in the same manner: If it happened that neither was thrown, after the contest had continued about a minute, they parted, either by consent or the intervention of their friends, and in this case each slapped his arm, as a challenge to a new engagement, either with the same antagonist or some other. While the wrestlers were engaged, another party of men performed a dance, which lasted also about a minute; but neither of these parties took the least notice of each other, their attention being wholly fixed on what they were doing. We observed with pleasure, that the conqueror never exulted over the vanquished, and that the vanquished never repined at the success of the conqueror; the whole contest was carried on with perfect good-will and good-humour, though in the presence of at least five hundred spectators, of whom some were women. The number of women indeed was comparatively small, none but those of rank were present, and we had reason to believe that they would not have been spectators of this exercise but in compliment to us.

This lasted about two hours; during all which time the man who had made a way for us when we landed, kept the people at a proper distance, by striking those who pressed forward very severely with his stick: Upon enquiry we learnt that he was an officer belonging to Tootahah, acting as master of the ceremonies.

It is scarcely possible for those who are acquainted with the athletic sports of very remote antiquity, not to remark a rude resemblance of them in this wrestling-match among the natives of a little island in the midst of the Pacific Ocean: And our female readers may recollect the account

given

given of them by Fenelon in his Telemachus, where, though
the events are fictitious, the manners of the age are faithfully transcribed from authors by whom they are supposed to
have been truly related.

When the wrestling was over, we were given to understand that two hogs, and a large quantity of bread-fruit,
were preparing for our dinner, which, as our appetites were
now keen, was very agreeable intelligence. Our host,
however, seemed to repent of his liberality; for, instead of
setting his two hogs before us, he ordered one of them to
be carried into our boat; at first we were not sorry for this
new disposition of matters, thinking that we should dine
more comfortably in the boat than on shore, as the crowd
would more easily be kept at a distance: But when we
came on board, he ordered us to proceed with his hog to
the ship: This was mortifying, as we were now to row four
miles while our dinner was growing cold; however, we
thought fit to comply, and were at last gratified with the
cheer that he had provided, of which he and Tubourai Tamaide had a liberal share.

Our reconciliation with this man operated upon the people like a charm; for he was no sooner known to be on
board, than bread-fruit, cocoa-nuts, and other provisions
were brought to the fort in great plenty.

Affairs now went on in the usual channel; but pork being
still a scarce commodity, our master, Mr Mollineux, and
Mr Green, went in the pinnace to the eastward, on the 8th.
early in the morning, to see whether they could procure any
hogs or poultry in that part of the country: They proceeded in that direction twenty miles; but though they saw
many hogs, and one turtle, they could not purchase either
at any price: The people every where told them, that they
all belonged to Tootahah, and that they could sell none
of them without his permission. We now began to think
that this man was indeed a great prince; for an influence so
extensive and absolute could be acquired by no other. And
we afterwards found that he administered the government
of this part of the island, as sovereign, for a minor whom
we never saw all the time that we were upon it. When
Mr Green returned from this expedition he said he had
seen a tree of a size which he was afraid to relate, it being
no less than sixty yards in circumference; but Mr Banks
and Dr Solander soon explained to him that it was a species
of

of the fig, the branches of which, bending down, take fresh root in the earth, and thus form a congeries of trunks, which being very close to each other, and all joined by a common vegetation, might easily be mistaken for one.

Though the market at the fort was now tolerably supplied, provisions were brought more slowly: A sufficient quantity used to be purchased between sun-rise and eight o'clock, but it was now become necessary to attend the greatest part of the day. Mr Banks, therefore, fixed his little boat up before the door of the fort, which was of great use as a place to trade in: Hitherto we had purchased cocoa-nuts and bread-fruit for beads; but the market becoming rather slack in these articles, we were now, for the first time, forced to bring out our nails: One of our smallest size, which was about four inches long, procured us twenty cocoa-nuts, and bread-fruit in proportion, so that in a short time our first plenty was restored.

On the 9th, soon after breakfast, we received a visit from Oberea, being the first that she had made us after the loss of our quadrant, and the unfortunate confinement of Tootahah; with her came her present favourite, Obadée, and Tupia: They brought us a hog and some bread-fruit, in return for which we gave her a hatchet. We had now afforded our Indian friends a new and interesting object of curiosity, our forge, which, having been set up some time, was almost constantly at work. It was now common for them to bring pieces of iron, which we suppose they must have got from the Dolphin, to be made into tools of various kinds; and as I was very desirous to gratify them, they were indulged, except when the smith's time was too precious to be spared. Oberea having received her hatchet, produced as much old iron as would have made another, with a request that another might be made of it; in this, however, I could not gratify her, upon which she brought out a broken axe, and desired it might be mended; I was glad of an opportunity to compromise the difference between us: Her axe was mended, and she appeared to be content. They went away at night, and took with them the canoe, which had been a considerable time at the point, but promised to return in three days.

On the 10th, I put some seeds of melons and other plants into a spot of ground which had been turned up for the purpose: they had all been sealed up by the person of

whom

whom they were bought, in small bottles, with rosin; but
none of them came up except mustard; even the cucum-
bers and melons failed, and Mr Banks is of opinion that
they were spoiled by the total exclusion of fresh air.

This day we learned the Indian name of the island, which
is *Otaheite,* and by that name I shall hereafter distinguish
it: But after great pains taken we found it utterly impossible to teach the Indians to pronounce our names; we had,
therefore, new names, consisting of such sounds as they
produced in the attempt. They called me *Toote;* Mr
Hicks, *Hete;* Mollineux they renounced in absolute despair,
and called the master *Boba,* from his christian name Robert; Mr Gore was *Toarro;* Dr Solander, *Torano;* and
Mr Banks, *Tapane;* Mr Green, *Eteree;* Mr Porkinson,
Patini; Mr Sporing, *Polini;* Petersgill, *Petrodero;* and in
this manner they had now formed names for almost every
man in the ship: In some, however, it was not easy to find
any traces of the original, and they were perhaps not mere
arbitrary sounds, formed upon the occasion, but significant
words in their own language. Monkhouse, the midshipman, who commanded the party that killed the man for
stealing the musket, they called *Matte;* not merely by an
attempt to imitate in sound the first syllable of Monkhouse,
but because *Matte* signifies *dead;* and this probably might
be the case with others.

SECTION XII.

Some Ladies visit the Fort with very uncommon Ceremonies: The
Indians attend Divine Service, and in the Evening exhibit a
most extraordinary Spectacle: Tubourai Tamaide falls into
Temptation.

FRIDAY, the 12th of May, was distinguished by a visit
from some ladies whom we had never seen before, and who
introduced themselves with very singular ceremonies. Mr
Banks was trading in his boat at the gate of the fort as usual, in company with Tootahah, who had that morning paid
him a visit, and some other of the natives; between nine
and ten o'clock, a double canoe came to the landing-place,
under the awning of which sat a man and two women: The
Indians that were about Mr Banks made signs that he
should

should go out to meet them, which he hasted to do; but by the time he could get out of the boat, they had advanced within ten yards of him: They then stopped, and made signs that he should do so too, laying down about a dozen young plantain trees, and some other small plants: He complied, and the people having made a lane between them, the man, who appeared to be a servant, brought six of them to Mr Banks by one of each at a time, passing and repassing six times, and always pronouncing a short sentence when he delivered them. Tupia, who stood by Mr Banks, acted as his master of the ceremonies, and receiving the branches as they were brought, laid them down in the boat. When this was done, another man brought a large bundle of cloth, which having opened, he spread piece by piece upon the ground, in the space between Mr Banks and his visitors; there were nine pieces, and having laid three pieces one upon another, the foremost of the women, who seemed to be the principal, and who was called Ooiattooa, stepped upon them, and taking up her garments all around her to the waist, turned about, with great composure and delibe-ration, and with an air of perfect innocence and simplicity, three times; when this was done, she dropped the veil, and stepping off the cloth, three more pieces were laid on, and she repeated the ceremony, then stepping off as before; the last three were laid on, and the ceremony was repeated in the same manner the third time. Immediately after this the cloth was rolled up, and given to Mr Banks as a present from the lady, who, with her friend, came up and saluted him. He made such presents to them both as he thought would be most acceptable, and after having staid about an hour they went away. In the evening the gentlemen at the fort had a visit from Oberea, and her favourite female at-tendant, whose name was Otheothea, an agreeable girl, whom they were the more pleased to see, because, having been some days absent, it had been reported she was either sick or dead.

On the 13th, the market being over about ten o'clock, Mr Banks walked into the woods with his gun, as he gene-rally did, for the benefit of the shade in the heat of the day: As he was returning back, he met Tubourai Tamaide, near his occasional dwelling, and stopping to spend a little time with him, he suddenly took the gun out of Mr Banks's hand, cocked it, and holding it up in the air, drew the trig-
ger ·

ger· Fortunately for him it flashed in the pan: Mr Banks immediately took it from him, not a little surprised how he had acquired sufficient knowledge of a gun to discharge it, and reproved him with great severity for what he had done. As it was of infinite importance to keep the Indians totally ignorant of the management of fire-arms, he had taken every opportunity of intimating that they could never offend him so highly as by even touching his piece; it was now proper to enforce this prohibition, and he therefore added threats to his reproof: The Indian bore all patiently; but the moment Mr Banks crossed the river, he set off with all his family and furniture for his house at Eparre. This being quickly known from the Indians at the fort, and great inconvenience being apprehended from the displeasure of this man, who upon all occasions had been particularly useful, Mr Banks determined to follow him without delay, and solicit his return: He set out the same evening, accompanied by Mr Mollineux, and found him sitting in the middle of a large circle of people, to whom he had probably related what had happened, and his fears of the consequences; he was himself the very picture of grief and dejection, and the same passions were strongly marked in the countenances of all the people that surrounded him. When Mr Banks and Mr Mollineux went into the circle, one of the women expressed her trouble, as Terapo had done upon another occasion, and struck a shark's tooth into her head several times, till it was covered with blood. Mr Banks lost no time in putting an end to this universal distress; he assured the chief, that every thing which had passed should be forgotten, that there was not the least animosity remaining on one side, nor any thing to be feared on the other. The chief was soon soothed into confidence and complacency, a double canoe was ordered to be got ready, they all returned together to the fort before supper, and as a pledge of perfect reconciliation, both he and his wife slept all night in Mr Banks's tent: Their presence, however, was no palladium; for, between eleven and twelve o'clock, one of the natives attempted to get into the fort by scaling the walls, with a design, no doubt, to steal whatever he should happen to find; he was discovered by the centinel, who happily did not fire, and he ran away much faster than any of our people could follow him. The iron, and iron-tools, which were in continual use at the armourer's forge, that

was

was set up within the works, were temptations to theft which none of these people could withstand.

On the 14th, which was Sunday, I directed that divine service should be performed at the fort : We were desirous that some of the principal Indians should be present, but when the hour came, most of them were returned home. Mr Banks, however, crossed the river, and brought back Tubourai Tamaide and his wife Tomio, hoping that it would give occasion to some enquiries on their part, and some instruction on ours : Having seated them, he placed himself between them, and during the whole service, they very attentively observed his behaviour, and very exactly imitated it, standing, sitting, or kneeling, as they saw him do : They were conscious that we were employed about somewhat serious and important, as appeared by their calling to the Indians without the fort to be silent; yet when the service was over, neither of them asked any questions, nor would they attend to any attempt that was made to explain what had been done.

In the evening of this day, an exhibition of the grossest lewdness was made by a young couple, in presence of Oberea and several women of superior rank, who indeed seemed to assist in it, by their advice to the female, a girl about eleven or twelve years of age. This was quite in conformity to the custom of the place, and did not appear to excite the least feeling of shame in either performers or spectators.[1]

On

---

[1] The relation of this incident is purposely varied from the copy. It is but justice to the Otaheitans to apprize the reader, that in the account of the missionary voyage, published in 1799, and hereafter to be noticed, this conduct as to immodesty is in no small degree explained, and they are acknowledged even to excel in some parts of delicacy of sentiment and behaviour. The testimony of that account, it may be remarked, is deserving the more credit, because the mission itself was avowedly founded on the conviction of the total depravity of these islanders, and was purposed as an attempt at reformation on religious principles. Still, however, it is most certain that the Otaheitans were much addicted to sensual indulgences, and that Oberea, as we have already seen, was noted for libidinous propensities. How far their peculiar circumstances may either account for or palliate their apparent immorality in this respect, is quite another question; one too, it is probable, which the prejudiced and erring mind of man is, of itself, incompetent to solve. One thing, however, is most certain : The Judge of all the earth will do what is right with his creatures, whether he take vengeance for transgression, or pardon in mercy, or reward in approbation.—E.

On the 14th and 15th, we had another opportunity of observing the general knowledge which these people had of any design that was formed among them. In the night between the 13th and 14th, one of the water-casks was stolen from the outside of the fort: In the morning there was not an Indian to be seen who did not know that it was gone; yet they appeared not to have been trusted, or not to have been worthy of trust; for they seemed all of them disposed to give intelligence where it might be found. Mr Banks traced it to a part of the bay where he was told it had been put into a canoe, but as it was not of great consequence, he did not complete the discovery. When he returned, he was told by Tubourai Tamaide, that another cask would be stolen before the morning: How he came by this knowledge it is not easy to imagine; that he was not a party in the design is certain, for he came with his wife and his family to the place where the water-casks stood, and placing their beds near them, he said he would himself be a pledge for their safety, in despight of the thief: Of this, however, we would not admit; and making them understand that a centry would be placed to watch the casks till the morning, he removed the beds into Mr Banks's tent, where he and his family spent the night, making signs to the sentry when he retired, that he should keep his eyes open. In the night this intelligence appeared to be true; about twelve o'clock the thief came, but discovering that a watch had been set, he went away without his booty.

Mr Banks's confidence in Tubourai Tamaide had greatly increased since the affair of the knife, in consequence of which he was at length exposed to temptations which neither his integrity nor his honour was able to resist. They had withstood many allurements, but were at length ensnared by the fascinating charms of a basket of nails: These nails were much larger than any that had yet been brought into trade, and had, with perhaps some degree of criminal negligence, been left in a corner of Mr Banks's tent, to which the chief had always free access. One of these nails Mr Banks's servant happened to see in his possession, upon his having inadvertently thrown back that part of his garment under which it was concealed. Mr Banks being told of this, and knowing that no such thing had been given him, either as a present or in barter, immediately examined the basket, and discovered, that out of

seven

seven nails five were missing. He then, though not with-out great reluctance, charged him with the fact, which he immediately confessed, and however he might suffer, was probably not more hurt than his accuser. A demand was immediately made of restitution; but this he declined, say-ing that the nails were at Eparre: However, Mr Banks appearing to be much in earnest, and using some threaten-ing signs, he thought fit to produce one of them. He was then taken to the fort, to receive such judgment as should be given against him by the general voice.

After some deliberation, that we might not appear to think too lightly of his offence, he was told, that if he would bring the other four nails to the fort, it should be forgotten. To this condition he agreed; but I am sorry to say he did not fulfil it. Instead of fetching the nails, he removed with his family before night, and took all his furniture with him.

As our long-boat had appeared to be leaky, I thought it necessary to examine her bottom, and to my great surprise, found it so much eaten by the worms, that it was necessary to give her a new one; no such accident had happened to the Dolphin's boats, as I was informed by the officers on board, and therefore it was a misfortune that I did not ex-pect: I feared that the pinnace also might be nearly in the same condition; but, upon examining her, I had the satisfaction to find that not a worm had touched her, though she was built of the same wood, and had been as much in the water; the reason of this difference I imagine to be, that the long-boat was paid with varnish of pine, and the pinnace painted with white lead and oil; the bottoms of all boats therefore which are sent into this country should be painted like that of the pinnace, and the ships should be supplied with a good stock, in order to give them a new coating when it should be found necessary.

Having received repeated messages from Tootahah, that if we would pay him a visit he would acknowledge the fa-vour by a present of four hogs, I sent Mr Hicks, my first lieutenant, to try if he could not procure the hogs upon easier terms, with orders to show him every civility in his power. Mr Hicks found that he was removed from Eparre to a place called *Tettahah*, five miles farther to the west-ward. He was received with great cordiality; one hog was immediately produced, and he was told that the other three, which were at some distance, should be brought in the

the morning. Mr Hicks readily consented to stay; but the morning came without the hogs; and it not being convenient to stay longer, he returned in the evening with the one he had got.

On the 25th, Tubourai Tamaide and his wife Tomio made their appearance at the tent, for the first time since he had been detected in stealing the nails; he seemed to be under some discontent and apprehension, yet he did not think fit to purchase our countenance and good-will by restoring the four which he had sent away. As Mr Banks and the other gentlemen treated him with a coolness and reserve which did not at all tend to restore his peace or good-humour, his stay was short, and his departure abrupt. Mr Monkhouse, the surgeon, went the next morning in order to effect a reconciliation, by persuading him to bring down the nails, but he could not succeed.

Section XIII.

Another Visit to Tootahah, with various Adventures: Extraordinary Amusement of the Indians, with Remarks upon it. Preparations to observe the Transit of Venus, and what happened in the mean Time at the Fort.

On the 27th, it was determined that we should pay our visit to Tootahah, though we were not very confident that we should receive the hogs for our pains. I therefore set out early in the morning, with Mr Banks and Dr Solander, and three others, in the pinnace. He was now removed from Tettahah, where Mr Hicks had seen him, to a place called *Atahourou,* about six miles farther; and as we could not go above half-way thither in the boat, it was almost evening before we arrived. We found him in his usual state, sitting under a tree, with a great crowd about him. We made our presents in due form, consisting of a yellow stuff-petticoat, and some other trifling articles, which were graciously received; a hog was immediately ordered to be killed and dressed for supper, with a promise of more in the morning. However, as we were less desirous of feasting upon our journey than of carrying back with us provisions, which would be more welcome at the fort, we procured a reprieve for the hog, and supped upon the fruits of the country

country. As night now came on, and the place was crowded with many more than the houses and canoes would contain, there being Obeiea with her attendants, and many
other travellers whom we knew, we began to look out for
lodgings.   Our party consisted of six : Mr Banks thought
himself fortunate in being offered a place by Oberea in her
canoe, and wishing his friends a good night, took his leave.
He went to rest early, according to the custom of the country, and taking off his clothes, as was his constant practice,
the nights being hot, Obeiea kindly insisted upon taking
them into her own custody, for otherwise, she said, they
would certainly be stolen.   Mr Banks, having such a safe
guard, resigned himself to sleep with all imaginable tranquillity : But waking about eleven o'clock, and wanting to
get up, he searched for his clothes where he had seen them
deposited by Obeiea when he lay down to sleep, and soon
perceived that they were amissing.   He immediately awakened Oberea, who starting up, and hearing his complaint,
ordered lights, and prepared in great haste to recover what
he had lost. Tootahah himself slept in the next canoe, and
being soon alarmed, he came to them, and set out with
Obeiea in search of the thief.   Mr Banks was not in a
condition to go with them, for of his apparel scarce any
thing was left him but his breeches ; his coat and his waistcoat, with his pistols, powder-horn, and many other things
that were in the pockets, were gone.   In about half an hour
his two noble friends returned, but without having obtained any intelligence of his clothes or of the thief.   At first
he began to be alarmed ; his musquet had not indeed been
taken away, but he had neglected to load it ; where I and
Dr Solander had disposed of ourselves he did not know,
and therefore, whatever might happen, he could not have
recourse to us for assistance.   He thought it best, however,
to express neither fear nor suspicion of those about him ;
and giving his musquet to Tupia, who had been waked in
the confusion and stood by him, with a charge not to suffer it to be stolen, he betook himself again to rest, declaring himself perfectly satisfied with the pains that Tootahah and Oberea had taken to recover his things, though
they had not been successful.   As it cannot be supposed
that in such a situation his sleep was very sound, he soon
after heard music, and saw lights at a little distance on
shore : This was a conceit or assembly, which they call a
Heiva ;

Heira, a common name for every public exhibition; and as it would necessarily bring many people together, and there was a chance of my being among them with his other friends, he rose, and made the best of his way towards it. He was soon led by the lights and the sound to the hut where I lay, with three other gentlemen of our party; and easily distinguishing us from the rest, he made up to us more than half naked, and told us his melancholy story. We gave him such comfort as the unfortunate generally give to each other, by telling him that we were fellow-sufferers; I showed him that I was myself without stockings, they having been stolen from under my head, though I was sure I had never been asleep, and each of my associates convinced him, by his appearance, that he had lost a jacket. We determined, nevertheless, to hear out the concert, however deficient we might appear in our dress; it consisted of three drums, four flutes, and several voices: When this entertainment, which lasted about an hour, was over, we retired again to our sleeping-places; having agreed that nothing could be done toward the recovery of our things till the morning.

We rose at day-break, according to the custom of the country; the first man that Mr Banks saw was Tupia, faithfully attending with his musquet; and soon after, Oberea brought him some of her country clothes as a succedaneum for his own; so that when he came to us he made a most motley appearance, half Indian and half English. Our party soon got together, except Dr Solander, whose quarters we did not know, and who had not assisted at the concert: In a short time Tootahah made his appearance, and we pressed him to recover our clothes; but neither he nor Oberea could be persuaded to take any measure for that purpose, so that we began to suspect that they had been parties in the theft. About eight o'clock, we were joined by Dr Solander, who had fallen into honester hands, at a house about a mile distant, and had lost nothing.

Having given up all hope of recovering our clothes, which indeed were never afterwards heard of, we spent all the morning in soliciting the hogs which we had been promised; but in this we had no better success: We therefore, in no very good humour, set out for the boat about twelve o'clock, with only that which we had redeemed from the butcher and the cook the night before.

As

As we were returning to the boat, however, we were entertained with a sight that in some measure compensated for
our fatigue and disappointment. In our way we came to
one of the few places where access to the island is not
guarded by a reef, and, consequently, a high surf breaks
upon the shore; a more dreadful one indeed I had seldom
seen; it was impossible for any European boat to have
lived in it, and if the best swimmer in Europe had, by
any accident, been exposed to its fury, I am confident that
he would not have been able to preserve himself from
drowning, especially as the shore was covered with pebbles and large stones; yet, in the midst of these breakers,
were ten or twelve Indians swimming for their amusement:
Whenever a surf broke near them, they dived under it,
and, to all appearance with infinite facility, rose again on
the other side. This diversion was greatly improved by
the stern of an old canoe, which they happened to find
upon the spot; they took this before them, and swam out
with it as far as the outermost breach, then two or three
of them getting into it, and turning the square end to the
breaking wave, were driven in towards the shore with incredible rapidity, sometimes almost to the beach, but
generally the wave broke over them before they got half
way, in which case they dived, and rose on the other side
with the canoe in their hands: They then swam out with
it again, and were again driven back, just as our holiday
youth climb the hill in Greenwich-park for the pleasure of
rolling down it. At this wonderful scene we stood gazing
for more than half an hour, during which time none of the
swimmers attempted to come on shore, but seemed to en-
joy their sport in the highest degree; we then proceeded
in our journey, and late in the evening got back to the
fort.

Upon this occasion it may be observed, that human nature is endued with powers which are only accidentally exerted to the utmost; and that all men are capable of what
no man attains, except he is stimulated to the effort by
some uncommon circumstances or situation. These Indians effected what to us appeared to be supernatural,
merely by the application of such powers as they possessed in common with us, and all other men who have no
particular infirmity or defect. The truth of the observation is also manifest from more familiar instances. The

rope-dancer and balance-master owe their art, not to any peculiar liberality of nature, but to an accidental improvement of her common gifts ; and though equal diligence and application would not always produce equal excellence in these, any more than in other arts, yet there is no doubt but that a certain degree of proficiency in them might be universally attained. Another proof of the existence of abilities in mankind, that are almost universally dormant, is furnished by the attainments of blind men. It cannot be supposed that the loss of one sense, like the amputation of a branch from a tree, gives new vigour to those that remain. Every man's hearing and touch, therefore, are capable of the nice distinctions which astonish us in those that have lost their sight, and if they do not give the same intelligence to the mind, it is merely because the same intelligence is not required of them : He that can see may do from choice what the blind do by necessity, and by the same diligent attention to the other senses, may receive the same notices from them ; let it therefore be remembered as an encouragement to persevering diligence, and a principle of general use to mankind, that he who does all he can, will ever effect much more than is generally thought to be possible.

Among other Indians that had visited us, there were some from a neighbouring island which they called *Eimeo* or *Imao*, the same to which Captain Wallis had given the name of the Duke of York's Island, and they gave us an account of no less than two-and-twenty islands that lay in the neighbourhood of Otaheite.

As the day of observation now approached, I determined, in consequence of some hints which had been given me by Lord Morton, to send out two parties to observe the transit from other situations, hoping, that if we should fail at Otaheite, they might have better success. We were, therefore, now busily employed in preparing our instruments, and instructing such gentlemen in the use of them as I intended to send out.

On Thursday the 1st of June, the Saturday following being the day of the transit, I dispatched Mr Gore in the long boat to Imao, with Mr Monkhouse and Mr Sporing, a gentleman belonging to Mr Banks, Mr Green having furnished them with proper instruments. Mr Banks himself thought fit to go upon this expedition, and several native tives, particularly Tuboutai Tamaide and Tomio, were also of the party. Very early on the Friday morning, I sent Mr Hicks, with Mr Clerk and Mr Petersgill, the master's mates, and Mr Saunders, one of the midshipmen, in the pinnace to the eastward, with orders to fix on some convenient spot, at a distance from our principal observatory, where they also might employ the instruments with which they had been furnished for the same purpose.

The long-boat not having been got ready till Thursday in the afternoon, though all possible expedition was used to fit her out, the people on board after having rowed most part of the night, brought her to a grappling just under the land of Imao. Soon after day-break, they saw an Indian canoe, which they hailed, and the people on board shewed them an inlet through the reef into which they pulled, and soon fixed upon a coral rock, which rose out of the water about one hundred and fifty yards from the shore, as a proper situation for their observatory: It was about eighty yards long and twenty broad, and in the middle of it was a bed of white sand, large enough for the tents to stand upon. Mr Gore and his assistants immediately began to set them up, and make other necessary preparations for the important business of the next day. While this was doing, Mr Banks, with the Indians of Otaheite, and the people whom they had met in the canoe went ashore upon the main island, to buy provisions; of which he procured a sufficient supply before night. When he returned to the rock, he found the observatory in order, and the telescopes all fixed and tried. The evening was very fine, yet their solicitude did not permit them to take much rest in the night: One or other of them was up every half hour, who satisfied the impatience of the rest by reporting the changes of the sky; now encouraging their hope by telling them that it was clear, and now alarming their fears by an account that it was hazy.

At day-break they got up, and had the satisfaction to see the sun rise, without a cloud. Mr Banks then, wishing the observers, Mr Gore and Mr Monkhouse, success, repaired again to the island, that he might examine its produce, and get a fresh supply of provisions: He began by trading with the natives, for which purpose he took his station under a tree; and to keep them from pressing upon him

hint

him in a crowd, he drew a circle round him, which he suffered none of them to enter.

About eight o'clock, he saw two canoes coming towards the place, and was given to understand by the people about him, that they belonged to *Tarrao*, the king of the island, who was coming to make him a visit. As soon as the canoes came near the shore, the people made a lane from the beach to the trading-place, and his majesty landed, with his sister, whose name was *Nuna*; as they advanced towards the tree where Mr Banks stood, he went out to meet them, and, with great formality, introduced them into the circle from which the other natives had been excluded. As it is the custom of these people to sit during all their conferences, Mr Banks unwrapped a kind of turban of Indian cloth, which he wore upon his head instead of a hat, and spreading it upon the ground, they all sat down upon it together. The royal present was then brought, which consisted of a hog and a dog, some bread-fruit, cocoa-nuts, and other articles of the like kind. Mr Banks then dispatched a canoe to the observatory for his present, and the messengers soon returned with an adze, a shirt, and some beads, which were presented to his majesty, and received with great satisfaction.

By this time, Tubourai Tamaide and Tomio joined them, from the observatory. Tomio said, that she was related to Tarrao, and brought him a present of a long nail, at the same time complimenting Nuna with a shirt.

The first internal contact of the planet with the sun being over, Mr Banks returned to the observatory, taking Tarrao, Nuna, and some of their principal attendants, among whom were three very handsome young women, with him: He showed them the planet upon the sun, and endeavoured to make them understand that he and his companions had come from their own country on purpose to see it. Soon after, Mr Banks returned with them to the island, where he spent the rest of the day in examining its produce, which he found to be much the same with that of Otaheite. The people whom he saw there also exactly resembled the inhabitants of that island, and many of them were persons whom he had seen upon it; so that all those whom he had dealt with, knew of what his trading articles consisted, and the value they bore.

The

The next morning having struck the tents, they set out on their return, and arrived at the fort before night.

The observation was made with equal success by the persons whom I had sent to the eastward, and at the fort, there not being a cloud in the sky from the rising to the setting of the sun, the whole passage of the planet Venus over the sun's disk was observed with great advantage by Mr Green, Dr Solander, and myself: Mr Green's telescope and mine were of the same magnifying power, but that of Dr Solander was greater. We all saw an atmosphere or dusky cloud round the body of the planet, which very much disturbed the times of contact, especially of the internal ones; and we differed from each other in our accounts of the times of the contacts much more than might have been expected. According to Mr Green,

	Hours.	Min.	Sec.	
The first external contact, or first appearance of Venus on the Sun, was	9	25	42	Morning.
The first internal contact, or total emersion, was	9	44	4	Morning.
The second internal contact, or beginning of the emersion,	3	14	8	Afternoon.
The second external contact, or total emersion,	3	32	10	Afternoon.

The latitude of the observatory was found to be 17° 29' 15"; and the longitude 149° 32' 30" W. of Greenwich. A more particular account will appear by the tables, for which the reader is referred to the Transactions of the Royal Society, vol. lxi. part 2 p. 397 et seq. where they are illustrated by a cut.

But if we had reason to congratulate ourselves upon the success of our observation, we had scarce less cause to regret the diligence with which that time had been improved by some of our people to another purpose. While the attention of the officers was engrossed by the transit of Venus, some of the ship's company broke into one of the store-rooms, and stole a quantity of spike-nails, amounting to no less than one hundred weight: This was a matter of public and serious concern; for these nails, if circulated by the people among the Indians, would do us irreparable injury, by reducing the value of iron, our staple commodity. One of the thieves was detected, but only seven nails were

were found in his custody. He was punished with two dozen lashes, but would impeach none of his accomplices.

SECTION XIII.

*The Ceremonies of an Indian Funeral particularly described.
General Observations on the Subject : A Character found
among the Indians to which the Ancients paid great Veneration : A Robbery at the Fort, and its Consequences ; with
a Specimen of Indian Cookery, and various Incidents.*

ON the 5th, we kept his majesty's birth-day ; for though it is the 4th, we were unwilling to celebrate it during the absence of the two parties who had been sent out to observe the transit. We had several of the Indian chiefs at our entertainment, who drank his majesty's health by the name of Kihiargo, which was the nearest imitation they could produce of King George.

About this time died an old woman of some rank, who was related to Tomio, which gave us an opportunity to see how they disposed of the body, and confirmed us in our opinion that these people, contrary to the present custom of all other nations now known, never bury their dead. In the middle of a small square, neatly railed in with bamboo, the awning of a canoe was raised upon two posts, and under this the body was deposited upon such a frame as has before been described : It was covered with fine cloth, and near it was placed bread-fruit, fish, and other provisions : We supposed that the food was placed there for the spirit of the deceased, and consequently, that these Indians had some confused notion of a separate state ; but upon our applying for further information to Tubourai Tamaide, he told us, that the food was placed there as an offering to their gods. They do not, however, suppose, that the gods eat, any more than the Jews supposed that Jehovah could dwell in a house : The offering is made here upon the same principle as the temple was built at Jerusalem, as an expression of reverence and gratitude, and a solicitation of the more immediate presence of the Deity. In the front of the area was a kind of stile, where the relations of the deceased stood to pay the tribute of
their

their sorrow; and under the awning were innumerable small pieces of cloth, on which the tears and blood of the mourners had been shed; for in their paroxysms of grief it is a universal custom to wound themselves with the shark's tooth. Within a few yards two occasional houses were set up, in one of which some relations of the deceased constantly resided, and in the other the chief mourner, who is always a man, and who keeps there a very singular dress in which a ceremony is performed that will be described in its turn. Near the place where the dead are thus set up to rot, the bones are afterwards buried.

What can have introduced among these people the custom of exposing their dead above ground, till the flesh is consumed by putrefaction, and then burying the bones, it is perhaps impossible to guess; but it is remarkable that Ælian and Apollonius Rhodius impute a similar practice to the ancient inhabitants of Colchis, a country near Pontus in Asia, now called Mingrelia; except that among them this manner of disposing of the dead did not extend to both sexes: The women they buried; but the men they wrapped in a hide, and hung up in the air by a chain. This practice among the Colchians is referred to a religious cause. The principal objects of their worship were the Earth and the Air; and it is supposed that, in consequence of some superstitious notion, they devoted their dead to both.[1] Whether the natives of Otaheite had any notion of

[1] If the Colchians, according to the assertion of Herodotus, Euter. 104, are to be considered as derived from the Egyptians, which some circumstances of resemblance render probable, it seems not irrational to imagine, that they had acquired from that people an abhorrence to the thought of becoming food for worms. This, Herodotus says, in Thal. 16. was the reason why they (the Egyptians) embalmed the bodies of the dead; for which the practice adopted by the Colchians, of wrapping them in hides of oxen for the purpose of preservation, was judged an adequate substitute. But though this be admitted as satisfactory with respect to the origin of the usage, it affords no explanation as to the difference observable in the treatment of the sexes after death, which must be looked for in some other circumstance, common to these two people, or peculiar to one of them. It can scarcely be imputed to the different estimation in which the sexes were held whilst living; for if any thing, at least in the opinion of Diodorus Siculus, the women were in higher authority in Egypt than the men, in so far as civil and political rights were concerned. On the other hand, it is certain from Herodotus, that men alone could officiate in the service of their gods, whether male or female, and that there were no priestesses in Egypt. No reason can be discovered for this exclusion.

It

of the same kind, we were never able certainly to determine; but we soon discovered, that the repositories of
their dead were also places of worship. Upon this occasion it may be observed, that nothing can be more absurd
than the notion that the happiness or misery of a future
life depends, in any degree, upon the disposition of the
body when the state of probation is past; yet that nothing
is more general than a solicitude about it. However cheap
we may hold any funeral rites which custom has not fami-
liarized, or superstition rendered sacred, most men grave-
ly deliberate how to prevent their body from being broken
by the mattock and devoured by the worm, when it is no
longer capable of sensation; and purchase a place for it
in holy ground, when they believe the lot of its future existence to be irrevocably determined. So strong is the association of pleasing or painful ideas with certain opinions
and actions which affect us while we live, that we involuntarily act as if it was equally certain that they would affect
us in the same manner when we are dead, though this is
an opinion that nobody will maintain. Thus it happens,
that the desire of preserving from reproach even the name
that we leave behind us, or of procuring it honour, is one
of the most powerful principles of action, among the inhabitants of the most speculative and enlightened nations.
Posthumous reputation, upon every principle, must be acknowledged to have no influence upon the dead; yet the
desire of obtaining and securing it, no force of reason, no
habits of thinking can subdue, except in those whom habitual baseness and guilt have rendered indifferent to honour

It is merely credible, that the Egyptians, though ascribing great excellence to the female sex in various particulars, nevertheless judged them to
be destitute of that principle which constituted the essence of the gods,
and therefore unfit for their society. Possibly they might in consequence
imagine them to be incapable of immortality and transmigration, a belief
which they so firmly maintained, as to be led to specify the various
changes which the soul underwent for the space of three thousand years,
when it re-assumed the human body. Now, if the Colchians credited
this doctrine of the immortality and transmigration of the soul, and at the
same time depreciated for any reasons whatever the dignity of women,
one may easily conceive why they should think of a difference in the mode
of disposing of male and female corpses. After all, however, such reasoning as this is very far from satisfactory; nevertheless, in the mind of the
judicious reader, accustomed to contemplate the minute circumstances,
which, though much modified, prove a connection betwixt different people,
yet cannot but have some weight.—E.

nour and shame while they lived. This indeed seems to be among the happy imperfections of our nature, upon which the general good of society in a certain measure depends; for as some crimes are supposed to be prevented by hanging the body of the criminal in chains after he is dead, so, in consequence of the same association of ideas, much good is procured to society, and much evil prevented, by a desire of preventing disgrace or procuring honour to a name, when nothing but a name remains.

Perhaps no better use can be made of reading an account of manners altogether new, by which the follies and absurdities of mankind are taken out of that particular connection in which habit has reconciled them to us, than to consider in how many instances they are essentially the same. When an honest devotee of the church of Rome reads, that there are Indians on the banks of the Ganges who believe that they shall secure the happiness of a future state by dying with a cow's tail in their hands, he laughs at their folly and superstition: and if these Indians were to be told, that there are people upon the continent of Europe, who imagine that they shall derive the same advantage from dying with the slipper of St Francis upon their foot, they would laugh in their turn. But if, when the Indian heard the account of the catholic, and the catholic that of the Indian, each was to reflect, that there was no difference between the absurdity of the slipper and of the tail, but that the veil of prejudice and custom, which covered it in their own case, was withdrawn in the other, they would turn their knowledge to a profitable purpose.

Having observed that bread-fruit had for some days been brought in less quantities than usual, we enquired the reason, and were told, that there being a great shew of fruit upon the trees, they had been thinned all at once, in order to make a kind of sour paste, which the natives call *Mahie*, and which, in consequence of having undergone a fermentation, will keep a considerable time, and supply them with food when no ripe fruit is to be had.

On the 10th, the ceremony was to be performed, in honour of the old woman whose sepulchral tabernacle has just been described, by the chief mourner; and Mr Banks had so great a curiosity to see all the mysteries of the solemnity, that he determined to take a part in it, being told, that he could be present upon no other condition. In the even-

ing

ing, therefore, he repaired to the place where the body lay, and was received by the daughter of the deceased, and several other persons, among whom was a boy about fourteen years old, who were to assist in the ceremony. Tubourai Tamaide was to be the principal mourner; and his dress was extremely fantastical, though not unbecoming. Mr Banks was stripped of his European clothes, and a small piece of cloth being tied round his middle, his body was smeared with charcoal and water, as low as the shoulders, till it was as black as that of a negro: The same operation was performed upon several others, among whom were some women, who were reduced to a state as near to nakedness as himself; the boy was blacked all over, and then the procession set forward. Tubourai Tamaide uttered something, which was supposed to be a prayer, near the body; and did the same when he came up to his own house: When this was done, the procession was continued towards the fort, permission having been obtained to approach it upon this occasion. It is the custom of the Indians to fly from these processions with the utmost precipitation, so that as soon as those who were about the fort, saw it at a distance, they hid themselves in the woods. It proceeded from the fort along the shore, and put to flight another body of Indians, consisting of more than an hundred, every one hiding himself under the first shelter that he could find: It then crossed the river, and entered the woods, passing several houses, all which were deserted, and not a single Indian could be seen during the rest of the procession, which continued more than half an hour. The office that Mr Banks performed was called that of the *Nineveh,* of which there were two besides himself; and the natives having all disappeared, they came to the chief mourner, and said *imitata,* there are no people, after which the company was dismissed to wash themselves in the river, and put on their customary apparel.

On the 12th, complaint being made to me, by some of the natives, that two of the seamen had taken from them several bows and arrows, and some strings of plaited hair, I examined the matter, and finding the charge well supported, I punished each of the criminals with two dozen lashes.

Their bows and arrows have not been mentioned before, nor were they often brought down to the fort: This day, however

however, Tubourai Tamaide brought down his, in consequence of a challenge which he had received from Mr Gore. The chief supposed it was to try who could send the arrow farthest; Mr Gore, who best could hit a mark; and as Mr Gore did not value himself upon shooting to a great distance, nor the chief upon hitting a mark, there was no trial of skill between them. Tubourai Tamaide, however, to shew us what he could do, drew his bow, and sent an arrow, none of which are feathered, two hundred and seventy-four yards, which is something more than a seventh, and something less than a sixth part of a mile. Their manner of shooting is somewhat singular; they kneel down, and the moment the arrow is discharged, drop the bow.

Mr Banks, in his morning walk this day, met a number of the natives, whom, upon enquiry, he found to be travelling musicians; and having learnt where they were to be at night, we all repaired to the place. The band consisted of two flutes and three drums, and we found a great number of people assembled upon the occasion. The drummers accompanied the music with their voices, and, to our great surprise, we discovered that we were generally the subject of the song. We did not expect to have found among the uncivilized inhabitants of this sequestered spot, a character, which has been the subject of such praise and veneration where genius and knowledge have been most conspicuous; yet these were the bards or minstrels of Otaheite. Their song was unpremeditated, and accompanied with music; they were continually going about from place to place, and they were rewarded by the master of the house, and the audience, with such things as one wanted and the other could spare.

On the 14th, we were brought into new difficulties and inconvenience by another robbery at the fort. In the middle of the night, one of the natives contrived to steal an iron coal-rake, that was made use of for the oven. It happened to be set up against the inside of the wall, so that the top of the handle was visible from without; and we were informed that the thief, who had been seen lurking there in the evening, came secretly about three o'clock in the morning, and, watching his opportunity when the centinel's back was turned, very dexterously laid hold of it with a long crooked stick, and drew it over the wall. I thought it of some consequence, if possible, to put an end to these practices at once, by doing something that should make it the common interest of the natives themselves to prevent them. I had given strict orders that they should not be fired upon, even when detected in these attempts, for which I had many reasons: The common centinels were by no means fit to be entrusted with a power of life and death, to be exerted whenever they should think fit, and I had already experienced that they were ready to take away the lives that were in their power, upon the slightest occasion; neither indeed did I think that the thefts which these people committed against us, were, in them, crimes worthy of death: That thieves are hanged in England, I thought no reason why they should be shot in Otaheite; because, with respect to the natives, it would have been an execution by a law *ex post facto:* They had no such law among themselves, and it did not appear to me that we had any right to make such a law for them. That they should abstain from theft, or be punished with death, was not one of the conditions under which they claimed the advantages of civil society, as it is among us; and I was not willing to expose them to fire-arms, loaded with shot, neither could I perfectly approve of firing only with powder: At first, indeed, the noise and the smoke would alarm them, but when they found that no mischief followed, they would be led to despise the weapons themselves, and proceed to insults, which would make it necessary to put them to the test, and from which they would be deterred by the very sight of a gun, if it was never used but with effect. At this time, an accident furnished me with what I thought a happy expedient. It happened that above twenty of their sailing canoes were just come in with a supply of fish: Upon these I immediately seized, and bringing them into the river behind the fort, gave public notice, that except the rake, and all the rest of the things which from time to time had been stolen, were returned, the canoes should be burnt. This menace I ventured to publish, though I had no design to put it into execution, making no doubt but that it was well known in whose possession the stolen goods were, and that as restitution was thus made a common cause, they would all of them in a short time be brought back. A list of the things was made out, consisting principally of the rake, the musket which had been taken from the marine when the Indian

dian was shot; the pistols which Mr Banks lost with his
clothes at Atahourou; a sword belonging to one of the
petty officers, and the water cask. About noon, the rake
was restored, and great solicitation was made for the release of the canoes, but I still insisted upon my original
condition. The next day came, and nothing farther was
restored, at which I was much surprised, for the people
were in the utmost distress for the fish, which in a short
time would be spoilt; I was, therefore, reduced to a disagreeable situation, either of releasing the canoes, contrary
to what I had solemnly and publicly declared, or to detain
them, to the great injury of those who were innocent, without answering any good purpose to ourselves: As a temporary expedient, I permitted them to take the fish, but still
detained the canoes. This very licence, however, was productive of new confusion and injury; for, it not being easy
at once to distinguish to what particular persons the several lots of fish belonged, the canoes were plundered, under
favour of this circumstance, by those who had no right to
any part of their cargo. Most pressing instances were still
made that the canoes might be restored, and I having now
the greatest reason to believe, either that the things for
which I detained them were not in the island, or that those
who suffered by their detention had not sufficient influence
over the thieves to prevail upon them to relinquish their
booty, determined at length to give them up, not a little
mortified at the bad success of my project.

Another accident also about this time was, notwithstanding all our caution, very near embroiling us with the Indians. I sent the boat on shore with an officer to get ballast for the ship, and not immediately finding stones convenient for the purpose, he began to pull down some part
of an enclosure where they deposited the bones of their
dead: This the Indians violently opposed, and a messenger
came down to the tents to acquaint the officers that they
would not suffer it. Mr Banks immediately repaired to the
place, and an amicable end was soon put to the dispute, by
sending the boat's crew to the river, where stones enough
were to be gathered without a possibility of giving offence.
It is very remarkable, that these Indians appeared to be
much more jealous of what was done to the dead than the
living. This was the only measure in which they ventured
to oppose us, and the only insult that was offered to any individual

dividual among us was upon a similar occasion.   Mr Monkhouse happening one day to pull a flower from a tree which
grew in one of their sepulchral enclosures, an Indian, whose
jealousy had probably been upon the watch, came suddenly behind him, and struck him : Mr Monkhouse laid hold
of him, but he was instantly rescued by two more, who
took hold of Mr Monkhouse's hair, and forced him to quit
his hold of their companion, and then ran away without offering him any farther violence.

In the evening of the 19th, while the canoes were still
detained, we received a visit from Oberea, which surprised
us not a little, as she brought with her none of the things
that had been stolen, and knew that she was suspected of
having some of them in her custody.   She said indeed, that
her favourite Obadee, whom she had beaten and dismissed,
had taken them away; but she seemed conscious, that she had
no right to be believed : She discovered the strongest signs
of fear, yet she surmounted it with astonishing resolution,
and was very pressing to sleep with her attendants in
Mr Banks's tent.   In this, however, she was not gratified;
the affair of the jacket was too recent, and the tent was besides filled with other people.   Nobody else seemed willing
to entertain her, and she therefore, with great appearance
of mortification and disappointment, spent the night in her
canoe.

The next morning early, she returned to the fort, with
her canoe and every thing that it contained, putting herself wholly into our power, with something like greatness of
mind, which excited our wonder and admiration.   As the
most effectual means to bring about a reconciliation, she
presented us with a hog, and several other things, among
which was a dog.   We had lately learnt, that these animals
were esteemed by the Indians as more delicate food than
their pork; and upon this occasion we determined to try
the experiment : The dog, which was very fat, we consigned
over to Tupia, who undertook to perform the double office
of butcher and cook.   He killed him by holding his hands
close over his mouth and nose, an operation which continued above a quarter of an hour.   While this was doing, a
hole was made in the ground about a foot deep, in which a
fire was kindled, and some small stones placed in layers alternately with the wood to heat; the dog was then singed,
by holding him over the fire, and, by scraping him with a
shell,

shell, the hair taken off as clean as if he had been scalded
in hot water : He was then cut up with the same instrument,
and his entrails being taken out, were sent to the sea, where
being carefully washed, they were put into cocoa-nut shells,
with what blood had come from the body : When the hole
was sufficiently heated, the fire was taken out, and some of
the stones, which were not so hot as to discolour any thing
that they touched, being placed at the bottom, were covered with green leaves : The dog, with the entrails, was then
placed upon the leaves, and other leaves being laid upon
them, the whole was covered with the rest of the hot stones,
and the mouth of the hole close stopped with mould : In
somewhat less than four hours it was again opened, and the
dog taken out excellently baked, and we all agreed that he
made a very good dish. The dogs which are here bred to
be eaten, taste no animal food, but are kept wholly upon
bread-fruit, cocoa-nuts, yams, and other vegetables of the
like kind : All the flesh and fish eaten by the inhabitants is
dressed in the same way.

On the 21st, we were visited at the fort by a chief, called
Oamo, whom we had never seen before, and who was treated by the natives with uncommon respect; he brought with
him a boy about seven years old, and a young woman about
sixteen : The boy was carried upon a man's back, which we
considered as a piece of state, for he was as well able to walk
as any present. As soon as they were in sight, Oberea, and
several other natives who were in the fort, went out to meet
them, having first uncovered their heads and bodies as low
as the waist: As they came on, the same ceremony was performed by all the natives who were without the fort. Uncovering the body, therefore, is in this country probably a
mark of respect; and as all parts are here exposed with
equal indifference, the ceremony of uncovering it from the
waist downwards, which was performed by Ooratooa, might
be nothing more than a different mode of compliment,
adapted to persons of a different rank. The chief came
into the tent, but no entreaty could prevail upon the young
woman to follow him, though she seemed to refuse contrary to her inclination : The natives without were indeed
all very solicitous to prevent her; sometimes, when her resolution seemed to fail, almost using force : The boy also
they restrained in the same manner ; but Dr Solander happening to meet him at the gate, took him by the hand, and
led

led him in before the people were aware of it: As soon, however, as those that were within saw him, they took care to have him sent out.

These circumstances having strongly excited our curiosity, we enquired who they were, and were informed, that Oamo was the husband of Oberea, though they had been a long time separated by mutual consent; and that the young woman and the boy were their children. We learnt also, that the boy, whose name was *Terridiri*, was heir-apparent to the sovereignty of the island, and that his sister was intended for his wife, the marriage being deferred only till he should arrive at a proper age. The sovereign at this time was a son of *Whappai*, whose name was *Outou*, and who, as before has been observed, was a minor. Whappai, Oamo, and Tootahah, were brothers: Whappai was the eldest, and Oamo the second; so that, Whappai having no child but Outou, Terridiri, the son of his next brother Oamo, was heir to the sovereignty. It will, perhaps, seem strange that a boy should be sovereign during the life of his father; but, according to the custom of the country, a child succeeds to a father's title and authority as soon as it is born: A regent is then elected, and the father of the new sovereign is generally continued in his authority, under that title, till his child is of age; but, at this time, the choice had fallen upon Tootahah, the uncle, in consequence of his having distinguished himself in a war. Oamo asked many questions concerning England and its inhabitants, by which he appeared to have great shrewdness and understanding.

SECTION XIV.

An Account of the Circumnavigation of the Island, and various Incidents that happened during the Expedition, with a Description of a Burying-place and Place of Worship, called a Morai.

ON Monday the 26th, about three o'clock in the morning, I set out in the pinnace, accompanied by Mr Banks, to make the circuit of the island, with a view to sketch out the coast and harbours. We took our route to the eastward, and about eight in the forenoon we went on shore, in
a district

a district called *Oahounue*, which is governed by *Alio*, a young chief, whom we had often seen at the tents, and who favoured us with his company to breakfast. Here also we found two other natives of our old acquaintance, *Tituboalo* and *Hoona*, who carried us to their houses, near which we saw the body of the old woman, at whose funeral rites Mr Banks had assisted, and which had been removed hither from the spot where it was first deposited, this place having descended from her by inheritance to Hoona, and it being necessary on that account that it should lie here. We then proceeded on foot, the boat attending within call, to the harbour in which Mr Bougainville lay, called *Ohidea*, where the natives shewed us the ground upon which his people pitched their tent, and the brook at which they watered, though no trace of them remained, except the holes where the poles of the tent had been fixed, and a small piece of potsheard, which Mr Banks found in looking narrowly about the spot. We met, however, with *Orette*, a chief who was their principal friend, and whose brother *Outorrou* went away with them.

This harbour lies on the west side of a great bay, under shelter of a small island called *Boourou*, near which is another called *Taawirrii;* the breach in the reefs is here very large, but the shelter for the ships is not the best.

Soon after we had examined this place, we took boat, and asked Tituboalo to go with us to the other side of the bay; but he refused, and advised us not to go, for he said the country there was inhabited by people who were not subject to Tootahah, and who would kill both him and us. Upon receiving this intelligence, we did not, as may be imagined, relinquish our enterprise; but we immediately loaded our pieces with ball: This was so well understood by Tituboalo as a precaution which rendered us formidable, that he now consented to be of our party.

Having rowed till it was dark, we reached a low neck of land, or isthmus, at the bottom of the bay, that divides the island into two peninsulas, each of which is a district or government wholly independent of the other. From Port Royal, where the ship was at anchor, the coast trends E. by S. and E.S.E. ten miles, then S. by E. and S. eleven miles to the isthmus. In the first direction, the shore is in general open to the sea; but in the last it is covered by reefs of rocks, which form several good harbours, with safe anchorage, in 16, 18, 20, and 24 fathom of water, with other conveniences. As we had not yet got into our enemy's country, we determined to sleep on shore: We landed, and though we found but few houses, we saw several double canoes, whose owners were well known to us, and who provided us with supper and lodging; of which Mr Banks was indebted for his share to Ooratooa, the lady who had paid him her compliments in so singular a manner at the fort.

In the morning, we looked about the country, and found it to be a marshy flat, about two miles over, across which the natives haul their canoes to the corresponding bay on the other side. We then prepared to continue our route for what Tituboalo called the other kingdom; he said that the name of it was *Tiarrabou* or *Otaheite Ete*; and that of the chief who governed it, *Waheatua*: Upon this occasion also, we learnt that the name of the peninsula where we had taken our station was *Opoureonu*, or *Otaheite Nue*. Our new associate seemed to be now in better spirits than he had been the day before; the people in Tiarrabou would not kill us, he said, but he assured us that we should be able to procure no victuals among them; and indeed we had seen no bread-fruit since we set out.

After rowing a few miles, we landed in a district, which was the dominion of a chief called *Maraitata*, the burying-place of men, whose father's name was *Pahairedo*, the stealer of boats. Though these names seemed to favour the account that had been given by Tituboalo, we soon found that it was not true. Both the father and the son received us with the greatest civility, gave us provisions, and, after some delay, sold us a very large hog for a hatchet. A crowd soon gathered round us, but we saw only two people that we knew; neither did we observe a single bead or ornament among them that had come from our ship, though we saw several things which had been brought from Europe. In one of the houses lay two twelve-pound shot, one of which was marked with the broad arrow of England, though the people said they had them from the ships that lay in Bougainville's harbour.

We proceeded on foot till we came to the district which was immediately under the government of the principal chief, or king of the peninsula, Waheatua. Waheatua had a son, but whether, according to the custom of Opoureonu, he administered the government as regent, or in his own right,

right, is uncertain. This district consists of a large and fertile plain, watered by a river so wide, that we were obliged to ferry over it in a canoe; our Indian train, however, chose to swim, and took to the water with the same facility as a pack of hounds. In this place we saw no house that appeared to be inhabited, but the ruins of many, that had been very large. We proceeded along the shore, which forms a bay, called *Oaitipeha*, and at last we found the chief sitting near some pretty canoe awnings, under which, we supposed, he and his attendants slept. He was a thin old man, with a very white head and beard, and had with him a comely woman, about five-and-twenty years old, whose name was *Toudidde*. We had often heard the name of this woman, and, from report and observation, we had reason to think that she was the *Oberea* of this peninsula. From this place, between which and the isthmus there are other harbours, formed by the reefs that lie along the shore, where shipping may lie in perfect security, and from whence the land trends S.S.E. and S. to the S.E. part of the island, we were accompanied by *Tearee*, the son of Waheatua, of whom we had purchased a hog, and the country we passed through appeared to be more cultivated than any we had seen in other parts of the island: The brooks were every where banked into narrow channels with stone, and the shore had also a facing of stone, where it was washed by the sea. The houses were neither large nor numerous, but the canoes that were hauled up along the shore were almost innumerable, and superior to any that we had seen before, both in size and make, they were longer, the sterns were higher, and the awnings were supported by pillars. At almost every point there was a sepulchral building, and there were many of them also in land. They were of the same figure as those in Opoureonu, but they were cleaner and better kept, and decorated with many carved boards, which were set upright, and on the top of which were various figures of birds and men: On one in particular, there was the representation of a cock, which was painted red and yellow, to imitate the feathers of that animal, and rude images of men were, in some of them, placed one upon the head of another. But in this part of the country, however fertile and cultivated, we did not see a single bread-fruit; the trees were entirely bare, and the inhabitants seemed to subsist

principally

principally upon nuts, which are not unlike a chesnut, and which they call *Ahee.*

When we had walked till we were weary, we called up the boat, but both our Indians, Tituboalo and Tuahow, were missing: They had, it seems, stayed behind at Waheatua's, expecting us to return thither, in consequence of a promise which had been extorted from us, and which we had it not in our power to fulfil.

Tearee, however, and another, embarked with us, and we proceeded till we came a-breast of a small island called *Otooareite;* it being then dark, we determined to land, and our Indians conducted us to a place where they said we might sleep: It was a deserted house, and near it was a little cove, in which the boat might lie with great safety and convenience. We were, however, in want of provisions, having been very sparingly supplied since we set out; and Mr Banks immediately went into the woods to see whether any could be procured. As it was dark, he met with no people, and could find but one house that was inhabited: A bread-fruit and a half, a few Ahees, and some fire, were all that it afforded; upon which, with a duck or two, and a few curlieus, we made our supper, which, if not scanty, was disagreeable, by the want of bread, with which we had neglected to furnish ourselves, as we depended upon meeting with bread-fruit, and took up our lodging under the awning of a canoe belonging to Tearee, which followed us.

The next morning, after having spent some time in another fruitless attempt to procure a supply of provisions, we proceeded round the south-east point, part of which is not covered by any reef, but lies open to the sea; and here the hill rises directly from the shore. At the southermost part of the island, the shore is again covered by a reef, which forms a good harbour; and the land about it is very fertile. We made this route partly on foot, and partly in the boat: When we had walked about three miles, we arrived at a place where we saw several large canoes, and a number of people with them, whom we were agreeably surprised to find were of our intimate acquaintance. Here, with much difficulty, we procured some cocoa-nuts, and then embarked, taking with us Tuahow, one of the Indians who had waited for us at Waheatua's, and had returned the night before, long after it was dark.

When we came abreast of the south-east end of the island,

island, we went ashore, by the advice of our Indian guide, who told us that the country was rich and good. The chief, whose name was *Mathiabo*, soon came down to us, but seemed to be a total stranger both to us and to our trade: His subjects, however, brought us plenty of cocoa-nuts, and about twenty bread-fruit. The bread-fruit we bought at a very dear rate, but his excellency sold us a pig for a glass bottle, which he preferred to every thing else that we could give him. We found in his possession a goose and a turkey-cock, which, we were informed, had been left upon the island by the Dolphin : They were both enormously fat, and so tame that they followed the Indians, who were fond of them to excess, wherever they went.

In a long house in this neighbourhood, we saw what was altogether new to us. At one end of it, fastened to a semi-circular board, hung fifteen human jaw-bones ; they appeared to be fresh, and there was not one of them that wanted a single tooth. A sight so extraordinary, strongly excited our curiosity, and we made many enquiries about it : But at this time could get no information, for the people either could not, or would not understand us.

When we left this place, the chief, Mathiabo, desired leave to accompany us, which was readily granted. He continued with us the remainder of the day, and proved very useful, by piloting us over the shoals. In the evening, we opened the bay on the north-west side of the island, which answered to that on the south-east, so as at the isthmus, or carrying-place, almost to intersect the island, as I have observed before ; and when we had coasted about two-thirds of it, we determined to go on shore for the night. We saw a large house at some distance, which, Mathiabo informed us, belonged to one of his friends ; and soon after several canoes came off to meet us, having on board some very handsome women, who, by their behaviour, seemed to have been sent to entice us on shore. As we had before resolved to take up our residence here for the night, little invitation was necessary. We found that the house belonged to the chief of the district, whose name was *Wiverou* : He received us in a very friendly manner, and ordered his people to assist us in dressing our provision, of which we had now got a tolerable stock. When our supper was ready, we were conducted into that part of the house where Wiverou was sitting, in order to eat it ;

Mathiabo

Mathiabo supped with us, and Wiveiou calling for his supper at the same time, we eat our meal very sociably, and
with great good humoui. When it was over, we began to
enquire where we weie to sleep, and a part of the house
was shewn us, of which we were told we might take possession for that purpose. We then sent foi oui clokes, and
Mr Banks began to undress, as his custoin was, and, with
a precaution which he had been taught by the loss of the
jackets at Atabouiou, sent his clothes aboard the boat, proposing to cover himself with a piece of Indian cloth. When
Mathiabo peiceived what was doing, he also pretended to
want a cloak; and, as he had behaved very well, and done
us some service, a cloke was oidered for him. We lay
down, and observed that Mathiabo was not with us; but
we supposed that he was gone to bathe, as the Indians always do before they sleep. We had not waited long, however, when an Indian, who was a stianger to us, came and
told Mi Banks, that the cloke and Mathiabo had disappeai-
ed together. This man had so far gained oui confidence,
that we did not at fiist believe the ieport; but it being
soon after confirmed by Tuahow, our own Indian, we knew
no time was to be lost. As it was impossible for us to pui-
sue the thief with any hope of success, without the assistance of the people about us, Mi Banks started up, and
telling our case, requiied them to iecover the cloak; and
to enfoice this requisition, shewed one of his pocket-pistols, which he always kept about him. Upon the sight of
the pistol, the whole company took the alarm, and, instead
of assisting to catch the thief, oi recover what had been
stolen, began with great precipitation to leave the place;
one of them, however, was seized, upon which he immediately offered to direct the chase: I set out therefore with
Mr Banks, and though we ran all the way, the alarm had
got before us, for in about ten minutes we met a man biing-
ing back the cloak, which the thief had relinquished in
great terror; and as we did not then think fit to continue
the pursuit, he made his escape. When we returned, we
found the house, in which there had been between two
and three hundred people, entirely deserted. It being,
however, soon known that we had no iesentment against
any body but Mathiabo, the chief, Wiveiou, our host, with
his wife and many others, returned, and took up their lodgings with us for the night. In this place, however, we
were

were destined to more confusion and trouble, for about five
o'clock in the morning our sentry alarmed us, with an account that the boat was missing: He had seen her, he said,
about half an hour before, at her grappling, which was not
above fifty yards from the shore; but, upon hearing the
sound of oars, he had looked out again, and could see nothing of her. At this account we started up greatly alarmed, and ran to the water-side: The morning was clear and
star-light, so that we could see to a considerable distance,
but there was no appearance of the boat. Our situation
was now such as might justify the most terrifying apprehensions; as it was a dead calm, and we could not therefore suppose her to have broken from her grappling, we
had great reason to fear that the Indians had attacked her,
and finding the people asleep, had succeeded in their enterprise: We were but four, with only one musquet and
two pocket-pistols, without a spare ball or charge of powder for either. In this state of anxiety and distress we remained a considerable time, expecting the Indians every
moment to improve their advantage, when, to our unspeakable satisfaction, we saw the boat return, which had been
driven from her grappling by the tide; a circumstance to
which, in our confusion and surprise, we did not advert.

As soon as the boat returned, we got our breakfast, and
were impatient to leave the place, lest some other vexatious accident should befall us. It is situated on the north
side of Tiarrabou, the south-east peninsula, or division, of
the island, and at the distance of about five miles south
east from the isthmus, having a large and commodious harbour, inferior to none in the island, about which the land
is very rich in produce. Notwithstanding we had had little communication with this division, the inhabitants every
where received us in a friendly manner; we found the
whole of it fertile and populous, and, to all appearance, in
a more flourishing state than Opoureonu, though it is not
above one-fourth part as large.

The next district in which we landed, was the last in
Tiarrabou, and governed by a chief, whose name we understood to be *Omoe.* Omoe was building a house, and
being therefore very desirous of procuring a hatchet, he
would have been glad to have purchased one with any
thing that he had in his possession; it happened, however,
rather unfortunately for him and us, that we had not one

                                                        hatchet

hatchet left in the boat. We offered to trade with nails, but he would not part with any thing in exchange for them; we therefore re-embarked, and put off our boat, but the chief being unwilling to relinquish all hope of obtaining something from us that would be of use to him, embarked in a canoe, with his wife *Whanno-ouda*, and followed us. After some time, we took them into the boat, and when we had rowed about a league, they desired we would put ashore: We immediately complied with his request, and found some of his people, who had brought down a very large hog. We were as unwilling to lose the hog, as the chief was to part with us, and it was indeed worth the best axe we had in the ship; we therefore hit upon an expedient, and told him, that if he would bring his hog to the fort at *Matavai*, the Indian name for Port Royal Bay, he should have a large axe, and a nail into the bargain, for his trouble. To this proposal, after having consulted with his wife, he agreed, and gave us a large piece of his country-cloth as a pledge that he would perform his agreement, which, however, he never did.

At this place we saw a very singular curiosity: It was the figure of a man, constructed of basket-work, rudely made, but not ill designed; it was something more than seven feet high, and rather too bulky in proportion to its height. The wicker skeleton was completely covered with feathers, which were white where the skin was to appear, and black in the parts which it is their custom to paint or stain, and upon the head, where there was to be a representation of hair: Upon the head also were four protuberances, three in front and one behind, which we should have called horns, but which the Indians dignified with the name of *Tate Etc*, little men. The image was called *Manioe*, and was said to be the only one of the kind in Otaheite. They attempted to give us an explanation of its use and design, but we had not then acquired enough of their language to understand them. We learnt, however, afterwards, that it was a representation of Mauwe, one of their Eatuas, or gods of the second class.

After having settled our affairs with Omoe, we proceeded on our return, and soon reached Opoureonu, the north-west peninsula. After rowing a few miles, we went on shore again, but the only thing we saw worth notice, was a repository for the dead, uncommonly decorated: The pave-
ment

ment was extremely neat, and upon it was raised a pyramid, about five feet high, which was entirely covered with the fruits of two plants, peculiar to the country. Near the pyramid was a small image of stone, of very rude workmanship, and the first instance of carving in stone that we had seen among these people. They appeared to set a high value upon it, for it was covered from the weather by a shed, that had been erected on purpose.

We proceeded in the boat, and passed through the only harbour, on the south side of Opoureonu, that is fit for shipping. It is situated about five miles to the westward of the isthmus, between two small islands that lie near the shore, and about a mile distant from each other, and affords good anchorage in eleven and twelve fathom water. We were now not far from the district called *Papurra*, which belonged to our friends Oamo and Obeiea, where we proposed to sleep. We went on shore about an hour before night, and found that they were both absent, having left their habitations to pay us a visit at Matavai : This, however, did not alter our purpose ; we took up our quarters at the house of Oberea, which, though small, was very neat, and at this time had no inhabitant but her father, who received us with looks that bid us welcome. Having taken possession, we were willing to improve the little day-light that was left us, and therefore walked out to a point, upon which we had seen, at a distance, trees that are here called *Etoa,* which generally distinguish the places where these people bury the bones of their dead : Their name for such burying-grounds, which are also places of worship, is *Morai.*[7] We were soon struck with the sight of an enormous pile, which, we were told, was the Morai of Oamo and Oberea, and the principal piece of Indian architecture in the island. It was a pile of stone-work, raised pyramidically, upon an oblong base, or square, two hundred and sixty-seven feet long, and eighty-seven wide. It was built like the small pyramidal mounts upon which we sometimes fix the

---

[7] " The sacred ground, around the Morais," says the missionary account, " affords a sanctuary for criminals. Thither, on any apprehension of danger, they flee, especially when numerous (human) sacrifices are expected, and cannot therein be taken by force, though they are sometimes seduced to quit their asylum." The reader will often have to notice with surprise the remarkable resemblance in certain customs of a religious nature, betwixt these people and others more known in history.—E.

the pillar of a sun-dial, where each side is a flight of steps; the steps, however, at the sides, were broader than those at the ends, so that it terminated not in a square of the same figure with the base, but in a ridge, like the roof of a house : There were eleven of these steps, each of which was four feet high, so that the height of the pile was forty-four feet; each step was formed of one course of white co-ral-stone, which was neatly squared and polished ; the rest of the mass, for there was no hollow within, consisted of round pebbles, which, from the regularity of their figure, seemed to have been wrought. Some of the coral-stones were very large ; we measured one of them, and found it three feet and a half by two feet and a half. The foun-dation was of rock stones, which were also squared ; and one of them measured four feet seven inches by two feet four. Such a structure, raised without the assistance of iron-tools to shape the stones, or mortar to join them, struck us with astonishment : It seemed to be as compact and firm as it could have been made by any workman in Europe, except that the steps, which range along its great-est length, are not perfectly straight, but sink in a kind of hollow in the middle, so that the whole surface, from end to end, is not a right line, but a curve. The quarry stones, as we saw no quarry in the neighbourhood, must have been brought from a considerable distance ; and there is no me-thod of conveyance here but by hand : The coral must also have been fished from under the water, where, though it may be found in plenty, it lies at a considerable depth, ne-ver less than three feet. Both the rock-stone and the coral could be squared only by tools made of the same substance, which must have been a work of incredible labour ; but the polishing was more easily effected by means of the sharp coral sand, which is found every-where upon the sea-shore in great abundance. In the middle of the top stood the image of a bird, carved in wood; and near it lay the broken one of a fish, carved in stone. The whole of this pyramid made part of one side of a spacious area or square, nearly of equal sides, being three hundred and sixty feet by three hundred and fifty-four, which was walled in with stone, and paved with flat stones in its whole extent ; though there were growing in it, notwithstanding the pave-ment, several of the trees which they call *Etoa,* and plan-tains. About a hundred yards to the west of this building,

was

was another paved area or court, in which were several
small stages raised on wooden pillars, about seven feet
high, which are called by the Indians *Ewattas*, and seem
to be a kind of altars, as upon these are placed provisions
of all kinds as offerings to their gods; we have since seen
whole hogs placed upon them, and we found here the skulls
of above fifty, besides the skulls of a great number of
dogs.[8]

The principal object of ambition among these people is
to have a magnificent Morai, and this was a striking memorial of the rank and power of Oberea. It has been remarked, that we did not find her invested with the same
authority that she exercised when the Dolphin was at this
place, and we now learnt the reason of it. Our way from
her house to the Morai lay along the sea-side, and we observed every-where under our feet a great number of human bones, chiefly ribs and vertebræ. Upon enquiring into the cause of so singular an appearance, we were told,
that in the then last month of *Owarahew*, which answered
to our December, 1768, about four or five months before
our arrival, the people of Tiarrabou, the S.E. peninsula
which we had just visited, made a descent at this place,
and killed a great number of people, whose bones were
those that we saw upon the shore: That, upon this occasion, Oberea, and Oamo, who then administered the government for his son, had fled to the mountains; and that
the conquerors burnt all the houses, which were very large,
and carried away the hogs, and what other animals they
found. We learnt also, that the turkey and goose, which
we had seen when we were with Mathabo, the stealer of
cloaks, were among the spoils; this accounted for their
being found among people with whom the Dolphin had
little or no communication; and upon mentioning the jaw-
bones, which we had seen hanging from a board in a long
house, we were told, that they also had been carried away
as trophies, the people here carrying away the jaw-bones
of their enemies, as the Indians of North America do the
scalps.

After

[8] The liberality of these people to their gods is particularly noticed in
the missionary account. " They offer to them all the products of their
island, hogs, fowls, fish, and vegetables ; and at every feast a portion is
presented to the Eatooa, before they presume to take their own repast."
—E.

After having thus gratified our curiosity, we returned to our quarters, where we passed the night in perfect security and quiet. By the next evening we arrived at Atahourou, the residence of our friend Tootahah, where, the last time we passed the night under his protection, we had been obliged to leave the best part of our clothes behind us. This adventure, however, seemed now to be forgotten on both sides. Our friends received us with great pleasure, and gave us a good supper and a good lodging, where we suffered neither loss nor disturbance.

The next day, Saturday, July the 1st, we got back to our fort at Matavai, having found the circuit of the island, including both peninsulas, to be about thirty leagues. Upon our complaining of the want of bread-fruit, we were told, that the produce of the last season was nearly exhausted; and that what was seen sprouting upon the trees, would not be fit to use in less than three months: This accounted for our having been able to procure so little of it in our route.

While the bread-fruit is ripening upon the flats, the inhabitants are supplied in some measure from the trees which they have planted upon the hills to preserve a succession; but the quantity is not sufficient to prevent scarcity: They live therefore upon the sour paste, which they call *Mahie,* upon wild plantains, and ahee-nuts, which at this time are in perfection. How it happened that the Dolphin, which was here at this season, found such plenty of bread-fruit upon the trees, I cannot tell, except the season in which they ripen varies.

At our return, our Indian friends crowded about us, and none of them came empty-handed. Though I had determined to restore the canoes which had been detained to their owners, it had not yet been done; but I now released them as they were applied for. Upon this occasion I could not but remark with concern, that these people were capable of practising petty frauds against each other, with a deliberate dishonesty, which gave me a much worse opinion of them than I had ever entertained from the robberies they committed, under the strong temptation to which a sudden opportunity of enriching themselves with the inestimable metal and manufactures of Europe exposed them.

Among others who applied to me for the release of a
canoe,

canoe, was one *Potattow*, a man of some consequence, well known to us all. I consented, supposing the vessel to be his own, or that he applied on the behalf of a friend: He went immediately to the beach, and took possession of one of the boats, which, with the assistance of his people, he began to carry off. Upon this, however, it was eagerly claimed by the right owners, who, supported by the other Indians, clamorously reproached him for invading their property, and prepared to take the canoe from him by force. Upon this, he desired to be heard, and told them, that the canoe did, indeed, once belong to those who claimed it; but that I, having seized it as a forfeit, had sold it to him for a pig. This silenced the clamour, the owners, knowing that from my power there was no appeal, acquiesced; and Potattow would have carried off his prize, if the dispute had not fortunately been overheard by some of our people, who reported it to me. I gave orders immediately that the Indians should be undeceived; upon which the right owners took possession of their canoe, and Potattow was so conscious of his guilt, that neither he nor his wife, who was privy to his knavery, could look us in the face for some time afterwards.

SECTION XV.

An Expedition of Mr Banks to trace the River: Marks of Subterraneous Fire: Preparations for leaving the Island: An Account of Tupia.

ON the 3d, Mr Banks set out early in the morning with some Indian guides, to trace our river up the valley from which it issues, and examine how far its banks were inhabited. For about six miles they met with houses, not far distant from each other, on each side of the river, and the valley was every where about four hundred yards wide from the foot of the hill on one side, to the foot of that on the other: but they were now shewn a house which they were told the last that they would see. When they came up to it, the master of it offered them refreshments of cocoa-nuts and other fruits, of which they accepted; after a short stay, they walked forward for a considerable time; in bad way it is not easy to compute distances, but they imagined that
they

they had walked about six miles farther, following the course
of the river, when they frequently passed under vaults,
formed by fragments of the rock, in which they were told
people who were benighted frequently passed the night.
Soon after they found the river banked by steep rocks, from
which a cascade, falling with great violence, formed a pool,
so steep, that the Indians said they could not pass it. They
seemed, indeed, not much to be acquainted with the valley
beyond this place, their business lying chiefly upon the declivity of the rocks on each side, and the plains which extended on their summits, where they found plenty of wild
plantain, which they called *Vae.* The way up these rocks
from the banks of the river, was in every respect dreadful;
the sides were nearly perpendicular, and in some places one
hundred feet high; they were also rendered exceeding
slippery by the water of innumerable springs which issued
from the fissures on the surface: Yet up these precipices
a way was to be traced by a succession of long pieces of the
bark of the *hibiscus tiliaceus,* which served as a rope for the
climber to take hold of, and assisted him in scrambling
from one ledge to another, though upon these ledges there
was footing only for an Indian or a goat.   One of these
ropes was nearly thirty feet in length, and their guides offered to assist them in mounting this pass, but recommended another at a little distance lower down, as less difficult
and dangerous.   They took a view of this " better way,"
but found it so bad that they did not chuse to attempt it,
as there was nothing at the top to reward their toil and hazard, but a grove of the wild plantain or vae tree, which
they had often seen before.

During this excursion, Mr Banks had an excellent opportunity to examine the rocks, which were almost every
where naked, for minerals; but he found not the least appearance of any.   The stones every where, like those of
Madeira, shewed manifest tokens of having been burnt;
nor is there a single specimen of any stone, among all those
that were collected in the island, upon which there are not
manifest and indubitable marks of fire; except perhaps
some small pieces of the hatchet-stone, and even of that,
other fragments were collected which were burned almost
to a pumice.   Traces of fire are also manifest in the very
clay upon the hills; and it may, therefore, not unreason-
ably be supposed, that this, and the neighbouring islands,
are either shattered remains of a continent, which some

have

have supposed to be necessary in this part of the globe, to preserve an equilibrium of its parts, which were left behind when the rest sunk by the mining of a subterraneous fire, so as to give a passage to the sea over it; or were torn from rocks, which, from the creation of the world, had been the bed of the sea, and thrown up in heaps, to a height which the waters never reach. One or other of these suppositions will perhaps be thought the more probable, as the water does not gradually grow shallow as the shore is approached, and the islands are almost every where surrounded by reefs, which appear to be rude and broken, as some violent concussion would naturally leave the solid substance of the earth.

On the 4th, Mr Banks employed himself in planting a great quantity of the seeds of water-melons, oranges, lemons, limes, and other plants and trees which he had collected at Rio de Janeiro. For these he prepared ground on each side of the fort, with as many varieties of soil as he could chuse; and there is little doubt but that they will succeed. He also gave liberally of these seeds to the Indians, and planted many of them in the woods: Some of the melon seeds having been planted soon after our arrival, the natives shewed him several of the plants, which appeared to be in the most flourishing condition, and were continually asking him for more.

We now began to prepare for our departure by bending the sails, and performing other necessary operations on board the ship, our water being already on board, and the provisions examined. In the mean time we had another visit from Oamo, Oberea, and their son and daughter; the Indians expressing their respect by uncovering the upper parts of their body as they had done before. The daughter, whose name we understand to be Toimata, was very desirous to see the fort, but her father would by no means suffer her to come in. Tearee, the son of Waheatua, the sovereign of Tiarrabou, the south-east peninsula, was also with us at this time; and we received intelligence of the landing of another guest, whose company was neither expected nor desired: This was no other than the ingenious gentleman who contrived to steal our quadrant. We were told, that he intended to try his fortune again in the night; but the Indians all offered zealously to assist us against him, desiring that, for this purpose, they might be permitted to lie in the fort. This had so good on effect, that the thief relinquished his enterpiise in despair.

On the 7th, the carpenters were employed in taking down the gates and pallisadoes of our little fortification, for firewood on board the ship; and one of the Indians had dexteiity enough to steal the staple and hook upon which the gate turned: He was immediately pursued, and after a chace of six miles, he appeared to have been passed, having concealed himself among some rushes in the brook; the rushes were searched, and though the thief had escaped, a scraper was found which had been stolen from the ship some time before; and soon aftei our old friend Tubourai Tamaide brought us the staple.

On the 8th and 9th, we continued to dismantle our fort, and our friends still flocked about us; some, I believe, sorry at the approach of our departure, and others desirous to make as much as they could of us while we staid.

We were in hopes that we should now leave the island without giving or receiving any other offence; but it unfortunately happened otherwise. Two foieign seamen having been out with my permission, one of them was robbed of his knife, and endeavouring to recover it, probably with circumstances of great provocation, the Indians attacked him, and dangerously wounded him with a stone; they wounded his companion also slightly in the head, and then fled into the mountains. As I should have been sorry to take any farther notice of the affair, I was not displeased that the offenders had escaped; but I was immediately involved in a quarrel which I very much regretted, and which yet it was not possible to avoid.

In the middle of the night between the 8th and 9th, Clement Webb and Samuel Gibson, two of the marines, both young men, went privately from the fort, and in the morning were not to be found. As public notice had been given, that all hands were to go on boaid on the next day, and that the ship would sail on the morrow of that day oi the day following, I began to fear that the absentees intended to stay behind. I knew that I could take no effectual steps to recover them, without endangering the harmony and good-will which at present subsisted among us; and therefore determined to wait a day for the chance ot their return.

On Monday morning the 10th, the marines, to my great
concern

concern, not being returned, an enquiry was made after them of the Indians, who frankly told us, that they did not intend to return, and had taken refuge in the mountains, where it was impossible for our people to find them. They were then requested to assist in the search, and after some deliberation, two of them undertook to conduct such persons as I should think proper to send after them to the place of their retreat. As they were known to be without arms, I thought two would be sufficient, and accordingly dispatched a petty officer, and a corporal of the marines, with the Indian guides, to fetch them back. As the recovery of these men was a matter of great importance, as I had no time to lose, and as the Indians spoke doubtfully of their return, telling us, that they had each of them taken a wife, and were become inhabitants of the country, it was intimated to several of the chiefs who were in the fort with their women, among whom were Tubourai Tamaide, Tomio, and Oberea, that they would not be permitted to leave it till our deserters were brought back. This precaution I thought the more necessary, as, by concealing them a few days, they might compel me to go without them; and I had the pleasure to observe, that they received the intimation with very little signs either of fear or discontent: assuring me that my people should be secured and sent back as soon as possible. While this was doing at the fort, I sent Mr Hicks in the pinnace to fetch Tootahah on board the ship, which he did, without alarming either him or his people. If the Indian guides proved faithful and in earnest, I had reason to expect the return of my people with the deserters before evening. Being disappointed, my suspicions increased; and night coming on, I thought I was not safe to let the people whom I had detained as hostages continue at the fort, and I therefore ordered Tubourai Tamaide, Oberea, and some others, to be taken on board the ship. This spread a general alarm, and several of them, especially the women, expressed their apprehensions with great emotion and many tears when they were put into the boat. I went on board with them, and Mr Banks remained on shore, with some others whom I thought it of less consequence to secure.

About nine o'clock, Webb was brought back by some of the natives, who declared that Gibson, and the petty officer and corporal, would be detained till Tootahah should be set at liberty. The tables were now turned upon me, but I had proceeded too far to retreat. I immediately dispatched Mr Hicks in the long-boat, with a strong party of men, to rescue the prisoners, and told Tootahah that it behoved him to send some of his people with them, with orders to afford them effectual assistance, and to demand the release of my men in his name, for that I should expect him to answer for the contrary. He readily complied; this party recovered my men without the least opposition; and about seven o'clock in the morning, returned with them to the ship, though they had not been able to recover the arms which had been taken from them when they were seized: These, however, were brought on board in less than half an hour, and the chiefs were immediately set at liberty.

When I questioned the petty officer concerning what had happened on shore, he told me, that neither the natives who went with him, nor those whom they met in their way, would give them any intelligence of the deserters; but, on the contrary, became very troublesome: That, as he was returning for further orders to the ship, he and his comrade were suddenly seized by a number of armed men, who having learnt that Tootahah was confined, had concealed themselves in a wood for that purpose, and, who having taken them at a disadvantage, forced their weapons out of their hands, and declared, that they would detain them till their chief should be set at liberty. He said, however, that the Indians were not unanimous in this measure; that some were for setting them at liberty, and others for detaining them: That an eager dispute ensued, and that from words they came to blows, but that the party for detaining them at length prevailed: That soon after Webb and Gibson were brought in by a party of the natives, as prisoners, that they also might be secured as hostages for the chief; but that it was after some debate resolved to send Webb to inform me of their resolution, to assure me that his companions were safe, and direct me where I might send my answer. Thus it appears that whatever were the disadvantages of seizing the chiefs, I should never have recovered my men by any other method. When the chiefs were set on shore from the ship, those at the fort were also set at liberty, and, after staying with Mr Banks about an hour, they all went away. Upon this occasion, as they had done upon another of the same kind, they expressed their joy by an undeserved
liberality.

liberality, strongly urging us to accept of four hogs. These we absolutely refused as a present, and they as absolutely refusing to be paid for them, the hogs did not change masters. Upon examining the deserters, we found that the account which the Indians had given of them was true: They had strongly attached themselves to two girls, and it was their intention to conceal themselves till the ship had sailed, and take up their residence upon the island. This night every thing was got off from the shore, and every body slept on board.

Among the natives who were almost constantly with us, was Tupia, whose name has been often mentioned in this narrative. He had been, as I have before observed, the first minister of Oberea, when she was in the height of her power: He was also the chief tahowa or priest of the island, consequently well acquainted with the religion of the country, as well with respect to its ceremonies as principles. He had also great experience and knowledge in navigation, and was particularly acquainted with the number and situation of the neighbouring islands. This man had often expressed a desire to go with us, and on the 12th in the morning, having with the other natives left us the day before, he came on board with a boy about thirteen years of age, his servant, and urged us to let him proceed with us on our voyage. To have such a person on board, was certainly desirable for many reasons; by learning his language, and teaching him ours, we should be able to acquire a much better knowledge of the customs, policy, and religion of the people, than our short stay among them could give us, I therefore gladly agreed to receive them on board. As we were prevented from sailing to-day, by having found it necessary to make new stocks to our small and best bower anchors, the old ones having been totally destroyed by the worms, Tupia said, he would go once more on shore, and make a signal for the boat to fetch him off in the evening. He went accordingly, and took with him a miniature picture of Mr Banks's, to shew his friends, and several little things to give them as parting presents.

After dinner, Mr Banks, being desirous to procure a drawing of the Morai belonging to Tootahah at Eparré, I attended him thither, accompanied by Dr Solander, in the pinnace. As soon as we landed, many of our friends came to meet us, though some absented themselves in resentment

of

of what had happened the day before. We immediately proceeded to Tootahah's house, where we were joined by Oberea, with several others who had not come out to meet us, and a perfect reconciliation was soon brought about; in consequence of which they promised to visit us early the next day, to take a last farewell of us, as we told them we should certainly set sail in the afternoon. At this place also we found Tupia, who returned with us, and slept this night on board the ship for the first time.

On the next morning, Thursday the 13th of July, the ship was very early crowded with our friends, and surrounded by a multitude of canoes, which were filled with the natives of an interior class. Between eleven and twelve we weighed anchor, and as soon as the ship was under sail, the Indians on board took their leaves, and wept, with a decent and silent sorrow, in which there was something very striking and tender: The people in the canoes, on the contrary, seemed to vie with each other in the loudness of their lamentations, which we considered rather as affectation than grief. Tupia sustained himself in this scene with a firmness and resolution truly admirable: He wept indeed, but the effort that he made to conceal his tears, concurred, with them, to do him honour. He sent his last present, a shirt, by Otheothea, to Potomia, Tootahah's favourite mistress, and then went with Mr Banks to the mast-head, waving to the canoes as long as they continued in sight.

Thus we took leave of Otaheite, and its inhabitants, after a stay of just three months; for much the greater part of the time we lived together in the most cordial friendship, and a perpetual reciprocation of good offices. The accidental differences which now and then happened could not be more sincerely regretted on their part than they were on ours: The principal causes were such as necessarily resulted from our situation and circumstances, in conjunction with the infirmities of human nature, from our not being able perfectly to understand each other, and from the disposition of the inhabitants to theft, which we could not at all times bear with or prevent. They had not, however, except in one instance, been attended with any fatal consequence; and to that accident were owing the measures that I took to prevent others of the same kind. I hoped indeed to have availed myself of the impression which had been made upon them by the lives that had been sacrificed in in their contest with the Dolphin, so as that the intercourse between us should have been carried on wholly without bloodshed ; and by this hope all my measures were directed during the whole of my continuance at the island, and I sincerely wish, that whoever shall next visit it, may be still more fortunate. Our traffic here was carried on with as much order as in the best regulated market in Europe. It was managed principally by Mr Banks, who was indefatigable in procuring provision and refreshments while they were to be had; but during the latter part of our time they became scarce, partly by the increased consumption at the fort and ship, and partly by the coming on of the season in which cocoa-nuts and bread-fruit fail. All kinds of fruit we purchased for beads and nails, but no nails less than forty-penny were current: After a very short time we could never get a pig of more than ten or twelve pounds, for less than a hatchet; because, though these people set a high value upon spike nails, yet these being an article with which many people in the ship were provided, the women found a much more easy way of procuring them than by bringing down provisions.

The best articles for traffic here are axes, hatchets, spikes, large nails, looking-glasses, knives, and beads, for some of which, every thing that the natives have may be procured. They are indeed fond of fine linen cloth, both white and printed; but an axe worth half-a-crown will fetch more than a piece of cloth worth twenty shillings.

END OF TWELFTH VOLUME

EDINBURGH:
Printed by James Ballantyne & Co.

Lightning Source UK Ltd.
Milton Keynes UK
UKOW01f0918071117
312328UK00007B/758/P